Ius Gentium: Comparative Perspectives on Law and Justice

Volume 89

Ius Gentium is a book series which discusses the central questions of law and justice from a comparative perspective. The books in this series collect the contrasting and overlapping perspectives of lawyers, judges, philosophers and scholars of law from the world's many different jurisdictions for the purposes of comparison, harmonisation, and the progressive development of law and legal institutions. Each volume makes a new comparative study of an important area of law. This book series continues the work of the well-known journal of the same name and provides the basis for a better understanding of all areas of legal science.

The *Ius Gentium* series provides a valuable resource for lawyers, judges, legislators, scholars, and both graduate students and researchers in globalisation, comparative law, legal theory and legal practice. The series has a special focus on the development of international legal standards and transnational legal cooperation.

More information about this series at http://www.springer.com/series/7888

Alan Uzelac • Stefaan Voet
Editors

Class Actions in Europe

Holy Grail or a Wrong Trail?

Springer

Editors
Alan Uzelac
Faculty of Law
University of Zagreb
Zagreb, Croatia

Stefaan Voet
KU Leuven
Leuven, Belgium

ISSN 1534-6781 ISSN 2214-9902 (electronic)
Ius Gentium: Comparative Perspectives on Law and Justice
ISBN 978-3-030-73035-2 ISBN 978-3-030-73036-9 (eBook)
https://doi.org/10.1007/978-3-030-73036-9

This Springer imprint is published by the registered company Springer Nature Switzerland AG.
The registered company address is: Gewerbestrasse 11, 6330 Cham, Switzerland

Preface

This book addresses one of the topical trends in contemporary judicial systems: the collectivization of dispute resolution in civil, commercial, and consumer matters. The contributors to this book were invited to evaluate how various methods of collective redress function in their social context and to give their assessment on the direction and the desirability of current developments. The principal motive for this book was the apparent switch in the general opinion on collective litigation in Europe. While class actions and similar collective redress procedures were for a long time dominantly rejected as "non-European" and unnecessary, the recent initiatives of the European policymakers embraced for the first time a more comprehensive approach with representative actions that provide both injunctive and compensatory redress measures. At the same time, the aftermath of some high-profile cases (e.g. Dieselgate) pointed to the importance of effective judicial processing of collective harm situations and caused another surge in the interest for European collective redress mechanisms. However, before an enthusiastic general acceptance, a number of other issues need to be resolved, both in Europe and in the rest of the world.

The contributions in this book are collected from leading authors who come not only from Europe but also from Asia and North and South America. In Europe, the contributors are covering different legal traditions and geographic locations, from North and West (Norway, Sweden, UK, Netherlands, and Belgium) to South and East (France, Italy, and Slovenia). The collected contributions were enriched by an exchange of views of the authors that took place in May 2019 at the Inter-University Centre Dubrovnik (IUC) within the Public and Private Justice (PPJ) series of seminars. The editors are grateful to the IUC and its staff, and in particular to Mr. Tomislav Kvesić, for their continuing support to high-quality, professional, and academic debates.

The original ideas and the first drafts of the chapters in this book date from pre-COVID-19, but most of the editing and production work happened when the pandemic was at its peak. While this certainly affected the speed of the process, it also demonstrated that new, innovative approaches to the way courts and judges deal with challenges of mass harm are sorely needed. In this sense, we believe that the pandemic made this book even more interesting and topical.

As editors, we would like to thank a number of people who helped in the production and editing of the present volume. Our gratitude goes in particular to Mr. Randolph W. Davidson and Mr. Edward Frisken for their help in revising the chapters of the non-native English speakers. Dr. Marko Bratković and Mr. Juraj Brozović provided valuable editing assistance. We also express our gratitude to the Springer team for their patience and support that helped us to continue and finalize our work on this project.

Zagreb, Croatia
Leuven, Belgium
February 2021

Alan Uzelac
Stefaan Voet

Contents

Editors and Contributors

About the Editors

Alan Uzelac Professor of Law at the University of Zagreb, Croatia, where he teaches Civil Procedure and Comparative Civil Procedure, Organization of the Judiciary and Alternative Dispute Resolution. He is Founding Member of the European Commission for the Efficiency of Justice (CEPEJ) in Strasbourg. He is Delegate in the UNCITRAL Working Group on Arbitration and Conciliation. He is Co-director of the Public and Private Justice seminar at the Inter-University Centre, Dubrovnik, Croatia. He is Director of the research project Transformation of Civil Justice Under the Influence of Global and Regional Integration Processes.

Stefaan Voet Associate Professor of civil procedure at the University of Leuven and a Host Professor at the University of Hasselt. He is Programme Affiliate at the CMS/Swiss Re Research Programme on Civil Justice Systems at the Centre for Socio-Legal Studies at the University of Oxford. He is Member of the Class Actions Exchange Network spearheaded by the Universities of Stanford, Oxford, and Tilburg and affiliate at the Class Action Lab of the University of Montréal. He is also a member of different working groups of the European Law Institute.

Contributors

Maria Astrup Hjort Faculty of Law, University of Oslo, Oslo, Norway

Maria José Azar-Baud University of Paris-Sud, Paris, France

Alexandre Biard Erasmus University Rotterdam, Rotterdam, The Netherlands

Laura Ervo Örebro University, Örebro, Sweden

Yulin Fu Peking University Law School, Beijing, China

Aleš Galič Faculty of Law, University of Ljubljana, Ljubljana, Slovenia

Christopher Hodges University of Oxford, Oxford, UK

Jasminka Kalajdzic Faculty of Law, University of Windsor, Windsor, ON, Canada

Xandra E. Kramer Erasmus Universiteit Rotterdam, Rotterdam, Netherlands
Universiteit Utrecht, Utrecht, Netherlands

Linda S. Mullenix University of Texas, Austin, TX, USA

Catherine Piché Faculty of Law, University of Montreal, Montreal, QC, Canada

Elisabetta Silvestri Department of Law, University of Pavia, Pavia, Italy

Jorg Sladič Faculty of Law, University of Maribor, Maribor, Slovenia

Ianika N. Tzankova Tilburg Law School, Tilburg, The Netherlands

Alan Uzelac Faculty of Law, University of Zagreb, Zagreb, Croatia

Ana Vlahek Faculty of Law, University of Ljubljana, Ljubljana, Slovenia

Stefaan Voet KU Leuven, Leuven, Belgium

Hermes Zaneti Jr Federal University of Espírito Santo, Vitória, Brazil

Part I
Introduction

Collectivization of European Civil Procedure: Are We Finally Close to a (Negative) Utopia?

Alan Uzelac and Stefaan Voet

Abstract Europe is unison in its rediscovered interest for collective and group litigation. New initiatives, legislative projects and model rules on collective redress emerge almost on a daily basis. In this chapter, the editors provide the background to this development and introduce the research presented in other chapters gathered in this book. Longstanding tradition of American class actions and their broad practical use are contrasted to the relatively recent European fascination with collective redress mechanisms and their limited reach. But, while incoherent and fragmented legislation on collective redress still does not produce spectacular results, many diverse initiatives demonstrate that the landscape of collective litigation is changing quickly. The trial and error approach that has so far characterized European attempts to introduce a workable collective redress system that is radically different from American-style class actions, did not so far produce a universal solution. However, a few important steps towards the Holy Grail of effective European collective redress have been made, both at the EU level, and at the level of its Member States. After a brief summary of the developments noted in the chapters which follow, the authors ask questions regarding the limits of collectivization of civil justice in a European context. Should the spread of collective procedures be embraced without reservations, or may it turn out to be a 'wrong trail'? The answer to this question depends on the ability to adjust collective redress mechanisms to urgent social needs and public purposes on one side, and to specific features of European legal systems on the other side. Recent global developments show that particular local circumstances play an important role in designing specific forms of collective redress. The enthusiasm about class and representative relief should take into account multiple risks entailed in the collectivization of civil procedure. Examples from Canada, Brazil and China indicate that local procedures may or may not work properly, but that none of them

A. Uzelac (✉)
Faculty of Law, University of Zagreb, Zagreb, Croatia
e-mail: auzelac@pravo.hr

S. Voet
KU Leuven, Leuven, Belgium
e-mail: stefaan.voet@kuleuven.be

A. Uzelac, S. Voet (eds.), *Class Actions in Europe*, Ius Gentium: Comparative Perspectives on Law and Justice 89, https://doi.org/10.1007/978-3-030-73036-9_1

can be simply exported to different environments with different social policies and institutional infrastructures.

1 Approaching the Elusive Target: The Rise of Collective Redress on the Old Continent

Can Europeans become Americans without American flaws? Can Americans export their virtues to Europe, free from specific flavours of their peculiar American character? In a nutshell, these two questions—asked in the context of collective legal procedures that involve a large number of people—summarize the contents of this book.

Ever since the global spread of Hollywood blockbuster movies featuring the successes and glories of judicial battles of lone fighters against collective injustice, Europe was infected with the virus of procedural collectivization. In the year 2000, Soderbergh's Erin Brockovich, a true story about a single mother that successfully initiated litigation against a powerful water polluter, and ultimately winning the largest settlement ever paid in a direct-action lawsuit in U.S. history, cashed in more money outside than inside America. Twenty years later, European filmmakers are still interested in the Agent Orange case, the story of several million people (including many American soldiers) who were exposed to toxic defoliant which was used during the Vietnam War.[1] The common denominator of these and many other mass harm situations, if litigated in the US, are class actions.

Class actions are generally considered to be a very specific American type of litigation, which partly spurred the interest for them in the rest of the world, and where they were largely felt as fascinating but strange. Difficult to define, they were described by the U.S. Supreme Court in a negative way, as 'an exception to the usual rule that litigation is conducted by and on behalf of the individual named parties only'.[2] In this feature of 'American civil procedural exceptionalism' (Marcus 2014) a representative acts on behalf of a large class, and the decision made in the process not only affects the representative and the sued party or parties, but also affects a whole class of other unnamed persons who do not directly participate in the process. In procedural terms, the latter persons are bound by the *res judicata* effect of the class action decision, although not being a party to the proceeding.

Such form of representative action for the benefit of a group or a class of unnamed litigants has been until recently unknown in Europe. But, the Old Continent, the cradle of Western legal civilization, over time developed a perplexed, love/hate relationship with class actions. For a long time class actions were considered incompatible with the European legal culture, so much that enforcing U.S. class action decisions was held incompatible with public policy. But, at the same time, the

[1] See for instance Agent orange, la dernière bataille, French-US documentary, 2020.

[2] *Wal-Mart v. Dukes*, 564 U.S. 338 (2011).

insufficiency of one-on-one civil litigation in the context of ever more complex and collective disputes triggered the original European attempts to introduce something similar to class actions, but at the same time different and truly European. The whole history of European collective redress development is marked by a pursuit of a such native European forms of class actions which would be powerful and effective, without being 'too American'. This book explores the fate of this pursuit.

In order to distinguish European forms of collective processes from their American counterpart, labels were changed. Instead of 'class actions', Europeans speak of 'collective redress' and 'representative litigation'. However, beyond such disguise, the fundamental structure remains the same, as well as the fundamental challenge: how to remain truly and authentically 'European' and at the same time reach at least a fraction of the efficiency of American class actions.

So far, the responses to this formidable challenge failed to produce spectacular results. As reported in 2014, in most European countries collective redress was a very much discussed topic, but in practice it resembled to the metaphor of 'squeaking mice' (Harsági and Van Rhee 2014). While in the U.S., collective litigation is ubiquitous, in many fields overtaking by importance (and even by volume) individual litigation, in Europe it has been largely an exception. However, things are moving at a fast pace, and some very recent developments seem to promise essential changes. Is Europe approaching the elusive target of effective collective litigation? This book explores the new developments, seeking to find whether the Holy Grail—a purely 'European' but still functional concept of collective redress that can be widely embraced and broadly used—is starting to emerge on the horizon.

2 Class Actions in Europe

For several decades, collective redress and class actions have been on the political and policy agenda of many European countries. There have always been three leagues. First, there are the self-proclaimed European frontrunners: jurisdictions that are supposed to have relatively long-standing class action procedures. The most notable examples are Portugal and the Scandinavian countries. Second, there are European countries that have adopted class action procedures more recently. Some of these regimes are limited to a specific sector, and are not of a universal or transsubstantive nature. Examples are Belgium, France, England and Wales and the Netherlands. Third and finally, one can distinguish countries which traditionally did not have class action procedures, in the sense of representative collective or group actions, save in very exceptional cases. This is for example the case in Eastern European countries. In other words, the class action landscape, on the Member States level, remains scattered and widely differing.

The European legislator also struggled for a long time with taking a clear position on collective redress and establishing a coherent legal framework. Over the years, piecemeal legislation was enacted, of which the effectiveness is limited. Reference can be made to the CPC (consumer protection cooperation) Regulation (which was revised in 2017)[3] and the 2009 Injunctions Directive.[4] In June 2013, and after a series of studies and preparatory policy documents, the European Commission published a Recommendation on common principles for injunctive and compensatory collective redress mechanisms in the Member States concerning violations of rights granted under Union Law.[5] The goal is not to harmonize the national systems, but to list some common, non-binding, principles relating both to judicial (compensatory and injunctive) and out-of-court collective redress that Member States should take into account when crafting such mechanisms.

In April 2018, the European Commission published its New Deal for Consumers package.[6] It aimed at stepping up the enforcement of EU law in a holistic way and securing more effective consumer redress in mass harm situations. It included a proposal for a Directive on representative actions for the protection of collective interests of consumers.[7] The latter intends to modernize and expand the scope of application of the 2009 Injunctions Directive. In December 2020, the new Directive of 25 November 2020 on representative actions for the protection of the collective interests of consumers was published.[8]

The new Directive will make it possible for Qualified Entities (such as consumer organisations and independent public bodies) to request injunctive and compensatory redress measures. The Directive will be the *leitmotiv* for the coming debate and development of European class actions.

This book wants to contribute to this forthcoming academic and policy debate by addressing collective redress from three different angels. The next part deals with the (still existing) critical perspectives on collective redress, followed by a part that looks at the many faces of collective litigation in Europe. The fourth and final part looks at the global perspectives of collective redress.

---

[3]Regulation 2017/2394 of the European Parliament and of the Council of 12 December 2017 on cooperation between national authorities responsible for the enforcement of consumer protection laws and repealing Regulation, 2017 O.J. (L 345) (EU).

[4]Directive 2009/22 of the European Parliament and of the Council of 23 April 2009 on injunctions for the protection of consumers' interests, 2009 O.J. (L 110) (EC).

[5]Recommendation of the European Commission of 11 June 2013 on common principles for injunctive and compensatory collective redress mechanisms in the Member States concerning violations of rights granted under Union Law, 2013 O.J. (L 201).

[6]https://ec.europa.eu/newsroom/just/item-detail.cfm?item_id=620435. Accessed 6 Nov 2020.

[7]European Commission (11 Apr 2018). Proposal for a Directive of the European Parliament and of the Council on representative actions for the protection of the collective interests of consumers, and repealing Directive 2009/22/EC. https://eur-lex.europa.eu/legal-content/EN/TXT/?uri=COM:2018:184:FIN. Accessed 6 Nov 2020.

[8]Directive 2020/1828 of the European Parliament and of the Council of 25 November 2020 on representative actions for the protection of the collective interests of consumers and repealing Directive 2009/22/EC, 2020 O.J. (L 409) (EU).

3 Critical Perspectives on Collective Redress

In the next chapter, entitled *Evaluating Collective Redress: Models, Evidence, Outcomes and Policy*, Christopher Hodges (Oxford University) asks two fundamental questions. What should the aims of collective redress be? Which mechanisms best deliver collective redress? The first is a normative question, and the second is an empirical question. The second question asks to what extent any particular technique or mechanism succeeds in satisfying the objectives set in the first question. According to Hodges, the answer to the first question is a matter of public policy and perhaps legal philosophy. The answer to the second can only be decided by empirical evidence. Hodges concludes that the empirical evidence indicates that a number of techniques are better than others. Current evidence is that mechanisms such as online independent ombudsmen and regulatory authorities with mass redress powers are particularly effective in delivering redress to consumers.

Another critical view on collective redress is expressed in the chapter *For the Defense: 28 Shades of European Class Actions*. Linda Mullenix (University of Texas) looks at the European collective redress developments from an American perspective. She states that throughout the twentieth century, virtually all European countries that had studied the American class action had rejected its implementation as a part of domestic law. In the early twenty-first century, however, several European countries reconsidered their longstanding antipathy to the American class action. In 2013, the European Commission launched its Recommendation for Injunctive and Compensatory Collective Redress Mechanisms. This was not a success. According to Mullenix, the 28 EU countries have developed a patchwork quilt of differing approaches to collective redress and largely have eschewed implementing procedural mechanisms that resemble the American class action rule, in efforts to preserve domestic cultural and legal norms, and to avoid American style class action abuses. Mullenix concludes that the overarching portrait that emerges from this chaotic assemblage of initiatives is one that is curiously cautious and decidedly non-revolutionary.

4 Many Faces of Collective Litigation: European Perspectives

The above conclusion is illustrated in the second part of this book that looks at the many faces of collective litigation in Europe.

In a fourth chapter of this book, *The Dawn of Collective Redress 3.0 in France?*, Maria José Azar-Baud (University of Paris—Sud) and Alexandre Biard (Erasmus University Rotterdam) describe the situation in France. France has limited experience when it comes to group actions. The instrument was formally adopted in 2014 after decades of debates and controversies. Subsequent developments have been patchy, and problems plaguing group actions remain multiple in practice. Azar-Baud and Biard conclude that the development of group actions in France has triggered several interesting evolutions: they have revitalised existing old procedural mechanisms, such as representative joint actions, and in parallel also indirectly led to the emergence of a myriad of new Legaltech actors attracted by an emerging mass litigation market, actors who use online tools and platforms for mobilising individual claimants and structuring mass claims.

In a fifth chapter, *From Injunction and Settlement to Action: Collective Redress and Funding in the Netherlands*, Xandra Kramer (Erasmus University and Utrecht University) and Ianika Tzankova (Tilburg University), explore the Dutch system. They start with the 2005 Dutch Collective Settlement Act which in a number of cases with a global outreach has proven to be effective. In 2019, a collective action procedure for compensation of damage was introduced. According to Kramer and Tzankova, a crucial aspect for the effectiveness of these collective redress mechanisms is the availability of funding. In particular, they pay attention to third party funding. Although highly controversial in Europe, they consider this kind of funding as a solution to enable inherently expensive collective actions.

In a sixth chapter, *Class Actions in Belgium: Evaluation and the Way Forward*, Stefaan Voet (KU Leuven) analyses the Belgian class action system. In 2014, Belgium introduced a consumer class action. In 2018, the procedure was expanded to disputes between SMEs and businesses. The chapter gives a description of Belgium's class action procedure (class action prerequisites, jurisdiction, opt-in or opt-out, procedure, redress and enforcement phase). It follows with an overview of the cases brought to date (nine in total). This (limited) case law allows to draw a number of conclusions about the pros and cons of the procedure. The chapter then draws attention to new and alternative ways to achieve collective redress (consumer dispute resolution (CDR) and regulatory redress). Voet concludes that the focus should be on exploring and optimising all options for mass harm situations and to connect these options so they can form an integrated dispute resolution framework.

In a seventh chapter, *Class Actions and Group Litigation—A Norwegian Perspective*, Maria Astrup Hjort (University of Oslo) looks at the class action system in Norway. Class actions were introduced with The Norwegian Dispute Act of 2005. Norwegian civil procedure already had several other types of collective litigation, but these procedures did not cover the catchment area for the class action rules. The chapter on class actions was a novelty when the act was passed and it represented something new in Norwegian civil procedure. The ability to decide on a legal question with effect for many individual claims reduces the costs of each claim and thus gives access to the courts for claims involving amounts or interests so small that they would otherwise not be brought as individual actions. Hjort gives an introduction to the Norwegian class action rules and discusses whether they have been a success or not.

In an eight chapter, *Group Actions in East-Nordic Legal Culture*, Laura Ervo (Örebro University) looks at the class action developments in Sweden and Finland. In Sweden, a system of group actions has been in force since 2003. Since then only 21 of these actions have been initiated. In Finland, public group actions, that can only be brought by the Consumer Ombudsman, are allowed by the 2007 Group

Action Act. To date, no such actions have been initiated. Thus, so far, Swedish and Finnish group actions have not been very successful. The question is why? In Sweden, there are proposals on how to make group actions more effective. In Finland, current discussions focus on expanding the scope of application. A frequent argument is the risk of US-style litigation that does not fit well into Nordic legal culture. Ervo tries to answer the question whether this is really true.

In a ninth chapter, *Rebooting Italian Class Actions*, Elisabetta Silvestri (University of Pavia), analyses the 2019 Italian statute providing for a new regulation of collective redress. The statute moved Italian group actions, both actions for compensatory relief (i.e. damages or restitution) and actions for injunctive relief, from the Consumer Code to the Code of Civil Procedure. According to Silvestri, this reflects a new vision of collective redress, namely a wider scope of application: no more references to consumers and users, but standing granted generically to bearers of 'homogenous individual rights', whether or not they are consumers or users. Furthermore, the new perimeter of class actions encompasses any claim arising out of both contract liability and tort liability, which signals another significant change aimed at designing class actions as general remedies. Yet, Silvestri concludes that nothing has changed as far as the procedure by which class members can join the action (via opt-in) is concerned. In spite of a few interesting features, the new rules sketch a procedure that is still cumbersome and excessively technical.

In a tenth chapter, *Challenges in Drafting and Applying the New Slovenian Collective Actions Act*, Aleš Galič and Ana Vlahek (University of Ljubljana), examine the 2017 Slovenian Collective Actions Act. The new legislation was perceived as an urgently needed piece of legislation and a top priority in guaranteeing access to justice. In the meanwhile, three collective actions have been filed with the courts under the new rules. Galič and Vlahek show the challenges faced and the decisions taken in drafting the act as well as the problems the parties and the judiciary have been facing in the application of new Act. They conclude that the Slovenian experience may serve as a model of the 'dos' and 'don'ts' for all drafters of such legislation in the EU Member States where collective redress has not yet been implemented.

Chapter 11, The *Lessons of Airfreight Cartel: Mechanisms of Coordination of Parallel Collective Lawsuits in Several Jurisdictions?*, is a case study by Jorg Sladič (European Faculty of Law, Ljubljana). Airfreight Cartel is a regulatory case being litigated before the Court of Justice of the EU. This case is an example of how to coordinate class actions in the United States, Canada, Australia, the Netherlands, the United Kingdom and France. The chapter assesses the stakes in coordination of parallel lawsuits in collective redress from a European point of view. According to Sladič, mechanisms of coordination of parallel lawsuits in collective redress are the cornerstone of any successful cross-border collective redress mechanism. These include mechanisms such as *forum non conveniens*, anti-suit injunctions, *lis pendens* and related actions doctrine. According to Sladič, a novel approach in coordination could be an international panel on cross-border collective redress.

In final chapter of this part, *Collective Redress in the EU: Will it Finally Come True?*, Alexandre Biard (Erasmus University Rotterdam) and Stefaan Voet

(KU Leuven) look at the new and forthcoming Directive for representative actions for consumers, which will allow Qualified Entities across the EU to collectively claim compensation in mass harm situations. Presented by the European Commission in April 2018 as part of its New Deal for Consumers package, the Directive intends to strengthen the enforcement of consumer rights and to ensure access to justice when large-scale damage arise. It also gives considerable leeway to the Member States when implementing the new rules into their national legislations. According to Biard and Voet, the effectiveness of the new EU instrument will therefore strongly depend on the procedural choices made at national levels. These issues are pivotal to ensure that the EU collective redress instrument fully meets its objectives.

5 Global Perspectives on Collective Redress

The fourth and final part looks at the global perspectives of collective redress.

In chapter 13, *The State of Reform in First and Second Generation Class Action Jurisdictions*, Jasminka Kalajdžić (University of Windsor) explores the state of reform in the first and second generation class action jurisdictions: the United States, Australia, Israel and Canada. Besides an outline of their respective class action procedures, she discusses the reform initiatives of the past 3 years in each of the four countries and explores common areas of concern as well as areas of divergence. Comparing and contrasting these reform efforts illustrates the evolution of class actions in these countries and provides useful insights for those studying and contributing to the development of newer collective redress systems.

In a 14th chapter, *Empirical Data and the Powerful Lessons Learnt about Class Actions in Quebec*, Catherine Piché (University of Montreal) evaluates the economic utility and effectiveness of class actions in Quebec based on empirical data obtained at the Class Actions Lab over a period of 25 years. The University of Montreal Faculty of Law's Class Actions Lab is conducting this study in the course of its 'Class Action Compensation Project'. The Project measures the end product of class action litigation, the value and benefit of this kind of litigation, and, incidentally, its costs as assumed by the parties and the system. This is the first Canadian study of its kind. Piché shows that class actions are instruments of compensation of class members, but that this compensation remains imperfect by way of the number of members compensated, the extent to which they are compensated and the exorbitant costs of bringing such actions.

In a 15th chapter, *Collective Redress in Brazil: Success or Disappointment?*, Hermes Zaneti Jr. (Federal University of Espírito Santo) recognizes that the Brazilian experience with class actions is one of the most developed in the civil law world. However, this experience is not only successful. The goal of this chapter is to sketch a broad and realistic view by looking at the good experiences (and by using some quantitative and qualitative data), but also by taking into account new trends and being aware of the evolution of the Brazilian system. Zaneti focuses on the emergence of aggregate litigation as a form of collective redress, in combination with Brazilian class actions, and what he calls 'the procedural law of disasters'.

In a 16th and final chapter, *Class Actions and Public Interest Litigation in China*, Yulin Fu (Peking Law School) looks at China's two major judicial reliefs against large-scale rights' infringement. On the one hand there is the 'mass private interest action' under which the victims of mass harm can opt in and join the class plaintiff in representative litigation. The plaintiffs are bound by the judgment. The victims who did not join the plaintiff's class may sue separately, but in separate litigation the class judgment is usually applied as a kind of 'model-litigation'. On the other hand, a new form of collective relief was created in 2012: 'public interest litigation'. In public interest litigation the procurator and some other legally authorized social organizations act as plaintiffs in cases of environmental harm and mass infringement of consumer rights. An individual consumer is not allowed to file a public interest lawsuit, in spite of the fact that the legally authorized plaintiff entities often lack motivation to file such claims.

6 A Wrong Trail? Some Concluding Remarks on the Risks of Collectivization

All developments described in this book give us right to conclude that a lot is going on, and even more is expected to happen in a very foreseeable future. Some invisible barriers in the European approach to collective redress are falling, or are just about to fall. Compensatory relief in collective mass claims has entered through the front doors of European legislators. Leading European academics gathered in the ELI-UNIDROIT project of model legislation for civil procedure included collective redress as a regular and standard feature for future national procedural codes.[9] But, how far can this process go, and should we applaud this development without reservations, accepting it only as a process that enhances access to justice and offers enforcement of claims that were previously regarded hopeless?

The answer to this question depends on the ability to adjust collective redress mechanisms both to pressing social needs and public purposes, and to specific features of European legal systems, which are otherwise much more prone to public enforcement of collective claims and public means for the resolution of mass harm situations.

Starting with the latter, Europe is not burdened with the deeply rooted American distrust of intrusive central government and its regulatory agencies (Kagan 2001). On the contrary, in most European countries there is a plentitude of administrative bodies authorized to deal with similar situations as the ones that occur in the American-style class actions. Maybe their effectiveness is limited, but the emergence

[9] https://www.unidroit.org/english/principles/civilprocedure/eli-unidroit-rules/200925-eli-unidroit-rules-e.pdf, Accessed 4 Dec 2020.

of collective redress in Europe can complicate the situation and could cause enforcement conflicts and/or an excuse for non-action. Further research on the juxtaposition of administrative and judicial means for enforcement of collective claims is needed, focusing on their coordination and interference. While collective redress mechanisms may be the best way to deal with particular issues, good administrative response may cover the others.

Where judicial response to collective claims is needed, it still remains to be seen where collective procedures are ultimately necessary. In the light of development of technology, advanced algorithms and the use of artificial intelligence provide unprecedented potential for making individual litigation cheaper, simpler and faster than ever before. Quick and easy access to online adjudication may provide an alternative to collective redress, especially for small value claims, such as consumer claims. A part of this potential, if only properly realized, could empower those litigants who would otherwise not be motivated to initiate judicial processes due to rational apathy or other reasons.

But why would collective redress schemes not be preferable to modern tech and ADR schemes, if they are faster and cheaper? Improvement of individual redress schemes is maybe worth the effort in itself, even if slightly more complex and expensive. Many of the often-cited grounds for the use of collective schemes are not motivated by their superiority, but by the weakness of conventional procedures used by national civil justice systems. If introducing collective procedures is a shortcut to bypass the clogged arteries of conventional litigation, would it not be better to undertake necessary reforms and address the very heart of the crisis? Class actions are not a panacea for the chronic diseases of our judiciaries. They can be useful, but they can also distract us from the real problems in the dispute resolution systems of our modern societies. So, instead of spending efforts and energy on the adoption of procedures developed for a different societal background, should we not focus on what is essential?

If we disregard the systemic objections, there may be another catch. Collective redress has found its broadest application in the common law world, and its driving forces were, as emphasized by its champions, in entrepreneurial lawyering, contingency fees and punitive damages (Klonoff 2015; Miller 2018). All these components seem to be missing in Europe. Even if we see some signs of their emergence, maybe we should not embrace them too eagerly. Some chapters in this book provide good examples why this is the case. Huge compensatory claims, aggressive law firms, explosive growth of new and underregulated litigation funding schemes and the erosion of the 'loser pays' rule are not necessarily the future which Europe should desire. Some, albeit not quite disinterested observers have already warned of 'very powerful indicators that all of the same incentives and forces that have led to mass abuse in other jurisdictions are also gathering force in the EU' (ILR 2017).

There are also other more structural problems. European judiciaries are quite diverse, but on the average, they are more prone to a positivistic way of thinking, and less trained to find innovative and flexible ways of dealing with complex situations, which arise in processing mass cases. The formation of a new generation of judges and training them to move away from their customary routines not only takes time, but also calls for a comprehensive change in attitude. It is feasible, but it is rather more probable that new ways of mass litigation will be given to old-school legal professionals, which is likely to result in a mismatch. European-style class actions have therefore rarely been very successful, especially when introduced in the more conservative judicial environments of Southern and Eastern Europe where modern case management techniques are only waiting to be put on the agenda. In an environment where individual actions need decades to be processed, it is hardly to expect that collective litigation will last any shorter. It is interesting, and somewhat paradoxical, that exactly those countries which otherwise experience inefficiency and problematic quality of their civil justice systems have expressed interest in the quick development of collective redress schemes, as demonstrated by the chapter of Galič and Vlahek in this book. For some, steering complex social issues to collective litigation in an inefficient court system can be compared to sending busses of clients to a restaurant that has a record of poor quality and slow service to individual guests.

All these doubts apply also to EU models of collective redress. So, before Brussels starts to cheerfully play the class action tunes, we need to ask more questions. Where is the proper balance between restrictive rules that keep collective litigation in the EU at its minimum, and the open regulatory opt-out invitation that may lead to an overflow of abusive litigation spilling over to the Old Continent? If some of us are lawyers, we may feel delighted by this prospect of expanding our business model. However, those who advocate a reasonable and fair system of dispute resolution that works for the benefit of citizens and businesses may have some doubts.

The potential issues of trans-border recognition of collective redress outcomes can also open interesting new horizons. Can we envisage that in the future EU-made class actions resulting in substantive awards of damages against American companies are enforced in the U.S., or that American class action decisions awarding punitive damages are regularly recognized in Europe? No matter whether Europe will steer its course towards a more comprehensive spectrum of collective litigation means (as it does at present), there will still be sufficient differences to cause frictions in transnational context, and we can only expect that arguments for and against recognition will become fuzzier.

But let us suppose that all these problems can be miraculously resolved by quick and comprehensive reforms (so rare in the past several centuries). What remains is the question of legitimacy of judicial collectivization. Maybe we can again disregard the fact that, according to EU Justice Scoreboard,[10] in at least one half of the Member States citizens and businesses do not have trust in their judiciaries, and assess their independence as fairly or very bad. However, if we accept that one of the goals of collective redress is the modification of behaviour affecting a large number of people, its function is eminently political (Scott 1975). For a policy-implementing judiciary (Damaška 1986), an impeccable record and high public level of support is

[10]https://ec.europa.eu/info/policies/justice-and-fundamental-rights/upholding-rule-law/eu-justice-scoreboard_en. Accessed 4 Dec 2020.

needed to allow it to make decisions with resolve and wisdom. In a political system that generally prefers that public policies are enforced by private means, it is easier to accept that judges play political roles. However, even there, as expressed by an influential judge, it is not unproblematic, since judicial legislation lacks democratic legitimacy, which is the essential glue that connects the fabric of a political community (Sumpton 2019).

In Europe, where Montesquieu's concept of judicial power is still resonating, acceptance of the potential political nature of judicial intervention may be even harder, just like the acceptance of the vision of economic liberalism according to which private plaintiffs will be the best representatives of public political goals. For that reason, in Europe, but also in other parts of the world (as showed by the chapters of Fu and Zaneti in this book) the crucial issue is who should have class action standing. Which individuals, public or private entities, organizations or bodies are/may be eligible to file collective suits? While in the U.S. the driving force behind class actions are private lawyers who, in a way, are understood as 'private attorneys general' (Miller 2018), this seems to be (still) unacceptable elsewhere. On the contrary, public attorney generals play a vital role in collective litigation in China and Brazil, and most European jurisdictions limit class action standing to selected associations and organizations.

The readers of this book will in the end decide for themselves the answer to the question indicated in the title of this book. Is collectivization of procedures in European civil justice systems desirable and inevitable? Is it a temporary fashion that threatens to jeopardize fundamental principles of European civil process? Is it going to spread, suppressing conventional litigation to a bare minimum, or will it continue to be a rare and ineffective road to justice? Is it a Holy Grail of a wrong trail? Progress or decay? Utopia or dystopia? We hope that we have provided sufficient food for thought based on a number of diverse examples from Europe and beyond. Factors that shape collective litigation are cultural, economic and political (Hensler et al. 2016), and they are quite diverse. Ultimately, the answer to these questions may depend on the ability to adjust collective redress mechanisms to urgent social needs in the context of specific features of each European legal system.

References

Damaška M (1986) The faces of justice and state authority. Yale University Press

Harsági V, van Rhee CH (2014) Multi-party redress mechanisms in Europe: squeaking mice? Intersentia

Hensler DR et al (2016) Class actions in context. how culture, economics and politics shape collective litigation. Elgar, Cheltenham and Northampton

ILR (2017) Institute for Legal Reform, 'The Growth of Collective Redress in the EU—A Survey of Developments in 10 Member States', March. 2017. www.instituteforlegalreform.com/uploads/sites/1/The_Growth_of_Collective_Redress_in_the_EU_A_Survey_of_Developments_in_10_Member_States_April_2017.pdf. Accessed 1 Dec 2020

Kagan R (2001) Adversarial legalism: the American way of law. Harvard University Press, Cambridge
Klonoff RH (2015) Why Most Nations Do Not Have U.S.-Style Class Actions?, Bloomberg BNA Class Action Litigation Report. https://news.bloomberglaw.com/class-action/why-most-nations-do-not-have-us-style-class-actions . Accessed 1 Dec 2020
Marcus R (2014) 'American Exceptionalism' in goals for civil litigation. In: Uzelac A (ed) Goals of civil justice and civil procedure in contemporary judicial systems. Springer, Cham, pp 123–141
Miller AR (2018) The American class action: from birth to maturity. Theor Inq Law 19:1–45
Scott K (1975) Two models of the civil process. Stanford Law Rev 27:937:950
Sumpton J (2019) Trials of the state. Law and the decline of politics. Profile Books, London

Alan Uzelac Professor of Law at the University of Zagreb, Croatia, where he teaches Civil Procedure and Comparative Civil Procedure, Organization of the Judiciary and Alternative Dispute Resolution. Founding Member of the European Commission for the Efficiency of Justice (CEPEJ) in Strasbourg. Delegate in the UNCITRAL Working Group on Arbitration and Conciliation. Co-director of the Public and Private Justice seminar at the Inter-University Centre, Dubrovnik, Croatia. Director of the research project Transformation of Civil Justice Under the Influence of Global and Regional Integration Processes.

Stefaan Voet Associate professor of civil procedure at the University of Leuven and a host professor at the University of Hasselt. Programme Affiliate at the CMS/Swiss Re Research Programme on Civil Justice Systems at the Centre for Socio-Legal Studies at the University of Oxford. Member of the Class Actions Exchange Network spearheaded by the universities of Stanford, Oxford and Tilburg and affiliate at the Class Action Lab of the University of Montréal. He is also a member of different working groups of the European Law Institute.

Part II
Critical Perspectives on Collective Redress

Evaluating Collective Redress: Models, Evidence, Outcomes and Policy

Christopher Hodges

Abstract This chapter asks two fundamental questions. What should the aims of collective redress be? Which mechanisms best deliver collective redress? The first is a normative question, and the second is an empirical question. The second question asks to what extent any particular technique or mechanism succeeds in satisfying the objectives set in the first question. The answer to the first question is a matter of public policy and perhaps legal philosophy. The answer to the second can only be decided by empirical evidence. The empirical evidence indicates that a number of techniques are better than others. Current evidence is that mechanisms such as online independent ombudsmen and regulatory authorities with mass redress powers are particularly effective in delivering redress to consumers.

1 The Objectives

Many academic or lobbying texts claim that class actions deliver the following benefits, and that these are the only relevant objectives: procedural economy in access to justice; upholding rights; and deterrence. On closer inspection, however, at least two of these objectives turn out not to be as fundamental as they are claimed to be, and they also obscure reality, thereby preventing a sound evaluation of the empirical question identified at the start.

It is suggested that the fundamental objectives are, in fact, the following:

- delivering collective redress when it is due;
- upholding the law;
- affecting future behaviour.

Research funding was provided by HM Government, the Swiss Reinsurance Company Limited and the European Justice Forum.

C. Hodges (✉)
University of Oxford, Oxford, UK
e-mail: christopher.hodges@csls.ox.ac.uk

A. Uzelac, S. Voet (eds.), *Class Actions in Europe*, Ius Gentium: Comparative Perspectives on Law and Justice 89, https://doi.org/10.1007/978-3-030-73036-9_2

Although there is not space to go into detail on these issues—which it is important to do—let us briefly examine them further.

1.1 Analysing the Objectives

1.1.1 Delivering Justice

The argument on procedural economy is ultimately about the economics of providing access to justice. The recognition is that individual claims may be too small for individual claimants rationally to bring them, given the costs in terms of finance, risk of liability for transactional costs, and investment of time. Therefore, it is logical that by aggregating individual small claims and processing them as a group, there should be savings. However, rational cost evaluation needs to take account of two other factors. First, is the intrinsic cost of the combined procedure still high because of innate complexities, such as in registering and validating all individual claims, case management of the entire group of cases, selecting common issues, processing test cases or preliminary issues, applying 'common' decisions to all individual cases, processing all individual cases? Costs would be likely to increase in those cases that involve different elements in individual cases, such as individual reliance on representations, individual causation, and individual extent of claimed and compensatable damages. There is also the issue of the cost of intermediaries (lawyers and funders) and the extent to which such costs have to be funded 'up front' and may be reclaimed at the end. Experience in Europe seems to be that, unlike in the USA, mass litigation does not settle after a case has been certified (with the possible exception of the Netherlands). Further, a comparison needs to be undertaken of the cost of class litigation against other available possible mechanisms. Almost no evaluations or comparisons have been undertaken on these wider bases.

So much talk has been about *access* to justice as justification for any mechanism. Too often, that slogan is used to justify the availability and use of a system from which certain intermediaries may earn rents. But the slogan obscures the fundamental policy objective that justice needs to be *delivered*. Surely the focus should be on having available, prioritising and using mechanisms that are proven to deliver justice to those who need it, with appropriate speed and cost. A system that does not *deliver* justice does not deserve respect—or to be allowed to continue. Too much debate about collective redress assumes a particular mechanism and process. There is widespread lack of vision and even knowledge about what options exist. The principal current options used in Europe are outlined below, together with findings on comparative evaluation.

1.1.2 Upholding the Law

People need to have confidence that the rules are applied fairly to everyone, without distortion through bribery, favouritism, or bias. That is the role of sports referees, judges, police, and regulators everywhere. It is the basis of how humans can sustain cooperative interaction of any kind, whether social or commercial. A level playing field has to exist, which means that those who are responsible for the playing field and keeping the game fair must act effectively and impartially in keeping the field and the game fair and level. The confidence of players and observers will only be sustained if that is seen to happen.

In safety-critical industries such as civil aviation, the concept that the rules must be seen to be observed and that consequences will follow if they are not is vital to achieving the engagement of all actors and is known as 'just culture'.[1] European Union legislation defines 'just culture' as meaning[2]

> a culture in which front line operators or others are not punished for actions, omissions or decisions taken by them that are commensurate with their experience and training, but where gross negligence, wilful violations and destructive acts are not tolerated.

Just culture draws a line between acceptable and unacceptable behaviour based on motivation. 'A wilful violation is not acceptable. An honest mistake is.'[3] Standards of behaviour require professional competence, openness, sharing, and taking responsibility for one's mistakes by correcting them and improving.[4] Critically, a 'just culture' complements and supports an 'open culture' which requires a complete absence of blame. There must be a just culture—i.e. accountability and appropriate consequences to improve safety—but there must be no blame. If there is blame, people will fear unfair consequences, and they will not share information.[5] People will not volunteer information if they fear that they might be criticised, blamed, ostracised, sanctioned or subject to retaliation whether by colleagues, employers, regulators, journalists, friends or family.[6] This policy is set out in the EU legislation:

> The sole objective of safety investigations should be the prevention of future accidents and incidents without apportioning blame or liability.[7]

[1]Dekker (2007).

[2]Commission Regulation (EU) No 691/2010 of 29 July 2010 laying down a performance scheme for air navigation services and network functions and amending Regulation (EC) No 2096/2005 laying down common requirements for the provision of air navigation services, Art. 2(k).

[3]Dekker (2007), p. 15.

[4]McCune et al. (2011), p. 195.

[5]Dekker (2007), p. 103: 'The sheer threat of judicial involvement is enough to make people think twice about coming forward with information about an incident that they were involved in.'

[6]Dekker (2007), p. 103; Helmreich (1999), pp. 39–43; McCune et al. (2011).

[7]Regulation (EU) No 996/2010, Recital 4. Even in 1994, it was provided that a safety recommendation shall in no case create a presumption of blame or liability for an accident or incident: Directive 94/56/EC, Art. 10.

> The civil aviation system is based on feedback and lessons learned from accidents and incidents which require the strict application of rules of confidentiality in order to ensure the future availability of valuable sources of information. In this context sensitive safety information should be protected in an appropriate way.[8]
>
> The civil aviation system should equally promote a non-punitive environment facilitating the spontaneous reporting of occurrences and thereby advancing the principle of 'just culture'.[9]
>
> The information provided by a person in the framework of a safety investigation should not be used against that person, in full respect of constitutional principles and national law.[10]

This open and just culture approach is increasingly being adopted by businesses and regulators in other sectors, as indicated below. Studies have supported the need for an absence of fear in situations varying from medical practice[11] to cleaning businesses.[12] It is critical that a just culture has to apply *throughout* the industry, in *all of* the regulatory, professional accreditation, commercial and social relationships. A risk of blame arising in any one of those relationships will make individuals fear to share information and thus risks the entire enterprise of sharing and learning. The approach must also apply *constantly*: the goal is to continuously ask oneself and others, and review all relevant information, to maintain and improve performance.[13]

Maintaining a just culture and a fair, level playing field means that consequences should occur when things go wrong but not that the only consequence is to blame an individual player who is supposed to have been a wrongdoer. If time is taken to identify the root cause of a problem, it may be concluded that the fundamental problems lie with the field, the system or other players, and that future risk will only be reduced if wider and more sophisticated action is taken than imposing a financial or liberty sanction on the proximate causer. This approach presents a challenge to some societies and lawyers who are familiar with the concepts of blame and punishment. Yet the scientific evidence is clear: cultures that rely on blame will be impeded from learning or improving their performance. So the rules need to be upheld, but how that is done is critical.

1.1.3 Affecting Behaviour

The two main categories of legal thought on how law affects future behaviour are private enforcement (encompassing tort law and civil procedure) and public law (administration and regulation). Orthodox theory in both these categories is based on

---

[8]Regulation (EU) No 996/2010, Recital 22.

[9]Regulation (EU) No 996/2010, Recital 24.

[10]Regulation (EU) No 996/2010, Recital 25.

[11]Gallagher et al. (2003), p. 1001; Studdert et al. (2010), p. 351; Professional Standards Authority (2018).

[12]Sykes et al. (2014), p. 16.

[13]The aviation industry accepts living with risk, so aims to maintain *performance* and not explicitly for *safety*.

the *assumption* that enforcement of law through imposing financial consequences (fines or damages) and public shaming (being adjudged to be in the wrong) increases deterrence. It is further assumed that deterrent sanctions affect future behaviour and avoid wrongdoing. The underlying objective, however, is to affect behaviour. It is not deterrence. Deterrence is one of several possible tools, the effectiveness of each of which needs to be evaluated by empirical evidence.

The most influential theory has been that all people who injure others are rational cost-avoiders, make decisions by calculating costs and benefits, and will be influenced in all future decisions (especially in choosing to avoid causing harm to others) by knowledge of the *ex post* imposition of financial or other sanctions on them or others.[14] Many objections have been tabled to that theory, not least from the findings of behavioural psychology on the reasons why human beings act or fail to act. For example, behavioural studies suggest that a key tenet that increasing a penalty will exert greater deterrent effect is incorrect.[15] The concept of deterrence carries an assumption that imposition of a sanction (such as the cost of remedying the harm caused) will *completely* prevent similar behaviour or harm in future: there is little empirical evidence for that assumption. Empirical evidence has been emerging over some decades that deterrence is an assumption that has at best questionable validity and in an extensive number of situations is virtually non-existent as a phenomenon. Further, imposing deterrent sanctions can adversely affect compliance.[16]

Classic economic theory that behaviour is affected by deterrent financial sanctions has now been eclipsed by extensive behavioural psychology on how people *actually* make decisions.[17] The scientific evidence illuminates the reasons why people and (public or private) organisations take decisions and act. The evidence is that individuals are *not* rational cost calculators and that actions are the result of many possible influences, biases, emotional impulses, or organisational factors and cultures, in which fear of the imposition of sanctions usually has little preventative effect.[18]

Decisions are taken for many reasons, and the supposed fear of legal penalties may have very limited or no effect on behaviour.[19] Deterrence theory struggles to explain how harm can be avoided where it is caused by complex interactions between multiple people, systems and cultures. Medical practice was for some time subjected to the assumption that training and punishment would eliminate all

[14]Leading texts are Pigou (1920), Allingham (1999), Archer and Tritter (2001), Becker (1968), Stigler (1971).

[15]Beres and Griffith (2001), Ehrlich (1996), Greenwood et al. (1994), p. 16. But see Kessler and Levitt (1999).

[16]Accessible books are Ariely (2008), Banaji and Greenwald (2016), Barrett (2017), Bazerman and Tenbrunsel (2011), Haidt (2012), Heffernan (2011), Kahneman (2011).

[17]Kahneman (2011) and Barrett (2017).

[18]For histories of individuals involved in corporate crime, see Soltes (2016) and Gentilin (2016).

[19]For a review see Hodges (2015a).

medical error (the 'perfectibility' model).[20] Emphasis on the incompetent doctor shifts the emphasis away from the more fundamental questions about systemic approaches to mishaps.[21] Leape noted that reliance on inspection as a mechanism of quality control was discredited long ago in industry,[22] because the technique is reactive. Product regulatory systems typically rely on continuous control and monitoring of design, manufacture, distribution and marketing functions by means of a permanent quality system.

The typical pattern of medical mishaps is not caused by a sole individual.[23] Safety issues and related incidents are often the result of complex local, organisational and system-wide processes, with similar events recurring repeatedly in different places across the healthcare system. The purpose of safety investigation is to understand the patterns of causality that produce harm, and to make recommendations that can address those causes across the healthcare system in order to improve the safety of all patients.

The vast majority of safety incidents are associated with inadvertent or unintentional errors on the part of caring and committed staff. These errors are typically provoked by poorly designed systems, equipment, or work contexts.[24]

The changes that may need to be made in organisations, procedures, ways of working, and social arrangements are many and varied. Assuming that all necessary changes will follow from imposing sanctions is an attitude that is uninformed by behavioural psychology and the culture of organisational groups. The United Kingdom's National Health Service (NHS) has accepted that imposing sanctions on an organisation is of little use and deflects scare resources needed for healthcare. What is needed is a 'no blame' open and just culture.[25]

The current author undertook an extensive review of the research evidence that either public or private enforcement produces deterrence.[26] He found many assertions or assumptions that deterrence exists, and a number that then tried to calculate assumed effects, but of the few studies that attempted to measure *whether* deterrence exists as a phenomenon, they add up to very little evidence that any effect exists.

Extensive evidence now exists that 'regulating through culture' offers the most effective way of affecting future behaviour, from areas as mixed as aviation safety (see above), workplace safety,[27] regulation of water pricing, regulation of essential

[20]Leape (1994), p. 851.

[21]Mulcahy and Rosenthal (1998), p. 8.

[22]Leape (1994), p. 851; citing Berwick (1989) and Deming (1982).

[23]Department of Health (2016), p. 21.

[24]Ibid, 25, 26, quoting National Advisory Group on the Safety of Patients in England (2013).

[25]See Department of Health (2015), Cm 9113; *NHS England Serious Incident Framework* (2015), Department of Health (2016), NHS England and NHS Improvement (2019).

[26]Hodges (2015a).

[27]Webster and Bolt (2016), RR1082; Blanc (2018).

services,[28] and financial services.[29] The Organisation for Economic Co-operation and Development (OECD) is following the same evolution of thought.[30] The UK's Water Services Regulation Authority (Ofwat) has inserted requirements on purpose, strategy, values and culture into its licence conditions.[31] Furthermore, commercial organisations that are based on an ethical culture can produce extremely good financial performance.[32]

The current author's evaluation of the enforcement policies adopted by many UK public regulatory authorities found that deterrence is rarely mentioned and instead other objectives and approaches are adopted.[33] Only a small number of public authorities aim to respond to wrongdoing by imposing financial penalties based on a theory of deterrence—and their results are not impressive. In contrast, many other regulators aim to affect future behaviour, and to do so by differentiating between those who break rules based on their motivations. In most cases, people and companies aim to obey the law, and their future compliance can be improved by being supported to do so. Imposing deterrent penalties on them will reduce future compliance rather than improve it. In some cases, people deliberately aim to break the law, in which case they deserve hard enforcement, but again deterrence will have limited effect on their future behaviour.

All of this thinking is based on extensive evidence from the findings of behavioural science and empirical studies on how people behave in groups. It overturns many theoretical assertions of legal philosophy and economic theory. Regulators are increasingly realising that the most effective results will be achieved where businesses adopt ethical cultures.[34] This is science, not assertion. Given the scientific findings, it is then necessary to re-evaluate the mechanisms and techniques that are needed to deliver the outcomes of delivering justice, upholding the rules, and affecting future behaviour. This may involve fundamental reforms in legal thinking and the mechanisms of historical legal systems.

1.2 Criminal Enforcement: Beyond Deterrence

A critical historical choice occurred in the United States in the middle of the twentieth century when private enforcement was encouraged over public enforcement. The drivers have been traced to academic preference for private enforcement

28Essential Services Commission of South Australia (2018).

29DeNederlandscheBank (2015) and G30 (2018); Financial Conduct Authority (2018).

30OECD (2010, 2013, 2014, 2015), G20/OECD (2015), OECD (2017), OECD, KDI (2017).

31Ofwat (2019).

32Godart et al. (2014); Sisodia et al. (2014) and EY (2016).

33Hodges (2015a). For government publications see Hodges (2016a), Committee on Standards in Public Life (2016), Scottish Government (2016).

34Hodges and Steinholtz (2017).

as a means of 'disciplining' large, diffuse investment markets[35] and a cultural and ideological preference for 'adversarial legalism'.[36] The critical reform of Rule 23 of the Federal Rules of Civil Procedure in 1966 was accompanied by, 'Much greater uncertainty [than the academic proposal] that the class action should be a private, market-driven supplement to governmental regulation'.[37] Yeazell's analysis was that[38]

> The courts have sanctioned the purely entrepreneurial litigator, perhaps because they fear the redistribution of political and economic power that might result from a whole-hearted embrace of the possibilities inherent in the concept.

The current rule thus embodies both the individualistic idea of a voluntary joinder device and the more expansive vision of a privately funded vindicator of legal rights. But by blending the two visions it denies to each the integrity of its conception. Interest, the crucial concept in the present rule, stands with one foot in each world; Mill and Burke would both recognise their ideas, though neither would be satisfied with their embodiment.

The American theory and practice of both regulatory and private enforcement remains stuck in a paradigm of deterrence, driving large fines, incentivisation for corporations to create large internal compliance systems by offering significant reductions in penalties, incentivisation of owning up, and incentivisation of whistleblowing. However, convincing empirical evidence that either external or internal autocratic command and enforcement systems is effective has yet to be produced. Private enforcement achieved political success in achieving the 1960s idealism of racial educational equality,[39] in which class actions operated as 'a form of political expression' and enabled 'a minority to petition for redress of grievances'[40] precisely because the public enforcement or any other mechanism was lacking or ineffective.

Elsewhere, ideas about regulation, compliance, enforcement and deterrence are all moving on. Many UK regulatory authorities seek to work *with* businesses, rather than to blame and shame them, still less to punish them. Serious sanctions will, of course, continue to be imposed on criminals—those who intend to break the rules, especially if for their own benefit, as opposed to people who make honest mistakes. The idea that imposing sanctions affects future behaviour has been significantly undermined by empirical evidence and in theorising.[41] These changes are of major significance and lessons need to be learned and applied.

---

[35]Kalven and Rosenfield (1941), p. 684, 687.

[36]Kagan (2001) and Farhang (2010).

[37]Yeazell (1987), p. 239.

[38]Ibid.

[39]Farhang (2010).

[40]*NAACP* v. *Button* 371 US 415 (1963) at 429 and 431.

[41]Hodges and Voet (2018), ch 7.

1.3 The Importance of Empirical Evidence

Any claim that any mechanism succeeds in achieving its objectives can only be objectively evaluated by empirical evidence, not by assertion. If there is more than one available mechanism, all options should be compared and evaluated. What is the evidence?

Two major reviews of the empirical evidence from the USA were published in 2015 that painted a picture of the reality of the US private enforcement system that was not only far from the idealistic image but also revealed its considerable failures to deliver justice or regulate markets. Coffee showed that different types of class actions had risen and fallen over time,[42] following fashions as entrepreneurs developed a new area and were then cut back by other forces. The current author reviewed the evidence on a sequence of features of US class actions:[43]

- Selection of case types strongly favoured those in which large money damages would be paid in settlements, especially securities cases, ignoring cases that had little monetary value but high social relevance.
- Transactional costs were consistently high, especially in claimant attorneys' fees as an incentive for them to pursue private enforcement and so avoid the need for public enforcement.
- Overall economic costs to all parties were high.
- Payments to individual claimants were low, compared with total settlement sums and reduced by lawyers' fees.
- Settlements occurred in which merits appeared to play very limited relevance; in many cases researchers were unable to establish whether settled claims had merit or not.
- Forum shopping was a recognised phenomenon.

Concerns were voiced (whether justified or not) over conflicts of interest, and abuse had led to a series of reforms, such as the Class Action Fairness Act of 2005, the Private Securities Litigation Reform Act (PSLRA) of 1995, a shift to Multi-District Litigation (MDL), and a US Supreme Court led shift from litigation to private arbitration. Many consumer and labour cases, if they continue to exist, are now invisible. It appears to be unknown to what extent people bother to claim or there may be any effect of defendant behaviour. The effect of private, unregulated online dispute resolution options is unclear, but they only operate in limited consumer cases.

---

[42]Coffee (2015).

[43]*US Class Actions: Theory and Reality* EUI Florence working paper 2015/36 (ERC ERPL 14), http://hdl.handle.net/1814/36536; in German at http://hdl.handle.net/1814/46464. A shorter version is: Hodges (2016b). The number of sources is large but see especially Hensler et al. (2000).

2 Evaluating the Collective Redress Mechanisms in Europe

Hodges and Voet undertook an evaluation of the empirical evidence of the principal collective redress mechanisms from reports from scholars and lawyers across European states.[44] The main mechanisms are:

1. A court-based class, collective or representative mechanism, however defined.
2. A mechanism that commences with a criminal trial, after which a linked consecutive procedure deals with compensation (the *partie civile* or 'piggyback').
3. Compensation paid as a result of the intervention of a public regulatory authority (regulatory redress).
4. A collective alternative dispute resolution (ADR) mechanism, of which the dominant model is a consumer Ombudsman.
5. For personal injury claims, an administrative redress scheme.

These mechanisms are discussed individually below. In evaluating the mechanisms, the following criteria were applied:

1. ***Advice***. To what extent does the mechanism enable consumers to access advice before or during the processing of their complaint? To what extent also does the system provide advice to traders, especially small traders who may not be familiar with the law or dispute resolution options or processes, so as to achieve swift, cost-effective and fair resolutions?
2. ***Identification of infringement and harm***. How is a problem involving the occurrence of breach of law and/or damage identified?
3. ***Identification of people harmed and due redress***. Must individuals come forward, or can they be identified without coming forward?
4. ***Access***. To what extent is the mechanism user-friendly for consumers or claimants to access?
5. ***Cost to access***. What cost must a person who claims to have suffered harm pay, and fund, in order to access the process? Or is access free?
6. ***Triage***. To what extent does the mechanism act as a triage to prevent unmeritorious cases or unnecessary cases proceeding further? This may include, at one extreme, preventing fraudulent claims being advanced and, at the other extreme, swiftly resolving cases that should be resolved one way or the other.
7. ***Duration***. How long does the mechanism take from start to finish? How long does it take to resolve issues, from when they first arose (i.e. when damage occurred, before a claim was made) to final resolution?
8. ***Costs***. How much are the gross transactional costs of a collective procedure, and the standing costs of a process? Who bears the costs, both initially and finally?

[44] Hodges and Voet (2018).

9. ***Outcomes***. What is achieved? Are the outcomes the ones desired by the parties, the law, or society?
10. ***Compensation for loss: making whole***. Is a person who has suffered harm fully recompensed? How much of an award is lost in transactional costs, e.g. of intermediaries? Are extra emotional or other costs incurred and recompensed?
11. ***Changes in Behaviour***. Does the mechanism directly produce changes in systemic behaviour that reduces the incidence or future risk of non-compliance with the law? To what extent does the mechanism, therefore, act as a regulatory mechanism?

The principal findings of the study were as follows.

First, the EU rejected the US model of maximising private enforcement in favour of a more balanced (public–private) approach involving safeguards.

Second, there has been extensive experimentation by EU Member States in collective action models for damages. The current position would present a huge challenge for harmonisation. There is no coherence in national class action laws, none of which correspond to the European Commission's 2013 blueprint. Each national system is tailored to domestic need, often uninfluenced by the Commission's blueprint, and the overview is of piecemeal development, which is uncontrolled.

Third, there has been a shift in the techniques by which redress is delivered. The 'old technology' of private litigation has been superseded in some Member States by a highly effective 'new technology'[45] involving regulators and consumer Ombudsmen. These techniques have been approved by the United Nations Conference on Trade and Development (UNCTAD) and deserve to be widely adopted.[46]

Fourth, the empirical evidence clearly shows that the regulatory redress and consumer Ombudsman models—especially where those two are combined—score far more highly than the collective litigation model across the criteria. The piggy-back technique is a logical development that attempts to sequence public and private enforcement so as to achieve some efficiency of process. But that first step has been eclipsed in efficiency and effectiveness by the two other techniques. Regulatory redress fuses private enforcement entirely into public enforcement. ADR in its traditional forms of arbitration or mediation can only deliver *individual* redress, absent a Dutch-style ability for a court to approve *ex post* a collective settlement. Both the Ombudsman model and the regulatory model, especially where they operate in a parallel coordinated fashion, deliver significantly more functions than just dispute resolution, but also act as effective mechanisms to support fair and competitive markets.

---

[45]This terminology of old and new technology was first used, to our knowledge, by Derville Rowland of the Central Bank of Ireland at the Law Reform Commission's annual regulatory conference, Dublin, 2016.

[46]UNCTAD (2016), ch 6 and 11, http://unctad.org/en/PublicationsLibrary/webditcclp2016d1.pdf. Accessed 10 February 2020.

2.1 Class Actions

A wide range of different mechanisms exist but all of them involve trying to process multiple individual claims by imposing some simplifications, such as by selecting common issues or illustrative lead cases that can be determined first, and the decisions applied to all the other cases.

The policy debates at EU and national levels have all been difficult, as they have sought to achieve a balance between two opposing concerns. One objective is to create a collective judicial mechanism for delivering mass redress to consumers, especially where the effects involve many consumers and small individual sums. The other objective is at the same time to avoid creating a system that could be captured by legal and financial intermediaries, which would result in unfounded or excessive claims that would risk 'defendants having to enter into blackmail settlements'. The outcome of trying to balance these opposing objectives has produced a different model in almost every country, as different combinations of procedures and safeguards emerge from the political law-making processes.

It is easy to get lost in the detail of comparing the differences in the design of different national class action models, and the sometimes tortuous histories of cases that are brought. Accordingly, it is easy to miss the simple basic point that virtually none of the mechanisms work well. The overwhelming impression from reading the cases is that they take years, cost a lot of money, sometimes deliver little tangible results to deserving claimants, whilst intermediaries often get rich. In many countries, there are few cases. An example is England and Wales, where the existence of three large group cases at the time of this writing,[47] whose lengthy journeys through the courts attract considerable publicity, can obscure the fact that many other mass redress cases are resolved extremely quickly by Ombudsmen and regulators on a regular basis. A now infamous case is the Deutsche Telekom action in Germany that led to the introduction of the KapMuG[48] procedure. Individual actions started in 2003 were not resolved 16 years later. Lawyers in Italy and Poland appear to start class actions enthusiastically, but only perhaps half survive certification. In Italy, litigation takes perhaps a decade in any event.

The interesting exception is the Netherlands, where public policy encourages settlement, and the 2005 Collective Settlements Act provides for settlement-only class actions.[49] Nine large cases were dealt with by this means between 2006 and the present although they took some time and the legal costs were considerable.

---

[47] Against Google on behalf of 4 million customers over alleged misuse of users' data, against Mastercard on behalf of some 46 million cardholders over charges, and against Lloyds TSB bank by 5000 shareholders over misleading statements in the acquisition of HBOS (the case was dismissed in December 2019).

[48] Capital Market Test Case Proceedings. Federal Law Gazette 2005 I (no 50), 2437.

[49] Dutch Civil Code, Arts. 7:900–7:910 and Dutch Judicial Code, Arts. 1013–1018. See Asser (2008), p. 17; Fleming and Kuster (2012), p. 286; Tzankova and Lunsingh Scheurleer (2009), p. 149; van der Heijden (2010), p. 197.

2.2 *Criminal-Civil Piggyback*

This technique adds a compensation process onto the end of a criminal process, thereby achieving some efficiency by aiming at a single fact-finding process and avoiding delay after the end of a successful criminal process in achieving civil compensation for those harmed. The piggyback achieves consecutive public then private enforcement, in which, it may be noted, the state's process takes precedence.

However, the disadvantages are that criminal proceedings must be brought, be against defendants with adequate financial resources, and be successful against defendants with adequate financial resources. The criminal judge must also be required to process the civil cases, which seems to be the case only in Belgium[50] and France, and it appears that in many other European states judges use their discretion to avoid accepting the damages cases. In Germany and the Netherlands, for example, a private party can become a formal party to the criminal proceedings only if allowed by the judge.

There have been some successful cases, such as in Belgium, where criminal judges have appointed a civil judge as a 'special master' to handle the damages cases. The cases still take a long time.

2.3 *Regulatory Redress*

Regulatory redress occurs where redress is ordered by, or brought about by the intervention of, public enforcers.[51] The redress element is typically just one of a number of elements that the regulator aims to resolve: cessation of breaches, root cause analysis of the problem, identification of actions necessary to avoid repetition or reduce risk, implementation of such actions by all relevant actors, payment of redress or other remedial activity (repair of the environment or a payment to an environmental charity), imposition of any relevant sanction(s), ongoing monitoring to ensure that actions are implemented and if further alterations are needed. A regulator would have power to ensure that each of these steps are taken, such as power to order or obtain an injunction, and power to order redress to be paid or to start a collective action.

The overriding objectives are to achieve resolution of *all* relevant aspects of wrongdoing efficiently and swiftly, in comprehensive holistic packages. Thus, the public and private law aspects of a problem should all be resolved together. The experience of regulators that operate in this fashion is that comprehensive solutions are in practice *negotiated* without the need for drawn-out court cases. Both defendants and regulators seek acceptable 'total peace' resolutions. Outcomes can therefore be achieved strikingly swiftly and with low transactional costs for all. Claimants

[50]Code of Criminal Procedure, Arts. 63, 67. Voet (2013), 280–281.

[51]Hodges and Voet (2018), ch 5.

Fig. 1 Market distortion due to illicit gains and losses

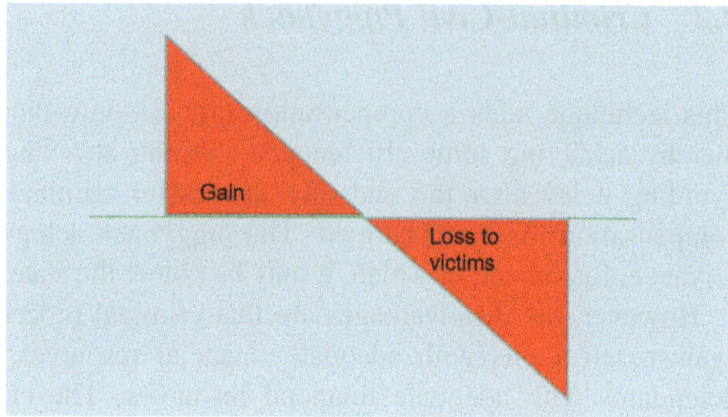

should receive 100% of their legally compensable losses, without deduction for the costs of intermediaries: they would typically not need intermediaries or have to take any or much action to lodge or verify a claim. The mechanism of course requires safeguards to protect the independence and disinterested actions of the public enforcement agencies, as with all their activities.

The change in approach by regulators and government has arisen from the realisation that it is a function of a market regulator to ensure that the market is maintained as a competitive level playing field. Illicit gains and losses distort the market, as shown in the diagram above (Fig. 1),[52] which need to be rectified. That requires public market authorities to ensure that redress is paid, as a distorted market would otherwise continue for perhaps years. Further, the promotion of swift resolution is good for businesses and their customers.

The nature of the redress elements of regulators' powers differ,[53] but the experience is consistent: swift, effective, full, cost-efficient redress, coupled with wider actions to achieve future fair market behaviour. Regulatory redress has been delivered by the Consumer Ombudsman of Denmark,[54] the Consumer Ombudsman of Finland,[55] the Italian regulatory authority for electricity gas and water (AEEGSI),[56] the Italian Central Bank,[57] and the Central Bank of Ireland. The Directorate-General for Competition (DG COMP) of the European Commission has agreed redress instead of a fine in rare cases, such as one involving Deutsche Bahn.[58]

---

[52]Hodges (2011), p. 383, Figure 1, adapted.

[53]A categorisation is at Hodges (2015b), p. 829. See Department for Business Innovation & Skills (2015).

[54]Hodges and Voet (2018), pp. 160–166.

[55]Ibid, 166–168.

[56]Ibid, 170–173.

[57]Ibid, 175–176.

[58]Press release: European Commission (2013). The company proposed to pay railway companies that it does not own a one-time retroactive refund of 4% of their latest annual traction current invoice, and to provide the Commission with the necessary data to assess whether the price levels charged under the new pricing system would lead to a margin squeeze.

In the UK, the technique has been used regularly by the financial regulator since 2000, and is now standard practice for the Financial Conduct Authority,[59] the regulators for energy,[60] communications, water, gambling,[61] and even the Competition and Markets Authority. Since 2015, all UK enforcers of consumer protection laws have been authorised to impose or agree 'Enhanced Consumer Measures' as part of a toolbox including traditional criminal measures and civil measures, with the objectives of delivering redress, improving compliance, and increasing information to consumers to enable exercise choice.[62] These powers give authorities considerable flexibility but are subject to requirements, such as that measures must be just, reasonable and proportionate.

An example of the change in policy is that of the UK energy regulator Ofgem. Before 2010, it used fines and ignored redress. Since then (Fig. 2), its fines have generally decreased, but it has reached agreements with operators in relation to their implementation of behavioural changes and voluntary payment of considerable sums in redress. Many of these cases involve overcharging, so implementing repayments to customers can be done in the next month's bill. In more complex cases, the criteria for implementing redress schemes can be agreed. The Financial Services Authority agrees schemes regularly, both under its statutory powers and through voluntary agreements if activities are technically outside its remit, and the schemes are usually operated by the Financial Ombudsman Service.

The focus on consumers and the shift in regulatory approach has been met with changes by businesses. Companies in the communications sector have agreed a scheme, approved by the regulator Ofcom, under which they pay voluntary compensation to customers for service quality events: loss of service (£8 per day after two days), delayed provisioning (£5 per day) and missed appointments (£25 per incident).[63]

Regulatory redress is almost by definition a procedure that should deliver redress automatically to all those who have been harmed. This transcends the opt-in or opt-out debate: it demonstrates that it is acceptable for a wide power to be exercised by a trusted public authority, in circumstances in which arguments about possible

[59]Financial Services and Markets Act 2000, s 404 [consumer redress scheme] and s 404F(7) [single firm scheme].

[60]Energy Act 2013, s 144 and Sch 14. In the financial year 2015–2016, nearly £43 million was secured as a result of Ofgem enforcement investigations.

[61]Regulatory systems that include the grant of licences to actors such as utilities or gambling enable licence conditions to be amended to require or approve of redress packages.

[62]Consumer Rights Act 2015, Sch 5, Art 14. The enforcers covered are: Competition and Markets Authority, Trading Standards Services in Great Britain, Department for Enterprise, Trade and Investment in Northern Ireland, Civil Aviation Authority, the Northern Ireland Authority for Utility Regulation, Ofcom, Ofwat, Ofgem, Phonepay Plus, The Information Commissioner, Office of Rail Regulation, the Financial Conduct Authority, community enforcers under the Injunctions Directive, Secretary of State for Health, Department of Health, Social Services and Public Safety in Northern Ireland.

[63]Ofcom (2017) and Communications' Providers' Voluntary Code of Practice for an Automatic Compensation Scheme (2017).

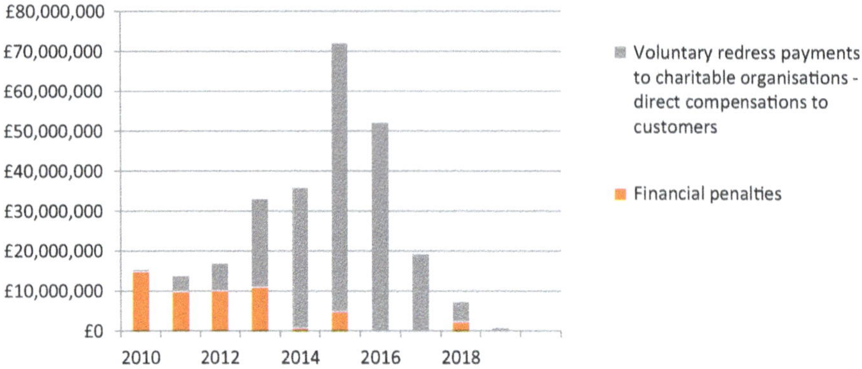

Fig. 2 Ofgem financial penalties and voluntary redress payments by companies 2010–2018

conflicts of interest or possible abuse do not arise in countries where public authorities are trusted, thereby avoiding concerns on whether any private intermediary might give rise to concern.

A *cy-près* equivalent also automatically arises. The energy and water regulators often agree that a company will make payments to charities where difficulties exist in making individual compensation payments. The Environment Agency agrees (technically as civil sanctions) that polluting companies should make payments to relevant charities that maintain areas (forests, rivers, coastlines, neighbourhoods) that have been polluted.

The European Commission's original proposal for revision of the Regulation on Cooperation between Member States for Consumer Protection (the CPC Regulation) was to give consumer enforcers across the EU a full regulatory redress power, but this was watered down in the legislative process. The 2017 CPC Regulation contains the following powers for consumer enforcement authorities:

(a) the power to *seek or obtain commitments* from the trader responsible for the infringement covered by this Regulation to cease that infringement;[64]
(b) the power to *receive* from the trader, on the trader's initiative, additional *remedial commitments* for the benefit of consumers that have been affected by the alleged infringement covered by this Regulation, or, where appropriate, to seek to obtain commitments from the trader to *offer adequate remedies to the consumers* that have been affected by that infringement;[65]

[64]Regulation (EU) 2017/2394 of the European Parliament and of the Council of 12 December 2017 on cooperation between national authorities responsible for the enforcement of consumer protection laws and repealing Regulation (EC) No 2006/2004, Art. 9.4(b).

[65]Ibid, Art. 9.4(c).

(c) where applicable, the power to *inform, by appropriate means, consumers* that claim that they have suffered harm as a consequence of an infringement covered by this Regulation about *how to seek compensation* under national law;[66]
(d) in a cross-border situation, one competent authority may request another to take necessary enforcement measures, and the requested authority shall take relevant action, and may receive from the trader, on the trader's initiative, *additional remedial commitments for the benefit of consumers that have been affected* by the alleged intra-Union infringement, or, where appropriate, may seek to obtain commitments from the trader to offer *adequate remedies to consumers* that have been affected by that infringement.[67]

It is also proposed that traders will be incentivised voluntarily to provide redress to consumers in order to benefit from leniency provisions for penalties.[68]

The Australian Law Reform Commission approved of the regulatory redress technique in its 2019 review of class actions and litigation funding and called for its wider adoption.[69]

2.4 Ombudsmen

ADR has become increasingly the preferred policy method for delivering consumer and commercial justice, even if mechanisms in some countries are not particularly advanced. However, ADR schemes that are based on arbitration-style models or mediation can only process individual cases and are challenged to process collective cases. Ombudsman-style ADR entities can, however, process multiple mass cases with little difficulty. A consumer Ombudsman should identify as part of normal processing of individual cases whether several involve similar facts or issues. The Ombudsman can then either adopt a case management approach (perhaps staying some cases temporarily whilst resolving key issues or test cases) or notify traders and regulators that they should consider taking action. The latter situation may lead to cessation of an underlying practice and to adoption of voluntary or imposed regulatory redress arrangements. Consumer Ombudsmen in all of the major market sectors in the UK and Belgium are well experienced in operating in this way, on a

[66] Ibid, Art. 9.4(d).

[67] Ibid, Art. 12.

[68] Proposal for a Directive of the European Parliament and of the Council amending Council Directive 93/13/EEC of 5 April 1993, Directive 98/6/EC of the European Parliament and of the Council, Directive 2005/29/EC of the European Parliament and of the Council and Directive 2011/83/EU of the European Parliament and of the Council as regards better enforcement and modernisation of EU consumer protection rules, COM(2018) 185 final, 11.4.2018.

[69] Australian Law Reform Commission (2018).

daily basis.[70] The UK is adopting a regulatory-plus-ombudsman model for property agents,[71] landlord-and-tenant issues[72] and social housing.

It will be seen that a highly effective model operates where an Ombudsman and a regulator exist and are able to work closely together, respecting each other's independence and different roles. The approach would be:

1. Ombudsman identifies a number of similar claims – a trend; applies a consistent approach to resolution
2. Ombudsman publishes information on complaints activity
3. Reactions:

   (a) Traders: ability to correct
   (b) Consumers: buying choices, switching
   (c) Competitors: market response
   (d) Media/market comment: reputation
   (e) Regulators: appropriate scrutiny and action

4. Regulator discussion with companies:

   (a) Power to make trader review records and pay redress, with claims over to the Ombudsman
   (b) Power to impose redress scheme
   (c) Oversight of voluntary/scheme redress: enforced
   (d) Consumers may go spontaneously to Ombudsman

That approach can be contrasted with many court-based collective actions, for example:

(a) A case in Belgium against an airline for a flight delayed by eight hours on 23 March 2015. The court certified the case in April 2016 and it was settled in July 2017, after which individual passengers were to be paid by the airline voluntarily.[73] An Ombudsman for aviation, such as exists in Germany, would have resolved the case swiftly.
(b) A case in France where the competition authority fined companies involved in a cartel €534 after which a consumer association initiated a class action for up to 20 million consumers' overpaid charges of up to €1.6 million. Only 12,521 consumers joined the action.[74] An effective regulator would have included redress in the enforcement package with the fine.

---

[70] Hodges and Voet (2018), ch. 6; Hodges and Stadler (2013).
[71] Ministry of Housing, Communities and Local Government (2019a).
[72] Ministry of Housing, Communities & Local Government (2019b).
[73] Hodges and Voet (2018), p. 47.
[74] Hodges and Voet (2018), p. 75.

2.5 *Personal Injuries: Administrative Schemes*

The equivalent ADR mechanism that works best for processing individual or mass personal injury claims is an administrative injury redress scheme. Macleod and Hodges investigated around 40 of these from across the world.[75] The most familiar scheme is the New Zealand Accident Compensation Scheme. Adjacent schemes for workplace injuries, motor injuries, patient insurance, and drug insurance operate highly effectively in all Nordic states. Vaccine damage schemes operate in most major countries. France has the ONIAM patient and product scheme.[76] A number of *ad hoc* schemes have been created by governments or industry.

Macleod and Hodges found models to be effective, efficient and to deliver fair and accurate redress. The major reason for adopting an administrative scheme in healthcare systems is to support an open culture in the healthcare system, as discussed above.

3 Conclusions: What Should Policy Be?

We need to ask the correct fundamental questions. How do we deliver redress, without huge cost and delay, encouraging claims that are valid and not excessive, and minimising the cost of transactions and intermediaries? How do we ensure that the rules are observed and that errors and mistakes are identified, that relevant information is shared swiftly without fear, and that lessons are learned and performance improved and risk reduced? How do we affect the future behaviour and culture of people and organisations? In addition to those 'How?' questions, there are 'What/Which?' questions. What are the best techniques and structures to deliver those objectives? That is an empirical issue that may change over time.

Stephen Yeazell asked: 'What is the most effective means of enabling the collective organisation of society?'[77] Are the answers about power and rents (of primary parties and of intermediaries), or more about means of engagement?

The main conclusion is that different mechanisms and intermediaries have evolved, and are continuing to evolve. The current author recently reviewed the means of resolving all major types of disputes in England and Wales, and concluded that the traditional court system is out of date and that pathways, intermediaries, techniques, structures and architectures have emerged.[78] The issue of collective redress is merely one example, although an important one, in which those who make public policy and those who comment on it (scholars) need to set out a new

---

[75]Macleod and Hodges (2017).

[76]Office National d'Indemnisation des Accidents Médicaux, des affections iathrogènes et des infections nosocomiales. Article L. 1142–22 of the French Public Health Code.

[77]Yeazell (1987), p. 41.

[78]Hodges (2019).

vision that actually *delivers* the desired objectives. Those who continue to use the language of procedural economy and deterrence will miss this point and miss the important debate on what the future should look like.

The empirical evidence is that litigation is grossly ineffective as a means of regulation of the behaviour of people in modern and complex organisations. If the choice is just between public and private modes, it might now be concluded:

- Efficiency: a private mechanism might save public revenues, but needs to incentivise private actors so has to permit huge cost and distorting incentives that produce abuse and are selective of cases pursued.
- Effectiveness: a public mechanism is far more effective than a private mechanism at affecting behaviour. However, it is now being realised that the economic theory that behaviour will be fully affected by imposing financial sanctions (irrespective of whether they are fines or damages) is incorrect and fails to address the real drivers of organisational behaviour. Other approaches such as affecting culture and making technical changes to systems are more effective.

The choice is no longer binary between public and private enforcement. We now know more about how to affect the behaviour of individuals and organisations. Current thinking locates the answer in new approaches to regulation, Ombudsmen and culture.

None of the above points to a conclusion that a court class action is not needed. But it should be restricted to its appropriate place. The finding of the Hodges and Voet study that in all but a small number of Member States there were few collective court actions is consistent with the observation by Yeazell that group litigation can historically be viewed not as a primary means of social control but as 'a legal avenue for grievances of marginal social groups'.[79] He highlighted that class actions have been used as adjuncts to mainstream litigation and the settlement of issues, whether by litigation, politics or otherwise. In other words, it is a long-stop mechanism. That is what the class action was in its great success in achieving social, human and educational access rights in the USA in the 1960s after other approaches had failed. Litigation options such as class actions should be available as a long-stop if the regulatory and Ombudsman mechanisms do not respond, but only accessible if other options do not exist or respond.

Class litigation is a fall-back mechanism when better solutions do not exist or respond. The priority, however, is to continue to create better mechanisms that respond well to the primary objectives and do so better than the fall-back mechanism.

The EU is pursuing disjointedly the multiple strategies of encouraging public enforcement in a strongly regulatory environment, encouraging ADR (but not Ombudsmen), and encouraging private enforcement and collective actions (confusing the issue by changing the name to representative actions). This is an almost comic situation, but one that is not evidence-based policy and may not lead to

[79] Yeazell (1987), p. 287.

coherent relations or economic health between citizens and markets. The EU has taken no steps to address the evidence on deterrence or any other enforcement policy.

The evidence points firmly to a new approach involving effective regulatory authorities and Ombudsmen (not other forms of ADR). The regulatory systems and approaches in some Member States need serious attention and capacity.

References

Allingham M (1999) Rational choice. St. Martin's Press Inc., New York

Archer MS, Tritter JQ (2001) Rational choice theory: resisting colonization. Routledge, New York

Ariely D (2008) Predictably irrational: the hidden forces that shape our decisions. HarperCollins

Asser WDH (2008) New trends in standing and res Iudicata in collective suits (the Netherlands). In: Jongbloed AW (ed) The XIIIth World Congress of Procedural Law: The Belgian and Dutch Reports. Intersentia

Australian Law Reform Commission (2018) Integrity, fairness and efficiency—an inquiry into class action proceedings and third-party litigation funders. Final Report

Banaji MH, Greenwald AG (2016) Blindspot: hidden biases of good people. Bantam Books

Barrett R (2017) The values-driven organization: cultural health and employee well-being as a pathway to sustainable performance, 2nd edn. Routledge

Bazerman MH, Tenbrunsel AE (2011) Blind spots: why we fail to do what's right and what to do about it. Princeton University Press

Becker G (1968) Crime and punishment: an economic approach. J Polit Econ 76:169

Beres LS, Griffith TD (2001) Habitual offender statutes and criminal deterrence. Connecticut Law Rev 34(55)

Berwick D (1989) EM Codman and the rhetoric of battle: a commentary. Milbank Q 320:262

Blanc B (2018) From chasing violations to managing risks. Origins, challenges and evolutions in regulatory inspections. Edward Elgar

Coffee JC (2015) Entrepreneurial litigation: its rise, fall and future. Harvard University Press

Committee on Standards in Public Life (2016) Upholding the Seven Principles of Public Life in Regulation

Communications' Providers' Voluntary Code of Practice for an Automatic Compensation Scheme (2017)

Dekker S (2007) Just culture. Balancing safety and accountability. Ashgate Publishing

Deming WE (1982) Quality, productivity and competitive position. MIT Press, Cambridge

DeNederlandscheBank (2015) Supervision of behaviour and culture: foundations, practice & future developments

Department for Business Innovation & Skills (2015) Enhanced consumer measures. Guidance for enforcers of consumer law

Department of Health (2015) Learning not blaming: The government response to the Freedom to Speak Up consultation, the Public Administration Select Committee report 'Investigating Clinical Incidents in the NHS', and the Morecambe Bay Investigation

Department of Health (2016) Report of the Expert Advisory Group; Healthcare Safety Investigation Branch

Ehrlich I (1996) Crime, punishment, and the market for offenses. J Econ Perspect 10:43

Essential Services Commission of South Australia (2018) Strategy 2018–2021

European Commission (2013) Antitrust: Commission market tests commitments proposed by Deutsche Bahn concerning pricing system for traction current in Germany. IP/13/780

EY (2016) Governing culture: practical considerations for the board and its committees

Farhang S (2010) The litigation state: public regulation and private lawsuits in the U.S. Princeton University Press, Princeton
Financial Conduct Authority (2018) Transforming Culture in Financial Services
Fleming J, Kuster JJ (2012) The Netherlands. In: Karlsgodt PG (ed) World class actions: a guide to group and representative actions around the globe. Oxford University Press
G20/OECD (2015) Principles of Corporate Governance. OECD Report to G20 Finance Ministers and Central Bank Governors
G30 (2018) Banking Conduct and Culture: A Permanent Mindset Change
Gallagher TH, Waterman AD, Ebers AG et al (2003) Patients' and physicians' attitudes regarding the disclosure of medical errors. JAMA 289:1001
Gentilin D (2016) The origins of ethical failures. Lessons for leaders. Routledge
Godart ON, Görg H, Hanley A (2014) Trust-based work-time and product improvements: evidence from firm level data' Kiel Institute for the World Economy, Working Paper No 1914
Greenwood PW et al (1994) Three strikes and you're out: estimated benefit and cost of California's mandatory new sentencing laws. RAND Corporation
Haidt J (2012) The righteous mind. Why good people are divided by politics and religion. Penguin Books
Heffernan M (2011) Wilful blindness. Why we ignore the obvious at our peril. Simon & Schuster
Helmreich RL (1999) Building safety on the three cultures of aviation. In: Proceedings if the IATA Human Factors Seminar, Bangkok
Hensler DR, Dombey-Moore B, Giddens B, Gross J, Moller EK, Pace NM (2000) Class action Dilemmas. Pursuing public goals for private gain. RAND Institute for Civil Justice
Hodges C (2011) European competition enforcement policy: integrating restitution and behaviour control. World Compet 3:383
Hodges C (2015a) Law and corporate behaviour: integrating theories of regulation, enforcement, culture and ethics. Hart
Hodges C (2015b) Mass collective redress: consumer ADR and regulatory redress. Eur Rev Priv Law 23(5):829
Hodges C (2016a) Ethical business practice: understanding the evidence. Better Regulation Delivery Office
Hodges C (2016b) US class actions: promise and reality. In: Micklitz HW, Wechsler A (eds) The transformation of enforcement. Hart
Hodges C (2019) Delivering Dispute resolution: a holistic review of models in England & wales. Hart
Hodges C, Stadler A (2013) Resolving mass disputes: ADR and settlement of mass claims. Edward Elgar
Hodges C, Steinholtz R (2017) Ethical business practice and regulation: a behavioural and values-based approach to compliance and enforcement. Hart
Hodges C, Voet S (2018) Delivering collective redress: new technologies. Hart
Kagan RA (2001) Adversarial legalism: the American way of law. Harvard University Press
Kahneman D (2011) Thinking, fast and slow. Allen Lane
Kalven H, Rosenfield M (1941) The contemporary function of the class suit. Univ Chicago Law Rev 8:684, 687
Kessler D, Levitt SD (1999) Using sentence enhancements to distinguish between deterrence and incapacitation. J Law Econ 42(34)
Leape LL (1994) Error in medicine. J Am Med Assoc 272(23):851
Macleod S, Hodges C (2017) Redress schemes for personal injuries. Hart
McCune D, Lewis C, Arendt D (2011) Safety culture in your safety management system. In: Stolzer AJ, Halford CD, Goglia JJ (eds) Implementing safety management systems in aviation. Ashgate, Farnham
Ministry of Housing, Communities and Local Government (2019a) Regulation of Property Agents Working Group. Final Report

Ministry of Housing, Communities and Local Government (2019b) Strengthening Consumer Redress in the Housing Market. Summary of responses to the consultation and the Government's response

Mulcahy L, Rosenthal MM (1998) Beyond blaming and perfection: a multi-dimensional approach to medical mishaps. In: Rosenthal MM, Mulcahy L, Lloyd-Bostock S (eds) Medical mishaps. Pieces of the puzzle. Open University Press, Buckingham

National Advisory Group on the Safety of Patients in England (2013) A promise to learn—a commitment to act. Department of Health, London

NHS England and NHS Improvement (2019) The NHS Patient Safety Strategy. Safer culture, safer systems, safer patients

NHS England Serious Incident Framework (2015)

OECD (2010) Risk and regulatory policy: improving the governance of risk

OECD (2013) OECD Guidelines for Multinational Enterprises, 2011 edition

OECD (2014) Consultation on Public Consultation Best Practice Principles for Improving on Enforcement and Inspections P Lunn, Regulatory Policy and Behavioural Economics

OECD (2015) OECD Best Practice Principles for Regulatory Policy: Regulatory Enforcement and Inspections (OECD, 2014); Corporate Governance and Business Integrity. A Stocktaking of Corporate Practices

OECD (2017) Behavioural Insights and Public Policy. Lessons from Around the World

OECD, KDI (2017) Improving Regulatory Governance. Trends, Practices and the Way Forward

Ofcom (2017) Automatic Compensation. Protecting consumers from service quality problems

Ofwat (2019) Board leadership, transparency and governance – principles

Pigou AC (1920) The economics of welfare. MacMillan, London

Professional Standards Authority (2018) Lessons Learned Review. The Nursing and Midwifery Council's handling of concerns about midwives' fitness to practise at the Furness General Hospital

Scottish Government (2016) Delivering better outcomes for consumers and businesses in Scotland

Sisodia R, Sheth J, Wolfe D (2014) Firms of endearment. How world-class companies profit from passion and purpose, 2nd edn. Pearson Education, Upper Saddle River

Soltes E (2016) Why do they do it: inside the mind of the White-Collar criminal. PublicAffairs

Stigler GJ (1971) The theory of economic regulation. Bell J Econ Manage Sci 2:3–21

Studdert D, Piper D, Iedema R (2010) Legal aspects of open disclosure II: attitudes of health professionals-findings from a national survey'. Med J Aust 193:351

Sykes W, Groom C, Desai P, Kelly J (2014) Coming clean: the experience of cleaning operatives. Equality and Human Rights Commission

Tzankova I, Lunsingh Scheurleer D (2009) The Netherlands. Ann Am Acad Polit Soc Sci 622:149

UNCTAD (2016) Draft Manual on Consumer Protection. http://unctad.org/en/PublicationsLibrary/webditcclp2016d1.pdf. Accessed 10 Feb 2020

US Class Actions: Theory and Reality EUI Florence working paper 2015/36 (ERC ERPL 14). http://hdl.handle.net/1814/36536; in German at http://hdl.handle.net/1814/46464. Accessed 10 February 2020

van der Heijden MJ (2010) Class actions. In: van Erp JHM, van Vliet PW (eds) Netherlands reports to the Eighteenth international congress of comparative law. Intersentia

Voet S (2013) Public enforcement and A(O)DR as mechanisms for resolving mass problems: a Belgian perspective. In: Hodges C, Stadler A (eds) Resolving mass disputes: ADR and settlement of mass claims. Edward Elgar

Webster M, Bolt H (2016) The effectiveness of HSE's regulatory approach: the construction example. Health & Safety Executive, 2016

Yeazell SC (1987) From medieval group litigation to the modern class action. Yale University Press, New Haven

Christopher Hodges Professor of Justice Systems and Head of the Swiss Re Research Programme on Civil Justice Systems, Centre for Socio-Legal Studies, University of Oxford. Supernumerary Fellow of Wolfson College, Oxford. Co-founder of the International Network for Delivery of Regulation.

For the Defense: 28 Shades of European Class Actions

Linda S. Mullenix

Abstract Throughout the twentieth century, virtually all European countries that had studied the American class action had rejected implementation of the class action as a part of domestic law. In the early twenty-first century, however, several European countries reconsidered their longstanding antipathy to the American class action. The EU Parliament in 2013 issued a Recommendation for Injunctive and Compensatory Collective Redress Mechanisms requesting that all EU countries—by 2017—implement some form of collective redress mechanism. In May 2018, the Commission issued a Report assessing the practical implementation of the Recommendation. The Commission's study reveals that the 28 EU countries have developed a patchwork quilt of differing approaches to collective redress. Although many EU countries have undertaken legislative initiatives and implemented some of the Commission's recommendations, in a number of countries, several of the Commission's principles have had little or no impact on domestic laws. Perhaps most significantly, the 28 EU countries largely have eschewed implementing procedural mechanisms that resemble the American class action rule, in efforts to preserve domestic cultural and legal norms, and to avoid American-style class action abuses. Thus, European initiatives towards implementing a class action device represent an American class action defense lawyer's dream.

1 Introduction

As is well known, the American class action rule has long dominated the worldwide procedural landscape as a means for achieving collective redress. Congress enacted the original American class action rule in 1938, and by 2018 U.S. courts had accumulated 80 years of class action experience. Other common law jurisdictions similarly embraced the class action procedure to resolve aggregate disputes; as early

L. S. Mullenix (✉)
University of Texas at Austin, Austin, TX, USA
e-mail: lmullenix@law.utexas.edu

A. Uzelac, S. Voet (eds.), *Class Actions in Europe*, Ius Gentium: Comparative Perspectives on Law and Justice 89, https://doi.org/10.1007/978-3-030-73036-9_3

as 1978 Quebec enacted a class action statute, followed in 1992 by the province of Ontario.[1] By 1991 Australia also had enacted a representative proceeding act.[2]

Although common law countries gradually warmed to the notion of class litigation, most civil law jurisdictions strenuously resisted the introduction of American-style class action procedure into their domestic law. This resistance to American-style class litigation was especially pronounced in European countries, where traditional forms of individual adjudication were jurisprudentially conceived as a form of natural law right, embodied in the notion that every person is entitled to his or her day in court. Jurisprudentially, then, the American concept of collective action or aggregate litigation, which subsumed or denied litigant autonomy, was something of an affront to European sensibilities.

European scholarly commentary in the 1980s and 1990s—when the specter of class litigation first appeared as a possibility in domestic conversations—was especially harsh in assessing American-style class litigation as anathema to continental jurisprudence.[3] Not only did continental scholars view American-style class litigation as theoretically flawed, but they also pointed out that Europe had no need for class litigation for several reasons. Perhaps most important, scholars could point to the robust domestic regulatory regimes that provided strong enforcement mechanisms for regulatory violations.

The existence of the strong regulatory state undercut or obviated the need for individuals to band together to redress injuries. In addition, class litigation was viewed as unnecessary because domestic law already provided existing means for collective redress through established associations that could, on behalf of their members, pursue relief if necessary. Labor associations provided an example of longstanding auspices for collective relief.[4] Other smaller associations served a similar function: for example, the French wine growers association could pursue relief on behalf of its members if price-fixing threatened their market.

Continental scholars and practicing lawyers also looked askance at the darker underside of American class litigation, contemplating deleterious professional and societal consequences inspired by class litigation. Among the negative aspects of American class litigation, continental observers could not help but note the interplay of class litigation with American litigiousness, problems of client solicitation, stirring-up litigation, entrepreneurial lawyering, and enormous transaction costs and attorney fees in these cases. Thus, after canvassing both the theoretical and the practical issues raised by American-style class litigation, European scholars

---

[1]See, e.g., Statutes of Ontario, An Act Respecting Class Proceedings; Statutes of Quebec, An Act Respecting the Class Action (1978).

[2]Acts of Parliament of the Commonwealth of Australia, Amendment Act of 1991 (Representative Proceedings).

[3]See, e.g., Cappalli and Consolo (1992), Cappelletti and Garth (1983), Fisch (1979), Koch (1986), Koch (1994), Parker (1995), Taruffo (1990).

[4]Ibid.

resoundingly replied to the prospect of the introduction of domestic class actions in Europe with resounding responses of "Nein!" and "Basta!" and "No!"[5]

The continental opposition to American-style class litigation persisted into the early twenty-first century. By the mid-1990s, however, European countries one-by-one began to rethink their resistance to the possibility of class litigation. Finland and Sweden led the way in studying and then drafting class litigation statutes.[6] Gradually, other European countries followed, either enacting complete class action rules—as did Italy[7]—or through gradual, limited class experiments embedded in consumer protection statutes—as did France.[8] It would be interesting to learn what inspired this rethinking of the possibility and the merits of class litigation that emerged in continental Europe in the opening years of the twenty-first century.

Nonetheless, with the gradual emergence of various forms of class litigation on the continent, an EU Parliament undertook a study of collective redress issues, as well as modalities for accomplishing collective relief.[9] In setting forth principles to undergird domestic redress mechanisms, the Commission notably eschewed the label "class action," preferring instead the nomenclature of "collective redress"—a continuing reflection, perhaps, of the continental distaste for American class actions.

Following the publication of its study outlining principles, the EU Parliament in 2013 issued a Recommendation for Injunctive and Compensatory Collective Redress Mechanisms in Member States (concerning violations of rights granted under Union law).[10] The Recommendation requested that all 28 EU countries—by 2017—implement some form of collective redress mechanism. The Recommendation set forth a comprehensive list of principles to guide legislative initiatives in developing collective redress law that largely followed the principles set forth in the EU Commission's earlier study.[11]

In 2017, a consortium of European research institutions, led by the Max Planck Institute for Procedural Law, issued a lengthy study of the effectiveness of national

---

[5]Ibid.

[6]Draft Proposal for a Class Action Act, Committee Report of the Legislative Department of the Ministry (January 1995) (proposed Finnish class action); Summary of Proposed Act on Class Actions (1995) (proposed Swedish class action); Official report, Proposed Act on Class Actions (1995) (proposed Swedish class action Act).

[7]Nashi (2010); see Legge 24 Dicembre, n 244, Art. 2, para 445–449, Dec. 24, 2007, in Gazz. Uff. 12 Gennaio 2008, n 8 [original draft] (providing the legal framework for collective actions in Italy); Legge 23 Luglio 2009, n 99, Art. 49, para 14, in Gazz. Uff. 31 Luglio 2009, n 176, Supplemento Ordinario, n 136 [final draft]. The final draft went into effect in January 2010.

[8]Class action litigation in France is situated in its consumer protection provisions and is limited to services provided, sales of products, and damages caused by unfair competition. See generally Lutfalla and Magnier (2006), Brouquier (2015), Lesur (2016), reporting that since October 1, 2014, when the law entered into force, only six class actions were brought through 2016.

[9]European Parliament Resolution of 2 February 2012 Towards a Coherent Approach to Collective Redress [2012](2011/2089 (INI)).

[10]2013/396 EU: Commission Recommendation of 11 June 2013 on Common Principles for Injunctive and Compensatory Collective Redress Mechanisms.

[11]Ibid.

procedural law and practices to ensure the effective procedural protection of EU consumers.[12] A segment of that report focused on the developing use of collective redress mechanisms in Member States to effectuate protection of consumers under EU law and the 2013 EU Recommendation.[13]

In May 2018, the Commission issued a Report to the European Parliament, the Council, and the European Economic and Social Committee assessing the practical implementation of the Recommendation 4 years after its publication.[14] The Commission's study reveals that the 28 EU countries have developed or enacted a patchwork quilt of differing approaches to class actions or collective redress. Although many EU countries have undertaken some legislative initiatives and implemented some of the Commission's recommendations, in a number of countries, several of the Commission's principles have had little or no impact on domestic laws. In addition, a separate study of the implementation of collective redress across the 28 EU countries concluded that the heterogeneity of procedures within the EU was problematic; not all EU citizens are afforded the same level of protection by domestic laws.[15]

Perhaps most significantly, the 28 EU countries largely (although not entirely) have eschewed implementing procedural mechanisms that resemble the American class action rule, in efforts to preserve domestic cultural and legal norms, and to avoid American-style class action abuses. Thus, the continental repugnance of American-style class litigation that was so prominent in scholarly commentary through the end of the twentieth century resonates today in the measures that EU countries have now enacted. The EU apparently desires to accomplish measures of collective redress, but at the same time to distance itself from American class action imperialism. Indeed, some countries, such as Austria and Germany, continue to manifest a strong opposition to the introduction of compensatory collective redress mechanisms, arguing that the current legal systems are sufficient to provide adequate redress.[16]

In its conclusion, the Commission recognized that its work is far from complete in its project to bring collective redress across the EU. Based on its assessment of the

---

[12]Consortium of European Universities, Max Planck Institute Luxembourg for Procedural Law, An Evaluation of National Procedural Laws and Practices in Terms of Their Impact on the Free circulation of Judgments and on the Equivalence and Effectiveness of the Procedural Protection of Consumers Under EU Consumer Law (June 2017) (report commissioned by the European Commission), JUST/2104/RCON/PR/CIVI/0082).

[13]Voet (2017).

[14]*Report from the European Commission to the European Parliament*, The Council and the European Economic and Social Committee on the Implementation of the Commission Recommendation of 11 June 2013 on common principles for injunctive collective redress mechanisms in the Member States concerning violations of rights granted under Union law (2013/396/EU) (January 25, 2018) (hereinafter 2018 EU Commission Report).

[15]See Directorate General for Internal Policies, Policy Department for Citizens' Rights and Constitutional Affairs, *Collective Redress in the Member States of the European Union*, PE 608.829 (October 2018).

[16]Voet (2017), p. 260.

current state of collective redress, the Report noted that "the potential of the principles of the Recommendation in facilitating access to justice for the benefit of the functioning of the single market is still far from being fully exploited."[17]

Perhaps the most significant consequence of the 28 EU collective redress enactments is the extent to which American class action defense lawyers may find comfort in these various initiatives. It should not be surprising that American businesses and multinational corporations, when the EU began considering the introduction of collective redress, viewed with alarm the prospect that American-style class action litigation would spread across continental Europe.

This chapter discusses the extent to which defense interests in confining class action or collective redress mechanisms influenced the ultimate enactments of the 28 EU countries, either consciously or not. As I argue, the initial EU Commission study that set forth the over-arching principles to guide EU countries in formulating collective redress measures was imbued with defense-favoring principles. In turn, the European Parliament adopted these defense-favoring principles wholesale into the EU Recommendation, which became the foundational document for the 28 EU countries. Despite local variations, the 28 EU countries have formulated collective redress mechanisms—in their antipathy to the American class action rule—that corporate defense attorneys could be comfortable with.

Part I of this chapter provides historical background describing the American defense bar's 40-year efforts at litigation and tort reform in the United States, which include class action litigation reform. Many of the reform principles advanced by the American defense bar have now been incorporated into the EU approaches to collective redress. Thus, to the extent that American defense attorneys were able to influence the European debate over instituting collective redress, then the corporate defense bar successfully confined the possibility of American-style class litigation in Europe, at least for the time being.

Part II examines the defense-favoring principles that were articulated in the EU Commission's initial study and report, that then became the core of the EU Recommendations to the 28 EU countries with the 4-year mandate to implement domestic law on collective redress.

Part III then surveys the extent to which the 28 EU countries have adopted defense-favoring collective redress measures after promulgation of the Recommendation. This portion of the chapter concludes with the observation that although the EU has marched into the twenty-first century embracing collective redress, the ways in which the EU countries have done so reflects much of the attitudes and concerns of the continental scholars of the 1980s and 1990s, who eschewed class litigation. Whether this persists into the future remains an open case.

[17]2018 EU Commission Report, 19–21.

2 A Brief History of Modern American Defense Efforts at Tort and Litigation Reform in the United States

2.1 The Tort and Litigation Reform Movement Generally

The contemporary limitations on collective redress mechanisms that are found in many of the 28 EU countries reflects an adverse attitude towards class litigation resonating in the tort reform movement in the United States that began in the 1980s and has extended four decades to the present. The American litigation and tort reform movement was part of a sweeping political agenda by conservative Republicans to remake American political institutions, including the judicial system and access to justice. The conservative reform platform found its definitive exposition of issues and aims in the so-called "Contract with America," signed by Republican party members on September 27, 1994.[18]

The Contract with America outlined promised legislative initiatives if Republican candidates became the majority party in Congress after the 1994 election season. These pledges included a promise to shrink the size of government, promote lower taxes and greater entrepreneurial activity, litigation and tort reform, and welfare reform.[19] Although the Contract with America included many social, political, and institutional platforms, the goal of litigation and tort reform played a major role in the conservative political agenda. Major organizations such as the United States Chamber of Commerce—joined by ad hoc groups such as the Citizens Against Law Suit Abuse and the Law Litigation Abuse Watch—began a public relations campaign to educate the public concerning the need for litigation and tort reform.[20] These organizations were financially underwritten by large businesses and wealthy conservative individuals such as the Koch brothers. Billions of dollars were poured into this public relations campaign; major corporations reportedly were contributing at least a million dollars a year to litigation and tort reform efforts.[21]

The litigation and tort reform movement was centrally based on the theory of a litigation explosion in the United States that negatively impacted corporations, the ability of businesses to compete in the international arena, and the economic welfare of the country generally. The corporate critique of the American legal system chiefly found expression in Walter Olson's 1991 book, *The Litigation Explosion: What Happened When America Unleased the Lawsuit*.[22]

---

[18]Vairo (2016). The groundwork for the Contract with America was first laid by the President's Council for Competitiveness, in "An Agenda for Civil Justice in America" (1991); Vice President Dan Quayle unveiled this agenda in a speech to the American Bar Association meeting in August 1991.

[19]Vairo (2016), n 8.

[20]Vairo (2016), p. 1743.

[21]Vairo (2016), 1743, n 10.

[22]See Olson (1991).

Olson argued that America had become an overly litigious society with too many lawsuits because Americans had become accustomed to a rights-based theory of justice that encouraged citizens to pursue legal relief for grievances that individuals otherwise would "have common sense to ignore."[23] Certain uniquely American features of the litigation landscape helped to fuel this litigation explosion, including lawyer advertising, contingency fee arrangements, and the American rule that each side in a litigation pay their own fees (rather than the continental civil law "loser pay" fee rule). In addition, litigation was further encouraged by media reports of large jury verdicts (publicized as "jackpot justice"), and "runaway juries" favoring plaintiffs' claims.[24]

Central to Olson's critique was the notion that, in contemporary society, this culture of litigiousness encouraged and incentivized plaintiffs to pursue frivolous lawsuits that required businesses to spend large sums of money defending weak or meritless claims. Corporate lawyers were also part of the problem: they encouraged their corporate clients to litigate against such lawsuits, rather than settle their disputes through negotiation. The incentives in the American legal system of dispute resolution provoked plaintiffs and corporate defendants alike either to pursue or defend against redress for small, sometimes even imaginary (or fraudulent) harms.[25] Corporate interests focused on certain types of lawsuits that were considered to be out of control, such as medical malpractice and tort and insurance litigation.[26] These types of litigation became targets of particular concern for corporate reform efforts.

Olson's critique and attack on the American legal system focused on procedural amendments that he believed encouraged the expansion of access to the courts and hence the late twentieth-century litigation explosion. These procedural changes included the relaxation of jurisdictional requirements, liberal notice pleading (eliminating the more exacting code pleading requirements), modern liberalized discovery rules that were the bane of corporate businesses defending lawsuits, as well as modern liberalized evidence rules. Olson argued that plaintiffs' attorneys, sympathetic legislators, and liberal judges had coalesced to design and implement modern liberal procedure which incentivized plaintiffs and their attorneys to pursue litigation. Consequently, the result of this litigation explosion redounded to the detriment of corporate America, which was forced to spend large sums of money to either settle or defend unmeritorious lawsuits.

As a consequence of the perceived litigation explosion and liberal procedural developments incentivizing litigation, various corporate interests and lobbying groups spearheaded numerous tort and litigation reform efforts throughout the United States. Many of these efforts were aimed at modifying substantive tort principles. By 1986, 41 states had enacted some form of tort reform, which included

---

[23]Hensler (1991) reviewing Olson (1991).

[24]Vairo (2016), p. 1743.

[25]Hensler (1991), p. 176.

[26]Note (1996) (state tort reform efforts at limiting potential malpractice liability of health-care providers).

non-economic damage caps in professional liability cases.[27] Other litigation and tort reform efforts aimed at changing the substantive law included modifications of joint and several liability rules, collateral source rules, and limits on punitive damages.[28]

2.2 *The Class Action Litigation Reform Movement*

Against the background of these substantive tort reform initiatives throughout the 1980s and 1990s, it was inevitable that corporate and defense interests eventually would focus attention on class action litigation abuse. Throughout the 1980s and 1990s, corporate defense attorneys waged an aggressive war against mass tort class litigation in federal courts. By the mid-1990s, the defense bar had largely and successfully accomplished this goal of defeating mass tort litigation in federal courts. Through a series of class action decisions that curbed mass tort class litigation in federal courts, it became increasingly difficult, if not impossible, for plaintiffs' attorneys to successfully seek certification of mass tort litigation classes in federal courts.[29] As a consequence of this metaphorical closing of the federal courthouse doors to mass tort class litigation, plaintiffs' attorneys decamped to state court to pursue mass tort class action litigation.[30]

With the movement of class litigation from federal courts to state court venues, plaintiffs' attorneys discovered that state courts were highly receptive to class litigation. Most state courts had lax class action rules and procedures, and under-developed class action jurisprudence that did not track the more restrictive class jurisprudence of federal courts. Thus, plaintiffs' attorneys found that in state court they could accomplish relatively easy class certification of proposed class actions.[31] In addition, plaintiffs' attorneys quickly discovered numerous plaintiff-friendly state jurisdictions and venues, which encouraged forum-shopping for optimal, speedy class certification and recovery on behalf of class claimants.

With the movement of class litigation into state court venues, corporate defense attorneys found themselves relatively disarmed and disadvantaged in anti-corporate

---

[27]Vairo (2016), p. 1743 nn 13–14, reports that by 2004, 23 states had capped non-economic damages in professional liability cases. See also Note (1996), p. 1768 (various tort reform initiatives).

[28]Vairo (2016), p. 1743.

[29]Castano v. Amer. Tobacco Co., Inc., 84 F.3d 734, 744 (5th Cir. 1996); In re American Medical Systems, Inc., 75 F.3d 1069, 1079 (6th Cir. 1996); In the Matter of Rhone-Poulenc Rorer, Inc., 51 F.3d 1293 (7th Cir. 1995).

[30]Forty-eight of the 50 states have state class action rules that permit class litigation in state court. The two states without class action rules are Mississippi and Virginia.

[31]These easily accomplished class certifications in obliging state court jurisdictions were dubbed "drive-by" certifications for the ease with which plaintiffs could receive class certification merely upon the filing of conclusory motions and pleadings, without evidentiary support or judicial hearings.

state courts. Moreover, corporate defendants discovered that many state court jurisdictions were amenable to certification of nationwide class actions that federal courts had long declined to certify for classwide resolution. Hence, class litigation in state court exposed corporate defendants to wide-ranging liability on a greater scale than had been possible in federal courts.

By the end of the twentieth century and into the early twenty-first century, the corporate defense bar became increasingly agitated at the developments of state class action litigation. Starting in 2002 the United States Chamber of Commerce's Institute for Legal Reform initiated a so-called "Judicial Hellhole" survey by asking defense lawyers which state jurisdictions they would label as "judicial hellholes"—obviously denoting terrible places for corporations to be compelled to defend class action litigation.[32]

As the deleterious trend of state class action litigation evolved and persisted, corporate defense attorneys and their institutional allies lobbied Congress to change jurisdictional rules to get class litigation out of state courts. Through an 8-year effort, defense-side interests successfully induced Congress to enact the Class Action Fairness Act of 2005 (CAFA).[33] CAFA accomplished two major goals for corporate defense interests: (1) it created new federal jurisdiction especially for class litigation based on relaxed diversity jurisdiction standards, and more importantly[34] (2) it created removal jurisdiction from state courts into federal courts, in which certification jurisprudence was more restrictive—and therefore defendant-favoring—than state courts.[35] In addition to CAFA, in the mid-1990s Congress also stepped in to reform securities class action litigation, by similarly tightening both the substantive and procedural rules relating to class litigation of securities and shareholder derivative litigation.[36]

Moreover, in addition to legislative lobbying efforts to restrict class litigation in state and federal courts, corporate interests scored several victories in major U.S. Supreme Court appeals which effectively curbed the ability of plaintiffs to utilize the class action vehicle to vindicate group rights. These cases involved classwide employment discrimination claims,[37] alleged antitrust violations,[38] and contractual class action waivers.[39]

---

[32]Vairo (2016), p. 1744 n 15.

[33]28 U.S.C. §§ 1332(d), 1453, 1711–1715: Pub. L. 10902 (Feb. 18, 2005).

[34]28 U.S.C. § 1332(d).

[35]28 U.S.C. § 1453.

[36]Private Securities Litigation Reform Act of 1995, Pub. L. 104-67, 109 Stat. 737 (codified as amended in scattered sections of 15 U.S.C.) (1995); see also Securities Litigation Uniform Standards Act of 1998, Pub. L. 105-353, 112 Stat. 3227 (1998).

[37]Wal-Mart Stores, Inc. v. Dukes, 131 S. Ct. 2541 (2011).

[38]Comcast Corp. v. Behrend, 133 S. Ct. 1426 (2013).

[39]AT&T Mobility LLC v. Concepcion, 131 S. Ct. 1740 (2011); American Express Co. v. Italian Colors Restaurant, 133 S. Ct. 2304 (2012).

2.3 The Class Litigation and Tort Reform Principles Developed in the American Conservative Reform Agenda

The litigation and tort reform movement in the United States has a long lineage reaching back at least four or five decades. As discussed above, the centerpiece of the reform movement can be traced back to the foundational 1994 document, the Contract with America. Tenet Nine of the *Contract* dealt with a variety of tort and litigation reform initiatives. When the Republican party successfully captured the Congress in 1994, within the first 100 legislative days the Republicans introduced four "Common Sense" reform bills designed to live up to the promises of the Contract with America: The Common Sense Product Liability Reform Act,[40] the Common Sense Product Liability Reform Act of 1995,[41] the Common Sense Legal Reform Acts of 1995,[42] and the Common Sense Legal Standards Reform Act of 1995.[43]

These bills proposed a series of reforms that capture the ways in which the defense bar has long sought to confine and restrict litigation, based on the premise of a litigation explosion of frivolous and wasteful litigation. As one commentator has noted, these common sense tort reform bills shared the major elements of the classical tort reform movement: "a strong pro-defendant leaning, the goal of eliminating pro-plaintiff common law rules, and in many cases the desire to award special protections to particular sectors of the economy."[44] All the tort reform bills shared a common statement of purpose and desire to deter frivolous litigation.[45] Some of the bills would allow sanctions to be directly imposed on plaintiffs that file frivolous suits.[46] Central to these legislative bills were provisions to institute punitive damage limitations or to eliminate defendant liability in certain areas; to eliminate joint or several liability of multiple defendants; and to adopt the British rule of fee-shifting (otherwise known as the "loser pay" rule).[47]

In its continuing litigation and tort reform efforts, Congress a decade later focused more narrowly on problems of class action abuse that Congress intended to remedy through enactment of the Class Action Fairness Act of 2005. The legislative history accompanying the CAFA bill set forth a long litany of class action abuses.[48] Among these were forum-shopping for desirable plaintiff-friendly venues (to the detriment of corporate defendants); excessive attorney fee awards in class litigation or

[40]H.R. 917, 104th Cong., 1st Sess. (1995); 141 Cong. Rec. H2486 (March 1995).

[41]H.R. 955, 104th Cong., 1st Sess. (1995); 141 Cong. Rec. H1849 (Feb. 15, 1995).

[42]H.R. 10, 104th Cong., 1st Sess. (1995).

[43]H.R. 956, 104th Cong. 1st Sess. (1995); 141 Cong. Rec. H1849 (Feb. 15, 1995).

[44]Note (1996), p. 1770.

[45]Ibid.

[46]Ibid.

[47]Ibid.

[48]Class Action Fairness Act of 2005, Senate Report 109-14, S. Rep. No. 14, 109th Cong., 1st Sess. 2005, 2005 WL 627977, 2005 U.S.C.C.A.N. 3 (leg. Hist.); Cong. Rec. 151 (Feb. 28, 2005).

settlements; class settlements that returned negligible benefits to class members, including so-called "coupon" settlements; judicial blackmail inducing defendants to settle frivolous lawsuits rather than litigate; due process violations of defendants' rights by denying out-of-state defendants the opportunity to contest plaintiffs' claims; wasteful copycat duplicative class actions; and easy, lax class certification requirements in state court venues.[49]

Thus, in the context of the American tort and class litigation reform movements, corporate defendants and their institutional allies—such as the U.S. Chamber of Commerce, the Defense Research Institute, the Cato Institute, the Products Liability Advisory Council—have long advocated for a series of defense-favoring principles for adjudication of aggregate class litigation: sanctions for frivolous litigation; stringent class certification requirements; capping or elimination of punitive damages; restrictions on excessive attorney fees; restrictions on or elimination of contingency fee arrangements; and loser pay rules. More recently, corporate interests involved in class litigation have lobbied against *cy pres* settlement provisions in class action settlements,[50] and the prospect of third-party financing of class litigation.[51] As recently as 2018, the House of Representatives was again "stirring up old tort reform" in a series of legislative initiatives, most notably the proposed Fairness in Class Litigation Act.[52] As will be seen, when the EU Commission and EU Parliament began considering the possibility of class actions or collective redress mechanisms for the EU, a similar set of principles and values permeated the discussion of future legislative initiatives.

3 The EU Principles to Guide Legislative Initiatives for Member States Collective Redress Mechanisms

It is difficult to know—let alone document—the extent to which American corporate interests influenced the developing EU conversation on the introduction of class action or collective relief in EU Member States. At best it is possible to observe that the American business community watched with interest (and perhaps growing alarm) at the prospect of class action litigation spreading through European countries, which inevitably would draw American multinational corporations into

[49]Ibid.

[50]See Brief for Petitioners, Frank v. Gaos, 2018 WL 3374998 (U.S. Appellate Briefs 2018); Brief of Chamber of Commerce of the United States of America as Amicus in Support of Petitioners, Frank v. Gaos, 2018 WL 3473993 (U.S. Appellate Brief 2018); Brief of the Cato Institute and Americans for Prosperity as Amici in Support of the Petitioners, Frank v. Gaos, 2018 WL 3455704 (U.S. Appellate Brief 2018). See also Beisner (2010), p. 3.

[51]See Beisner et al. (2009).

[52]See Steinman (2018) (commenting on HR 985, the Fairness in Class Action Litigation Act).

worldwide class action defense.[53] It is difficult to assess the degree to which knowledge and understanding of the American experience of tort and class action litigation informed the debates in the European Commission and Parliament in their recommendations for collective redress mechanisms. What is striking, however, is the degree to which the guiding principles for EU collective redress initiatives embraced so many aspects of American defense-oriented class litigation reform.

Between 2002 and 2012, the European Commission undertook "the best part of a decade of intense debate" concerning the possible introduction of class action or collective redress mechanisms into the domestic laws of EU countries.[54] The Commission issued a series of discussion papers along with extensive public consultation. In 2012, the Commission adopted a resolution calling for the introduction of a *Collective Redress Proposal* that would provide a "common set of principles providing uniform access to justice throughout the European Union."[55] The principles set forth in the Commission resolution were largely incorporated verbatim in the 2013 EU Commission *Recommendation on Collective Redress Mechanisms*.[56]

On June 11, 2013, the European Commission released its *Recommendation on Collective Redress Mechanisms*.[57] Echoing American concerns with abusive class action litigation that had been extensively canvassed during the years leading up to the enactment of the Class Action Fairness Act of 2005, the Recommendation included extensive references to the necessity for various safeguards that aim to curb what it described as "the development of an abusive litigation culture."[58] According to commentators, these cautionary notes concerning the need for collective redress safeguards reflected the intense lobbying efforts on the part of the business community and others who feared the introduction of a American-style class action regime.[59] The fact that the Recommendation's introductory rhetoric acknowledged class action abuse was to be avoided should have provided some comfort to concerned American corporate defense interests that were following class developments in the EU.

With due regard for local legal culture and national principles, the 2013 EU Recommendation called upon each of the 28 EU Member States to implement a national collective redress system based on common European principles within 2 years of the Recommendation. The proposed collective redress mechanisms were

---

[53]See, e.g., Harbour and Shelley (2007); Hensler (2016) (discussing the 2013 European Principles on Collective Redress); Clark et al. (2013) (commenting on the draft European Recommendation on Collective Redress Mechanisms).

[54]Clark et al. (2013), p. 425.

[55]European Parliament Resolution of 2 February 2012 Towards a Coherent Approach to Collective Redress [2012] (2011/2089(INI)).

[56]Ibid.

[57]Commission Recommendation on common principles for injunctive and compensatory collective redress mechanisms in the Member States concerning violations of rights granted under Union Law, Strasbourg, XXX COM (2013) 3539/3.

[58]2013 EU Commission Recommendation, 3.

[59]Clark et al. (2013), p. 425.

to apply to a range of substantive claims, including infringements of consumer protection, and violations of environmental, financial services, and competition law, where two or more persons were injured and suffered damage as a consequence of illegal activity. The Recommendation provided for a review of the operation of the collective redress system 4 years after its publication. Hence, in 2017–2018, the Commission was to assess whether the EU Parliament should take any further steps to introduce or modify collective redress in Member States, including mandating the proposals set out in the Recommendation.

In addition to its cautionary notes about avoiding class action abuse, the heart of the Recommendation was the "common principles" the Commission recommended to guide Member States in establishing their individual collective redress regimes.[60] Several of the EU common principles embraced values and tenets that clearly resonated in American defense-oriented views on class litigation:

Certification The 2013 EU Recommendation did not include a specific procedure for class certification (American-style), but did include a requirement that there be "verification at the earliest possible stage of litigation that cases in which conditions for collective actions are not met, and manifestly unfounded cases, are not continued." The Recommendation also required that "courts should carry out the necessary examination of their own motion." In discussing the implementation of some form of early verification, the Recommendation did not address the extent of the common issue or issues that would be required to bring a claim under the proposed regime, and did not discuss a requirement that the common issues predominate over the individual issues, as required for certification of American damage class litigation.

As will be seen, many EU Member States adopted a so-called "admissibility" standard as the threshold consideration for proceeding with a collective redress. Although these admissibility standards are variously (and loosely) defined, they provide a threshold screening mechanism by which Member States can terminate unmeritorious class actions at an early stage in the proceedings.

The Representative Party The 2013 EU Recommendation confined representative actions by providing that such actions should only be brought by "designated representative entities" that were not-for-profit and that had a direct relationship between their main objectives and the rights claimed to have been violated, and had adequate resources and expertise to properly represent the claimants.

Contingency Fees The 2013 EU Recommendation embraced the European continental repugnance towards contingency fees, stating that Member States should not permit the use of contingency fee agreements because of the risk that contingency fee arrangements create an incentive to litigation. However, the Recommendation did not completely bar the use of contingency fee arrangements, indicating that some Member States might choose to allow them.

[60] 2013 EU Commission Recommendation, 5–10.

The Loser Pay Rule The 2013 EU Recommendation endorsed as a general principle the so-called English rule to the effect that the loser pays the winner's costs of the proceedings.

Punitive Damages Consistent with continental practice, the 2013 EU Recommendation prohibited the use of punitive damage remedies in collective redress actions.

Pre-Trial Discovery The 2013 EU Recommendation did not expressly provide guidance concerning pre-trial discovery. However—undoubtedly cognizant of American-style liberal discovery and its impact on American class litigation—the Recommendation's introductory material stated that "intrusive pre-trial discovery procedures . . . should be avoided as a general rule."

Third-Party Funding The 2013 Recommendation allowed for third-party funding in collective redress actions, with significant safeguards for such litigation financing. Thus, third-party financing could be approved provided that there was no conflict of interest between the funder and the claimants, the funder had sufficient resources to meet the cost of the proceedings, and the claimants had sufficient resources to meet any adverse costs. Moreover, the Recommendation mandated the disclosure of the third-party funding arrangements at the commencement of the proceedings. In addition, the Recommendation imposed a prohibition on the funder who might seek to "influence procedural decisions of the claimants," including on settlements, and a prohibition on the charging of excessive interest.

Opt-In Regime The 2013 EU Recommendation generally endorsed the continental approach to collective actions based on an opt-in, as opposed to the American-style opt-out, class regime. However, the Recommendation provided for an exception to the general opt-in principle by allowing for adoption of an opt-out regime if a Member State justified this choice by reasons of sound administration of justice.

Cross-Border Litigation Contemplating the prospect of cross-border collective actions, the 2013 EU Recommendation envisaged a single action in a single national forum for cases involving claimants in more than one Member State.

In summary, American and non-American defense lawyers could take comfort in the major guiding principles that the EU Commission set forth to instruct Member States in legislating and implementing collective redress mechanisms. The EU basically set forth ground rules for collective redress mechanisms that would allow for creation of collective redress mechanisms that would be unlike American class actions in most respects. The principles mandated some sort of threshold admissibility requirement; confined who might serve as a collective representative; largely eschewed contingency fee arrangements; required a loser pay rule; prohibited punitive damages; and strongly cautioned against pre-trial discovery (on an American model). In some respects, American class action defense attorneys might even take comfort in the continental opt-in requirement, which empirically has been shown to reduce participation in class proceedings. Perhaps the single worrisome aspect of the 2013 EU Recommendation was its endorsement of third-party financing, a funding mechanism that has not been embraced and has largely been resisted to date in U.S. class action litigation.

Finally, the American corporate class action defense bar could take great comfort in the extensive rhetorical warnings from the Commission describing the potential for class action abuse, which various abuses were to be strenuously avoided by Member States in adopting their domestic collective redress procedures. The 2013 EU Recommendation fundamentally abjured American-style entrepreneurial lawyering, and concomitant lawyer-driven class litigation.

4 The 28 EU Member States Enact Collective Redress Mechanisms: Legislative Initiatives That American Defense Lawyers Could Appreciate

The publication of the 2013 EU Recommendation should have provided defense-oriented interests with some measure of comfort, because behind-the-scenes lobbying efforts of the business community—to avoid or forestall the institution of American-style class litigation—seems to have had an impact on the articulation of the guiding principles for EU Member States. It then remained to be seen what the 28 EU Member States would enact in the ensuing 4 years from the publication of the Recommendation to the implementation of those guiding principles and recommendations.

In the several 2017–2018 studies reporting on the implementation of the 2013 EU Commission Recommendation, the 28 Member States have produced 28 shades of EU class actions. Collectively, the Member States have somewhat hewed to the guiding principles, which again should provide some provisionary comfort to the concerns of the defense bar. Nonetheless, although the report card on implementation of the Commission's 2013 EU Recommendation documents a largely defense-favorable landscape, there are some cautionary notes among Member States in the procedures they have adopted which have departed from the recommended principles.

4.1 Availability of Collective Redress Through Injunctive or Compensatory Mechanisms

Of initial note is the fact that the institution or implementation of collective redress legislation has been slow among the EU countries, a finding perhaps of some solace to defense-oriented parties.[61] After canvassing the various legislative initiatives of

[61] 2018 EU Commission Report, 2: "Legislative activities affected by the Recommendation have remained somewhat limited in the Member States."

Member States, the Commission Report generally concluded that its findings demonstrated "that in spite of the Recommendation several Member States have not introduced collective redress mechanisms in their national system."[62] The Commission findings also noted the persistence of great divergence of collective redress mechanisms among the Member States.[63] The Commission Report generally documented the very limited institution and scope of collective redress mechanisms even after the Recommendation encouraged Member States to enact such collective measures.[64]

Since the Commission issued its 2013 Recommendation, seven EU Member States have enacted reforms of their collective redress laws, and the reforms in these countries have not always follow the Recommendation's principles.[65] Belgium and Lithuania enacted compensatory redress mechanisms for the first time, and France and the UK modified their existing laws to improve procedures that were not considered effective.[66] The Commission reported that new legislation was advancing in the Netherlands and Slovenia, with possible new legislation in Germany.[67]

Significantly, most collective redress mechanisms that Member States have enacted or are in the process of enacting are largely restricted to consumer matters.[68] The 2018 Report indicated that all Member States have injunctive relief mechanisms in place for consumer actions.[69] While some Member States have embraced injunctive relief class actions for all types of substantive claims,[70] other Member States

---

[62]Ibid, 4.

[63]Ibid.

[64]The Report concluded, with regard to the institution of collective redress mechanisms by Member States:

> The replies to the call for evidence show that collective redress, where available, is mainly used in the area of consumer protection and related areas such as passenger rights or financial services. Another area where several cases were reported is competition law, especially where alleged cartel victims claim compensation after the decision on an infringement by a competition authority (follow-on actions). The relative absence of recourse to collective redress in other fields is due not only to the fact that in many Member States compensatory or indeed injunctive relief is available only for consumers or in competition law; it also appears to be linked to other factors such as the complexity and length of the proceedings or restrictive rules on admissibility, often relating to legal standing.

[65]Ibid, 2.

[66]Ibid.

[67]Ibid. The Netherlands enacted a collective damage action for monetary damages on March 19, 2019. The legislation applies to harmful events that took place on or after November 15, 2016.

[68]Ibid.

[69]Ibid, 3.

[70]Ibid. The countries that have embraced a complete horizontal approach to injunctive relief collective actions are Bulgaria, Germany, Lithuania, the Netherlands, and Sweden.

have made injunctive relief collective actions available for competition cases,[71] environmental violations,[72] employment issues,[73] or antidiscrimination claims.[74]

The fact that many EU countries have taken a cautious, limited approach to the substantive types of claims for which such relief is available—or have confined the nature of the remedy to injunctive relief—should be of some comfort to defense-oriented interests fearful of a more broad-ranging scope for collective redress initiatives. And, the fact that the remedy in consumer cases has largely been confined to injunctive relief reflects EU countries' embrace of the most common pre-existing form of collective remedy familiar to EU countries prior to the EU Commission's 2013 Recommendation*:* the injunctive relief action.

The 2013 Recommendation had stressed that all Member States should have collective redress mechanisms "both injunctive and *compensatory*" available in all cases where rights granted under EU law were or had been violated "to the detriment of more than one person."[75] Defense interests—in anticipation of collective action procedures being instituted in EU countries—perhaps most feared the introduction of *compensatory* class relief. For American corporate defense attorneys and their clients drawn into class litigation, the prospect of compensatory class litigation presented the greatest threat because of the potential enormous compensatory damage exposure to the class claimants as well as significant attorneys' fees as a consequence of a classwide settlement.

The 2018 EU Commission Report noted that the availability of compensatory collective redress mechanisms varies widely across the EU countries' procedures. In general, 19 Member States offer compensatory relief through their collective redress procedures,[76] but in half these countries, compensatory redress is limited to certain types of claims such as consumer, competition, financial services, labor, environmental and antidiscrimination claims.[77] Significantly, nine Member States do not offer any form of compensatory collective redress.

Surveying the availability of collective redress mechanisms post-Recommendation should supply some consolation to defense-oriented interests anxious about the arrival of collective redress mechanisms throughout the EU. First, the institution of collective redress procedures has been slow and gradual.

---

[71]Ibid. The countries that have injunctive relief collective actions available in competition (antitrust) collective actions are Hungary, Luxembourg, and Spain.

[72]Ibid. The countries that have made injunctive relief collective actions available for environmental violations are France, Hungary, Portugal, Slovenia, and Spain.

[73]Ibid. The countries that have made injunctive relief collective actions available in employment cases are Hungary and Spain.

[74]Ibid. The countries that have made injunctive relief collective actions available for antidiscrimination claims are Croatia, France, and Spain.

[75]2013 EU Commission Recommendation, para 2.

[76]2018 EU Commission Report, 3. The countries which permit compensatory relief collective actions are Austria, Belgium, Bulgaria, Denmark, Germany, Finland, France, Greece, Hungary, Italy, Malta, the Netherlands, Poland, Portugal, Romania, Spain, Sweden, and the UK.

[77]Ibid, 3.

Second, collective redress has chiefly been directed towards injunctive remedies, often narrowly confined to certain types of cases. In essence, many EU Members States have defaulted to the pre-existing form of collective redress with which they already are familiar and comfortable. Third, compensatory relief collective redress actions have been similarly slow to be introduced and have been limited in scope and application. Most notable for American corporate and defense interests, EU Member States to date have shown little interest in permitting compensatory mass tort personal injury collective actions—the bane of the American defense bar.

4.2 Standing and Admissibility Criteria: Relation to the American Certification Requirement

The 2013 EU Recommendation called for Member States to set forth procedures for designing entities that would have legal standing to bring a representative action, "where the parties directly affected by an infringement are represented by an organization which alone has the status of claimant in the proceedings."[78] The 2018 Commission Report found that all Member States had set forth some conditions for legal standing collective redress to act as representative entities in both injunctive and compensatory actions.[79] Collective redress in the form of representative actions was present in almost all Member States, predominantly in environmental and consumer injunctive relief actions.[80]

Among Member States, the most common requirements to establish entity standing include the non-profit character of the entity and the relevance of the litigation's subject matter to the organization's aims. Other Member States have articulated additional specific requirements pertaining to the designated entity's experience and expertise.[81] The Commission Report concluded that the variations with regard to standing were of some significance "since more stringent rules for representative entities could potentially lead to a limitation of the right to seek collective redress and thereby access to courts."[82]

The standing requirements for EU collective redress actions differ significantly from the standing issue in American class action jurisprudence, which focuses on whether the individual class representative plaintiff has suffered injury-in-fact, traceable to the defendant's conduct, that is redressable at law. EU Member States,

---

[78]2013 EU Commission Recommendation, paras 4–7. The Recommendation set out specific minimum criteria for such designation: the non-profit character of the entity, a direct relation between its objectives and the violated rights and a sufficient capacity to represent multiple claimants acting in their best interests.

[79]2018 EU Commission Report, 5.

[80]Ibid, 4.

[81]Ibid, 5.

[82]Ibid.

in lodging the standing criterion in representative entities and associations, focus the standing requirement on adequacy issues similar to the adequacy requirement in American class litigation.

Nonetheless, the EU standing requirement offers defense interests the opportunity at the threshold of collective redress a means to challenge the ability of the designated entity to serve in a representative capacity. Moreover, the fact that the Commission recognized that the imposition of stringent standing requirements could frustrate the ability of injured parties to seek collective redress and thereby access to the courts resonates in the same policy argument long advanced by class action proponents in the United States.

The 2013 EU Recommendation urged Member States to ensure that "admissibility" of the asserted claims was verified at the earliest possible stage of litigation and that proposed cases that did not meet the conditions for collective action and were "manifestly unfounded" were not to be continued as collective actions.[83] The 2018 Commission Report concluded that the civil procedure rules of many Member States that provided for early dismissal of manifestly unfounded claims applied with equal force to proposed collective actions. Only Spain and Sweden did not set forth specific rules on admissibility for collective actions, and therefore defaulted to their general civil procedure rules. Moreover, for injunctive relief collective actions, the main admissibility criterion was the standing of the entity.[84] The Report also found that Member States typically set forth more specific admissibility criteria for compensatory damage collective actions.[85]

The standards for admissibility of a proposed collective action varied across Member States. All Member States require a showing of the homogeneous nature (commonality) of the joined claims.[86] In addition, other Member States variously require a showing that proceeding as a collective action is more efficient[87] or the capacity of the representative entity to protect the interests of affected persons.[88] These EU admissibility criteria resonate in certain similar requirements for class certification pursuant to the American class action rule,[89] but are far less elaborate or demanding than the class certification jurisprudence that has developed in the United States. In surveying the varying criteria on admissibility set forth by Member States, the Commission noted its concern that "existing divergences in conditions on admissibility may still result in unequal access to justice in compensatory collective

[83] 2013 EU Commission Recommendation, paras 8–9.

[84] 2018 EU Commission Report, 6.

[85] Ibid.

[86] Ibid.

[87] Ibid. The countries that require a showing of efficiency to satisfy admissibility are Belgium, Denmark, Finland, Italy, and Lithuania.

[88] Ibid. The countries that require a showing of the capacity of the representative entity to protect the interests of affected persons are Finland, Italy, the Netherlands, Romania, and the UK.

[89] Fed. R. Civ. P. 23(a) and (b) (requirements for class certification).

actions as overly restrictive rules on admissibility could limit access to procedure."[90]

The varying EU admissibility criteria—from an American defense perspective—offers the most substantial means for easy access to collective actions in EU jurisdictions because of the loose, vague definition of admissibility criteria. Notably, although EU admissibility requirements universally mandate a finding of commonality of joined claims, the nature of the required commonality (and what satisfies this requirement) is undefined. As American class action litigators are well aware, judicial construction of the American requirement of "common questions of law and fact" has been much contested in class action jurisprudence.[91] In addition, no EU country—following U.S. class action jurisprudence in damage class actions—has super-imposed a requirement that common questions predominate over individual common questions.[92]

4.3 The Loser Pay Rule

The 2013 EU Commission Recommendation urged that, "(T)he party that loses a collective action should reimburse necessary legal costs to the winning party," thereby adopting the English loser pay rule.[93] In its 2018 Report, the Commission found that all EU Member States, with the exception of Luxembourg, follow the loser pay principle in their domestic civil procedure law. With regard to collective mechanisms, the Report found that the overwhelming majority of Member States applied the exact same loser pay rule to collective actions.[94]

The EU Commission, however, cautioned that Member States differed in their understanding of what constituted reimbursable costs, and that the application of different domestic law could lead to substantial divergences in the actual reimbursement of the costs of the winning party in very similar proceedings, depending on the forum. "Therefore, the Commission concluded, the aim of preventing abusive litigation through the loser pay principle, in reality, is not equally achieved in all Member States."[95]

The universal acceptance of the loser pay rule throughout EU Member States as applied to collective actions of course is advantageous to defense-oriented litigants,

---

[90]2018 EU Commission Report, 7. The Commission further recommended that as admissibility was a preliminary phase of the collective action, "expeditious decisions on admissibility are important for the legal certainty of all the parties involved."

[91]See, e.g., Wal-Mart Stores, Inc. v. Dukes, 563 U.S. 338 (2011) (extensive discussion of Rule 23 (a)(2) commonality requirement).

[92]Fed. R. Civ. P. 23(b)(3) (predominance requirement).

[93]2013 EU Recommendation, para 13.

[94]2018 EU Commission Report, 8. The Report noted limited exceptions in some jurisdictions for exemptions from court fees for representative entities and public authorities in consumer cases. The countries with such exemptions were Croatia, Hungary, Malta, Poland, and Romania.

[95]Ibid, 9.

who have long lobbied for the institution of a loser pay rule in the United States. However, the Commission's caveat concerning individual forum definition of what constitutes reimbursable "costs" may, as the Commission suggests, somewhat undermine the utility of the loser pay principle for preventing the abusive litigation that concerns American defense attorneys.

4.4 Attorneys' Fees

The 2013 EU Commission Recommendation solidly counseled against the introduction of attorney contingency fee arrangements into EU collective redress regimes.[96] The Recommendation provided that attorney remuneration and the method of calculating attorney fees should not create unnecessary incentives to litigation not in the interest of the parties. Member States were to prohibit contingency fees that risked creating such incentives. The Commission further recommended that if Member States were to allow contingency fee arrangements, then such attorney fee schemes should be appropriately regulated in collective redress cases.[97]

The 2018 EU Commission Report generally found that Member States did not regulate lawyers' fees in non-collective cases. Similarly, the Report found that Member States did not regulate lawyers' fees in collective redress cases. However, Member States that followed the 2013 Recommendation almost universally had not adopted contingency fee regimes. As of 2018, only nine Member States allowed for some form of contingency fee,[98] with the amount ranging from 15% under the Slovenia draft legislation, to 50% of the value of the award in the UK.[99] The Report noted that not all forms of contingency fees were likely to incentivize litigation. For example, in Germany contingency fees were allowed only in exceptional circumstances where the alleged victim lacked financial means and could only pursue relief with a contingency fee arrangement.[100] On the other hand, the UK (with permitted 50% contingency awards) and Spain (with permitted 33% contingency awards) were viewed as "more likely to incentivize unnecessary litigation."[101]

Other Member States allowed for performance fees: upward fee awards in the case of successful prosecution, or a reduction of fee awards where litigation goals

[96] 2013 EU Commission Recommendation, paras 29–30.

[97] Ibid.

[98] 2018 EU Commission Report, 16. The nine Member States permitting some form of contingency fee arrangements are Bulgaria, Cyprus, Czech Republic, Germany, Greece, Poland, Slovenia, Spain, and the UK.

[99] Ibid.

[100] Ibid.

[101] Ibid.

were not achieved.[102] In particular, two Member States—the Netherlands and Finland—noted that attorney fees were problematic and a factor that contributed to the high cost of redress proceedings.[103] The Commission generally concluded that the prevailing systems of attorney fees that were embedded in national procedural law traditions were followed for collective actions, and there was no evidence that any changes were contemplated to modify such systems for collective redress cases.[104]

The fact that EU Member States almost universally have eschewed instituting contingency fee arrangements to pay attorney fees in collective redress mechanisms again reflects a European default to longstanding, historical repugnance to contingency fee arrangements. That Member States have not adopted contingency fee arrangements wholesale—with limited exceptions—should provide additional reassurance to defense-oriented actors that the lure of high contingency fee awards in European collective actions will incentivize American-style entrepreneurial lawyering. EU Member States seem to have received the American critique that contingency fee arrangements for collective redress actions incentivize lawyer-driven litigation, which leads to abuse of process.

4.5 *Punitive Damages*

Similar to the European distaste for contingency fee arrangements, European civil law jurisdictions have long abjured punitive damages. Consequently, the 2013 Commission Recommendation called for a prohibition on punitive damages in collective redress cases, as well as "of other awards exceeding the compensation that would have been obtained in individual litigation."[105]

The 2018 EU Commission Report noted that the concept of overcompensation in the form of punitive damages was alien to the majority of Member States in their domestic law. The majority of countries did not award punitive damages, and there were no reports where punitive damages were requested or granted in collective redress cases. Only Greece and England and Wales admitted some form of punitive damages in very limited form.[106]

The continued European non-recognition and resistance to punitive damages—now transposed into the collective redress arena—is another victory for defense

[102]Ibid. The countries with performance fees in their collective redress legislation were Austria, Belgium, France, Italy, Lithuania, Luxembourg, Poland, and Sweden.

[103]Ibid. A respondent from the UK submitted an example of a collective redress case where the national court had held was an abuse of process where attorneys were working on a contingency fee basis.

[104]Ibid.

[105]2013 EU Commission Recommendation, para 31.

[106]2018 EU Commission Report, 17.

interests in containing European-style class litigation. In America class litigation, the possibility of large-scale punitive damages for wrongdoing has served as an additional incentive to pursue classwide relief.

4.6 Third-Party Financing

The 2013 EU Commission Recommendation addressed the nascent movement in several common law countries that currently allows for third-party financing of class action litigation. While not prohibiting third-party financing arrangements, the Recommendation sought to confine the implementation of third-party financing schemes so as not to create incentives for abusive litigation and conflicts of interest. To this end, the Recommendation set forth a series of obligations of parties entering into third-party financing arrangements, and considerations that courts should take into account in managing litigation supported by third-party financers.[107]

The 2018 EU Commission Report indicated that no Member State had implemented the Recommendation's several prescriptions to govern the implementation of third-party financing schemes,[108] and that the Commission's recommendations with regard to regulating third-party financing had almost no impact on Member States.[109] No Member States, in their collective redress regimes, had any provisions regulating third-party financing. Only two Member States—Greece and Ireland—prohibited third-party financing.[110]

The EU Commission Report further noted that third-party financing had already been utilized in three Member States (Austria, the Netherlands, and the UK) and was largely implemented without significant regulation.[111] Reviewing those instances where third-party financing had been utilized, the Commission concluded that third-party financing was increasingly being used in several Member States. The Commission noted that the growing possibility of third-party financing had implications for cross-border disputes, "as funds to initiate litigation can be easily provided across borders."[112] Consequently, the Commission warned that, "(T)his general lack of implementation means that unregulated and uncontrolled third-party financing can proliferate without legal constraints, creating potential incentives for litigation in certain Member States."[113]

---

[107]2013 EU Commission Recommendation, paras 14–16, 32.

[108]2018 EU Commission Report, 9.

[109]Ibid, 10.

[110]Ibid, 9. The Report noted that Slovenia is in the process of enacting legislation that would regulate third-party financing in accordance with the limitations on third-party financing set forth in the Recommendation.

[111]Ibid.

[112]Ibid, 10.

[113]Ibid, 9.

The Commission's concerns about third-party financing and the apparent unregulated acceptance of third-party financing by some Member States embody defense apprehensions about this form of litigation financing. The Commission clearly has stated its concerns about the potential for litigation abuse in the collective redress context when such financing is unaccompanied by regulation. As such, third-party financing is one problem where defense interests apparently did not prevail in the introduction of collective redress regimes in the EU. On a forward-going basis, the prospect of third-party financing should be a cause of concern for defense-oriented interests.

4.7 *The Continental Opt-In Preference*

As is well known, American class action procedure operates on an opt-out principle for damage class actions.[114] The American preference for the opt-out procedure is rooted in the jurisprudential theory that by declining to affirmatively exit the class, the class member has given consent to be bound by the class judgment.[115] The American preference for the opt-out procedure also is grounded in the pragmatic knowledge that few class members will opt-out of the class, thereby maximizing the class size for plaintiffs' counsel. In addition, optimizing the size and scope of the class helps to assure global peace for settling defendants. Although American class action procedural law has long maintained the opt-out preference, in recent reform circles the possibility of reverting to the continental opt-in principle has received some support.[116]

The European civil law preference has long been the opposite of the American opt-out preference: consent can only be conferred by affirmatively opting into a proceeding. The 2013 EU Commission Recommendation, consistent with this longstanding jurisprudential precept, strongly urged Member States to introduce the opt-in principle for their collective redress mechanisms.[117] Thus, a natural or legal person should be able to join or withdraw from a collective action until a judgment or settlement of the case.[118] This problem of consenting to collective redress cases primarily implicates compensatory damage actions where there is a

[114]Fed. R. Civ. P. 23(b)(3); Fed. R. Civ. P. (c).

[115]See Phillips Petroleum Co. v. Shutts, 472 U.S. 797 (1985) (consent by declining to opt-out of Rule 23(b)(3) damage class action).

[116]See ALI (2010) para 2.10, 176–178 & Reporter's Note to Cmt. a (Am. Law. Inst. 2010) (encouraging opt-in aggregation in certain cases and "provid[ing] courts with authority to create opt-in mechanisms for voluntary aggregation of claimants by their affirmative consent"); see generally Dodson (2016).

[117]2013 EU Commission Recommendation, paras 21–24. The Recommendation noted that natural or legal persons joining an action should do so based on their express consent only.

[118]Ibid.

possibility of high individual damages (and of less concern in injunctive relief classes with homogeneous interests in the remedy).

In enacting collective redress mechanisms, the Member States reflected a diversity of approaches to the opt-in or opt-out principles. Thirteen Member States enacted collective redress schemes that apply the opt-in principle.[119] Four Member States adopted a combination of opt-in and opt-out procedures, depending on the type of action or the specifics of the case.[120] Two Member States adopted an opt-out principle only.[121] Given the diversity of approaches that Member States adopted with regard to giving consent to a collective proceeding, the Commission concluded that its firm recommendation of the opt-in procedure had a limited effect on Member States as they enacted domestic legislation.

The implications for defense-minded actors of the EU opt-in/opt-out procedure are unclear. At a minimum, the diversity of procedures complicates the resolution of cross-border collective actions. For American defense attorneys schooled in the opt-out procedure, the presence of EU opt-in rules may serve to undermine the defense goal of achieving global peace. On the other hand, empirical studies have shown that opt-in procedures tend to minimize class participation—a result that defense-minded litigants may desire. However, with the American reform movement now supporting the importation of the continental opt-in preference, it is unclear the extent to which defense attorneys might be satisfied or dissatisfied with the current state of affairs in EU Member States with regard to this aspect of class procedure.

5 Conclusion

The introduction of collective redress mechanisms into the 28 EU Member States reflects 28 shades of European class actions. It is fair to suggest that no two countries' enactments are the same, instead presenting a dizzying array of complicated procedures and rules. But the overarching portrait that emerges from this chaotic assemblage of initiatives is one that is curiously cautious and decidedly non-revolutionary. Indeed—ironically—the content of the EU collective redress initiatives harkens back to the twentieth-century European attitudes of disapproval towards American class litigation. Thus, Europe appears to have made itself safe from the American class action; what EU Member States have enacted might be characterized as "class action lite."

A prominent theme that emerges from an appreciation of what EU Member States have accomplished is the extent to which their collective redress mechanisms

[119]2018 EU Commission Report, 13. The Member States adopting the opt-in principle are Austria, Finland, France, Germany, Greece, Hungary, Italy, Malta, Poland, Romania, Spain, and Sweden.

[120]Ibid. The Member States adopting a combination approach are Belgium, Bulgaria, Denmark, and the UK.

[121]Ibid. The Member States adopting an opt-out procedure are only the Netherlands and Portugal.

embody the chief platforms of American tort and class litigation reform. It can hardly escape notice the number of times that the EU Commission, in its study and recommendations, sounded the alarm about potential class action abuses and the societal evils of frivolous, unmeritorious litigation. These passages could well have been written by the U.S. Chamber of Commerce. For corporate defense attorneys (and their clients) who were apprehensive about the introduction of American-style class litigation in Europe, there is much relief to be found in the EU enactments.

To a large extent, the EU countries have chiefly confined collective redress cases to injunctive relief actions, a form of collective remedy with which many EU countries were already familiar and comfortable. The EU Recommendation and national enactments manifest a strong preference for recourse to alternative dispute resolution auspices, where available, to resolve collective disputes. Compensatory damage collective actions have been slower to gain traction in the EU, have been limited in many respects, and there has been virtually no discussion or embrace of mass tort personal injury class actions that have so dominated the American legal landscape. The EU countries largely have undermined the prospect of entrepreneurial, lawyer-driven class litigation by rejecting contingency fee arrangements. Most EU countries have endorsed the loser pay rule, a longtime favorite reform of the American corporate defense bar. The EU countries have rejected the availability of punitive damages, another incentive to class litigation.

Although American-style class litigation largely has been circumscribed throughout the EU, some novel (and un-American) innovations may prove problematic for corporate defense interests in coming years. It remains to be seen the extent to which the allowance of unregulated third-party financing will incentivize European collective actions. The vagueness of the "admissibility" requirements of EU countries may prove vexing precisely because of their uncertainty and fluidity. Finally, the jury is out concerning the implications of the opt-in/opt-out procedures that inform various EU collective redress regimes.

Finally, the EU collective redress initiatives and their foundational principles reflect a curious flashback to the continental scholarship of the late twentieth century, when European academics roundly rejected the American class action rule and said "Nein!" and "Basta!" to class litigation. Decades later, *Plus ça change, plus c'est la même chose.*

References

ALI (2010) Principles of the law. Aggregate Litigation

Beisner JH (2010) Cy Pres: a not so charitable contribution to class action practice. U.S. Chamber Institute for Legal Reform

Beisner JH et al (2009) Selling lawsuits, buying trouble: third-party litigation funding in the United States. U.S. Chamber Institute for Legal Reform

Brouquier E (2015) Class Actions in France – What You Need to Know. GEN RE. Available via http://de.genre.com/knowledge/blog/class-actions-in-france-what-you-need-to-know.html

Cappalli RB, Consolo C (1992) Class actions for continental Europe? A preliminary inquiry. Temp Int Comp Law J 6:217
Cappelletti M, Garth B (1983) The Protection of Diffuse, Fragmented and Collective Interests in Civil Litigation
Clark SS et al (2013) Is the class action 'centre of gravity' moving away from the United States? Def Couns J 80:420
Dodson S (2016) An Opt-in option for class actions. Mich Law Rev 115:171
Fisch WB (1979) European analogues to the class action, group action in France and Germany. Am J Comp Law 27:51
Harbour LJ, Shelley ME (2007) The emerging European class action: expanding multi-party litigation to a shrinking world, Prac. Litigator 18(4):23
Hensler DR (1991) Diagnosing the nation's legal ills. Judicature 75:176
Hensler DR (2016) From sea to shining sea: how and why class actions are spreading globally. Univ Kan Law Rev 65:965
Koch H (1986) Class and public interest actions in German Law. Civil Just Q 66
Koch H (1994) Mass Torts in Germany. German National Reports in Civil Law Matters for the XIV Congress of Comparative Law in Athens
Lesur (2016) French class action has less impact than expected. McDermott Will & Emery. Available via https://www.mwe.com/en/thought-leadership/publications/2016/02/french-class-action-law-has-less-impact
Lutfalla E, Magnier V (2006) French legal reform: what is at stake if class actions are introduced in France? Def Couns J 73:301
Nashi R (2010) Italy's class action experiment. Int Law J 43:147
Note (1996) "Common sense" legislation: the birth of neoclassical tort reform. Harv Law Rev 109:1765
Olson WK (1991) The Litigation Explosion: What Happened When America Unleased the Lawsuit
Parker D (1995) Standing to litigate "Abstract Social Interests" in the United States and Italy: reexamining "Injury in Fact". Colum J Transnatl Law 33:259
Steinman S (2018) Tort 'Reform' stew. JTLA Trial 54:18
Taruffo M (1990) Group Actions in Civil Procedure. Italian National Report to the XIII International Congress of Comparative Law
Vairo G (2016) The role of influence in the arc of tort "reform". Emory Law J 65:1741
Voet S (2017) Actions for Collective Redress. In: Consortium of European Universities, Max Planck Institute Luxembourg for Procedural Law (2017) An Evaluation of National Procedural Laws and Practices in Terms of Their Impact on the Free circulation of Judgments and on the Equivalence and Effectiveness of the Procedural Protection of Consumers Under EU Consumer Law (report commissioned by the European Commission). JUST/2104/RCON/PR/CIVI/0082

Linda S. Mullenix Holder of the Rita and Morris Atlas Chair in Advocacy at the University of Texas School of Law. Served as a U.S. Supreme Court Fellow; a scholar-in-residence at the Rockefeller Foundation Bellagio Study and Conference Center in Italy; and held the Fulbright Senior Distinguished Chair in Law, in Trento, Italy. An elected Life Member of the American Law Institute, an elected Life Fellow of the Texas Bar Foundation, an elected Life Fellow of the American Bar Foundation, and an elected member of the International Association of Procedural Law. She teaches civil procedure, mass tort litigation, class action litigation, federal courts, and conflict of laws.

Part III
Many Faces of Collective Litigation: European Perspectives

The Dawn of Collective Redress 3.0 in France?

Maria José Azar-Baud and Alexandre Biard

Abstract France is a country with a long tradition of collective proceedings in general but has only a limited experience when it comes to group actions in particular (which are called in French '*actions de groupe*'). This procedural instrument was formally adopted in 2014 after decades of tense debates and controversies. Its subsequent developments have been patchy and the problems plaguing its functioning and its added value for harmed individuals remain multiple in practice. Unexpectedly, the development of group actions in France has triggered several interesting evolutions. They have first revitalised old and pre-existing procedural mechanisms, which were until now rarely used. Second, they have indirectly contributed to the emergence of a myriad of new Legaltech actors attracted by an emerging mass litigation market in France. These actors use online tools and platforms for mobilising individual claimants, hence structuring mass claims. In parallel, the recent EU initiatives, and in particular the adoption in November 2020 of Directive 2020/1828 on representative actions for the protection of the collective interest of consumers, are likely to have an important impact on the French collective redress landscape. In other words, France may be at the dawn of a new era, the one of 'collective redress 3.0'.

1 Introduction

Collective redress and collective litigation have been a geographical, legal and societal adventure.[1] Their roots can be traced back to medieval England,[2] but they developed in the United States and in most other common law jurisdictions in the

[1]Hensler et al. (2016).
[2]Yeazell (1977, 1987).

M. J. Azar-Baud
University of Paris-Sud, Paris, France
e-mail: maria-jose.azar-baud@u-psud.fr

A. Biard (✉)
Erasmus University Rotterdam, Rotterdam, The Netherlands
e-mail: biard@law.eur.nl

A. Uzelac, S. Voet (eds.), *Class Actions in Europe*, Ius Gentium: Comparative Perspectives on Law and Justice 89, https://doi.org/10.1007/978-3-030-73036-9_4

twentieth century, before flourishing worldwide in the first decades of the twenty-first century under different terminologies (class action, group action, etc.).[3]

The underlying reasons for the global rise of collective redress proceedings are multiple, complex, often intertwined and shaped by domestic considerations. Consequently, they significantly diverge across countries.[4] They may have been dictated by contexts, as the ever-increasing digitalisation and globalisation of goods and services have nowadays multiplied the risks of mass harm situations, while the tools for compensating individuals in such situations may often still be lacking. They may have been dictated by a desire to save resources and to facilitate economies of scale for all parties when mass claims arise. They may have been adopted as tools for deterring wrongdoers and fostering behavioural changes. They also may have been introduced under the pressure of other countries, and be explained by a desire to stay competitive in the new mass litigation global market currently emerging. Regardless of their peculiar procedural design and respective policy rationales, the global development of collective redress mechanisms makes the topic highly interesting for scholars and policymakers, as it encourages experience-sharing and, where possible, exchanges of best practices.

In this chapter, we will focus on the state of affairs in France, a country which has a long tradition with collective proceedings (understood in their broader sense), but only a recent one when it comes to group actions (a mechanism formally known as '*action de groupe*' in France), since the latter was formally adopted in 2014. Using a musical comparison, one may say that group actions have followed a Sirtaki tempo in France.[5] They first started with slow and lengthy policy discussions in the 1980s. In the following discussion, we will refer to this first phase as 'Collective redress 1.0' (Sect. 2). Then, when the new *action de groupe* was finally introduced in 2014, subsequent developments turned out to be quick and multiple but also patchy and disorganised. To date, group actions have not managed to get into a groove yet: problems plaguing the instrument are multiple and their results remain limited. We will refer to this phase as 'Collective redress 2.0' (Sect. 3). Finally, two recent observeable trends may importantly shape the future of the French collective redress landscape. First, a constellation of new players using the internet and new technologies for mobilising people, aggregating individual claims and structuring mass cases are nowadays emerging. They operate outside and alongside the existing procedural framework for group actions that is traditionally led by associations. Second, and in parallel, recent EU initiatives—in particular the new EU Directive 2020/1828 of 25 November 2020 on representative actions for the protection of the collective interests of consumers—may also importantly shape the future of collective redress. Consequently, we may be at the dawn of a new era hereafter referred to as 'Collective redress 3.0' (Sect. 4). In the field of collective redress, exchanging experience is pivotal. Insights collected about France may thus be

[3]Hensler (2017).

[4]Ibid.

[5]Biard and Pato (2019).

interesting for other countries as well since similar developments are likely to quickly spread to other jurisdictions in the coming years.

2 Collective Redress 1.0 (1980s–2014): The Tortuous Search for a 'French-Style' Group Action

France has a long history with representative proceedings. Different instruments (judicial and extrajudicial) have been in place for several decades. However, the toolbox was for long incomplete as it did not contain suitable tools to deal with mass claims (Sect. 2.1). To fill in this gap, a group action mechanism ('*action de groupe*') was finally adopted in 2014 after many years of discussions (Sect. 2.2).

2.1 An Incomplete Toolbox for Handling Mass Litigation

Let's first consider some of the judicial options available in France when mass harm situations occur. At the beginning of the twentieth century, the French Court of Cassation acknowledged the admissibility of compensatory actions brought by associations defending the individual interests of their members provided that their articles of association include such a possibility (the so-called and today well-established '*Ligues de défense*' case law). Originally, such actions were intended to right a wrong affecting small and circumscribed groups of individuals who usually knew each other and were aware that they were entitled to obtain compensation (e.g. creditors of the same bankrupt company, employees working in the same company, etc.).[6] Today, this technique still appears to be an important tool when it comes to pleading by proxy on behalf of groups of people.[7]

At the same time, other tools for dealing with ever-increasing, multifaceted mass harm situations have multiplied. However, their effectiveness for compensating claimants has remained inconclusive in practice. For example, one of these tools—known as the *action en représentation conjointe*—gives the possibility to accredited associations to start actions to defend the individual interests of persons who have suffered from the same misconduct in similar circumstances. Initially introduced into consumer law in the 1990s, the scope of the action was then extended to other fields such as environmental and securities issues. Yet, the mechanism suffers from many procedural hurdles, which in practice have considerably limited its use and effects.[8] For example, associations are neither authorised to advertise their actions nor allowed to approach individual claimants directly. Also, individual claimants must

[6]Biard and Amaro (2016).

[7]Crim., 20 May 2015, n° 14-81.147, JurisData n° 2015-011901.

[8]Patetta (2010).

give their express consent in writing before the start of the proceedings. In 2006, a report highlighted that fewer than 10 representative actions had been filed by associations since 1992. Furthermore, it pointed out the procedural complexities arising out of the management of the individual mandates, which ultimately led to a paralysis of the action.[9] Finally, as several observers noted, the *action en représentation en conjointe* has sometimes been viewed with some scepticism within the judiciary.[10]

In parallel, France has substantial experience with extrajudicial tools for solving mass harm situations. First, several ad hoc compensation funds (e.g. funds for victims of medical accidents (ONIAM), asbestos (FIVA) and terrorism (FGTI)) have multiplied when mass harm situations arise. Yet, in practice their effectiveness for compensating claimants remains controversial. For example, proceedings before the ONIAM have been described as lengthy and complex.[11] In 2013, the ONIAM expert Committee rejected 86% of applications submitted by victims involved in the 'Mediator' scandal.[12] At the time, this was criticised by a number of associations.[13] Conversely, the FGTI (special fund for victims of terrorism) has brought several positive results and facilitated victims' compensation.[14]

Second, rules supporting collective settlements of mass claims have progressively emerged from practice.[15] For example, in 2009 CMAP (the Paris Mediation and Arbitration Centre) conducted a mediation process between a bank and several associations. The dispute dealt with erroneous and misleading information on variable rates for housing loans. The parties reached an agreement in only six months, which was at that time perceived as a success.[16] Based on this experience, CMAP then developed a set of rules aimed at facilitating the collective settlement of mass claims.

2.2 *Group Actions in France: Mission Possible, Finally!*

As early as the 1980s, the absence of an effective mechanism for compensating individuals involved in mass harm situations fuelled discussions on the necessity to

[9]Hyest (2006). The report highlighted (in French): 'ce système très peu utilisé est tombé en désuétude ... Les associations ont signalé l'extrême lourdeur de la gestion des mandats individuels reçus conduisant à une paralysie de l'action'.

[10]Dupont (2011).

[11]Bacache (2013).

[12]Moracchini-Zeidenberg (2013).

[13]See, e.g., http://www.victimes-isomeride.asso.fr/.

[14]Bechu and Kaltenbach (2019).

[15]Ascenci and Bernheim-Desvaux (2012).

[16]See 'Médiation du Crédit Foncier: un « accord exemplaire » selon l'AFUB', nov. 2009, www.cbanque.com/actu/13284/mediation-du-credit-foncier-un-accord-exemplaire-selon-afub.

adopt a French-style group action.[17] In parallel, the multiplication of big scandals ('PIP breast implants' and 'Mediator', just to name two) and their wide media coverage made the need for reforms a pressing issue. Discussions sought to adopt a 'virtuous' group action model that would protect the system from the purported excesses of the US class actions.[18] However, debates turned out to be very complicated and polarised between stakeholders. For decades, the topic fuelled political statements,[19] was supported by successive governments, defended by regulatory bodies, and discussed many times before Parliament.

Until 2014, all these attempts fell apart due notably to the strong opposition of lobbies using the US class action model as a threat, and arguing that this instrument could ultimately harm the competitiveness of the country. These successive failures led some scholars to compare the thorny emergence of group actions in France to the myth of Sisyphus, the legendary Greek figure sentenced by the gods to roll a boulder to the top of a hill only to see it roll down again, and being forced to endlessly perform this same task all over again.[20]

Yet, in 2014 group actions finally became a reality with Act no. 2013-344 of 17 March 2014, also called '*Loi Hamon*'. Their scope was initially limited to consumer and competition law.[21] Group actions started effectively on 1 October 2014, and on the very first day the consumer organisation *UFC Que Choisir* started an action against the real estate company Foncia alleging unfair contractual terms.[22] In the single month of October 2014, three different actions were engaged,[23] which showed that after years of waiting, consumer organisations were on their marks and ready to fully embrace the new instrument.

---

[17]Calais Auloy (1985).

[18]Veillard and Volders (2008), Azar-Baud (2013), Biard (2014).

[19]See, e.g., Discours aux forces vives de la Nation, January 2005. Available at www.actiondegroupe.com/chirac-classaction/. Accessed November 2019.

[20]Du Chastel (2008), Martinet and Du Chastel (2009), Amrani-Mekki (2012).

[21]Azar-Baud and Carval (2015).

[22]See www.quechoisir.org/action-ufc-que-choisir-l-ufc-que-choisir-lance-la-premiere-action-de-groupe-contre-foncia-groupe-44-millions-d-euros-doivent-etre-reverses-aux-locataires-n12371/. Accessed November 2019.

[23]Namely, UFC Que Choisir v. Foncia (1 October 2014), Confédération Syndicale des Familles (CSF) v Paris Habitat- OPH (13 October 2014), Consommation, Logement et Cadre de Vie (CLCV) v. Axa and AGIPI (28 October 2014).

3 Collective Redress 2.0 (2014–2019): Fast Developments But Mixed Results

The procedural format of the French group action is atypical in many aspects (Sect. 3.1). Its successive developments have been quick but also patchy (Sect. 3.2). Yet, up to today it has remained an instrument with a limited effectiveness for resolving mass claims (Sect. 3.3).

3.1 A New Instrument: The 'Action de Groupe'

In 2014, the *'Loi Hamon'* introduced a peculiar and complex form of group action sometimes described as a 'procedural monster',[24] in which associations and the courts play central roles. Associations have a monopoly for standing, and lawyers (*avocats*) cannot start group actions at their own initiative. This limitation was strongly criticised by the Bar.[25] In practice, however, lawyers remain important players since they assist and represent associations during the proceedings (group actions are filed before High Courts of First Instance—now called "Tribunal judiciaire" and previously "Tribunal de grande instance"—where representation by lawyers is compulsory). As further discussed below, the legal requirements applying to associations depend on the sector at stake. As regards consumer group actions, for example, associations must be representative at the national level, have at least 1 year of existence, show evidence of effective and public activity with a view to the protection of consumer interests, and have a threshold of individually paid-up members. In practice, this covers approximately 15 associations to date.

Schematically, the procedure follows a two-stage process, which can be described as follows: a duly registered association initiates a group action lawsuit before the High Court of First Instance of the domicile of the defendant (unless the defendant is located outside France; in this case, the Paris High Court of First Instance has exclusive jurisdiction). During the liability phase (or Phase 1), the court decides both on the admissibility of the claim and on the liability of the defendant(s) through the review of individual cases presented by the association. These individual cases act as a cornerstone, since there is formally no group of claimants at the beginning of the procedure. The decision of the court is thus based only on the review of those individual cases. In doing so, policymakers wanted to avoid a too-early 'massification' of the dispute.[26] The individual cases must be representative enough of the entire group, and the court needs to be confident that the underlying facts and legal issues can be extrapolated to other individuals who find themselves in similar circumstances. During this first phase, the court defines the scope of the defendant's

[24] Molfessis (2014), Claudel (2014), Haeri and Javaux (2014).

[25] Bretzner (2013) and Portmann (2019).

[26] Beteille and Yung (2019).

liability, the damage to be compensated, and available remedies. It also defines the scope of the group, the parameters that individuals must meet to join the group, and sets cut-off dates for joining the group. Furthermore, the court specifies how the case should be publicised in the media (publicity is done at the expense of the defendant). As regards group actions in competition law, they can be 'follow-on' group actions only, and have to be initiated within a period of 5 years from the date the administrative decision or the review court judgment has become final. Interestingly, the French group action model follows a peculiar 'late opt-in' system, since the group is only constituted after the court decision on liability has been handed down. This system has pros and cons. On the one hand, it is attractive for individual claimants since the likely success of their individual claims will be clarified beforehand by the court. In theory, this should incentivise individual claimants to join the action. The association alone bears the litigation risks. On the other hand, the late opt-in system also creates some uncertainty. For example, the court has no clear view as to the actual size of the group (apart from the estimates and numbers brought forward by the association). Also, in some cases, defendants may not have clear views on the total loss and expected damages. During the award distribution phase (Phase 2), claimants fulfilling the criteria set down by the court can join the group within the set timeframe. Once the award has been distributed, the court terminates the proceeding and, if necessary, may address any unresolved issues arising out of the award distribution.

In parallel, the new framework has also introduced rules for the collective settlement of mass claims.[27] The association and defendant(s) can agree to settle their case, and the settlement agreement must be submitted to the court for review. The court must conduct an in-depth evaluation of the proposed agreement. Judges should in particular ensure that the interests of all potential group members are adequately protected. The settlement agreement is then advertised in the media to allow individuals to opt in.

In practice, it appears that the existence of a group action mechanism has led a few associations to reach settlement agreements on behalf of (limited) groups of individuals. The contents of those agreements remain confidential. As a consequence, their benefit is often limited to those members of the group the association was already aware of (e.g. pre-paid members of the organisation or individuals who may be connected to the organisation in some way).

3.2 Patchy Developments

After consumer and competition law (in 2014), the scope of group actions was then expanded to health (Act no. 2016-41 of 26 January 2016),[28] environmental issues,

[27]Brochier (2014).

[28]Bacache (2016).

discrimination,[29] privacy and data protection (Act no. 2016-1547 of 18 November 2016).[30] The lawmaker followed a sectoral approach, and built a taxonomy based on the specifics of the rights at stake.[31] The lawmaker also adopted a 'common procedural framework' enshrined in the Code of Civil Procedure and the Code of Administrative Justice. However, this 'common procedural framework' did not replace the special rules, which (for most of them) are also reiterated in the relevant codes (e.g. the Environmental Code, Public Health Code, Consumer Code, etc.). For the sake of simplicity and visibility, group actions certainly would have justified a more uniformed legislative treatment.

Furthermore, the lawmaker failed to take full stock of the experience with group actions before expanding their scope to new domains.[32] Ultimately, this approach today tends to jeopardise the system as a whole and makes it unnecessarily over-complicated.

Many procedural differences exist between sectors. A first example regards divergences in the types of remedies that can be claimed by associations. Group actions in consumer law can exclusively be used to claim compensation for material damage affecting consumers' assets but not for non-material damage. This limitation had until September 2020 deterred French consumer organisations from launching group actions in the context of the Dieselgate scandal, as the proof of a material damage turned out to be difficult to establish.[33] Conversely, group actions in the healthcare sector can be used to claim compensation for personal injuries, and data-related group actions as well as environmental ones can be used for moral damage. A second example regards the standing requirements for associations. As highlighted earlier, for consumer group actions, associations must (among other things) be representative at the national level. On the contrary, in the healthcare sector, the action can be initiated by accredited associations of users of the healthcare system that are representative at the national or local level. This covers approximately 500 associations to date. Again broadening the rule, trade unions also have standing to sue in discrimination-related group actions provided that the discriminatory practices took place within the scope of work relationships or within a public service. A third example regards the opt-in period, which can be between two and six months for consumer group actions but between six months and 5 years for health-related group actions. Arguably, sectoral specificities can indeed justify some procedural differences (e.g. a longer opt-in period for health-related group actions appears necessary, as the materialisation of damage in this specific context may take time in practice). Yet a simpler and more coherent approach would certainly

[29]Bugada (2017).

[30]Azar-Baud (2017a).

[31]Azar-Baud (2017b), Mainguy (2016), Amrani-Mekki (2015).

[32]Azar-Baud (2017a).

[33]In September 2020, the French consumer organisation CLCV finally started a group actions against Volkswagen seeking compensation on behalf of French consumers (see: Biard 2021).

have been beneficial for all stakeholders. In addition, this sectoral approach ignores the fact that, beyond each particular field, the rights to be defended throughout group actions often present a number of key similarities.[34]

3.3 *A Half-Full Glass*

A public register listing and detailing ongoing and past group actions is still missing in France.[35] Only the State Council (*Conseil d'Etat*) keeps a register with group actions filed before the administrative courts. To fill this gap, private initiatives—such as, notably, the *Observatoire des actions de groupe*[36]—have been launched to facilitate visibility and the tracking of past and on-going group actions. Between 2014 and 2019, approximately 20 group actions started before judicial courts (a majority of cases being consumer group actions), and around 20 before the administrative courts. Before judicial courts, group actions were directed against banks (e.g. BNP Paribas), pharmaceutical companies (e.g. Sanofi), real estate companies (e.g. Foncia, Immobilière 3F), telecom companies (e.g. SFR, Free), or tech companies (e.g. Google). Before administrative courts, claims were directed against the Ministry of Internal affairs or the Ministry of Education. The largest (expected) group of claimants brought together up to one to two million individuals, and only 36 individuals for the smallest one, which means that group actions have also been used to deal with very local issues. To date, most of the cases are still pending, several, however, have been rejected, and three have been settled.[37] Not a single cross-border group action has started to date.

Evaluating group actions requires setting a benchmark. In this respect, the number of actions cannot as such represent a good and sufficient indicator showing the success or the failure of the instrument. Indeed, only a few cases might have been successful and brought positive results, whereas multiple individual actions might have failed or had only a limited impact in practice. In other words, the quality of the mechanism does not rest solely on the quantity of the actions initiated. As a general observation, it is usually common place to say that the first results with group actions in France have been nuanced,[38] if not disappointing.[39] To begin on a positive note, contrary to early criticisms, group actions have neither weakened the foundations of the French economy nor led to abuses or frivolous lawsuits. Many of the initial fears have not materialised in practice. However, it also appears that group actions are still

[34] Ibid.

[35] Azar-Baud (2018).

[36] See www.observatoireactionsdegroupe.fr. Accessed November 2019.

[37] CSF v. Paris Habitat OPH was settled for €2 million distributed to 100,000 individuals. UFC v. Free Mobile was settled for an amount of €1.7 million (group members individually received between €1 and €12. Familles Rurales v. SAS Manoir de Ker an Poul was also settled.

[38] Azar-Baud (2019).

[39] Abad and Kemel (2016), Cour des Comptes (2017), Biard (2018a), Javaux and Haeri (2019).

to date a poor mechanism for compensating individuals. Six years after their introduction, several weaknesses continue to plague their functioning.

A first problem regards the length and complexity of the procedure. Group actions are costly for associations, and in practice only a few of them have sufficient resources to start an action.[40] A report issued by the National Assembly in October 2016 highlighted that only a few associations have the capacity (both financial and human) to launch and handle group actions, as they are often time-consuming.[41] To date, no group actions have reached Phase 2 (the compensation phase). In practice, Phase 1 (the liability phase) is lengthy: experience has shown that between three and 4 years are usually needed on average for the court to issue its decision, which then may be appealed. For example, it took 4 years for the Paris High Court of First Instance to hand down its decision on Phase 1 in the very first group action *UFC Que Choisir v. Foncia* filed in October 2014. In total, it might take not less than 7 or 8 years to the court before delivering a final decision for Phase 1 that would no longer be subject to appeal or cassation. Challenging the representativeness of the individual cases brought forward by associations has been a key step in the litigation strategies of defendants and has contributed to delays during the proceedings.[42]

Furthermore, even though no group actions have reached Phase 2 yet, it is expected that Phase 2 will also be lengthy and burdensome for all stakeholders, in particular for associations when organising the award distribution. Realistically, individual plaintiffs may eventually be compensated only after many years. Noteworthy, proposals aimed at broadening legal standing have multiplied in the past few years. For example, the 2016 report cited above suggested authorising group actions initiated by ad hoc associations and by the Directorate General for Fraud Prevention and Competition (DGCCRF) that is linked to the Ministry of Economy.[43] In October 2018, a legislative proposal also suggested allowing groups of individuals to start mass claims on their own motion. As the authors of the bill highlighted, this evolution should be seen as part of a broader movement supporting a greater participation of the civil society.[44]

Another issue regards a certain judicial scepticism—or at least, should we say, a cautious behaviour among certain judges—when it comes to the use of the instrument. This was for instance exemplified in the case *CNL v. Société 3F*. The consumer association CNL started a group action against the real estate company 3F arguing the existence of an unfair contractual penalty clause for delay in payments. The association sought compensation for the damage suffered by the tenants. One key issue was whether housing law could be interpreted as falling within the scope of consumer group actions. As evidenced by the parliamentary

---

[40] Biard (2018b).

[41] Abad and Kemel (2016).

[42] Javaux (2017).

[43] Abad and Kemel (2016).

[44] Proposition de loi n°1327 pour ouvrir les actions de groupe aux citoyens, 17 octobre 2018 (in French: 'cette proposition de loi s'inscrit dans le mouvement d'une plus grande inclusion de la société civile dans l'accès au droit').

discussions that preceded the adoption of the *Loi Hamon* in 2014, it was clear that housing was not a sector that had been excluded from the scope of group actions.[45] At first instance, the Paris High Court of First Instance declared the action admissible, recognising the field of housing law as falling within the scope of consumer group actions. Yet, the same court rejected the claim on the merits while considering that the organisation had failed to prove the company's breach of its legal or contractual obligations. Conversely, for the Paris Court of Appeal[46] the group action was not admissible. This court considered social housing to be excluded from the scope of consumer law, as it is governed by specific rules. The claimant organisation challenged the decision before the Court of Cassation, which ultimately upheld the position of the Court of Appeal. In the interim, the lawmaker enacted a new Act (*Loi portant évolution du logement, de l'aménagement et du numérique*—'ELAN'), this time explicitly expanding group actions to the field of housing.[47] Arguably, there may be plenty of reasons explaining the decision of the Court of Appeal (and of the Court of Cassation) declaring the group action inadmissible. Nevertheless, the narrow judicial interpretation can ultimately be viewed as a sign of cautious judicial behaviour, judges being ultimately unwilling to expand the scope of group actions on their own motion in the absence of clear legal provisions allowing them to do so.

From the perspective of associations, one added value of group actions has been their media impact. In theory, publicity about the group action is only possible when the court decision in Phase 1 is no longer subject to appeal or cassation. In practice, however, associations have often accompanied the start of their group actions with broad media coverage, sometimes several months before the formal start of the procedure. For example, in *CNL v. Immobilière 3F*, the launch of the group action was extensively reported in off-line and online newspapers in November 2014 even though the claim was formally registered in January 2015. In the same vein, the association APESAC announced the launch of a group action against the pharmaceutical company Sanofi in December 2016, but the action officially started only in the spring of 2017. This situation—not anticipated by the lawmaker—was criticised by businesses and led many of them to adapt their early communications strategies. In this respect, group actions may have succeeded in triggering behavioural changes among companies.[48] The early publicity generated by associations can be seen as a by-product of the multi-stage design of the French group action. It is indeed necessary for associations to inform potential claimants at the early stages of the procedure in order to ensure a preservation of evidence, which will allow individual claimants to ultimately join the group during Phase 2.

Finally, data protection may rapidly become a promising field for French group actions.[49] Initially, data protection group actions were only possible for injunctive

---

[45] See Rapp. AN n°1574, p. 40.

[46] CA Paris, Pole 4, Chamber 3, Nov. 9, 2017, No. 16/05321: D. 2017. 2368; JA 2018, n°571, p. 11, obs. X. Delpech; RTD civ. 2018. 149, obs. P.-Y. Gautier.

[47] Danon (2019).

[48] Coignac (2015).

[49] Biard and Pato (2019).

relief. In 2018, the possibility to start group actions for compensatory purposes was finally adopted with Act no. 2018-493 of 20 June 2018 (in particular thanks to an amendment brought by the National Assembly). In November 2018, the organisation Internet Society France started a group action against Facebook in the context of its 'E-Bastille' initiative launched in 2017. In a formal notice letter sent to Facebook,[50] the organisation listed seven grievances, including notably a failure to secure the personal data of Facebook's users, the unauthorised collection of user information, and several security breaches. The organisation asked for €1000 per plaintiff, an amount described by the association as a 'fair compensation in view of the massive and continuous nature of the violation',[51] which would correspond to an amount of approximately €100 million in total. Moreover, after the €50 million fine issued by the French Data Protection Authority (CNIL) to Google in January 2019 for violations of the EU General Data Protection Regulation (GDPR), the consumer association *UFC-Que Choisir* started an action against Google on behalf of 200 'dissatisfied consumers'.[52]

4 Towards Collective Redress 3.0 (2020 and Beyond): Digitalisation and Europeanisation

Two trends are likely to considerably shape the future of collective redress in France. They are, namely, first, the increased digitalisation of procedures, the use of artificial intelligence (AI) and the growing role of Legaltech for resolving mass claims (Sect. 4.1), and, second, the growing influence of the EU on the existing regulatory framework for collective redress (Sect. 4.2).

4.1 Digitalisation: Legaltech for Mass Litigation

As in other countries, Legaltech platforms have mushroomed in France in the past few years. They now offer a wide range of services ranging from assistance with court filings, assembly of legal documents, big data for legal research, tools of predictive justice, legal chatbots and online legal advice to online dispute resolution services through mediation and other extrajudicial tools.[53] These new entrepreneurs also have started to embrace the field of mass litigation (we named these new players

---

[50]See https://www.isoc.fr/wp-content/uploads/2018/11/2018-11-MED-Facebook.pdf. Accessed November 2019.

[51]Ibid.

[52]See www.quechoisir.org/decryptage-action-de-groupe-contre-google-vos-questions-nos-reponses-n68427/. Accessed November 2019.

[53]Biard (2019a).

'mass litigation entrepreneurs').[54] It is noteworthy that this new phenomenon is not limited to France but is also observable in other countries, such as, for example, the Netherlands (e.g. *claimshare*) and Germany (e.g. *myrights*).[55] In France, many of these platforms have been created by lawyers in collaboration with IT specialists. Lawyers indeed have viewed mass litigation as an emerging market with new business opportunities.[56] In parallel, initiatives from lawyers in this sector have been facilitated by a progressive relaxation of the rules on advertising and communication traditionally applying to lawyers' activities. As early as 2015, the Paris Bar set up its own digital platform for collecting and aggregating individual claims.[57] Between November 2015 and November 2016, the platform *avocat-action-conjointe.fr* (now closed) hosted up to 25 actions in various domains.[58]

Importantly, these platforms do not launch group actions (*action de groupe*) in the narrow sense described above but merely aggregate individual claims into more classical joint actions. In other words, they 'produce' mass claims through an aggregation of individual claimants. In parallel, interest groups are also developing new marketing tools for raising awareness and mobilising people, which ultimately has facilitated new methods for acting collectively.[59]

The internet and new technologies offer several advantages when it comes to mass litigation: they facilitate the adhesion of individuals who can join a claim by simply clicking on a weblink,[60] structure 'communities' of claimants, facilitate communication and knowledge-sharing between claimants and counsels, but also within the group through discussion forums and other online discussion tools, reduce costs thanks to a dematerialisation of documents, and, finally, ensure a wide publicity and mediatisation of the action, as the information is often extensively reported on social media. Some platforms also have argued that their priority has been to replace the individual claimant at the heart of the procedure. They consider that under the current group action framework the voices and individual circumstances of claimants are lost and diluted within the group and behind the actions of associations.[61]

---

[54]Biard and Kramer (2019), Biard and Javaux (2019).

[55]See also Rott (2016).

[56]Biard and Javaux (2019).

[57]Dufour (2015), Barreau de Paris (2017).

[58]Barreau de Paris (2015).

[59]van Elten and Rehder (2018). For example, in 2018 four NGOs launched a campaign called the 'Century's Affair' ('L'Affaire du siècle') to obtain signatures for a petition forcing the government to act against climate change.

[60]Some of these platforms have been depicted as (in French): 'un véritable supermarché d'actions, dans lequel le client-justiciable n'a plus qu'à se servir. La justice à portée de clic' (Médiacités, 'Plateformes d'actions collectives: la Justice à portée de clic?',13 novembre 2019. www.mediacites.fr/enquete/national/2019/11/13/plateformes-dactions-collectives-la-justice-a-portee-de-clic/. Accessed November 2019.

[61]The platform mysmartcab states (in French): 'à l'inverse dans le cadre d'une action collective le justiciable garde sa liberté d'action. Par ce biais, vous êtes à l'origine de l'action et vous devenez coproducteur de la décision judiciaire. Au final, la décision vous appartient et elle ne dépend pas

It is noteworthy that the first generation of internet platforms has until now essentially been used for structuring mass claims and mobilising people. In other words, they have mainly focused on communication and exchanges of information. However, it is likely that a second generation of platforms will soon use AI, machine learning and other predictive justice tools to also facilitate and speed up the resolution of mass claims. This is already happening with some ODR (online dispute resolution) platforms using automated decision-making for the resolution of disputes. Some of these online tools exist in France even though their activities are still limited to individual disputes today.[62]

Let's focus on specific examples to illustrate how mass litigation entrepreneurs operate in practice. The platform *mysmartcab* launched by a law firm has initiated several joint actions, which have attracted hundreds of claimants. In particular, one of the joint actions brought together thousands of individuals against the pharmaceutical company Merck with regard to an alleged lack of information concerning the new formula of one of its blockbuster products (Levothyrox), used for the treatment of thyroid hormone deficiency. A group of four lawyers represented the whole group of claimants, and they asked for €10,000 per plaintiff. The first hearings took place in December 2018 in Lyon and had to be relocated outside the courtroom because the number of attendees exceeded the capacity of the room. Through mysmartcab, counsels are remunerated with a flat-rate contribution of €96 paid by each individual claimant participating in the action, plus a share of 10% of the final award in the event of success. Occasionally, additional expertise fees also may apply.

Another example is the platform *V pour Verdict*, which, according to its website, has initiated approximately 15 actions to date in various sectors.[63] In Fall 2019, V Pour Verdict announced the launch of an action against the car manufacturer Renault in the context of the Dieselgate scandal. The platform charges a flat-rate fee of €30 to €50 to individual claimants, and it retains up to 15–20% of the final award in the event of success. At the end of 2019, the platform also announced the launch of a new online service dedicated to the settlement of mass claims (called *cessez le feu*).[64] The objective of this service is to promote out-of-court settlements through a dematerialised mediation procedure organised by a professional mediator.[65] Participation is free for claimants. The platform will retain 20% of the final award if an agreement is reached between the parties.

The rise of Legaltech platforms for resolving mass claims remains controversial for several reasons.[66] A first issue regards the likely difficult cohabitation between platforms launched by lawyers and associations, as the latter normally have a

d'une décision prise par une association de consommateurs ou une majorité dans laquelle votre voix se trouve perdue'.

[62]See, e.g., www.justice.cool/la-mediation-avec-justice-cool/. Accessed November 2019.

[63]See https://actions.vpourverdict.com/. Accessed November 2019.

[64]See https://cessezlefeu.com/. Accessed November 2019.

[65]See https://cessezlefeu.com/foire-aux-questions/. Accessed November 2019.

[66]Biard and Javaux (2019).

monopoly to initiate group actions. Several associations have viewed the activities of these platforms as a form of unfair competition. In addition, the coexistence of platforms and associations tends to contribute to a certain confusion since individuals may not fully understand the differences existing between the group action procedure (*action de groupe*), which is free of charge for claimants and for which associations bear all the risks, and other classic joint actions structured by online platforms, which remain costly for claimants (indeed all these platforms apply some kind of success fees). Moreover, the financial risks borne by individual claimants in the event of failure of the action remain often unclear.

A second issue regards the current lack of a regulatory framework applying to the activities of these platforms. Arguably, lawyers operating behind online platforms are regulated by their professional code of ethics. However, simply put, unlike associations starting group actions, actions initiated by online platforms are not regulated, thus the latter are not subject to the same procedural constraints and safeguards. For example, in the context of group actions, to ensure that the association adequately protects the interests of all individual claimants, the lawmaker has required a prior accreditation (*agrément*) of the association showing (among other things) that it is adequately representative at the national (or local) level. Yet, nothing comparable exists for online platforms, and the scope of the judicial supervision remains unclear when it comes to actions initiated by online platforms or settlements they may conclude on behalf of groups of people.

One could argue that the competition between associations and platforms can also be positive, and ultimately incentivises associations to scale up, specialise and diversify their activities. Associations may collaborate and ultimately gain advantage from these online platforms. Some platforms seem open to collaboration with associations.[67] For example, the association CLCV explicitly mentions on its website its partnership with the online platform *demanderjustice.org*.[68] Some associations have also developed online tools for structuring mass claims.[69] However, such examples tend to remain scarce.

4.2 *Europeanisation: The (Likely) Effects of the EU Initiative in France*

Besides the impact of new technologies, the new EU Directive 2020/1828 on representative actions for consumers may importantly (re)shape the future of

---

[67]See mysmartcab (in French: pour autant, la plateforme n'entend pas opposer actions de groupe et actions collectives conjointes. Nous souhaitons mettre au point un outil commun de l'action collective et la plateforme a vocation à s'ouvrir à tous ceux (avocats, associations, ONG, syndicats, etc.) soucieux de défendre, via la justice, l'intérêt général')(emphasis in original).

[68]See http://www.clcv.org/communiques-de-presse/litige-de-consommation-demander-justice-avec-la-clcv.html. Accessed November 2019.

[69]Biard and Javaux (2019).

collective redress in France.[70] The Commission presented its proposal as part of its 'New Deal for Consumers' package,[71] which aims at stepping up consumer protection and the enforcement of consumer law in the EU. The proposal builds on the 2016–2017 Fitness Check of EU consumer and marketing law[72] and the 2018 evaluation report of the Commission on the implementation of the 2013 Recommendation on collective redress.[73] In 2013, the EU Recommendation set down several common principles that all collective redress mechanisms should follow (e.g. no opt out, no contingency fees, no punitive damages, conditions for starting an action, etc.).[74] Yet, the EU Recommendation was quickly criticised.[75] Doubts materialised in 2018, and in its report of the same year the EU Commission ultimately acknowledged the limited practical impact of the Recommendation in the Member States. For example, in 2018, nine Member States still did not provide for any compensatory collective redress mechanisms.[76] When these mechanisms were available, they still varied significantly in terms of design and effectiveness.[77] In parallel, mass harm situations had multiplied and affected millions of EU citizens, the Volkswagen scandal or Ryanair's massive flight cancellations in 2017 being among the most notorious ones. As former EU Justice Commissioner Jourová highlighted, the fact that, unlike in the USA, in the EU many consumers did not obtain compensation in the Dieselgate scandal, which was felt as 'a cold shower'.[78] The Commission was thus pressed to take action.[79]

The Commission's proposal expanded and renewed the framework laid down in the Injunction Directive of 2009.[80] 'Qualified Entities' (e.g. consumer organisations, public independent bodies, etc.) complying with strict criteria may, within a single representative action ('one-stop shop'), seek as an interim measure an injunction order establishing an infringement as well as measures aimed at eliminating the continuing effects of the infringement, including a redress order. The proposed Directive also sets down rules for the collective settlement of mass claims, subject to close scrutiny by the court or the administrative authority. Throughout 2018, the Commission organised meetings in the Member States (known as 'Consumer dialogues') with the intention of presenting the New Deal for Consumers package, and reaching out to national stakeholders. The proposal was finally adopted by the EU

[70]EU Commission (2018a); Biard (2018a); Azard-Baud (2020), pp. 233–268; Azar-Baud (2021).

[71]EU Commission (2018b).

[72]EU Commission (2017a, b).

[73]EU Commission (2018a).

[74]EU Commission (2013).

[75]Stadler (2013), Hodges (2014), Sorabji (2014), Nagy (2015), Voet (2014a, b).

[76]Trans Europe Experts (2018).

[77]EU Commission (2018b), Biard (2018b), Trans Europe Experts (2018).

[78]Citizens' Dialogue in Vienna, 25 September 2018. Available at https://ec.europa.eu/info/events/citizens-dialogues/citizens-dialogue-vienna-commissioner-vera-jourova-new-deal-consumers-2018-sep-25_en. Accessed November 2019.

[79]EU Parliament (2017), BEUC (2017).

[80]Biard (2018b), Biard and Kramer (2019).

Parliament in March 2019 with several amendments. In particular, the Parliament added more stringent standing criteria for Qualified Entities (e.g. it ruled out the possibility to have actions brought by ad hoc entities). The draft was then adopted by the Council of the EU in Fall 2019. The Council brought several changes to the proposal of the Commission. A political deal on the new EU Directive was finally reached in June 2020 and the text was finally adopted by the EU in November 2020.[81]

France, like the other EU Member States, has now until December 2022 to implement the new rules. Let's try to already foresee its potential impact in France. First, an important question is whether the new EU mechanism will replace, complement or amend the French group action regime as it exists today. As regards the first option (replacement), the EU Commission has made it very clear on several occasions that the proposed instrument is not intended to replace existing collective redress mechanisms existing at national levels. Instead, the proposed redress system would either be integrated into existing instruments or exist in parallel. In practice, this means that the French lawmaker will have the possibility to either create a new instrument based on the criteria of the Directive or to amend the existing group action rules. It is likely (of course with some uncertainty) that the French lawmaker will decide to amend the existing rules. Indeed, in many aspects, the EU instrument resembles the French group action regime (i.e. a two-step process with a first phase focusing on the merits followed by a compensation/redress phase). This does not come as a surprise given that the French group action has been one of the sources of inspiration (among others) of the EU lawmaker when designing the EU instrument. It seems, therefore, that some limited changes might be sufficient to make the French group action compliant with the requirements of the EU Directive. All in all, the EU initiative could be an interesting opportunity for revising and upgrading the collective redress framework nowadays existing in France.

Second, the draft Directive intends to strengthen the activities of 'Qualified Entities' by notably encouraging Member States to take 'the necessary measures to ensure that procedural costs do not constitute financial obstacles for Qualified Entities' to effectively start collective redress proceedings. In this view, Member States should consider 'limiting applicable court or administrative fees, granting them access to legal aid where necessary, or by providing them with public funding for this purpose'. This provision is important, as several scholars have pointed out that a proper financing for mass claims is one of the key factors of their success.[82] In France, the costs associated with group actions have limited their use by associations. The French rules did not provide for public funding. The court may order the defendant to provide the association with an advance on payment with regard to the costs and expenses arising out of Phase 2. The amount is left to the court's discretion and must reflect the nature and the complexity of the diligences borne by the association. In practice, this option has never materialised to date. In November

[81]Several Member States have indeed sent reasoned opinions (e.g. Czech Republic) or expressed concerns (e.g. Germany).

[82]Hodges (2008), Tzankova (2017).

2017, the association APESAC requested from the pharmaceutical company Sanofi an advance on payment of legal fees of approximately €660,000, but the request was ultimately rejected by the court. The provisions of the EU Directive may therefore trigger changes in France where civil society organisations have usually only limited funds for bringing actions.

Third, the Directive intends to introduce rules regulating the third-party funding of mass claims. According to the Directive, third-party funding should be fully transparent in order to avoid conflicts of interest and abusive litigation. In 2013, the EU Recommendation already sought to introduce a framework for third-party funding, and set down several transparency requirements.[83] However, as the EU Commission highlighted in 2018, '[T]his [was] one of the points where the Recommendation had almost no impact in the laws of the Member States (. . .) This general lack of implementation means that unregulated and uncontrolled third-party financing can proliferate without legal constraints, creating potential incentives for litigation in certain Member States'.[84] In France, third-party funding emerged in the early 2010s.[85] Since then, several players have started to offer their services (e.g. *actoowin*, *alterlitigation*, *des-thirdpartyfunding*, etc.).[86] Today, the field is still largely unregulated[87] despite several soft law initiatives focusing notably on third-party funding in the context of international arbitration.[88] In parallel, other forms of financing, such as crowdfunding platforms (*wejustice*; *citizencase*, etc.) are also progressively emerging for financing litigation.[89] In this context, the EU Directive might be the first one to introduce rules regulating third-party funding in France.

Fourth, the Directive provides that it neither affects private international law rules (in particular EU Regulation 'Brussels Ibis',[90] EU Regulation 'Rome I',[91] and EU Regulation 'Rome II')[92] applying to representative actions nor establishes new ones. The legal framework remains therefore incomplete. This gap was already pointed out by several scholars as regards the 2013 Recommendation.[93] For example, the plaintiff-friendly choice of jurisdiction provided by Article 18 of Brussels Ibis is not available for collective redress, and the general choice of jurisdiction designating

---

[83] EU Commission (2013).

[84] EU Commission (2018a).

[85] Les Échos, 'Le financement de contentieux aiguise l'appétit des fonds, 27 August 2019. Available at www.lesechos.fr/finance-marches/marches-financiers/le-financement-de-contentieux-aiguise-lappetit-des-fonds-1126728. Accessed November 2019.

[86] Babonneau (2013).

[87] Barreau de Paris (2016).

[88] ICC (2014), Barreau de Paris (2017).

[89] See www.wejustice.com/comment-ca-marche. Accessed November 2019.

[90] Regulation n°1512/2012 on jurisdiction and the recognition and enforcement of judgments in civil and commercial matters.

[91] Regulation n°593/2008 on the law applicable to contractual obligations.

[92] Regulation n°864/2007 on the law applicable to non-contractual obligations (Rome II).

[93] Stadler (2013), Kramer (2014).

the courts of the Member State of the defendant's domicile (Art. 4) should not be the only ground of jurisdiction available for collective redress.[94] As for applicable law, the complexity of multi-party litigation makes the choice of law difficult. Therefore, to avoid forum-shopping, one single forum should have jurisdiction when possible, namely the one of the territory of which the centre of the group's main interest is located[95] or if it is not possible to be determined, it should be the court of the Member State within the territory of which the defendant is located.[96] Inspiration could be drawn from the EU Insolvency Regulation as it allows representative actions on behalf of individuals residing in different Member States.[97]

Finally, one may wonder whether the new EU rules on collective redress will have an impact on the activities of the so-called 'mass litigation entrepreneurs' and other Legaltech platforms previously described. When presenting the draft Directive, former Justice Commissioner Jourová highlighted that 'representative actions, in the European way, will bring more fairness to consumers, not more business for law firms'.[98] However, it is noteworthy that the requirements imposed on Qualified Entities for starting actions are strict (some requirements have even been strengthened during the discussions before the European Parliament). Paradoxically, the strict standing conditions imposed on Qualified Entities might—as a side-effect—feed the activities of mass litigation entrepreneurs whose actions are less affected by heavy regulatory burden. Consequently, whereas Qualified Entities may be encumbered by strict conditions for starting actions, online platforms whose functioning is simpler may become tools for resolving mass harm situations. This unbalanced state of affairs may ultimately call for a policy intervention to level the playing field between associations and online platforms. To date, a legislative act (*Loi n° 2019-222 of 23 March 2019 de programmation 2018–2022 et de réforme pour la Justice*) and a decree (*Décret n° 2019-1089 of 25 October 2019 relatif à la certification des services en ligne de conciliation, de médiation et d'arbitrage*) have introduced a new voluntary certification scheme for internet platforms offering online dispute resolution services.[99] It is, however, unclear whether the new scheme could also apply to the situation of mass litigation entrepreneurs.

[94]Trans Europe Experts (2018).

[95]Azar-Baud (2013), Biard and Kramer (2019).

[96]Trans Europe Experts (2018).

[97]Trans Europe Experts (2018).

[98]Euractiv, 'EU clear path for collective law suits', 11 April 2018. Available at www.euractiv.com/section/eu-priorities-2020/news/eu-clears-path-for-collective-law-suits. Accessed November 2019.

[99]Biard (2019b).

5 Concluding Remarks

Interestingly, the rise of group actions in France has had several unexpected effects: it notably contributed to revitalising some existing old procedural mechanisms such as representative joint actions, and, in parallel, also triggered the rise of new (Legaltech) actors attracted by the developments of a new mass litigation market. It remains to be seen whether these different players will manage to collaborate or whether they will compete. Ultimately, it appears that a myriad of tools is slowly emerging in France besides group actions. All together, they create a new private enforcement toolkit. One may legitimately ask the question of where the plaintiffs stand in this complex situation. Some of them may be confused by the multiplication of instruments. Alternatively, others may find the possibility of having multiple instruments ultimately beneficial. In any case, consumers' attitudes and expectations vis-à-vis the tools that today exist for resolving mass claims will need to be carefully analysed in the future. At this stage, let's hope that a fair and positive competition between actors will take place, and that synergies between them will eventually emerge. Only time will tell.

References

Abad D, Kemel P (2016) Rapport d'information sur la mise en application de la loi 2014-344, n°4139, 19 octobre 2016. Available at www.assemblee-nationale.fr/14/rap-info/i4139.asp. Accessed Nov 2019

Amrani-Mekki S (2012) La rengaine de l'action de groupe. Gazette du Palais 252

Amrani-Mekki S (2015) L'action groupe du 21e siècle - un modèle réduit et réducteur. La semaine juridique, november 2015

Ascenci & Bernheim-Desvaux (2012) La médiation collective, solution amiable pour résoudre les litiges de masse. Contrats, concurrences, consommation, n°8-9, étude 9

Azar-Baud MJ (2013) Les actions collectives en droit de la consommation, Etude de droit français et argentin à la lumière du droit comparé. Nouvelle Bibliothèque de thèses, Dalloz

Azar-Baud MJ (2017a) De l'inaction aux actions de groupe: nouveaux enjeux. Entretien Dalloz 19 janvier 2017

Azar-Baud MJ (2017b) 3 questions: Actions de groupe: nouveaux enjeux, JCP E 26 janvier 2017

Azar-Baud MJ (2018) En attendant un registre d'actions de groupe et autres actions collectives - Une revue de presse 1637

Azar-Baud MJ (2019) Actions de groupe: Perspectives et pistes d'amélioration, Dalloz, Juris associations 591

Azard-Baud MJ (2020) French Group Action Lawsuits – between tradition and modernity. REDC, Revue européenne de droit de la consommation/Eur J Consumer Law 2:233–268

Azar-Baud MJ (2021) The effects of the directive on representative actions for the protection of the collective interest of consumers on the French group action regime. Rev. Italo-española de Derecho procesal, 2021/1, Marcial Pons, 2/2021

Azar-Baud MJ, Carval S (2015) L'action de groupe et la réparation des dommages de consommation: bilan d'étape et préconisations, Dalloz

Babonneau M (2013) Alter Litigation ou le financement de contentieux par des tiers. Dalloz Actualité 4 avril 2013

Bacache M (2013) L'indemnisation des victimes de contaminations sanguines: le casse-tête. Revue Trimestrielle de Droit Civil

Bacache M (2016) Les spécificités de l'action de groupe en droit de la santé. Dalloz

Barreau de Paris (2015) Actions conjointes des justiciables: les avocats mises sur le numérique. Available at www.avocats.paris/actualites-evenements/actions-conjointes-des-justiciables-les-avocats-misent-sur-le-numerique. Accessed November 2019

Barreau de Paris (2016) Le financement de l'arbitrage par les tiers ('Third-Party Funding'). Available at www.avocatparis.org/system/files/publications/rapport_et_projet_resolution_tpf_0.pdf. Accessed November 2019.

Barreau de Paris (2017) Résolution sur le financement de l'arbitrage par les tiers, 21 February 2017. Available at http://www.avocatparis.org/system/files/publications/resolution_financement_de_larbitrage_par_les_tiers.pdf. Accessed November 2019

Bechu C, Kaltenbach P (2019) Rapport d'information fait au nom de la Commission des lois du Sénat sur l'indemnisation des victimes, No 107, 2013. Available at https://www.senat.fr/rap/r13-107/r13-1071.pdf. Accessed November 2019

Beteille L, Yung R (2019) Rapport d'information fait au nom de la Commission des lois du Sénat sur l'action de groupe, n°499, 26 Mai 2010. Available at: www.senat.fr/rap/r09-499/r09-4991.pdf. Accessed November 2019

Beuc (2017) Letter sent to President Juncker and Commissioner Jourova 'Time for the European Commission to legislate on Collective Redress', 10 October 2017. Available at www.beuc.eu/publications/beuc-x-2017-107_time_for_the_european_commission_to_legislate_on_collective_redress.pdf. Accessed November 2019.

Biard A (2014) Judges & Mass Litigation from a (Behavioural) Law & Economics Perspective (PhD thesis, Erasmus Universiteit Rotterdam, Hamburg Universität, Università di Bologna. Available at http://ediss.sub.uni-hamburg.de/volltexte/2016/8204/pdf/BIARD_Manuscript_2014.pdf. Accessed November 2019

Biard A (2018a) Sale temps pour l'action de groupe... la nécessaire recherche d'outils alternatifs pour résoudre les litiges de masse. 157 Revue Lamy Droit Civil

Biard A (2018b) Collective redress in the EU: a rainbow behind the clouds? ERA Forum 19

Biard A (2019a) Justice en ligne ou nouveau Far Www.est? La difficile régulation des plateformes en ligne de règlement extrajudiciaire des litiges, Revue internationale de droit économique 2

Biard A (2019b) Ensuring the quality of ODR platforms: a new (voluntary) certification scheme in France', Conflict of Laws Blog, 13 November 2019. Available at: http://conflictoflaws.net/2019/ensuring-quality-of-odr-platforms-a-new-voluntary-certification-scheme-in-france/. Accessed November 2019

Biard A (2021) Retour sur 6 ans de Dieselgate en Europe du point de vue des consommateurs. D.C.C.R. (forthcoming)

Biard A, Amaro R (2016) Resolving Mass Claims in France: Toolbox & Experience. BACT-RILE Working Paper Series

Biard A, Javaux B (2019) Recours collectifs à l'heure de la Legaltech: l'initiative européenne serait-elle déjà obsolète? Revue Lamy Droit Civil, Septembre 2019

Biard A, Kramer X. (2019) The EU directive on representative actions for consumers: a milestone or another missed opportunity, Zeitschrift für Europäisches Privatrecht (ZEuP)

Biard A, Pato A (2019) Dancing Cheek-to-Cheek: Collective Redress & Data Protection, Leuven Blog for Public Law, 16 August 2019. Available at: www.leuvenpubliclaw.com/dancing-cheek-to-cheek-collective-redress-data-protection/. Accessed November 2019

Bretzner JD (2013) Ombres et Lumières autour de la Qualité pour Agir dans l'Action de Groupe. Gazette du Palais 16 May 2013, n°136

Brochier M (2014) La "transaction de groupe", Les particularités de la transaction dans l'action de groupe. Semaine Juridique Entreprise

Bugada A (2017) L'action de groupe en matière de discrimination dans les relations de travail', JCP S 4

Calais Auloy J (1985) Rapport de la Commission pour la codification du droit de la consommation - Proposition pour un code de la consommation
Claudel E (2014) Action de groupe et autres dispositions concurrence de la loi consommation: un dispositif singulier. Revue trimestrielle de droit commercial
Coignac A (2015) Action de groupe: quelle stratégie pour les entreprises? Dalloz Actualité 16 février 2015
Cour des comptes (2017) Référé S2017-3839, 18 Decembre 2017. Available at www.ccomptes.fr/sites/default/files/2018-02/20180305-refere-S2017-3908-DGCCRF-protection-eco-consommateur.pdf. Accessed November 2019
Danon A (2019) Logement: avant ELAN, l'action de groupe était impossible. Dalloz juillet 2019
Du Chastel A (2008) L'action de groupe ou le mythe de Sisyphe. Petites Affiches 23 juin 2008, n°125
Dufour O (2015) Actions de groupe: la riposte du Barreau de Paris. Gazette du Palais 28 novembre 2015
Dupont N (2011) L'Action en Représentation Conjointe des Associations de Consommateurs ou l'Action Mal-Aimée des Juges. Recueil Dalloz
Elten K, Rehder B (2018) Demand justice and Dieselgate: how a transnational civil society coalition rocks the legal systems in Europe'. Paper prepared for the ECPR Standing Group, Sciences Po, Paris SGEU conference, 13–15 June 2018. Available at https://ecpr.eu/Filestore/PaperProposal/c803b862-4eab-4620-aea8-07c6a8293f5b.pdf. Accessed November 2019
EU Commission (2013) Recommendation of 11 June 2013 on common principles for injunctive and compensatory collective redress mechanisms in the Member States concerning violations of rights granted under Union Law, OJ L 201
EU Commission (2017a) Report on the fitness check on EU consumer and marketing Law, SWD (2017)209 final, 23 May 2017
EU Commission (2017b) Report on the implementation of the Commission Recommendation of 11 June 2013 on common principles for injunctive and compensatory collective redress mechanisms in the Member States concerning violations of rights granted under Union Law, COM(2018)40 final, 25 January 2018
EU Commission (2018a) Proposal for a directive of the European Parliament and the Council on representative actions for the protection of the collective interests of consumers, and repealing Directive 2009/22/EC, COM (2018)184 final, 11 April 2018
EU Commission (2018b) A New Deal for Consumers, COM (2018)183 final, 11 April 2018
EU Parliament (2017) Recommendation following the inquiry into emission measurements in the automotive sector, P8-TA (2017)0100, 4 April 2017
Haeri K, Javaux B (2014) L'action de groupe à la française, une curiosité. La Semaine Juridique edition générale 31 mars 2014
Hensler D (2017) From sea to shining sea: how an why class actions are spreading globally. Univ Kansas Law Rev 65:965
Hensler D, Hodges C, Tzankova I (eds) (2016) Class actions in context: how culture, economics and politics shape collective litigation. Edward Elgar Publisher
Hodges C (2008) The Reforms of class and representative actions in European legal systems. A new framework for collective redress in Europe. Hart, Oxford
Hodges C (2014) Collective redress: a breakthrough or a damp sqibb? J Consum Policy 37:67–89
Hyest JJ (2006) Rapport d'information fait au nom de la Commission des lois du Sénat sur les Class Actions, n°249, 14 mars 2006. Available at www.senat.fr/rap/r05-249/r05-2490.html. Accessed November 2019
ICC (International Chamber of Commerce), Guide pratique sur le financement de l'arbitrage par les tiers, 2014. Available at www.icc-france.fr/chambre-de-commerce-internationale-page-6-64-506-Arbitrage.html. Accessed November 2019
Javaux B (2017) De la difficulté d'obtenir la nullité de l'assignation en action de groupe. Revue Lamy Droit Civil 154:6388

Javaux B, Haeri K (2019) Action de groupe: quatre ans après, un bilan en demi-teinte, Dalloz avocats 4
Kramer X (2014) Securities collective action and private international law issues in Dutch WCAM settlements: global aspirations and regional boundaries. Pac McGeorge Glob Dev Law J 27:235
Mainguy D (2016) L'élargissement des actions de groupe. Revue Lamy Droit Civil 136
Martinet L, Du Chastel A (2009) Du retour de l'action de groupe et du mythe de Sisyphe. Petites Affiches 49
Molfessis N (2014) L'exorbitance de l'action de groupe à la française. Recueil Dalloz
Moracchini-Zeidenberg M (2013) Mediator: la bataille du lien de causalité continue. Responsabilité civile et assurances 2
Nagy C (2015) The European collective redress debate after the European Commission's Recommendation—one step forward, two steps back? Maastricht J Eur Comp Law 22:530–552
Patetta G (2010) Une illustration flagrante des limites du système français. Revue Lamy Droit civil 70
Portmann O (2019) Il est inacceptable de réserver l'action de groupe à 17 personnes morales. Dalloz actualité
Rott P (2016) Claims management services: an alternative to ADR? Eur Rev Priv Law 1
Sorabji J (2014) Reflections on the commission communication on collective redress. IJEL 17:58
Stadler A (2013) The Commission's Recommendation on common principles of collective redress and private international law issues. Ned Int Privaatr 4:483–488
Trans Europe Experts (2018) Collective Redress in the Member States of the European Union
Tzankova I (2017) Wetsvoorstel collectieve schadevergoedingsactie: een oplossing voor welk probleem ook alweer? TVP
Veillard I, Volders B (2008) La consécration des actions de groupe en Europe – La traversée de l'Atlantique aurait-elle adouci le Monstre à la Frankenstein? Revue de jurisprudence commerciale 2
Voet S (2014a) European collective redress: a status quaestionis. Int J Proc Law 4:97
Voet S (2014b) Where the wild things are. Reflections on the state and future of European collective redress. In: Keirse A, Loos M (eds) Waves in contract and liability law in three decades of Ius Commune. Intersentia
Yeazell S (1977) Group litigation and social context: toward a history of the class action. Columbia Law Rev 77:866
Yeazell S (1987) From medieval group litigation to the modern class action. Yale University Press

Maria José Azar-Baud Associate Professor at University of Paris-Saclay and lecturer at several national and international Universities (University Paris 1 Panthéon-Sorbonne, University Paris 2 Panthéon-Assas), where she teaches Consumer law, Class actions, International Contracts and Comparative law. Funder and chair of the Observatory of Group Actions and other forms of Collective Redress (since 2017). International counsel, serving on the Executive Board of two European non-profit organisations acting as plaintiffs in mass tort cases.

Alexandre Biard Affiliated senior researcher at Erasmus University Rotterdam. His research focuses on consumer rights, enforcement, collective redress and access to justice.

From Injunction and Settlement to Action: Collective Redress and Funding in the Netherlands

Ianika N. Tzankova and Xandra E. Kramer

Abstract The Netherlands is internationally known for its collective settlement mechanism that was introduced in 2005. In a small number of cases with a global outreach this settlement regime has proven to be effective. However, its application relies on the willingness to conclude a settlement agreement and to have it declared binding by the court. A collective action regime had been in place for decades, but was limited to injunctive and declaratory relief. After years of discussion the collective redress system was 'upgraded' by introducing a collective action procedure for damages in 2020. While the intention behind this latest addition can be welcomed as an effective collective action system in this regard was lacking, some of its features are also subject to criticism and have raised doubts as to whether the new Act is an improvement. That is especially the case with respect to actions filed for declaratory and injunctive relief by so called 'ideological claimants'. Another crucial aspect for the effectiveness of collective redress mechanisms in general, but particularly with respect to monetary relief, is the availability of funding. The different modes of financing litigation, are the topic of extensive debate. In particular third-party funding as a solution to enable expensive collective actions to take place, has gained critical attention in Europe, even though it may prove to be the only available or viable funding option in the international context. This chapter discusses

The authors are grateful to Dennis van Gulik, Huguette Knolsfor, and Wouter Hoogeveen for their research assistance and thank Willem Visser for his input on an earlier draft of paragraph 3.4. Mistakes however are of the authors. For Xandra Kramer the research has received funding from the European Research Council (ERC) under the European Union's Horizon 2020 research and innovation programme (grant agreement No 726032), ERC consolidator project 'Building EU Civil Justice: challenges of procedural innovations - bridging access to justice'; see www.euciviljustice.eu.

I. N. Tzankova
Tilburg University, Tilburg, Netherlands
e-mail: i.n.tzankova@tilburguniversity.edu

X. E. Kramer (✉)
Erasmus Universiteit Rotterdam, Rotterdam, Netherlands

Universiteit Utrecht, Utrecht, Netherlands
e-mail: kramer@law.eur.nl

A. Uzelac, S. Voet (eds.), *Class Actions in Europe*, Ius Gentium: Comparative Perspectives on Law and Justice 89, https://doi.org/10.1007/978-3-030-73036-9_5

developments in collective redress in the Netherlands with a focus on the issue of funding and on the position of the Netherlands collective redress regime in the European and international context. It concludes that if the Netherlands is to continue to hold its predominant position in Europe in relation to collective redress, that will not be because of the new law, but because of the creativity of lawyers, the pragmatism of the Dutch courts and the willingness of funders to rely on both.

1 Introduction

The Netherlands holds a special position in the European and global debate on collective redress. While seen by some as exemplary for its collective settlement mechanisms in particular, the Dutch collective procedures and their wide territorial reach have also been debated and even fiercely criticised. Since 1 January 2020, the Netherlands has three collective redress regimes in place. First, the more traditional collective action regime (WCA) that was introduced in 1994, allowing non-profit organisations that meet certain criteria to file collective actions for injunctive or declaratory relief.[1] Secondly, in 2005, the much-discussed collective settlement regime (WCAM) was introduced, inspired by the US settlement-only classes. This regime has enabled a number of global settlements to be declared binding on an opt-out basis by the Amsterdam Court of Appeal.[2] These include the well-known *Shell* and *Converium* global settlements. Thirdly, after years of political and academic debate, a new statutory regime was enacted on 1 January 2020, complementing the injunctive relief and settlement regime with a collective damages actions statute (WAMCA).[3] The WAMCA is available for claimants domiciled in the Netherlands if the matter has a sufficient link with the jurisdiction and—as the WCAM—generally operates on an opt-out basis. While quite a few legal bloggers and internationally-oriented law firms reported about the structure and main features of the new law, so far only few critical assessments have been made informing the international legal audience about the implications of the new Act, both in terms of challenges and opportunities. By contrast, the enactment of WAMCA was preceded by a large number of (critical) comments from the Dutch legal (academic and practitioners) community of varying nature.[4] In addition, on 24 November 2020

[1]Tzankova (2015). Another mechanism would be the assignment or power of attorney model, but although facilitating access to justice and wildly used in competition matters, this procedural device is not a 'proper' representative collective redress mechanism.

[2]Arons and Van Boom (2010), Kramer (2013) and Tzankova and Hensler (2013).

[3]Wet afwikkeling massaschade in collectieve acties (Stb. 2019,130).

[4]E.g. Kortmann (2018), Van Boom and Weber (2017), De Bie Leuveling and Van de Velden (2017), Tzankova (2017), Bosters (2017), Arons and Koster 2017, Pavillon and Althoff (2017), Bauw and Voet (2017).

the EU Directive on Representative actions for consumers was adopted.[5] That raises additional questions with respect to the application of WAMCA in the international context.

The goal of this paper is twofold. First, it aims to inform the international (legal) community involved in mass claims dispute resolution in the international context about the latest legislative developments and the context in which the WAMCA was introduced. That history is useful to appreciate how the thinking in the Netherlands evolved and why the law took its current shape. It is also still relevant, because the old regime will remain applicable for a while, in addition to the WAMCA and WCAM. Moreover, the Netherlands not only has one of the oldest collective redress regimes in the EU and may offer lessons for other civil law jurisdictions with younger collective redress systems, but it is expected to remain an important jurisdiction in the evolving European and global legal markets in the future, at least in the area of competition, securities and consumer law. The question is, however, whether that expectation is justified also after the introduction of the WAMCA, which has a limited temporal and territorial scope. Secondly, the paper will address two main topics: the funding of collective redress and in particular the new costs and fee regime under the WAMCA and the interaction between the WAMCA and the pre-existing WCA and WCAM on the one hand and its international implications in view of the forthcoming EU legislation on the other.

This paper is organised as follows. Section 2 discusses the background of the new law, focusing on the changes that have been made to the existing mechanism over the years in order to fix emerging problematic issues and as the practice became more mature. Section 3 focuses on the main features of the new collective regime for damages and will assess to what extent there could be a role for the Netherlands Commercial Court in collective redress in the international context. Section 4 explores the new costs and fee regime under WAMCA and to what extent WAMCA facilitates or restricts the use of third-party funding since that is the major (if not sole) funding source of international collective redress in the Netherlands. In Sect. 5 Dutch collective redress will be assessed against the background of the latest legislative EU developments and in the private international law context, and discusses the limitations that the WAMCA has imposed on the global reach of the regime. Section 6 will conclude with a summary and a reflection on the findings.

[5]November 2020 on representative actions for the protection of the collective interests of consumers and repealing Directive 2009/22/EC, OJ L 409/1.

2 Collective Redress in the Netherlands: Something Old, Something New

This section focuses on two pre-existing systems, the collective action for injunctive and declaratory relief and the collective settlement mechanism, and revisions—both regulatory and self-regulatory 'fixes'—that have been made to these over the years to address shortcomings. These provide the background necessary to understand the latest addition to the Dutch collective redress system, the WAMCA will be discussed in more detail in Sect. 3.

2.1 Pre-Existing Collective Redress Mechanisms and Its Shortcomings

The Netherlands has had a collective action regime since 1994 when the case law of the Dutch Supreme Court[6] allowing for collective actions by non-profit organisations (that protected certain public or collective interests) was codified. Under the old regime there was no formal certification test and the standing threshold was in practice fairly low: (i) a non-profit making character, (ii) a certain legal structure and (iii) adequate articles of association. The Netherlands is one of the few civil law jurisdictions that allows for ad hoc established non-profit entities to have standing in collective redress, in addition to longstanding associations. Twenty six years of experience in collective redress suggests that the existence of such organisations has not led to more collective actions in comparison to the ones brought by other types of institutional representative claimants[7] and in any event do not support claims of increased frivolous litigation, in fact they suggest the opposite.[8] The Dutch experience also demonstrates that ad hoc foundations are needed in a mature civil (law) justice system:[9] over time longstanding associations may suffer from agency issues as well and struggle to properly fulfil their role due to constraints of various types.[10] Ad hoc organisations make sure that a proper system of checks and balances with respect to longstanding associations in collective redress remains in place. As collective actions became more frequent as a result of globalisation,

[6]Supreme Court of the Netherlands, 27 June 1986, ECLI:NL:PHR:1986:AD3741.

[7]Tillema (2019), p. 273: "The number of cases brought by entrepreneurial representative organisations starts to gradually climb from 2008 onwards, but remains (well) under the level of the number of cases brought by the other representative organisations."

[8]Tillema (2019), p. 274: "The findings did support the claim that there is an increased detection of mass wrongdoings, although the number of collective actions appears to have remained modest."

[9]Tzankova (2016).

[10]Tzankova (2020).

industrialisation and the wider spread of social media,[11] a number of shortcomings in the existing system of collective redress in the Netherlands became apparent.

First, the existing system would not allow for collective actions for damages. It required for claimants to file an individual suit to claim for their losses once a declaratory relief had been successfully obtained. Secondly, it was not possible for a defendant to obtain 'global peace' and reach closure: the judgment was binding only on the organisation initiating the action, parallel collective actions could co-exist absent the availability of an adequate formal concentration mechanism and if one of the collective actions was unsuccessful, a new organisation could appear and try again. Finally, as the number of parallel actions increased, it was unclear for group members which initiative to support. There were no specific governance requirements for ad hoc established foundations and the quality of the various initiatives with varying governance structures was difficult to assess and compare. Gradually a number of legislative and self-regulatory initiatives were introduced to address the shortcomings of this legislation. These will be briefly identified below.

2.2 *First Fix: Damages Scheduling Via Collective Settlements*

The first noteworthy legislative initiative was the introduction of WCAM in 2005: the collective settlement statute that provides defendants with a tool to obtain closure, by exclusively appointing the Amsterdam Court of Appeal to declare a settlement binding on an opt out basis, if a defendant prefers a final resolution of a mass claim over protracted litigation.[12] Compensation is provided via damages scheduling where claimants receive compensation based on common key characteristics of the subgroup they belong to rather than the particularities of their individual claim. Although the WCAM was not intended to deal with international matters, it soon proved to fill a gap in the global dispute resolution market, that is inhabited by creative (and opportunistic) lawyers and clients.[13] That was not met without criticism from academics and experts on private international law,[14] but offered at least some (pragmatic) solutions to pressing societal issues and mass claims with an international outlook.[15] Moreover, the Dutch judiciary did not shy away from its daunting task and was willing to play a facilitative role.[16] Despite of the fact that the WCAM enables the distribution of compensation in a mass claim setting and in a way aims to remedy the lack of collective damages actions, the fact that it can only be invoked if the alleged defendant(s) are willing to settle when they want 'global

[11]For a more extensive discussion of the drivers of collective litigation see: Hensler (2011).

[12]For the background of WCAM see: Frenk (2005).

[13]See for the background of the Shell-settlement: Hensler (2016).

[14]Van Lith (2010), Kramer (2013) and Halfmeier (2012).

[15]Dexia, Shell, Converium and Fortis were resolved using WCAM in an international context.

[16]Los (2013).

peace' contributed to the perception that it is first and foremost a defendant-friendly device. Such criticism was especially fuelled after a collective settlement in the Dexia mass claim was approved under WCAM,[17] but resulted in a large number of opt outs by consumers dissatisfied with the settlement. Critics claimed that it was most of all favourable for the settling Dexia bank, absent a proper collective damages action. Although subsequent tweaks on the WCAM were introduced in 2011/12[18] they did not address the main criticism that a WCAM settlement needs to be voluntary.

2.3 Second Fix: Better Collective Settlements Via Supreme Court Oversight

Since the introduction of a collective regime for damages was politically an overly sensitive topic, other legislative initiatives were launched to facilitate qualitative collective settlements under some form of judicial oversight. The lower courts were given the power in mass claim disputes to request, at their own initiative, or at the request of the parties, the Dutch Supreme Court to answer questions about the interpretation of certain points of law. The lower court can do that without handing down a final judgment, but instead rule halfway through the proceedings, via interim judgments. The ratio of this provision is pragmatic and inspired again by the experiences in Dexia where the defendant was able to defer a final unfavourable judgment of the Supreme Court for a long time. It was believed on the consumer side, that it negatively influenced the quality of the collective settlement. When there is an uncertainty on a question of law that stands in the way of an out of court or court supervised settlement, parties do not need to file an appeal and litigate all the way to the Supreme Court, losing time and resources. The Supreme Court rules on the matter with priority and in that way facilitates fast resolution ending in a settlement at a level playing field or by a judgment that is less likely to be appealed.[19] That was at least the legislative philosophy behind this fix. Interestingly, there is one important exception in that law: the Amsterdam Court of Appeal, when acting under WCAM, is not allowed to pose pre-judicial questions to the Supreme Court when assessing collective settlements for approval, the fear being that this would jeopardise the speedy process under WCAM. Although the evaluations of this law (relating to prejudicial questions) suggest that it offers a useful tool in the toolkit of courts and parties and is filling a gap in some need of legal practice,[20] it is unclear to what extent, if at all, it has produced quicker and fairer *collective settlements* either out of

[17]Court of Appeal Amsterdam, 25 January 2007, ECLI:NL:GHAMS:2007:AZ7033.

[18]One of which was to postpone the start of related individual proceedings after the expiry of the opt out period and not after the binding declaration date: *Kamerstukken II* 2011/12, 33,126, no. 3.

[19]*Kamerstukken II* 2008/09, 31,762, no. 1, p. 5.

[20]Giesen et al. (2016).

court or under WCAM.[21] It is ironic that the proceedings that resulted from the opt outs in Dexia, 10 years later are still pending, despite a number of pre-judicial questions obtained in relation to this specific mass claim that triggered this particular legislative reform. In any event, this measure did not prove adequate to counterbalance the absence of a collective damages action under WCA.

2.4 *Third Fix: Better Settlements Under Court Supervision*

Another legislative initiative in a similar line of thinking as the one above concerns the introduction of a pre-trial case management conference that could be initiated at the request of an organisation that would have standing in a collective action or at the request of a potential defendant who anticipates being sued in a collective action. The pre-trial case management conference could be used either to explore an out of court settlement, under a court's direction or supervision that might result in a subsequent WCAM approval or to agree on a sensible litigation plan moving forward. Again, that was the legislative philosophy behind this provision. The procedure could also be invoked by a defendant who anticipates being sued by more than one organisation and who pro-actively wants to manage that. Such a use would address another issue identified under the old collective action regime—parallel actions. However, the pre-trial case management conference procedure, that was introduced in 2012 was invoked only twice at the request of non-profit organisations: the potential claimants in collective actions. Both times it was invoked unsuccessfully: the defendants objected and the court rejected the request.[22] This fix can hardly be viewed as a success either, since it did not meet its goal to contribute to a level playing field for claimants with respect to unwilling defendants.

2.5 *Fourth Fix: Claim Codes for Ad Hoc Foundations*

While the Dutch legislature was working on the above, there were also self-regulatory initiatives to cope with the issue of 'quality control' of ad hoc foundations. The expectation was that while that would not prevent parallel or competing initiatives in collective actions, it would offer at least some guidance to the courts and group members, when assessing the governance and activities of ad hoc

[21]It was invoked in relation to a pending collective action only once or twice: e.g. Supreme Court of the Netherlands March 28, 2014, ECLI:NL:HR:2014:766, to clarify whether a letter sent by a non-profit organisation could bar the statute of limitation for the whole group. Many of the referrals to the Supreme Court seem to involve individual matters that concern questions of law relevant for Banks and similar institutions when dealing repeatedly with these in individual cases.

[22]Art. 1018a DCCP; District Court Den Haag, 5 October 2015, ECLI:NL:RBDHA:2015:11469, District Court Amsterdam, 29 March, 2018, ECLI:NL:RBAMS:2018:1681.

foundations. In 2011, a self-regulatory initiative resulted in a Claim Code providing (comply or explain) rules for the governance of ad hoc foundations acting in collective actions.[23] For example, the Claim Code 2011 provided guidelines for the composition and remuneration of board and supervisory board members, conflicts of interest and communications by the foundation with the public and its constituency. Although the idea behind the Claim Code (improvement of governance and accountability) was generally endorsed, there was also criticism. The Claim Code increased further the financial burden on non-profit organisations in collective actions, without recognising the commercial litigation funding reality; litigating collective actions is costly, whilst the free rider issue is not addressed under WCA. Class members can profit from the outcome, but cannot be forced to contribute to the costs of the action. Adding an extra layer of governance costs does not solve the free rider and funding issues of non-profit organisations. Commercial litigation funders will only be interested in funding collective actions if their business model is appreciated and adequately integrated into the Claim Code.

To address the latter, in 2019 the Claim Code was revised and a new version was published recognising that commercial litigation funding plays a meaningful role in collective redress, but also needs to be scrutinised. The revised Claim Code 2019[24] attempts to strike a balance between accountability and the administrative burden for the foundations by stipulating that Board members need to be adequately remunerated and have to be independent, but at the same time to allow the appointment of a representative of the funder to sit on the supervisory board. WAMCA[25] codifies some of the principles laid down in the Claim Code 2011, but the timing of the issuing of the Claim Code 2019 was such that the WAMCA legislature could not take that into account. The legislature deviated in any event from the Claim Code 2011 by stipulating that ad hoc representative entities acting under WAMCA have mechanisms in place to consult their constituency about material developments in relation to the action.

2.6 On the Way to a New Regime

Whilst the Dutch legislature has not been sitting still since 1994, when the WCA was introduced, the subsequent measures discussed above have only had a limited, or in any event at best, unintended success for defendants in international mass claims. After a long period of national consultations and drafting, finally, a proposal was put forward by a self-appointed working group. This consisted of lawyers acting for plaintiffs and defendants. Eventually a bill ended up before parliament and after a number of amendments this became the WAMCA. Following a Parliamentary

[23]Tillema (2019), p. 272.

[24]Van Delden et al. (2019).

[25]Wet Afwikkeling Massaschade in Collectieve Actie (Stb 2019,130).

motion in 2011 calling for more efficiency in collective actions,[26] a draft bill was presented for public consultation in 2014.[27] In the consultation paper the aim was described as aiming to "*enhance the efficient and effective redress of mass damages claims and to strike a balance between a better access to justice in a mass damages claim and the protection of the justified interests of persons held liable*". The legislative proposal was brought before Parliament on 15 November 2016, and after a number of revisions, the proposal was adopted in January 2019. The WAMCA came into force on 1 January 2020 and is applicable on claims filed after that date in relation to events that occurred on or after 15 November 2016 (the date that the new law Bill was submitted with Parliament) or that took place before that date, but continued afterwards, that would typically be the case in competition or securities litigation where there is typically a fact complex that spans a longer time period. This explains why for a while the WCA and WAMCA will be parallel in place.

3 The New Collective Action for Damages: WAMCA

As explained above, the WAMCA's original aim was to address the absence of a regime for collective action for damages and the res judicata effect of judgments in collective actions, the phenomenon of parallel national proceedings and to improve the governance standards for ad hoc foundations. The WAMCA seems to achieve all of that (Sects. 3.1 and 3.2), but various concerns have been raised, including ones related to the price that has been paid by non-profit organisations and consumers in the end (Sect. 3.3). Another noteworthy development is the establishment of the Netherlands Commercial Court that could play a role in the WAMCA as well (Sect. 3.4).

3.1 Four Stages

Under the WAMCA collective actions for damages can be claimed, parallel or overlapping national actions for the same facts will no longer be possible, and any judgment will be binding on the certified class. The new collective action regime came into force on 1 January 2020.[28] As mentioned above, the WAMCA is applicable to collective actions in any field of law filed after that date in relation to wrongdoings that took place after 15 November 2016. The process at first instance can be roughly divided into four stages:

---

[26]The so-called motion Dijksma, *Kamerstukken II* 2011/12, 33,000-XIII, no 14.

[27]See for a brief English outline: Kramer (2014b).

[28]Wet afwikkeling massaschade in collectieve acties (Stb. 2019,130).

1. An admissibility test and a certification process, consisting of a number of sub-stages resulting in a ruling on jurisdiction, a test of sufficient link with the Netherlands, a ruling on the suitability of the action for collective resolution, the suitability of the candidate representative entity to run the case and, if there are multiple candidates: the selection and appointment of an Exclusive Representative. This stage could easily take a few years;
2. After the first stage that defines the scope of the action, in the second stage the scope of the class is further defined as being opt out, opt in or a hybrid. The default position is that the action is opt out for claimants domiciled in the Netherlands and opt in for claimants domiciled outside of the Netherlands, but the court can rule otherwise at the request of one of the parties and certify the entire class on an opt out or opt in basis;
3. After certification, further definition of the class via opt in and or opt out and the notification of the class, what follows is the ordering by the court of either negotiations or mediation;
4. The last stage ends either with a court approved collective settlement, resulting from the negotiations/mediation, or with a court order in favour of one of the parties. If the court orders in favour of the claimants, the damages awarded are distributed by damage scheduling process.

3.2 Main Features

Below follows a brief description of the noteworthy features of the four stages identified above. First, the writ needs to be published on a publicly accessible website so that the public is informed and other competing initiatives can express their intent to also serve as a representative in the same or a related action. If there are multiple candidates and they cannot agree on a role division, an Exclusive Representative (ER) will be appointed by the court. Standing is still limited to non-profit entities, but when appointing the ER or when selecting from amongst multiple candidates, the court needs to take a number of factors into account with respect to the governance, representativity and financial capacity of the entity in order to assess whether the interests of the (absent) group members are adequately protected. For example, with respect to governance, adherence to the relevant Claim Codes is considered. With regard to representativity, decisive factors include the size of the constituency, the size of the claim value of the represented group and other activities that the organisation carries out. Furthermore, prior relevant activities and expertise of the ER (or its (supervisory) board members) in relation to collective actions can also be taken into account. The organisations that are not selected to act as an ER can remain involved in the proceedings by monitoring the conduct of the ER. In addition to the 'review' of the suitability of the ER, the ER also needs to demonstrate that a collective resolution of the matter at hand is more efficient and effective than an individual action and that the claim is not lacking a proper legal basis at the outset. If that be the case, the ER runs the risk of being ordered to pay to the defendant(s) five times the applicable fixed cost award.

As part of the certification stage the court needs to examine whether there is a sufficient connection with the Netherlands, the so-called 'scope rule'.[29] That is the case if one of three alternatives grounds apply.[30] After the appointment of the ER, which at the same time marks the end of the debate on certification, there is an opportunity for group members domiciled in the Netherlands to opt out[31] and for other group members to opt in if that is within the scope of the action.[32]

Appeal against the appointment of an ER is not possible. Appeal is possible against the ruling on certification.

After certification there is a court directed negotiations/mediation phase.[33] If that leads to a collective settlement, then there is a similar settlement approval procedure as under WCAM, with a within the WAMCA context, a second opt out window.[34] If there is no settlement, parties have the opportunity to amend their statements of claim and defence and, at the request of the court, to submit proposals for a damages distribution plan.[35] The court rules on the basis of these proposals or at its own motion. How an appeal of that ruling would work is not entirely clear. The burdensome process surrounding the appointment of the ER suggests that in principle, this is the only party on the claimant side that is entitled to file an appeal if the claims are dismissed by the lower courts.

3.3 *Some Criticism and Challenges*

A first and obvious challenge arises from the parallel applicability of three collective redress regimes for an uncertain time period, especially with respect to continuous infringements (e.g. in shareholder, competition, general consumer and product liability matters) having an international component, which concerns most of the substantial mass claims. The differences between the three regimes are substantial and are expected to invoke strategic behaviour and satelite litigation on the part of litigants.

[29] Article 3:305a paragraph 3 sub b DCC.

[30] The representative entity should be able to show that (i) the majority of the individuals on behalf of whom the collective claim is brought (the "class"), reside in the Netherlands; or (ii) the defendant resides in the Netherlands; or (iii) the event or events on which the collective action is based, took place in the Netherlands. However, the mere fact that the defendant resides in the Netherlands may not be sufficient if there is no other circumstance that connects the case to the Dutch jurisdiction.

[31] Article 1018f paragraph 1 DCCP.

[32] Article 1018f paragraph 5 DCCP.

[33] Article 1018g DCCP.

[34] Article 1018h DCCP.

[35] Article 1018i Dutch Code of Civil Procedure.

Another issue concerns the increased admissibility criteria that will negatively impact the availability of collective redress for idealistic non-monetary actions and plaintiffs.[36] Under WAMCA they will be struggling even more than they already did under WCA. It has been pointed out by the legislature that such claimants can be exempted from some of the admissibility criteria[37] and the first case law under WAMCA seems to validate that assumption, but it has also revealed that it has added a whole new layer of admissibility discussions with related uncertainty, delay and costs for these organisations.[38]

The co-existence of the WAMCA, which may result in a settlement, and the WCAM also creates friction as the rules are not fully aligned. There are two different certification regimes in place, where the WAMCA regime is stricter than that of the WCAM. In addition, the WAMCA introduces a scope rule restricting territorial reach, whereas a similar rule in the WCAM is lacking. This scope rule, which will be discussed in greater detail in Sect. 5, is problematic in itself and has been criticised for not being compatible with EU legislation.[39]

Serious doubts can also be raised with respect to the cost-efficiency of the WAMCA generally. The new admissibility criteria require from the candidate ER extensive book building activities and substantial investments prior to the filing of collective claims. In the end one party is bound to pay an excessive price for this and that is likely to be either class members or the defendants. An example: some of the bookbuild efforts may turn out to have taken place unnecessarily or in vain. Once the ER is appointed and the class is identified, class members do not need the non-appointed candidate organisations anymore, but will be nevertheless paying for signing up with them, because they will be contractually obliged to do so to the respective funders.

Another point of concern relates to the lack of clarity concerning damages calculation under WAMCA. Whilst the legislative history of the Act states that WAMCA does not alter the substantive law, it suggests that the only way to award and assess damages is via damages scheduling (as also calculated and accepted under WCAM, also on aggregated basis). It is unclear however, how the two principles (aggregate calculation required versus not altering substantive law) relate to and interact with each other in the context of WAMCA.

The above uncertainty can be expected to also have an immediate negative impact on the availability of commercial funding under WAMCA. Commercial funding arrangements are often based on the expected outcome of a matter and uncertainties or lack of clarity in the law on such topics that are essential for funders, will at the very least negatively influence the terms under which they will be willing to provide funding. Funding issues will be further discussed under Sect. 4.

---

[36] Van Boom and Weber (2017).

[37] Article 3:305a (6) DCC.

[38] District Court Amsterdam, 28 October 2020, HA ZA 20-284.

[39] Van der Plas (2019).

These are just some of the anticipated concerns and challenges under WAMCA that may question the extent to which the new regime is going to make a difference and should be considered an improvement in comparison to the current situation. On its face, WAMCA seems to make a difference for consumers only in relation to straightforward large scale small claim matters, with a sufficiently large Dutch claimant base that is financially attractive for a funder to become engaged on commercially lucrative terms for both the funders and the ER. That is likely to be only a fairly limited number of cases.

3.4 WAMCA and the Netherlands Commercial Court

One year before the enactment of WAMCA, on 1 January 2019, the English speaking Netherlands Commercial Court (NCC) was launched.[40] The establishment of the NCC is part of a strong development in recent years to establish specialised courts equipped to deal with complex international business cases.[41] The NCC resides in Amsterdam and rules in two instances: it consists of a District Court and a Court of Appeal. The judges have been carefully selected from the 11 District Courts and 4 Courts of Appeal in the Netherlands based on their experience and expertise with cases with an international dimension and their command of the English language. Unlike some other English-speaking commercial courts in other non-English speaking jurisdictions, under the NCC not only are the proceedings conducted in English, but English is also the language of all procedural documents, hearings and the judgment. The proceedings are conducted electronically, whilst oral hearings can take place in person or via video facilities. Interestingly, the NCC welcomes lawyers from non-Dutch jurisdictions as well. Lawyers admitted to practice elsewhere are allowed to draft documents and speak on behalf of their clients at NCC hearings, but they need to use a local lawyer for the formal representation of the clients and the electronic filing of documents. Electronic filings and swift proceedings in English by experienced judges do come at a price. For example, where the ordinary court fees are in the range of EUR 600–4000 depending on the value of the claim, the NCC charges fixed court fees for filing, ranging from EUR 15,000 to EUR 20,000 per party. Absent agreement, the unsuccessful party is typically responsible for lawyers' fees that are assessed on the basis of fixed rates ranging from EUR 1000—EUR 12,000 for each act of process which is also higher as compared to the regular Dutch fixed costs regime, but still very 'competitive' when compared to the court fees and costs of litigation before English and German courts and arbitral tribunals, such as the ICC.

[40] *See* among others Schelhaas (2019), Bauw et al. (2018), Bauw (2019).

[41] See Kramer and Sorabji (2019), including analyses from 12 jurisdictions as well as comparative views.

Although the NCC aims to compete with arbitration as a dispute resolution mechanism for commercial disputes, soon after the enactment of WAMCA the NCC announced that it should also be viewed as a viable option in relation to collective actions with an international dimension.[42] NCC can become involved under WAMCA if, in addition to the requirements discussed above, and under Sect. 3.1 the Amsterdam court has not only international jurisdiction, but also jurisdiction under the national rules of Dutch civil procedure. For example, if Dutch courts have international jurisdiction, but the Hague, Den Bosch or Rotterdam District court have to hear the case according to the domestic jurisdictional rules, then the NCC cannot be invoked, unless there is a choice-of-court clause, which typically will not be the case. Additional NCC requirements are that the collective action needs to concern an international civil or commercial matter within the autonomy of the parties and the parties to the collective action—the claimants' foundation or association and the defendant(s)—agree on the proceedings to be in English before the NCC (the 'NCC agreement'). The "civil or commercial matter" test is easily met. The dispute needs to relate to civil law in a broad sense.

The "international dispute" test is also broad in scope.[43] It is met not only where one or more of the parties have their domicile in a foreign jurisdiction, but also where the dispute otherwise involves a relevant cross-border element, such as shareholders, employees or revenue located in or linked to a foreign jurisdiction. The last criterium that needs to be met is that both parties need to agree to conduct the proceedings in English. The NCC agreement can be included in a clause, either before or after the dispute arises. It can be implicit (because the defendant does not oppose the jurisdiction of the NCC) and potentially only partial: for example only with respect to the determination of the international jurisdiction of the Dutch courts or another key preliminary issue. One can imagine that a multinational company sued as a defendant before the NCC acknowledges the advantages of conducting in English the proceedings related to the jurisdiction of the Dutch court. It might partially submit to its jurisdiction, only to dispute it, but in English: the legal debate in court on jurisdiction would otherwise be conducted in Dutch before the ordinary Dutch courts. The translation and coordination costs of the international legal team of a multinational defendant will arguably be lower when proceedings are conducted before the NCC.

In addition to meeting the specific NCC requirements, another complication in the context of WAMCA arises when there are competing initiatives for the exclusive representative position. Even if the action is first filed with the NCC and the defendant has not disclosed its formal position on the jurisdiction of the NCC court, the second filed action needs to follow the first one and to also agree with the jurisdiction of the NCC.[44] It is unclear what happens if that is not the case. The

---

[42] The NCC announcement is to be found here: https://www.rechtspraak.nl/SiteCollectionDocuments/factsheet-netherlands-commercial-court-and-class-actions.pdf.

[43] Antonopoulou (2019).

[44] Article 1018c paragraph 6 and article 1018d paragraph 1 DCCP.

NCC will need to rule on the matter, but it will not be a predictable and a straightforward decision, because its implication will be that higher court fees and potential higher adverse cost awards are imposed on the parties. It would be wise if claimant initiatives intending to file a WAMCA-action with the NCC, to the extent possible, coordinate their efforts on that point beforehand. Whether WAMCA defendants will submit to a (partial) NCC-jurisdiction in view of the advantages pointed out above, remains uncertain.

Despite of the willingness of the Dutch judiciary to facilitate litigating under the WAMCA before the NCC and its obvious advantages in complicated international matters, it remains to be seen how realistic that proposition is in view of the many requirements that an action needs to meet, the cooperation required from all parties involved and their tendency to deploy strategic behavior that optimises their legal position, even when that is not in line with principles of procedural efficiency and economy.

4 Financing Collective Redress

This section starts in Sect. 4.1 with a brief explanation of the phenomenon of TPF. Section 4.2 will discuss TPF under the old collective redress regime and WCAM, while Sect. 4.3 will focus on the position of TPF under the WAMCA.

4.1 Introduction

There are a number of ways to finance the various forms of mass claim dispute resolution, including collective redress, in the Netherlands. In the early days, collective actions were financed via a combination of funding sources varying from individual contributions, legal aid and legal expense insurance.[45] Nowadays, absent the general availability[46] of contingency fees for lawyers in the Netherlands, collective actions are increasingly funded via TPF arrangements. The latter are funding facilities that a third party unrelated to the litigation provides on a 'non-recourse basis' to cover all or part of the litigation costs, in exchange for a success fee related to the outcome of the litigation. The non-recourse nature of the funding facility indicates that, unlike a bank loan, it only needs to be 'repaid' if the action is successful and unlike with a bank loan, the 'debtor' is not required to provide a

[45]For a more general discussion of the topic of funding in mass claims in the Dutch context see: Tzankova (2012).

[46]No win no fee arrangements are currently allowed for lawyers only with respect to individual personal injury cases, thus outside the context of collective redress. The 5 year pilot initiated by the Dutch Bar Association in 2014, was positively evaluated and extended in 2019 for another 5 years, until and including 2024: Nederlandse Orde van Advocaten (2018).

guarantee for the funding. Hence the interest rates of bank loans cannot serve as benchmarks for the success fees of TPF: they are two entirely different instruments with entirely different mechanics. Comparisons of TPF funding facilities with a bank lending and with the interest rate paid on bank lending are therefore misleading and should be avoided.

The success fee of a third-party funder can be calculated in different ways: as a percentage of the outcome, as a multiplier of the investment or as a combination of the two. Traditionally, third-party funders were spin-offs from insurers and re-insurers[47] or entities financially supported by the family offices of high net worth individuals, hedge funds and private equity. Some of these legal finance providers are publicly listed entities,[48] with many pension funds and institutional investors among their shareholders. Investing in TPF by institutional investors is not only attractive, because of reported high returns on investment, but also because it adds to the diversification of investment portfolios in a unique way. Litigation is an asset class the performance of which does not correlate to activity in the international financial markets. For that reason, TPF investments are a good addition to an investment portfolio from a risk management point of view, and institutional investors and their risk and investment managers have recognised that.

Whilst traditionally TPF was known for providing financing to impoverished clients with strong claims in high value stand alone or single cases (the ‘David v. Goliath’-type of disputes), in recent years the menu of this category of litigation finance providers has expanded drastically. TPF nowadays provides finance facilities for the litigation portfolios of large multinational corporate clients, which could even include the litigation costs of defending a claim. It has become clear that there are substantial financial bookkeeping advantages for corporate clients to make use of litigation financing. TPF also finances the work stream of law firms acting on contingency fee basis, the enforcement of arbitral awards and related asset tracing or asset recovery activities and can also buy claims (at any stage of the proceedings). TPF can take over a latent litigation risk in the context of merger and acquisition negotiations or provide for ‘seed facility’ for book building and litigation project management facilities in relation to collective actions. Sometimes it provides the latter services in kind, for which the client pays only later, in the event of success. Last but not least, TPF finances many legal tech platforms and companies active in the dispute resolution space. Although TPF can certainly be viewed as innovators and pioneers in litigation finance and legal services, they are typically not legal pioneers. TPF prefer to avoid risky and speculative cases that are based on novel liability theories. While in the past there was a tendency to specialise and focus on the funding of certain type of claims e.g. arbitration, competition, shareholder disputes, collective actions, common law markets, civil law markets etc., nowadays TPF diversify their investment portfolios to mitigate risks and search ways and

[47]That was especially the case on the German market with Munich Re, Allianz and Fortis backing litigation funding activities on the German (speaking) market.

[48]Examples are Burford Capital, LCM, Omni Bridgeway.

avenues to expand their market share. Proper due diligence remains key for the success of any TPF and different funders have deployed different ways to deal with that, varying from setting up experienced specialised in-house legal due diligence departments to retaining on an ad hoc or permanent basis high profile external experts.

The use of terminology of TPF in legislative documents and policy discussions on national and EU level suggests that an universal understanding exists together with agreement about the uniformity, form, shape and activities of third-party funders. But that is arguably not the case, as was demonstrated above. More research is needed to appreciate the implications of these developments that challenge the traditional view of TPF as facilitators of 'modern Robin Hoods' and its influence on the David v. Goliath perspectives on collective redress. That influence may not be as straightforward as one may think and be further affected by regulatory measures put forward by legislators who are unaware of the scope and penetration of third-party funders in the legal and corporate markets. Does TPF make sure that David becomes Goliath? Or does it help Goliath to grow even bigger? Or does it make them equals? To what extent do unregulated TPF contribute to the principle of equality of arms? What is an appropriate or optimal scope and nature of potential regulation of TPF in view of all of these questions? These topics will be some of the key research themes of the future in relation to access to justice and collective redress.[49]

4.2 *TPF Under the Old Regime and WCAM*

The Netherlands applies the English rule on costs (loser pays) which, absent the general availability of contingency fees for lawyers as explained above (Sect. 5.1), makes the availability of TPF in large and complex matters necessary.[50] That is especially the case in relation to collective actions after the introduction of the Claim Codes (see Sect. 2.5 above) that increased not only the level of governance, but also the costs of running an ad hoc foundation. For a long time there was little academic and public policy attention and appreciation for the difficulties that 305a-entities generally experience when funding collective redress and even more so after the introduction of Claim Code 2011. A quantitative empirical study that looked at the

[49]Although the attention of academia and practice with respect to TPF are to be considered overwhelming in recent years (only in the Netherlands, e.g. De Mot et al. 2017; Luiten 2017; Van der Krans 2018; Solas 2019), there is still an universe that needs to be explored, partly because both phenomena are moving targets: TPF and collective redress are continuously evolving.

[50]Art. 6:96 lid 2 DCC provides for a very limited loser pays rule. Traditionally, only fixed litigation costs are awarded, and actual lawyer's fees are no part of it. These are dependent on the amount at stake, the number of legal motions and submissions filed with and heard by the courts. For a more detailed description of how that system works see Tzankova et al. (2014).

compliance with the Claim Code 2011 by ad hoc claim entities deploying TPF concluded in 2016 that there were major compliance issues.[51] However, the applied quantitative research method failed to explain the reasons behind that non-compliance, which was crucial to appreciate what was actually going on.[52] The subsequent revision of Claim Code 2011 that included consultations also of third-party funders has in any event contributed to an increased awareness of the existence and nature of the funding issues of ad hoc claim foundations. Under the Claim Code 2019 (principle VII), a litigation funder is entitled to appoint one of the members of the supervisory board. According to Principle III the claiming entity will need to do due diligence into the capitalisation and any potential track record, as well as the reputation of the TPF. Noteworthy is also the requirement that the agreement should contain a choice of Dutch law and a choice of forum for the Dutch court or an arbitration body domiciled in the Netherlands in case of disputes with the funder. Also, the funder is in principle not allowed to terminate the agreement before judgment has been rendered in first instance. The representative entity should also have the sole control of the litigation and settlement strategy. Its lawyer and any other providers of services engaged by it will have to act exclusively on its behalf of and for the benefit of its members. Information about the identity and place of domicile of the external lender, the main features of the system of remuneration(s) and the services that have been agreed with the external lender need to be communicated via the website of the organisation. It remains to be seen how that will evolve in practice and under WAMCA since the Claim Code 2019 was announced just before the enactment of WAMCA and the legislature could not take it into account.

Apart from the principles for ad hoc foundations laid down in Claim Code 2019, TPF was and still is unregulated in the Netherlands. The Dutch legislature has consistently taken the view that it is still early days and there are too many unknowns with respect to the scope and nature of the phenomenon generally to make any sensible suggestions about regulatory measures.[53] In view of what was discussed in § 4.1 this seems to be a valid argument, although it does have negative implications for the use of TPF in the context of collective redress, absent a pre-existing statutory or judicially developed 'common fund'-theory[54] in the Netherlands. A TPF contract

[51] Bauw and Van der Linden (2016).

[52] This is in itself an interesting research topic from legal methodology point of view and illustrates the virtues and vices of the application of different empirical research methods; while quantitative research is useful to illustrate certain trends or development, it fails to explain underlying issues and causes. A qualitative research method would be more suitable for that purpose.

[53] E.g. in *Kamerstukken II* 2016/17, 34,608, no. 3, p. 12.

[54] A common fund-doctrine insures that in class actions every group member who benefits from collective litigation or settlement ultimately contributes in the litigation costs, including the potential success fees of the funders, absent a (pre-)existing contractual agreement between the respective 'free riding'- group member and the funder.

is categorised under Dutch law as a private contract 'sui generis',[55] where the starting point is that the principle of contractual freedom applies.

Today there are at least four Netherlands-based litigation funders,[56] whilst many internationally operating litigation funding providers also finance mass claim[57] dispute resolution in the Netherlands. It is on public record that investor,[58] consumer[59] and competition[60] matters are financed via TPF and there is an increasing reluctance to rely on individual contributions from group members, partly because that raises free rider issues and risks born by the contributing class members, especially in the context of a collective settlement under WCAM. Absent a common fund doctrine in the Netherlands, these risks have now been transferred to the TPF, whose Dutch lawyers will need to come up with ways to construe if not a common fund theory, at least to resemble a common fund-result under WAMCA.

Under the old collective action regime potential funding issues could be brought by defendants in the context of the discussion of the requirement, whether 'the interests of the group are sufficiently protected'.[61] Sometimes such motions were successful and the courts seem to have gradually grown into a more active role.[62]

A similar development is to be observed under WCAM. Whilst there was originally little attention for the interaction between funders' fees and the settlement approval process,[63] since the Fortis settlement there is no longer doubt what the court's attitude will be. By declaring a commercial entity admissible as petitioner, whilst being critical about the role and attitude of the non-profit association VEB in the litigation and settlement process, the Court demonstrated a pragmatic approach with respect to standing and conflict of interest: a profit motive does not automatically disqualify a collective initiative, as having a non-profit profile does not automatically mean that there are no issues.[64] Furthermore, the court ruled that fees must always be part of the court's review of a proposed WCAM settlement, regardless of whether the parties have expressly included fee provisions in the

[55]Van Boom and Luiten (2015). The doctrines of 'champerty and maintenance' that lead to doctrinal issues and require statutory or case law solutions in common law jurisdictions are uncommon in the Netherlands.

[56]Liesker Procesfinanciering, Redbrest, Capaz, Weiss Capital and Omni Bridgeway.

[57]We speak of 'mass claim' because not all of them concern collective actions in the Netherlands.

[58]E.g. Shell, Converium and Fortis settlements.

[59]E.g. Dexia and VW litigations.

[60]E.g. follow on-damages litigations in relation to Air cargo, Sodium Chlorate and Trucks cartels.

[61]Article 3:305a(2) Dutch Civil Code.

[62]District Court Oost-Brabant, 29 June 2016, ECLI:NL:RBOBR:2016:3383; Court of Appeal Amsterdam, 14 April 1 2020, ECLI:NL:GHAMS:2020:1157.

[63]In Shell and Converium the Amsterdam Court of Appeal applied a fairly passive approach to the topic.

[64]See Tzankova (2020) on the topic of agency issues under various standing models in collective redress.

settlement documents submitted for approval.[65] Also the issue of 'free riding' was recognised by the court. The court's attempt to remedy this via implementation of the norm that 'active participants' (the group members that actively came forward to register with and support a foundation), should be reimbursed for their participation by receiving extra compensation to cover the success fee they own to the TPF. However, that is arguably not a proper 'remedy', since it only neutralises the negative financial effects of their participation. It does not motivate them to be 'active' and sign up in future cases, which has become even more relevant and problematic under WAMCA as was discussed under Sect. 3. Indeed, the size of the constituency is a relevant factor when obtaining external financing and subsequently, when assessing the admissibility of competing claiming initiatives. Another noteworthy and possibly controversial development[66] in the Fortis settlement in relation to funding, is the court's informal use of 'amicus curiae' to collect views and information on accepted funding practices and success fees rates, to be able to better assess the funding arrangements of the parties in that case. Last but not least, the practice of parties appearing as an objector and as a result of that obtaining a payment from the settling parties of their objections succeed, seems to have received the court's blessing in principle. A practice that can be problematic in jurisdictions with a more developed class actions jurisprudence,[67] because of the potential for coercion.[68]

4.3 TPF and Cost Orders Under WAMCA

With effect from 1 January 2020 and as part of WAMCA a separate costs and fee regime was introduced for collective damages actions, and special attention is given to the situation where TPF is involved. There are differing views on the utility of the legislative measures.[69] Moreover, there are different categories and sets of rules that are relevant for TPF backing collective actions under the new law. Some of the rules concern the relationship between the funder and the representative entity, others relate to potential cost and fee awards, including the success fee of the funder, and relate to the position of the defendant.

As discussed above, under WAMCA the financial capacity of the exclusive representative is part of the admissibility test and plays a role in the certification of the action, but the focus in that stage is to ensure that there are sufficient means to fund the action and to cover potential adverse cost awards. Nothing more and

[65] Court of Appeal Amsterdam. 13 July 2018, ECLI:NL:GHAMS:2018:2422 consideration 5.20 & 5.21.

[66] Tzankova (2018).

[67] Lopatka and Brooks Smith (2012), Karlsgodt (2011).

[68] Kalajdzic (2018).

[69] Tzankova (2017) and Weterings (2020).

nothing less. The focus in that stage is also on the potential role of the funder in the litigation and on the safeguards for preventing inappropriate influence from the funder on the course of the action. To that end the court might require disclosure to the court of the funding agreement. Whether the defendants should be allowed to review the funding agreement as well, is considered controversial, since such a disclosure will provide the other side with key strategic information and jeopardise the principle of equality of arms. The courts are provided with very little guidance when reviewing funding agreements. Since the Claim Code 2019 lays down explicitly in Principles III and VII and the accompanying notes guidelines for avoiding conflicts of interest, it is likely that the WAMCA courts will take these into account, when interpreting the new law and ruling on the appropriate role of funders.

With respect to the new cost and fee regime it is, first, important to note that a claimant that brings a manifestly unfounded claim can be 'fined' by the court by awarding the defendant five times the regular and applicable fixed cost award.[70] In addition, it has become possible for the lead plaintiff to demand compensation of all costs incurred, "unless fairness dictates otherwise".[71] Apart from this 'fairness-criterion', there is no pre-set determination mechanism for the basis or scope of the calculation of the funders fee. It goes without saying that with regard to the availability of TPF and the willingness of funders to back collective actions, it is key that they have sufficient comfort that any contractually agreed success fees are awarded. Furthermore, it is key that in the opt out context, the calculation of their success fee is based on the compensation of the total of class and not only of the class members who registered with the respective claiming entity, to prevent free rider issues. That, in combination with the fairly broad 'fairness criterion' when reviewing success fees and the court ruling in Fortis, suggest that success fees that meet market standards can be awarded separately, on top of damages not just in the context of a collective settlement, but also (and even more so one would expect) in the context of a successful collective action. Moreover, it appears from the WAMCA legislative history that the legislator explicitly had in mind the current practice of including claimant's costs in settlement and intended to open up the opportunity to claim for such compensation in the event that no settlement would be agreed upon. The legislator made clear that this also concerns the lead claimant's third-party litigation funder's costs.[72] Absent a settlement, the success fee of the funder becomes part of a debate in court at the very end of the proceedings, unless this kind of discussion is somehow triggered at an earlier stage, for instance in the context of admissibility and certification.

Still, many questions with respect to the position and remuneration of the TPF remain unanswered. For example, whether it should be appropriate for defendants to comment on the percentage of the success fee of the funder in the context of certification or when an ER needs to be appointed, if there are multiple candidates

[70] Article 1018l DCCP.

[71] Article 1018i DCCP and article 6:96(2)(b) and (c) DCC.

[72] *Kamerstukken II* 2017/18, 34,608, no. 9, p. 5.

to choose from. These are puzzling questions. Whilst the defendant has a self-interest to keep that percentage as low as possible, one may wonder whether that is a legitimate interest to take into account when deciding what is in the best interest of the class and who is the best ER. Furthermore: the 'cheapest' funder or the 'cheapest representation' is not necessarily the better one for the class.

Similarly, although the defendant might have a self-interest in the appointment of one ER over another, again: it is in our view not necessarily a legitimate one, and it would be inappropriate to give defendants that opportunity when assessing funding agreements and selecting ER. It is counterintuitive to let defendants have a say in who is to be viewed as the best representative of their counterparts. This does not mean that defendants cannot have legitimate interests in these discussions, but their scope and timing are in our view limited. The legitimate interests of defendants end with the establishment that the funder is capable of covering potential adverse cost awards. They can re-emerge or revive again in a later stage, after an award of the claim and when discussing the 'fairness' of full cost awards to be then paid by the defendant.

Allowing such fee discussions in an earlier stage (in the context of the admissibility or certification test) would in our view be appropriate only at the request of the funder and/or the candidate ER to clarify and verify whether certain assumptions about the applicable cost and fee regime are correct, if that is a pre-condition for providing funding for the respective claim, which otherwise would not be available. The justification there lays in procedural economy: if the assumptions turn out to be incorrect and/or the funder is not prepared to provide funding, potentially under amended or adjusted conditions, the collective action is off the table. It would then be better to have clarity on that rather sooner than later.

Another key question that remains unanswered is the interaction between the ER and its TPF and the potential candidate ER (and their funders)—the ones who were not appointed. To the extent they are not entitled to a full cost award, their constituency will need to pay the success fee out of the damages they will receive. Since the ER is already acting and funding the action also on their behalf and for their benefit, the constituency of the 'monitoring' entities seem to be paying a high price for that monitoring. Equally, if a defendant is considering negotiating a 'global settlement', it will also have to incorporate and anticipate the financial consequences, resulting from the fact that there is a whole chain or group of 'monitoring' entities and their funders out there. The experiences in Fortis have revealed that this is not an unrealistic scenario. This is not a cost-efficient system and one will have to wait and see, how parties and courts deal with these issues and the creative solutions they might need invent to make collective redress work. It would be disappointing after all these years of legislative efforts if the WAMCA would turn out to be a 'damp squib' or in the best case a Rolls Royce that only a happy few can afford.

5 Dutch Collective Redress in an International Perspective

This section turns to the European and international dimension of collective redress. The Dutch WCAM mechanism has been subject of discussion both in the EU and global context. Topics of debate concern in particular the opt-out system and the wide territorial reach the Amsterdam Court of Appeal has allowed itself in declaring WCAM settlements binding in a number of high impact cases. As this has been the topic of a substantial number of papers,[73] this section will only briefly discuss the global reach of these settlements (Sect. 5.1), before turning to the rules included in the WAMCA resulting in limitations to the global outreach (Sect. 5.2) and the importance of recent EU developments for Dutch collective redress (Sect. 5.3).

5.1 Global Aspirations of the WCAM and Criticism

The majority of the WCAM settlements so far have involved foreign parties. While originally conceived as an instrument to settle a product liability case, it proved to be a useful instrument for transnational security cases in particular. This has led the Dutch Ministry of Justice to have a study carried out on private international law aspects.[74] This focused on international jurisdiction and cross-border enforcement in particular, whilst also addressing aspects of the applicable law and the cross-border service of documents. The particularities of the WCAM mechanism, where a joint request to declare the settlement binding is made by the representatives, on behalf of the victims (designated as "interested parties" or "beneficiaries"), and the allegedly responsible party make the application of the existing jurisdiction rules complicated. These are to a great extent based on the domicile of the defendant—most notably Article 4 Brussels I-bis Regulation–, but it is questionable who can be considered as defendant in these cases, as it concerns a joint request for settlement without an underlying action.

In two cases that have attracted attention worldwide, the *Shell* and the *Converium* case, the Amsterdam Court of Appeal addressed the issue of international jurisdiction extensively.[75] Both concerned securities cases regarding misleading information provided to the investors and these settlements were in part complementary to US settlements. The boost of and attention for the Dutch WCAM 10^{10} years ago also resulted from the landmark case of *Morrison v. Nat'l Australian Bank* in which the U.S. Supreme Court limited securities class actions to U.S. litigants or shares bought

[73]See, *inter alia*, the extensive study by Van Lith (2010), Arons and van Boom (2010), Tzankova and van Lith (2012), Kramer (2013, 2014a).

[74]Dutch Ministry of Justice/WODC (2010), also published as a book: Van Lith (2010).

[75]Court of Appeal Amsterdam. 29 May 2009, ECLI:NL:GHAMS:2009:BI5744 (*Shell Petroleum NV/Dexia Bank NV Netherlands*) [hereinafter Shell]; Court of Appeal Amsterdam, 17 January 2012, ECLI:NL:GHAMS:2010:BO3908 (*Scor Holding*) [hereinafter Converium].

on the U.S. stock exchange.[76] In the *Shell* case, the Amsterdam Court of Appeal ruled that the *interested parties/beneficiaries* are to be considered as defendants, meaning that for those victims on whose behalf the settlement is concluded living in the Netherlands, Article 4 of the Brussels I-bis will provide jurisdiction. In relation to the non-Dutch interested parties/defendants, the Court resorted to Article 8(1) Brussels I-bis, providing jurisdiction in case of multiple defendants and connected claims. For parties not domiciled in the EU, similar rules in the Lugano Convention (EFTA States) and the international jurisdiction rules of the Dutch Code of Civil Procedure were used.[77]

In the *Converium* case, the Amsterdam Court of Appeal went a step further. In this case the allegedly responsible party, Converium, was a Swiss company and only 3% of the beneficiaries were domiciled in the Netherlands. The Court provided an extensive reasoning to justify accepting jurisdiction, emphasising the aim of the settlement, that the settlement was complimentary to the US actions and settlements, which excluded non-U.S. parties and those not having bought shares on the NYSE, and that the right of access to justice and the right to be heard had to be respected. As in the *Shell* case, the court used the domicile of the defendant and the multiple defendants rule, but added the place where the contract has to be carried out within the meaning of Article 7(1) Brussels I-bis Regulation.[78] The Court argued that the place of performance of the obligation to pay compensation was in the Netherlands, since the representative organisations (VEB, the Dutch shareholders association and the *ad hoc* Converium foundation) were seated in the Netherlands. Despite the legitimations and using multiple heads of jurisdiction the link with the Netherlands was very weak in this case.[79] This ruling has been criticised in doctrine and even led to questions in Parliament.[80] One commentator went as far as to call the Dutch system a 'judicial hellhole' referring to the *Converium* case.[81]

In a collective action under the WCA—the first Dutch instrument—preliminary questions have been referred to the European Court of Justice. These regard the interpretation of Article 7(2) and the place of financial damage in the context of a collective action, where damage arises in different countries.[82] While this does not relate to a WCAM settlement, the outcome of the case will be relevant for the international jurisdiction under the new WAMCA.

Apart from the jurisdictional issue, doubt has also been expressed as to whether WCAM settlements would be eligible for recognition and enforcement under the

[76]Morrison v. Nat'l Australian Bank Ltd.,130 S. Ct 2869, 2883 (2010); *see* Silberman (2012); *see* Kaal and Painter (2012).

[77]Shell, supra note 42. See Kramer (2014a), pp. 254–256.

[78]Converium, supra note 77.

[79]Kramer (2014a), pp. 256–258.

[80]*See* inter alia Van Lith (2010), Gidi (2012), p. 953; Allemeersch (2012) and Kramer (2014a).

[81]Gidi (2012), p. 953.

[82]Request for a preliminary ruling, Case C-709/19 (*Vereniging van Effectenbezitters*). Zaak C-709/19xxx.

Brussels I-bis Regulation and globally.[83] In particular the opt-out system coupled with the wide jurisdictional reach adopted in practice has been mentioned as perhaps violating procedural public policy.[84] It is submitted that judicial activism to secure the right to be heard, the reasonableness of the settlement, increased attention for representativeness and funding aspects[85] as well as other regulatory fixes[86] in fact do overall provide a balanced system of collective settlement.

5.2 Scope Rule: The End of Global Dutch Collective Redress?

Aware of the criticism that has been voiced in relation to the wide casting of the jurisdictional net by the Amsterdam Court of Appeal and the opt-out approach of the WCAM, the Dutch legislator took precautionary measures in the WAMCA.

First, as was briefly mentioned in Sect. 3.1 above, a scope rule limiting the extraterritorial reach of collective actions was implemented. Secondly, the opt-out mechanism that is also adopted in the WAMCA is reversed in relation to foreign parties.

The most remarkable provision implemented by the WAMCA is the scope rule securing a close link with the Netherlands. According to the Explanatory report, the scope rule aims to strike a balance between enabling a collective action and the legitimate interests of the party against whom the action is directed. It should also prevent too many cases being brought in the Dutch court and limit the burden this puts on the judicial system as well as to diminish the negative effects on the business climate.[87] This rule is not intended as a rule on international jurisdiction, as the Parliamentary documents explicate, but regulates the legal standing of representatives. The new Article 3:305a (3)(b) of the Dutch Civil Code provides that a representative only has legal standing if the claim has a sufficiently close relationship with the Netherlands. A sufficiently close relationship with Dutch jurisdiction exists if:

1. the legal person can make a sufficiently plausible claim that the majority of persons whose interests the legal action aims to protect have their habitual residence in the Netherlands; or
2. the party against whom the legal action is directed is domiciled in the Netherlands, and additional circumstances suggest that there is a sufficiently close relationship with Dutch jurisdiction; or
3. the event or events to which the legal action relates took place in the Netherlands.

---

[83]Van Lith (2010), Hess (2012), Halfmeier (2012), Wautelet (2011), Bariatti (2012) and Muir Watt (2010).

[84]*See* for a more detailed discussion Kramer (2014a), pp. 262–271.

[85]Supra, Sect. 4.

[86]Supra, Sect. 2.

[87]*Kamerstukken* II 2016–2017, 34 608, no 310.

The first draft did not include sub (2)[88] which was added during the legislative process as the other two criteria were considered to be too narrow. This scope rule aims to prevent bringing before the Dutch court in cases such as the *Converium* case in which only a small minority of the interested parties reside in the Netherlands and where the settling company is situated abroad.

While this rule is phrased as a rule on legal standing, the use of territorial criteria that resemble those of international jurisdiction rules raises the question as to their compatibility with the Brussels I-bis Regulation in particular. This question was also addressed early in the legislative process and by the Dutch advisory committees on private international law and civil procedure.[89] Their advice was to frame the territorial criteria as a domestic rule regarding legal standing, while these should at the same time not impede the functioning of the Brussels I-bis Regulation. Rightfully, in doctrine it has been concluded that this rule is nevertheless doubtful in view of the EU jurisdiction rules.[90] It is submitted that application of the territorial criteria on legal standing may in fact be at odds with the Brussels I-bis rules. While sub (1) and (3) may tie in with Article 7(2) Brussels I-bis Regulation depending on how these will be interpreted in practice,[91] the requirement of 'additional circumstances' in sub (2) can undermine the functioning of Article 4 Brussels I-bis. The latter is, as are the other rules of the Regulation, a hard and fast rule and the Court of Justice has made it very clear that there is no room for forum non-conveniens defences.[92] These rules also leave little room for the application of Article 8(1) on multiple defendants, or—though not likely in collective action cases—a choice of court. Should a (preliminary) defence regarding the inadmissibility of the claim in view of the legal standing scope rule and a jurisdictional defence be raised simultaneously, the Dutch court could of course decide that while having international jurisdiction, the claim is inadmissible, or decide on the admissibility first and leave the question of international jurisdiction aside if the requirements of Art. 3:305a (3)(b) are not met. However, this seems to be somewhat artificial and would lead to the undesirable result that parties' access to the Dutch judge is restricted. In addition, one may also wonder how this scope rule operates in the context of the new Representative Actions Directive (*infra* Sect. 4.3) which requires that cross-border claims in consumer cases can be brought by Qualitative Entities from another Member State.[93]

---

[88]Kramer (2014b).

[89]Advice Standing Committee on Private International Law and Advisory Committee Civil Procedure (*Staatscommissie voor Internationaal Privaatrecht en Adviescommissie voor Burgerlijk Procesrecht*), a April 2016, available at https://zoek.officielebekendmakingen.nl/blg-789395.pdf (visited 25 November 2020), at 3.4.1.

[90]van der Plas (2019), Bosters (2017).

[91]Though as van der Plas (2019), pp. 545–546 argues, in case a claim is based on breach of contract within the meaning of Article 7(1) Brussels I-bis the legal standing rules may be more limited than the international jurisdiction rules.

[92]CJEU 1 March 2005, Case C-281/02, ECR I-1383 (*Owusu v Jackson*).

[93]Article 4b Representative Actions Directive. See further Sect. 4.3.

The second limitation in cross-border cases is that the opt-out regime does in principle not apply to foreign parties. While opt-out mechanisms make a settlement obviously much more attractive for companies and increases the efficiency of collective actions, the WAMCA makes an exception for collective actions involving foreign parties. Dutch parties can make use of an opt-out within a period to be set by the court of 1 month at least. However, for foreign parties the new act provides for a general opt-in regime for foreign parties. Article 1018f (5) of the Dutch Code of Civil Procedure provides that persons who are not domiciled or resident in the Netherlands are only bound if they have informed the court registry within the period set by the court that they agree to having their interests represented in the collective action. There is some leeway to deviate from this rule. The court may, at the request of a party, decide that non-Dutch domiciles and residents belonging to the precisely specified group of persons whose interests are being represented in the collective action, are subject to the opt-out rule.

What is remarkable is that these rules seem to result from the criticism raised in relation to the WCAM, but do not concern the WCAM itself. They are part of the WAMCA regime, and while perhaps the scope rule and particularly coupled with EU developments (see Sect. 5.3) may eventually influence the operation of the WCAM as well, the legislator seems not to have considered aligning both regimes in this respect.

5.3 Dutch Collective Redress and EU Developments

For Dutch collective redress and in particular the cross-border dimension, the EU developments are also of importance. Collective redress has been a topic of debate for almost 20 years and considering the huge discrepancies in policy, legislation, and practice between the Member States, it has proven difficult to establish an EU wide instrument so far. Collective redress is also a politically sensitive issue that has fuelled fierce reactions across the EU and at national level, where consumer and civil society groups have lobbied for stronger and collective enforcement mechanisms while business representatives have had a strong voice against EU harmonisation.[94]

The 2013 Recommendations on collective redress were adopted by way of compromise.[95] These non-binding Recommendations have had little practical influence in the Member States, but were nevertheless a clear sign of where the EU stands on some aspects of collective redress.[96] Most relevant for the Dutch context is that the Recommendation clearly favours an opt-in mechanism, though it does not fully

[94]See on the EU legislative history also Tzankova (2020).

[95]Commission Recommendation of 11 June 2013 on common principles for injunctive and compensatory collective redress mechanisms in the Member States concerning violations of rights granted under Union Law, OJ L 201 pp. 60–65.

[96]*See* in relation to the WCAM, Kramer (2014a), pp. 245–248.

shut the door on opt-out mechanisms. It states that exceptions to the opt-in principle 'should be duly justified by reasons of sound administration of justice'.[97] The Dutch government took the position that the WCAM, being a settlement mechanism and not a collective action, was not at odds with the Recommendation.[98] The Recommendation unfortunately provides little guidance on cross-border aspects and does not address the above mentioned questions regarding international jurisdiction and recognition and enforcement as stakeholders had different opinions. The Commission stated that the 'existing rules laid down in the Brussels I Regulation should be fully exploited',[99] while in relation to recognition and enforcement, the Commission remarked that a future report on the application of the Brussels I Regulation should include information on the effective enforcement of cross-border collective redress actions.[100] In relation to applicable law—not addressed in the present paper[101]–, the Commission stated that it is not convinced that special conflict of law rules are required to avoid the application of multiple laws and referred to the existing rules of the Rome I and Rome II Regulations. A last point that is particularly relevant in the Dutch context is the reluctance in relation to third party funding in the EU. The Recommendation, however, does not prohibit third-party financing, but laid down a number of transparency requirements.[102]

A step forward has been made by the Directive for representative actions for consumers introducing minimum requirements for the availability of collective actions. The proposal for this directive was put forward in April 2018 as part of the New Deal for Consumers.[103] After intensive negotiations and many amendments the Directive was adopted on 24 November 2020. The Representative Actions Directive (RAD) introduces Qualified Entities (QEs) that will be able to collectively claim compensation for mass harm. The RAD gives Member States considerable freedom in the implementation of the rules. For the Dutch context, it is important that following the amendments negotiated by the Council, a distinction is made between domestic and cross-border cases. The Member States—including the Netherlands—did not want their domestic mechanisms to be impeded by EU rules. Cross-border representative actions are defined as those brought by a qualified entity in a Member State other than that in which the qualified entity is designated.[104] As regards domestic cases, the Member States are free to either have opt-in or opt-out collective redress mechanisms in place pursuant of Article 9 RAD. For cross-borders cases

[97]Recommendation, No 21.

[98]Kamerstukken II 2012–2013, 22,113, no 1663.

[99]Communication from the Commission to the European Parliament, the Council, the European Economic and Social Committee and the Committee of the Regions, Towards a European Horizontal Framework for Collective Redress', COM (2013) 401/2 final, 11 June 2013, p. 13.

[100]European Commission Communication (*supra* footnote 2), pp. 13–14.

[101]See in relation to the WCAM, Van Lith (2010); Kramer (2014a), pp. 271–277.

[102]Recommendation, No 15-16.

[103]Biard and Kramer (2019).

[104]Article 3 (4d) RAD.

only opt-in actions are allowed. This is in line with the WAMCA, as discussed in the previous subsection. In addition, QEs designated for bringing cross-border cases are subject to additional requirements.[105] One of these is that the legal entity should demonstrate 12 months of actual public activity in the protection of consumer interests prior to its designation request. It is clear that this rule deviates from those of the WCAM and WAMCA, and the importance of *ad hoc* claim vehicles in Dutch legal practice. At this moment it is not clear how these rules will be implemented in the Netherlands.

Lastly, the RAD allows third party litigation funding under certain conditions, if national law allows this. Article 10 contains conflict of interest provisions that seem to be in line with the provisions set up in the Claim Code 2019 and with the admissibility requirements under WAMCA. Article 12 governs the implementation of the loser pays rule, but stipulates also that individual consumers who in case of success would profit from the action, in principle cannot be held liable for potential adverse cost orders. It is unclear whether losing defendants also need to cover the success fee of the TPF, but the Directive does not seem to exclude that so the current Dutch practice seems to be compatible with the Directive here too. Last but not least, Article 20 makes explicit that there should be attention for the funding of collective redress and that Member States can take various measures to that end. In that context is promising the recognition of the potential of 'cy pres distribution' in Article 9(7): Member States can use proceeds that remain unclaimed to feed into a Legal Aid or Public/Private collective redress fund.

As in the 2013 Recommendation, rules on private international law are lacking in the RAD.[106] The absence of dedicated rules on international jurisdiction and recognition and enforcement in particular—which should ideally be included in the existing private international law instruments—will continue to create uncertainty as to cross-border collective redress. The existing rules on the applicable law are not well suited for complex cross-border mass harm case either. Considering that most situations of mass harm do not confine themselves to national borders, adequate private international rules are pivotal for the effectiveness of EU collective redress. For instance, the *Volkswagen* case has led to litigation in many different countries in Europe and globally, and without proper coordinating mechanisms this will continue to be problematic.

[105] Article 4(3) RAD.

[106] Article 2(3) RAD provides that this directive is without prejudice to EU private international law rules.

6 Concluding Remarks

Dutch collective redress has been developing and fine-tuning over the past 15 years, with varying degree of success. Smaller and bigger fixes to the existing system have been put in place, and apart from legislative amendments, active judges, practitioners and self-regulation have played an important role. After years of intensive deliberations, the system of Dutch collective redress was completed when the WAMCA became applicable on 1 January 2020. However, it is not only completed, but also made more complicated as a result of the co-existence of different regimes. These differences play out in the certification requirements and the scope rule implemented in the WAMCA in particular. Whereas there may be good reasons to maintain the WCAM, or perhaps even to have different scopes and requirements, these should have been explicated and justified at the least.

To what extent WAMCA will meet the high expectations of the consumer lobby, remains to be seen. One thing is clear: the WAMCA has brought a significant layer of complexity into the mass claim dispute resolution process in the Netherlands in many ways. Candidates exclusive representatives will need to spend more time and resources on the filing of a claim: either to meet the stricter admissibility and certification requirements or to demonstrate that they can be exempted from some of these. Because of WAMCA's temporal scope and maintaining the WCAM, there will be (for quite some time) three collective redress schemes in place with sufficient scope for overlap and accompanying judicial battles and protracted litigation. Running a WAMCA action via the NCC adds yet another layer of complexity in international cases. While the introduction of the 'scope rule' can be explained against the criticism that has been raised in relation to the wide international jurisdiction that the Amsterdam Court of Appeal had afforded itself under the WCAM, this rule limits the global reach of the new Dutch collective redress regime considerably. The legislature seems to have 'fixed' what was not broken (yet), whilst it did not take the measures with respect to WCAM that the international community felt needed to be taken. In addition, while framed as a legal standing rule in the WAMCA certification test, it is questionable whether this 'fix' is compatible with the international jurisdiction rules of the Brussels I-bis Regulation.

The new European legislation in relation to consumer collective redress with its distinction between domestic and cross-border actions and rejection of the ad hoc designation entities, brings additional challenges in the international context. Last but not least, the critical factor that can make or break the use of WAMCA is the availability of TPF and the extent to which it is attractive for funders to invest in such actions and for consumer to afford their services. Whether WAMCA provides funders with sufficient comfort to ultimately collect reasonable success fees within a reasonable time frame, the future will tell. It seems fair to conclude that if the Netherlands is to continue to hold its predominant position in Europe in relation to collective redress, that will be as a result of the creativity of Dutch lawyers, the pragmatism of Dutch courts and the reliance of TPF on the two. It will not be thanks to, but in fact, despite of the introduction of the WAMCA. To end on a more cheerful note, one thing is certain: this will be a lawyers' paradise!

References

Allemeersch B (2012) Transnational class settlements: lessons from "Converium". In: Wrbka S, Van Uytsel S, Siems M (eds) Collective actions: enhancing access to justice and reconciling multilayer interests? Cambridge University Press, Cambridge, pp 364–384

Antonopoulou G (2019) Requirements upon agreements in favour of the NCC and the German chambers - crashing with the Brussels ibis regulation? Erasmus Law Rev 12(1):56–69

Arons T, Koster G (2017) Op weg naar collectief schadeverhaal in het Nederlands recht. Ondernemingsrecht 86(10/11):485–493

Arons T, van Boom W (2010) Beyond tulips and cheese: exporting mass securities claim settlements from the Netherlands. Eur Bus Law Rev 21(6):857–883

Bariatti S (2012) Recognition and enforcement in the EU of judicial decisions rendered upon class actions: the case of U.S. and Dutch judgments and settlements. In: Pocar F et al (eds) Recasting Brussels I: proceedings of the conference held at the University of Milan on November 25–26, 2011. CEDAM, Padova, pp 31–61

Bauw E (2019) Commercial litigation in Europe in transformation: the case of the Netherlands commercial court. Erasmus Law Rev 12(1):15–23

Bauw E, van der Linden T (2016) Onderzoek 'Naleving Claimcode'. https://www.uu.nl/sites/default/files/rebo-rgl_vervolgonderzoek-nalevingclaimcode-2016.pdf Accessed 22 Nov 2020

Bauw E, Voet S (2017) Van Stok achter de deur tot keurslijf. NJB 2006(4):240–247

Bauw E, Koster H, Kruisinga SA (2018) De kansen voor een Netherlands Commercial Court. Boom Juridisch, Den Haag

Biard A, Kramer XE (2019) The EU Directive on representative actions for consumers: a milestone or another missed opportunity? ZEuP 27:249–260

Bosters M (2017) Het wetsvoorstel collectieve schadevergoedingsactie: de scope rule nader bekeken. NTHR 5:246–256

de Bie Leuveling J, van de Velden J (2017) Collectief schadeverhaal vanuit de optiek van de aangesproken partij. Ondernemingsrecht 85(10/11):82–92

De Mot J, Michael Faure M, Louis Visscher L (2017) Third party financing and its alternatives: an economic appraisal. In: van Boom W (ed) Litigation, costs, funding and behaviour. Routledge, Abingdon, pp 31–54

Frenk N (2005) Privaatrecht Actueel. De wet collectieve afwikkeling massaschade en de aandelenlease-affaire. WPNR 6629(569):569–570

Gidi A (2012) The recognition of U.S. class action judgments abroad: the case of Latin America. Brook J Int Law 37(3):893–965

Giesen I, Kristen FGH, de Jong ER et al (2016) De Wet prejudiciële vragen aan de Hoge Raad: een tussentijdse evaluatie in het licht van de mogelijke invoering in het strafrecht. WODC report 2016

Halfmeier A (2012) Recognition of a 'WCAM' settlement in Germany. NIPR 2:176–184

Hensler D (2011) How economic globalisation is helping to construct a private transnational legal order. In: Muller S et al (eds) The law of the future and the future of law. Torkel Opsahl Academic EPublisher, Oslo. http://www.fichl.org/fileadmin/fichl/documents/FICHL_11_Web.pdf

Hensler D (2016) A class action 'mash-up': in re Royal Dutch/Shell transport securities litigation. In: Tzankova I, Hensler D, Hodges C (eds) Class actions in context: how culture, economics and politics shape collective litigation. Edwar Elgar Publishing, Cheltenham, pp 170–188

Hess B (2012) A coherent approach to European collective redress. In: Fairgrieve D, Lein E (eds) Extraterritoriality and collective redress. Oxford University Press, Oxford, pp 6.01–6.31
Kaal WI, Painter RW (2012) Forum competition and choice of law competition in securities law after Morrison v. National Australia Bank. Minn Law Rev 97, 132:165–185
Kalajdzic J (2018) Class actions in Canada. The promise and reality of access to justice. UBC Press, Vancouver/Toronto, pp 101–106
Karlsgodt P (2011) Warding off "professional" objectors to class action settlements. https://classactionblawg.com/2011/03/31/warding-off-professional-objectors-to-class-action-settlements/. Accessed 20 Nov 2020
Kortmann J (2018) Wetsvoorstel afwikkeling massaschade in collectieve actie (34608). Aanzienlijk verbeterd, maar het moet nog beter! NJB 407(8)
Kramer XE (2013) Enforcing mass settlements in the European judicial area: EU policy and the strange case of Dutch collective settlements (WCAM). In: Hodges C, Stadler A (eds) Resolving mass disputes: ADR and settlement of mass claims. Edward Elgar, Cheltenham, pp 63–90
Kramer XE (2014a) Securities collective action and private international law issues in Dutch WCAM settlements: global aspirations and regional boundaries. Pac McGeorge Glob Bus Dev J 27(2):235–279
Kramer XE (2014b) Dutch draft bill on collective action for compensation – a note on extraterritorial application, Conflictoflaws.net, 20 November 2014, https://conflictoflaws.net/2014/dutch-draft-bill-on-collective-action-for-compensation-a-note-on-extraterritorial-application/
Kramer XE, Sorabji J (eds) (2019) International business courts: a European and global perspective. Eleven International Publishing, Den Haag
Lopatka J, Brooks Smith D (2012) Class action professional objectors: what to do about them? Fla State Univ Law Rev 39:865–930
Los W (2013) Toepassing van de WCAM – bespiegelingen over de rol en taak van de rechter. In: Los W et al (eds) Collectieve acties in het algemeen en de WCAM in het bijzonder. Bju, Den Haag
Luiten (2017) Third party litigation funding. Een korte introductie, Boom Juridische Uitgeverij
Nederlandse Orde van Advocaten (2018) Experiment resultaatgerelateerde beloning verlengd. https://www.advocatenorde.nl/nieuws/experiment-resultaatgerelateerde-beloning-verlengd. Accessed 22 Nov 2020
Netherlands Commercial Court Factsheet Netherlands commercial court and class actions. https://www.rechtspraak.nl/SiteCollectionDocuments/factsheet-netherlands-commercial-court-and-class-actions.pdf. Accessed 21 Nov 2020
Pavillon C, Althoff D (2017) Wijze raad is halve daad of veel raad maar weinig baat? De impact van de Aanbevelingen van de Juristengroep op het wetsvoorstel Afwikkeling massaschade in een collectieve actie. MvV 2017(3):104–115
Schelhaas HN (2019) The brand new Netherlands commercial court: a positive development? In: Kramer XE, Sorabji J (eds) International business courts. Eleven International Publishing, Den Haag, pp 45–64
Silberman LJ (2012) Morrison v. National Australia Bank: implications for global securities class actions. In: Fairgrieve D, Lein E (eds) Extraterritoriality and collective redress. Oxford University Press, Oxford, pp 123–138
Solas GM (2019) Third party funding: law, economics and policy. Cambridge University Press
Tillema I (2019) Entrepreneurial mass litigation: balancing the building blocks. Erasmus University Rotterdam, Rotterdam
Tzankova I (2012) Funding of mass disputes: lessons from the Netherlands. J Law Econ Policy 8 (3):549–591
Tzankova I (2015) Everything you wanted to know about Dutch foundations but never dared to ask: a check list for investors part 1. VbR 5(2):149–153
Tzankova I (2016) Collective redress in Vie d'OR: a reflection on a European cultural phenomenon. In: Tzankova I, Hensler D, Hodges C (eds) Class actions in context: how culture, economics and politics shape collective litigation. Edwar Elgar Publishing, Cheltenham, pp 117–134

Tzankova I (2017) Wetsvoorstel collectieve schadevergoedingsactie: Een oplossing voor welk probleem ook alweer? Tijdschrift voor Vergoeding Personenschade 16(4):107–119

Tzankova I (2018) Noot bij Gerechtshof, 13 July 2018, ECLI:NL:GHAMS:2018:2422 (Wet collectieve afwikkeling massaschade Fortis/Ageas). Jurisprudentie Onderneming & Recht 6(10)

Tzankova I (2020) Legal standing in collective redress. In: Stadler A, Jeuland E, Smith V (eds) Collective and mass litigation in Europe. Edward Elgar, Cheltenham, pp 127–152

Tzankova I, Hensler D (2013) Collective settlements in the Netherlands: some empirical observations. In: Hodges C, Stadler A (eds) Resolving mass disputes: ADR and settlement of mass claims. Edward Elgar Publishing, Cheltenham, pp 91–105

Tzankova I, van Lith H (2012) Class actions and class settlements going global: the Netherlands. In: Fairgrieve D, Lein E (eds) Extraterritoriality and collective redress. Oxford University Press, Oxford, pp 4.01–4.76

Tzankova I, Maanen v M, Rijnhart M (2014) A Dutch view on discovery: short and sweet. Def Couns J 81(3):229–238

van Boom W, Luiten L (2015) Procesfinanciering door derden. RM Themis 2015(5):188–199

van Boom W, Weber F (2017) Collectief procederen – Ontwikkelingen in Nederland en Duitsland. WPNR 2017(7145):291–299

van Delden AH, Bauw E, Lemstra JH, Okhuijsen RW, Polak RW, Tonkens-Gerkema W, van Mourik J (2019) Claimcode2019. BJU, Den Haag

van der Krans A (2018) Third party litigation funding. Onderneming en Financiering 26(2):30–41

van der Plas CG (2019) De collectieve actie 2.0 in grensoverschrijdende zaken: het territoriaal ontvankelijkheidsvereiste onder de loep. NIPR 3:537–552

van Lith H (2010) The Dutch collective settlements act and private international law; Aspecten van het Internationaal Privaatrecht in de WCAM. Maklu, Apeldoorn

Watt HM (2010) Brussels I and aggregate litigation or the case for redesigning the common judicial area in order to respond to changing dynamics, functions and structures in contemporary adjudication and litigation. IPRAX 30(2):111–116

Wautelet P (2011) Art 33. In: Magnus U, Mankowski P (eds) Brussels IIbis regelation. Sellier European Law Publishers, München, pp 634–644

Weterings W (2020, 2020) Procesfinanciering door derden bij collectieve schadevergoedingsclaims: Op zoek naar een balans. AV&S (3):81–84

Case Law

CJEU 1 March 2005, Case C-281/02, ECR I-1383 (*Owusu v Jackson*)

Morrison v. Nat'l Australian Bank Ltd.,130 S. Ct 2869, 2883 (2010)

Supreme Court of the Netherlands, 27 June 1986, ECLI:NL:PHR:1986:AD3741

Supreme Court of the Netherlands, 28 March 2014, ECLI:NL:HR:2014:766

Court of Appeal Amsterdam, 25 January 2007, ECLI:NL:GHAMS:2007:AZ7033

Amsterdam Court of Appeal, 29 May 2009, ECLI:NL:GHAMS:2009:BI5744 (*Shell Petroleum NV/Dexia Bank NV Netherlands*)

Court of Appeal Amsterdam, 17 January 2012, ECLI:NL:GHAMS:2010:BO3908 (*Converium*)

Court of Appeal Amsterdam, 13 July 2018, ECLI:NL:GHAMS:2018:2422

District Court Den Haag, 5 October 2015, ECLI:NL:RBDHA:2015:11469

District Court Oost-Brabant, 29 June 2016, ECLI:NL:RBOBR:2016:3383

District Court Amsterdam, 29 March 2018, ECLI:NL:RBAMS:2018:1681

District Court Amsterdam, 28 October 2020, HA ZA 20–284

Court of Appeal Amsterdam, 14 April 2020, ECLI:NL:GHAMS:2020:1157

Parliamentary Documentation

Kamerstukken II 2008/09, 31762, no. 1
Kamerstukken II 2011/12, 33000-XIII, no 14
Kamerstukken II 2011/12, 33126, no. 3
Kamerstukken II 2012-2013, 22113, no 1663
Kamerstukken II 2016/17, 34608, no. 3
Kamerstukken II 2016–2017, 34 608, no 310
Kamerstukken II 2017/18, 34608, no. 9

Ianika N. Tzankova Holder of the first European chair in the field of Class Actions and Mass Claim Dispute Resolution, established in 2007. Academic Co-Director of the Global Law Bachelor where she developed and teaches the course on Civil Procedure and Global Dispute Resolution. Academic Director of the university's Honours Outreach Program. Author of numerous articles on civil procedure, mass claims and collective redress. Former member of the Working Group of the European Law Institute and current member of a working group of the ALI/UNIDROIT project on Transnational Civil Procedure that drafted the model rules on collective redress.

Xandra E. Kramer Professor of civil justice at the Erasmus University Rotterdam and of private international law at Utrecht University, as well a deputy judge in the District Court of Rotterdam. Her research focuses on access to justice and justice innovation, the functioning of civil justice systems, international contracts, and transnational complex litigation. She has been involved in multiple studies for the European Parliament, the European Commission, and the Dutch Ministry of Justice, and was a reporter and a co-reporter of working groups resulting in the ELI-UNIDROIT Model European Rules of Civil Procedure (2020). Elected member of the Dutch Royal Academy of Arts and Sciences (KNAW).

Class Actions in Belgium: Evaluation and the Way Forward

Stefaan Voet

Abstract In 2014, Belgium introduced a consumer class action. In 2018, the procedure was expanded to disputes between SMEs and businesses. This chapter opens with a description of Belgium's class action procedure (class action prerequisites, jurisdiction, opt-in or opt-out, procedure, redress and enforcement phase). It follows with an overview of the cases brought between September 2014 and April 2020 (nine in total). This (limited) case law allows us to draw a number of conclusions about the pros and cons of the procedure. The chapter then draws attention to new and alternative ways to achieve collective redress (consumer dispute resolution (CDR) and regulatory redress). The conclusion arrived at is that our focus should be on exploring and optimising all options for mass harm situations and to connect these options so they can form an integrated dispute resolution framework.

1 Introduction

In April 2018, the European Commission launched its New Deal for Consumers.[1] Besides strengthening consumer rights online, introducing effective penalties for violations of EU consumer law, tackling the dual quality of consumer products and improving conditions for businesses, one of the cornerstones of the New Deal is to give consumers better and more efficient tools to enforce their rights and to get compensation. The Commission aims to do so by amending the existing Injunctions

[1] European Commission (2018) Press Release A New Deal for Consumers: Commission strengthens EU consumer rights and enforcement. https://ec.europa.eu/commission/presscorner/detail/en/IP_18_3041. Accessed 15 Mar 2020.

S. Voet (✉)
KU Leuven, Leuven, Belgium
e-mail: stefaan.voet@kuleuven.be

A. Uzelac, S. Voet (eds.), *Class Actions in Europe*, Ius Gentium: Comparative Perspectives on Law and Justice 89, https://doi.org/10.1007/978-3-030-73036-9_6

Directive.[2,3] The idea is to allow qualified entities, such as a consumer organisation, to seek not only injunctive relief but also compensatory redress, such as compensation, replacement or repair, on behalf of a group of consumers that have been harmed by an illegal commercial practice. In December 2020, the new Representative Actions Directive (RAD) was published.[4,5] Member States have to transpose the Directive by December 2022.

Belgium introduced a class action system in 2014. On 1 September 2014, the Act of 28 March 2014 introducing a consumer collective redress action in the Code of Economic Law entered into force.[6] This act introduced a class action in Belgian law, i.e. a representative action brought about by a representative acting on behalf of a group of persons facing the same or similar factual and/or legal issues, who are not parties to the procedure but who are ultimately bound by the *res iudicata* effect of the final decision. In 2018, the scope of application was extended to SMEs.[7]

In this chapter, I begin with a description of the Belgian class action procedure (Sect. 2). Next I give an overview of the cases brought to date. This (limited) case law allows making a number of remarks about the pros and cons of the procedure (Sect. 3). I then detail several other ways to achieve collective redress that could be an alternative for, or that could exist in conjunction with, class actions (Sect. 4). I end the chapter with some concluding comments (Sect. 5).

[2]Directive 2009/22 of the European Parliament and of the Council of 23 April 2009 on injunctions for the protection of consumers' interests, 2009 O.J. (L 110) (EC).

[3]Proposal for a Directive of the European Parliament and of the Council on representative actions for the protection of the collective interests of consumers, and repealing Directive 2009/22/EC, COM/2018/0184 final – 2018/089 (COD).

[4]Directive 2020/1828 of the European Parliament and of the Council of 25 November 2020 on representative actions for the protection of the collective interests of consumers and repealing Directive 2009/22/EC, 2020 O.J. (L 409) (EU).

[5]Council of the European Union (2019) Proposal for a Directive of the European Parliament and of the Council on representative actions for the protection of the collective interests of consumers, and repealing Directive 2009/22/EC—General Approach. https://data.consilium.europa.eu/doc/document/ST-14600-2019-INIT/en/pdf. Accessed 15 Mar 2020.

[6]Loi portant insertion d'un titre 2 'De l'action en réparation collective' au livre XVII 'Procédures juridictionnelles particulières' du Code de droit économique et portant insertion des définitions propres au livre XVII dans le livre 1er du Code de droit économique [Act Introducing a Consumer Class Action in the Code of Economic Law] of 28 March 2014, Moniteur belge [Official Gazette of Belgium] of 29 April 2014, 35201.

[7]Loi portant modification, en ce qui concerne l'extension de l'action en réparation collective aux P.M.E., du Code de droit économique [Act Expanding the Scope of Application of the Class Action in the Code of Economic Law] of 30 March 2018, Moniteur belge [Official Gazette of Belgium] of 22 May 2018, 41950.

2 Belgium's (Consumer) Class Action

In this section I describe the procedural features of the Belgian class action mechanism:[8] the three class action prerequisites (Sect. 2.1), the exclusive competence of the Brussels courts (Sect. 2.2), the opt-in or opt-out regime (Sect. 2.3), the class action procedure (Sect. 2.4), the nature of collective redress (Sect. 2.5) and the role of the collective claims settler (Sect. 2.6).

2.1 Class Action Prerequisites

2.1.1 Consumer Law and SMEs Disputes

The first class action certification criterion is that the cause of action must be a possible[9] infraction by the defendant of his contractual obligations or of one of the (now) 33 European or Belgian consumer regulations or acts that are specifically enumerated in the act.[10] These regulations and acts relate to provisions regarding competition law and banking, market practices, consumer protection, payment and credit services, product safety, intellectual property, privacy, electronic signature, prices, insurance and professional liability, travel, energy and transport of passengers.[11] The class representative has to base his claim on one or more of these regulations or acts.[12]

In 2014, the procedure only applied to C2B (consumer-to-business) disputes. Amendments to expand the scope of application, for example, to shareholder disputes, were rejected.[13] The Minister clarified that the act was a modest first

[8]This chapter is largely based on (and is an update of) Voet (2015).

[9]This implies a difficult prima facie judgment on the merits of the case. 'Possible' does not mean certain. It means that, in all reasonableness, there has to be sufficient evidence showing a violation by the defendant.

[10]Article XVII.36, 1° Code of Economic Law.

[11]Article XVII.37 Code of Economic Law. In June 2017, Articles 101 and 102 of the Treaty on the Functioning of the European Union were added (Article XVII.37, 33°). In May 2018, Regulation 2016/679 of the European Parliament and of the Council of 27 April 2016 on the protection of natural persons with regard to the processing of personal data and on the free movement of such data, and repealing Directive 95/46/EC (the General Data Protection Regulation) was added (in Article XVII.37, 10°/1).

[12]The class representative cannot base his claim on general tort law (Article 1382 Belgian Civil Code: 'any act whatever of man which causes damage to another obliges him by whose fault it occurred to make reparation'). He has to invoke the breach of one or more of the aforementioned regulations or acts.

[13]Chambre des représentants de Belgique, Rapport – Projet de loi portant insertion d'un titre 2 "De l'action en réparation collective" au livre XVII "Procédures juridictionnelles particulières" du Code de droit économique et portant insertion des définitions propres au livre XVII [Report of the Proposal to Introduce a Consumer Class Action in the Code of Economic Law], Doc. 3300/004, 17 February 2014, available at https://www.dekamer.be/FLWB/pdf/53/3300/53K3300004.pdf (accessed 20 Mar 2020), pp. 41, 51, 63, 66, 68, 69, 71, 72 and 75.

step. If this turned out positive, the procedure might be expanded to other fields of substantive law.[14]

In 2018, the procedure was expanded to disputes between SMEs (small and medium-sized enterprises) and businesses.[15] The direct cause of the expansion of the scope of application of the procedure was the 2017 Fipronil crisis.[16] The crisis developed in European countries, including Belgium, and involved Fipronil insecticide whose use and spread had contaminated chicken eggs and egg products sold and distributed for consumption. As a consequence of the contamination, dozens of poultry companies were blocked by the Belgian Federal Agency for the Safety of the Food Chain because there was the possibility that they had produced eggs that were contaminated with Fipronil. The Belgian government set up a task force to contain the crisis. One of the measures it took was the expansion of the class procedure to SMEs. This meant that not only consumers, but also SMEs could go to court (collectively) to obtain redress for the damage they suffered as a result of the same incident.

The expansion is limited to SMEs in the sense of the Commissions' Recommendation of 6 May 2003 concerning the definition of micro, small and medium-sized enterprises.[17,18] It concerns only enterprises which employ fewer than 250 persons and which have an annual turnover not exceeding EUR 50 million, and/or an annual balance sheet total not exceeding EUR 43 million.[19] This is about 98% of all Belgian companies.[20]

2.1.2 Standing

The second certification prerequisite is that the class action can only be brought by an adequate class representative.[21] In the case of consumers, the action can only be brought by:[22]

[14]Ibid., pp. 16–17, 22, 40 and 42–43.

[15]Loi portant modification, en ce qui concerne l'extension de l'action en réparation collective aux P. M.E., du Code de droit économique [Act Expanding the Scope of Application of the Class Action in the Code of Economic Law] of 30 March 2018, Moniteur belge [Official Gazette of Belgium] of 22 May 2018, 41950.

[16]https://en.wikipedia.org/wiki/2017_Fipronil_eggs_contamination. Accessed 25 Apr 2020.

[17]2003 O.J. (L 124).

[18]Article XVII.38, §1/1 Code of Economic Law.

[19]Article 2.1 of the Annex of the Recommendation of 6 May 2003.

[20]Lambrecht (2017).

[21]Article XVII.36, 2° Code of Economic Law.

[22]Article XVII.39, first two paragraphs Code of Economic Law.

- a consumer association having legal personality and represented in the Special Advisory Commission on Consumption (*Commission Consultative Spéciale Consommation*) or authorised by the Minister of Consumer Affairs;
- a non-profit association having legal personality,[23] whose statutory aim corresponds with the collective harm and authorised by the Minister of Consumer Affairs;
- the Consumer Mediation Service; this Service only has standing to initiate a class action and to negotiate a collective settlement; if a settlement cannot be reached, and the court has to decide the merits of the case, a consumer association has to step in to continue the procedure;[24] in 2014, Belgium implemented the Consumer ADR Directive;[25] the Act of 4 April 2014 set up the Consumer Mediation Service;[26] this Service receives all requests for the out-of-court resolution of consumer disputes and transfers them to an existing ADR entity; if there is no such entity, it handles the dispute itself;[27] it is Belgium's residual ADR entity and, as mentioned above, has standing to bring a class action for the purpose of negotiating a collective settlement;
- a representative entity authorised by an EU Member State to act as a representative and meeting the criteria as set out in Article 4 of the Recommendation of the European Commission of 11 June 2013 on common principles for injunctive and compensatory collective redress mechanisms in the Member States concerning violations of rights granted under Union Law.[28]

In the case of SMEs, the action can only be brought by:[29]

- an inter-professional association having legal personality and represented in the High Council for Self-Employed and SMEs (*Conseil supérieur des Indépendants et des PME*) or authorised by the Minister of Consumer Affairs;
- a non-profit association having legal personality,[30] whose statutory aim corresponds with the collective harm and authorised by the Minister of Consumer Affairs;

[23]On the day this association brings a class action it needs to have legal personality for at least 3 years.

[24]Article XVII.40 Code of Economic Law.

[25]Directive 2013/11 of the European Parliament and of the Council of 21 May 2013 on alternative dispute resolution for consumer disputes and amending Regulation (EC) No 2006/2004 and Directive 2009/22/EC, 2013 O.J. (L 165) (EU).

[26]Loi portant insertion du Livre XVI, "Règlement extrajudiciaire des litiges de consommation" dans le Code de droit économique [Act Introducing an Out-Of-Court Settlement Procedure for Consumers in the Code of Economic Law] of 4 April 2014, Moniteur belge [Official Gazette of Belgium] of 12 May 2014, 38262.

[27]See Voet (2016a).

[28]2013 O.J. (L 201).

[29]Article XVII.39, last two paragraphs Code of Economic Law.

[30]On the day this association brings a class action it needs to have legal personality for at least 3 years.

- a representative entity authorised by an EU Member State to act as a representative and meeting the criteria as set out in Article 4 of the Recommendation of the European Commission of 11 June 2013 on common principles for injunctive and compensatory collective redress mechanisms in the Member States concerning violations of rights granted under Union Law.[31]

Belgian law explicitly, and correctly, states that the representative also has to be adequate.[32] Standing has to be distinguished from adequacy of representation.[33] An association or organisation having class action standing is not automatically adequate to be a class representative in a specific case. When multiple associations present themselves as class representative, the class action mechanism forces the court to determine which association or body is most adequate to represent the class in that particular case. There should be no 'first come, first served' principle.

2.1.3 Superiority

The third and final condition is that the class action be more suitable than (or superior to) an individual civil action.[34] In assessing this condition, the court may take into account the following elements: the potential group size, the existence of individual injury in connection with the collective harm, the complexity and judicial efficiency of the class action mechanism, and the legal certainty for the group of consumers on whose behalf the action is brought. The size of the individual injury cannot be a decisive factor, in the sense that a judge cannot deny certification simply because the injury suffered by the class members differ while they all face the same or similar factual or legal issues.[35]

[31]2013 O.J. (L 201).

[32]Article XVII.36, 2° *in fine* Code of Economic Law.

[33]See Gidi (2003), pp. 367–372 and Micklitz (2007), p. 21.

[34]Article XVII.36, 3° Code of Economic Law.

[35]Chambre des représentants de Belgique, Projet de loi portant insertion d'un titre 2 "De l'action en réparation collective" au livre XVII "Procédures juridictionnelles particulières" du Code de droit économique et portant insertion des définitions propres au livre XVII [Proposal to Introduce a Consumer Class Action in the Code of Economic Law], Doc. 3300/001, 17 January 2014, available at www.dekamer.be/FLWB/PDF/53/3300/53K3300001.pdf (accessed 20 Mar 2020), pp. 8–9 and 21.

2.2 Brussels Courts

The Brussels Commercial Court, and in appeal the Brussels Court of Appeals, have exclusive jurisdiction to decide class actions that will be binding on the whole country.[36]

2.3 Opt-In or Opt-Out

There is no default rule in Belgium. In its certification decision, the Belgian court can freely choose between an opt-in or opt-out system.[37] The court will make the decision in light of the underlying facts and claims of the case. In some (limited) cases, the court must impose an opt-in system: when the class members are not residing in Belgium,[38] and when physical or moral damages are claimed.[39]

In order for class members to make an informed decision whether to remain in the class or opt out, they should be notified of the key decisions, including about certification and the merits of the case. In Belgium, the certification decision and other key decisions (judicial approval of a collective settlement, decision on the merits of the case and the decision closing the procedure) are published on the website of the Federal Public Service Economy, SMEs, Self-Employed and Energy and a link to this website is published in the Official Gazette of Belgium (*Moniteur belge*).[40] In exceptional cases, the court can order other forms of notice (e.g. in newspapers, magazines or on websites), including individual notice.[41]

2.4 Procedure

The Belgian legislature prioritises and facilitates the out-of-court resolution of mass harms. A settlement is possible in each phase: before the proceedings (in which case the parties can ask the court to approve the collective settlement),[42] during the

[36]Article 633*ter* Belgian Judicial Code.

[37]Article XVII.43, §2, 3° Code of Economic Law.

[38]Articles XVII.38, §1, 2° (consumers) and XVII.38, §1/1, 2° (SMEs) Code of Economic Law.

[39]Article XVII.43, §2, 3° Code of Economic Law.

[40]Articles XVII.43, §3, XVII.50, XVII.55 and XVII. 62 Code of Economic Law. See https://economie.fgov.be/fr/themes/protection-des-consommateurs/action-en-reparation/decisions-rendues-dans-le. Accessed 10 Apr 2020.

[41]Articles XVII.43, §2, 9° and XVII.54, §1, 6° Code of Economic Law.

[42]Article XVII.42, §2 Code of Economic Law.

mandatory negotiation phase after the class action has been certified[43] or during the procedure on the merits of the case.[44]

2.4.1 Settlement Before the Proceedings

If the parties reach a collective settlement before the start of the proceedings, they jointly submit it to the court to have it approved (homologated).[45] The agreement has to contain the following information:[46] a detailed description of the collective harm; a description of the class; information about the class representative and the defendant(s); the extent and the forms of collective redress; the reasons for using the opt-in or opt-out system; in the case of an opt-out system, the amount of time the class members who will not opt out will have after the settlement approval to come forward to obtain individual compensation; the amount of costs the defendant (s) will pay to the class representative; which party will pay the costs of notice; a possible revision procedure; additional forms of notice and the text of the collective settlement as it will appear when provided to the class members. If one of these elements is missing or unclear, the court will send the agreement back to the parties, who will have to complete it within eight days.[47] The joint petition must contain evidence that the certification criteria are met.[48]

The court must make a decision within two months.[49] If it refuses to approve the settlement, the procedure will end; it will not proceed as a litigation class action. There is no pro forma approval. The law states that the court will refuse approval if the agreed redress is evidently unreasonable.[50] Approval will also be refused if the amount of time that the class members who will not opt out will have after the settlement approval to come forward in order to obtain individual compensation is evidently unreasonable; if the additional forms of notice are evidently unreasonable; or if the amount of costs that the defendant(s) will pay to the class representative exceed the real costs the latter has incurred.[51] Again, and if necessary, the court can send the agreement back to the parties to have it amended on one or more of these

---

[43] Article XVII.45-48 Code of Economic Law.

[44] Article XVII.56 Code of Economic Law.

[45] Article XVII.42, §2 Code of Economic Law.

[46] Article XVII.45, §3, 2°-13° Code of Economic Law.

[47] Article XVII.42, §3 Code of Economic Law.

[48] See Sect. 2.1 above. The cause of action is a possible infraction by the defendant of his contractual obligations or of one of the (now) 33 European or Belgian consumer regulations or acts that are enumerated in the Act; the class action is brought by an adequate class representative and is more suitable than (or superior to) an individual civil action.

[49] Article XVII.44, §1 Code of Economic Law.

[50] Article XVII.49, §2 Code of Economic Law.

[51] Ibid.

grounds.[52] If the settlement is ultimately approved, the court will appoint a collective claims settler.[53] Neither the collective settlement nor the judicial approval decision implies a recognition of liability by the defendant.[54] The approval decision and the complete text of the settlement will be published on the website of the Federal Public Service Economy, SMEs, Self-Employed and Energy and a link to this website is published in the Official Gazette of Belgium (*Moniteur belge*).[55]

2.4.2 No Settlement Before the Proceedings

If the parties do not reach a collective settlement before the proceedings, the class action procedure will be initiated by the class representative, who will submit a petition to the clerk of the court. The complaint must contain the following information:[56] evidence that the certification criteria are met; a description of the collective harm; a detailed description of the class; and the reasons for using the opt-in or opt-out system. If one of these elements is missing or unclear, the court will send the petition back to the class plaintiff, who will have to complete it within eight days.[57]

The court has to make a certification decision within 2 months.[58] If the class action is not certified, the lawsuit will be dismissed without prejudice. Otherwise, the court renders a certification decision that has to contain the following elements:[59] a description and the cause of the collective harm; the applicable opt-in or opt-out system and its modalities (including the opt-in or opt-out period); a detailed description of the class; information about the class representative and the defendant(s); the period during which the parties have to negotiate a collective settlement; and additional forms of notice. The certification decision will be published on the website of the Federal Public Service Economy, SMEs, Self-Employed and Energy and a link to this website is published in the Official Gazette of Belgium (*Moniteur belge*).[60]

[52] Ibid. There are no indications in the preparatory works of the Act of 28 March 2014 that the court could ask the parties to amend the agreement on grounds other than those mentioned in Article XVII.49, §2 Code of Economic Law.

[53] Article XVII.49, §3 Code of Economic Law. See Sect. 2.6 below.

[54] Articles XVII.46 and XVII.51 Code of Economic Law.

[55] Article XVII.50 Code of Economic Law.

[56] Article XVII.42, §1 Code of Economic Law.

[57] Article XVII.42, §3 Code of Economic Law.

[58] Article XVII.43, §1 Code of Economic Law.

[59] Article XVII.43, §2 Code of Economic Law.

[60] Article XVII.43, §3 Code of Economic Law. See https://economie.fgov.be/fr/themes/protection-des-consommateurs/action-en-reparation/decisions-rendues-dans-le. Accessed 10 Apr 2020.

In its certification decision, the court must set a time limit during which the parties have to negotiate a collective settlement.[61] This cannot be shorter than three months and not longer than six months.[62] The court can prolong the time limit once by a maximum of six months.[63] During this mandatory negotiation phase, the parties can use an accredited mediator.[64] If a settlement is reached, the approval procedure as described above will apply.

If a settlement cannot be reached within the allotted time frame, the procedure will continue so that the court can decide the merits of the case.[65] Within a month after the court has been notified of the fact that no collective settlement could be reached, it will order a hearing, where the parties agree on a procedural calendar or one is imposed by the court.[66] If the parties reach a collective settlement during the procedure on the merits of the case, they can ask the court to approve it, and the procedure as described above will apply.[67] If no settlement is reached, the court will decide the merits of the case. If it finds the class claim valid, the decision will contain the same elements as a collective settlement.[68] The court will also appoint a collective claims settler.[69] The decision will be published in the same manner as the approval decision.[70]

2.5 *Collective Redress in Kind or by Monetary Payment*

Any collective settlement and decision on the merits of the case will have to determine the extent and forms of collective redress. This redress can be in kind (e.g. replacement of a deficient product) or by monetary payment. The amount of payment can be determined on an individual basis, meaning that the defendant (s) will have to pay an individualised amount of money to every consumer coming forward, or, when this is impossible or impracticable, on a global basis.[71]

Every consumer wanting to be compensated has to come forward, even in an opt-out system. In the event of a low take-up rate, the court will determine the

[61] Article XVII.45, §1 Code of Economic Law.

[62] Article XVII.43, §2, 8° Code of Economic Law.

[63] Article XVII.45, §1 Code of Economic Law.

[64] Article XVII.45, §2 Code of Economic Law. On mediation in Belgium and the accreditation of mediators see Taelman and Voet (2015).

[65] Article XVII.52 Code of Economic Law.

[66] Article XVII.53 Code of Economic Law.

[67] Article XVII.56 Code of Economic Law.

[68] Article XVII.54, §1 Code of Economic Law.

[69] Article XVII.54, §2 Code of Economic Law.

[70] Article XVII.55 Code of Economic Law.

[71] Articles XVII.45, §3, 6° and XVII.54, §1, 7° Code of Economic Law.

allocation of the residual funds. The court has a wide range of options: the funds can flow back to the defendant or the defendant can be ordered to set up a *cy-près* scheme (e.g. an invoice discount or the distribution of coupons or a free product).[72]

Common Belgian liability law applies,[73] in the sense that the guiding principle remains full and individual compensation of the injury suffered. It is by no means the intention of the legislature to introduce punitive damages that could lead to overcompensation.[74]

2.6 *Enforcement Phase: Collective Claims Settler*

Finally, there is a phase during which the settlement or the decision on the merits of the case is enforced under the supervision of a collective claims settler.[75] The claims settler is appointed by the court from a list drawn up by the general assembly of the Brussels Commercial Court or the Brussels Court of Appeals. Only attorneys, ministerial public servants or judicial mandataries who are competent in settling claims can be appointed.[76]

The enforcement procedure is very complicated and governed by short time limits. In the case of an opt-out system, the court determines a time frame during which the class members who have not opted out have to come forward before the clerk of the court in order to obtain individual compensation. In the case of an opt-in system, consumer class members have already opted in with the clerk of the court. Based on the information received from the clerk of the court, and within a reasonable time, the claims settler draws up a provisional list of class members who will receive compensation. When a member does not meet the class description, this is mentioned on the list.[77] The claims settler sends the list to the judge, the class representative, the defendant and the class members he proposes to exclude. Within 30 days, the class representative or the defendant can challenge the inclusion or

---

[72]Article XVII.61, §2 Code of Economic Law and Chambre des représentants de Belgique, Projet de loi portant insertion d'un titre 2 "De l'action en réparation collective" au livre XVII "Procédures juridictionnelles particulières" du Code de droit économique et portant insertion des définitions propres au livre XVII [Proposal to Introduce a Consumer Class Action in the Code of Economic Law], Doc. 3300/001, 17 January 2014, available at www.dekamer.be/FLWB/PDF/53/3300/53K3300001.pdf (accessed 20 Mar 2020), p. 42. On *cy-près*, see Mulheron (2006).

[73]Chambre des représentants de Belgique, Projet de loi portant insertion d'un titre 2 "De l'action en réparation collective" au livre XVII "Procédures juridictionnelles particulières" du Code de droit économique et portant insertion des définitions propres au livre XVII [Proposal to Introduce a Consumer Class Action in the Code of Economic Law], Doc. 3300/001, 17 January 2014, available at www.dekamer.be/FLWB/PDF/53/3300/53K3300001.pdf (accessed 20 Mar 2020), p. 37.

[74]Ibid.

[75]Article XVII.57, §2 Code of Economic Law.

[76]Article XVII.57, §1 Code of Economic Law. There are no detailed legal criteria to determine this competence.

[77]Article XVII.58, §1 Code of Economic Law.

exclusion of a class member on the provisional list with the clerk of the court. No more than 14 days later, the clerk informs the concerned class members and the claims settler. Within 14 days, the class representative, the defendant(s), the class members whose enlistment is challenged and the claims settler have the opportunity to communicate their views to the clerk of the court.[78] Within 30 days, the court orders a hearing. The claims settler, the class representative, the defendants and the class members concerned are heard, after which the court makes up the final list of class members entitled to compensation.[79] This list is provided to all parties.

If conflicts occur during the enforcement phase, the parties and the claims settler can always ask the court to resolve them.[80]

Every three months, the claims settler reports to the judge. A copy of this report is sent to the class representative and the defendant(s). The report contains all useful information regarding the progress of the enforcement of the settlement or decision and a detailed overview of the costs and elements allowing determination of the remuneration of the claims settler. The court approves or disapproves the report. In the event of approval, the decision is considered to be an enforceable title for the claims settler to claim his costs and fees from the defendant(s).[81]

When the settlement or the decision is fully enforced, the claims settler deposits a final report, a copy of which is sent to the class representative and the defendant(s). The final report contains all information for the court to decide on the closure of the procedure, (if applicable) an overview of the funds that were not distributed among the class members and a detailed outline of the costs and fees of the claims settler.[82]

The court decides on the final report and determines the allocation of the residual funds. By approving the report, the court closes the enforcement procedure. The approval of the final report is considered to be an enforceable title for the claims settler to claim his costs and fees from the defendant(s).[83] The decision is published on the website of the Federal Public Service Economy, SMEs, Self-Employed and Energy and a link to this website is published in the Official Gazette of Belgium (*Moniteur belge*).[84]

A Royal Decree of 6 December 2018 regulates the fees of the claims settler.[85] His fee is calculated on an hourly basis. The hourly rate cannot be more than €140 per

[78]Article XVII.58, §3 Code of Economic Law.

[79]Article XVII.58, §4 Code of Economic Law. The question arises whether an excluded class member can challenge the decision that excludes him. Because he is not a party to the proceedings, he cannot appeal the decision. The fact that the class member concerned is heard by the court does not make him a party.

[80]Article XVII.60 Code of Economic Law.

[81]Article XVII.61, §1 Code of Economic Law.

[82]Article XVII.61, §1/1 Code of Economic Law.

[83]Article XVII.61, §2 Code of Economic Law.

[84]Article XVII.62 Code of Economic Law.

[85]Arrêté royal relatif à l'indemnité du liquidateur dans le cadre de l'action en réparation collective [Royal Decree Regarding the Remuneration of the Claims Settler in the Context of a Class Action] of 6 December 2018, Moniteur belge [Official Gazette of Belgium] of 17 December 2018, 99084.

hour. In exceptional cases, the court can permit a higher rate if the case is complicated and after hearing the claims settler and the defendant. The claims settler has to substantiate his costs and fees. To limit the costs, the claims settler has to use, as much as possible, electronic means.

3 Case Law and Evaluation

3.1 Case Law

The class action procedure entered into force on 1 September 2014. Between then and 1 April 2020—i.e. five and a half years—nine cases were brought (see Table 1).[86]

The following conclusions can be drawn:

- all cases were consumer class actions; there are no SME class actions;
- eight consumer class actions were brought by Test-Achats, Belgium's biggest consumer association; one consumer class action was brought by the Consumer Mediation Service;
- four consumer class actions were finished; five consumer class actions are still pending;
- of the four consumer class actions that were finished, there was:
  - one collective settlement (*Groupon*), although not homologated by the court in the sense of the law;
  - one settlement only on the costs and fees of the class representative (*Thomas Cook Airlines Belgium*);
  - one case that was declared unfounded on the merits (*Proximus*);
  - one case that was stopped before any judicial decision (*NMBS/SCNB*);
- in one still pending consumer class action there was a partial collective settlement (illegal resale of concert tickets), although not homologated by the court in the sense of the law;
- in three cases there was a formal certification decision (*Thomas Cook Airlines Belgium*, *Proximus* and *Volkswagen*); in every case the class action was certified;
- in one case there was a decision on the merits of the case (*Proximus*); the case was declared unfounded;
- in all consumer class actions the class representative asked for the opt-out regime; in the three cases where there was a certification decision, the court imposed the opt-in regime in two cases (*Thomas Cook Airlines Belgium* and *Proximus*) and the opt-out regime in one case (*Volkswagen*);

[86] My thanks go to Laura Marcus of Test-Achats and Eric Houtman, Energy Ombudsman for providing me some additional information.

Table 1 Overview of all Belgian class action procedures between September 2014 and April 2020

Defendant	Nature of the case	Number of class members	Opt-out or opt-in	Status
Test-Achats as class representative				
Thomas Cook Airlines Belgium 2 October 2015[a]	Delayed plane	183	Test-Achats asked for an opt-out; the court imposed an opt-in	**Finished** Certification decision on 4 April 2016[b] and final judgment on 29 May 2017 Settlement about the costs and fees of Test-Achats[c]
NMBS/SNCB (National Railway Company of Belgium) 23 November 2015	Delayed trains	44,000 registered complainants	Test-Achats asked for an opt-out	**Finished** No judicial decision Test-Achats could cooperate with NMBS/SNCB to improve the existing compensation mechanism for delays
Proximus (telecom operator) 30 November 2016	Misleading information about decoders	± 30,000 potential victims	Test-Achats asked for an opt-out; the court imposed an opt-in	**Finished** Certification decision on 4 April 2017, confirmed in appeal on 10 January 2018; final judgment in appeal on 30 January 2019[d] Claim was unfounded
Groupon (e-commerce marketplace) (https://www.test-achats.be/actions-collectives/action-collective-groupon-compensation) 26 October 2017	Defective delivery of diaper boxes	1200	Test-Achats asked for an opt-out	**Finished** No certification decision Collective settlement (€200 cash and €100 in the form of credits on the Groupon-account)

Volkswagen and d'Ieteren Auto (Belgian importer and distributor of Volkswagen cars) (https://www.test-achats.be/mobilite/autos/dossier/dieselgate-faites-vous-partie-des-gens-trompes) 30 June 2016	Emissions scandal	± 11,000 registered victims; ± 400,000 involved cars	Test-Achats asked for an opt-out; the court imposed an opt-out	**Ongoing** Certification decision on 18 December 2017[e] (after interlocutory decision on 27 February 2017),[f] negotiation phase is finished; court will deal with merits of the case in February 2022
5 companies exploiting 8 websites 8 December 2016	Illegal resale of concert tickets	2650 registered victims	Test-Achats asked for an opt-out	**Ongoing** Collective settlement with one company (Events Belgium) in 2018 (for 450 victims)[g] There was an interlocutory judgment regarding jurisdictional matters;[h] this decision was appealed; the court of appeal referred the case back to the first judge, where the case is currently pending
Facebook (https://www.test-achats.be/actions-collectives/facebook)30 May 2018	Data breach	42,708 (beginning of April 2020)	Test-Achats asked for an opt-out	**Ongoing** Certification hearing on 2 March 2020
Ryanair (https://www.test-achats.be/actions-collectives/ryanair) 11 July 2019	Strikes in the summer of 2018	1299 (beginning of April 2020)	Test-Achats asked for an opt-out	**Ongoing** No certification decision yet (there was an introductory hearing on 13 September 2019)

(continued)

Table 1 (continued)

Defendant	Nature of the case	Number of class members	Opt-out or opt-in	Status
Consumer Mediation Service as class representative				
8 energy companies[i] 3 August 2018	Unfair subscription fees[j]	± 40,000 victims	Consumer Mediation Service asked for an opt-out	**Ongoing** On 9 November 2019 there was an interlocutory judgment regarding procedural matters;[k] this decision was appealed; the case is currently pending before the Court of Appeals

[a]This is the date on which the petition was submitted to the court
[b]https://economie.fgov.be/fr/themes/protection-des-consommateurs/action-en-reparation/decisions-rendues-dans-le. Accessed 10 Apr 2020
[c]The settlement was not disclosed. All passengers were compensated voluntarily by Thomas Cook before or shortly after the procedure
[d]https://economie.fgov.be/fr/themes/protection-des-consommateurs/action-en-reparation/decisions-rendues-dans-le. Accessed 10 Apr 2020
[e]Ibid
[f]This decision was not appealed by Volkswagen
[g]The settlement was not disclosed
[h]Some of the defendants, having their seat in the Netherlands, disputed the jurisdiction of the Belgian courts. The court claimed it has jurisdiction. This decision was confirmed in appeal. The Court of Appeals sent the case back to the lower court
[i]Essent, Luminus, Octa+, Mega, Energy People (in the meantime bankrupt) and Zeno (now Energy2Business but not active anymore on the residential market)
[j]Clients have to pay subscription fees for one full year even when they terminate the contract before that year starts
[k]Regarding the capacity and adequacy of the Consumer Mediation Service to bring the class action

- in the ‘smallest’ consumer class action there were 183 class members (*Thomas Cook Airlines Belgium*), in the ‘biggest’ consumer class action there were 44,000 class members (*NMBS/SNCB*);
- in two consumer class actions there was a formal final decision ending the procedure (*Thomas Cook Airlines Belgium* and *Proximus*); it took the court on average 698 days (a little bit less than two years) to come to this final decision (605 days in *Thomas Cook Airlines Belgium* and 791 days in *Proximus*);
- in three consumer class actions there was a formal certification decision (*Thomas Cook Airlines Belgium*, *Proximus* and *Volkswagen*); in two cases (*Thomas Cook Airlines Belgium* and *Volkswagen*) the decision was not appealed, here it took the court on average 360.5 days (about a year) to come to the certification decision (185 days in *Thomas Cook Airlines Belgium* and 536 days in *Volkswagen*); in one case (*Proximus*) the decision was appealed, here it took the court(s) 406 days (a little bit over a year) to come to the certification decision.

3.2 Evaluation

3.2.1 Scope

European policymakers recommend that all Member States should have collective redress mechanisms in *all* areas where Union law grants rights to citizens and companies: consumer protection, competition, environmental protection, protection of personal data, financial services legislation and investor protection. The principles set out in the 2013 Recommendation should be applied horizontally and equally in those areas, but also in any other areas where collective claims for injunctions or damages in respect of violations of the rights granted under Union law would be relevant.[87]

Conversely, most European class actions are of a sectoral nature, in the sense that their scope is limited to, for example, consumer or competition law. At first sight this is at odds with the access to justice goal of the Recommendation.[88] For some disputes collective access to justice is provided, while for other disputes, falling outside the scope of the law, there is only individualised access to justice.

In Belgium, where the class action regime originally was limited to consumer law cases, the Constitutional Court held that the act’s limited scope of application did not render it unconstitutional.[89] The Court stated that most mass cases are consumer cases and that the list of European and Belgian consumer regulations and acts

[87]Recital (7) of Recommendation of the European Commission of 11 June 2013 on common principles for injunctive and compensatory collective redress mechanisms in the Member States concerning violations of rights granted under Union Law, 2013 O.J. (L 201).

[88]Ibid., recitals (9) and (10).

[89]Belgian Constitutional Court 17 March 2006, case 41-2016, available at http://www.const-court.be/en/common/home.html. Accessed 20 Apr 2020.

(forming the scope of the Belgian class action procedure) was sufficiently comprehensive. Moreover, the Court found that because it concerns a novel and complicated procedure, the Belgian legislature was right to limit, in the first instance, its scope to consumer cases.

This reasoning is not convincing. The fact that most mass cases are consumer cases (which is not substantiated by empirical evidence) and that the class action procedure is 'complicated' (whatever that means) are not reasonable (even fallacious) grounds to exclude other kinds of cases from the procedure. Nevertheless, there might be another plausible and more acceptable reason why Member States limit their class action procedures to specific sectors, namely the existence of other (more efficient) means of resolving (mass) disputes in other sectors. This will be discussed below.[90]

In 2018, the scope of application of the class action procedure was expanded to disputes between SMEs and businesses.[91] The direct cause for this was the 2017 Fipronil crisis. Two remarks can be made. On the one hand, the Minister declared, back in 2014, that the consumer class action act would be a modest first step. If this turned out positive after an evaluation in 2017, the procedure might be expanded to other fields of substantive law. Although the preparatory works of the Act of 30 March 2018 mention 'an evaluation',[92] this was never published (Who did this evaluation? What methodology was used? What were the conclusions?). Moreover, in 2017 only five cases were brought. On the other hand, the procedure was (surprisingly) expanded to 98% of all Belgian companies because of one single mass case, the 2017 Fipronil crisis.[93] All of this is not an example of efficient policy-making.

[90]Section 4 below.

[91]Section 2.1.1 above.

[92]Chambre des représentants de Belgique, Projet de loi portant modification, en ce qui concerne l'extension de l'action en réparation collective aux P.M.E., du Code de droit économique [Proposal to Expand the Scope of Application of the Class Action in the Code of Economic Law], Doc. 2907/001, 22 January 2018, available at https://www.lachambre.be/FLWB/PDF/54/2907/54K2907001.pdf (accessed 20 Mar 2020), p. 4: 'l'accord de gouvernement a prévu l'évaluation de la loi après deux ans, dans le but, en particulier, de déterminer s'il était opportun d'en étendre le bénéfice à d'autres catégories de justiciables. Cette évaluation a conduit à la conclusion que son extension aux PME est souhaitée par de nombreux acteurs'.

[93]The legislative proposal was submitted to Parliament on 22 January 2018. Two months later, on 22 March 2018, the proposal was already accepted by Parliament. See https://www.dekamer.be/kvvcr/showpage.cfm?section=flwb&language=fr&cfm=/site/wwwcfm/flwb/flwbn.cfm?dossierID=2907&legislat=54&inst=K. Accessed 20 Mar 2020.

3.2.2 Class Representative

The Belgian legislature chose for an associational plaintiff, who has no private cause of action or grievance against the defendant.[94] This choice can be applauded.[95] When such a plaintiff initiates a class action, the focus will, from the outset, be on the class and not on the personal claim of an individual class member.[96] The collective interests of the class members as a whole will be the motivating reason for initiating a class action. During the proceedings, these interests will always come first, not those of an individual representative class member or his attorney. Therefore, one may expect associational plaintiffs to pursue class actions more strongly, with more commitment and enthusiasm, which will benefit the class members. Moreover, time-consuming procedural problems will not occur when the individual claim of the class representative becomes moot or is settled by the defendant.

On the other hand, there is a danger of market monopolisation, which can be detrimental to the interests of potential class members. Limiting, or even constraining, standing to a certain number of players can lead to a possible lack of enforcement. Bringing a class action will depend on the financial willingness of these, usually non-profit, entities. The question arises, and this will be discussed below, how great this willingness is under a loser pays system and in the absence of external funding sources.

Moreover, the fact that in some jurisdictions, such as Belgium, only authorised or accredited associations or organisations have standing can also be criticised because this could mean too much government dependency.[97] The possibility to initiate a class action would de facto depend on ministerial authorisation.[98] The Minister replied that there are legal conditions he has to obey and that in the event of arbitrariness his decision could be annulled by the Belgian Council of State (the highest administrative court).[99]

As mentioned above,[100] a Belgian consumer class action can be brought (a) by a consumer association having legal personality and represented in the Special Advisory Commission on Consumption (*Commission Consultative Spéciale Consommation*) or authorised by the Minister of Consumer Affairs or (b) a non-profit association having legal personality whose statutory aim corresponds

[94]Mulheron (2004), p. 303 (referring to an ideological plaintiff).

[95]Voet (2013a), pp. 457–464.

[96]This refers to the class-entity or class-as-client theory (Shapiro (1998)).

[97]This criticism was also raised in Parliament (Chambre des représentants de Belgique, Rapport – Projet de loi portant insertion d'un titre 2 "De l'action en réparation collective" au livre XVII "Procédures juridictionnelles particulières" du Code de droit économique et portant insertion des définitions propres au livre XVII [Report of the Proposal to Introduce a Consumer Class Action in the Code of Economic Law], Doc. 3300/004, 17 February 2014, available at https://www.dekamer.be/FLWB/pdf/53/3300/53K3300004.pdf (accessed 20 Mar 2020), p. 13).

[98]Ibid., pp. 11 and 14.

[99]Ibid., p. 18.

[100]Section 2.1.2 above.

Table 2 Overview of all Belgian associations having standing to bring a consumer class action

Name	Nature of the association	Class action standing
Verbraucherschutzzentrale VoG (Consumer Protection Center of East Belgium)[a]	Consumer association	Represented in the *Commission Consultative Spéciale Consommation* (Special Advisory Commission on Consumption)[b]
Test-Achats[c]	Consumer association	
Collectif Solidarité contre l'Exclusion : Emploi et Revenus pour tous (CSCE) (Solidarity Collective Against Exclusion: Work and Income for Everyone)[d]	Association against exclusion	Authorised by Ministerial Decree of 9 October 2014 to bring a class action on behalf of energy consumers
Syndicat National des Propriétaires et Copropriétaires (SNPC) (National Syndicate of Owners and Co-owners)[e]	Association defending the interests of (co-)owners	Authorised by Ministerial Decree of 21 October 2015 to bring a class action on behalf of consumers suffering injury regarding their movable or immovable property
Netwerk van verenigingen waar armen het woord nemen (Flemish Anti-Poverty Network)[f]	Anti-poverty association	Authorised by Ministerial Decree of 20 June 2018

[a]https://www.vsz.be/. Accessed 25 Apr 2020
[b]https://www.ccecrb.fgov.be/c/fr/25/presentation. Accessed 25 April 2020
[c]https://www.test-achats.be/. Accessed 25 Apr 2020
[d]http://www.asbl-csce.be/. Accessed 25 Apr 2020
[e]https://www.snpc-nems.be/. Accessed 25 Apr 2020
[f]https://www.netwerktegenarmoede.be/nl. Accessed 25 Apr 2020

with the collective harm and authorised by the Minister of Consumer Affairs. To date, five associations have consumer class action standing (see Table 2 above).[101]

Of the nine consumer class actions, eight were brought by Test-Achats. This indicates that this consumer association has indeed a de facto market monopoly in bringing consumer class actions in Belgium. This can largely be explained by the fact that Test-Achats, as the biggest consumer association,[102] has the most means—in the sense of staff and financial resources—to bring such a procedure.

It is regrettable that Belgian law does not allow ad hoc associations or special-purpose foundations, under the form of a legal entity and created after a specific mass

[101]I focus only on associations that can bring consumer class actions and not on associations that can bring SME class actions, since no such actions were brought to date.

[102]For example in 2018, Test-Achats made a profit of €3,328,960.73 (see https://cri.nbb.be/bc9/web/catalog;jsessionid=F7C4467C63DF113260524C64196CC7D2?execution=e1s2 (accessed 25 Apr 2020)).

case, to bring a class action. Amendments in that respect were rejected.[103] As mentioned above,[104] non-profit associations need to have legal personality for at least 3 years and they have to be authorised by the Minister of Consumer Affairs.

Again,[105] Belgian law states that the representative also has to be adequate because standing has to be distinguished from adequacy of representation. The adequacy of representation test can obviate potential conflicts of interest. If it is clear from the beginning that the associational interests of the plaintiff prevail over the economic interests of the class, the judge can rule that the plaintiff is not adequate as a class representative. If the conflict of interest occurs during the procedure, the judge can replace the class representative at the request of a class member or even the defendant.

3.2.3 Funding and Financing[106]

The biggest obstacle to the effectiveness of many European class action regimes, including the Belgian one, is the funding and financing controversy, which goes to the heart of any class action system. At the outset it should be noted that most jurisdictions, Belgium included, assume that class action procedures can and will be financed in the same way as individual procedures. This is not the case.

Funding and financing class actions is a complex issue. It is challenging to embed this kind of procedure in the existing one-on-one litigation funding rules. In individual litigation, the costs and lawyer fees are (pre)financed by the identifiable plaintiff pursuing his individual claim, or a third party (e.g. a lawyer, a legal-expenses insurer, a legal-aid scheme or a third-party litigation funder) directly connected with that plaintiff. In class action litigation, and at least at the outset of the procedure, the plaintiff acts on behalf of a group of unquantifiable and unidentified class members. Rational apathy and free-rider problems minimise the incentive for those members to invest in the litigation, leaving the funding to be paid for or organised by their agent (i.e. the class representative) who will in most cases be confronted with wealthy and sophisticated repeat players as counterparties in the litigation. This results in an investment asymmetry.[107]

The fees and costs in question are also substantial. Collective redress procedures not only entail court costs and lawyer fees, but also specific class action-related costs

---

[103]Chambre des représentants de Belgique, Rapport – Projet de loi portant insertion d'un titre 2 "De l'action en réparation collective" au livre XVII "Procédures juridictionnelles particulières" du Code de droit économique et portant insertion des définitions propres au livre XVII [Report of the Proposal to Introduce a Consumer Class Action in the Code of Economic Law], Doc. 3300/004, 17 February 2014, available at https://www.dekamer.be/FLWB/pdf/53/3300/53K3300004.pdf (accessed 20 Mar 2020), p. 57.

[104]Section 2.1.2 above.

[105]Ibid.

[106]See Voet (2016b).

[107]Tzankova (2012), p. 554.

connected to: an intensive preparation stage, a complicated certification phase, multiple individual or non-individual notifications to class members, reaching a settlement, court ordered investigations, a possible elaborate trial on the merits of the case, internal administration and communication processes, potential distribution procedures, etc. All these costs and fees need to be pre-financed, irrespective of the outcome of the case.

Due to the loser pays rule, which is well entrenched in the European legal tradition,[108] the final outcome of the case will ultimately determine who will have to bear some or all of these costs and fees.

In a one-on-one setting, there are two principal actors on the initiator side: the plaintiff pursuing his individual claim and his (representing) counsel. Collective redress procedures are, from the plaintiff's side, characterised by a triangular structure. In addition to the class representative and the class lawyer, there are a number of unquantifiable and unidentified class members. Although they are not formal parties to the procedure, it is their rights that are being adjudicated in a decisive manner, in the sense that they are directly bound by the *res iudicata* effect of the decision, unless they have not opted in or have opted out. Therefore, the funding issue should be approached from this triangular structure: funding by the class representative (an individual class member, a governmental body or an association/foundation), funding by the class counsel and funding by a third party (public funding, legal aid, legal-expenses insurance and third-party litigation funding). I have analysed this elsewhere.[109] My conclusion was that there is no clear-cut answer to the question of how collective redress actions should best be financed. The most sustainable solution seems to be a mixture of options: direct funding by a governmental body or organisational plaintiff, a governmental fund, tailor-made designed legal aid and legal-expenses insurance, regulated third-party litigation funding, and one-way cost shifting.

3.2.4 One Exclusive Class Action Court

The Belgian legislature, rightfully, chose one exclusive class action court: the Brussels Commercial Court, and in appeal the Brussels Court of Appeals.[110]

One exclusive class action court can lead to a specialised and experienced court and can pave the way for an efficient resolution of class actions.[111] Uniform and predictable case law can develop in a specialised area of the law. Moreover, a specialised and more experienced court is able to deal with these cases more

[108] Including Belgium, see Article 1017 Belgian Judicial Code.

[109] Voet (2016b).

[110] Section 2.2 above.

[111] Choi (2004), p. 1517 ('specialized judges may develop expertise in distinguishing between frivolous and meritorious claims and therefore become more willing to sanction frivolous suits'). This is also in the best interests of defendants.

efficiently and swiftly. Because the total number of mass cases in European countries seems to be fairly limited, even in jurisdictions that already have class actions or class action-like tools, it would be inefficient to give jurisdiction to multiple courts in a small country such as Belgium. One competent court also avoids time-consuming litigation over jurisdictional issues, as well as the disadvantages of forum shopping.

3.2.5 Procedure

Finally, three remarks can be made regarding the procedure.

At first instance, the Brussels Commercial Court has exclusive jurisdiction to hear class action cases. The class action certification decision can be appealed. According to Belgian law,[112] when a decision is appealed all the (factual and legal) issues that were not decided by the first court are transferred to the appellate court that will decide them. There is no referral back to the court of first instance in the event the appellate court affirms the decision. However, there are some exceptions to this rule. For example, when the appellate court affirms, on the same grounds, an investigative measure ordered by the first court, it will refer the case back to the first court. This exception does not apply when the Brussels Court of Appeals affirms a class action certification decision. In that event, the Court of Appeals has jurisdiction to deal with the rest of the procedure. This was for example the situation in the *Proximus* case where the Brussels Court of Appeals rendered the final judgment declaring the claim unfounded. Because the stakes in class action procedures are usually high, one would expect that the certification decision will almost always be appealed, meaning that the procedure at first instance will be de facto limited to the certification issue. It will then be the Brussels Court of Appeal that will approve a collective settlement reached after certification or that will render a decision on the merits of the case. However, the limited case law shows that this is not always what happens. Only in the *Proximus* case was the certification decision appealed. In the *Thomas Cook Airlines Belgium* and *Volkswagen* cases there was no appeal against the certification decision.

In the Belgian class action procedure, the class member has to opt in or opt out after receiving notification of the certification decision.[113] This choice is irrevocable. If a consumer has opted in or has not opted out, and afterwards disagrees with a collective settlement or the decision on the merits of the case, he will be bound by the *res judicata* effect of that settlement or decision. This allows determination of the definite size of the group at an early stage of the proceedings, which can facilitate and encourage a collective settlement. The legislature also wants to avoid class

[112]Article 1068 Belgian Judicial Code.

[113]Articles XVII.38, §1 (consumers) and XVII.38, §1/1 (SMEs) Code of Economic Law.

members making their opt-in or opt-out decision based on the result of the procedure.[114] An amendment allowing class members to opt out at any stage of the proceedings—to avoid the possible adverse effect that class members will simply not opt in or will opt out because their choice will be final—was rejected.[115]

Finally, many class action regimes struggle with devising a coherent and clear (back-end) framework for the distribution of damages after a collective settlement or decision. Problems of individual quantification of loss can present huge difficulties. Usually specific tailor-made techniques are missing.[116] Most jurisdictions, including Belgium, start from the naïve premise that the traditional civil law rules can simply be applied. Moreover, complicated sub-procedures exist where one of the parties or a claims settler has to distribute the funds among the class members. To date, the enforcement phase in the Belgian class action procedure has not been used. The future will show whether this is a workable framework.

4 Alternative Ways to Achieve Collective Redress

4.1 CDR

In this final section, several alternative ways, other than class actions, to achieve collective redress receive our attention. They have come to the fore in a number of jurisdictions, Belgium among them. The first is the out-of-court resolution of (mass) consumer disputes.[117]

[114] Chambre des représentants de Belgique, Projet de loi portant insertion d'un titre 2 "De l'action en réparation collective" au livre XVII "Procédures juridictionnelles particulières" du Code de droit économique et portant insertion des définitions propres au livre XVII [Proposal to Introduce a Consumer Class Action in the Code of Economic Law], Doc. 3300/001, 17 January 2014, available at www.dekamer.be/FLWB/PDF/53/3300/53K3300001.pdf (accessed 20 Mar 2020), pp. 23 and 31.

[115] Chambre des représentants de Belgique, Rapport – Projet de loi portant insertion d'un titre 2 "De l'action en réparation collective" au livre XVII "Procédures juridictionnelles particulières" du Code de droit économique et portant insertion des définitions propres au livre XVII [Report of the Proposal to Introduce a Consumer Class Action in the Code of Economic Law], Doc. 3300/004, 17 February 2014, available at https://www.dekamer.be/FLWB/pdf/53/3300/53K3300004.pdf (accessed 20 Mar 2020), p. 52.

[116] In Belgium, Falla proposed a Quebecian-inspired toolbox to deal with the distribution of damages under the Belgian class action regime (Falla (2014)).

[117] Hodges and Voet (2018), pp. 211–260 and Voet (2017), pp. 131–133.

On the one hand, this is embedded in the Belgian class action procedure.[118] As mentioned earlier,[119] the procedure is construed around reaching a collective settlement. Such a settlement is possible in each phase: before the proceedings (in which case the parties can ask the court to approve the settlement), during the mandatory negotiation phase after the class action has been certified or during the procedure on the merits of the case.

On the other hand, a new world is emerging in the field of consumer redress: consumer dispute resolution (CDR).[120] CDR uses the traditional ADR techniques, but within the context of a dispute resolution structure that is entirely separate from the courts. The CDR architecture encompasses a number of possible structures: arbitration, sometimes with mediation as a first stage; official quasi-arbitration but non-binding adjudication; regulated arbitration; complaint functions within public regulatory authorities; private sector ombudsmen, sometimes regulated; and statutory ombudsmen. CDR also encompasses online dispute resolution (ODR), which uses technology (the internet) to facilitate ADR.[121] The model here is usually binding arbitration, although the process, arbitrators and systems are not always transparent. However, online platforms also usually provide a direct communications channel between consumer and trader, which has a high success rate of negotiated and voluntary redress where the platform includes a self-regulatory feedback feature.

CDR gained momentum in 2013 when the European Parliament and the Council adopted a new Consumer ADR Directive and a Consumer ODR Regulation.[122] The Regulation establishes a free and interactive pan-European ODR platform through which consumers and traders can initiate ADR in relation to disputes concerning online transactions (offline transactions are excluded). National ADR entities receive the complaint electronically and seek to resolve the dispute through ADR. The ODR

[118]This is also the preferred option of the European policymakers: 'The Member States should ensure that the parties to a dispute in a mass harm situation are encouraged to settle the dispute about compensation consensually or out-of-court, both at the pre-trial stage and during civil trial . . .'; 'The Member States should ensure that judicial collective redress mechanisms are accompanied by appropriate means of collective alternative dispute resolution available to the parties before and throughout the litigation . . .' (Articles 25 and 26 of Recommendation of the European Commission of 11 June 2013 on common principles for injunctive and compensatory collective redress mechanisms in the Member States concerning violations of rights granted under Union Law, 2013 O.J. (L 201)).

[119]Section 2.4 above.

[120]Creutzfeldt (2013) and Hodges (2014).

[121]Hörnle (2009).

[122]Directive 2013/11 of the European Parliament and of the Council of 21 May 2013 on alternative dispute resolution for consumer disputes and amending Regulation (EC) No 2006/2004 and Directive 2009/22/EC (Directive on consumer ADR), 2013 O.J. (L 165) (EU) and Regulation 524/2013 of the European Parliament and of the Council of 21 May 2013 on online dispute resolution for consumer disputes and amending Regulation (EC) No 2006/2004 and Directive 2009/22/EC (Regulation on consumer ODR), 2013 O.J. (L 165) (EU).

platform was launched in the spring of 2016.[123] The Consumer ADR Directive promotes ADR by encouraging the use of approved ADR entities that ensure the following minimum quality standards: the entities should be impartial and provide transparent information, offer their services at no or nominal cost, and hear and determine complaints within 90 days of referral. The Directive applies to domestic and cross-border disputes concerning complaints by a consumer resident in the EU against a trader established in the EU.

CDR has two added values. First, although not particularly designed for this, many CDR regimes have the potential of processing mass problems. They are capable of identifying and processing multiple (similar or identical) claims and have developed aggregation techniques—similar to how courts aggregate bulks of claims—that deliver consistency of outcomes. For example, in the Netherlands the Consumer Complaint Commissions regularly allocate a series of similar cases for hearing on the same day, thereby providing consistency of adjudication. The results of these cases are then communicated to the parties of other (suspended) cases and these parties are invited to settle their case.[124] Second, if well designed, CDR can go beyond mere dispute resolution. Hodges identified the five functions of CDR: (1) consumer advice, (2) dispute resolution, (3) aggregation of data, (4) publication of the aggregated data, as feedback to traders/sectors and information to consumers, competitions, regulators and investors and (5) improving market behaviour.[125]

In the meantime, almost all Member States have implemented the Consumer ADR Directive,[126] including Belgium. As mentioned previously,[127] the Directive was implemented by the Act of 4 April 2014.

The Directive set up the Consumer Mediation Service, Belgium's residual ADR entity.[128] This is an autonomous public body with legal personality and is composed of a front office and a service for the out-of-court resolution of consumer disputes. The Consumer Mediation Service has a particular structure, in the sense that it is composed of the existing federal economic ombudsman services and two private ombudsman services.[129] The latter two were chosen not only because they administer a large number of complaints, but also because their services are similar to the public ombudsman services.

Every year the Consumer Mediation Service publishes an activity report. Besides statistical information about the number of complaints, this report can contain recommendations about systematic or significant problems that occur frequently

[123] https://webgate.ec.europa.eu/odr. Accessed 29 Apr 2020.

[124] Weber and Hodges (2012), p. 148.

[125] Hodges (2016), p. 353.

[126] For an overview see Cortés (2016a).

[127] Section 2.1.2 above.

[128] https://consumerombudsman.be/en. Accessed 29 Apr 2020.

[129] Two members of the Telecom Mediation Service, two members of the Ombudsman Service for the Postal Sector, two members of the Ombudsman Service for Energy, two members of the Mediator for Rail Passengers, the Ombudsman in Financial Matters and the Insurance Ombudsman.

Table 3 Most important data (2016–2018) of Belgium's Consumer Mediation Service

Total number of new cases					
2016		**2017**		**2018**	
7105		9574		9081	
Requests for information					
2016		**2017**		**2018**	
174		844		1115	
Total number of cases referred to another CDR entity or falling outside CDR scope					
2016		**2017**		**2018**	
2763		3677		3013	
Total number of residual cases (dealt with by the CMS)					
2016		**2017**		**2018**	
4342		5053		4890	
Admissible	Not admissible	Admissible	Not admissible	Admissible	Not admissible
2838	1504	2581	2472	2542	2352
Closed residuals cases by the CMS					
2016		**2017**		**2018**	
Settlement: 50% Recommendation: 37% Closure: 13%		Settlement: 48% Recommendation: 22% Closure: 13%		Settlement: 55% Recommendation: 33% Closure: 12%	
Average duration of a case					
2016		**2017**		**2018**	
38 days		36 days		44 days	

and lead to consumer disputes. These structural recommendations can indicate how such problems can be avoided or resolved in the future. The goal is to enhance traders' performance and facilitate the exchange of information and best practices. This statistical information can also play a key role in detecting mass cases and exposing rogue traders. They can also give rise to regulatory interventions (i.e. investigations, the imposition of (administrative) sanctions or criminal prosecution).[130]

Table 3 above gives an overview of the most recent data.[131]

[130]The exchange of data is facilitated by Article 17 of the Consumer ADR Directive dealing with the 'cooperation between ADR entities and national authorities enforcing Union legal acts on consumer protection'.

[131]This was compiled on the basis of the 2016, 2017 and 2019 annual reports. https://mediationconsommateur.be/fr/publications/2. Accessed 29 Apr 2020.

4.2 Regulatory Redress

Within the broader context of the transformation of (public and private) enforcement,[132] new trends and approaches emerge. One example is regulatory redress, which is redress that is ordered or brought about by the intervention of public enforcers.[133] Its strength is the combined weight of public/regulatory enforcement tools and civil/compensatory tools. The advantage, and at the same time incentive, for businesses is that all aspects of a (mass) harm situation are resolved in one process, thereby avoiding sequential public (i.e. criminal and/or regulatory) and private procedures and costs. Doing the right thing in providing redress can be incentivised by leniency in enforcement policies or by the advantage of maintaining high commercial reputation. It goes without saying that in order for regulatory redress to work, there needs to be sufficient resources and, more importantly, safeguards to protect the independence of the public enforcement agencies (such as publication of enforcement policies, fair procedural rules, a predictable and transparent process, ministerial and stakeholder oversight, the possibility for courts to impose more serious sanctions and a mechanism for appeals, etc.).

There are multiple public enforcers or regulators in Belgium, but generally their powers regarding restitution or civil sanctions are limited.[134] The focus is on deterrence rather than restitution. Nevertheless, victims can claim compensation following a public enforcement decision (*follow-up*), arguing that the tort (or at least the fault element) has been proven by the findings of a violation.

However, some remarks have to be made regarding two important regulators and their link with redress: the Financial Services and Markets Authority (FSMA)[135] and the Commission for the Regulation of Electricity and Gas (CREG).[136] A first remark relates to the general finding that restitution and civil sanctions are not the main focus of public regulators or enforcers. One could take the example of the FSMA. When a supervised trader does not comply with the regulations in place, the FSMA has a wide array of instruments to deal with this non-compliance and to sanction the trader.[137] The (administrative) sanctioning has to be situated in the relationship

[132]See Micklitz and Wechsler (2016).

[133]Hodges and Voet (2018), pp. 153–210 and Voet (2017), pp. 133–135. For a typology see Hodges (2015), pp. 841–845 (removing illicit profits, ordering redress to be paid, bringing a collective action, piggybacking civil claimants in public enforcement proceedings, referring assessment of loss to the court, ordering an infringer to create a restoration scheme, ordering an infringer to propose a compensation scheme, approving a compensation scheme proposed by one or more parties, referring a proposed compensation scheme to a court for approval, ordering an infringer to negotiate, etc).

[134]Voet (2013b), p. 274.

[135]http://www.fsma.be/. Accessed 29 Apr 2020.

[136]https://www.creg.be/en. Accessed 29 Apr 2020.

[137]For instance, require the publishing of a correction, inspections, publishing warnings, suspend trading, striking an intermediary from the register, revoking authorisation, imposing fines or penalties.

between the FSMA and the supervised trader, not vis-à-vis the financial consumer. Although a consumer's complaint might trigger an investigation and administrative action, a harmed financial consumer will need to have recourse to other instruments outside the regulatory framework.

One should nevertheless pay attention to the possibility of including the consumer indirectly in a settlement between the FSMA and the non-complying trader. The fact that the consumer is not a party to that settlement does not imply that the consumer cannot be kept in mind when drafting the terms of the settlement. A settlement concerning interest rate derivatives to cover variable rate loans to SMEs between the FSMA and a number of financial institutions provides an excellent example.[138] After inspection, the FSMA concluded that not all of the rules regarding the duty of care and the supply of information were observed by the financial institutions concerned, so the FSMA pressed for several interventions. Some only related to the institutions, such as their duty to make sure that their employees are qualified to assume the responsibility imposed on them. Yet, the consumer was not forgotten. The financial institutions concerned agreed to pay each client a certain amount of money by way of commercial compensation. In that way, compensation is provided to the consumers although the settlement was only reached between the FSMA and a number of financial institutions.

In addition to including consumers' redress in settlements, the statutory framework can also provide some assistance to financial consumers. In that regard, Article 30*ter* of the Act of 2 August 2002[139] comes to mind. It contains a rebuttable presumption that in the event a financial consumer is harmed by a transaction and a trader listed in the next paragraph of the provision has committed a certain breach as a result of that transaction, the transaction at hand is presumed to be the result of the breach. This means the presumption entails that the investor would not have made the same decision without the breach.

A second remark concerns the CREG. The statutory framework provides for the creation of a Dispute Resolution Chamber (*Chambre d'appel*) which would resolve disputes between the network administrator and the network users regarding the duties of the network administrator, the distribution network administrators and the administrators of closed industrial networks within the context of the act on the organisation of the electricity market (and its implementing orders), except for disputes regarding contractual rights and obligations.[140] The *law in the books* certainly leaves room for offering redress to consumers, but the *law in practice*

[138]https://www.fsma.be/sites/default/files/public/sitecore/media%20library/Files/fsmafiles/news/2015-05_rentederivaten.pdf. Accessed 29 Apr 2020.

[139]Loi relative à la surveillance du secteur financier et aux services financiers [Act Regarding the Surveillance of the Financial Sector and Financial Services] of 2 August 2002, Moniteur belge [Official Gazette of Belgium] of 4 September 2002, 39121.

[140]Article 29 of the Loi relative à l'organisation du marché de l'électricité [Act Regadering the Organisation of the Electricity Market] of 29 April 1999, Moniteur belge [Official Gazette of Belgium] of 11 May 1999, 16264.

has not yet developed, since the Dispute Resolution Chamber is currently unable to operate due to a lack of appointment of its members.[141]

5 Conclusion

It is clear that class action mechanisms, as components of private enforcement, are gaining momentum in Europe. This is also the case in Belgium where the Act of 28 March 2014 introduced a consumer class action. In 2018, the procedure was expanded to disputes between SMEs and businesses.

Five and a half years later, nine cases have been brought. Four have been concluded, with only one collective settlement (*Groupon*). Perfection is not of this world. Certainly, Belgium's class action procedure has a number of deficiencies: the limited scope of application, the market monopoly of Belgium's biggest consumer association, the complete lack of appropriate and suitable funding and financing mechanisms in addition to several procedural design flaws. The fear of abusive or frivolous litigation forced the Belgian legislator to build in safeguards, yet thereby possibly inducing a catch-22 situation.

There are two possible solutions to deal with this. On the one hand, one can plead for (another) procedural reform. This might be a naïve solution. Most class action reforms are the result of a political compromise trying to reconcile the diverging interests of opponents and proponents. In other words, achieving the most optimal and efficient device is usually not the primary goal. After all, class actions will remain a controversial issue and devising them requires one to perform a delicate balancing act.

On the other hand, one should not throw the baby out with the bathwater. One should take a step back and look at the broader conceptual (dispute resolution) framework. In light of the alternative and new approaches that have come to the fore, the way forward seems to be to re-orient the private collective redress model. Class actions should be molded and adjusted so they can fit into an integrated national framework.

Consumer dispute resolution has become, or is becoming, the mainstream method of resolving small consumer disputes. If well designed, CDR can capture and resolve mass problems. Because many CDR schemes can aggregate data, which can be exchanged with regulators, the mechanism can go beyond mere dispute resolution. Regulatory redress, which is redress that is ordered or brought about by the intervention of public enforcers, is still terra incognita. Nevertheless, the examples mentioned in this chapter show that it works and that in some contexts it can offer real, sustainable and impressive solutions—again, if it is well designed. There need

[141]CREG (2015), p. 82 ('d'autre part, la Chambre des litiges, qui constitue un organe de la CREG, n'a pas encore pu fonctionner en 2015, faute d'un arrêté de nomination de ses membres').

to be sufficient resources and safeguards to protect the independence of the public enforcement agencies.

Although one may criticise these changes, and despite the existence of caveats, these techniques are here to stay. In many jurisdictions CDR and regulatory redress were not the consequence of a well-targeted policy, but developed and implemented by the sectors and actors themselves, making them market-driven, and thus unstoppable.

The focus should be on exploring and optimising *all* options for mass harm situations. Even more important is to connect these options so they can form an integrated (dispute resolution) framework. Only a broad and integrated instrumentarium, as a 'dispute resolution continuum',[142] which can avoid empty enforcement gaps, can tackle mass harm situations effectively and efficiently.

Many models are possible. In the CDR orbit, statutory forms of cooperation exist. Article 16 of the Consumer ADR Directive provides for cooperation and exchanges of experience between CDR entities. Member States have to ensure that CDR entities cooperate in the resolution of cross-border disputes and conduct regular exchanges of best practices as regards the settlement of both cross-border and domestic disputes. A network of national CDR entities has already been set up. Article 17 focuses on the cooperation between CDR entities and public regulatory authorities, including the exchange of information on practices in specific business sectors about which consumers have repeatedly lodged complaints. It also supports feedback on market behaviour to traders, competitors and customers. The latter function can be vital in the resolution of mass consumer disputes. If a CDR entity or an ODR provider detects a collective problem—which they can easily do because they receive and store complaints electronically—and provides timely feedback to a regulator, the latter can intervene quickly to avoid an escalation of the dispute, or the CDR entity can itself apply a consistent generic approach to all of the similar individual complaints it receives. Such a scheme allows an integrated approach. If the regulator concludes that collective restitution should be provided, then it could cooperate with the relevant CDR entity.

One of the conclusions of a 2016 study analysing the implementation of the Consumer ADR Directive in the various Member States is the need for interconnection between the courts, the enforcement bodies and the CDR.[143] In this study, Hodges noted that 'A pathway should be built between [CDR] entities and the courts as well as regulators when statutory interpretation is at stake. A system of preliminary reference between [CDR] entities and regulators, which could in turn trickle up from regulators to national courts, should be put in place to ensure an adequate application of consumer law'.[144]

[142]Stuyck (2007), p. 5.

[143]Cortés (2016b), p. 465.

[144]Hodges (2016), p. 351.

References

Choi S (2004) The evidence on securities class actions. Vand Law Rev 57:1465–1526
Cortés P (2016a) The new regulatory framework for consumer dispute resolution. Oxford University Press, Oxford
Cortés P (2016b) Conclusion. Ensuring the provision of consumer dispute resolution. In: Cortés P (ed) The new regulatory framework for consumer dispute resolution. Oxford University Press, Oxford, pp 447–468
CREG (2015) Rapport Annuel 2015. https://www.creg.be/sites/default/files/assets/Publications/AnnualReports/2015-creg-ar-fr.pdf. Accessed 29 Apr 2020
Creutzfeldt N (2013) The origins and evolution of consumer dispute resolution systems in Europe. In: Hodges C, Stadler A (eds) Resolving mass disputes. ADR and settlement of mass claims. Edward Elgar, Cheltenham, pp 223–246
Falla E (2014) Les dommages de masse. Propositions pour renforcer l'efficacité de l'action en réparation collective. Thèse visant à l'obtention du titre de docteur en sciences juridiques. Unpublished (on file with author). See http://difusion.ulb.ac.be/vufind/Record/ULB-DIPOT:oai:dipot.ulb.ac.be:2013/239308/Details. Accessed 27 Apr 2020
Gidi A (2003) Class actions in Brazil: a model for civil law countries. Am J Comp Law 51:311–408
Hodges C (2014) Unlocking justice and markets: the promise of consumer ADR. In: Zekoll J, Bälz M, Amelung I (eds) Formalisation and flexibilisation in dispute resolution. Brill, Leiden, pp 336–368
Hodges C (2015) Mass collective redress: ADR and regulatory techniques. ERPL 23:829–873
Hodges C (2016) Consumer redress. Implementing the vision. In: Cortés P (ed) The new regulatory framework for consumer dispute resolution. Oxford University Press, Oxford, pp 351–370
Hodges C, Voet S (2018) Delivering collective redress. New technologies. Hart, Oxford
Hörnle J (2009) Cross-border internet dispute resolution. Cambridge University Press, Cambridge
Lambrecht P (2017) La "class action" pour les PME: un remède ultime. https://www.feb.be/domaines-daction/droit%2D%2Djustice/class-action/la%2D%2Dclass-action%2D%2Dpour-les-pme%2D%2Dun-remede-ultime_2017-09-06/. Accessed 10 Apr 2020
Micklitz H (2007) Collective private enforcement of consumer law: the key questions. In: van Boom WH, Loos M (eds) Collective enforcement of consumer law. Securing compliance in Europe through private group action and public authority intervention. Europe Law Publishing, Groningen, pp 13–36
Micklitz H, Wechsler A (2016) The transformation of enforcement. European economic law in a global perspective. Hart, Oxford
Mulheron R (2004) The class action in common law legal systems: a comparative perspective. Hart Publishing, Oxford
Mulheron R (2006) The modern Cy-Près Doctrine. Applications & Implications. Routledge Cavendish, London
Shapiro D (1998) Class actions: the class as party and client. Notre Dame Law Rev 73:913–962
Stuyck J et al (2007) An Analysis and Evaluation of Alternative Means of Consumer Redress other than Redress through Ordinary Judicial Proceedings. Final Report. http://www.eurofinas.org/uploads/documents/policies/OTHER%20POLICY%20ISSUES/comparative_report_en.pdf. Accessed 10 Apr 2020
Taelman P, Voet S (2015) Mediation in Belgium: a long and winding road. In: Esplugues C, Marquis L (eds) New developments in civil and commercial mediation. Springer, pp 89–112
Tzankova I (2012) Funding of mass disputes: lessons from the Netherlands. J Law Econ Policy 8:549–591
Voet S (2013a) Cultural dimensions of group litigation: the Belgian case. Ga J Int Comp Law 41:433–480
Voet S (2013b) Public enforcement and A(O)DR as mechanisms for resolving mass problems: a Belgian perspective. In: Hodges C, Stadler A (eds) Resolving mass disputes. ADR and settlement of Mass Claims. Edward Elgar, Cheltenham, pp 270–292

Voet S (2015) Consumer collective redress in Belgium: class actions to the rescue. EBOR 16:121–143

Voet S (2016a) The implementation of the consumer ADR directive in Belgium. In: Cortés P (ed) The new regulatory framework for consumer dispute resolution. Oxford University Press, Oxford, pp 125–147

Voet S (2016b) The crux of the matter: funding and financing collective redress mechanisms. In: Hess B, Bergström M, Storskrubb E (eds) EU civil justice: current issues & future outlook. Hart, Oxford, pp 201–222

Voet S (2017) Where the wild things are'. Reflections on the state and future of European collective redress. In: Keirse A, Loos M (eds) Waves in contract and liability law in three decades of Ius Commune. Intersentia, Cambridge, pp 105–140

Weber F, Hodges C (2012) The Netherlands. In: Hodges C, Benöhr I, Creutzfeldt-Banda N (eds) Consumer ADR in Europe. Hart, Oxford, pp 129–165

Stefaan Voet Associate professor of civil procedure at the University of Leuven and a host professor at the University of Hasselt. Programme Affiliate at the CMS/Swiss Re Research Programme on Civil Justice Systems at the Centre for Socio-Legal Studies at the University of Oxford. Member of the Class Actions Exchange Network spearheaded by the universities of Stanford, Oxford and Tilburg and affiliate at the Class Action Lab of the University of Montréal. He is also a member of different working groups of the European Law Institute.

Class Actions and Group Litigation: A Norwegian Perspective

Maria Astrup Hjort

Abstract Class actions were introduced in Norwegian civil procedure with the Norwegian Dispute Act of 2005, inspired by the United States' federal rule on class actions. Norwegian civil procedure already had several other types of collective litigation, but these procedures did not cover the catchment area for the class action rules. The chapter on class actions was a novelty when the act was passed and it represented something new in Norwegian civil procedure. The ability to decide on a legal question with effect for many individual claims reduces the costs of each claim and thus gives access to the courts for claims involving amounts or interests so small that they would otherwise not be brought as individual actions. This chapter gives an introduction to the Norwegian class action rules and discusses whether the rules have been a success or not. The rules are compared with the source of inspiration. The importance of the origin of the rules and its influence on the interpretation of Norwegian rules is examined.

1 Introduction

Norway is part of a Nordic legal culture. The Nordic legal family has elements from both common law and civil law, but is traditionally considered closer to the civil law tradition.[1] The roots of the class action rules are located in the common law countries, but this legal institute has inspired countries from other legal cultures to introduce similar rules.[2] Norway is one of them.

When the Norwegian Civil Procedure Act was to be reformed 20 years ago, it was explicitly stressed in the mandate that the reform committee preparing the thorough

[1] Zweigert and Kötz (2019), p. 285. Nylund and Sunde (2019) introduce further the Nordic courts and court proceedings.

[2] NOU 2001: 32, 468, 484.

M. A. Hjort (✉)
Faculty of Law, University of Oslo, Oslo, Norway
e-mail: m.a.hjort@jus.uio.no

A. Uzelac, S. Voet (eds.), *Class Actions in Europe*, Ius Gentium: Comparative Perspectives on Law and Justice 89, https://doi.org/10.1007/978-3-030-73036-9_7

revision of the previous act should consider whether class action rules were suitable for Norwegian conditions. One of the goals for the procedural reform was to make the procedure more flexible and more adapted to different needs of actions.[3] Introducing class action rules in Norwegian civil procedure was considered one way to achieve this goal.

The Committee went on several study trips to the United States and attended American conferences on class actions.[4] On the basis of these experiences, the Committee concluded that rules on class actions should be introduced in Norwegian civil procedure. The Ministry of Justice and Public Security came to the same conclusion. They emphasized that many small claims remained unresolved although they could legally be well founded. Individual court proceedings for such small claims were disproportionately expensive.[5] A separate chapter on class actions was introduced in the Dispute Act (DA) of 2005, the act replacing the former Civil Procedure Act of 1915.

The class action rules were one of the main substantive changes in the civil procedure reform and one of the changes that attracted the most attention. The act came into force in 2008. With more than 10 years of experience with these rules, it is time to make an evaluation and consider whether this rule set has been a success or not. First, let me introduce the rules.

2 Dispute Act Chapter 35: Class Actions

The rules on class actions are located in the Dispute Act chapter 35, and section 35-2 lists the four prerequisites for class actions.

First, there is a prerequisite that

> several legal persons have claims or obligations for which the factual or legal basis is identical or substantially similar (DA sec. 35-2 letter a).

The prerequisite consists of two elements. One requirement is that the class consists of 'several' legal persons and the other is that 'the factual or legal basis is identical or substantially similar'. When a class consists of many members it is not difficult to imagine that there could be individual differences within the class. The prerequisite is set to ensure that the claims or obligations can be subject to a joint processing. The more prominent the individual circumstances are, the clearer it will be that the prerequisite is not met. However, it is not necessary to find the exact limit on how vast the differences can be, as the necessary limitation will result from the *second* prerequisite: class actions can only be brought if

> class procedure is the most appropriate method of hearing the claims (DA sec. 35-2 letter c.).

[3]NOU 2001: 32, 243–244.

[4]NOU 2001: 32, 85.

[5]Ot.prp. no. 51 (2004–2005), p. 330.

The court will have to make a total assessment of the entire case-complex and consider whether class procedure will provide the most appropriate method of hearing compared to other collective or individual options. Both the first and the second prerequisite are a rewrite and adaptation of Rule 23 (a)(1)-(2) of the US Federal Rules of Civil Procedure.

The *third* prerequisite demands that

> the claims can be heard by a court with the same composition and principally in accordance with the same procedural rules ... (DA sec. 35-2 letter b)

This prerequisite also contains two separate elements. Firstly, the court must be competent for all the requirements, and, secondly, the requirements must be able to follow the same procedural track.

The last and *fourth* prerequisite is that a group representative can be appointed. The group representative is either someone fulfilling the conditions of being a member of the group or an organisation, an association or a public body with a purpose that includes the litigation issue (DA sec. 32-3(1)). The group representative is designated by the court. It may be worth noting that according to the US rules, the group representative is required to have a 'typical case' of the class. According to Norwegian law, appointment as group representative requires considerably more. The representative shall safeguard the group's rights and obligations in the class action and ensure that the group members are kept properly informed.

The second paragraph of the provision contains a restriction on the right to be group members. Only those who could bring or join an ordinary lawsuit before Norwegian courts can be group members. Without such a restriction, Norwegian courts would have international authority, which they do not.

Rule 23 of the US Federal Rules of Civil Procedure establishes three different types of class actions, and there are different terms related to each type. The lawsuit must fulfil the terms of one of these types in order to constitute a class action. This scheme is not incorporated into Norwegian law, which means that Norway has only imported *part* of the US class action procedure.

3 Opt In and Opt Out

The US class actions rules are based on an opt-out solution, where potential group members who do *not* want to participate in the lawsuit must opt out of the lawsuit. The advantage of such a solution is that there is no risk of anyone losing their rights because they do not have knowledge of the lawsuit. This also relieves individuals of the burden of signing up.

In Norway, however, the opposite approach was chosen. The main rule is that potential group members must actively sign up to be part of the lawsuit through an opt-in solution. According to the preparatory work to the Dispute Act, the choice was based on the fact that the Norwegian legal tradition has always emphasised that it is up to the individual whether he or she will file a case with the courts. The

Committee saw no reason to change this freedom of choice. They argued that there may be different reasons why one chooses not to go to court. In addition, it was pointed out that by the opt-out solution, there was a risk of being bound by a judgment that was not known, and that such a judgment could be an obstacle for a later individual lawsuit.

However, it was recognised that in some situations an opt-out solution might be more appropriate. This was especially true for cases where the claim was so small that the group members would not see the value of bringing an individual lawsuit. Those who did not wish to participate in the lawsuit would have the opportunity to decline participation. It was assumed that the possibility of notifying group members would be relatively good in a small country like Norway.[6] Thus, the risk of intervention in the individual's freedom of choice will be less. The Norwegian rules therefore also allow the opt-out solution for class actions. The premise is that the claims individually involve amounts or interests that are so small that it must be assumed that a considerable majority of them would not be brought as individual actions, and that the court considers the opt-out solution to be the best (DA sec. 35-7).

4 Costs

US lawyers have to cover the costs of the case themselves and only recover them if they win the case. A group member in a class action will therefore not risk being charged for the counterparty's case costs, nor is there a risk of paying legal costs for the individual group member. If the lawyer wins the case, he or she will in return receive a significant proportion of the group's award. This scheme means that the lawyer will have a self-interest in winning the case. Although the Norwegian rules on class actions are inspired by US law, it was never the intention to incorporate US rules on legal costs into the class action procedure. The Committee also mentioned the Canadian system with funds covering the legal costs.[7] The funds allow the classes to bring the matter to trial and winning class actions must waive some of the compensation awarded back to the fund, enabling the fund to cover legal costs in upcoming class actions. However, this scheme too did not provide the solution to the question of legal costs in the Norwegian Dispute Act.

In Norway, the starting point is that every party is responsible for their own legal costs, but only to the degree that the party who loses the case pays the legal costs of the winning party, as well as his or her own costs. Thus, parties in a lawsuit carry the risk of having to pay significant legal costs. The issue of legal costs is always decided independently of the substantive outcome of the case, which means that Norwegian lawyers have no self-interest in the substantive result in the case.

[6]NOU 2001: 32, 493.

[7]NOU 2001: 32, 491.

For class actions, the responsibility for, and the right to have the costs covered lies with the group representative. For *opt-out* class actions, the Committee considered it to be a rather hopeless situation to claim legal costs from the individual group members if the case failed. This, of course, limits the possibility of being a group representative, and most opt-out class actions have so far been filed by organisations or government agencies such as the Norwegian Consumer Council.[8]

For *opt-in* class actions, it is possible for the group representative to claim coverage of the costs. The representative may require all group members to pay a stipulated maximum liability for costs. Upon request, the stipulated maximum liability is determined by the court, and it can also be determined that the amount or part of it must be paid before registration as a group member. Through this payment, the group representative can secure funds to cover costs in the case, primarily those relating to the lawyer(s).

5 The Use of the Norwegian Rule Set

An important factor in assessing whether the Norwegian rule set on class actions is a success or not is to what extent these rules are used. I surveyed all registered decisions from the district courts, courts of appeal and the Supreme Court that mention the Dispute Act chapter 35 on class actions. From the time the Dispute Act came into force on 1 January 2008 until today, 49 decisions have been made related to class actions.[9] A case complex can lead to several decisions, and of the 49 decisions I found that they originated from 27 case complexes based on class action procedure. However, in more than one-third of these case complexes, the conclusion was that the prerequisites for class actions were not met. Recurring problems are the assessment of whether ‘class action is the best method of hearing the claims’ (cf. sec. 35-2, second para., letter c). This is a discretionary assessment in which class actions are compared to the other alternative methods for obtaining claims with a collective element.

An example of this is a case from the Oslo District Court regarding the royalties on books after a publisher had gone bankrupt.[10] The main issue in the case, the royalties, was similar for everyone in the group, but the group members did not have identical publishing agreements. In addition, some of the group members had paid royalties in advance while others had not. Some of the group members were heirs of an author, and for these cases questions about inheritance was also part of the

[8]See, e.g., the case between DNB Asset Management AS vs. the unit holders of the mutual fund DNB Norway, LB-2018-43087. The case is further described in Sect. 5 below.

[9]Search made 16.01.2020 on ‘LOV-2005-06-17-90-§35-*’ in the following databases at www.lovdata.no: HRSIV, LASIV, LBSIV, LESIV, LGSIV, LFSIV, LHSIV, LXSIV and TRSIV, ie. decisions of the Supreme Court, courts of appeal and district courts. It should be noted that decisions from the district courts are only occasionally registered in the databases.

[10]See decision TOSLO-2013-7802.

picture. The court did not consider the prerequisite in section 35-2, second para., letter a—whether the factual and legal bases were 'identical or substantially similar'—but concluded that class actions were not 'the best method of hearing the claims' (cf. sec. 35-2 second para., letter c).

The assessment on whether class actions are the best method of hearing the claims was also up for discussion in a case before the Borgarting Court of Appeal in Oslo. Here, 21 buyers of apartments in a new building had filed a lawsuit claiming day fines, due to delayed completion.[11] The main issue in the case—the day fine—was similar for all group members, and the claims were based on identical contract provisions. However, the size of the fine varied from buyer to buyer, partly because the apartments had different sizes and partly because the number of days of delay varied from apartment to apartment. The court pointed out that other methods than class actions could have been used, but nevertheless concluded that class actions were 'the best method of hearing the claims'. It was emphasised that there was a clear and limited group and that it would be easier for the group members to use class action procedure.

Since a number of cases do not fulfil the prerequisites for class actions, only 13 cases have so far been registered using the opt-in procedure and four cases the opt-out procedure. With so few cases one may ask whether the rules have had any function whatsoever. However, for many of these cases, the class action rules have been crucial.

One case that has attracted attention in the media is the case between the Norwegian bank DNB and approximately 180,000 fund customers.[12] These customers had bought shares in mutual funds and the agreement between the bank and the customers was based on actively managed funds. However, the bank only managed the funds passively through so-called index-based management. Thus, the customers did not get the service they paid for. For each customer, the difference between what the customers should have got and what they actually received was less than €400, but in total it amounted to €700 million. The judgment handed down by the Court of Appeal fully upheld the claims of the fund customers.[13]

Another important case is Westerdals School of Communication vs. 474 previous students at the school. The students claimed that over a period of more than 10 years they had been charged too much in tuition fees. The students filed an opt-in class action, and the total claim came to nearly €2.9 million. Each student had a claim of nearly €5000. Unlike in the DNB case, individual cases could have been brought. However, a class action was regarded as the most appropriate method of filing the claims.

[11] See decision LB-2018-28008.

[12] DNB Asset Management AS vs. the unit holders of the mutual fund DNB Norway, LB-2018-43087.

[13] The case is allowed before the Supreme Court, see HR-2019-1654-U, and the hearing will take place in January 2020.

6 Collective Litigation

With the introduction of the class action rules in the Dispute Act, the Committee emphasised that the new rules would not lead to any restrictions on the other forms of collective litigation. In addition to class actions, Norwegian civil procedure has three different ways of handling collective litigation. First, and probably most important, cases can be united through subjective cumulation.[14] This solution is ideal if the claim affects several parties, or if there is a close relationship between the parties' claims or obligations. However, each party acts independently, and in the judgment the court will assess each party individually. The collectiveness and the coordination of the common interest in the case will therefore be weaker than with a class action. Nor are the rules on subjective cumulation expedient when the claims involve amounts or interests so small that they would not be brought as individual actions. For these cases, a class action would be the only possibility for giving the claims a hearing before the ordinary courts.

The second type of collectively characterised litigation relates to cases where an organisation or association acts to safeguard specific interests on behalf of a group.[15] A case concerning pollution could typically be brought before the courts by a nature or environmental protection organisation, and claims regarding calculation of salary of a profession may be brought by a trade union organisation. Such litigation may have an effect on the members of the organisation, but the members are not parties to the case and cannot be attributed anything in the judgment. Thus, the procedure is not expedient in tort claims concerning the members of the organisation.

The third type is referred to as so-called 'pilot cases'. One case is selected as a single representative of many similar cases, with the assumption that the outcome of this single case will be decisive for the other similar cases. The disadvantages of pilot cases are that procedural rights are limited to only the parties of the single case and there is uncertainty as to how far the legal effects of the judgment actually reach and are respected. Still, this solution is regularly used and functions well in situations where the legal question is similar, but where the facts of the cases differ to such an extent that the court nevertheless will have to assess the cases individually.

Subjective cumulation, cases raised by an organisation or association or getting the legal question settled through a pilot case give opportunities for a common solution of many similar claims, but still does not cover the catchment area for the class action rules. In class actions the group will act as a unit, the court assesses the legal question once, and the judgment is *res judicata* in all the individual claims. This makes the litigation cheaper and gives access to the courts for claims involving amounts or interests so small that they would otherwise not be brought as individual actions. From this perspective, the Norwegian class action rules have a mission.

---

[14] See DA sec. 15-1 to 15-3.

[15] See DA sec. 1-4.

7 Have the Class Action Rules Been a Success?

There are several ways of evaluating whether the Norwegian class action rules have been a success or not. One way is to consider whether the introduction of the class action rules has changed people's confidence in the courts. Unfortunately, there are no statistics on people's confidence in the courts based specifically on the class action rules, but, in general, the Norwegian citizens' confidence in the courts is very high. Nine out of ten people have very or quite high confidence in the courts.[16] What we can conclude, at least, is that class action rules have not diminished people's confidence in the courts.

Another way of evaluating the success of the Norwegian class action rules is to consider whether the rules fulfil a function previously not covered in the legislation. Based on the discussion above, the conclusion seems clear. The class action rules constitute another procedure for collectively characterised litigation, and the procedure widens the access to the courts. This especially applies to claims involving amounts or interests so small that they would otherwise not be brought as individual actions.

A third way of evaluating the success is to consider the use of the rules. During the preparation of the Dispute Act the Norwegian Bar Association and several other respondents to the act proposal argued that the need for class action rules in Norwegian civil procedure was not present. To the extent that there was a need for a legal procedure for these types of cases, they argued that alternative dispute resolution in consumer cases would be a satisfactory alternative.[17] Some of the consultative bodies feared that the class action rules would lower the litigation threshold and argued that the rules could create the basis for legal extortion. They emphasised that while a loss may be trivial to each class member, it will often be significant for the defendant.[18] Just the threat of being sued in a class action may create a very uncertain situation for a business, and the respondents were concerned that the class action could be abused to force a settlement.

However, none of these concerns have turned into practice. Extortion or threats on the basis of the class action has not been reported, and case law shows a need for the rules. As my survey of the case law showed in Sect. 5 above, the use of the rules is quite limited, approximately four decisions per year, and approximately one final class action judgment per year.[19] However, a determination as to the success of the rules should not necessarily rest on the number of hearings by the courts. One might very well argue that the low number of cases reflects the actual need for the class action rules and that the rules work as intended in these cases.

A procedure is used only if people find it expedient. If a more convenient way to assert one's rights exists, that will be the one preferred. Protection of rights does not

[16]The Norwegian courts (2017).

[17]Ot.prp. no. 51 (2004–2005), p. 327.

[18]Ot.prp. no. 51 (2004–2005), p. 328.

[19]Cases not registered in Lovdata's databases are not included in this calculation.

necessarily have to be found in the court system. If media coverage makes the wrongdoer stop his or her behaviour and the one concerned pays redress to the offended parties, the need for class action will be limited. People will not choose the class action system if easier and less expensive systems offering a legal settlement of the claim exists. Norway has several dispute resolution boards handling cases within a specific field. An implication of the scheme of these boards is the reduced need for legal proceedings in the ordinary courts, and this also affects the need for class actions. That said, the class action procedure has been crucial for several cases found in the case law.

8 Cherry-Picking from the Common Law Tradition

As mentioned already, the main source of inspiration is the United States. The Committee preparing the Dispute Act even commented in their own work, stating:

> In particular, there is reason to take a relatively close look at regulations and case law in the United States. This is where one has the longest and broadest experience with modern class action.[20]

On the basis of the US regulation and case law, class actions were introduced as a new element in Norwegian civil procedure, primarily aimed at increasing access to the courts for claims involving amounts or interests so small that they would not be brought as individual actions. The legislature's intention is honourable, but the source of inspiration is worth some comments.

There is a strong connection between legislation and society, and they mutually influence each other. The strong connection has, *inter alia*, an impact on changes.[21] Changes in society lead to changes in the legislation, and changes in legislation lead to changes in the society. Changes in the legislation may originate in an expressed desire in the society, but there are also many examples where the initiative comes from the legislature. The class action rules are an example of the latter.

When introducing new elements in a country's legislation, the legislature may look for inspiration abroad before designing the act or the amendment. In this way, the legislature can examine the effect of the rules from which it is relevant to source inspiration. The premise for examining the effect of the rules is, however, a similarity between the legal system potentially sourced from and the legal system to be reformed. Alan Watson emphasised in his book *Legal Transplants* the importance of good systematic knowledge of foreign law before sourcing from it. He points out that

---

[20]NOU 2001: 32, 468.

[21]The relation between legislation and society also appears in Knoph (1998), p. 1 (later editions of the book have omitted this paragraph), and in Mathiesen (2011), p. 26 ff.

> [a] rule of Swedish law which is successful at home might be a disaster in the different circumstances existing in Scotland; a rule of French law which there works badly might provide an ideal rule for Scotland.[22]

The American class action rules fit into an American legal tradition, and this tradition differs from the Norwegian tradition in many ways. There are differences in legal thinking, differences in people's trust in the court system, differences in compensation disbursement, differences in the legal cost system and differences when it comes to other possibilities to have small claims, typically consumer claims, resolved. The United States does not offer litigation at different dispute resolution boards in the same way as Norway does, and the class action procedure is therefore necessary in a completely different way than in Norway. Extensive use of class actions in the United States will not necessarily imply corresponding use in Norway.

The main factor regarding the use of class actions is probably the compensation disbursement. In Norway, compensation measurement is based on the loss suffered by the injured party. Small and limited damage will never lead to any large amount of compensation. In the United States, compensation measurement is based on the company's financial situation. This means that the amount of compensation can exceed the loss suffered by the injured party. This opens up a business for lawyers, and a lawyer may enter into an agreement whereby he or she receives a percentage of the compensation amount if the case succeeds. The lawyer's self-interest in the proceedings and the question whether the lawyer or the parties take the initiative to the file the case influence the use of class actions.

Even though the Norwegian class action rules are a legal transplant inspired by and based on US class action rules, the Norwegian rules get a quite different expression. The American rules are taken out of their original context and placed in the Norwegian legal culture. In Norway, the rules work on different premises and the interaction with the other Norwegian procedural rules affects both the use of the class action rules and their interpretation. Even though the wording resembles its origins, the connection to the society it works in gives the rules another content. One might ask whether it is possible to have a bite without eating the whole cake. To me, it seems as the (selection of) US class action rules have turned into something else in the Norwegian Dispute Act. In that sense, it may actually be misleading to emphasise that Norwegian rules on class actions are a legal transplant from the United States. It is more of a cherry-picking from the common law tradition.

References

Knoph R (1998) Knophs oversikt over Norges rett, 11th edn. Universitetsforlaget, Oslo
Mathiesen T (2011) Retten i samfunnet – en innføring i rettssosiologi, 6th edn. Pax forlag, Oslo
NOU 2001: 32 Rett på sak. Lov om tvisteløsning (tvisteloven)

[22] Watson (1974), p. 17.

Nylund A, Sunde JØ (2019) Courts and Court Proceedings. In: Letto-Vanamo P, Tamm D, Mortensen BOG (eds) Nordic law in European context, 1st edn. Springer
Ot.prp. no. 51 (2004-2005) Om lov om mekling og rettergang i sivile tvister (tvisteloven)
The Norwegian Courts (2017). https://www.domstol.no/nyheter/nyhetsarkiv2/2017/rekordhoy-tiltro-til-domstolene1/
Watson A (1974) Legal Transplants – an approach to comparative law, 1st edn. University Press of Virginia, Charlottesville
Zweigert K, Kötz H (2019) Introduction to comparative law (trans: Weir T), 3rd revised edn. Clarendon Press, Oxford

Maria Astrup Hjort Professor at the University of Oslo, Norway, where she holds the Chair for Civil Procedure. Her teaching and research cover issues in national and comparative civil and criminal procedure, legal history and ethics.

Group Actions in East-Nordic Legal Culture

Laura Ervo

Abstract In Sweden, a system of group actions has been in force since 2003. The original aim was to see about 20 such actions a year. In actual fact, in the 17 years of the existence of the system, 21 group action cases have been initiated, a number of which ended successfully for the plaintiffs. In Finland, only a public group action is allowed by the Group Action Act and the only authority that can bring the action is the Consumer Ombudsman. Up to the present time, there have been no group actions filed in Finland, even though the Act has been in force since late 2007. This cautious start was made in order to guarantee safeguards against the abuse of the group action system and to reach consensus to accept group actions in the country. Thus, so far East-Nordic (ie Swedish and Finnish) group actions have not been very successful. This has led to discussions in both countries as to the reasons why. In Sweden, discussions examine how to make the group action procedure more effective in the future. In Finland, discussions explore the scope of group actions and the possibilities to make them broader. However, those who are opposed to the group action system per se and its widening repeat the argument that the American way of litigation brings risks and does not fit well into Nordic legal culture. This argument was already common at the time the group action system was adopted in Sweden and in Finland as well. Does, in fact, this argument hold true? Or, can group actions actually correspond with East-Nordic culture? This contribution explores—and offers answers—to these questions.

The term "East-Nordic" refers to Sweden and Finland.

L. Ervo (✉)
Örebro University, Örebro, Sweden
e-mail: laura.ervo@oru.se

A. Uzelac, S. Voet (eds.), *Class Actions in Europe*, Ius Gentium: Comparative Perspectives on Law and Justice 89, https://doi.org/10.1007/978-3-030-73036-9_8

1 Introduction

In Sweden, a system of group actions has been in force since 2003 under the Group Action Act (Lag om grupprättegång 2002:599). The scope of group actions is open, covering all civil cases that fall within the competence of general courts and environmental damages in environmental courts. Furthermore, the scope is not limited to consumer cases only. All three forms of group actions are allowed, namely public, private and organizational. While the original aim was to see about 20 actions per year,[1] during the entire 17 years of the existence of the system there have been only 21 group actions,[2] mainly private suits,[3] a number of which ended successfully for the plaintiffs.; the others were dismissed, cancelled or ended with a friendly settlement or arbitration. Clearly, the original aim has not been achieved.

In Finland, the situation is the opposite. There, only a public group action is allowed by the Group Action Act (Ryhmäkannelaki 13.4.2007/444) and the only authority that can bring the action is the Consumer Ombudsman. This extremely cautious start was made in order to guarantee safeguards against the abuse of the group action system and to reach consensus to accept group actions in the country. However, the cautious start also means that a group action is merely the law on the books. Up to the present time, there have been no group actions filed in Finland even though the Act has been in force since late 2007.[4] The Consumer Ombudsman has come in for a lot of criticism because he has not started any group actions yet.[5] His reply is that the *possibility* to bring a group action has been an effective threat and thus there has been no need to initiate an action, for the disputes have been resolved by other means.[6]

---

[1]Lindblom (2008), p. 260.

[2]Anna Wallerman Ghavanini, 2021, United we stand, divided we sue: collective access to court in Sweden, particularly for labour and social security claims. European Labour Law Journal, unpublished manuscript.

[3]Ervo and Persson (2008).

[4]https://yle.fi/uutiset/3-10155371. Accessed 2 May 2020.

The Finnish Consumer Ombudsman is considering filing a class action against two credit plans that feature unreasonable credit costs. The preliminary period to opt in ended on 22 November 2019 for the class action that the Ombudsman is considering bringing against two instant credit companies. In total, over 1500 consumers have preliminarily opted in or requested that the Consumer Ombudsman assist them in the court proceedings. The next step will be for the Ombudsman to initiate negotiations with the opposing parties. The actual opt-in period will begin in 2020 if the class action progresses to the District Court. This would be the first group action in Finland. https://www.kkv.fi/en/current-issues/press-releases/2019/23.10.2019-finnish-consumer-ombudsman-intervenes-in-unreasonable-instant-credit-plan-costs/ and https://www.kkv.fi/en/current-issues/press-releases/2019/26.11.2019-class-actions-on-instant-credit-move-forward/. Accessed 1 May 2020.

[5]https://yle.fi/uutiset/3-8205579, https://www.ts.fi/tstv/1074810990/Miksi+Suomessa+ei+ole+nostettu+ryhmakanteita and https://www.kaleva.fi/mielipide/paakirjoitukset/merkittava-ennakkotapaus-oikeuden-ratkaisu-ryhmakanteesta-olisi-hyva-saada/828998/. Accessed 2 May 2020.

[6]https://yle.fi/aihe/artikkeli/2008/11/13/ryhmakanne-jai-suutariksi. Accessed 2 May 2020.

Summa summarum: so far, East-Nordic (ie Swedish and Finnish) group actions have not been as successful as hoped for.

This has led to discussions in both countries as to the reasons why. In Sweden, discussions have taken place on how to make the group action procedure more effective in the future.[7] In Finland, discussions have taken place on the scope of group actions and the possibilities to make them broader. However, those—and especially the Finnish Chamber of Commerce—against the group action system and its widening repeat the argument that the American way of litigation brings risks and will change Finnish law in dramatic and undesirable ways.[8]

2 East-Nordic Legal Culture

2.1 Starting Point

An argument often heard in the East-Nordic countries is that group actions do not fit well into local legal culture and traditions, full stop, but without defining the legal culture. In principle, it is true that legal transplants need to fit into the context and legal culture if they are to work well in their new environment. However, to be credible the legal culture and its contents should be described first. Additionally, not only the contents but also the objectives of group action should be taken into consideration when discussing the legal culture. Namely, is it not the case that access to justice and access to the courts belong to East-Nordic legal culture and traditions just as consumer protection and environmental protection do? Group actions have been adopted in East-Nordic countries to guarantee and facilitate access to justice and the courts, especially in small consumer cases where the risks involved in going to court otherwise is too high. In addition, group actions have been found to be effective in protecting the environment. At the very least, these objectives of group action fit very well into the East-Nordic legal culture where the aim of justice, protection of the weak and living in harmony with nature are essential cultural elements.[9]

Additionally, especially in Finland, there are problems with access to the courts because civil cases no longer go to the courts: because the risks associated with the costs is simply too high. Delays are also a problem in Finland.[10] Group action is one possibility to solve these problems, particularly in small consumer cases.

In this context, there really is only one question: Should legal culture and traditions be accepted as a barrier preventing legal development? Legal culture should not be used as a vague and hollow argument without contents.

---

[7]Justitiedepartementet (2008).

[8]https://kauppakamari.fi/2018/04/13/eun-ajama-amerikkalaistyylinen-ryhmakanne-ei-sovi-suomeen/. Accessed 2 May 2020.

[9]See Ervo (2015), p. 138.

[10]Autio (2014), pp. 32–34.

In what follows, the author's aim is to study the current East-Nordic legal culture and, by doing so, explore whether group action in fact fits into the local culture or collides with it.

2.2 *Folksy Legal Culture*[11]

Nordic legal culture is democratic, transparent, human, flexible, pragmatic and reformistic. In the other words, it is folksy.[12] Swedish legal culture is very discussion-oriented, while in comparison Finnish legal culture is quite executive. Finns run things quickly and in a creative way instead of embedding them with detailed plans and discussions with all actors first.[13] In addition, discretion has in many cases been delegated from the legislator to adjudication in the form of open norms and concepts in laws to guarantee flexible solutions in new situations of application. However, even this type of flexible legal culture has still been found to be too restrictive in Finland. Syrjänen has paid attention to the problem. According to him, there should be more creative solutions made by courts in the name of justice.[14] Siltala argues that there are two different "trends" in Finnish adjudication, namely, the legalistic one and the more creative one. The latter is used especially whenever European legislation has to be applied in order to find the more corresponding interpretation between "Finnish" and European rules.[15] Hautamäki, in turn, thinks that judicial activism is increasing in Finland due to more open norms that delegate more discretion to the courts.[16] Tuori shares the opinion of Hautamäki and Siltala that activism is increasing and affecting more issues in EU legislation.[17]

What is interesting is that Björn Bertilsson in Sweden has reached similar conclusions and stated that earlier very cautious Swedish courts, which were extremely bound to *travaux preparatoires* and wording, have now become more active thanks to Europeanization. He stresses how this more creative way of interpretation and application is strange to Swedish judges, who are traditionally not used to these types of instruments in their adjudication.[18] Elisabet Fura-Sandström too shares this opinion on the diminished significance of *travaux preparatoires* in Sweden. According to her, the case law has grown more important and judges have become more creative and willing to solve the problem within the courts.[19]

[11]Ervo (2015).

[12]Hirschfeldt (2011), pp. 5–6 and Wilhelmsson (2003), p. 85.

[13]Ervo (2015), p. 145.

[14]See Syrjänen (2012), pp. 335–388.

[15]Siltala (2003), p. 294.

[16]Hautamäki (2003), p. 172.

[17]Tuori (2000), p. 1051.

[18]Bertilsson (2010), pp. 29–31.

[19]Fura-Sandström (2004), pp. 264–265.

In the field of law, this means that individual solutions are rare in Sweden and courts wait for the legislator's reaction whenever new solutions are needed.[20] In Finland, it is not considered that risky to make fair and rational decisions in the situation where the law seems to be old-fashioned or otherwise lacking or to include the possibility for discretion.

The reason for this can be found in Finland's history. Namely, in Finland, legislative reforms were not easy to realize during the period when Finland was an autonomous part of the Russian empire between 1809 and 1917. Due to political reasons, Finnish legislation was for some time static and not subject to development. The Russian period and its challenges led to rapid developments in independent Finland and to some flexibility in applying and interpreting laws to correspond with the demands in the society at that time. These legal reforms have usually been realized quickly, without extensive and broad societal discussion. One of the main goals has been effectiveness.[21] Therefore, Finnish legal culture is still today characterized by quick solutions and rapid reforms, which can be realized whenever needed through new interpretations in the case law if the legislator has not reacted to relevant new and pressing needs in the society. This makes flexibility, creative solutions and common sense trademarks of Finnish legal culture; a legal culture that has previously been referred to as "folksy".[22]

Apart from that, the main pillars of the Nordic model are a tradition of dynamic constitutional principles, active popular movements and civic organizations, freedom of expression, equality, solidarity and affinity with nature. Combined with hard work and enterprise, these elements form the basis of a society that promotes productivity, a sense of security and a balanced connection between the individual and the community.[23] Often neighborhood, nature, history, languages, religion, the special Nordic mentality and common legal habits have been seen as a basis on which it is possible to say that Nordic law is a "legal family" in the true sense of the term.[24]

Group action fits well into this way of thinking and those values mentioned above. As long as group actions are used as a tool to promote access to justice, it is a democratic, transparent and human instrument just as the Nordic culture is. The Nordic culture is also folksy, in other words, flexible, pragmatic and reformistic. As a tool group actions not that flexible, so there are many procedural hindrances to be tackled before a group action can be successful. At the same time, it is a reformistic way of solving the access to the courts and access to justice problem in consumer and

[20]See, for instance, Tuori (2000), pp. 1049–1050.

[21]Kekkonen (1998), p. 936 and Saarnilehto (2003), p. 74. In the latter source it is said that those problems were solved between 1917 and 1995.

[22]Sallila (2011), p. 466.

[23]www.formin.fi/public/default.aspx?contentid=81004&nodeid=35435&contentlan=2&culture=en-US. Accessed 2 May 2020.

[24]Lando (2011), pp. 10–11.

environmental cases. The aim has been to find a pragmatic solution to these named problems.

Group action fits well into the tradition of active popular movements and civic organizations, equality and solidarity, too. Where environmental group actions are concerned, they serve the affinity with nature. Hard work and enterprise, which promote productivity, a sense of security and a balanced connection between the individual and the community, are not that far removed from the group action culture, either.

When comparing legislative procedures and court culture in Finland and Sweden we find that in Finland courts are more creative and legislative procedures are more a matter of action than discussion. In Sweden, courts are more bound to the *travaux preparatoires* and there are comprehensive discussions before legal reforms. From that perspective, is a bit surprising that group actions have been more successful in Sweden compared with the very cautious start in Finland. From the cultural perspective, the situation could have been just the opposite.

2.3 Current Effects in Legal Culture

Certainly, there are differences in the legal culture of the East-Scandinavian countries. To begin with, Swedish society is more *multicultural* compared with Finland. At the end of 2019, about 19.56% of the Swedish population was foreign born[25] whereas in Finland, in 2018, it was only 7%.[26] How this affects the legal culture is an interesting question. As a matter of fact, its impact is visible in daily life, for instance, in court proceedings where foreigners are parties and should be met in the same way as Swedes. How to realize this is one of the current challenges.[27] In addition, there may be latent effects, for instance, in the form of stereotypes.[28] Multiculturalism can cause problems with access to the courts because of a lack of knowledge and information. Group actions could be one good solution to promote access to justice and access to the courts in all groups of the society. By doing so, group actions also can promote equality before the law. Therefore, there is a need to develop and adopt group actions also in Swedish daily life.

[25]https://www.scb.se/hitta-statistik/statistik-efter-amne/befolkning/befolkningenssammansattning/befolkningsstatistik/. Accessed 20 Feb 2020.

[26]https://www.tilastokeskus.fi/tup/maahanmuutto/maahanmuuttajat-vaestossa/ulkomailla-syntyneet.html. Accessed 20 Feb 2020.

[27]https://www.domstol.se/globalassets/filer/gemensamt-innehall/styrning-och-riktlinjer/strategier-och-riktlinjer/bemotandestrategi-for-sveriges-domstolar.pdf. Accessed 2 May 2020. Also, Ökat förtroende för domstolarna – strategier och förslag – Betänkande av Förtroendeutredningen Stockholm 2008, SOU 2008:106, p. 62.

[28]Torstensson (2010), pp. 95–100.

The other main cultural difference is based on the ideology of *folkhemmet*,[29] which illustrates recent Swedish societal history. It still profoundly affects the self-image[30] of Swedes today. Something similar did not occur in Finland even if both countries are welfare states. The idea of *folkhemmet* strongly affects Swedish culture and the way of living, especially concerning social connections such as working environment and labor law, for instance. It is, namely, important that we all feel well, participate, for instance, in decision-making at the work place and no one is left on their own. This type of social way of thinking comes from the *folkhemmet* ideology and that idea is very well embedded throughout society in Sweden. On the other hand, in Finland, individual lifestyle is more common, and the bottom-up way of thinking is not that important either.[31] For instance, at work, hierarchy is accepted as a matter of fact. This deep difference in society and social life clearly affects legal culture, too, and, for instance, the way in which legal tools are used and laws interpreted.

To me, group action presents something similar. It means to act together so that no one is left on their own, but justice will reach each and every individual in the same circumstances. There is also a need for a volunteer spirit to start the group action and to reach the group members. Often, associations are used to initiate the group action in practice. This type of spirit is close to *folkhemmet* ideology.

2.4 Group Action as a Legal Transplant

There is always also a link between the law and morals. To be justifiable, the law should correspond with the common morality in the area where it is applicable.[32] If not, there are problems in legislative democracy. Where legal transplants—such as group actions—are concerned, the differences in societal morals can cause problems when the morals of the country of origin do not correspond with the morals of the host country.

The more law includes moral concepts such as "fair" or "reasonable" or other types of discretion in the form of open norms, the more difficult it is to place it in the new context as a "legal transplant". Or perhaps it is indeed easier, because in that case the transplant can be fulfilled with contents that are valid in its new home.

[29] *Folkhemmet* is a political concept that played an important role in the history of the Swedish Social Democratic Party and the Swedish welfare state. The core of the "Folkhem" vision is that the entire society ought to be like a small family where everybody contributes. See more about the concept, for example, in Dahlqvist (2002), pp. 445–465.

[30] Bertilsson (2010), p. 28.

[31] https://www.hs.fi/ulkomaat/art-2000006493608.html. Accessed 2 May 2020.

[32] Ervo (1996), p. 15.

Nevertheless, there is no guarantee that the transplant will work in the identical way in its new surroundings whenever there is a strong connection to moral aspects.[33]

Where group actions are concerned, the moral thinking of the original, American style of class action with punitive damages and so on does not correspond with the East-Nordic morals where revenge, sanctions or profit and winning are not number one in the ranking. More important is to win the case on principle and to attain justice. It is also important that the poor, the weak and the otherwise vulnerable can get access to justice. The fairness and feeling of fairness should be fulfilled not only in books, but also in practice. Still, group actions can be a tool that promotes both type of values. Therefore, they can work very well in both types of moral contexts.

The role of foreign law has changed in the current legal culture. Recently, it seems to have become a trend to exchange experiences internationally, and even to quote foreign cases in domestic case law. This leads to new possibilities that fit well into our East-Scandinavian pragmatic, flexible and situationally sensitive legal culture. Finally, this exchange of inspiration underpins the notion that new ideas develop alongside real problems and the need to solve them, and not as inanimate systems.[34] The trend to adopt and develop group actions in Europe not only corresponds but also comes easier together with this more general trend.

There have been problems in access to the courts and access to justice especially in consumer cases in the East-Nordic countries.[35] One solution to this problem has been group actions, which have been adopted as legal transplants from American legal culture to the Scandinavian legal family. However, these transplants have been adapted before adoption. East-Nordic group actions are not copies of American class actions, but a stripped-down version that has been said to fit better into the East-Nordic legal culture. The most radical tools such as punitive damages are not in the Nordic toolbox. Still, the stripped-down version also loses its original power despite the fact that this version can reduce transplant rejection, and make adoption and use of the instrument easier.

2.5 Nordic Law

Nordic law is a term that is often used to refer to the legal unity of the Nordic countries. The reason for this is partly found in the common history, language, culture and cooperation at the legislative level. The term "Nordic law" can be used as a synonym for the Scandinavian legal family. However, to me, Nordic law refers more to the contents of the Nordic or Scandinavian law, whereas the term

[33] As Tuulikki Mikkola has written, it is impossible to import the domestic morality together with the transplants from country to country, which means that the moral concepts will obtain different contents whenever transplanted. Mikkola (2010), p. 830.

[34] Wilhelmsson (2003), p. 87.

[35] Autio (2014), pp. 32–34; Ervo and Persson (2015), pp. 461–463.

"Scandinavian legal family" mainly is the term to classify the location of Nordic law as a civil law system but with its own specific characteristics based in local history and culture.[36]

"Nordic" can be used also so that geographically it is the correct. Scandinavia is geographically a smaller area and does not cover all those countries that belong to the Scandinavian legal family.[37] Therefore "Nordic" is more correct. Still, the Scandinavian legal family is an institute, whereas Nordic law is a concept that can be used instead of that. The combination "the Nordic legal family" is seldom or never used whereas Scandinavian law can be used instead of Nordic law. Still, to me the Scandinavian legal family term refers to the placing of legal orders and putting Scandinavian law in the civil law countries but, at the same time, stressing its original speices. Nordic or Scandinavian law refers to the contents of that legal family, that is, uniform systematics, principles of law as well as common legal culture as a background of legal interpretation and legal sources of law.[38]

The Nordic countries lack a general civil code and use a system of less comprehensive statutes supplemented by analogies from statutory provisions, established case law and legal doctrine filling the gaps, which is a factor of particular importance.[39]

Nordic law is characterized by its specific legal method, its mixture of statutory law and case law, and its less theoretical and conceptualized approach to legal problems. Also, Nordic law often has its own special features when it comes to the basic legal values and solutions chosen. At the same time, though, it is seldom uniform. When looking into the details, there are quite often notable differences between the exact position of the law on a specific point in the different Nordic countries. Nevertheless, it is a common experience among Nordic lawyers taking part in international legal work or conferences that there is a discernible Nordic legal way of approaching and treating legal problems characterized by realism and pragmatism.[40]

Nordic law is normally based on pragmatism and practical needs instead of concentrating on a theoretical and conceptualized approach. Thus, legislation has a clear focus and concentrates on issues of importance. Legal reform is for the benefit of the economy and welfare of the citizens, and unnecessary legal formalism is avoided.[41]

The realism and pragmatism of Nordic lawyers and their sound sense of what is useful and necessary in practice, their tendency to avoid undue conceptualism and the construction of large-scale integrated theoretical systems, the less intense influence of Roman law, the lack of large, systematically constructed private law

[36]See Bernitz (2007), pp. 17–23.

[37]Ibid., at pp. 15–16.

[38]Ibid.

[39]Bernitz (2018), p. 387.

[40]Ibid.

[41]Ibid., at p. 386.

codifications and the more limited use of all-embracing legal principles are all characteristics of Nordic law.[42]

Additionally, what is of decisive importance for the scope of legal unity between the countries is the degree of congruity between the fundamental premises of their legal theory, consistency in the formation of their basic legal concepts, uniformity in their methodology of codification, the doctrine of precedent and the choice of the sources of law.[43]

Legal dynamics is exceptionally strong in Nordic law. Additionally, instrumentalism often plays a strong role in legal interpretation, which means that the results of the interpretation are paid attention to. Different possible interpretations are compared with each other from the point of view of the results. After that, the interpretation is chosen, which leads to the best results from a practical perspective.[44] Accordingly, legal science needs to take into account the practical consequences that judicial decisions produce. Legal sources can no longer be limited to statutory and customary law: economic factors, social usefulness and people's sense of justice also have to be considered.[45] Both the legal dynamics and the instrumental way of thinking is especially typical in Finnish legal culture.

3 Scandinavian Realism

3.1 Background

From the historical perspective, the main phenomenon shaping East-Nordic legal culture is Scandinavian realism. Scandinavian realism was the Nordic reply to the critique of legal formalism. This paradigm shift dates back to the time of the so-called Uppsala School of philosophy in the 1920s and is regarded as a significant legal movement in the Scandinavian countries, most particularly in Sweden.[46]

Scandinavian legal realists abandoned natural law theories as metaphysical and legal positivism as unscientific. Jurisprudence was to be understood as social theory and legal policy as social technology. With the help of legal realism it was hoped that the problems caused by the late nineteenth-century industrialization and urbanization could be remedied.[47] The influence of intellectual history and philosophy, the social sciences and European anti-conceptualist legal thinking were the reasons for the birth of Scandinavian realism, where the main point lies in denying the

[42]Ibid.

[43]Ibid., at p. 385.

[44]Hänninen (2009), pp. 1063–1064.

[45]Pihlajamäki (2004), p. 474.

[46]Sreeparvathy G. Scandinavian Realists (May 2, 2011). Available at SSRN: https://ssrn.com/abstract=1829163 or https://doi.org/10.2139/ssrn.1829163.

[47]Pihlajamäki (2004), pp. 472–474 and Sreeparvathy (2011), pp. 15–16.

possibility of a science of justice or values.[48] It was up to the sociology of law to describe the relations between law and society, on the one hand, and the "cultural values" of law, on the other. Dogmatic scholarship, a normative science, could then decide between the alternatives thus brought to the fore.[49] These are purely subjective reactions or reflective of class or political ideology, and it is impossible to construct a science on such a basis.[50]

Especially, the Uppsala School is influenced by Axel Hägerström and his critical philosophical writings. The philosophical pragmatism of Charles Peirce and John Dewey is given as the philosophical framework underlying legal realism in general. Both Peirce and Dewey as pragmatists and realists despised metaphysical constructions and demanded that philosophy and law need to be made to serve social needs. In Scandinavia, Alf Ross shared the same perspectives and wanted to see law as social policy.[51] This was most explicitly developed in the final chapter of *Om ret og retfærdighed* where Ross claimed that the task of a legal scientist is to function as a "rational technician", assisting the political decision makers by elaborating on the most appropriate means by which a given end can be realized.[52]

If Scandinavian legal realism could be reduced to one basic dogma, the idea that the law is a social phenomenon ultimately relying only on the sanction of man himself would probably be the suggestion. This was a basic line of thought for Axel Hägerström (1868–1939), as well as for his followers Vilhelm Lundstedt (1882–1955), Karl Olivecrona (1897–1980), Alf Ross (1899–1979) and Ingemar Hedenius (1908–1982).[53] Especially, Olivecrona's *Law as Fact* (1939) has been characterized as a milestone in the development of Scandinavian legal realism.[54]

Sometimes Danish-Norwegian, elder realism is separated from this younger version of Scandinavian realism which has its roots in the Uppsala School. Danish-Norwegian realism and Scandinavian realism differ from the methodological point of view. However, in single questions both versions can again be quite similar. Otherwise, the main common issue is to see constructivism as an enemy. The objective with Scandinavian realism was not to counter Danish-Norwegian realism. Rather, it was more like a rational reconstruction of that. In addition, Danish-Norwegian realism was a pragmatically oriented version, whereas Scandinavian realism was a theoretical variant.[55]

In Finland, legal theory based on Scandinavian realism did not take hold that strongly. For instance, the inheritance handed down from Alf Ross was mainly in understanding the legal terms, in an analytical way, instead of incorporating his

[48]Pihlajamäki (2004), p. 471 and Sreeparvathy (2011), pp. 13–14.

[49]Pihlajamäki (2004), p. 474.

[50]Ibid., at p. 471 and Sreeparvathy (2011), pp. 13–14.

[51]Pihlajamäki (2004), p. 471 and Sreeparvathy (2011), pp. 13–14.

[52]Ross (2013), p. 466 and Strang (2009), p. 74.

[53]Strang (2009), p. 62.

[54]Olivecrona (1971), p. 67.

[55]Helin (2009), pp. 69–70.

empiricist ontology.[56] Especially in the 1930s, it was not that trendy in Finland to refer to Scandinavian realism in a positive sense. It was even said to be scientific suicide at that time to confess to being a follower of that idea. However, the effects of Scandinavian realism in Finland were quite significant later.[57]

In Sweden, the supporters of Scandinavian realism were often radical leftists, whereas in Finland the most important scholar, Kaila, stressed that politics should not be linked with this approach of a legal theory. It is not that common in Finland to find academics who were radical leftists, but in Sweden many of the supporters of the Uppsala School were Social Democrats and politically active, too.[58] Later on, to give more space to the analytical philosophy in Finland, Scandinavian realism was peeled from the radical politics first. This was important due to the existing Finnish political climate in the 1920s through the 1960s. Still, it is important to keep in mind that Scandinavian realism was not only about the ideology of the welfare state, but had other political connections, too.[59]

3.2 Compared with American Realism

The connection between both American and Scandinavian realist thought and the belief in rationality, science, technology and social planning was common to the entire Western world in the early twentieth century. Functionalism and social engineering characterize the worldview of the realists and their way of conducting legal research. This *social engineering* means progressive public measures taken to remedy the social problems caused by laissez faire capitalism. It coincides with the building of the social welfare state.[60]

What did the United States and Scandinavia have in common, what made legal scholars in both of these parts of the world devote their energies to legal realism? There must be something similar in the Scandinavian and American way of legal thinking. In the other words, there are common cognitive elements in both American and Scandinavian legal thinking.[61]

Namely, American law and legal science has maintained much of the original common law pragmatism. At the same time, space has been provided for a European-type scientific approach towards law. The "first wave" realists combined traditional common law pragmatism with a newer thinking that was inspired by

[56]Tuori (2000), p. 1004.

[57]Helin (2009), pp. 71–72.

[58]Malminen (2010), p. 321.

[59]Ibid., at p. 323. See also Hänninen (2009), pp. 1063–1064.

[60]Malminen (2010), p. 321 and Pihlajamäki (2004), p. 473.

[61]Pihlajamäki (2004), p. 478.

social science. There is much the same kind of an intellectual blend in Scandinavian law and legal science.[62]

Traditionally, also Scandinavian law is lay-dominated. In addition, in the Nordic countries there is no experience of feudalism. Historically, Swedish legal literature was intended for readers with little or no training in law. Therefore, difficult legal concepts and doctrines were avoided. Against the traditional pragmatist background of Swedish law, the ways in which the social welfare state worked its way into Swedish legal scholarship become understandable. The pragmatist, policy-oriented solutions that legal realism promoted, fell on fertile ground in Sweden. There, law had never lost its connection with normal people's normal lives. There, legal professionals had never managed to monopolize their language and culture in the way their colleagues in the more southerly parts of Europe had been able to do.[63]

American and Scandinavian jurists do not share a common tradition. However, American and Scandinavian jurists, much more so than continental ones, share a common attitude towards law as a practical enterprise. They also share a common conception of their role as mediators of the law to laymen in courts. Additionally, they do share the thought of the practical that concerns the society with the law. In other words, a legal solution has to work in practice. Otherwise it is not valid. In this sense, not only the life of America, but also Scandinavian law has been more about the experience than the logic. Both Scandinavian and American jurists are, by tradition, pragmatists. The pragmatic tradition is reflected in the way the judiciary has been constructed. In both areas this way of thinking is strong, additionally in the legal literature. The pragmatist tradition still prevails. It is reflected in the relatively slight interest in a theoretical approach among practitioners of mainstream positivist legal science. This is true in both areas, America and Sweden. As a result, and because of their similar understanding of law's basic nature, American and Scandinavian legal scholars made similar choices when it came to channeling progressivist ideology into law.[64] The common tradition of realism has its natural reasons and roots in the American and Swedish society.

3.3 The Connection with Pragmatism

Legal realism has quite pragmatical starting points. The American legal realist was skeptical of the prevailing legal formalism with its fixed concepts and principles. The theory had to be adapted to the facts. When people live according to rules and customs, it is not a categorical imperative but a relationship of power. This power is dominant. Law cannot be deduced from the concept of justice only. Therefore, it was demanded that the judiciary must be scientific, in other words, the impact assessment

[62]Ibid., at p. 484.
[63]Ibid., at p. 486.
[64]Ibid., at p. 487.

is needed and empirical where the actions are predicted. Namely, judicial resolution is not entirely rational.[65]

The pragmatist is also future-oriented. The will of the legislator, precedents and analogous reasoning are not central. The pragmatist ignores sources of law and method as long as it is possible without compromising the credibility of the judiciary. In a sense, a pragmatic attitude is a search for an equitable solution.[66] That is the reason why pragmatism fits very well into the common law tradition where equity plays a significant role. Somehow all that fits well not only into Scandinavian legal culture but Scandinavian realism, too.

The common lawyer instinctively mistrusts abstract speculation. S/he believes that general principles have a role to play in the law. At the same time, s/he doubts that most serious disputes can be decided by reference to them alone. In addition, s/he insists that hard cases require the exercise of practical wisdom. The good old common lawyer solves practical problems. In solving them, s/he proceeds step by step, not within grandiose theoretical frameworks, just like the common law itself. The portrait of the common lawyer is as a pragmatist where s/he is proceeding empirically.[67]

As described earlier, Scandinavian legal culture is very practical. It is practical by tradition, and remains so today. It can be described even as pragmatical, at least in Finland, where judges sometimes make quite creative decisions in the face of practical needs, and find fair and well-working solutions. There are no hindrances to filling in the gaps in the norms or the lack of details where the legislator has not reacted or has delegated discretion to the courts. A natural part of the thinking in daily life is that it is a duty and a right of a judge to make a solution that is fair and one that works well, in other words, one that is practical.[68] Is that not pragmatism? Maybe, the relation between Scandinavian legal realism and pragmatism is clearer than often admitted. Perhaps this link has gotten stronger recently, as Europeanization sometimes requires quick solutions and new interpretations. This is the case in situations where European law suddenly needs to be put into the national context in circumstances where a proper incorporation is lacking. Often, European law is more or less deposited into national law, at least in the East-Scandinavian jurisdictions, where national law is not always reformed, but European law is just added into the national context more or less as it stands.[69]

Therefore, the way of legal thinking and interpreting the law in the common law and in the East-Scandinavian contexts is perhaps not that far apart, as is generally assumed. One reason lies in realism and its link to the pragmatism that both areas share.

---

[65] Kulla (1999), p. 3.

[66] Ibid.

[67] Pihlajamäki (2004), p. 480.

[68] Ervo (2015), p. 145.

[69] Ervo (2020), pp. 58–63.

3.4 Group Actions in This Context

It was typical of both American and Scandinavian realism to see law from the perspective that law can change society.[70] Because the group action system has been adopted in Scandinavian countries, for instance, to grant access to the courts and, thereby, access to justice in small consumer cases, there is hope for change. By adopting the group action system, the legislator wished also to change the law more. In other words, the aim was to promote consumers' rights to access the courts and thus access to justice, too. And in particular, because group actions are not used that much in Scandinavia, the fact of their existence itself seems to be enough.[71] Their very existence is often enough to promote access to justice even in such situations where the more traditional procedural tools are not effective. In the long run, the change and the effects it brings about will probably no longer be limited to single cases where the result often has been that the defendant has voluntarily made compensation so as to avoid group actions, but that consumer protection becomes more effective in the preventive sense. Therefore, one may easily see that the law on group actions does change the society. In that sense, it realizes Scandinavian realism.

Group actions are also a pragmatically approached and instrumental solution to the issue of providing access to justice and access to the courts. All of that is appreciated in Nordic law and fits well into Scandinavian realism, too. From that perspective, it is not surprising that group actions are adopted into Scandinavian law and this system of legal protection should correspond with the legal culture, too, especially where the historical development of Nordic legal theory is concerned.

4 Sustainability

4.1 Sustainability in Proceedings

Sustainability is a current global trend. In the Nordic countries it is taken very seriously because it belongs to the Nordic culture and mentality to carefully follow norms and standards. This sense of duty is culturally strong in the Nordic countries. Therefore, there are good grounds to say that sustainability is currently one of the leading aims in the Nordic societies. If this trend and development continues also in the near future as strongly as it has so far, there are also good grounds to claim that sustainability is the main current phenomenon that will shape the East-Nordic legal culture in a quite radical way.

[70]Malminen (2010), p. 319.

[71]Of course, there are also other reasons why group actions are not used more.

As is well known, "sustainability" embraces ecological, economic and social as well as cultural sustainability[72] of which ecological sustainability is the best known and traditionally the oldest ingredient of sustainable development. Just recently, the other ingredients have come into focus and discussions, for instance, on the contents of social and cultural sustainability have gotten more attention.

Also recently, there have been discussions on sustainability in respect of procedures. Two main concepts of sustainability that apply in a legal context have been identified: sustainability functionalism and sustainability factualism. The first concept refers to those procedures whose purpose and task is to preserve existing resources; for instance, environmental cases even if, according to Linna, procedure as such does not produce functional sustainability because results depend on the substantive law. Thus, according to her, procedure in itself is based on sustainability-factualism, where a party can choose a type of procedural tool that allows sustainable solutions. Other types of procedure can also conserve resources even if doing so is not their principal purpose. In such cases, sustainability is a by-product.[73]

At the same time, there might also be functional sustainability whenever procedural tools are seen from practical, sustainable perspectives. Dispute resolution processes can be considered from a sustainability point of view. Process principles, such as the principle of the appropriateness of the process (cost, time, certainty), which will speed up dispute resolution and diminish the increase in costs, also result in sustainability. The same goes for the principle of certainty. Sustainability is not only about time and costs, but also about sustainable content, which may be deemed certain and fulfill the requirements of fairness and quality. Technical solutions help bring about sustainability in practice, examples being witness attendance at a distance and electronic document service. These are examples of real and pragmatic sustainability at its best. Therefore, the line between functional and factual sustainability in proceedings is changeable. I think that the sustainable procedure can fulfill the demands of functional sustainability, as such, and not only factual sustainability as a by-product, especially when one of the main aims in the proceedings is to organize the way of handling matters in a sustainable way. In addition, substantive law cannot be fulfilled without procedures. Therefore, the proceedings are the first step in achieving the goal of sustainability by substantive law. That is why procedures are included infunctional sustainability. There is no procedure without substantive laws, but there is also no realization of substantive laws without procedures in the event the laws are not fully followed on a voluntary basis.[74]

In a later article, Linna also talks about procedures that produce sustainability and procedures where it is a by-product. She seems to have softened this dichotomy of functional/factual sustainability even by herself now. She also talks about internal

[72]https://www.ym.fi/fi-fi/ymparisto/kestava_kehitys/mita_on_kestava_kehitys. Accessed 4 May 2020.

[73]Linna (2018), p. 658.

[74]Ervo (2020), pp. 75–76.

and external sustainability where internal refers to outcomes such as functional sustainability and external refers to sustainable procedures as such.[75]

According to empirical studies, it is common that lawyers consider matters of sustainability when counselling their clients and choosing the way to resolve the dispute. However, they do not always know exactly what sustainability factually means and includes. It is also normal that the aims and choices that are nowadays called sustainable correspond with the traditional objectives in a lawyer's work. Actually, how modern is the concept of sustainability? Many of its ingredients have been followed for decades, but earlier it was called economy or reasonableness. Still, the difference is that earlier the reasons for "sustainable" choices were egoistic and individual, whereas nowadays sustainability refers to global common-wealth and societal benefits instead of egoistic winning.[76]

According to the Sustainable Development Goals, also known as the Global Goals, which were adopted by all United Nations Member States in 2015 as a universal call to action to end poverty, protect the planet and ensure that all people enjoy peace and prosperity by 2030, peace, justice and strong institutions are included as goals in sustainability.[77] Goal number 16 has been translated into Finnish using words such as *rauha* (peace), *oikeudenmukaisuus* (fairness) and *hyvä hallinto* (good governance).[78] In Swedish, the same Goal number 16 has been expressed by the English words "peaceful and inclusive communities" (*fredliga och inkluderande samhällen*). Justice has not been translated literally. Who knows whether it is included in "peaceful and inclusive communities" as one main component?[79]

The variety of words in translations is interesting. The first ingredient, peace, is almost identical in all studied languages, but in Swedish it is not only about peace as such for it has been put into the context of society that should be not only peaceful but also inclusive. This approach is very context-based and typically Swedish. Namely, everyone's participation is culturally and socially a very typical way of doing things and a widely accepted goal in Sweden, sometimes even at the expense of individuality. In Finnish, the term has been translated by stressing fairness and good governance. Fairness and good governance are the main contents in the procedural human and fundamental rights to which Finnish case law and doctrine has strongly paid attention since the 1990s, and up to the present. It is interesting how the cultural context can be seen in the choice of words. How to approach sustainability seems to be partly a cultural question.

---

[75]Linna (2020).

[76]De Savornin Lohman (2011), pp. 3–4.

[77]https://um.fi/agenda-2030-sustainable-development-goals. Accessed 5 May 2020.

[78]https://www.ykliitto.fi/yk-teemat/kestava-kehitys/kestavan-kehityksen-tavoitteet. Accessed 5 May 2020.

[79]https://www.regeringen.se/regeringens-politik/globala-malen-och-agenda-2030/agenda-2030-for-hallbar-utveckling/. Accessed 5 May 2020.

In every case, this aspect of social and cultural sustainability, namely peace, fairness and good governance as well as peaceful and inclusive communities are highly connected with proceedings. Procedures and ways to resolve disputes are needed to reach peace and to keep the society peaceful. Justice, fairness and good governance are as such legal and mainly procedural terms. To fulfill Goal number 16 in to the East-Nordic style, procedures that are based on justice and fairness are needed, including good governance in administrative bodies. In addition, all this should be organized in a way which fulfills the goal of inclusive communities. How to fulfill this goal then?

Group action is one good example. It is inclusive: all who have been suffering can attain a fair solution. By doing so it promotes justice, not only procedural fairness but also justice in the form of substantive laws. To put it in a bit of a provocative way: through one case alone, inclusive people get justice. In addition, group action is often used in environmental cases that directly seek functional sustainability.

4.2 Dimensions of Sustainable Justice

It is said that justice in the context of sustainability includes three dimensions, as follows:

1. Justice among people of different generations ("intergenerational" justice);
2. Justice among different people of the same generation ("intragenerational" justice); and
3. Justice between people and nature ("physio centric ethics").[80]

Legal procedures mainly link the intragenerational aspect of justice. Dispute resolution is a good example of intragenerational justice among different people of the same generation. However, group actions as a type of procedure includes sustainable dimensions also in the first and third sense. Namely, justice among people of different generations can be touched by the threat effect of group actions. For instance, in consumer protection or environmental cases, the successful group action case effectively prohibits companies from doing the same in the future. In addition, this effect is not only felt by the losing party but also by other actors in the same field. For instance, the group actions against Volkswagen (in regard to VW's diesel engines pollution emissions scandal) probably prohibit not only Volkswagen but also other actors in the car industry from trying anything similar in the near future. Therefore, there can even be intergenerational justice effects in the context of group actions, at least in the short run. As is well known, memory is short, and I would not overestimate this effect where time is concerned. In the same way, group actions can realize justice between people and nature whenever environmental cases are in question. That is why the sustainable nature of group actions covers more

[80] Linna (2018), p. 656. See also Stumpf et al. (2015), pp. 7439–7450.

compared with traditional dispute resolution one-on-one. Additionally, by using group actions instead of individual cases, the costs of proceedings can be reduced. As a whole, group actions can be seen as the most sustainable way of dispute resolution. Only mediation can compete with group actions in respect of the expenses, time-consumption and perhaps fairness, depending on one's view, are concerned. But also mediation is a type of procedure and, therefore, not as sustainable as group actions.

Nonetheless, the characteristics of adversarial proceedings, which also cover group actions, have also been found to be unfavorable from the ecological (sustainable) perspective. According to De Savornin Lohman, the following systems and power interventions are favorable to the ecology:[81]

- Promotion of cooperation and improvement of relationships
- Promotion of mutual respect
- Strengthening of the sense of responsibility
- Keeping problems in context
- Finding resolutions to causes of problems
- Encouragement for the parties
- Strengthening of the morality of the parties and taking that to a higher level
- Focusing on the positive aspects
- A future-oriented focus
- Focus on opportunities and new perspectives
- Focus on reintegration and rehabilitation

Whereas the following systems and power interventions are unfavorable for the ecology:[82]

- Causing harm to mutual relationships
- Conflict escalation or promotion (sometimes contradiction is needed to provide clarity)
- Removing material interests from the connection between material and immaterial interests that they form a part of (eg: juridification of a conflict to become a legal dispute)
- Monitoring, assessment, judgment condemnation, retributive punishment
- Imposing a solution (such as court decisions) that is not connected to the ecosystem or that does not secure the ecosystem
- Imposing or pressing solutions (what could, for instance, happen during a hearing—after—defense)
- Materialist strengthening

[81]De Savornin Lohman (2011), p. 5.

[82]Ibid.

- Focusing attention on negative aspects or on what went wrong (except where this is necessary as a part of a forward-looking perspective, such as the strengthening of a sense of responsibility and mutual respect, creating good relationships, rehabilitation and reintegration)
- Focusing on the past

These lists correspond mainly with adversarial dispute resolution and mediation processes. Mediation, restorative justice and therapeutic jurisprudence are seen as procedures, which correspond with sustainability. Group actions are not different from the traditional litigation in this sense. If this is a measure of sustainability, group actions are not fulfilling the requirements. However, the lists above seem to cover mainly societal, psychological, moral and other types of soft values that are, of course, extremely important in justice, fairness and sustainability. Therefore, sustainability or egological justice is discussed in a bit different context by Lohman. His report was published before the United Nations 2030 Agenda for Sustainable Development as well. Therefore, the point of view and terms used are different from the present and the cited lists cannot be fully compared with the current discussion on sustainability and justice as its component. Still, sustainability in justice can also be found in its hard contents such as I introduced above. In that context, group actions fulfill the requirements quite well. From the 2030 Agenda perspective, group action is an adequate tool to promote sustainable justice.

Because sustainability is affecting the Nordic countries very strongly just now and shaping the current Nordic culture too, and due to the fact that group actions fulfill the requirements of justice as a piece in the puzzle of sustainability, it can be said that from the sustainability perspective group actions fit very well into the current Nordic culture.

5 The Legal Culture of Group Actions and Group Actions in the Legal Culture

Group actions could be one good solution to promote access to justice and access to the courts not only in general but in all groups of society, in particular. At their best, group actions can promote equality before the law. From that perspective, group actions correspond very well with the East-Nordic legal culture and values.

Group action is all about doing things together. The aim is to reach each and every individual to provide justice. Often, associations are used to start a group action and reach the group members. This mentality is close to the Swedish *folkhemmet* ideology. All this reflects, somehow, also a volunteer spirit, which is said to be typical for the Nordic culture.

The American style of class action with punitive damages does not correspond with East-Nordic values where revenge, sanctions or profit and winning are not number one in the ranking. More important are principles, justice and equality among the poor, the weak and otherwise vulnerable groups in society. Fairness and a feeling of fairness should be fulfilled. Group actions can be used for promoting not only profit, wining and sanctions but also the Nordic values of justice and equality. Therefore, they can work very well also in the East-Nordic type of moral context especially if they are not copied as such but adapted into the local culture before adoption.

It has been the wish and objective of the East-Nordic legislators to change the society by adopting group actions. By doing so the access to justice and access to the courts are promoted especially in consumer and environmental cases. Group action is a pragmatic instrument in the fight for a better legal reality. From this point of view group actions can even be seen as fruits of the historical development in the Nordic countries where Scandinavian realism gained a foothold between 1920 and 1950.[83]

To sum up, the culture of group actions is not that far away from Scandinavian and especially East-Nordic legal culture as sometimes thought at first sight. The above-described cultural fragments are good examples of that. It is just about putting pieces together in a fitting way. To successfully adopt legal transplants often means some adapting first, instead of copying directly. By doing so, legal transplants can be fitted well into the new context. And thereby, legal transplants can be planted in a fruitful way in different contexts. Different contexts are not always so different either, and legal transplants are not always as exotic as thought at the moment they are imported. Keeping this in mind, group actions can be expansive and easily grown plants also in the soil of the East-Nordic environment.[84]

References

Autio A (2014) Lainkäyttö yritysten riidanratkaisussa. Lakimiesliiton Kustannus

Bernitz U (2007) What is scandinavian law? Concept, characteristics, future. Scand Stud Law 50:14–29

Bernitz U (2018) Nordic law: position and possibilities. JFT 5:385–391

Bertilsson B (2010) Förändringstendenser i svensk rättskultur, Rättskipningens funktion och domarens roll. Svensk Juristtidning, pp 23–32

Dahlqvist H (2002) Folkhemsbegreppet: Rudolf Kjellén vs Per Albin Hansson. Historisk Tidskrift 3:445–465

De Savornin Lohman A (2011) Working Document on Sustainable Justice for the Expert Meeting on Sustainable justice organized by the Montaigne Center for Justice and conflict resolution at the University of Utrecht, December 2, 2011. https://papers.ssrn.com/sol3/papers.cfm?abstract_id=2210027m. Accessed 5 May 2020

Ervo L (1996) Ylimmät prosessiperiaatteet – oikeudenmukaisen oikeudenkäynnin osatekijät. Lakimiesliiton Kustannus

Ervo L (2015) Comparative analysis between East-Scandinavian countries. Scandinavian Legal Studies. Stockholm Institute for Scandinavian Law, Stockholm

[83]https://tieteentermipankki.fi/wiki/Oikeustiede:skandinaavinen_realismi. Accessed 5 May 2020.

[84]See Lindblom (1989).

Ervo L (2020) The Finnish Way of understanding procedural autonomy: a practical approach to implementing EU civil procedural law. In: Nylund A, Krans B (eds) Procedural autonomy across Europe. Intersentia, pp 57–80
Ervo L, Persson AH (2008) Focus on collective redress, Sweden. https://www.collectiveredress.org/collective-redress/reports/sweden/overview. Accessed 2 May 2020
Ervo L, Persson AH (2015) Finnish and Swedish legislation in light of the ADR Directive – Boards and Ombudsmen. In: Lein E, Fairgrieve D, Otero Crespo M et al (eds) Collective Redress in Europe – Why and How?. British Institute of International an Comparative Law: London, pp 455–478
Fura-Sandström E (2004) Rättsbildning i en ny miljö — hur har domstolarnas roll och betydelse förändrats? Domstolarnas roll då, nu och sedan. Svensk Juristtidning, pp 263–269
Hänninen S (2009) Axel Hägerström ja pohjoismaisen oikeuden haaste EU-oikeudelle. Lakimies 7–8:1053–1070
Hautamäki V (2003) Tuomioistuin aktivismi tutkimuskohteena. Oikeus 2:170–180
Helin M (2009) Pohjoismaisen oikeusrealismin historia. Oikeus 38:68–72
Hirschfeldt J (2011) Domstolarna som statsmakt – några utvecklingslinjer. Juridisk Tidskrift 1:3–20
Justitiedepartementet (2008) Utvärdering av lagen om grupprättegång. Ds 2008(74):002–1013. Available at https://data.riksdagen.se/fil/A564E315-04B6-4C7E-8581-428AD4011606. Accessed 2 May 2020
Kekkonen J (1998) Suomen oikeuskulttuurin historiaa ja paikannusta. Lakimies 6–7:929–936
Kulla H (1999) Pragmatismi hallinto-oikeudessa. Lakimie 4:1–12
Lando O (2011) Nordic countries, a legal family? A diagnosis and a prognosis. Global Jurist Adv 2:1–15
Lindblom PH (1989) Grupptalan. Det anglo-amerikanska class actioninstitutet ur svenskt perspektiv. Norstedts, Stockholm
Lindblom PH (2008) Grupptalan i Sverige. Norstedts Juridik, Stockholm
Linna T (2018) Sustainability ja prosessit – kestävää siviiliprosessioikeutta? Lakimies 6:651–676
Linna T (2020) Business sustainability and insolvency proceedings—the EU perspective. J Sustain Res 2(2):e200019. https://doi.org/10.20900/jsr20200019. Accessed 4 May 2020
Malminen T (2010) Upsalan koulukunnan jalanjäljillä. Oikeus 39:318–324
Mikkola T (2010) Oikeudellisten siirrännäisten perusteista: esimerkkinä fidusiaarivastuu. Lakimies 5:816–834
Olivecrona K (1971) Law as fact, 2nd edn. Stevens & Sons, London
Pihlajamäki H (2004) Against metaphysics in law: the historical background of American and Scandinavian is compared. Am J Comp Law 52(2):469–487
Ross A (2013) Om ret og retfaerdighed. Hans Reitzels Forlag, Köpenhamn
Saarnilehto A (2003) Kansallisen oikeuskulttuurin uhat. Lakimies 1:74–80
Sallila J (2011) Eurooppalainen oikeuskulttuuri, pohjoismainen perinne ja juristi-identiteetti. Oikeushistoria Suomen oikeustieteellisissä aikakauslehdissä. Oikeus 4, pp 457–475
Siltala R (2003) Oikeustieteen tieteenteoria. Suomalainen Lakimiesyhdistys
SOU 2008:106, Ökat förtroende för domstolarna – strategier och förslag, Betänkande av Förtroendeutredningen Stockholm 2008
Sreeparvathy G (2011) Scandinavian Realists. Available at SSRN: https://ssrn.com/abstract=1829163 or https://doi.org/10.2139/ssrn.1829163. Accessed 13 April 2020
Strang J (2009) Two Generations of Scandinavian Legal Realists. Retfaerd 32 NR. 1/124
Stumpf KH, Baumgärtner S, Becker CU, Sievers-Glotzbach S (2015) The Justice dimension of sustainability: a systematic and general conceptual framework Sustainability 7:7438–7472. Available at https://papers.ssrn.com/sol3/papers.cfm?abstract_id=2579346. Accessed 4 May 2020
Syrjänen J (2012) Tuomarin harkinnan rajat - irti legalismin taakasta? Oikeustiede – Jurisprudentia XLV:335–388

The Justice Dimension of Sustainability: A Systematic and General Conceptual Framework: Sustainability 7: pp 7438–7472. https://papers.ssrn.com/sol3/papers.cfm?abstract_id=2579346. Accessed 4 May 2020
Torstensson N (2010) Judging the immigrant: accents and attitudes. Umeå University
Tuori K (2000) Tuomarit ja tuomioistuimet suomalaisessa oikeuskulttuurissa. Lakimies 7–8:1049–1059
Wilhelmsson T (2003) Suomen kansanomaisen oikeuskulttuurin uhat. Lakimies 1:81–89

Laura Ervo Head of the Law Unit and Professor of Law at the University of Örebro, Sweden, where she teaches Civil and Criminal Procedure and Alternative Dispute Resolution. Docent (Adjunct Professor) at the Finnish Universities of Helsinki, Turku and Easter Finland.

Rebooting Italian Class Actions

Elisabetta Silvestri

Abstract On April 12, 2019, the Italian Parliament passed a statute providing for a new regulation of collective redress. For the first time in the relatively short life of Italian group actions, both actions for compensatory relief (i.e. damages or restitution) and actions for injunctive relief are governed together and moved from the Consumer Code to the Code of Civil Procedure. This reflects a new vision of collective redress, namely a wider scope of application: no more references to consumers and users, but standing granted generically to bearers of 'homogenous individual rights', whether or not they are consumers or users. Furthermore, the new perimeter of class actions encompasses any claims arising out of both contract liability and tort liability, which signals another significant change aimed at designing class actions as general remedies. Yet, nothing has changed as far as the procedure by which class members can join the action is concerned: the opt-in option has been preserved even though the timeframe for opting in has been extended. In spite of a few interesting features, the new rules sketch a procedure that is still cumbersome and excessively technical. It should be interesting to see whether this attempt at reinvigorating group actions will be successful.

1 Introduction

I think that most readers are familiar with the expression 'American exceptionalism', and with the fact that, absent a specific definition of this expression, it can be interpreted as making reference to either positive or negative features of the American legal system, as well as to the political and societal system of the United States. Today, I would like to advance the theory that, on the other side of the Atlantic Ocean and within the European Union, we should begin to speak of 'Italian exceptionalism', but solely in a negative sense. Italians (and, in particular, Italian legislators) have the uncommon ability to obsess over minor details and, in the case

E. Silvestri (✉)
University of Pavia, Department of Law, Pavia, Italy
e-mail: elisabetta.silvestri@unipv.it

A. Uzelac, S. Voet (eds.), *Class Actions in Europe*, Ius Gentium: Comparative Perspectives on Law and Justice 89, https://doi.org/10.1007/978-3-030-73036-9_9

of legislators, to pass statutes and regulations concerning very specific sectors while the so-called 'big picture' is left untouched. Typically, that is what happens in the field of the administration of justice, most of all civil justice.

On April 12, 2019, a new statute on class actions for damages and injunctive relief was passed by the Italian Parliament.[1] A few days later the EU Justice Scoreboard for 2019 was published[2] showing again that Italy has the dubious honor of recording the worst performance within the EU as far as the delay of civil proceedings is concerned. As a matter of fact, in 2017 the average length of a civil or commercial case, from its inception until its end (that is to say, when all the available appeals have been exhausted), was estimated at no fewer than 1299 days (approximately three and a half years). In light of that, one may wonder whether the choice of reforming class actions (meaning, a very specific type of remedy) is reasonable while what we can define as 'common' adjudication for the judicial enforcement of individual rights appears to be in a very critical state. Truth be told, the reason for this choice has nothing to do with legitimate concerns over the possibility of receiving compensation for a group of individuals equally affected by the wrongful behavior perpetrated by a tortfeasor. The reform of class actions is only an exercise in legislative engineering aimed at overcoming the widespread opinion that considers the experience of class actions in Italy to be an absolute failure.[3] This is the background against which the new rules on Italian collective redress[4] must be tested in order to determine whether or not these very rules will be able to reboot Italian class actions.

2 Setting the Scene

Since 2010, the year when the rules governing class actions for damages entered into force, the number of class actions commenced and successfully brought to an end (meaning, with an award of damages granted, in general, to a small group of subjects) is just a handful. There are no official records. One can assume that probably 20 or 30 class actions were instituted, but the majority did not overcome the initial stage of the procedure, when the admissibility of actions is tested, and therefore it is impossible to track cases unless one has access to the records of the courts where they were brought. In any event, the story of Italian class actions for damages can still be described by expanding on the title of an essay this author

---

[1]See statute no. 31 of April 12, 2019, *Gazzetta Ufficiale* (Official Journal of the Italian Republic) no. 92 of April 18, 2019.

[2]The 2019 EU Justice Scoreboard, https://ec.europa.eu/info/sites/info/files/justice_scoreboard_2019_en.pdf.

[3]See, in particular, Afferni (2016), p. 99.

[4]Commentaries written in English on the new regulation of group actions are not yet available. For those who are brave enough to approach the flowery language of Italian scholars, here are some suggestions: Amadei (2019), p. 1049; Carratta (2019), p. 2297; Consolo (2019a), p. 737.

published in 2014.[5] When the rules governing class actions for damages finally entered into force, great expectations were nurtured not only by the legal community, but by the Italian society at large, since a huge number of individuals had been affected by financial scandals and, up till then, no forms of collective redress suitable to provide compensation for the harm caused by mass torts were available. Unfortunately, great expectations were met by big disappointment. On the one hand, past events were not included in the scope of class actions, which were designed to be available only for future occurrences. On the other hand, the procedural features of the new actions made them cumbersome and difficult to manage. Furthermore, the effectiveness of collective redress was hindered by the opt-in system adopted by the Italian legislator and made quite abstruse insofar as it required class members to join the proceeding by lodging a special motion previously unheard of and mysteriously called 'statement of adhesion'. More could be said to provide evidence of the fact that mass harm situations did not find an adequate protection in the form of collective compensatory redress provided for by the Italian rules, but it seems sufficient to emphasize the following point alone: the whole model of the Italian class action for damages was such that, from the very beginning, it was clear that things could not work. Not that the collective actions for injunctive relief were more successful, but in this case the excuse for their limited use was that they were established following the pattern designed by EU directives, so the national legislators could not be blamed for their failure.

Prior to the passage of the new statute, class actions for damages and the collective actions for injunctive relief were regulated by the Consumer Code[6] or, as one scholar unfortunately described it, both types of actions were confined in the 'ghetto' of the Consumer Code,[7] a piece of legislation that can hardly be seen as state of the art in consumer protection. The new statute has moved both actions to the Code of Civil Procedure, adding a new Title (Title VIII-*bis* on collective procedures) to Book Four of the Code.[8] Just for information, readers should know that Book Four of the Code is a true hodgepodge of procedural rules. In Book Four one may find a variety of non-contentious procedures, but also the summary *ex parte* proceeding leading to orders for payment, the eviction proceeding, a wide assortment of provisional remedies, divorce proceedings and—last but not least—arbitration. In

[5]See Silvestri (2014), pp. 197–208. Excerpts of court rulings concerning class actions for damages can be read (in Italian) in Brazzini, Muià (2019), pp. 52–62.

[6]The relevant rules of the Consumer Code were Arts. 139 and 140 (governing the collective actions for injunctive relief) and Art. 140-*bis* (governing the class action for damages). These rules are included in a special section of the Code devoted to access to justice for consumers and their associations. An extensive set of rules concerns the so-called consumer ADR following the implementation of Directive 2013/11/EU of the European Parliament and of the Council of 21 May 2013 on alternative dispute resolution for consumer disputes.

[7]See Pardolesi (2019), p. 305.

[8]The addition of a new Title V-*bis* on collective procedures appears also in the regulations for the implementation of the Code: they represent an annex to the Code whose purpose is to govern the practical aspects that may result from the enforcement of the Code's articles.

other words, Book Four of the Code of Civil Procedure is conceived as a legal 'department store',[9] in which one can find the judicial proceeding that fits one's needs. It is as if the legislators, after having abided by strict analytical accuracy in the preparation of the previous three books of the Code, had given up and decided to toss into Book Four all the leftover proceedings, the ones that could not be properly located anywhere else. And now, the assorted legal 'merchandise' of Book Four includes collective procedures, too.

The new location of the amended rules on both class actions for damages and the collective actions for injunctive relief does not represent just a formal change, for it is connected to the fact that—as will be clarified further in this contribution—the availability of the actions has been extended so that, on the one hand, standing to sue is granted to unnamed individuals who claim 'homogenous individual rights' (whether or not they are consumers or users, as was required by Art. 140-*bis* of the Consumer Code) and, on the other hand, the remedy (specifically, an injunction or an award of damages or a restitution order) can be sought against any possible type of misconduct that is legally relevant (and not only, as the old rules provided for, in case of breach of contract, unfair or anti-competitive commercial practices and product or service liability).

The changes just described are a positive feature, since they mean that now the scope of application of collective procedures is much wider than before. As a matter of fact, the failure of class actions could be blamed on their availability being restricted to consumers and users only, on the one hand, and to selected categories of contract and tort liability, on the other. In this regard, the new Italian act seems in line with the Commission Recommendation of 2013 on common principles for collective redress mechanisms,[10] insofar as this legal instrument connects collective redress loosely to 'mass harm situations',[11] without any further specifications; furthermore, for the first time in an official text the expression 'collective redress' (in Italian, *procedimenti collettivi*) appears and, as in the Recommendation, injunctive and compensatory mechanisms are regulated by a single act.[12]

[9]This is the definition of Book Four of the Code given by a prominent Italian scholar, the late Virgilio Andrioli: see Andrioli (1979), p. 52.

[10]Commission Recommendation of 11 June 2013 on common principles for injunctive and compensatory collective redress mechanisms in the Member States concerning violations of rights granted under Union Law (2013/396/EU), https://eur-lex.europa.eu/legal-content/EN/TXT/PDF/?uri=CELEX:32013H0396&from=EN.

[11]Ibid., Art. 3 (b): a 'mass harm situation' occurs when 'two or more natural or legal persons claim to have suffered harm causing damage resulting from the same illegal activity of one or more natural or legal persons'.

[12]The Recommendation is one of the documents included in a package of measures aimed at laying down the 'minimum standards' that Member States hopefully should apply in the domestic regulation of collective redress. The 'minimum standards' are principles common to both injunctive and compensatory collective actions, and they are supplemented by more principles applicable either to the former actions or to the latter. On the Recommendation, see, for instance, Silvestri (2016), pp. 203–214; Voet (2014), p. 97. In spite of the Recommendation, the findings of a relatively recent study commissioned by the European Parliament's Policy Department for Citizens'

3 The New Regulation of Italian Collective Redress: The Scope of Application

The reformed rules on class actions are quite complex and show a number of features worth mentioning. In spite of that, a detailed analysis of any rule is beyond the purpose of this contribution, which is intended to present only a general overview of the new group actions, hoping that it is enough to help the reader get the gist of the reform. One must also keep in mind that quite a number of the new features require a serious consideration in order to be judged so as to determine whether there is a chance for them to make the new forms of Italian collective redress successful. Furthermore, this kind of evaluation is not very useful when it is conducted *in vitro*, since what seems to make sense in theory may not be workable in practice. In view of the fact that the new rules will enter into force only in April 2020, at least a few years will have to pass before an educated judgment of the effectiveness of the new Italian collective redress can be made.

One of the most significant changes brought about by the new rules is the enlargement of standing to sue. While Article 140-*bis* of the Consumer Code mentioned only consumers and users as potential plaintiffs, according to the new Article 840-*bis* of the Code of Civil Procedure, standing is granted to the bearers of 'homogenous individual rights', whether or not they are consumers or users. With a good measure of approximation one may say that the class consists of individuals equally affected by harmful misconduct perpetrated by business entities or public services providers. The legislators missed the opportunity to clarify the meaning of the expression 'homogenous individual rights' (*diritti individuali omogenei* in Italian) that was already present in the text of Article 140-*bis* of the Consumer Code and does not appear in any other legal rule in force.[13] According to dictionaries of the Italian language, the lemma '*omogeneo*' ('homogenous' in English) means 'of the same nature or kind' and, by extension, similar or akin to something else. Yet—one may wonder—what makes two or more rights identical or at least similar? And according to which criteria can a court decide that individuals can be included in the class because their rights are 'homogenous'? Furthermore, when the procedure reaches the stage at which prospective class members take steps to join the action, what is the role played by the issues that are specifically connected with each

Rights and Constitutional Affairs show that the existing types of domestic collective redress are quite different among Member States, and therefore there are arguments to support a plea for a European legislative instrument aimed at harmonizing national legislations. That said, in light of the accentuated divergences in the Member States' approaches to collective redress, 'a horizontal compensatory collective redress mechanism with detailed procedural rules is desirable but unrealistic': see Directorate General for Internal Policies—Policy Department for Citizens' Rights and Constitutional Affairs—Legal Affairs, 'Collective Redress in the Member States of the European Union', https://www.europarl.europa.eu/RegData/etudes/STUD/2018/608829/IPOL_STU(2018)608829_EN.pdf.

[13]On the problems related to the interpretation of the expression 'homogenous individual rights', see Donzelli (2019), p. 11.

individual claim, besides the questions of fact or law that supposedly are common to the whole class? And finally, which type of evidence is required to satisfy the court that all the claims are 'homogenous', but at the same time a few class members are entitled to damages higher than the rest of the class? Wrestling with such questions and resolving them will be necessary in order to figure out which individuals are the real bearers of homogenous individual rights and thereby properly design the boundaries of the class. This will not be an easy task for the courts.

As far as the possible claims that can be commenced following the procedural pattern of compensatory class actions are concerned, as mentioned earlier, even from this angle the scope of application of class actions is wider than before, since the relevant rule only provides that the action can be instituted against business entities and public services providers 'for any acts performed in the course of their activities'. That seems to point to the fact that any claim arising out of both contract liability and tort liability can be litigated as a class action. In other words, the new class action for damages is conceived as a true general remedy, a highly positive feature that hopefully will allow stakeholders to resort to it in areas in which collective redress, as governed by the Consumer Code, was not available (for instance, in the field of environmental law or in the domain of financial instruments).[14]

The action can by commenced by any member of the class or—and this is new—by non-profit entities or organizations whose mission is the protection of the rights claimed by the class and supposedly affected by the alleged wrongdoer, provided that the entity or the organization has been included in a registry the Ministry of Justice is supposed to establish. The establishment of this registry, as well as the creation of a dedicated portal on the website of the Ministry of Justice for the dissemination of a variety of information concerning pending class actions, is one of the reasons why the new act will enter into force in April 2020—at least this is the official justification for such a long *vacatio legis*.

4 The Procedure

The new forms of Italian collective redress fall within the jurisdiction of the so-called 'business courts' (in Italian, *Tribunali delle imprese* or *sezioni specializzate in materia di impresa*). They are not autonomous courts, but specialized units established within ordinary courts that are in operation in the largest judicial districts. Probably, the idea of entrusting class actions to the care of these courts is not a wise one, for they already have a wide jurisdiction that includes disputes in the field of intellectual property law, cases arising out of antitrust law (domestic and European) as well as an extensive list of disputes concerning company law. In 2020, the jurisdiction of the 'business courts' will be extended not only to group actions but

[14]See, in particular, Ponzanelli (2019), p. 306.

also to a variety of proceedings provided by the reformed rules on bankruptcy and other insolvency procedures. These future developments raise legitimate concerns over the ability of these courts to handle efficiently the new cases, too. As a matter of fact, while one can estimate that class actions are not likely to crowd the courts' dockets, the same does not hold true for insolvency proceedings, whose number has been constantly increasing in recent years due to the economic downturn.

The proceeding develops through two stages, the first one devoted to testing the admissibility of the action and the second one (which takes place if the action has been declared admissible as a class action) for the decision on the merits. From a procedural point of view, a new and significant feature is the fact that class actions will be handled according to the rules of the so-called 'summary proceeding' (in Italian, *procedimento sommario di cognizione*), a simplified type of first instance proceeding that was introduced in 2009 and advances, although modestly, the cause of a managerial treatment of cases. In fact, from the point of view of judicial case management, the summary procedure is quite significant (at least in the Italian landscape), since the court, 'taking into account the introductory pleading and having heard the parties, can decide how the case will develop, dispensing with any formalities that are not essential to safeguarding the due process rights of the parties' (Art. 702-*ter*, sec. 5, Code of Civil Procedure; my translation). Therefore, the court can adapt the procedure to the needs of the case with a flexible approach that is the exact opposite of the rigid approach typical of the structure of an ordinary first instance proceeding. Unfortunately, the summary proceeding has not been very successful in practice (for a variety of reasons). In spite of that, the Government has been entrusted by the Parliament to enact new rules for the reform of the Code of Civil Procedure, rules that will have to include the generalization of the summary proceeding, which would become the basic model of proceedings before first instance courts.[15]

Returning to the treatment of class actions in the first stage of the proceeding, the court must decide whether the action is admissible within 30 days from the date of the first hearing; the decision can be appealed against, but the court of appeal, too, must decide within a strict deadline.

The court will reject the action as inadmissible first of all when the action is 'manifestly groundless'. At an intuitive level, it is easy to say that an action is 'manifestly groundless' when it is grossly devoid of any merit, but beyond this statement it is hard to venture possible examples of 'manifestly groundless' actions, since it is a type of evaluation largely dependent on the specific circumstances of the case at stake. The action is also inadmissible when the court finds that the rights of the prospective class members are not 'homogenous' and, in this regard, one may recall the observations made earlier on the ambiguous meaning of the adjective 'homogenous' when it is supposed to have a legal connotation. Furthermore, the inadmissibility of the action may ensue from a conflict of interest between the

[15]These new winds of change in the field of civil procedure have not been well received by the legal community: see Costantino (2019), Carratta (2020).

plaintiff and the defendant, as well as from the court's opinion as to the inability of the plaintiff to take care of the individual rights belonging to class members in a satisfactory way. This final reason making the action inadmissible can be related to, for instance, a lack of financial resources or the apparent deficiency of subjective requirements that are not easy to list in theory and that seem to be strictly connected with the circumstances of the case at hand.[16]

4.1 The Opt-in Option

The new Italian class action, like the old one, adopts an opt-in principle. Members of the class can join the claimant through an opt-in mechanism that is called 'adhesion' (*adesione* in Italian) to the lawsuit. They can opt in immediately after the court has certified that the lawsuit can proceed as a class action; in fact, the certification order sets the deadline for the adhesion. Group members who opt in do not become parties to the lawsuit even though they have the right to receive all the relevant information concerning the action. But the opt-in procedure is also available afterwards, meaning after the court has decided the case on the merits, finding for the class. This two-layered opt-in procedure is quite complicated and misleading. Probably, it was devised in an attempt to increase as much as possible the chances for class members to join the lawsuit. In any event, opt-in does not require the assistance of an attorney even though the formalities to be complied with seem to require a level of legal proficiency that ordinary people certainly lack.

Since class members can join the action through an 'adhesion' to the lawsuit, exactly as was provided for by the Consumer Code, one may still wonder what this mysterious object called 'adhesion' is. Nowhere else in the Italian laws in force does the word appear, and therefore an effort of imagination is required to understand why the legislators felt bound to connect the opt-in procedure to a mechanism that has no equal. One might think that the 'adhesion' is just another way to point to a permissible intervention in a proceeding already pending. The problem, though, is that intervention is expressly forbidden, which explains why opt-in does not grant the rights pertaining to the parties to a lawsuit. That said, the lack of clarity for understanding the legal nature of the 'adhesion' remains, and probably a reasonable decision is not to elaborate further on this aspect of the opt-in option. What is clear, however, is the idea of the legislators to design class actions replicating the traditional structure of individual actions, meaning actions with two parties only: one plaintiff (the class member or the non-profit entities or organizations that instituted the proceeding, together with the class members who opted in) and one defendant.

---

[16]See De Santis (2019), p. 90.

4.2 The Procedure After the Certification Stage. New Features of the Evidence-Taking Phase

As mentioned earlier, the court enjoys a good measure of discretion in molding the development of the proceeding as it deems suitable for the case at stake. According to the new Article 840-*quinquies* of the Code of Civil Procedure, the court, 'dispensing with the formalities that are not essential to safeguarding the due process rights of the parties, may proceed in the way that appears to be the most convenient for the preparation of the case taking into account the subject matter of the dispute' (my translation). Therefore, the court is free to decide which evidence it can take and how to gather it. The rule, though, deals specifically with the appointment of an expert witness, as well as with the use of statistical data and presumptive evidence.

There are some new interesting rules concerning the evidence-taking stage. In particular, the court can issue a disclosure order against the defendant concerning the evidence that the court considers relevant and that is in the defendant's possession or control. Detailed provisions are aimed at guaranteeing the rights of the defendant, most of all when the disclosure order could jeopardize confidential information and trade or professional secrets. The defendant has the right to be heard before the disclosure order is issued; furthermore, special rules are laid down with regard to specific problems that in common law jurisdiction would fall within the attorney-client privilege and the work-product doctrine.[17]

The court can impose monetary sanctions on the defendant who fails to comply with the order or destroys the evidence he was supposed to disclose. The fine can be hefty, since it can range from €10,000 to €100,000, and it is left to the court's discretion. Furthermore, the court can draw adverse inferences against the defaulting party and consider the fact for which the disclosure of evidence was ordered proved, just as if it had been admitted by the party himself. This is what in Italy we call *ficta confessio*.

4.3 Further Procedural Novelties

The final judgment, whether it finds for the class or for the defendant, must be made public in the open access section of the dedicated portal on the website of the Ministry of Justice. The purpose of this feature can be understood if one recalls

[17]Simply put, the attorney-client privilege can be defined as a shield protecting the communications between an attorney and his client when the communications are made in confidence for the purpose of providing legal assistance for the client: see American Law Institute (2000), para 68. As far as the work-product doctrine, one may cite Rule 26 (b)(3) of the American Federal Rules of Civil Procedure, according to which, 'Ordinarily, a party may not discover documents and tangible things that are prepared in anticipation of litigation or for trial by or for another party or its representative (including the other party's attorney, consultant, surety, indemnitor, insurer, or agent).'

that if the court finds for the class, class members who have not opted in yet, for instance because they were not even aware of the commencement of an action through which they could obtain compensation or restitution, can still join the proceeding within a deadline set by the court.

The judgment finding for the class shows another noteworthy feature, namely the appointment of two new *dramatis personae*: the judge in charge of the opt-in procedure and the class representative. These two appointments are listed by the rule governing the mandatory content of the judgment, which must also define the elements that qualify the individual homogenous rights. These elements are the requirements necessary to be included in the class and to justify the opt-in; in addition, the court's judgment must specify which evidence each class member is supposed to provide.

The judge in charge of the opt-in procedure is the judge who evaluates the position of each class member who opted in. If the judge is satisfied that a class member is the bearer of the right he claims, the judge decides the amount of money the class member is entitled to receive as damages or restitution. But the role of the judge in charge of the opt-in procedure is intertwined with the role of the class representative. In fact, the class representative (who becomes an officer of the court) is supposed to prepare a draft that will work as an allotment project for each class member. In other words, the rule providing for this 'project of individual homogenous rights' (this is the literal translation of the Italian expression) seems to hint at the fact that the representative is expected to jot down a sort of ranking list of the class members, who can object to the ranking, but only by offering written evidence to support their challenges. The project must then be submitted to the judge in charge of the opt-in procedure; if the judge approves it, the amount that each class member is entitled to receive is settled.

A number of new rules have appeared in the field of legal fees. While a cursory reading of the statute leads one to believe that the traditional principle according to which the 'loser pays' principle still applies, a peculiar rule concerning the remuneration that the class representative is entitled to claim from the defendant must be taken into account, which is, the remuneration is calculated as a percentage of the whole amount the defendant is supposed to pay to the class members. The percentage varies according to the number of the class members who opted in, but in the inverse proportion. In practice, the higher the number of the class members, the lower the bonus granted to the class representative. Furthermore, the attorney assisting the individual who instituted the proceeding and acted as lead plaintiff can be granted by the court a 'reward payment' (in Italian, *compenso premiale*, an expression that is challenging to translate) on top of his attorney's fees. In a legal system that is not keen to admit contingent fee arrangements, these new rules on litigation costs are almost revolutionary. Scholars have stated that these financial incentives (and, in particular, the one for the attorney of the lead plaintiff) will be the driving force of the new Italian group action,[18] the driving force that up to now has

[18]See, for instance, Consolo (2019b).

been missing and making class actions ineffective as instruments in the service of defending collective rights. At the same time, one cannot help emphasizing that Italian legislators seem to have disregarded what the Recommendation suggested in the field of costs. In fact, the Recommendation on common principles for collective redress[19] provided that Member States should make sure that 'the lawyers' remuneration and the method by which it is calculated do not create any incentive to litigation' (Art. 29). In addition, Member States 'should not permit contingency fees which risk creating such an incentive' (Art. 30). To strike a balance between promoting class actions as instruments for a better and more efficient judicial enforcement of collective rights and the need to avoid measures—in particular, financial measures—that could encourage abusive and frivolous actions is a goal that is difficult to achieve. It will be interesting to see whether the new Italian rules are able to hit the target.

The class representative can also begin the enforcement procedure on behalf of all the class members if the defendant fails to comply spontaneously with the court judgment. The rules governing collective enforcement include a few 'variations on the theme' of individual enforcement. These rules are extremely technical, and to expand on them would not help the reader to understand what is new in the reformed regulation of group actions. The same holds true for the rules on the appeals available against both the various orders the court can issue as the procedure progresses through its different stages and the final judgment on the merits of the action. The rules on collective settlements, too, are the source of a multitude of doubts as to their effectiveness and, most of all, their ability to guarantee the class member an adequate compensation. Ultimately, it is fair to say that all in all it is not easy to disentangle the many knots of the new rules, which is likely to have a bearing on the future success of the (allegedly) revamped class actions.

5 Collective Actions for Injunctive Relief

A word or two on the updated rules governing collective actions for injunctive relief seems appropriate. These actions are no longer available to consumers only, but to 'all those who are interested' (Art. 840-*sexiesdecies*, Code of Civil Procedure), meaning both individuals and non-profit entities or organizations whose mission is the protection of the interests adversely affected by the conduct the action is aimed at enjoining, provided that the entity or the organization has been included in a registry the Ministry of Justice is supposed to establish (the same registry mentioned earlier discussing standing to bring class actions for damages). Like class actions for damages, collective actions for injunctive relief can be instituted against business entities or public services providers with a view to preventing harmful acts or

[19]See n. 10 above.

omissions perpetrated in the course of their operation. Actions must be commenced before one of the so-called 'business courts', also already mentioned.

The procedure is quite straightforward since it follows the pattern of proceedings in non-contentious matters: simplified forms, ample powers of the court to take evidence *ex officio*, and limited avenues of appeal. In order to ensure enforcement of injunctions, incremental pecuniary sanctions vaguely resembling French *astreintes* can be imposed on the defaulting defendant at the discretion of the court, so as to persuade the defendant to comply with the court order. It is not clear, though, whether the money paid by the defendant will end up in the hands of the plaintiff or be allotted to the public purse. Furthermore, the court, when finding for the plaintiff, may order the defendant to adopt all the measures deemed necessary to remove (if possible) or to mitigate the prejudicial consequences of previous wrongful conduct.

6 Final Remarks

Speaking on the dramatic reform that in 1966 changed Rule 23 of the American Federal Rules of Civil Procedure and made class action an immensely powerful legal device thanks to the new provisions according to which decisions would bind all members of the represented class who did not opt out of the suit, Professor Benjamin Kaplan said, 'It will take a generation or so before we can fully appreciate the scope, the virtues and the vices of new Rule 23.'[20] Professor Kaplan's words can easily be adapted to the new Italian statute on collective redress.

A long time will have to pass before the pros and cons of the reformed rules on compensatory class actions and collective actions for injunctive relief can be properly understood. For the time being, though, one can say that many features of the new group actions seem redundant and convoluted. In short, they do not appear to justify any optimistic predictions concerning a more frequent use of collective redress in Italy, which, unfortunately, will continue the futile exercise of setting up judicial remedies just for show, without paying the slightest attention to their effectiveness in practice.

References

Afferni G (2016) 'Opt-in' class actions in Italy: why are they failing? J Eur Tort Law 7:82–100

Amadei D (2019) Nuova azione di classe e procedimenti collettivi nel codice di procedura civile. In: Cian G et al (eds) Le nuove leggi civili commentate, Anno XLII, n. 5. Wolters Kluwer, Milan, pp 1049–1090

American Law Institute (2000) Restatement (third) of the law governing lawyers. ALI, Philadelphia

[20]Professor Kaplan's quote is mentioned in Hensler et al. (2000), p. 49.

Andrioli V (1979) Diritto processuale civile. Jovene, Naples
Brazzini S, Muià PP (2019) La nuova class action alla luce della legge 12 aprile 2019, n. 31. G Giappichelli Editore, Turin
Carratta A (2019) La class action riformata. Giurisprudenza italiana, n. 10. UTET, Milan, pp 2297–2334
Carratta A (2020) Sull'ennesima ed inutile riforma del processo civile. http://www.treccani.it/magazine/diritto/approfondimenti/diritto_processuale_civile_e_delle_procedure_concorsuali/Sull_ennesima_ed_inutile_riforma_del_processo-civile.html. Accessed 13 Feb 2020
Consolo C (2019a) La terza edizione della azione di classe è legge ed entra nel c.p.c. Uno sguardo d'insieme ad una amplissima disciplina. Il corriere giuridico, n. 6. Ipsoa, Milan, pp 737–743
Consolo C (2019b) La terza generazione di azione di classe all'italiana fra giuste articolate novità e qualche aporia tecnica. http://www.dirittobancario.it/editoriali/claudio-consolo/la-terza-generazione-di-azione-di-classe-all-italiana-fra-giuste-articolate-novita-e-qualche-aporia. Accessed 13 Feb 2020
Costantino G (2019) Sulle proposte di riforma del processo civile di cognizione: contro la pubblicità ingannevole. http://www.questionegiustizia.it/articolo/sulle-proposte-di-riforma-del-processo-civile-di-cognizione-contro-la-pubblicita-ingannevole_11-12-2019.php. Accessed 13 Feb 2020
De Santis AD (2019) Il procedimento. In: Sassani B (ed) Class Action – Commento sistematico alla legge 12 aprile 2019, n. 31. Pacini Giuridica, Pisa, p 90
Donzelli R (2019) L'ambito di applicazione e la legittimazione ad agire. In: Sassani B (ed) Class Action – Commento sistematico alla legge 12 aprile 2019, n. 31. Pacini Giuridica, Pisa, pp 1–41
Hensler DR et al (2000) Class action dilemmas. Pursuing public goals for private gain. RAND Corporation, Santa Monica
Pardolesi R (2019) La classe in azione. Finalmente. Danno e responsabilità. Ipsoa, Milan, pp 301–305
Ponzanelli G (2019) La nuova class action. Danno e responsabilità. Ipsoa, Milan, pp 306–308
Silvestri E (2014) Class actions in Italy: great expectations, big disappointment. In: Harsági V, Van Rhee CH (eds) Multi-party redress mechanism in Europe: squeaking mice? Intersentia, Antwerp, pp 197–208
Silvestri E (2016) Group actions à la mode Européenne: a kinder, gentler class action for Europe? In: Picker CR, Seidman GI (eds) The dynamism of civil procedure – global trends and developments. Springer, Berlin, pp 203–214
Voet S (2014) European collective redress: a status of quaestionis. Int J Procedural Law 4:97–127

Elisabetta Silvestri Served as Associate Professor of Italian Civil Procedure, Comparative Civil Procedure, and Arbitration, Mediation and Assisted Negotiation at the Department of Law, University of Pavia, Italy until October 1, 2020. Scientific Director of the postgraduate programs for the training of mediators and ADR professionals accredited by the Italian Ministry of Justice. Economics. She has been lecturing in many Italian and foreign University on a wide variety of subjects in the field of civil procedure and related matters, such as evidence, judicial organization, collective redress, and ADR. Since 2010 she is co-director of the annual seminar 'Public and Private Justice', held in Dubrovnik, at the Inter-University Centre (IUC).

Challenges in Drafting and Applying the New Slovenian Collective Actions Act

Aleš Galič and Ana Vlahek

Abstract The Slovenian Collective Actions Act (CAA) was enacted in September 2017 and came into effect in April 2018. Collective redress available in Slovenia before the enactment of the CAA did not provide for any collective compensatory actions for any group of victims. Only collective injunctive relief was available for safeguarding the interests of consumers under the Consumer Protection Act of 1998 that implemented the EU Injunctions Directive. As more and more mass harm cases were detected in Slovenia, and as collective redress became one of the focal topics within the EU, the CAA was perceived as an urgently needed piece of legislation and a top priority of the Slovenian Government in guaranteeing access to justice. The CAA was drafted in 2016 taking into account the European Commission's Recommendation of 11 June 2013 on common principles for injunctive and compensatory collective redress mechanisms in the Member States concerning violations of rights granted under EU law, as well as best legislative solutions and practices of various foreign models. It introduced collective settlements, and compensatory and injunctive collective actions. Since the start of the application of the CAA, three collective actions have been filed with the courts under its rules. The purpose of this contribution is to show the challenges faced and the decisions taken in drafting the act as well as the problems the parties and the judiciary have been facing in the application of the CAA. The Slovenian experience may serve as a model of the "dos" and "don'ts" for all drafters of such legislation in the EU Member States where collective redress has not yet been implemented.

The text was submitted in November 2019.

A. Galič · A. Vlahek (✉)
University of Ljubljana, Faculty of Law, Ljubljana, Slovenia
e-mail: ales.galic@pf.uni-lj.si; ana.vlahek@pf.uni-lj.si

A. Uzelac, S. Voet (eds.), *Class Actions in Europe*, Ius Gentium: Comparative Perspectives on Law and Justice 89, https://doi.org/10.1007/978-3-030-73036-9_10

1 Introduction

The Slovenian Collective Actions Act (CAA)[1] was enacted on 26 September 2017 and came into effect on 21 April 2018 (Art. 67 CAA). Collective redress available in Slovenia before the enactment of the CAA did not provide for collective compensatory actions for any group of victims. Only collective injunctive relief was available for safeguarding the interests of consumers under the Consumer Protection Act 1998 (CPA)[2] that implemented the Injunctions Directive (Directive 98/27/EC[3] and later Directive 2009/22/EC[4]) and set out the rules on actions for the cessation of illegal practices and actions for a declaration of nullity.

As more and more mass harm cases were detected in Slovenia, and collective redress became one of the focal topics within the EU, the adoption of collective redress legislation was perceived as an urgently needed piece of legislation and a top priority of the Slovenian Government in guaranteeing access to justice. The CAA was drafted in 2016 taking into account the European Commission's Recommendation of 11 June 2013 on common principles for injunctive and compensatory collective redress mechanisms in the Member States concerning violations of rights granted under Union law,[5] as well as best legislative solutions and practices of various foreign models. It introduced collective settlements and collective actions including compensatory and injunctive collective actions. In the year and a half since the start of the application of the CAA, three collective actions have been filed with the courts under its rules.

Having been entrusted with the task of drafting the CAA by the Slovenian Ministry of Justice,[6] we had direct insight into the drafting and legislative processes. Within the Ministry's working group and the debates with the stakeholders, we experienced intense synergetic cooperation that led to support for the CAA from all political parties and eventually to the unanimous enactment of the CAA in the Slovenian Parliament.

The purpose of this contribution is to show the challenges faced and the decisions taken in drafting the act as well as the problems the parties and the judiciary have been facing in its application. The Slovenian experience may serve as a model of the "dos" and "don'ts" for all drafters in the EU Member States where collective redress has not yet been implemented.

---

[1]*Zakon o kolektivnih tožbah* (ZKolT), Official Gazette of RS, No. 55/17.

[2]*Zakon o varstvu potrošnikov (ZVPot)*, Official Gazette of RS, No. 20/98, with further amendments.

[3]Directive 98/27/EC of the European Parliament and of the Council of 19 May 1998 on injunctions for the protection of consumers' interests, OJ L 166, 11.6.1998, pp. 51–55.

[4]Directive 2009/22/EC of the European Parliament and of the Council of 23 April 2009 on injunctions for the protection of consumers' interests (codified version) Text with EEA relevance, OJ L 110, 1.5.2009, pp. 30–36.

[5]2013/396/EU.

[6]Draft CAA, No. EVA: 2016-2030-0007, p. 16.

2 Collective Redress Available in Slovenia Before the CAA

2.1 Collective Redress *Stricto Sensu*

Collective redress available in Slovenia before the enactment of the CAA did not provide for any general or specific collective compensatory actions scheme.[7] Only specific types of non-compensatory collective redress were available in the fields of protection of consumers, health and the environment. The object of these actions was not the protection of the rights of the plaintiff, but of a certain third person, or the rights of an unidentified circle of persons.[8]

The Code of Obligations (CO)[9] regulates the so-called popular action (*actio popularis*) for the protection of a *healthy living environment*. Pursuant to Article 133 of the CO, *anyone* may require another person to remove a source of danger that threatens him or her or an unspecified number of persons with significant damage, and to refrain from the activity producing disturbance or danger of harm if the disturbance or harm cannot be prevented by appropriate measures. At the request of *the interested person*,[10] the court shall order appropriate measures to prevent the occurrence of harm or disturbance, or to remove the source of the danger at the expense of its possessor if the possessor does not do so personally. Claims under Article 133 of the CO do not require damage to be sustained, a concrete injury risk or disturbance suffices.[11] Similarly, Article 14 of the Environmental Protection Act (EPA)[12] gives *citizens and their organizations* the right to require—in their exercise of the right to a healthy living environment—before the court that the holder of an environmental intervention stop such intervention if it causes or threatens to cause excessive negative effects to the environment or imminent threat to human life or health. The holder may also be prevented from launching environmental interventions if they are likely to cause such negative consequences.[13]

Collective organizational actions were available also for safeguarding the interests of consumers under the Consumer Protection Act of 1998 (CPA) that implemented the Injunctions Directive (Directive 98/27/EC and later Directive 2009/22/EC) already prior to entering the EU in 2004.[14]

In Chapter X on Pecuniary Protection, the CPA first set out the rules on actions for the cessation of a company's illegal practices (Arts. 74 and 75 of the CPA).

---

[7] Galič and Vlahek (2018), p. 25.

[8] Galič (2008), para 200.

[9] *Obligacijski zakonik (OZ)*, Official Gazette of RS, N. 83/01, with further amendments.

[10] It is not entirely clear whether this reference to *interested person* indicates that the action pursuant to Art. 133 of the CO is not a popular action. For further details, see Damjan (2011), pp. 243–270, 406–407.

[11] See ibid.

[12] *Zakon o varstvu okolja (ZVO-1)*, Official Gazette of RS, N. 41/04, with further amendments.

[13] For further details, see Damjan (2011), pp. 243–270, 406–407.

[14] For further details, see Vlahek (2020) (in press).

Article 74 stated that a company applying its general terms and conditions or submitting pre-printed contracts (formulary contracts) or applying business methods or advertisements contrary to law or good business practices in B2C relationships may be sued to cease with such illegal activities. In 2002, Article 74 was supplemented by a rule allowing the court to decide to publish the judgment at the company's expense. In doing so, the court was to decide to what extent it was necessary to also publish the reasoning of the judgment.[15] A new Article 74a was added in 2002 stating that in a dispute over misleading or comparative advertising under Article 74 of the CPA, the court may, on the request of the applicant, issue a provisional order pursuant to the Enforcement and Provisional Measures Act[16] ordering the cessation of misleading advertising or illicit comparative advertising, or prohibiting the publication of misleading or illicit comparative advertising, if the latter is about to be published. According to Article 75 (which was also supplemented in 2002), the action under Article 74 could be filed by *any organization which is a legal person established for the protection of the rights and interests of consumers, and which has actually operated for at least a year prior to filing the action*. Legal standing was also given to *a chamber or a business association of which the defendant company is a member*. If the conduct covered by the action was likely to affect the position and rights of consumers in an EU Member State, it could also be brought by *an organization or an independent public body (e.g. a consumer ombudsman) established under the law of that Member State for the protection of the rights and interests of consumers, and actually operating at least one year prior to filing the action*. Such persons could bring an action only after consulting the national consumer protection authority or directly if the national consumer authority would not reply to a request for consultation within 14 days.

Provisions on actions for a declaration of nullity were also added in 2002. Article 76 of the CPA gave the *organizations listed in Article 75 of the CPA* standing to file an action seeking the declaration of invalidity of certain B2C contracts or their individual provisions or of the general conditions included in B2C contracts. A favorable final judgment declaring the invalidity would have an *erga omnes* effect so that anyone could invoke it against the company. A dismissal of the action would, on the other hand, have effect only between the parties and would not prevent the filing of a new action with the same claim, either by another organization entitled to bring the action, or by persons having a legal interest in bringing such declaratory action.[17] As long as the lawsuit was pending, no new lawsuit could be instituted between the same parties or between the same defendant and another organization entitled to bring the action. Another organization entitled to bring the action under Article 76 of the CPA could join the plaintiff in the ongoing litigation throughout the proceedings

---

[15] *Zakon o spremembah in dopolnitvah Zakona o varstvu potrošnikov (ZVPot-A)*, Official Gazette of RS, No. 110/2002.

[16] *Zakon o izvršbi in zavarovanju (ZIZ)*, Official Gazette of RS, No. 51/98, with further amendments. See Galič (2008) para 289 ff.

[17] See Galič (2011), pp. 215–229, 402–403.

until the final decision and would have the status of an intervener in accordance with the general rules of civil procedure.[18]

From 1998 when collective injunctive relief was introduced by the CPA to 2018 when the CPA's provisions on organizational collective actions were replaced by similar provisions of the CAA, no actions under Articles 74–76 of the CPA were filed by representative consumer organizations or chambers having legal standing under the CPA.[19] The lack of interest and activity by those who have standing and the necessary resources (some of them having been, *inter alia*, financed by the Government) to request such relief for the benefit of the victims could be perceived as an obstacle to effective use of available injunctive relief mechanisms. The CAA of 2017 repealed the CPA's chapter on injunctive relief, but its provisions applied until 21 April 2018 when the CAA and its novel provisions on collective injunctive relief started to apply (Art. 66 CAA).

Before the decision to draft the CAA was taken, the Ministry for Economic Development and Technology started to draft a new CPA which would cover also consumer compensatory collective actions. This CPA draft has still not been finalized and will obviously not include the provisions on consumer collective redress, as they are already set out in the CAA.

2.2 General Procedural Mechanisms

According to the general rules of Slovenian civil procedure, an action may be filed by a person who asserts that he or she personally suffered a direct violation of his or her rights (*legitimatio ad processum*).[20] For an action to be admissible (as a matter of procedural law), it is not necessary to prove that the rights of a plaintiff were violated (*legitimatio ad causam*), but it is necessary to assert such a violation.[21] Hence, an action is in principle admissible only if a plaintiff seeks to protect his or her own (asserted) rights and not the rights of third persons.[22] A statute can, however, provide for a possibility to file an action, the object of which is not a protection of the rights of the plaintiff but of a certain third person, or of an unidentified circle of persons. As explained earlier, such statutes have existed already prior to the enactment of the CAA and have regulated specific types of non-compensatory collective redress in the fields of protection of consumers, health and the environment.

The Civil Procedure Act (CPrA),[23] however, regulates general procedural mechanisms that could have to an extent served as substitutes for inexistent compensatory

[18]For further details, see Galič (2008), para 315 ff.

[19]See also Galič and Vlahek (2018), p. 217.

[20]Galič (2008), para 200.

[21]Ibid.

[22]Ibid.

[23]*Zakon o pravdnem postopku (ZPP)*, Official Gazette of RS, No. 26/99, with further amendments.

collective redress *stricto sensu*: joinder of parties,[24] joinder of actions[25] and model case procedure.[26] Special rules on model case procedure in social disputes are laid down in the Labor and Social Courts Act,[27] while special rules on joinder of actions are laid down in the Prevention of Restriction of Competition Act.[28] It must be stressed that—in contrast to collective actions *stricto sensu*—all of these mechanisms require the filing of individual actions by the victims themselves and are not designed to meet the procedural needs in mass harm cases.[29]

Before the enactment of the CAA, Slovenian consumers and businesses took part in two group out-of-court actions aimed at forcing the (alleged) infringers to compensate them for damage (allegedly) sustained. These actions were promoted by different organizations and their attorneys in order to avoid filing burdensome and ineffective individual actions under the existent general rules of civil procedure.

The out-of-court actions were launched following two decisions finding antitrust infringements issued by the Competition Protection Office of the Republic of Slovenia (RS) (now the Public Agency of RS for the Protection of Competition). In the notorious 'electricity cartel' case, a refund of overcharges was requested from four Slovenian electricity companies that colluded on electricity prices.[30] The Society for the Refund of Electricity Overcharges campaigning for follow-on private enforcement[31] was established. Tens of thousands of consumers in Slovenia joined the Society, which was assisted by a law firm and a number of volunteers.[32] Under pressure from the Society and the media, the companies decided to voluntarily refund a certain amount of the overcharges before any lawsuits were filed.[33] The other out-of-court action assembled under the organization of the Slovene Consumers' Association[34] and tackled the issue of sums paid by the customers of Telekom Slovenije d.d. as a consequence of allegedly illegal tying/bundling of

[24] *Sosporništvo*, Arts. 191–198 CPrA. For further details, see Pogorelčnik Vogrinc (2018), pp. 35–36.

[25] *Združitev pravd*, Art. 300 CPrA.

[26] *Vzorčni postopek*, Art. 279b CPrA. For further details, see Betteto (2011) 231–241.

[27] Art. 79 of the Labor and Social Courts Act, Official Gazette of RS, No. 2/04, with further amendments. In labour disputes, the general rules of the CPrA on the model case procedure apply.

[28] Art. 62c of the Prevention of Restriction of Competition Act, Official Gazette of RS, No. 36/08, with further amendments.

[29] Galič and Vlahek (2018), p. 26.

[30] For further details, see Vlahek (2016), p. 381.

[31] Later renamed Society for the Rule of Law (www.dzp.si).

[32] The Society obtained over 70,000 authorizations from citizens to address to the companies the claims, in their names, for refund of the overcharges. A law office was also engaged in the project in the event actions had to be filed with the court. Vlahek (2016), p. 381.

[33] It amounted to approx. €30–€300 per household. Ibid.

[34] *Zveza potrošnikov Slovenije (ZPS)*, a non-governmental organization established in 1990 whose task is to protect and represent consumer interests.

ISDN and ADSL telecommunications services.[35] As public enforcement proceedings before the Slovenian competition authority and the courts had already continued for several years, the Slovene Consumers' Association—having regard to the fact that the limitation period with regard to these repayments might soon expire—publicly requested Telekom Slovenije d.d. to repay each of their customers a sum of €105.20 (mirroring approx. the sum paid for the ISDN as determined by the competition authority in its decision) or to promise in a notarial statement that it would refund the customers the amounts paid for and/or because of the ISDN in the event the final decision was in their favor. The company replied that as the case was still pending in the courts, no out-of-court settlements or other agreements were possible. The Slovenian Government, which was also requested to intervene and force Telekom Slovenije d.d. to submit its statement, allegedly did not respond.[36] The Association thus drafted lawsuits against Telekom Slovenije d.d. and invited all interested consumers to become members of the Association and thereby receive assistance and guidance as to filing their individual lawsuits. Some attorneys and law offices also offered legal assistance to consumers in advancing with their claims against Telekom Slovenije d.d.[37]

Similar out-of-court actions by the Slovene Consumers' Association took place between 2007 and 2011 for the protection of approximately 40,000 consumers who had entered into savings agreements with two Slovenian banks (NLB and Abanka Vipa) that did not pay interest as per the agreements. Being assisted by the Association and its attorneys, some of the consumers settled with the banks for compensation (est. total €13 million) while others (more than 160) filed individual lawsuits against the banks for the full amounts owed.[38] In these cases, too, the majority of the plaintiffs accepted the banks' offers to settle after the courts found infringement had occurred.

2.3 Assignment of Claims

Assignment of claims ('collection of claims') has also been available under the general rules of civil law laid down in the CO[39] enabling victims to transfer (by sale or other financial arrangement) their claims to a person collecting them in order to

[35]For details as to the proceedings before the competition authority and the courts, see Vlahek (2016), pp. 381–382.

[36]See https://www.zps.si/index.php/nasveti-in-zakonodaja-topmenu-235/mobilniki-tv-splet/7300.

[37]Vlahek (2016), pp. 382–383.

[38]See https://www.zps.si/index.php/osebne-finance-sp-1406526635/varevanja/4601-uspeen-zakljuek-akcije-modro-varevanje; https://www.zps.si/index.php/osebne-finance-sp-1406526635/varevanja/4717-zps-v-imenu-dveh-svojih-lanov-iztoila-abanko-za-20000-premalo-plaanih-obresti.

[39]*Cesija* or *prenos terjatve*. Arts. 417–426 CO.

pursue them in his or her own name.[40] As is the case with the general procedural mechanisms, the assignment, too, does not enable the filing of class or representative actions.

Assignment of claims was an instrument used in the Slovenian VW case that took place right before the start of application of the new CAA. An estimated 45,000 cars were affected in Slovenia. More than 6000 consumers joined the Slovenian VW campaign, which lasted from September 2017 to January 2018 and was led by the Slovene Consumers' Association, and assigned their claims to a German company (Financialright GmbH).[41] The action against VW AG was filed in Germany with the District Court in Braunschweig in March 2018. It stipulates that at least 65% of any repayment will go to the consumers, while the rest will cover the costs of the proceedings (costs of the campaign, the attorneys and the courts). If the action is unsuccessful (the case is still pending), the consumers will not bear any of the costs of the campaign or the proceedings.[42]

3 CAA Drafting Process

The CAA was drafted taking into account the European Commission's 2013 Recommendation on injunctive and compensatory collective redress mechanisms, as well as best legislative solutions and practices from various foreign models (e.g. those in Belgium, the Netherlands, Sweden and the UK).[43] One obstacle to drafting an efficient and workable piece of legislation was the lack of experience regarding collective actions in practice in the countries where such redress has been available on paper. The system of awarding and distributing damages was perceived as particularly ambiguous and underdeveloped. Another obstacle the drafters faced was the rather general and at times ambiguous provisions of the Recommendation. A result of the fact that the Commission failed to address all relevant questions of collective redress sufficiently and did not anticipate all plausible problems arising when the Recommendation was being put in practice is that some of the provisions of the CAA, such as those on third-party funding, are not drafted perfectly.[44]

The following common principles for collective redress mechanisms in the Member States concerning violations of rights granted under EU law were set out in the Commission's 2013 Recommendation:

---

[40]For further details, see Juhart (1996).

[41]See www.preVWara.si.

[42]Ibid.

[43]For details on these models, see Draft CAA, No. EVA: 2016-2030-0007, pp. 17–53.

[44]See Sect. 4.9.

- standing to be given to a (i) group of two or more natural or legal persons harmed in a mass harm situation,[45] and to (ii) representative non-profit entity (designated either in advance or ad hoc but having the administrative and financial capacity to be able to represent the interest of claimants in an appropriate manner) and/or to a public authority;
- a certification phase is required in order to avoid an abuse of the system and to guarantee the sound administration of justice;
- a national registry of collective actions is to be established;
- opt-in to be set as a rule (any exception to this principle, by law or by court order, should be duly justified by reasons of sound administration of justice);[46]
- elements such as punitive damages, intrusive pre-trial discovery procedures and jury awards, most of which are foreign to the legal traditions of most Member States, should be avoided as a general rule;
- the "loser pays principle" applies;
- third-party funding (TPF) is allowed but strictly regulated so that it does not lead to an abuse of the system or a conflict of interest;
- contingency fees are not desirable (they must not create any incentive to litigation that is unnecessary from the point of view of the interest of any of the parties).

These recommendations are largely mirrored in the CAA. Even the provision of Article 1/2 of the CAA on the purpose of the act corresponds to that of recital 1 of the Recommendation: to facilitate access to justice, stop and prevent illegal practices and enable injured parties to obtain compensation in mass harm situations caused by violations of rights arising out of civil, commercial and employment relationships, while ensuring appropriate constitutional procedural safeguards to avoid abusive litigation.[47] One of the parts where Slovenia has partially deviated from the Recommendation is the definition of standing (see Sect. 4.4). The other mechanism not corresponding fully to the recommendations is contingency fees, where the legislator has instead given preference to the Slovenian legal tradition and legal order.[48] Contingency fees are generally allowed in the Slovenian civil procedure and were additionally regulated by the CAA for cases of collective redress (see Sect. 4.9). It must be underscored that the Recommendation is an act of EU soft-law and is not binding upon the Member States. The Recommendation did, however, foresee that the Member States would implement it on a voluntary basis at the latest 2 years after

[45] Ambiguity of this provision is explained in Sect. 4.4.

[46] Ambiguity of this provision is explained in Sect. 4.7.

[47] Rec. 1 of the Recommendation reads as follows: "The purpose of this Recommendation is to facilitate access to justice, stop illegal practices and enable injured parties to obtain compensation in mass harm situations caused by violations of rights granted under Union law, while ensuring appropriate procedural safeguards to avoid abusive litigation."

[48] The importance of taking due account of the national legal tradition and legal order is emphasized in various EU acts on collective redress. See, e.g., the European Parliament's resolution of February 2012 titled 'Towards a Coherent European Approach to Collective Redress', 2011/2089(INI); para 13 of the Commission 2013 Recommendation.

its publication, i.e. by 26 June 2015. Slovenia did so with more than a 2-year delay. It was nevertheless one of the first Member States to react to the Recommendation.[49] The Commission announced in the Recommendation that it would monitor and assess the measures taken by the Member States, and decide by 26 June 2017 whether any further action, including legislative measures, was needed in order to ensure that the objectives of the Recommendation were fully met. In April 2018, the Commission published a proposal for a new directive on representative actions for the protection of the collective interests of consumers[50] signaling its discontent with the implementation of the 2013 Recommendation. The Proposal Directive resulted from the Commission's decision in 2017 to adopt a "New Deal for Consumers", a revision of consumer directives laying down substantive rules for consumer protection that would be complemented by strengthened procedural rules for enforcing consumers' rights.[51] Since at the time of drafting and adopting the CAA[52] the Commission's Proposal Directive was not yet available, the Proposal's novelties have not been addressed and inserted in the CAA's text. The CAA was adopted on 26 September 2017, entered into force on 21 October 2017 and started to apply on 21 April 2018, while the Proposal Directive was published on 11 April 2018, i.e. ten days prior to the application date of the already enacted CAA.

Although the Recommendation did not limit the areas in which collective redress should be available (it mentions EU law in general and lists some of the typical areas for the introduction of collective redress), the initial pragmatic idea of the CAA drafters was—following the Belgian model[53]—to cover only collective compensatory actions and settlements for a rather limited scope of consumer disputes. Redress other than compensatory would not be covered, as it had already been regulated in specific legislation, while compensatory collective redress was not yet available and had been perceived as the missing procedural mechanism guaranteeing access to

[49]Despite that, the reports on collective redress in Europe have to date rarely mentioned the Slovenian CAA. See, e.g., the Commission's own Report of 2018 on the implementation of the 2013 Recommendation that mentions only the drafting activities in Slovenia, albeit the CAA was enacted already in 2017. Report from the Commission to the European Parliament, the Council and the European Economic and Social Committee on the implementation of the Commission Recommendation of 11 June 2013 on common principles for injunctive and compensatory collective redress mechanisms in the Member States concerning violations of rights granted under Union law (2013/396/EU), COM/2018/040 final.

[50]COM (2018) 184: Proposal for a Directive of the European Parliament and of the Council on representative actions for the protection of the collective interests of consumers, and repealing Directive 2009/22/EC.

[51]See the European Parliament's Recommendation following *Dieselgate* issued in April 2017, Study for the Fitness Check of EU consumer and marketing law issued in May 2017, the Commission Work Program for 2018, etc.

[52]This contribution was submitted in September 2019, i.e. before the amendment activities took place within the Council. For further details on the contents of the directive, see Vlahek (2020) (forthcoming).

[53]For details on the Belgian regulation, see Draft CAA, Government of RS, No. EVA: 2016-2030-0007, pp. 32–37; Voet (2015a), pp. 121–143; Voet (2015b), pp. 202–222.

justice. Additionally, only a limited scope of disputes, i.e. only some types of consumer disputes where many persons are typically harmed by the same illegal practices, and that are suitable to being resolved within collective proceedings, were to be regulated by the CAA. This would serve as a test area that could always be broadened should the application of the existent collective redress give positive results. As the introduction of collective compensatory actions in the Slovenian civil procedure was a complete novelty and an experiment, it was felt that, initially, only a very narrow scope of the most typical disputes was to be covered by the new act.

After receiving feedback from various stakeholders,[54] redrafting within the Ministry's working group followed. The scope of the act's application was broadened, and the regulation of other types of collective proceedings was added. Consequently, the structure and the text of the draft were significantly amended leading also to a somewhat lower quality of the draft's text. Additional amendments to the draft (i.e. regarding application of the act to existent cases of mass harm, and the jurisdiction of the courts in collective proceedings) were made in the final stage during the parliamentary proceedings.[55]

The eventually adopted version of the CAA has 67 articles and comprises the following chapters: I. General provisions; II. Collective settlement; III. Collective damages action;[56] IV. Collective injunction actions; V. Costs of collective proceedings, third-party funding; and VI. Final provisions. The Slovenian CPrA applies *mutatis mutandis*. The CAA also states that it does not interfere with the rules of private international law. As the legislator decided that injunctive relief, too, is to be covered by the CAA, the CAA repealed the CPA's chapter on injunctive actions for the protection of consumers' interests and regulated them within the CAA's chapter on collective injunctive actions (Arts. 1/3 and 66 CAA).

The CAA called for two acts of delegated legislation to be issued by the Minister of Justice until the end of February 2018 (Art. 64 CAA): a Decree on the Registry of Collective Actions was adopted on 16 April 2018 and entered into force on 21 April 2018,[57] i.e. the day the CAA started to apply, while the Notaries' Tariff that had to cover anew the tariff for the notaries performing their tasks under the CAA was adopted only on 20 September 2019 and entered into force on 19 October 2019.[58]

---

[54]The following entities reacted to the draft by submitting their written comments: The Supreme Court of RS, Labor and Social Court in Ljubljana, State Attorney's Office, Ministry for Economic Development and Technology, Slovenian Bar, Slovenian Chamber of Commerce, Slovenian Consumers' Association, Slovenian Health and Social Security Union, Legal-Informational Center of NGOs. In order to make the drafting process as transparent as possible, the Ministry of Justice also organized a public meeting where the draft was presented and additional exchange of views on the draft could take place.

[55]Galič and Vlahek (2018), p. 27.

[56]Art. 3 CAA explains in this regard that a "collective damages action" within the meaning of the CAA is not to be understood *stricto sensu* as purely an action requesting damages, but also as an action requesting the return of unjustified enrichment or an action requesting performance.

[57]*Pravilnik o registru kolektivnih tožb*, Official Gazette of RS, No. 26/18.

[58]*Notarska tarifa*, Official Gazette of RS, No. 59/19.

4 Main Provisions of the CAA

4.1 Scope of Application

The initial idea was to cover only consumer collective compensatory actions and settlements under the Belgian model[59] in order to first test the appropriateness of the new concepts and procedural solutions within a rather narrow field of law where mass violations are most common, and where collective redress has developed most and is a suitable mechanism for resolving disputes.[60] Later in the drafting process, additional areas of law were added broadening the scope of application of the CAA to an almost horizontal level as advocated also by the Commission Recommendation.[61] The insistence of many stakeholders on inserting their field of operation under the CAA's scope of application (even if within these fields collective assessment is not the (most) appropriate means[62] showed that collective redress mechanisms were perceived as extremely important procedural tools despite the fact that they in no way jeopardized the existent mechanisms of individual legal protection. A general application of the CAA against the Republic of Slovenia was also called for.[63]

The CAA provides for collective settlements and collective actions in the following areas: consumer law, labor law, financial instruments market law, antitrust, environmental accidents and (only in the form of injunctive relief) within anti-discrimination law. These areas correspond largely to the areas expressly mentioned by the Recommendation as being typical areas where collective redress is of particular value. The CAA has, of course, not focused only on infringements of EU law, but also on the relevant infringements of Slovenian law. Various types of relief (compensatory, injunctive, to some extent even declaratory) are regulated, but the focus is clearly placed on actions for damages and other types of compensatory relief.

Collective compensatory and injunctive actions and settlements are available for the following claims (Art. 2 CAA):

---

[59]See Voet (2015a), pp. 121–143.

[60]Galič and Vlahek (2018), pp. 29–30.

[61]Para 7: "Amongst those areas where the supplementary private enforcement of rights granted under Union law in the form of collective redress is of value, are consumer protection, competition, environment protection, protection of personal data, financial services legislation and investor protection. The principles set out in this Recommendation should be applied horizontally and equally in those areas but also in any other areas where collective claims for injunctions or damages in respect of violations of the rights granted under Union law would be relevant."

[62]Galič and Vlahek (2018), p. 30.

[63]Galič and Vlahek (2018), p. 31.

1. claims of consumers arising from contractual relationships with businesses as specified by the legislation on consumer protection;[64]
2. claims arising from the violations of other consumer rights set out in the act on consumer protection;[65]
3. claims arising from the violations of Slovenian or EU antitrust laws;[66]
4. claims regarding the violations of the rules regulating the trade on organized markets and regarding the prohibited actions of market abuse under the act regulating the financial instruments market;[67]
5. claims of workers in individual labor disputes;[68]
6. damages claims in cases of environmental disasters as defined in the environmental protection act.[69]

In the field of protection against discrimination,[70] only collective injunctive actions are available (Art. 2/2 CAA), whereas compensatory redress is available only on an individual basis.

4.2 Temporal Application

The CAA applies from 21 April 2018 not only to cases falling under the CAA's scope of application where damages were sustained or other deprivations occurred

---

[64]A set of different acts protecting consumers falls under this category, such as the CPA, the Consumer Credit Act (*Zakon o potrošniških kreditih (ZPotK-2)*, Official Gazette of RS, No. 77/16), etc. However, only contractual relationships are covered in this category.

[65]E.g. in the CPA. Here, however, not just contractual breaches but also violations of other consumer rights are covered (if these are regulated in the CPA, not elsewhere).

[66]See Arts. 101 and 102 TFEU and/or Arts. 6 and 9 of the Prevention of Restriction of Competition Act (*Zakon o preprečevanju omejevanja konkurence (ZPOmK-1)*), Official Gazette of RS, No. 36/08, with further amendments.

[67]See the Market in Financial Instruments Act (*Zakon o trgu finančnih inštrumentov (ZTFI)*), Official Gazette of RS, No. 67/07, with further amendments.

[68]See the Labor and Social Courts Act (*Zakon o delovnih in socialnih sodiščih (ZDSS-1)*, Official Gazette of RS, No. 2/04, with further amendments). See also Vlahek (2018), pp. 495–515. This category was added to the list later in the drafting process. It is one of the rare categories where an action can be filed against the State. In this case, special rules of the CAA on standing and on jurisdiction apply. See how these rules were applied in the first Slovenian collective action (see Sect. 5) which was an action in a labor dispute.

[69]See the Environmental Protection Act (*Zakon o varstvu okolja (ZVO-1)*), Official Gazette of RS, No. 41/04, with further amendments. It is to be stressed that according to the CAA, only "environmental disasters" as defined in Art. 3 of the Environmental Protection Act, and no other forms of pollution of the environment, are covered by the CAA. This category was added to the CAA draft rather late in the drafting process after a fire in the Kemis company in May 2017 that resulted in the pollution of a nearby river, the air, etc.

[70]See the Act on the Protection against Discrimination (*Zakon o varstvu pred diskriminacijo (ZVarD)*), Official Gazette of RS, No. 33/16, with further amendments.

after the CAA's entry into force (i.e. after 21 October 2017), but also to those damages sustained or deprivations having occurred before the CAA's entry into force (as long as the limitation period has not run out) (Art. 6 CAA).

The question of the CAA's temporal application was one of the highly debated topics during the adoption of the act. Similar to the debate before the UK Competition Appeal Tribunal in *Dorothy Gibson v Pride Mobility Products Limited*,[71] discussions took place on the act's retroactive applicability. The initial CAA draft opted for a cautious approach and provided for the act to apply only to cases where the harm was sustained after the act's entry into force. This decision was taken mainly due to the fear of possible over-burdening of the courts with novel collective actions and settlements should the act apply also to existent cases. The majority of the stakeholders and the Members of the Slovenian Parliament, however, favored its broader application in order to cover the already known Slovenian cases of mass harm that could otherwise not have been assessed in collective proceedings. Within this debate, the focus was placed particularly on the *Dieselgate* case and the cases of environmental accidents that took place before the enactment of the CAA. It must be noted here, however, that due to a narrow definition of the scope of application of the CAA, these cases would not necessarily fall under the CAA. Eventually, the final provision of the CAA on its temporal application was amended in the final stage of the parliamentary proceedings to cover the cases irrespective of whether the harm was sustained before or after the act's entry into force. The CAA was perceived by the stakeholders as purely procedural law that does not set out any new substantive rights and obligations (but merely offers a set of rules on procedure to enforce the existent rights) and thus does not have the prohibited retroactive effect.[72] All three cases pending before the Slovenian courts under the rules of the CAA (they are presented in Sect. 5) cover mass harm sustained before the CAA's entry into force.

4.3 Jurisdiction

Collective actions and settlements are assessed by four (out of 11) district courts, i.e. the District Courts in Ljubljana, Maribor, Celje and Koper with the exception of labor disputes that are assessed by first instance labor courts at their seats in Ljubljana, Maribor, Celje and Koper (Art. 6 CAA). At the district courts, the decisions are in principle made by a single judge,[73] whereas at the labor courts

[71]Case number: 1257/7/7/16.

[72]For further details on such argument, see the UK Competition Appeal Tribunal's reasoning in the *Gibson* case.

[73]Exceptionally, the single judge may ask the president of the respective high court to transfer the case to senate of three judges if the case raises complex legal or factual questions.

decisions are made by a three-member senate constituted in accordance with the Labor and Social Courts Act.[74]

The initial idea within the working group was to give exclusive jurisdiction to only one of the district courts (and thus to only one out of four high courts in Slovenia to assess the appeals) and to only one of the labor courts.[75] The purpose of such exclusive jurisdiction was to guarantee a unified approach when applying the CAA.[76] The final stage of the parliamentary proceedings nevertheless led to an amendment giving jurisdiction to four district courts having their seats in the places of the four high courts (Ljubljana, Maribor, Celje and Koper) and to four labor courts of first instance also having their seats in Ljubljana, Maribor, Celje and Koper. This was in line with the general critique of the legislation giving exclusive jurisdiction, in cases where such jurisdiction is provided for, only to the District Court in Ljubljana. The Members of Parliament stressed the need to decentralize judicial activities and guarantee that also smaller courts have their own workload and, consequently, their own employees (while at the same time the Members of Parliament opted for jurisdiction of only the four largest district courts). They also opined that giving jurisdiction to multiple courts might assist in the evolution of court practice.[77] Having regard to a small number of class action cases that are extremely complex and far-reaching, exclusive jurisdiction of only one district court would in our opinion be a better solution for guaranteeing the proficient carrying out of collective proceedings. Irrespective of the number of the courts applying the CAA, this goal cannot be reached without the specialization of the judges.

When applying the CAA, the judges are faced with a high level of judicial discretion and with novel legal standards, such as "fair and adequate", "similar or connected factual or legal issues", "common issues prevail", "so numerous that", "not obviously unfounded" and "the agreement with the attorney is reasonable". The judges, *inter alia*, must decide on opt-in or opt-out, on individual damages or aggregate damages, and on personal delivery of mail or publication in the media. This higher level of discretion given to the judges is a *conditio sine qua non* for effective collective redress.[78] The 2013 Recommendation also stresses that the key role must be given to the courts in protecting the rights and interests of all the parties involved in collective redress actions as well as in managing the collective redress actions effectively.[79]

---

[74]See Art. 14 of this act. In the first Slovenian proceedings under the CAA, which was a labor dispute (see Sect. 5), the senate of the Labor and Social Court in Ljubljana was comprised of a professional judge and two jury judges, one from the list of employers, the other from the list of employees.

[75]Galič and Vlahek (2018), p. 34.

[76]General rules on jurisdiction of the courts in Slovenia are presented in Pogorelčnik Vogrinc (2018), pp. 27–29.

[77]Pogorelčnik Vogrinc (2018), pp. 27–29.

[78]See Galič and Vlahek(2018), pp. 34–35.

[79]Para 21 of the Preamble to the Recommendation.

Collective proceedings can also have an effect on the workload of other courts. Namely, if individual actions have been filed before a collective action was filed, the courts assessing such individual claims must, as a rule, stop the proceedings and wait for the outcome of the collective proceedings.[80]

4.4 *Standing and Representation*

The 2013 Recommendation advocates that collective actions should be brought either (i) jointly by those who claim to have suffered harm,[81] or (ii) in the case of a representative action, by ad hoc certified entities, by designated representative entities that fulfil certain criteria set by law,[82] or by public authorities,[83] whereby the representative entities should be required to prove the administrative and financial capacity to be able to represent the interests of the claimants in an appropriate manner.[84] The Recommendation states that representative actions are brought by such entities on behalf and in the name of two or more natural or legal persons who claim to be exposed to the risk of suffering harm or to have been harmed in a mass harm situation while those persons are not parties to the proceedings.[85] Such a procedural constellation, i.e. that the proceedings have effects on third parties who are not parties to the proceedings, is typical for collective proceedings. It is, however, not entirely clear what the Commission meant by saying that the action is brought in the name of two or more victims. It is also not entirely clear what the

[80]See Art. 7 CAA.

[81]Para 17 of the Preamble and point 3(a) of the Recommendation: "... a legal mechanism that ensures a possibility to claim compensation collectively by two or more natural or legal persons claiming to have been harmed in a mass harm situation".

[82]Point 4 of the Recommendation explains in this regard that the Member States should designate representative entities to bring representative actions on the basis of clearly defined conditions of eligibility. These conditions should include at least the following requirements: (a) the entity should have a non-profit character; (b) there should be a direct relationship between the main objectives of the entity and the rights granted under Union law that are claimed to have been violated in respect of which the action is brought; and (c) the entity should have sufficient capacity in terms of financial resources, human resources and legal expertise to represent multiple claimants and to act in their best interests. Point 5 adds that the Member States should ensure that the designated entity will lose its status if one or more of the conditions are no longer met. According to point 6, the Member States should also ensure that representative actions can only be brought by entities which have been officially designated in advance as recommended in point 4 or by entities which have been certified on an ad hoc basis by a Member State's national authorities or courts for a particular representative action. Additional rules for cross-border cases are set out in points 17 and 18 of the Recommendation.

[83]Point 7 of the Recommendation explains in this regard that in addition, or as an alternative to designating representative entities in accordance with points 4–6 of the Recommendation, the Member States should empower public authorities to bring representative actions.

[84]Paras 17 and 18 of the Preamble and point 3(a) and (d) of the Recommendation.

[85]Point 3(d) of the Recommendation.

Commission meant by defining as collective redress also collective actions brought jointly by those who have suffered harm. The Commission explained in the Preamble that

> [l]egal standing to bring a collective action in the Member States depends on the type of collective redress mechanism. In certain types of collective actions, such as group actions where the action can be brought jointly by those who claim to have suffered harm, the issue of standing is more straightforward than in the context of representative actions, where accordingly the issue of legal standing should be clarified.[86]

The most plausible interpretation is that in this case the Commission is referring to a joinder of parties, and not to a collective action proceedings *stricto sensu*, such as in the US-style class action. In the case of a joinder of parties, the victims are to file a lawsuit jointly and have the status of a party to the proceedings, whereas in cases of collective actions *stricto sensu* the lawsuit need not be filed by all the persons for whom the judgment will have effect, but is filed by a representative entity, a public authority or by some of the victims, but for the benefit of all the victims, and the judgment will have effect on all those victims who opt in or do not opt out. Additional ambiguity stems from points 21–24 of the Recommendation explaining how the "claimant party", as the Recommendation calls it, is to be constituted by the "opt-in" principle. It is not clear whether in these cases those opting in are merely class members for the benefit of whom the claimant party has filed the lawsuit, or in fact constitute the claimant party filing the lawsuit.

To a large extent, the CAA follows the 2013 Recommendation. In general, two types of persons may initiate proceedings under the CAA: (i) an existent or ad hoc non-profit private law entity with a direct connection between its main goals of action and the rights which were allegedly violated and regarding which the action is being filed; and (ii) a higher state attorney (in Slovene, *višji državni odvetnik*)[87] (the latter not against the Republic of Slovenia) (Art. 5 CAA). In contrast to the Recommendation, representative entities need not be officially designated in advance as entities having standing in collective actions.[88] US-style class actions filed by individual class members for the benefit of the whole class are not available, while the joinder of parties is available as a general procedural mechanism and is not regarded as a collective redress mechanism *stricto sensu* (see Sect. 2.1). The drafters opined that a public authority listed in the 2013 Recommendation as a potential person having standing in collective proceedings is also an appropriate person to initiate collective proceedings, as these are, in the opinion of the drafters, carried out

[86]Para 17 of the Preamble to the Recommendation.

[87]See http://www.dodv-rs.si/en/.

[88]The first Slovenian collective action (see Sect. 5) was filed by a union of the Ministry of Defense. As the action was filed against the Republic of Slovenia, it could not have been filed by a higher state attorney. One of the reasons for not limiting standing to pre-designated entities was the negative experience with collective actions under the CPA that could be filed by designated consumer organizations and other existent bodies. To our knowledge, they have not filed any such actions. Galič and Vlahek (2018), p. 31.

also in the public interest.[89] In deciding which public authority would best serve the collective interests of the victims, the legislator eventually opted for higher state attorneys, and not for state prosecutors, the Ombudsman or other persons suggested in the course of the drafting process.

Collective injunctive relief may—in addition to the persons listed above—also be sought by a body designated by the State to safeguard specific groups or interests. However, due to the requirements of the EU Injunctions Directive, only listed consumer organizations or chambers or business associations of which the defendant is a member, or EU listed organizations or public authorities from other Member States, may file a consumer collective injunctive action. In discrimination cases, collective injunctive actions may only be filed by the Slovenian Equal Rights Ombudsman or by an NGO with a recognized status of acting in the public interest in the field of protection against discrimination or protection of human rights.

If the claimant does not have standing, the court must reject the action as inadmissible. However, even if the claimant has standing, it will have to show its representativeness in order for the action to be certified (Arts. 5 and 28 CAA). Namely, the claimant (who has standing) must be deemed able to represent the group adequately and fairly (Art. 5 CAA). The court determines this in the certification phase taking into account all of the circumstances of the case, in particular: (i) the existing financial means, human resources and legal knowledge for representing the group; (ii) the activities already accomplished regarding the preparation of the collective settlement or collective action, as well as the organizing of the injured persons and the communications with them; (iii) the number of victims supporting its activities; (iv) media involvement of the claimant and its activities in disseminating information on the intended collective proceeding; and (v) possible prior experience in collective proceedings.[90] If more than one person acts as the claimant and each of the claimants represents only a part of the class or an individual sub-class, the representativeness must be assessed taking into account all of these persons together.[91]

[89]Galič and Vlahek (2018), p. 31.

[90]Ibid. See how this rule was applied in the first Slovenian collective action (see Sect. 5) where the court determined without any doubt that the union of the Ministry of Defense shows representativeness as required by the CAA. In its decision, the court stated that the claimant has sufficient financial resources to finance collective proceedings and added that the defendant has not even disputed this.

[91]Ibid.

4.5 *Certification Criteria for Compensatory Collective Actions*

After the court has established that the lawsuit (i) contains all the required elements,[92] (ii) falls under the CAA's scope of application, (iii) is filed by a person having legal standing under the CAA[93] and (if relevant) (iv) was not filed before the competition authority has decided on the antitrust infringement,[94] it proceeds to a so-called certification stage (*faza certifikacije*) within which the court will assess whether the lawsuit is to be certified, i.e. to be assessed in collective actions proceedings. The lawsuit is first forwarded to the defendant, who replies to the lawsuit only as regards the criteria for its certification (not yet as to the merits of the case) (Art. 27/2 CAA).

The CAA lists the following certification criteria for compensatory collective actions (Art. 28 CAA):

1. The claims are of the same nature, they are filed on behalf of a determinable group of persons and they concern the same, similar or connected factual or legal issues; they concern the same case of mass damage and they are suitable for being decided in collective proceedings. In determining suitability, the court takes into account the following: Do collective proceedings enable effective resolution of common legal and factual issues? What are the costs and benefits of advancing with collective proceedings? Have any individual claims already been filed? What are the size and the characteristics of the class? What are the options for determining class membership? Are the amounts suitable to be awarded as aggregate damages? and Are ADR and other means for resolving the dispute available?[95]
2. There are more common legal and factual issues for the whole group than questions relating only to individual members of the group.
3. The group is so numerous that the filing of individual claims or another manner of joining its members, e.g. joinder of claims or joinder of actions, would be less efficient than the filing of a collective compensatory action.
4. The plaintiff is representative (see Sect. 4.4).
5. The collective compensatory action is not manifestly ill-founded.
6. The conditions regarding the agreements on costs and funding are fulfilled (see Sect. 4.9).

[92]See Art. 26 CAA and the general rules of the CPrA, presented in Pogorelčnik Vogrinc (2018), p. 30.

[93]See Art. 27/1 CAA. If this is not established, the court rejects the action.

[94]Art. 9 CAA. If the competition authority has initiated infringement proceedings after the collective action was filed, the court stays the collective proceedings until the administrative/judicial proceedings assessing the antitrust infringement are finalized.

[95]See how in the first collective proceedings under the CAA (see Sect. 5) the court assessed these criteria.

7. The court deems that the eventual agreement with the attorney on contingency fees is reasonable (see Sect. 4.9).

After receiving the defendant's reply to the lawsuit as to whether the certification criteria are met or not, the court invites the parties to a hearing.[96] If the court decides that the certification criteria are not met, it rejects the collective action;[97] otherwise, it issues a decision approving the collective action (*sklep o odobritvi kolektivne tožbe*) (Art. 29 CAA). In this decision, it determines, *inter alia*, whether the system is an opt-out or an opt-in one, and sets the defendant a deadline for submitting a reply to the action as to the merits of the case. After the collective action is approved (the same rule applies in the case of confirmation of the collective settlement), the filing of another collective action in the same case is not allowed.[98]

Establishing a certification stage in collective proceedings is in line with the 2013 Recommendation which stresses that in order to avoid an abuse of the system, and in the interest of the sound administration of justice, no judicial collective redress action should be permitted to proceed unless the admissibility conditions set out by law are met.[99] The Commission explains that the Member States should provide for verification at the earliest possible stage of litigation so that cases in which conditions for collective actions are not met, and manifestly unfounded cases, are not continued. To this end, the courts should carry out the necessary examination on their own motion.[100]

4.6 Registry of Collective Actions

The courts currently publish data and documents regarding collective actions and settlements in a newly established Registry of Collective Actions (*Register*

[96]According to Art. 28/3 CAA, class members and other interested parties may send the court their written opinion on certification criteria. The court may, if it so wishes, invite such persons to a hearing and enable them to present their opinion. This was also the case in the first Slovenian collective action proceedings (see Sect. 5) where the Confederation of Slovenian Unions (CSU) was granted the status of an interested party in accordance with the CAA. The CSU provided its written opinion and was present at the hearing.

[97]In this case, the court issues a decision rejecting the collective action (*sklep o zavrženju kolektivne tožbe*). This was the situation in the first Slovenian collective action proceedings (see Sect. 5) where the court established that the criteria under points 1, 2 and 3 were not met (whereas those under points 4 to 7 were met or were not relevant to the case at hand).

[98]If more than one collective action is filed before the start of the certification stage with regard to the same mass harm case, the court decides which of the actions it will approve. If individual actions were filed before a collective action was filed, the courts assessing such individual claims must stop the proceedings and wait for the outcome of the collective proceedings. See Art. 7 CAA. Art. 8 CAA lays down the rules on the effects of collective proceedings on the limitation periods.

[99]Para 20 of the Preamble to the Recommendation.

[100]Points 8 and 9 of the Recommendation.

kolektivnih tožb). The registry was set up following the European Commission's 2013 Recommendation[101] and by taking into account some of the foreign models, such as the Quebecois Registry of Class Actions[102] and the publications on the web pages of the UK Competition Appeal Tribunal.[103] The initial idea of the drafters was to establish the registry on the web pages of the Agency of the Republic of Slovenia for Public Legal Records and Related Services,[104] where, *inter alia*, the Slovenian Business Register and data on insolvency proceedings are published. At the insistence of the Slovenian Supreme Court, the final decision taken within the working group was to publish the registry on the web pages of the Slovenian judiciary.

The class actions registry was launched in April 2018, in fact on the exact day when the CAA started to apply, and is managed by the Slovenian Supreme Court. It is available free online on the web pages of the Slovenian judiciary.[105] It is in electronic form, in the Slovene language, and contains data on all types of CAA collective proceedings.[106] In addition to the general rules on the registry laid down in the CAA,[107] a separate Decree on the Registry of Collective Actions was announced by the Minister of Justice setting out detailed rules on the functioning of the registry.[108] As three collective actions have already been filed with the Slovenian courts (see Sect. 5), the registry is already fully functioning.[109]

4.7 Opt-in or Opt-out

The 2013 Recommendation favors, so it seems, the opt-in system. It has not, however, prohibited the opt-out system. The problem with the relevant provisions of the Recommendation is that they are so poorly drafted that it is not even clear what exactly is meant by the term "opt-in" used by the Commission. Namely, point 21 states that "[t]he claimant party should be formed on the basis of express consent of the natural or legal persons claiming to have been harmed ('opt-in' principle). Any

[101] See paras 35–37 of the Recommendation.

[102] See https://www.registredesactionscollectives.quebec/en#.

[103] See https://www.catribunal.org.uk/.

[104] *Agencija Republike Slovenije za javnopravne evidence in storitve (AJPES).*

[105] See http://www.sodisce.si/sodni_postopki/javne_obravnave/kolektivne_tozbe/. The first page of the web pages of the judiciary offers a link to the registry ("*register KOLEKTIVNIH TOŽB*") where all collective actions/settlements cases are listed. Each of the cases then offers a link to the details of the proceedings.

[106] Its name suggests that it covers only collective actions, but it applies also to collective settlements.

[107] Arts. 10, 18, 27, 32, 33, 35, 37, 38, 42 CAA.

[108] *Pravilnik o registru kolektivnih tožb*, Official Gazette of RS, No. 26/18.

[109] The first entries show, however, that there is room for improvement. For example, second instance decisions are not being published in the register (only the appeal case number is stated) and have to be searched for in the general caselaw database.

exception to this principle, by law or by court order, should be duly justified by reasons of sound administration of justice." Paragraph 22 then states that

> [a] member of the claimant party should be free to leave the claimant party at any time before the final judgement is given or the case is otherwise validly settled, subject to the same conditions that apply to withdrawal in individual actions, without being deprived of the possibility to pursue its claims in another form, if this does not undermine the sound administration of justice.

Paragraphs 23 and 24 add that

> [n]atural or legal persons claiming to have been harmed in the same mass harm situation should be able to join the claimant party at any time before the judgement is given or the case is otherwise validly settled, if this does not undermine the sound administration of justice [and that] [t]he defendant should be informed about the composition of the claimant party and about any changes therein.

The Commission obviously regarded the victims, i.e. the class members, as the claimants, i.e. the parties to the proceedings.[110] Collective actions are, on the other hand, aimed exactly at omitting the need for the victims to file actions, i.e. to become the claimant parties to the proceedings.

Following the experience in the Member States where only the opt-in mechanism was available and did not give positive results,[111] and the fact that some of the Member States had opted for the opt-out system, the CAA allows for both opt-in and opt-out mechanisms (Arts. 3, 33 and 41 CAA). In the case of the opt-in system (*sistem vključitve*), only those victims will form the class that will willingly enter the group the way instructed by the courts and by the deadline set by the court. In the case of the opt-out system (*sistem izključitve*), all the victims will form the class unless they willingly exit the group the way instructed by the court and by the deadline set by the court (Art. 3 CAA). Once the victims opt in or are part of the class because they have not opted out, it is up to the court or the administrator to establish whether they are in fact entitled to compensation. In both systems, class members do not hold the procedural position of the claimant (party to the proceeding) (Art. 34/1 CAA) nor can they intervene on the part of the claimant party (Art. 34/4 CAA). They need not file any action, their only task is to opt in or opt out and, if pertinent, request the relevant sums to be paid to them (or any other remedy dependent on the type of action) if the action filed by the person having standing (who is not a class member; see Sect. 4.4) is successful. The CAA, however, states that the rules of the CPrA on the taking of evidence that apply to the parties to the proceedings apply also to class members despite their not having the position of parties to the proceedings.[112]

---

[110]This ensues also from the wording of para 17 of the Preamble on legal standing and para 3 of the Recommendation defining "collective redress".

[111]Galič and Vlahek (2018), p. 39; Vlahek (2017), pp. 546–554.

[112]Art. 34/2 CAA. According to Art. 37 CAA, persons showing probability that they are class members, and other justified persons, have the right to submit written opinions and may, under the conditions set out in the CAA, take part in the hearing on the merits of the case.

In the CAA collective actions proceedings, the claimant must suggest the type of mechanism (opt-in or opt-out) in the collective action and also must state the reasons for the choice (Art. 26 CAA). It is, however, the court that eventually decides on the type of mechanism on the basis of the circumstances of the case, in particular the value of the individual class member's claims and circumstances essential for approving the collective action (Arts. 29 and 30 CAA). The court is, however, not entirely free in setting the type of mechanism. Namely, in the following cases, only opt-in may be set out: (i) if non-pecuniary damages are requested; and (ii) if, according to the estimate made in the collective action, 10% or more of the claims are higher than €2000.[113] In addition, for class members without a permanent address in Slovenia, opt-in is the only available option, because, in reality, there is a greater possibility that such persons would not be informed of the collective proceedings.[114] The CAA does not state what the system might be in cases of mixed class members, i.e. when some members have a permanent address in Slovenia and some do not. It has been suggested in scholarly debates that in such cases a combination of opt-in (for those without a permanent address in Slovenia) and opt-out (for the rest of the class) could be plausible.

If the court approves the collective action, it decides on the system and sets a deadline of 30–90 days for opting in/opting out (Arts. 29 and 33 CAA). The court then informs the victims, *inter alia*, of the opt-in/opt-out option and its effect (Art. 31 CAA). The declaration on opting in/opting out cannot be revoked (Art. 34/3 CAA). The list of the members opting in or opting out is kept by the court.[115] The number (not the names or other personal data) of the class members who opted in or opted out must be published in the class actions registry (Arts. 10 and 33 CAA); the final judgment must also state which system was opted for (Art. 38 CAA). After the judgment (awarding damages on a non-individual basis) is issued, the administrator of the awarded damages (i.e. the notary; see Sect. 4.8) makes a list of class members on the basis of the declarations of the persons opting in/opting out and the evidence they submitted in support of their declarations (Art. 44 CAA). It is thus the administrator who decides on who of the declared class members in fact forms the class or sub-class. In case of refusal, he or she must state the reasons for that. The administrator sends the list to the court, the parties and the persons whose listing in the class/sub-class was denied. The parties have 30 days to object to the administrator's individual listing of class members.[116] The court then sets a hearing for the

---

[113] Galič and Vlahek (2018), pp. 40–41.

[114] This solution was copied from the UK CAT's proceedings.

[115] Art. 33 CAA. The court may deny putting a person opting in on the list only if it is obvious that he or she is not a class member. The final factual assessment of whether those put on the list (by way of opting in) or not opting out and submitting their statement that they are class members are in fact class members is made in the final stage of collective proceedings.

[116] Such objection is delivered to the other party, the administrator and the person whose listing is being objected to.

assessment of the list.[117] After the hearing, the court issues a decision containing the final list of the victims and their corresponding amounts to be received. A person not on the list is not a class member and is not bound by the effects of the collective judgment (Art. 45 CAA). As the CAA does not require that these activities take place only after the judgment becomes final, the drafting of the list and the assessment of the appeal may take place simultaneously.

In collective settlements, the parties set the type of mechanism (opt-in or opt-out) and must state the reasons for their choice. In the case of opt-in, the declarations of class members opting in coupled with the evidence of their status must be attached to the settlement (Art. 13 CAA). If the court confirms the settlement (in contrast to the proceedings with a collective action, here the court does not decide on the system), it sets a deadline of 30–90 days for opting in/opting out vis-à-vis the effects of the collective settlement (Art. 18 CAA). The court then informs the victims, *inter alia*, of the opt-in/opt-out option and its effect (Arts. 19 and 20 CAA). The collective settlement may stipulate that any party may cancel the settlement within a period not exceeding 30 days from the expiration of the period set for opting in/opting out if, when a settlement has been concluded under the system of opt-in, more than a certain number of class members opt out, or if, when a settlement has been concluded under the system of opt-in, less than a certain number of class members opt in (Art. 21/2 CAA).

4.8 Awarding and Distribution of Damages

The 2013 Recommendation does not set out the rules on awarding damages in collective actions proceedings. The only provision regulating damages is point 31 stating that the compensation awarded to natural or legal persons harmed in a mass harm situation should not exceed the compensation that would have been awarded if the claim had been pursued by means of individual actions. In particular, punitive damages leading to overcompensation should be prohibited. Although this is probably one of the focal elements of the collective redress proceedings, the Recommendation does not offer any explanation as to how the awarding system is to function. The drafters of the CAA thus analyzed the existent foreign models and attempted to set a rational awards system. Many questions have arisen as to how this system should function in a plethora of different types of claims, actions and judgments available under the CAA. That is why, unfortunately, only practice will show whether the set rules correspond fully to the purpose of the collective proceedings.

The CAA provides for two main options of awarding the damages depending on whether all of the class members are known or not: (i) individual award, where the

[117] It invites the administrator, the parties, the persons not listed and the persons whose listing was objected to. Art. 45 CAA.

judgment lists all the victims by name and the amounts granted to them (in such cases, the judgment itself represents an enforcement title and each of the class members, who must be determined already in the judgment, may start enforcement proceedings);[118] and (ii) non-individual award, where either aggregate damages (*agregatna odškodnina*) (Art. 3 CAA) are set or a per capita amount or other value or obligation to be fulfilled to each (not yet determined) class member is awarded, and an estimate of the total amount is made (Art. 40 CAA). In the latter two cases, the awarded/estimated amount is paid (after the judgment is final)[119] to a fiduciary bank account of the notary who acts as an administrator of collective damages (*upravitelj kolektivne odškodnine*) with the main task of determining who of the persons who opted in or that had not opted out is in fact entitled to damages.[120] If the amount is not paid to the notary's account in accordance with the judgment, the notary and the claimant party (not class members) may start enforcement proceedings. If class members form subgroups, the judgment must set the repayment for each of the subgroups. In the case of the opt-out system, the judgment must also set out the rules on the filing of individual requests by class members who have not opted out[121] (whereas in the case of an opt-in system, class members have to file a request already at the moment of opting in, i.e. after the collective action is approved).

If the awarded aggregate damages do not suffice for repayment of all determined class members, the amounts to which they are entitled are to be lowered accordingly (Art. 45/5 CAA). According to the initial cautious approach of the new Slovenian regime of collective actions, the CAA does not provide for any *cy-pres* solutions. Any surplus of the awarded damages is returned to the defendant (Art. 46/3 CAA), thus emphasizing the compensatory effect of the CAA. Despite not offering any mechanisms of punishment in the form of *cy-pres* or fines, the CAA is supposed to have a deterrent effect already by introducing collective actions and easing access to justice.

The administrator of collective damages is nominated by the court in the final judgment (i.e. the judgment on the merits). Before the nomination, the court gives the parties the opportunity to express their views on the circumstances relevant for choosing the notary, or to suggest which notary should be selected. The notary is entitled to reimbursement of his or her expenses and a fee for performing tasks in accordance with the CAA. The calculation of the notary's fee is set out in the Notary

[118]Art. 39 CAA. Such award is available only if individual assessment in collective proceedings would not require long-term assessment of class members' particularities.

[119]The CAA's provisions dealing with the collective judgment, its effects and further steps in collective proceedings do not always refer to a final judgement, making it somewhat difficult to understand whether specific effects of the judgment take place already when it is issued or only once it becomes final. The context and the CPrA's rules that apply *mutatis mutandis* have to be taken into account in such cases.

[120]The first Slovenian collective action proceedings (see Sect. 5) showed that the claimant had difficulties in delimiting the task of the court from that of the administrator.

[121]The deadline for that must be set between 90 days and 6 months.

Tariff (Tariff No. 16).[122] In the event of a settlement, however, the parties have the autonomy to determine any person or body to act as administrator of collective damages,[123] aggregate/estimated damages must, however, be paid to a fiduciary account of a notary (Art. 13 CAA).

4.9 Costs and Funding

The CAA lays down specific rules on the costs of collective proceedings and third-party funding that derogate or supplement the general regime on the costs of the proceedings.

First, it must be stressed that class members do not have to participate in collective proceedings and do not have to cover any of the costs of the parties in these proceedings irrespective of the outcome of the case. If they nevertheless decide to participate in the proceedings, they must bear their own costs sustained in the proceedings (Art. 37 CAA).

Specific regulation determines the amount in dispute in compensatory collective actions to 20% of the aggregate/estimated monetary value of all claims[124] and thus lowers the costs of collective proceedings and renders collective redress in Slovenia more accessible. In the case of injunctions, the amount may not exceed €10,000 irrespective of the actual value of the dispute (Art. 58/2, 3 CAA).

The CAA states expressly that "the loser pays principle" applies.[125] This is also a general principle of Slovenian civil procedure, as well as of the 2013 Recommendation.[126] The CAA adds that also the indispensable costs incurred by the claimant party before the filing of the collective action for the purposes of organizing and informing class members on the intent to file the action fall within the category of recoverable costs. The CAA gives the court discretion to order the claimant to lodge security for costs as a prerequisite for certification of a collective action (Art. 29/4 CAA).

Contingency fees are generally allowed in Slovenia, which is why the CAA does not adhere fully to the 2013 Recommendation which is not benevolent towards

[122] See Sect. 3.

[123] Art. 22 CAA. The CAA is silent on how and how much such person or body is to be paid for the service (unless he or she is a notary).

[124] Art. 58/1 CAA. See how this rule was applied in the first Slovenian collective action (see Sect. 5) where the requested damages amounted to €500,000, and the amount in dispute was thus set to €100,000.

[125] Art. 60 CAA. See how this rule was applied in the first Slovenian collective action (see Sect. 5) where the claimant who was unsuccessful already in the certification stage had to pay the defendant the costs in the amount of €1,703.65.

[126] See Rec. 13 of the Recommendation.

contingency fees.[127] According to the Slovenian Attorneys Act,[128] contingency fees may be set up to 15% of the awarded amount (Art. 17/3,4 of the Attorneys Act), whereas according to the specific regulation of the CAA (Art. 61/1,2,3), in collective actions contingency fees may be set up to 30% of the awarded amount if the attorney takes on the risk, not only to work for free if the action fails, but also to cover all costs in that case. This unique provision has been characterized as a "*sui generis* attorney third party funding", as it very much resembles third-party funding *stricto sensu*.[129] There is a safeguard in place in cases where the opt-out system applies: the awarded amount in the formula for calculating contingency fees in this case is the actual amount claimed by the members (and not the total aggregate/estimated amount) that, however, cannot be lower than 30% of the attorney's fee calculated on the basis of the total awarded amount.[130] The aim of this provision is obviously to prevent an attorney from collecting an unreasonable amount in contingency fees in an opt-out, low-claim scenario. The amount to which the attorney is entitled irrespective of the number of class members who have actually claimed the awarded compensation must be paid to the attorney immediately, and the remaining balance (if any) after the expiration of a minimum 90-day deadline for claiming the awarded compensation by the remaining class members. It was foreseen that this contingency fee regime would represent a realistic stimulus for attorneys to take the risk of financing certain collective claims. If the agreed contingency fees of a successful claimant's attorney are not covered by the amount to be paid for attorneys' fees by the defendant, the fees are paid from the awarded damages, thus lowering the class members' amounts (Art. 61/4 CAA). Balancing the goal of guaranteeing access to justice, on the one hand, and full compensation, on the other, the legislator gave preference to the first and created a sort of "statutory waterfall" giving priority to the attorneys' financial interests (which, admittedly, enabled in the first place compensation to the victims), over the interests of the class members to receive full compensation.[131] The CAA requires court scrutiny in the certification stage as to the reasonableness of a contingency fee arrangement with the attorney (Art. 28/4 CAA). It also requires that the court's notification to the class members that it has certified the collective action includes information on any contingency fee arrangements between the claimant and the attorney (Art. 32/1 CAA).

---

[127]See recs. 29 and 30 of the Recommendation: "The Member States should ensure that the attorneys' remuneration and the method by which it is calculated do not create any incentive to litigation that is unnecessary from the point of view of the interest of any of the parties. … The Member States should not permit contingency fees which risk creating such an incentive. The Member States that exceptionally allow for contingency fees should provide for appropriate national regulation of those fees in collective redress cases, taking into account in particular the right to full compensation of the members of the claimant party."

[128]*Zakon o odvetništvu* (ZOdv), Official Gazette of RS, No. 18/93, with further amendments.

[129]U.S. Chamber Institute for Legal Reform (2019), p. 73.

[130]Ibid.

[131]Ibid.

Slovenian general rules of civil procedure do not regulate genuine third-party funding. It is, though, expressly admissible under the CAA. Slovenia is to date the only EU Member State that has adopted specific statutory regulation of third party litigation funding (TPLF) in collective actions. It did so by implementing the majority of the provisions on TPLF as set out in the 2013 Recommendation as well as its safeguards in pursuit of sound administration of justice. To date, only two Member States have specific regulation of TPLF in place, Slovenia in its 2017 CAA and the Netherlands in the 2019 Claimcode—a soft-law instrument.[132] The CAA requires upfront disclosure to the court of the source of (third-party) funding to be used for bringing a collective action.[133] The CAA attempts to address conflicts of interest by: (i) empowering the court to refuse certification of a collective action if a conflict of interest exists between the funder and the claimant and the members of the collective (Art. 59/2 CAA); (ii) explicitly prohibiting the funder from financing a collective action against a funder's competitor or a defendant on whom the funder is dependent (Art. 59/3 CAA); and (iii) forbidding the funder to exert "decisive" control over the proceedings or the settlement.[134] The CAA mandates the financial capability of the funder to meet its financial obligations under the funding agreement towards the funded party (Art. 59/2 CAA). It requires that the claimant be financially capable of meeting a potential adverse cost order should the action fail (Art. 59/2 CAA). The CAA caps the funder's maximum return (or "interest", in the wording of the CAA) at the statutory interest rate in Slovenia.[135] Compared to the attorney contingency fees arrangements that enable attorneys to gain significantly by assuming very moderate cost-risks, such third party litigation funding seems financially non-viable.[136]

[132] For further details, see ibid., 72–74.

[133] Arts. 26/1 and 59/1 CAA. What exactly should be disclosed apart from the identity of the funder is not clear nor whether the litigation funding agreement must be produced. Also questionable is whether the disclosure obligation could be interpreted beyond the limits of *ex parte* and *in camera* principles, since the CAA requires the funded party to make the disclosure to the court and does not mention other parties. U.S. Chamber Institute for Legal Reform (2019) p. 72.

[134] U.S. Chamber Institute for Legal Reform (2019), p. 71 ff.

[135] Art. 59/3 CAA. This provision obviously stems from the prohibitive language of the 2013 Commission Recommendation, para 32. Since the CAA uses the word "interest" and omits the word "remuneration", it is unclear whether the Slovenian legislature has inadvertently structured TPLF as a loan (i.e. recourse debt instrument). The CAA has thus not copied fully rec. 32 of the 2013 Recommendation requiring the Member States to ensure that, in addition to the general principles of funding, for cases of private third-party funding of compensatory collective redress, it is prohibited to base remuneration given to or interest charged by the fund provider on the amount of the settlement reached or the compensation awarded unless that funding arrangement is regulated by a public authority to ensure the interests of the parties. U.S. Chamber Institute for Legal Reform (2019), p. 71 ff.

[136] U.S. Chamber Institute for Legal Reform (2019), p. 71 ff.

4.10 Collective Settlement

Following mainly the Dutch model,[137] the CAA foresees a special procedure of court assessment and approval of collective settlement (*kolektivna poravnava*) concluded by a representative claimant and a defendant and submitted jointly to the court for assessment and approval.[138] The stages are similar to those in cases of collective compensatory actions with the exception of the taking of a decision on the merits of the dispute. The assessment of the formalities of the settlement[139] is followed by the assessment of the substance of the settlement after holding a court hearing.[140] Within this assessment, the court checks: whether the person entering a settlement represents the interests of the class members; whether the amount of the damages to be paid is reasonable taking into account the actual sustained harm, and whether the repayment would be performed in a fast and simple manner; what the causes and liability are for the damage, while taking into account the fact that the settlement is concluded with mutual indulgence and in the circumstances of uncertainty, as well as the cost of litigation that would otherwise be incurred; whether the time limit within which individual claims have to be made is not manifestly unreasonable; whether the costs to be paid to the other party do not exceed the real costs incurred by that party; whether there is sufficient guarantee that the agreed amount will suffice to compensate all the injured parties; whether the agreement contains an independent and appropriate mechanism for determining the eligibility of claims by the members under the agreement, including an independent out-of-court dispute settlement mechanism; and whether the interests of the persons on whose account the agreement was concluded are sufficiently secured. If these prerequisites are not met, the court must dismiss the settlement (Art. 17 CAA).[141] Before doing so, the court may give the parties the opportunity to correct or amend the settlement, advising them and assisting them where necessary. If the court approves the settlement,[142] it sets out the rules for opting in or opting out (Art. 18 CAA). Listing of class members and distribution of the settled amounts by the person nominated in the settlement follows (Art. 19 CAA).

A collective settlement binds, if concluded under the opt-out system, all injured parties, except those who opted out from the effects of the settlement, and those who

[137]Wet Collectieve Afwikkeling Massaschade – WCAM 2005, see https://www.collectiveredress.org/collective-redress/reports/thenetherlands/legislation. The Belgian and British models were also analyzed. See Galič and Vlahek (2018), p. 37.

[138]See Arts. 12 to 25 CAA.

[139]The court may even offer the parties its assistance in redrafting their settlement if the court deems the wording of the settlement inappropriate and does not find the settlement evidently inadmissible. To this end, the court may conduct a hearing. See Arts. 13 and 14 CAA.

[140]To this end, the court has to inform the class members according to Art. 15 CAA.

[141]The decision dismissing the settlement may be appealed jointly by the parties. Art. 24 CAA.

[142]The decision approving the settlement may not be appealed but can be set aside according to the rules on court settlement.

are not domiciled or established in the Republic of Slovenia and have not opted in. If the settlement is concluded under the opt-in system, all of the injured parties who have opted in share in the effects of the settlement.[143] The CAA stresses that the conclusion of a collective settlement and its approval shall not constitute recognition of the unlawfulness of the conduct and liability of the person who undertakes to pay compensation under the settlement (Art. 20/3 CAA). Unless the settlement states otherwise, the parties must cover the costs in equal sums (Art. 25 CAA).

Conclusion of a conditional collective settlement is not permissible (Art. 21/1 CAA). The settlement may, however, stipulate that the claimant may withdraw from the collective settlement if the aggregate compensation has not been paid as agreed (Art. 21/2 CAA). The settlement may also stipulate that any party may cancel the settlement within a set period (which must not exceed 30 days) from the expiration of the period for opting in or opting out if more than a certain number of class members opt out or less than a certain number of group members opt in (Art. 21/3 CAA). A collective settlement may specify that payment of compensation under the settlement can no longer be claimed if more than 1 year has elapsed since the injured party learned of the right to claim the payment (Art. 21/4 CAA).

If it turns out that aggregate damages will not suffice for repayment of all the injured parties, the amounts paid to them shall be reduced pro rata unless the collective settlement provides for a different mechanism which the court deems to adequately protect the rights of the injured parties (Art. 23/2 CAA). The part of the damages which is not paid to the individual injured parties within the period agreed in the collective settlement shall be returned to the debtor (Art. 23/3 CAA). Injured persons who prove that they were unable to claim the payment within the set deadline may request from the debtor the payment from the funds that are to be, or have been, returned to the debtor (Art. 23/4 CAA).

In line with the principle of peaceful settlement of disputes, the CAA allows for the conclusion and approval of a collective settlement during the pending proceedings initiated by filing a collective action (Art. 36 CAA). The court may also direct the parties to a mediation in accordance with the Act on Alternative Dispute Resolution in Judicial Matters.[144]

---

[143]Notwithstanding this rule, a person who, at the time of the approval of the collective settlement, did not know and could not have known that the damage had occurred to him or her, may—after learning that the damage had occurred—be excluded from the collective settlement which was concluded under the opt-out system. A person who has undertaken to pay compensation under the settlement may give such injured party a period of at least six months within which to make a decision on whether he or she wishes to remain in the class or not. Art. 20/1, 2 CAA.

[144]*Zakon o alternativnem reševanju sporov (ZARSS)*, Official Gazette of RS, No. 97/09, with further amendments.

4.11 Collective Injunctive Actions

In case of injunctive actions (requiring cease and desist measures), the CAA requires a pre-judicial phase to be initiated by the potential future claimant. The representative person wishing to file a collective injunctive action (*kolektivna opustitvena tožba*) must first submit a written warning to the alleged infringer revealing its intention to sue the infringer unless he or she ceases with the infringement. After the addressee has received the warning, the claimant must wait 15 days before filing the action. Temporary injunctive measures may, however, always be requested for already performed activities, and also for planned activities.

If the claimant is successful with the injunctive action, the court determines the infringement, requires the defendant to cease with the infringement and forbids any such future activity. The court may also decide that the judgment or correction of inappropriate advertising must be published at the expense of the defendant if it deems this necessary to mitigate or eliminate the harmful effects of the infringement. In doing so, the court decides to what extent the *obiter dictum* of the judgment is to be published.

For cases of infringements of consumer interests, the CAA additionally states that judgments prohibiting the use of general terms and conditions or pre-drafted contractual provisions include also a prohibition against referring to such clauses with regard to already concluded contracts. The filing of collective consumer injunctive actions does not prevent a consumer from filing an individual action against the defendant for the protection of his or her rights. Furthermore, the CAA explicitly states that a final judgment finding infringement is binding upon other courts assessing individual consumer claims.

In cases of infringements of the Protection against Discrimination Act, the CAA provides for actions requesting the cessation, or prohibition of commencement, of discriminatory practices.

5 CAA in Action

The closer the date for the application of the CAA approached, the more the questions and fears about its application increased. Since the CAA would apply to existent mass harm cases,[145] something which had at the time become a hot topic in the media and political debate, compensatory actions and settlements were expected immediately after its start. To this end, the Ministry of Justice had organized various education activities for judges and lawyers already before the CAA's enactment.

To date, three compensatory collective actions have been filed with Slovenian courts in accordance with the CAA. No collective settlements as well as no claims

[145] See Sect. 4.2.

for collective injunctive relief are reported. In spring 2019, the Ministry of Justice called upon Slovenian attorneys to make more use of the CAA in practice.[146]

The first collective action was filed by the Ministry of Defense Union against the Republic of Slovenia on 23 July 2018 with the Labor Court in Ljubljana.[147] The claimant wanted the State to pay the ministry's employees (est. 250 victims categorized in two sub-classes) for non-payment of overtime work during shift handovers, and for lunch breaks that were not guaranteed (est. €0.5 million setting the amount in dispute at €0.01 million). The claimant stated that a formula for the calculation of individual amounts should be set by the court. After requesting the claimant to supplement and correct its action, and after carrying out a hearing on certification on 6 December 2018, the court issued the same day a decision denying certification of the action.[148] The plaintiff had to pay the defendant its costs of the proceedings in the amount of €1,703.65. The reason for denying certification was that in the opinion of the court the prerequisites laid down in Article 28/4/1, 2, 3 of the CAA had not been met, stressing in particular that in the case at hand common legal and factual issues for the whole group do not dominate over questions relating only to individual members of the group.[149] The claimant appealed the decision to the High Labor and Social Court, which on 4 July 2019 confirmed the first instance decision.[150]

The second collective action was filed on 8 April 2019 with the District Court in Ljubljana by the Institute for Seeking of Justice for Cheated Investors against multiple defendants, natural and legal persons, some of whom are domiciled in Slovenia and others abroad.[151] The institute was established in May 2018 by a number of investors and was active in media operations. According to available information, the institute claimed that more than 100 investors in the financial instruments market had lost all their savings (at least €9.3 million from 2007–2010) due to alleged fraud.[152] The case is still in the initial phase at the first instance. It should be interesting to see how the court will handle the questions of the scope of the CAA, representativeness, suitability for assessment under the CAA as well as the security for costs taking into account the number of the defendant parties and the status of the claimant party.

The third case reported in the Collective Actions Registry regards a case in which three individual lawsuits were already filed with the Local Court in Ljubljana and the

---

[146]No. 007-230/2017/4 of 16 April 2019.

[147]Pk 1/2018.

[148]See the data and documents available in the Collective Actions Registry (available in Slovene only): http://www.sodisce.si/sodni_postopki/javne_obravnave/kolektivne_tozbe/321S83201800001/.

[149]Pages 4–12 of the decision.

[150]Pdp 185/2019, available (in Slovene only) at http://sodnapraksa.si/?q=Pdp%20185/2019.&database[VDSS]=VDSS&_submit=i%C5%A1%C4%8Di&rowsPerPage=20&page=0&id=2015081111432920.

[151]I Pk 2/2019. See the data available in the Collective Actions Registry (available in Slovene only): http://www.sodisce.si/sodni_postopki/javne_obravnave/kolektivne_tozbe/321S03201900002/.

[152]See https://zavodipov.wixsite.com/zavodipov.

District Court in Ljubljana.[153] The collective action was filed by the Slovene Consumers' Association (*Zveza potrošnikov Slovenije*) against Banka Sparkasse d. d.,[154] which had allegedly breached the law on consumer credit contracts by inappropriately calculating interest.[155]

The filing of another collective compensatory action was for a certain time contemplated in 2019 with regard to infringements of passengers' rights by the Slovenian air carrier Adria Airways, which was facing financial problems.[156] As the company was already in bankruptcy proceedings, the filing of any collective action was ultimately not considered to be pragmatic.

6 The Future of Collective Redress in Slovenia

Slovenian collective redress is still in its formative phase. We are waiting to see whether its formula set out in the CAA will give proper results in practice. The first lawsuits have already been filed, and the judges and attorneys have started applying the CAA. By so doing, certain ambiguities and shortcomings of the CAA have been detected, and many new questions have arisen. The Slovenian legal environment now needs the time to detect the potential pitfalls of the new system, introduce the required improvements and enable the practice to evolve. Chaotic EU-level activities certainly do not assist us in achieving this goal. The latest piece of EU legislation, i.e. the 2018 Commission's draft directive on consumer collective actions, which lacks important definitions and an understanding of how civil procedure operates in practice, and is not based on any serious research on regulation and practice as well as the challenges faced in collective redress proceedings in and outside the EU, will sooner or later become hard law and will have to be implemented in our legal system. When that day comes, we fear that—unless the directive is properly redrafted—the infant and fragile Slovenian collective redress body of law that has just started to boost its immune system will collapse and have to be built anew. The lesson is, instead of being a Member State that is eager to arrive first at the party, it may sometimes be prudent, and worthwhile, to be fashionably late when it comes to implementing EU ideas.

[153] Pg 651/2019, P 891/2017 and P 891/2017. See http://www.sodisce.si/sodni_postopki/javne_obravnave/kolektivne_tozbe/321S03201900003.

[154] I Pk 3/2019. See http://www.sodisce.si/sodni_postopki/javne_obravnave/kolektivne_tozbe/321S03201900003/.

[155] See https://www.zps.si/index.php/osebne-finance-sp-1406526635/krediti/8157-zps-poziva-sparkasse-k-spostovanju-sklenjenih-pogodb.

[156] See, e.g., https://novice.svet24.si/clanek/novice/slovenija/5d09016c7d48e/se-obeta-skupinska-tozba-zoper-druzbo-adria-airways.

References

Betteto N (2011) Vzorčni postopek. Pravni letopis:231–241

Damjan M (2011) Množični zahtevki zaradi posegov v zdravo življenjsko okolje. Pravni letopis 243–270:406–407

Galič A (2008) Slovenia, international Encyclopaedia of laws, civil procedure, Suppl. 49. Kluwer Law International, The Hague

Galič A (2011) Skupinske tožbe na področju potrošniškega prava. Pravni letopis 215–229:402–403

Galič A, Vlahek A (2018) Zakon o kolektivnih tožbah. Pravosodni bilten 2:25–48

Juhart M (1996) Cesija, pogodbeni odstop terjatve. GV, Ljubljana

Pogorelčnik Vogrinc N (2018) Der Zivilprozess in Slowenien. Jahrbuch für Ostrecht, bd. 59, hb. 1:25–68

U.S. Chamber Institute for Legal Reform (2019) Uncharted Waters, An Analysis of Third Party Litigation Funding in European Collective Redress. Available at https://www.instituteforlegalreform.com/research/analysis-of-tplf-funding-in-the-european-collective-redress. Accessed 15 Oct 2019

Vlahek A (2016) Challenges of private enforcement of antitrust in Slovenia. In: Kovač M, Vandenberghe A-S (eds) Economic evidence in EU competition law. Intersentia, Cambridge, pp 375–428

Vlahek A (2017) Razvoj kolektivnega varstva na področju antitrusta v Združenem kraljestvu. In: Pavliha M et al (eds) Izzivi prava v življenjski resničnosti = Challenges of law in life reality: liber amicorum Marko Ilešič. Pravna fakultetav Ljubljani, Ljubljana, pp 541–554, 600–601

Vlahek A (2018) Kolektivne tožbe kot novo pravno sredstvo zoper množične kršitve pravic iz delovnopravnih razmerij. Delavci in delodajalci, 2/3/2018:495–515

Vlahek A (2020) Development of consumer collective redress in the EU: a light at the end of the tunnel? (forthcoming)

Voet S (2015a) Consumer collective redress in Belgium: class actions to the rescue? Eur Bus Org Law Rev 16:121–143

Voet S (2015b) The crux of the matter: funding and financing collective redress mechanisms. In: Hess B, Bergström M, Storskrubb E (eds) EU Civil Justice: current issues and future outlook, Swedish studies in European law. Hart, Oxford, pp 202–222

Aleš Galič Professor of civil procedure and international private law at the Faculty of Law, University of Ljubljana, Slovenia.

Ana Vlahek Associate Professor of civil and commercial law at the Faculty of Law, University of Ljubljana, Slovenia.

The Lessons of *Airfreight Cartel*: Mechanisms of Coordination of Parallel Collective Lawsuits in Several Jurisdictions?

Jorg Sladič

Abstract *Airfreight Cartel* is a regulatory case currently being litigated before the Court of Justice of the EU for infringement of Article 101 of the Treaty on the Functioning of the European Union (Consolidated Version of the Treaty on the Functioning of the European Union, OJ EU C 326, 26.10.2012, pp. 47–390.). While competition litigation in EU law is a topic of interest, the far more interesting issue from the point of view of civil litigation is the coordination of pending class actions in the United States, Canada, Australia, the Netherlands, the United Kingdom and France. The infringement of competition law in the airfreight cartel is challenged by collective redress lawsuits in these different jurisdictions (Sect. 1) (In this study, only European regulatory responses will be assessed. Decisions and rulings of Australian, Korean and US Competition Authorities will not be assessed in depth. At the regulatory level (prosecution by authorities of infringement of competition law, i.e. in Europe, Art. 101 TFEU) there are two European Commission decisions and several judgments annulling the first decision by the General Court of the EU.). This paper assesses the stakes in coordination of parallel lawsuits in collective redress from a European point of view (Sect. 2). Mechanisms of coordination of parallel lawsuits in collective redress are the cornerstone of any successful cross-border collective redress mechanism. There are several mechanisms that can be applied in coordination of collective redress (Sect. 3). These include mechanisms unknown in the EU such as the doctrine of toleration of foreign-related class actions (Sect. 4). A novel approach in coordination would be an international panel on cross-border collective redress (Sect. 5). *Forum non conveniens* and anti-suit injunction will be explored in the class action context (Sects. 6 and 7). The European answer to such mechanisms are described as the *lis pendens* and related actions doctrine (Sects. 8, 10 and 11). *Lis pendens* as a mechanism of coordination of parallel lawsuits in collective redress has already been explored in Quebec (Sect. 9). In conclusion, the possibility of agreements on prorogation of jurisdiction will be assessed within a collective redress framework (Sect. 12).

J. Sladič (✉)
European Faculty of Law, Ljubljana, Slovenia
e-mail: jorg.sladic@epf.nova-uni.si

A. Uzelac, S. Voet (eds.), *Class Actions in Europe*, Ius Gentium: Comparative Perspectives on Law and Justice 89, https://doi.org/10.1007/978-3-030-73036-9_11

1 The Complexity of the International Airfreight Cartel

The international airfreight cartel is the embodiment of the legal imbroglio of the modern "massified" and globalized economy. The cartel is described in detail in the decisions of the European Commission and the General Court of the EU.[1] In short, Air Canada, Air France-KLM, British Airways, Cargolux Airlines International, Cathay Pacific Airways, Deutsche Lufthansa, Japan Airlines, KLM, LAN Cargo, Latam Airlines Group, Lufthansa Cargo, Martinair Holland, Quantas, SAS and SAS Cargo Group, Scandinavian Airlines System Denmark-Norway-Sweden, Singapore Airlines Cargo, Singapore Airlines Limited and Swiss International Air Lines participated in a worldwide cartel to fix the level of fuel and security surcharges. This arrangement originated as a means to tackle rising fuel costs and the security surcharge that had been specially introduced to allegedly address the costs of certain security measures imposed following the terrorist attacks of 11 September 2001 and amounted to a price-fixing cartel spanning a 6-year period, from December 1999 to February 2006, in the airfreight services market covering flights from, to and within the European Economic Area. US authorities found that in addition to a fuel surcharge, a war-risk-insurance surcharge, a security surcharge, and a US customs surcharge were levied. The contacts between the airlines initially began with a view to discussing fuel surcharges. The carriers communicated with each other to ensure that worldwide air cargo carriers imposed a flat rate surcharge per kilo for all shipments. The cartel members extended their cooperation by introducing a security surcharge and refusing to pay a commission on surcharges to their clients (freight forwarders).[2]

In Europe, the international airfreight cartel met with civil litigation as seen, for example, in a 2011 torpedo action (i.e. an action for negative declaration under Art. 27 of the repealed Regulation 44/2001) in the Netherlands lodged by Air France/KLM against Deutsche Bahn, a corporation harmed by the cartel.[3] In 2015, the time was ripe for collective redress, as seen in the Netherlands where *Stichting Cartel*

---

[1]See the Summary of Commission Decision of 17 March 2017 – Relating to a proceeding under Article 101 of the Treaty on the Functioning of the European Union, Article 53 of the EEA Agreement and Article 8 of the Agreement between the European Community and the Swiss Confederation on Air Transport (Case AT.39258 – Airfreight) (notified under document C(2017) 1742) (Text with EEA relevance, OJ EU C 188, 14. 6. 2017, p. 14); Commission's decisions are available at http://ec.europa.eu/competition/elojade/isef/case_details.cfm?proc_code=1_39258; see also the General Court press release No 147/15.

[2]The aim of these contacts was to ensure that these surcharges were introduced by all of the carriers involved and that increases (or decreases) of the surcharge levels were applied in full without exception. By refusing to pay a commission, the airlines ensured that surcharges did not become subject to competition through the granting of discounts to customers. Such practices are in breach of the EU competition rules, European Commission Press Report IP/10/1487, Brussels, 9 November 2010, http://europa.eu/rapid/press-release_IP-10-1487_en.htm.

[3]Regulation (EU) No 1215/2012 of the European Parliament and of the Council of 12 December 2012 on jurisdiction and the recognition and enforcement of judgments in civil and commercial matters OJ EU L 351, 20. 12. 2012, p. 1 and Council Regulation (EC) No 44/2001 of 22 December

Compensation lodged an Austrian-style class action against the members of the cartel.[4] The pendency of the case before EU authorities (the Commission and the Court of Justice) was one of the reasons (perhaps even the main reason) why the Dutch Court of Cassation refused to rule on a request for clarification on the applicable law. It has not yet been definitively established why the Court did not make a ruling in the case as an infringement of Article 101 TFEU by the members of the cartel.[5] During the pendency of the case, it cannot be argued that the cartel was already proven. Dutch proceedings therefore interact with EU law.

In England, a group action by some 64,000 Chinese companies was dismissed in 2014, at the first instance, and then in 2015 at the appellate instance on a question of procedure.[6]

However, there were also class actions in Canada, Australia and the United States with "global classes".[7] In Australia, a class action was started in 2007 and closed in 2014 when the Federal Court of Australia (a higher Australian court) approved an agreement between the applicants and the members of the cartel, for the settlement of the Australian Air Cargo class action for 38 million Australian dollars. Class proceedings in the United States were commenced in November 2006, and a class action

---

2000 on jurisdiction and the recognition and enforcement of judgments in civil and commercial matters, OJ EC L 12, 16. 1. 2001, p. 1.

[4]In Austria, collective redress vehicles were developed autonomously (class action Austrian-style) by assignment of claims for collection by a special purpose vehicle that happens at the same time to also be a qualified entity under implementing measures of Directive 2009/22/EC. Collection of claims assigned to an agent has a long tradition in Austria, where the first cases of such litigation by private agents as a special purpose vehicle for collection of assigned claims were reported in 1926 (Klauser 2005, p. 744 with reference to the Austrian Supreme Court [Oberster Gerichtshof] case 3 Ob 479/26, ECLI:AT:OGH0002:1926:RS0037628). The assignment of claims for their enforcement in Austrian law is not conditioned by the fact that the assignee must be the entity qualified to bring a representative action for injunction. As a consequence, one can speak of a semi-private (in cases of assignment to a qualified entity) and of an entirely private and autonomous (in cases of Rechtsverfolgungsgesellschaft) collective redress. The quality to initiate such an action for collection of assigned claims does not lie in § 29(1) KschG, i.e. the national provision on qualified entities implementing Art. 3 of Directive 2009/22/EC. It lies rather in autonomous transactions made vis the special purpose vehicle. The same model as in Austria seems to be applied also in the Netherlands and Slovenia (Tzankova and Kortmann 2010, p. 119). Dutch law was modified in 2019 by a new law on collective redress.

[5]Dutch Supreme Court [Hoge Raad], case ECLI:NL:HR:2018:345, decision No 18/00298 of 16 March 2018, available at https://www.rechtspraak.nl/.

[6]Bao Xiang International Garment Centre & Ors v. British Airways Plc [2015] EWC 3071 (Ch) (27 October 2015).

[7]A global class (also transnational class) is a class in US class action composed of absent class members who are US residents and non-residents. A global class "encompasses a sizeable proportion of non-citizens" of the US (Clopton 2015, p. 1388, Oquendo 2017, p. 72). It could be contended that due to comity reasons global class actions are to be dismissed in common law jurisdictions on *forum non conveniens* grounds. In civil law jurisdictions such classes should operate under the opt-in system. Such class actions can "be filed in courts of more than one country" (see e.g. a recent Canadian decision Leon v Volkswagen AG, 2018 ONSC 4265 (CanLII), http://canlii.ca/t/htjgm. Accessed 16 Oct 2018).

was certified on behalf of persons who purchased airfreight shipping services for shipments directly from or to the country. In other words, a global class was certified, including domestic and foreign purchasers of airfreight services. The US *forum* declared it had jurisdiction for adjudicating the claims for inbound and outbound shipments, but dismissed claims for shipments to, from or within the European Union (excluding from or to the USA), because they were based on alleged violations of European law. The US *forum* declined to exercise jurisdiction over the claims brought under European law on the grounds of *forum non conveniens* and international comity. However, it assumed jurisdiction for claims brought under US law that involved shipments between the European Union and the United States. The US *forum* specifically considered whether plaintiffs who were non-resident in the United States had standing under the applicable US law and concluded that this was the case.[8]

In Canada, a class action against Lufthansa and Swiss International Airlines was settled in 2008 for a "global class". Class actions were lodged in courts in Ontario, Quebec and British Columbia. Class actions achieved settlements without any admission of liability by the defendants also for foreign absent class members who purchased airfreight services on shipments to/from Canada (excluding to/from the United States). Class action settlements for global classes were approved for several Canadian provinces.[9] In the Canadian branch of the case:

> [P]rior to the US certification motion, the defendants in the American proceeding brought a motion to dismiss the claims of the representative plaintiffs on a number of grounds. In an order resulting from that motion, the US court maintained the claims for inbound and outbound shipments, but dismissed claims for shipments to, from, or within the European Union (excluding from or to the United States), because they were based on alleged violations of European law. The US *forum* declined to exercise jurisdiction over the claims brought under European law on the grounds of *forum non conveniens* and international comity. However, it assumed jurisdiction of claims brought under US law that involved shipments between the European Union and the United States.[10]

In Australia, Canada and the United States the defendants pleaded lack of jurisdiction. The US *forum* then rejected the defendants' argument that charging fixed prices for airfreight services occurred outside the United States.

In conclusion, it appears that several courts in several jurisdictions can adjudicate collective redress actions with global classes. Canadian decisions dealing with (international) jurisdiction in class actions explain, on the one hand, that "it is difficult to reconcile class actions that include unidentified claimants with traditional approaches to jurisdiction"[11] and, on the other hand, that "a class action format is not a procedural structure that entitles a court to entertain the litigation of matters not

---

[8] Airia Brands Inc. v. Air Canada, 2017 ONCA 792, § 17, available at https://www.canlii.org/en/; see also the American case In re Air Cargo Shipping Services Antitrust Litigation, MDL No. 06-1775, 2008 WL 5958061 (E.D.N.Y. Sept. 26, 2008).

[9] http://www.aircargosettlement2.com/courtCa.

[10] Airia Brands Inc. v. Air Canada, 2017 ONCA 79, § 17.

[11] Airia Brands Inc. v. Air Canada, 2017 ONCA 792, § 69.

within the jurisdiction or competence of the certifying court".[12] "To allow for jurisdiction, either the members must be identified and present or consent to jurisdiction or there must be another doctrinal mechanism available to anchor jurisdiction."[13] However, an error would be made by "simply anchoring [the] jurisdiction analysis in a negation of the traditional bases for jurisdiction".[14] Special procedural characteristics of collective redress (representativeness) do not mean that traditional rules on allocation and coordination of international jurisdiction have been discarded.

2 Stakes in Coordination of Parallel Collective Lawsuits

From a European point of view, in practice there are only two stakes in coordination of allocation of international jurisdiction in collective redress. The first is: Can European claimants initiate legal action (individual or collective) before a European *forum* while there is a pending US class action litigation with a certified international class including the same non-resident European absent class members? The second stake from the point of view of coordination of lawsuits is: Can the European defendant successfully bar European absent class members from being included in a pending US class action as absent class members of an international class?

In Europe, the international coordination of pending collective lawsuits seems to operate under opt-in mechanisms explicitly providing that non-residents are required to opt-in in a pending lawsuit.[15]

It is clear that European non-resident absent class members can plead the defects in international jurisdiction of a US *forum* deemed contrary to *ordre public* of the European *forum* where *exequatur* is requested.[16] Spanish legislation on recognition of foreign judicial decisions in collective redress (Art. 47(2) of *Ley 29/2015, de 30 de julio, de cooperación jurídica internacional en materia civil*[17]) even contains a special provision barring the *exequatur* of foreign judicial decisions in collective redress given where international jurisdiction is based on criteria not foreseen in Spanish legislation (i.e. mirror image assessment of indirect jurisdiction).[18] In the

[12]Walter v. Western Hockey League, 2018 ABCA 188 (CanLII), http://canlii.ca/t/hs196, § 8.

[13]Airia Brands Inc. v. Air Canada, 2017 ONCA 792, § 69.

[14]Airia Brands Inc. v. Air Canada, 2017 ONCA 792, § 103.

[15]See for Canada e.g. Piché and Saumier (2019), p. 255, and for Belgium and Slovenia, Sladič (2017b), pp. 145 and 146 with reference to Art. XVII.38(1, 2) of Belgian Code of Economic Law and Art. 30(3) of Slovenian Law on Collective Actions.

[16]In such a case the class action is not a superior device to individual actions.

[17]BOE-A-2015-8564, https://www.boe.es/eli/es/l/2015/07/30/29.

[18]In collective redresss ... *la resolución extranjera no se reconocerá cuando la competencia del órgano jurisdiccional de origen no se hubiera basado en un foro equivalente a los previstos en la legislación española.*

following analysis, a number of open questions on international class or group will be assessed (Sect. 2.1) and then put in the jurisdictional framework (Sect. 2.2).

2.1 International Class or Group as the Main Issue in Coordination of Parallel Collective Lawsuits

According to US law, where a non-resident can join an international class, a US *forum* also has international adjudicatory jurisdiction over non-resident absent class members in a manner that is not known in other countries. However, a decision given in the United States or Canada including European absent class members for example on assessment (especially in Canada) of a real and substantial connecting factor might not be recognized in European states applying the assessment of mirror image in indirect jurisdiction. On the other hand, the question seems to be also whether there is a *res iudicata* effect (preclusion) of a US class action judgment for foreign class members in their jurisdiction of origin (Johnson 2012, pp. 970 and 971).[19]

The US Federal Rule of Civil Procedure 23 "is silent on the inclusion of foreign plaintiffs in US classes" and "on its geographical scope", "thus leaving courts with little direction on whether or, under what circumstances, to include foreign claimants in a US class action" (Monestier 2011, 5 and 8).[20] "Given a favourable territorial reach of substantive law and an otherwise proper class action, the proposed class might include, in addition to American plaintiffs, some foreigners who dealt with the foreign defendant outside the United States" (Clermont 2015, p. 69).

The "question is whether there is also [international] jurisdiction over absent class members or potential plaintiffs" (Halfmeier 2012, p. 177). If the idea of an absent class member benefiting from the protection of legal order of the domicile or residence against proceedings abroad is to be taken as the underlining guidance in assessing the international jurisdiction over absent class members, then international jurisdiction over absent class members is indeed neither easy to understand nor easy to endorse. Traditionally "there is no such thing as a court lacking personal jurisdiction over a plaintiff" (Andrews 2013, p. 331).

[19]The question of *exequatur* of a US class action from one State in another US State according to the case Ansari v. New York University "is usually not an issue when the class members are United States citizens, as courts in this country recognize the preclusive effect of a fairly noticed class action suit".

[20]Admittedly, in 1966 when Rule 23 was drafted no one could foresee "international" classes in US class actions. US *fora* are nevertheless quite often confronted with class actions comprising class members from several other states or jurisdictions. The Texas Supreme Court had to deal in *Citizens Ins. Co. of America v. Daccach* with a class action "brought by residents of 35 foreign countries who bought securities from defendant, a corporation that had its principal place of business in Texas" (Symeonides 2008, p. 38).

In order to give a decision on the merits in a global class action, a *forum* must also have jurisdiction over all of the international members of the group or class (Glenn 1999, p. 35). It would appear that as far as US law is concerned, a US "court can bind absent class members without having jurisdiction over them" (Winters 1985, p. 182). The international adjudicatory jurisdiction by a US *forum* hearing a class action could be based on the finding that where a US *forum* has jurisdiction in a class action over a resident absent class member, it also has jurisdiction over a non-resident absent class member. Non-resident absent class members are treated as though they were resident absent class members due to commonality of factual and legal issues in a class action applicable to both types of absent class members. Canadian legal writers explain that in Canadian common law "commonality itself [as the main characteristics of class actions] supplies the real and substantial connection sufficient to assert jurisdiction over non-resident class members" (Monestier 2010, p. 538). It is also said that common issues are "to be considered as a presumptive connecting factor in the real and substantial connection test" (Monestier 2010, p. 538). As such, in Canada "The real and substantial connection test has been a dominant, although not exclusive, test governing the issue of jurisdiction" (Monestier 2010, p. 538). Indeed, "commonality itself supplies the real and substantial connection sufficient to assert jurisdiction over non-resident class members" (Monestier 2010, p. 538). However, relying on the sufficient commonality as the real and substantial connection blurs the limits between the merits and the jurisdiction. Jurisdiction depends on the commonality, which itself depends on an early assessment of the merits (Monestier 2010, p. 550).[21] In comparative law of collective redress, Canadian case law, for example, confirmed, in 2015 and 2017, the commonality criterion as the real and substantial connecting factor in a class action with international class in the airfreight cartel.[22]

2.2 *Jurisdictional Stake in Coordination of Parallel Collective Redress*

A study prepared for the European Parliament put the problems in cross-border lawsuits very succinctly:

> The lack of common system of dispute resolution at the transnational level results in uncertainty, furthers the costs of exchanges, and may even deter economic actors from entering into cross-border exchanges (de Miguel Asensio et al. 2018, p. 6).

---

[21]In other words, the commonality is both the connecting factor in allocating the jurisdiction to adjudicate and the criterion for certification.

[22]*Airia Brands v. Air Canada,* 2015 ONSC 5332 and *Airia Brands Inc. v. Air Canada*, 2017 ONCA 79; see the summary at https://gavclaw.com/2018/01/09/airia-brands-inc-v-air-canada-jurisdiction-and-certification-of-global-classes/.

In assessing collective redress in European competition law, it has been observed that "failure to consolidate an action concerning all victims of the anticompetitive conduct may result in the risk of parallel proceedings. This creates the risk of irreconcilable judgements" (Telfer 2017, p. 70). Parallel proceedings occur when the same parties bring the same or closely related complaint simultaneously before multiple *fora* (Erk-Kubat 2014, p. 17). If this finding is applied *a maiore ad minus* also to collective redress, the logical conclusion is that parallel collective redress refers to at least two collective redress lawsuits pending against the same defendant in at least two different jurisdictions for redressing the same wrongs (George 2002, pp. 500 and 501). In this study, the term "parallel proceedings" refers to proceedings involving the same cause of action and between the same parties brought in the courts of different states.

Collective redress is said to be a technique of regulation through litigation, or, in other words, the state of the *forum* where a collective redress lawsuit is pending has a vested interest in the outcome of such a lawsuit. The *forum* where a collective lawsuit with an international class or group of absent class members is pending will therefore export the *forum's* considerations of what correct regulation should be. However, the existing framework of coordination of individual cross-border lawsuits will also have to be used in international collective redress. Traditionally, the rule *actor sequitur forum rei* applied in civil law Europe gives an advantage to the defendant, for in cross-border lawsuits he will have the advantage of the "home ground", i.e. the language, *usus fori* and knowledge of procedural law of the *forum*. As a consequence, any lack of coordination of pending parallel cross-border collective redress will be used and perhaps even abused by the representatives of the group or class.[23]

Due to the territorial nature of international civil procedure, problems in allocation of international jurisdiction between *fora* of several states will continue to exist (Franzina 2014a, p. 71). The nature of collective redress is related to a multitude of claims, i.e. in jurisdictional terms to the necessity of aggregation and coordination of parallel lawsuits (Hess 2010, p. 119). Due to the "massification" of damages and massive harm events, it is quite possible that there will be a class action pending in the United States and certain European members of the international class will lodge individual or even collective lawsuits against the same defendant before the European *forum* having international jurisdiction by virtue of registered or head office in the given European state (Heß 2000, p. 378). As many European laws of civil procedure provide for an action for negative declaration, there is always a possibility that the defendant may also choose his defence against a pending US class action in lodging an action for negative declaration (i.e. declaration that there is no liability or no fault) before a European *forum* against the international class or even only one plaintiff in the United States (Heß 2000, p. 378).

[23]However, the principle *abusus non tollit usum* shall be applied.

3 Overview of Mechanisms of Coordination of Parallel Cross-Border Lawsuits

In collective redress, there are several techniques of dealing with parallel proceedings that will also have to be applied in international litigation. Techniques of do-nothing, transfer and consolidation, stays, dismissals and anti-suit injunctions are enumerated in US legal writing (George 2002, pp. 502–506, 1999, pp. 777–782). However, such an enumeration does not cover the EU or civil law approach. Transfers and consolidations are fully known in internal (collective) litigation in EU Member States with no *extra muros* effects. Stay is known in *lis pendens* doctrine under the Brussels Ia Regulation. Assessing stay of proceedings as being a separate remedy in international lawsuits outside the *lis pendens* doctrine makes no sense to civil law lawyers. The consequence of *lis pendens* in cross-border lawsuits is namely the stay of proceedings of the later (second or younger) lawsuit. Instead of the US division of tools to coordinate parallel, simultaneous, concurrent and even related actions in collective redress, another division is proposed, namely the do-nothing remedy (toleration), the *forum non conveniens* doctrine, anti-suit injunctions, *lis pendens* and related actions doctrine and the agreements on prorogation. It will, however, be said that agreements on prorogation in consumer-oriented collective redress face an *ex ante* bar in recognition in substantive EU consumer protection law.[24]

The first option is letting parallel, simultaneous or concurrent national and foreign pending proceedings involving the same cause of action and the same parties exist and continue (the do-nothing approach) which seems to be the US approach in cross-border collective redress (George 2002, p. 502 and 503). The opposite approach is the pure and simple interdiction of any parallel proceedings abroad via an anti-suit injunction. This is a technique that seems to be much cherished in common law jurisdictions. However, such a technique suffers from the inconvenience of territoriality, i.e. the limits imposed on such an injunction by international law. It is also not likely that a foreign *forum* will accept an anti-suit injunction under the international *ordre public* assessment in any case (see the development on anti-anti-suit injunctions in European jurisdictions).

Another option is the application of the *lis pendens* rule based on the chronological principle of priority, or to be more exact, seniority based on the tradition of Roman law (*prior tempore, potior iure*) (Egea 2014, p. 148). Such a rule is sometimes described by common law lawyers as a first-to-file rule. Closely connected to *lis pendens* is the doctrine of related actions combined with consolidation of similar proceedings. Yet another option of coordination appears to be prorogation by virtue of an agreement (prorogation of jurisdiction). The final option is the judicial discretion to decline jurisdiction (*forum non conveniens*) (McLachlan 2008, pp. 243–253; Wautelet 2002, pp. 56–399). Provided that there is a conclusion

[24] CJEU, Sales Sinués and Drame Ba, C-381/14 and C-385/14, ECLI:EU:C:2016:252.

of a corresponding treaty or convention, the allocation of jurisdiction in collective redress could also be solved by having recourse to the upgraded and modified international multi-district litigation process.

The doctrines of toleration, *lis pendens*, anti-suit injunctions and *forum non conveniens* are used to coordinate parallel proceedings also in collective redress. *Lis pendens* and *forum non conveniens* are assessed in the 2008 International Law Association Resolution on Transnational Group Actions, adopted in Rio de Janeiro at the 73rd conference (§§ 54 and 57) as mechanisms of coordination of parallel lawsuits in collective redress. Recent case law on the application of the *forum non conveniens* doctrine in class actions is to be found in Canada.[25] Case law on anti-suit injunctions in class actions is to be found in antipodean common law.[26]

4 Toleration of Foreign Proceedings and "Related Class Actions"

Toleration will be understood in the framework of international civil procedure as a doctrine according to which there can be several simultaneous proceedings concerning the same parties and having the same cause of action pending before *fora* of several states. Any individual proceedings are not a bar to each other proceedings. In collective redress, a branch of the doctrine of toleration of parallel cross-border class actions—not necessarily involving the same plaintiff or the same absent class members—was largely discussed and developed by practitioners in common law jurisdictions in order to facilitate the management of multi-jurisdictional class actions who even speak of informal collaboration (Clopton 2018, p. 134).

A development in cross-border US-Canadian class actions will be mentioned and highlighted. The US and Canadian IMAX case paved the way for the new development of cross-border collective redress and related class actions (Clopton 2015, p. 1421).[27] Concurrent[28] Canadian and US securities fraud class actions against the corporation IMAX for alleged misrepresentations to the secondary market in respect

[25]Kaynes v. BP P.L.C, 2016 ONCA 601 and Paniccia v. MDC Partners Inc., 2017 ONSC 7298 (CanLII), https://www.canlii.org/en/.

[26]Federal Court of Australia, Jones v. Treasury Wine Estates Limited [2016] FCAFC 59, https://www.austlii.edu.au.

[27]See In re IMAX Sec. Litig., 283 F.R.D. 178 (S.D.N.Y. 2012), In re IMAX Sec. Litig., 272 F.R.D. 138, 142 - 44 (S.D.N.Y. 2010), In re IMAX Sec. Litig., 587 F. Supp. 2D 471, 474 - 78 (S.D.N.Y. 2008), Silver v. IMAX Corp., 2013 ONSC 1667 (Can.); Silver v. IMAX Corp., (2012) 110 O.R. 3d 425 (Can. Ont. Sup. Ct. J.); Silver v. IMAX Corp., (2011) 105 O.R. 3d 212 (Can. Ont. Sup. Ct. J.); Silver v. IMAX Corp., 2009 O.J. No. 5585 (Can. Ont. Sup. Ct. J.) (QL).

[28]Overlapping class proceedings according to a Canadian *forum*, Silver v. IMAX, 2013 ONSC 1667.

of financial reporting were initiated in 2006.[29] The certification in the Canadian class action comprised "a global class and included all persons that had acquired IMAX securities on the Toronto Stock Exchange and the NASDAQ regardless of where they lived".[30] The class in the US class action "consisted of all persons that had acquired IMAX securities on the NASDAQ during the relevant class period".[31] "Motions practice, discovery, and settlement negotiations proceeded in parallel until parties to the U.S.-side of the litigation reached a settlement" (Clopton 2015, p. 1421). The US *forum* approved the settlement with the condition that the Canadian *forum* adopt "an order amending the class definition in the related Canadian proceedings to carve out the class members who were included in the US settlement".[32] The Canadian *forum* approved the US settlement and only then did the US *forum* issue a consent decree (Clopton 2015, p. 1421).

Such an approach will be regarded both as an upgrade of traditional international legal assistance (*auxiulium iuris*) and as a development of the phenomenon of negotiations between courts in two sovereign nations (Westbrook 2003, p. 567).

The test field in toleration in cross-border collective redress is the multi-jurisdictional class action litigation between Canada and the United States. Both countries have their own approach to class actions. Canada applies a derivative of Rule 23 FRCP. However, cross-border class actions are deemed extremely complicated in both legal systems.[33] This is the case since:

> Courts in both countries have thus far been adept and adaptable in developing *ad hoc* procedures to deal with these types of issues. ... Here the settlement is global in scope crossing provincial and international boundaries and the jurisdictions in which the underlying proceedings have been commenced include two countries and several provinces. It would be useful if more formal protocols were developed to facilitate the courts and the parties in dealing with these types of cases.[34]

In 2011, the American Bar Association adopted a Protocol on Court-to-Court Communications in Canada-U.S. Cross-Border Class Actions and a Notice Protocol: Coordinating Notice(s) to the Class(es) in Multijurisdictional Class Proceedings. In 2011, the Canadian Bar Association adopted and then later in 2018, modernized

[29]The shares of the defendant IMAX had traded on both the Toronto Stock Exchange and the NASDAQ.

[30]https://www.internationallawoffice.com/Newsletters/Litigation/Canada/Dentons/Silver-v-IMAX-avoiding-war-on-two-fronts.

[31]https://www.internationallawoffice.com/Newsletters/Litigation/Canada/Dentons/Silver-v-IMAX-avoiding-war-on-two-fronts.

[32]https://www.internationallawoffice.com/Newsletters/Litigation/Canada/Dentons/Silver-v-IMAX-avoiding-war-on-two-fronts.

[33]*Frohlinger v. Nortel Networks Corporation*, 2007 CanLII 696 at §30 (Ont. S.C.J.), see also "Cross-border class actions raise due process and litigation preclusion issues of significance to United States counsel seeking to either implement multi-jurisdictional settlements or to select the most favourable venue for trial." http://blg.com/en/News-And-Publications/Documents/publication_1932.pdf, p.1.

[34]*Frohlinger v. Nortel Networks Corporation*, 2007 CanLII 696 at §30 (Ont. S.C.J.).

similar Canadian Class Actions Judicial Protocols. All of these protocols also deal in the coordination of tolerated, concurrently pending "related class actions" in the United States and Canada. Such protocols appear to be a modern development in "contractual" international legal assistance (Segovia González 2018, p. 315). "The Protocols set out "best practices" to assist in litigation of cross-border cases involving United States federal courts and Canadian courts."[35] It has been noted that, "However, adoption of this protocol by any court remains the decision of that court, absent legislative or regulatory direction."[36] In addition, "The Protocols are not intended to (and do not) interfere with or limit any court's authority or discretion, or supersede rules of procedure or other governing law, or adversely affect any rights of any parties or class members."[37]

The negotiations and coordination by virtue of the said protocols between two courts in two states are based on the idea of managerial judges in collective redress requiring information exchange. The essence of both protocols is contained in the class action management conferences. As noted by a Canadian *forum* in the event of a parallel US-Canadian class action, "It would seem ... that the various class proceedings would benefit from cooperation and coordination—using the three Cs of the Commercial List (communication, cooperation and common sense). Otherwise, they will be faced with the practical problem of fighting amongst themselves as to a turf war and running the risk of being divided and thereof susceptible to being conquered."[38]

Such applications of the doctrine of toleration are unknown in Europe and are rather an unexplored research field on the other side of the Atlantic.

5 Coordination by a Special Panel Allocating (International) Jurisdiction

In the United States, civil actions pending before different federal *fora* involving one or more common questions of fact can be transferred to any federal *forum* of first instance for coordinated or consolidated pretrial proceedings (George 1999, p. 815; Nagareda et al. 2013, p. 404). Therefore, "In practical terms, much of the action surrounding the MDL panel concern the selection of the district court in which a given body of related litigation is to be concerned" (Nagareda et al. 2013, p. 405).

[35]Report on Protocol on Court-to-Court Communications in Canada-U.S. Cross-Border Class Actions and a Notice Protocol: Coordinating Notice(s) to the Class(es) in Multijurisdictional Class Proceedings, p. 1.

[36]Resolution 18-03-A - Annex 1, Canadian Judicial Protocol for the Management of Multi Jurisdictional Class Actions and the Provision of Class Action Notice.

[37]Report on Protocol on Court-to-Court Communications in Canada-U.S. Cross-Border Class Actions and a Notice Protocol: Coordinating Notice(s) to the Class(es) in Multijurisdictional Class Proceedings, p. 1.

[38]Grace Canada Inc. (Re) (2005), 17 C.B.R. (5 th) 275 (Ont. Sup. Ct.).

The aim of such a referral is the promotion of just and efficient conduct of such actions. Such coordinated or consolidated pretrial proceedings will be conducted by a judge or judges to whom such actions are assigned by the judicial panel on multidistrict litigation. Proceedings for the transfer of an action may be initiated by the judicial panel on multidistrict litigation of its own initiative or following a motion filed with the panel by a party in any action in which transfer for coordinated or consolidated pretrial proceedings may be appropriate.[39] The MDL litigation has taken extreme proportions in the US massified economy and one US legal writer reported that Apple, Google, Facebook and corporate leviathans alike are heavily involved in massive class actions and face MDL litigation (Dodge 2014, p. 331).

In the United States, the Judicial Panel on Multidistrict Litigation is a chamber composed of seven judges having jurisdiction to aggregate civil actions pending in federal district courts into a single, transferee district court for coordinated or consolidated pretrial proceedings. The purposes of this transfer also referred to as the "centralization process" are to avoid duplication of discovery, to prevent inconsistent pretrial rulings and to conserve the resources of the parties, their counsel and the judiciary. Transferred actions not terminated in the transferee district are remanded to their originating transferor districts by the Panel at or before the conclusion of centralized pretrial proceedings.[40] The crucial ruling "the Panel has to make is the selection of the judge to whom an MDL case is transferred" (Sherman 2008, p. 10). As far as the selection, i.e. the allocation of the appropriate courts, is concerned, "Formally, the law permits the MDL Panel to select any federal district court for this purpose. In practice, the Panel's choice of transferee fora appears to be strongly influenced by the location of the filed cases and the defendant's *forum* preference" (Nagareda et al. 2013, p. 405), and "it is often availability and experience that leads to the transfer to a particular judge" (Sherman 2008, p. 10).

A very interesting proposal on international coordination is the setting-up or instituting of an international version of the judicial panel for international MDL. However, the US Judicial Panel on Multidistrict Litigation operates within one nation alone. From an international point of view, it is a US *forum* much the same way as the US Supreme Court is. It is a judicial authority of the United States. On the international level, this finding means that such a coordination of litigation is feasible only where a corresponding treaty or convention is adopted and incorporated in the national laws of contracting states.[41] It is the contention of this section that there is no such treaty and that the nearest equivalent of such a coordination is found in the European Brussels Ia regime. It is also contended that continental Europe will not accept any other solution than a foreseeable and perhaps strict and clear allocation of international jurisdiction. For a civil law-trained lawyer, on the other hand, multidistrict litigation operates on the basis of the assessment of the class action

---

[39] 28 U.S. Code § 1407 – Multidistrict litigation.

[40] http://www.jpml.uscourts.gov/overview-panel-0.

[41] See e.g. on failure of setting up a Canadian body coordinating multi-jurisdictional class procedure in Chabrny (2019), p. 137 and 138.

on the *forum non conveniens* doctrine and not on clear and foreseeable criteria. Consideration of equity and even perhaps efficiency found in the *forum non conveniens* doctrine are deemed offensive to the continental doctrine of the natural judge (*le juge naturel*) or legal judge (*gesetzlicher Richter*).

6 Coordination by the Doctrine of *Forum Non Conveniens*

In short, *forum non conveniens* is a common law doctrine originating in Scotland allowing courts to refuse "to hear cases when the ends of justice would best be served by trial in another *forum*" (Barrett 1947, p. 387).[42] In legal orders belonging to civil law legal systems some effects of the *forum non conveniens* doctrine can be achieved by application of the jurisdictional norm of *forum necessitatis* (Hess and Mantovani 2019, p. 5). However, it is too early to say whether the *forum* of necessity can be used to coordinate parallel collective lawsuits in several nations.

In the *Lernout and Hauspie* class action, US courts applied the *forum non conveniens* doctrine for the European (i.e. Belgian) share owners harmed who had bought the shares on EASDAQ (the Brussels stock exchange) (Kafi-Cherrat 2018, § 29). A Belgian *forum*—the Court of Appeal of Ghent [Hof van Beroep Gent]—recognized, by a judgment of 23 March 2017, the L&H class action approved settlement in Belgium.[43] Lernout & Hauspie Speech Products, N.V. was a Belgian IT enterprise specialized in speech recognition software. At the peak of its commercial activities, it was listed both on the NASDAQ and on the EASDAQ exchanges. L&H had its US executive offices in Massachusetts and as a consequence the international jurisdiction and venue in the US class action was vested in the US District Court for the District of Massachusetts.[44] European (i.e. Belgian) victims of

[42]On the introduction of that doctrine in English case law, see Beaumont (2018), p. 449, see on introduction of that doctrine in English case-law in Beaumont (2018), p. 449, see on two exceptions in civil law jurisdictions Goldstein (2016), pp. 51–83.

[43]The Dutch text is available at https://www.rechtbanken-tribunaux.be/sites/default/files/public/content/lh_-_geanonimiseerd.pdf.

[44]L&H went bankrupt on 25 October 2001 due to a securities fraud scheme. A Belgian criminal investigation was opened and concomitantly several class actions proceedings in the United States were lodged before US courts either by US or by Belgian prejudiced investors. The US *forum* in Massachusetts and the Belgian Court of Appeal of Ghent refer to 16 class actions. On 8 August 2000, *The Wall Street Journal* published a critical article about L&H. Based on that article a first US class action was lodged already on 9 August 2000. The first L&H class action in the USA was lodged only one day after the report of financial fraud in *The Wall Street Journal*. The Belgian criminal case with the civil private tort litigation annexed as an accessory to a criminal case appears to have started at a later time in 2001. The L&H class action ended with a negotiated settlement approved by the US *forum*. The defendants used the US-approved settlement in Belgium as a defence against the judgment to pay compensation to civil parties in Belgian criminal proceedings. As a consequence of the objection by the civil parties, the Belgian *forum* had to deal with the plea that the US class judgment approving the settlement was not binding on the civil parties in Belgian proceedings. The Court of Appeal of Ghent acknowledged the modernized legal landscape in

the wrongdoing, having bought their shares and other equity on the European EASDAQ market (i.e. European stock exchanges), could not initiate or join the class action in the United States. US class actions remained available only for shares bought on US stock exchanges. The result of the L&H class action seems to confirm the practice established already in the Dutch *Converium* case.[45] In that Dutch case, a certain number of shareholders harmed by the Swiss *Converium* had bought shares on the SWX Swiss Exchange. They were excluded from the US class action settlement approved by the US *forum* because it lacked jurisdiction over shareholders who bought shares on the SWX Swiss Exchange. *Forum non conveniens* doctrine is slowly becoming, if not an insurmountable, then at least quite an important obstacle for European lead plaintiffs and absent class members in the EU.

An interesting, newer case on the application of the *forum non conveniens* doctrine is to be found in Canadian class action case law.[46] As far as class actions are concerned, according to both cases, "the principle of comity underlies the *forum non conveniens* analysis".[47] From the point of view of a lawyer educated in the spirit of the Brussels Ia Regulation applying the *lis pendens* doctrine, there is indeed a real problem in conciliating the judicial comity doctrine with the *forum non conveniens* doctrine: "In the *forum non conveniens* analysis, juridical advantage is a problematic factor because ... assessing the merits of rival jurisdictions is inconsistent with the principles of comity."[48] Where a *forum non conveniens* is to be applied in a class action, a common law court will consider a list of discretionary factors

---

Belgium (collective redress in Book XVII of the CdE/WER) and concluded that US judicial decisions and the settlement approved by the US *forum* in the L&H class action are foreign enforceable judicial decisions within the meaning of the Belgian *lex fori* (Art. 22 of the Belgian Code of Private International Law). The plea according to which a class action settlement is solely a contract with *inter partes* effect was rejected as a judicial decision in a US class action confirms the settlement between the plaintiffs and the defendant(s). As a consequence, such a decision can be opposed to all the absent class members who did not duly opt-out (Court of Appeal of Ghent [Hof van Beroep Gent], judgment of 23 March 2017, § 66). Investors who effectively participated in the settlement are bound by it; the investors who timely opted out are not bound by the settlement. A class action judgment and settlement will be recognized *de plano* if they are not contrary to Belgian international *ordre public*. In comparing the Belgian collective redress under Book VII CdE/WER and the US class action, the Belgian *forum* concluded that US law guarantees more rights to absent class members than the Belgian legislation. The opt-out system is justified by reason of sound administration of justice. The fact that not all individual absent class members were personally informed does not vitiate the class action settlement (ibid. § 93.). The rights of the defence of the non-resident absent class members in the US class action were not violated. The salient point of the recognition refers to a certain lack of finality.

[45]Court of Appeal of Amsterdam [Gerechtshof Amsterdam], 12 November 2010, NJ 2010/683, LJN: BO3908 ECLI:NL:GHAMS:2010:BO3908.

[46]*Kaynes v. BP P.L.C*, 2016 ONCA 601 and *Paniccia v. MDC Partners Inc.*, 2017 ONSC 7298 (CanLII).

[47]*Paniccia v. MDC Partners Inc.*, 2017 ONSC 7298 (CanLII), §41 and also §42.

[48]*Paniccia v. MDC Partners Inc.*, 2017 ONSC 7298 (CanLII), §44.

> in determining the most appropriate forum for an action; including: (a) the location of the majority of the parties; (b) the location of the key witnesses and evidence; (c) contractual provisions that specify applicable law or accord jurisdiction; (d) the avoidance of multiplicity of proceedings; (e) the applicable law and its weight in comparison to the factual questions to be decided; (f) geographical factors suggesting the natural forum; (g) juridical advantage; i.e., whether declining jurisdiction would deprive the plaintiff of a legitimate juridical advantage in the domestic court; and (h) the existence of a judgement in the competing forum.[49]

In the EU, the *forum non conveniens* doctrine is deemed incompatible with European international *ordre public* and the Brussels Ia Regulation. The *forum non conveniens* doctrine is expressly deemed incompatible with the doctrine of the natural judge or legal judge according to which the court having jurisdiction to hear a case must be known in advance (*ex ante* predictability much cherished in civil law legal systems) (Picardi 2010, pp. 27–73). This fallacy of the *forum non conveniens* doctrine is sometimes also acknowledged in class actions in common law jurisdictions. As such, "If a party seeks out a jurisdiction simply to gain a juridical advantage rather than by reason of a real and substantial connection of the case to the jurisdiction, that is ordinarily condemned as *forum* shopping."[50]

The judicial rejection of the *forum non conveniens* doctrine by the Court of Justice of the EU in the case *Owusu* (C-281/02) was a surprise only for lawyers in common law legal systems.[51] It is contended that the *Owusu* case is the natural and foreseeable end of the doctrines of the natural judge or legal judge (Schack 2017, pp. 217–219; Briggs 2013, p. 101). The essence of that doctrine is a general and abstract and perhaps rigid predictability in the allocation of jurisdiction.

However, the *forum non conveniens* doctrine is applied in cross-border collective redress in common law legal orders. The Canadian case *Kaynes v. BP* refers to a Canadian securities class action against British Petroleum. An "Ontario class action, claiming damages for alleged misrepresentations made to shareholders by the respondent BP" was lodged; and, "The moving party purchased his BP securities on the New York Stock Exchange and the proposed Ontario class includes worldwide purchasers of BP securities." The Canadian *forum* first stayed proceedings against BP by virtue of a pending US class action in the District Court, Southern District of Texas. In addition, "The class in that proceeding includes the moving party and other Canadian investors who purchased BP securities on the" New York Stock Exchange. Later on, the Canadian *forum* lifted the stay and resumed the case against BP.[52] Much in the same way, in 2017 the Canadian Ontario Superior Court of Justice in the case *Yip v. HSBC Holdings plc* also applied the *forum non conveniens* doctrine in a securities class action.

---

[49] *Kaynes v. BP P.L.C*, 2016 ONCA 601, §39.

[50] *Paniccia v. MDC Partners Inc.*, 2017 ONSC 7298 (CanLII), §44.

[51] CJEU, *Owusu*, C-281/02, ECLI:EU:C:2005:120.

[52] *Kaynes v. BP P.L.C*, 2016 ONCA 601.

7 Coordination by Anti-Suit Injunctions

In short, an anti-suit injunction is a judicial decision ordering a party not to litigate before a different jurisdiction (Dowers 2013, p. 960). Anti-suit injunctions are usually an unknown legal figure in civil law jurisdictions. From a European point of view, a minority opinion states that such an injunction could be compatible with the Brussels Ia Regulation (Michaels 2006, pp. 1063 and 1064). However, as far as anti-suit injunctions in civil law legal orders are concerned, Germany appears to be an exception. German case law, since the *Reichsgericht* in the times of the Third Reich, developed an action on injunction to cease proceedings abroad (*Klage auf Unterlassung ausländischer Prozessführung*) (Schütze 2009, p. 52).[53] There is a possibility of the application of anti-suit injunctions under § 826 BGB (prohibition of causing damages by an act *contra bonos mores*) by a German defendant in a US class action (Heß 2000, p. 378.).

However, modern anti-suit injunctions are definitely a child of common law. A common law anti-suit injunction is directed to the defendant in a pending proceeding before a common law forum. Even though not directly directed at the foreign *forum*, it represents an indirect infringement of the jurisdiction of the foreign court, causing incompatibility with the international *ordre public* of the *forum* where the second case is pending (Nagel and Gottwald 2013, p. 365). The incompatibility with EU law and scope *ratione materiae* of licit anti-suit injunctions in parallel judicial proceedings was cleared by the CJEU in the cases *Turner*, *West-Tankers* and *Gazprom*.[54]

US class action litigation can encounter some anti-suit measures typical for civil procedure in common law jurisdictions. This development in common law legal systems refers to antipodean common law.[55] In 2016, the Federal Court of Australia in the case *Jones v. Treasury Wine Estates Limited* granted an anti-suit injunction addressed at group members in a class action pending in the United States where they sought to invoke the power of a US *forum* to obtain compulsory oral discovery. The case referred to a US class action pending against Treasury Wine Estates Limited before the US District Court, Southern District of New York. The Australian *forum* ordered several parties in the class action pending before a US *forum* to refrain from participating in the US proceedings.

In continental Europe, anti-suit injunctions are deemed not to be compatible with Article 6(1) ECHR, i.e. with fair trial requirements. Effective access to court is the essence of the fair trial requirement and will not pertain in the country where the second case was initiated. Continental courts usually declare such an injunction

[53]For the reason of such development (so-called Latvian divorces), see Coester-Waltjen (2017), pp. 1073 and 1074.

[54]CJEU, Turner, C-159/02, ECLI:EU:C:2004:228, Allianz, C-185/07, ECLI:EU:C:2009:69, Gazprom, C-536/13, ECLI:EU:C:2015:316.

[55]*Federal Court of Australia, Jones v. Treasury Wine Estates Limited* [2016] FCAFC 59, https://www.austlii.edu.au.

incompatible with Article 6(1) ECHR. Under the case law developed by the ECtHR, there might indeed be a latent incompatibility of anti-suit injunctions with Article 6 (1) ECHR. The Court

> reiterates that, according to its well-established case-law, Art. 6 §1 of the Convention may be relied on by individuals who consider that an interference with the exercise of one of their (civil) rights is unlawful and complain that they have not had the possibility of submitting that claim to a court meeting the requirements of Art. 6 § 1. In the words of the Court's Golder judgement, Art. 6§1 embodies the "right to a court", of which the right of access, that is the right to institute proceedings before courts in civil matters, constitutes one aspect.[56]

There is also the fully practical problem that a foreign *forum* will not easily enforce and give extra-territorial effect to an anti-suit injunction where there is no agreement on prorogation or arbitration clause. In civil law legal systems, traditionally an anti-suit injunction is viewed contrary to international law.

8 Coordination by the Rule of *Lis Pendens*

In national proceedings the *lis pendens* and its effects are clear. The *lis pendens* as a mechanism of protection against parallel and concurrent lawsuits is a bar to proceedings and a negative condition of admissibility barring a new lawsuit between the same parties involving the same cause of action during the pendency of the first lawsuit (Sladič 2017a, p. 222). The second court seized will decline jurisdiction where there are the same parties in both actions which are based on the same cause of action (object and cause). In the absence of the same law binding the *fora* of several states (such as e.g. the Brussels Ia Regulation), the *lis pendens* is determined by the *lex fori* of the state where the action was lodged. The virtue of the European doctrine of *lis pendens* is the simple *ex ante* avoidance of clash of parallel civil proceedings. The UNIDROIT Principles of Transnational Civil Procedure consider the *lis pendens* together with *res iudicata*. Both rules are designed to avoid repetitive litigation, whether concurrent (*lis pendens*) or successive (*res iudicata*) (Rule 28). In Europe the *lis pendens* doctrine is considered to be characteristic of the Brussels Regulations (Ballarino et al. 2016, p. 48), i.e. it is typical for civil law jurisdictions.

Even though *lis pendens* appears to be characteristic of EU private international law, EU law nevertheless appears to treat the said doctrine in the case of conflicts of individual and collective lawsuits in consumer collective redress in a negative way (Stürner and Wendelstein 2018, p. 1083). In collective redress under national *lex fori*, a European *forum* where the *lis pendens* defence is made will have to assess the mutual effects of an individual lawsuit and collective lawsuits. Whereas national laws might apply the technique of stay of national individual lawsuits in cases of national collective redress, the issue at the European and international stage is quite

[56] ECHR, *Golder v. United Kingdom*, ECLI:CE:ECHR:1975:0221JUD000445170, § 36, and Athanassoglou a.o. v. Switzerland, ECLI:CE:ECHR:2000:0406JUD002764495, § 43.

different (Voet 2017, pp. 270–272). In the EU (already at the national stage), Article 7 of Directive 93/13 precludes a provision of national law which requires a court—before which an individual action has been brought by a consumer seeking a declaration that a contractual term binding him to a seller or supplier is unfair—automatically to suspend such an action pending a final judgment concerning an ongoing collective action brought by a consumer association seeking to prevent the continued use, in contracts of the same type, of terms similar to those at issue in that individual action.[57] Where a national *forum* of the EU Member State court is required by virtue of a national Code of Civil Procedure to stay the individual action brought before it, pending a final judgment concluding the collective action, the outcome of which is likely also to be applied in the individual action and, on that basis, such a situation is liable to undermine the effectiveness of the protection intended by that directive, in view of the differences in the purpose and nature of the consumer-protection mechanisms given specific expression by individual action and collective redress.[58] The *Sales Sinués* case might be linked to national specifics of Spanish law of civil procedure (Voet 2017, p. 263);[59] however, in the EU at the international level the coordination of individual redress and collective redress makes the application of the *lis pendens* doctrine a very uncertain matter. *A simili ad simile*, an argument that the staying of individual lawsuits in a pending collective redress infringes EU consumer protection legislation will have to be extended to *lis pendens*. It could indeed be argued that the recognition of the effects of a pending US class action under the *lis pendens* doctrine goes against the *effet utile* of EU consumer protection law. Where substantive law, as in cases of EU consumer protection directives, bars the application of collective redress, then *lis pendens* will only be a one-way instrument. A defendant will be able to claim that the individual lawsuit brought by a consumer constitutes a *lis pendens*. However, there will be no *lis pendens* in case of a lawsuit brought by a qualified entity (i.e. the European lead plaintiff or collective or ideological party under Directive 2009/22/EC).[60]

A truly international *lis pendens* means that there is a lawsuit pending outside the EU involving the same cause of action as a lawsuit pending before the European *forum* (Virgós Soriano and Garcimartín Alférez 2007, p. 361; Kastanidis 2015, p. 579). In other words, the international *lis pendens* involves a parallel lawsuit pending between the same parties with the same cause of action (cause and object) in a third country outside the EU. However, parallel "proceedings involving a court in a third country raise substantially different issues from those raised by intra-European

[57]CJEU, Sales Sinués and Drame Ba, C-381/14 and C-385/14, ECLI:EU:C:2016:252, §43.

[58]CJEU, Sales Sinués and Drame Ba, C-381/14 and C-385/14, ECLI:EU:C:2016:252, §§35 and 36.

[59]CJEU, Sales Sinués and Drame Ba, C-381/14 and C-385/14, ECLI:EU:C:2016:252.

[60]Directive 2009/22/EC of the European Parliament and of the Council of 23 April 2009 on injunctions for the protection of consumers' interests (Codified version), OJ EU L 110, 1.5.2009, p. 30. This Directive was repealed by the Directive (EU) 2020/1828 of the European Parliament and of the Council of 25 November 2020 on representative actions for the protection of the collective interests of consumers and repealing Directive 2009/22/EC,OJ EU L 409, 4.12.2020, p. 1.

cases" (Franzina 2014b, p. 24). If under the horizontality principle the import of judicial proceedings abroad is to be considered to be based on the principle of equality (i.e. every *forum* is equal, there is no superiority of the *fora* of one state over the *fora* of another state), then the proceedings pending abroad are entitled to be acknowledged also in the *forum* of the title import state (Schack 2017, p. 315; McLachlan 2008, p. 229).

However, there is a latent mistrust of proceedings abroad, with the main reason being the unknown compliance with minimum procedural requirements in civil justice set by Article 6(1) ECHR. In addition, "In modern civil procedure fundamental rights must be respected also cases where such a procedure is regulated by EU regulations" (Sladič 2013, p. 337). Procedural guarantees offered in Europe under Article 6(1) ECHR or Article 47 of the Charter of Fundamental Rights of the EU might not be identical in third countries. In order to give a pending US class action the effects of *lis pendens*, the right to a fair trial under Article 6(1) ECHR must have roughly the same contents as the due process clause of the US Constitution.

The enormous advantage and advancement in international civil procedure in the EU since the entry into force of the Brussels Ia Regulation is a clear and uniform set of rules on *lis pendens* where an earlier lawsuit with the same cause of action is pending between the same parties in a third state that is not an EU member state (Kastanidis 2015, p. 579). In other words, where a lawsuit in a third country, e.g. the United States, will be deemed to fall within the scope of application *ratione materiae* of the Brussels Ia Regulation (i.e. a US class action will have to be a civil and commercial matter), uniform rules on *lis pendens* will apply in the EU (with the exception of Denmark). Private international law in the EU is no longer entirely closed solely within European dimensions (Franzina 2014a, p. 39).

The Hague Convention of 2 July 2019 on the Recognition and Enforcement of Foreign Judgments in Civil or Commercial Matters indirectly applies the international *lis pendens* doctrine in Article 7(2).[61]

Even before the entry into force of the Brussels Ia Regulation, issues of *lis pendens* of parallel European lawsuits in the case of a Canadian class action were already discussed in the Dutch case law. In October 2013 the court of first instance (Rechtbank Amsterdam) declined jurisdiction to hear a case against a Canadian defendant based on allegations of financial fraud (a Ponzi scheme) as there was already a class action pending.[62] The declining of jurisdiction was also based on the *res alibi pendens* as a subsidiary criterion.

Judges in Quebec, Canada already had experience with the *lis pendens* doctrine in class actions also in Canadian intra-provincial class actions requiring the application of private international law (i.e. inter-regional private law) and the law of international civil procedure. However, as long as Europe has recourse to qualified entities in the sense of Directive 2009/22/EC or Directive 2020/1828 in representative collective redress, the Canadian solution will have only partial interest in Europe.

[61] See https://www.hcch.net/en/instruments/conventions/full-text/?cid=137.

[62] Rechtbank Amsterdam, ECLI:NL:RBAMS:2013:7936, § 4.5.

Case law in Quebec principally deals with questions of *lis pendens* at the stage of certification in a single nation.[63] Where there are qualified entities such Canadian case law is indeed solely information of comparative importance. A *lis pendens*, i.e. a subsequent lawsuit before a European *forum*, while the first lawsuit is pending before a court of a third state can only be seen after the expiry of the opt-out period.[64]

From the US or Canadian point of view (or from the point of view of any collective redress operating under opt-out systems), the lodging of a parallel lawsuit in Europe will have to be assessed as implied opt-out. Where the second lawsuit in Europe was initiated by the absent European class members during the notice period for opting-out, there is indeed a direct opt-out. Not acknowledging such an opt-out would certainly lead to the bar to recognition of the US class action judgment or approved settlement. The manner for requesting exclusion is to be understood broadly. The direct manner is indeed the sending of information in compliance with the opt-out notice. However, lodging a lawsuit before a European *forum* is also an implied request for exclusion of any class action proceedings before the US *forum*. The lead plaintiff and the US *forum* are probably not aware of the pending European lawsuit. However, the defendant is only too well aware of a pending lawsuit before the European *forum*. It is argued that a lack of information by the defendant on pending European lawsuits where the certification order includes absent European class members amounts to infringement of the procedural duty imposed on parties to cooperate with the court hearing the case. Assuming that the period of time for opting-out has expired, the crucial provision in the EU is undoubtedly Article 33(1) of the Brussels Ia Regulation (Hess 2010, p. 119). Under Article 33(1), in cases where the international jurisdiction of the non-EU *forum* is based on the general rule of *actor sequitur forum rei* (Art. 4) or on the rules on special jurisdiction (Arts. 7, 8 or 9) and proceedings are pending before a court of a third state at the time when a court in a Member State is seized of an action involving the same cause of action and between the same parties as the proceedings in the court of the third state, the court of the Member State may stay the proceedings if:

- it is expected that the court of the third state will give a judgement capable of recognition and, where applicable, of enforcement in that Member State; and
- the court of the Member State is satisfied that a stay is necessary for the proper administration of justice. Legal writers speak of the application of the traditional triple identity in *lis pendens* doctrine (same object, same cause and same parties) (Kastanidis 2015, pp. 582 and 583).

Several other questions remain open in recognition of a pending US class action under the *lis pendens* doctrine in EU Member States (Romy 1999, p. 792):

[63]See e.g. Superior Court of Quebec, in case *Labrecque v. General Motors of Canada Ltd.*, 2011 QCCS 266, JG1876.

[64]See for a different solution in Quebec, in case *Hotte v. Servier Canada Inc.* [1999] R.J.Q. 2598 (C.A.).

- identity of parties (the same parties),
- the same cause of action (subject-matter of a civil lawsuit, i.e. object and the cause),
- capacity of recognition in the EU (the avoidance of irreconcilable final judicial decisions),
- discretionary power in the interest of proper administration of justice.

The question of the same *causa petendi* (cause of action) between a pending US class action and a consequent European lawsuit opens new horizons of international civil lawsuits. Under the current doctrine of the CJEU, "The cause of action comprises the facts and the rule of law relied on as the basis of the action."[65] While "most parallel proceedings will involve the same mass damage event giving rise to proceedings" (van Lith 2010, p. 56), it cannot be definitely said that the second part of the cause of action, the legal basis, is always identical. The identity in *lis pendens* in traditional lawsuits is not the same as the requirement of commonality in US class actions. The identity also requires the *idem ius* postulate; such a postulate could be given where subclasses are certified. Systems of collective redress operating under the opt-out system offer a striking similarity to the *litisconsortium necessarium*, a type of joinder in civil law legal systems where the principle *idem factum, idem ius* is applied. A ruling on the merits cannot be given to the members of the group in application of different substantive laws; there can solely be a split in subgroups requiring the application of similar law. Where the legal basis (the *lex causae*) and the facts are identical as in the pending US class action, one condition for international *lis pendens* is complied with. However, even if one condition is met, other conditions are not necessarily met.

Could there be cases where a partially same cause of action could also trigger a defence of *lis pendens*, as far as the same facts and the same rule of law relied on as the basis of the action are concerned? Where either the law or the facts are not identical, there is no *lis pendens*. A case could easily be construed. There is a pending consumer class action in the United States based on liability for defective products for personal injury. However, a single European international class member of a certified international class not having opted out lodged a civil lawsuit before an EU *forum* for material damages in his apartment due to defective product. There is no identity of facts or of legal basis (different damages). The assessment of the same cause of action in the defence of *lis pendens* under Article 33(1) of the Brussels Ia Regulation will therefore require a very detailed assessment of the US class action. The US certification order will have to be a very detailed one. Where an international class is certified, with e.g. subclasses of Europeans, the legal basis will also be explained if there is to be no relitigating of the case in the EU Member States.

The importance of the definition of parties in US class actions will certainly be raised in assessing the *lis pendens* of US class actions and European individual or collective redress. The situation is complicated in systems of collective redress

[65] CJEU, Tatry, C-406/92, ECLI:EU:C:1994:400, § 38.

operating under the opt-out system, as there is no express consent by the represented parties (implied consent by virtue of silence and not opting-out) (Hess 2010, p. 119). Under Article 33(1), there can be recognition of *lis pendens* solely where a lawsuit is pending between the same parties. The essence of any doctrine of *lis pendens* is the identity of the *causa petendi* and the parties.

In collective redress, the condition of same parties seems not to be complied with in any case. It has been noted that, "This is because class actions create a new type of claimant—one that did not exist when the traditional" rules on *exequatur* were created and developed (Brown 2008, p. 222). Which entity capable of bringing proceedings is a party to legal proceedings is determined by the *lex fori* of the European *forum*. The said *lex fori* also compromises the Brussels Ia Regulation. In Switzerland, the consequence of the *lex fori* approach to the *lis pendens* leads to the finding that the Swiss *forum* hearing the individual action, initiated by an individual who is a member of the certified international class against the defendant in a pending US class action, will have to determine in application of the *lex fori* whether the US class action and the individual action are litigated by the same parties (Romy 1999, p. 792).

As far as the defendant in a consumer-initiated international action is concerned, there are usually no problems. The defendant is for example one multinational corporation. However, the plaintiff seems to be in a completely different position. In an opt-in system of collective redress, even the absent class members express their intent to be parties to a collective redress lawsuit. Therefore, where the international representative collective redress operates under the opt-in system it would be difficult to deny the *lis pendens* effect in case of a second individual lawsuit by a class member having opted in.

However, the representative collective redress like a US class action operates under an opt-out system. In such systems, three types of plaintiffs will have to be distinguished: the lead plaintiff (named), members of the class having opted out in time and the absent and passive group members. Members of the class having opted out are not bound by the US class action judgment or approved settlement. In other words, they are not a party to the US class action lawsuit. No *lis pendens* defence can be used against them. The certified class is to be treated under the entity model as a litigant, i.e. a collective party to pending class action proceedings in the United States.[66] Therefore, the certification of collective party will also be capable of triggering the defence of *lis pendens*. However, if the *lex fori* of the requested EU Member State does not recognize the standing of a collective party, i.e. where the

[66]See for the doctrine of collective party e.g. Cappelletti 1975, pp. 591–593. In class actions, the class is "the litigant and the client" (Shapiro 1998, p. 919; Piché 2016, p. 299; Romy 1999, p. 796). The merit of such an approach is a very simple compatibility with the subjective *res iudicata* effect (*res iudicata ius facit inter partes*). In other words, in the USA a class action by a lead plaintiff representing a class is the result of the legislature's preference for class members as a collective party (Piché 2016, p. 299). As a consequence, there is a distinction between the traditional party in binary proceedings, on the one hand, and the ideological or collective party, on the other (Cappelletti 1975, pp. 587–593).

certified class—including the absent class members—is not accepted as a party to a pending US class action, there will be no identity of parties and consequentially no risk of *lis pendens*. Traditionally the "*lis pendens* rule applies to situations in which parties are themselves participants to proceedings" (van Lith 2010, p. 57; Romy 1999, p. 793). In other words, an active party's role is required. The said required active role for triggering the *lis pendens* defence in US class actions is indeed given solely to the representatives, i.e. lead plaintiffs. The lead plaintiff is named in the pending US class action lawsuit. Were the European lead plaintiff to initiate an individual lawsuit against the same defendant in the EU, the condition of same parties would be complied with. If the idea of collective party, i.e. the litigative entity, is pursued, an assessment of the term of party in civil procedure under the *lex fori* of the *forum* where *exequatur* is sought will have to be performed. The preferred option in Europe nevertheless seems to be a very traditional one. The party is solely the subject suing or being sued (Braun 2014, pp. 334 and 335).

As far as the absent and passive class members of a certified international class are concerned, the *lis pendens* defence will have to be denied to the defendant. In the Netherlands the question of identity of the parties was asked in the framework of the now repealed WCAM opt-out collective redress settlements. The question is indeed "whether applicants requesting a binding declaration of a WCAM group settlement are the "same parties" as an interested person instituting individual proceedings or requesting a declaratory judgement against the alleged responsible party, or even whether they are the same parties as class members against the alleged responsible party" (van Lith 2010, p. 57). As already mentioned, the traditional answer given is that, "the standard *lis pendens* rule applies to situations in which parties are themselves participants to proceedings" (van Lith 2010, p. 57; Romy 1999, p. 793). *A contrario*, therefore absent and passive class members do not even fall within the scope *ratione personae* of the pending US class action proceedings (Romy 1999, p. 793).

As far as the first condition of *lis pendens*, namely the "same parties", is concerned, there might be a problem with the definition of a party. It has been noted that, "The current differences among group litigation … suggest that foreign courts may hesitate before concluding that a class action and a follow-up action by an individual absent class member against the same defendant involve the "same parties" for purposes of claim preclusion" (Wasserman 2011, p. 380). While the statement in US legal writing is naturally not made in the framework of *lis pendens*, the idea used by US legal writing is indeed correct. The defence of *lis pendens* is an early and prior stage to the *res iudicata* defence. Both defences are used in different stages of a lawsuit and are based on the rule *bis de eadem re ne sit actio* (Štempihar 1953, p. 30; Romy 1999, pp. 792 and 794). Further:

> While American constitutional law and preclusion law permit absent class members to be bound by judgements against the class even if they never were afforded an affirmative opportunity to opt in, a review of the European class action and collective action vehicles reveals a deep reluctance to bind those who neither commence litigation in their own name nor affirmatively choose to opt in." [Wasserman 2011, p. 380]

The CJEU recalled in the *Tatry*[67] and *Drouot* assurances[68] on the *lis pendens* that the "terms used ... in order to determine whether a situation of *lis pendens* arises must be regarded as independent". A possibility of extending the *lis pendens* also to intra-EU collective redress is envisaged in the Brussels Ia Regulation (van Lith 2010, pp. 56 and 57). Such an opinion is rather to be considered acknowledging the scope (also *ratione loci*) of the autonomous meaning of legal terms in the EU. The CJEU recalled, in the recent *Axa Belgium* case

> that it follows from the need for a uniform application of EU law, and the principle of equality, that the terms of a provision of EU law, which make no express reference to the law of the Member States for the purpose of determining its meaning and scope, must normally be given an autonomous and uniform interpretation throughout the European Union, which must take into account the context of the provision and the objective pursued by the legislation in question.[69]

Therefore, the extension of the *lis pendens* via the autonomous interpretation by the CJEU also to US class actions would also require the acknowledgement on the *Henkel* and *Schrems* case law.[70] The non-recognition of the status of a consumer to an assignee of the rights of a private final consumer without itself being party to a contract between a professional and a private individual, even where the assignee is a qualified entity under the repealed Directive 2009/22/EC or now Directive 2020/1828, clearly shows the limits of the autonomous interpretation as a means of extension of (now) Brussels Ia Regulation to US class actions. The conclusion seems to be that under the Brussels Ia Regulation pending US class actions do not fall within the scope of the *lis pendens* under Article 33(1). The argumentation that the concept of party inherent to Brussels Ia Regulation is not adapted to collective redress seems wholly conclusive in the assessment of the Regulation (Perucchi 2008, p. 120).

However, the main objection to the autonomous application of the term party under the Brussels Ia Regulation is the finding in the case law of the US Supreme Court according to which it is not clear which class members have the status of party to a US class action lawsuit (Perucchi 2008, p. 120). The case referred to the capacity of bringing an appeal by an absent class member in a class action lawsuit. In US law, absent class members are not parties to the litigation; however, they are bound by the ruling or settlement (Lahav 2011, p. 1943). According to the US Supreme Court, the legal question was "whether petitioner should be considered a "party" for the purposes of appealing the approval of the settlement. ... Only parties to a lawsuit, or those that properly become parties, may appeal an adverse judgement" and "Nonnamed class members, however, may be parties for some purposes and not for others. The label "party" does not indicate an absolute characteristic, but rather a

[67] CJEU, Tatry, C-406/92, ECLI:EU:C:1994:400, § 30.

[68] CJEU, Drouot assurances, C-351/96, ECLI:EU:C:1998:242, § 16.

[69] CJEU, Axa Belgium, C-494/14, ECLI:EU:C:2015:692, § 21.

[70] CJEU, Henkel, C-167/00, ECLI:EU:C:2002:555, §13 and Schrems, C-498/16, ECLI:EU:C:2018:37.

conclusion about the applicability of various procedural rules that may differ based on context".[71] In other words, there is the renewed clash of paradigms: the Brussels Ia Regulation, based on the civil law legal tradition, requires certainty and *ex ante* predictability on the status of a party, while common law legal traditions in US class actions try to acknowledge justice in each individual case. If even US law does not determine the exact status of absent class members, international classes including absent class members from EU Member States in pending US class actions will not be able to trigger the *lis pendens* in parallel European lawsuits. Arguments according to which the US class action does not deal with the status of the party and that therefore any questions in civil law legal systems based on the status of the party cannot stand against US class actions seem to be at odds with the *lis pendens* doctrine, which deals *expressis verbis* with the status of a party (Perucchi 2008, p. 120). In other words, the regulatory nature of a US class action in the framework of the *lis pendens* will have to be made compatible with the purely individual nature of the *lis pendens* rule.

The last condition of the *lis pendens* is the performance of discretionary power in the interest of proper administration of justice, the said uncertainty of status and quality of party of European absent members in a pending US class action involving an international class with European absent members. Such an approach is wholly consistent with the procedural guarantees of Article 6(1) ECHR and Article 47 Charter of Fundamental Rights of the EU (Franzina 2014b, p. 35). The first guidance explaining the interest of proper administration of justice is the Recital (24) of the Brussels Ia Regulation (Franzina 2014b, p. 35). There should be an assessment of "all the circumstances of the case before" the European *forum*. In addition:

> Such circumstances may include connections between the facts of the case and the parties and the third state concerned, the stage to which the proceedings in the third State have progressed by the time proceedings are initiated in the court of the Member State and whether or not the court of the third State can be expected to give a judgement within a reasonable time.

The argumentation according to which circumstances are to be taken into account when assessing the position of European absent class members are their passive role and an uneasy status of a party in the pending US class action. This will probably lead to the conclusion that the proper administration of justice is best served by not staying the proceedings pending before the *fora* of EU Member States. The second guidance—in cases of consumer-oriented class action—will have to be the EU consumer protection law. "The general rule (the discretion of the court) seems to work well, no legislative action is needed. Usually, the court makes an individual assessment based on the circumstances concerned. Best to leave the matter to the discretion of the national courts" (Voet 2017, p. 279).

---

[71]US Supreme Court, *Devlin v. Scardelletti*, 536 U.S. 1 (2002).

9 *Lis Pendens* in Collective Redress: A Quebec Experience

It would appear that Quebec, a Canadian province said to be under civil law influence in Canada, is also applying by virtue of Article 3137 Civil Code of Quebec[72] the *lis pendens* doctrine with the discretionary power of the *forum* to stay the subsequent lawsuit in collective redress where there is a lawsuit pending in other jurisdictions. Yet such a discretionary stay is nevertheless repugnant to purely internal situations of the *forum* state. Discretionary stay is to be applied solely in international cases. A very interesting finding can be drawn from Quebec law and case law in *lis pendens* in class actions (Duquette 2003, pp. 88–93).

In 1999, the Quebec Court of Appeal started applying the *lis pendens* provision of Article 3137 of the Civil Code of Quebec to Canadian class action proceedings. The Code requires identity of the parties, identify of the object and identity of the material facts.[73] Basically, the result will be that the first party to file a class proceeding with respect to a particular defendant and proposed class will prevail under the doctrine of prior *tempore, potior iure*. Any subsequent class proceedings will be suspended given the appearance of *lis pendens*.

The question opened in 1999 before the Quebec appellate *forum* was simple: Can the doctrine of *lis pendens* be applied to collective redress in case of parallel class actions (*doit-on rejeter une demande d'autorisation d'exercer un recours collectif pour cause de litispendance lorsque trois requêtes sont présentées à quelques jours d'intervalle*)? The Quebec *forum* started its assessment by a finding according to which "*la litispendance . . . doit être analysée en fonction des règles particulières au recours collectif*". The term "the same parties" refers to every member of the class/group. Indeed,

> c'est l'identité juridique des parties qui est exigée pour l'application de la présomption de la chose jugée. Cela ne signifie pas que les parties doivent être physiquement identiques dans les deux cas. C'est l'identité juridique des parties qui est exigée pour l'application de la présomption de chose jugée, ... Et par identité des personnes, il faut entendre l'identité juridique et non pas l'identité physique. ... . Pour la chose jugée, il faut l'identité juridique des parties et non leur simple identité physique. L'une peut exister sans l'autre. Il y a identité juridique chaque fois qu'une personne représente une autre personne ou est représentée par elle. ... À cette étape de la demande d'autorisation, les requérants n'ont pas le statut de représentant du groupe. C'est précisément cette reconnaissance qu'ils recherchent. C'est cependant en leur qualité de membre d'un groupe qu'ils formulent leur requête ... Cette qualité de «membre d'un groupe» constitue leur véritable identité juridique. Conclure autrement permettrait à chaque membre d'un groupe de présenter sa propre requête sans qu'on puisse lui opposer la litispendance ou la chose jugée pour les requêtes ou les jugements obtenus par les autres membres du groupe. Je conclus donc à l'identité des parties.[74]

[72]On the application of a party, a Québec authority may stay its ruling on an action brought before it if another action, between the same parties, based on the same facts and having the same object is pending before a foreign authority, provided that the latter action can result in a decision which may be recognized in Québec, or if such a decision has already been rendered by a foreign authority.

[73]Court of Appeal of Quebec, *Hotte v. Servier Canada Inc.*, [1999] R.J.Q. 2598 (C.A.), § 6; see also Superior Court of Quebec, case Parker c. Apotex Inc., 2015 QCCS 1210 (CanLII).

[74]No official English translation seems to be available on CanLII.

However, how can one speak of the same parties, a prerequisite of *lis pendens*, if no class or group has been created? Can there be a *lis pendens* already before the certification of the class action? The answer given by the Superior Court of Quebec is that "the appearance of *lis pendens* is sufficient" where the "object of the dispute is to seek authorization" for a class action.[75] Probably the appearance will have to be assessed by comparing the proposed definition of classes or groups in parallel class actions. The difference between the physical identity of the parties and the legal identity of the parties could mean that the doctrine of collective party is the solution to be applied in private international law.

In 2012, the Quebec Court of Appeal seemed to have set up a continuation of *lis pendens* doctrine.[76] The rule of *prior tempore, potior iure* was qualified as occasionally having "*des effets préjudiciables pour les membres du groupe représenté*". It offered a *lis pendens* rule mitigated by common law considerations, a technique creating a legal hybrid that is theoretically satisfactory neither to civil nor to common law. The result is nevertheless interesting: the first motion to be filed is, in principle, the one that will be heard in priority; subsequent class actions will be stayed and will be heard, in the order they were filed, only if the preceding class action is ultimately dismissed. This is indeed the classic solution of *lis pendens*. However, the priority of the first class action filed may be challenged by the attorneys responsible for any subsequent class actions filed; the party challenging the priority of a previously filed class action has the burden of establishing that the prior class action is not in the best interests of the putative members, but rather constitutes an abuse of the first-to-file rule such that the subsequent action should proceed instead.[77] From a European point of view the possibility of challenge of the first motion could mean the end of the *lis pendens* doctrine, as there is always a possibility of disregarding a clear rule based on priority of filing by considerations of flexibility and procedural justice.

As far as the cause of action is concerned, the Supreme Court of Canada clarified the application of the *lis pendens* doctrine to cross-border lawsuits with the following words:

> In private international law matters, the nature of the required identities is altered somewhat in the Civil Code of Quebec in the case of *lis pendens*. In particular, in Art. 3137, as in Art. 3155(4), the Code retains identity of the parties and identity of the object but substitutes identity of the facts on which the actions are based for identity of the cause of action. This change takes into account the problems involved in reconciling the specific features of legal systems that come into contact with each other, as well as the diversity in their substantive law concepts and procedural rules. The Quebec judge therefore considers the facts on which the actions are based and does not go beyond the differences in the legal systems in question to try to find an identity of the cause of action. The analysis thus focuses more on the respective objects of the two actions . . . .[78]

---

[75] *Labrecque v. General Motors of Canada Ltd.*, §12.

[76] *Schmidt v. Johnson & Johnson* e.a, 2012 QCCA 2132 (Schmidt).

[77] English translation of the French original taken from https://www.dwpv.com/en/Insights#/article/Publications/2012/Quebec-Court-of-Appeal-Nuances-First-to-File-Rule-in-Class-Actions.

[78] *Canada Post Corp. v. Lépine*, 2009 SCC 16, [2009] 1 S.C.R. 549, §§ 51 and 52.

Where both pending class actions allege the same facts and ask for the same type of damages, and many of the allegations made and conclusions sought in *forum* A are very similar if not identical to the ones in *forum* B, there is clearly identity of the material facts and the object.[79] In a class action of international scope, the criteria for finding *lis pendens* were eased, identity of facts being substituted for identity of the cause of action.[80]

10 *Lis Pendens* and Directive 2009/22/EC and Directive (EU) 2020/1828

Injunctive collective redress under the repealed Directive 2009/22/EC and now Directive 2020/1828 is not covered *ratione materiae* by the intra-EU *lis pendens* (Art. 29 Brussels Ia Regulation). As in the case of international *lis pendens*, there is the requirement of the same cause of action and the same parties. Legal scholars even found that no case of *lis pendens* in intra-EU collective redress has yet been reported.[81]

There is no application of the *lis pendens* under Article 30 of the Brussels Ia Regulation in a legal action brought by a Spanish qualified entity against an Austrian enterprise for infringement of consumer protection legislation in Spain before Austrian courts. It will not be barred by a legal action brought by an Austrian qualified entity before Austrian courts against the same Austrian enterprise for infringement of consumer protection legislation in Austria. The Spanish qualified entity has no standing in a lawsuit for similar or same infringement of consumer protection legislation against Austrian consumers. Both actions are heard by the Austrian *forum*. However, one of the conditions of *lis pendens* under Article 30 of the Brussels Ia Regulation is also bringing an action in the courts of different Member States. Where both legal actions are pending before *fora* of the same EU Member State, there is no intra-EU *lis pendens*.

Even assuming (where applicable) that a legal action is brought by a Spanish qualified entity against an Austrian enterprise for infringement of consumer protection legislation in Spain before a Spanish *forum* and a parallel legal action brought by an Austrian qualified entity before an Austrian *forum* against the same Austrian enterprise for infringement of consumer protection legislation in Austria, there will be no identity of the parties. A qualified entity from Austria cannot be considered to be the same party as a qualified entity from Spain. The requirement of a qualified entity under Article 3 of Directive 2009/22/EC (now Art. 4 of Directive (EU) 2020/1828) actually means that any qualified entity is empowered solely to initiate

[79] Superior Court of Quebec, case *Parker c. Apotex Inc.*, 2015 QCCS 1210 (CanLII), § 7.
[80] Superior Court of Quebec, case *Labrecque v. General Motors of Canada Ltd.*, §13.
[81] Chabrny (2019), p. 203.

collective redress for infringement of EU legislation on consumer protection solely in a defined, single EU Member State. The conferral of such an auhtorisation to litigate certifies the qualified entity exclusively for infringements on the territory of the EU Member State where the status of qualified entity was conferred (Carballo Piñeiro 2009, p. 73 [according to the cited author, "la autorización estatal implica ineludiblemente su carácter territorial"]).

The collective redress lawsuit pending before a Spanish and an Austrian *forum* also does not have a same cause of action. Under Article 4 of Directive 2009/22/EC and Art. 6 of Directive (EU) 2020/1828 referring to intra-EU infringement refer to qualified entities from different EU Member States in order to protect the collective interests of consumers in different EU Member State. The limitation to the place of interests protected by the qualified entity means that the requirement of the same cause of action will not be met, as facts might be similar but are not identical, so no *lis pendens* will be triggered. There is the same rule of law concerned, but the protection of interests limited to a given territory makes it impossible to speak of a *lis pendens*.

11 Related Actions

Related actions will have a much more important role to play in collective redress in the EU (van Lith 2010, p. 57; Amaro et al. 2018, p. 101). It has been noted that, "For instance, in the Dieselgate case, one could argue that collective actions brought against Volkswagen in two different Member States by local plaintiffs, are related actions in the sense of Art. 30 [of Brussels Ia Regulation], if a risk of irreconcilability exists" (Amaro et al. 2018, p. 101). Related actions and the *lis pendens* are intrinsically connected. Where the *lis pendens* is given a broad interpretation, there is necessarily an unwanted spillover effect on the related actions (Bureau and Muir Watt 2010, pp. 219 and 220). Under EU law the term "related actions" means the absence of the same cause of action or of the same parties; however pending proceedings are so closely connected that it is expedient to hear and determine them together to avoid the risk of irreconcilable judgments resulting from separate proceedings. A caveat will be given: the definition of a related action is given solely within the intra-EU scope of the Brussels Ia Regulation; the purely international actions in Article 34 do not have a definition. However, there is no reason to consider that the definition of a related action is different in Article 34 than in Article 30(3). As in purely European connected actions, the aim of Article 34 seems to be the prevention of irreconcilable judicial decisions.

The discretionary staying of proceedings in a European *forum* where a US class action is pending is allowed under Article 34 of the Brussels Ia Regulation. A European *forum* is empowered either on the application of one of the parties or, where possible under national law, of its own motion to stay an action which is related to the action in the court of the third state if:

(a) it is expedient to hear and determine the related actions together to avoid the risk of irreconcilable judgments resulting from separate proceedings;
(b) it is expected that the court of the third state will give a judgment capable of recognition; and
(c) the court of the Member State is satisfied that a stay is necessary for the proper administration of justice.

In the *Royal Dutch Shell* case, a US class action was already certified when a request for declaring a WCAM settlement binding *erga omnes* was lodged (van Lith 2010, p. 57). The facts could be an excellent example of related actions; however, due to legislative development—the adoption and entry into force of the new Brussels Ia Regulation—the narrative of the *Shell* case only has a historical worth, as it deals with national Dutch-related actions. Nevertheless, any possibility of applying the related action doctrine will end in the question of recognition of the US class action ruling.

12 Agreements on Prorogation of Jurisdiction

In international consumer collective redress outside the United States there seems to be a movement towards setting agreements on jurisdictions (prorogation of jurisdiction) in consumer contracts with big US multinational corporations aside. The words "consumer collective redress" are to be stressed.[82]

In consumer contracts at the international level concluded by consumers resident in the EU and US enterprises (B2C contracts), Council Directive 93/13/EEC has to be acknowledged. In the *Océano Grupo Editorial* case, the consumer contracts contained a term conferring jurisdiction on the courts in Barcelona, a city in which none of the consumers were domiciled but where the plaintiffs had their principal place of business.[83] The CJEU ruled that, "The protection provided for consumers in consumer contracts entails the national court being able to determine of its own motion whether a term of a contract before it is unfair when making its preliminary assessment as to whether a claim should be allowed to proceed before the national courts." The Court stated, in reference to the clauses of prorogation of jurisdiction, that:

[82]In comparative law in other branches of law such as, for example, labour law, there seems to be an acceptance of traditional instruments of steering access to the courts in international lawsuits also in class actions or collective redress. Instruments of steering access to the courts in international lawsuits are arbitration clauses and prorogation clauses. They seem to be applied also in collective redress. A Canadian court recently gave a decision—in the case *Heller v. Uber Technologies Inc.*, 2018 ONSC 718 (CanLII), concerning the Uber employment case in a single Canadian province—that enforced an arbitration clause.

[83]CJEU, Océano Grupo Editorial, C-240/98 to C-244/98, ECLI:EU:C:2000:346.

> In disputes where the amounts involved are often limited, the lawyers' fees may be higher than the amount at stake, which may deter the consumer from contesting the application of an unfair term.
>
> [The Court further stated:] There is a real risk that the consumer ... will not challenge the term pleaded against him on the grounds that it is unfair. It follows that effective protection of the consumer may be attained only if the national court acknowledges that it has power to evaluate terms of this kind of its own motion.[84]
>
> It is hardly conceivable that, in a system requiring the implementation of specific group actions of a preventive nature intended to put a stop to unfair terms detrimental to consumers' interests, a court hearing a dispute on a specific contract containing an unfair term should not be able to set aside application of the relevant term solely because the consumer has not raised the fact that it is unfair.[85]

In practice, an agreement on prorogation of jurisdiction detrimental to consumers will have to be declared void by the *forum* hearing the case of its own motion already in the preliminary assessment of jurisdiction or objection of jurisdiction.

Such considerations are also to be encountered in non-European legal orders in class action litigation. In an Israeli class action lodged against Facebook for violation of compulsory Israeli data protection laws (breach of privacy under Israeli common law), the agreement on prorogation in favour of a California *forum* was not given effect.[86] Israeli users, i.e. Israeli consumers, express their agreement when registering Facebook and consent to application of California law and consent to jurisdiction of a California *forum*.[87] The Israeli *forum* hearing the case applied Israeli contract law on unfair terms in consumer contracts in the assessment of jurisdiction and held that it was a proper forum. The defence raised by Facebook that California law should be applied to determine the validity of the clause on prorogation of jurisdiction was rejected. If Facebook's contention were accepted, namely

> that the forum selection clause [should] be evaluated based upon the [choice of] law [clause] set forth therein, [then] the result would be that, with respect to a standard contract, no forum selection clause or choice of law clause could be examined under Israeli law, and it would be impossible to determine that they constitute unduly disadvantageous provisions. Doing so would thwart the possibility of filing a class action in Israel against defendants of this type.[88]
>
> [This case involves] a standard contract, that services a large population in Israel, where it is clear that Facebook conformed its website for the use of users in Israel in Hebrew. [It does not matter] whether we are dealing with a personal suit, the value of which is not high, in

---

[84]CJEU, Océano Grupo Editorial, C-240/98 to C-244/98, ECLI:EU:C:2000:346, § 26.

[85]CJEU, Océano Grupo Editorial, C-240/98 to C-244/98, ECLI:EU:C:2000:346, § 28.

[86]See on that agreement on prorogation in the European context, Stürner & Wendelstein (2018), pp. 1084 and 1085.

[87]http://www.sherby.co.il/blog/2016/06/29/israeli-court-requires-facebook-to-litigate-claims-in-israel-despite-forum-selection-and-choice-of-law-clauses/#comment-164. See also Israeli Supreme Court case PCA 5860/16 Facebook Inc. v. Ohad Ben Hamo. The Israeli *forum* stressed that Facebook exempts some Facebook users from a jurisdiction clause and found that Facebook allows residents of Germany to litigate against Facebook in Germany under German law.

[88]Ibid.

which case it would be appropriate to allow it to be heard in Israel, because otherwise it would not be brought before any tribunal, or whether [we are dealing with] a collective suit regarding consumer matters. . . . The burden that would be placed on [consumers] to litigate abroad or pursuant to California law would be significant, and it would likely prevent the litigation in many cases.[89]

13 Conclusion

Massification and globalization give rise to a number of negative developments among which may be counted international cartels, which can lead to collective litigation in more than one jurisdiction by the same parties for the same complaint and at the same time. Virtually every foreign enterprise present in the United States has been subject to class actions. In recent times, collective redress has also been applied in other countries. Cases where the same wrongful act is adjudicated in not one but several countries via collective redress are more and more common. However, the same wrongful act means the same mass-delict, infringement of isomorphic rights, similar harms and the same tortfeasor. In procedural terms, it could be said that the same defendant, same facts and the same cause of action (cause and object) in litigation pending in several countries are encountered. Such parallel and concurrent cross-border litigation is traditionally coordinated by mechanisms of toleration of foreign proceedings, anti-suit injunctions, *forum non conveniens* doctrine, *lis pendens* and related actions. Yet, whereas such coordination functions well in individual lawsuits, it is not clear whether such mechanisms will also work in the framework of collective redress.

It would appear that in collective redress—due to its specific nature—the issues of coordination of parallel lawsuits will have to operate under the doctrine of toleration of parallel proceedings. *Forum non conveniens* and anti-suit injunctions, even though applied in class actions of countries belonging to common law legal orders, actually try to avoid any internationalization of collective redress. On the other hand, *lis pendens* as a doctrine of coordination of collective redress in Europe suffers from the inconvenience caused by the requirement of an exact definition of the parties to the proceedings. It is not known how, for example, absent class members are to be treated in a pending collective redress. Are they a party in collective litigation? At the same time, the inconvenience of the approach of toleration is to move the question of parallel proceedings to the recognition stage (irreconcilable judicial decisions as a bar to recognition). Where one lawsuit is closed by a final decision (*res iudicata*) the judicial decision given by another *forum* in another state will not be recognized, and will have no effects (McLachlan 2008, p. 243).

[89]Ibid.

References

Amaro R, Azar-Baud MJ, Corneloup S, Fauvarque-Cosson B, Jault-Seseke F (2018) Study: collective redress in the Member States of the European Union. European Parliament, Brussels, Available at http://www.europarl.europa.eu/thinktank/en/document.html?reference=IPOL_STU(2018)608829

Andrews DC (2013) Personal Jurisdiction and choice of law in the cloud. Maryland Law Rev 73:313–384

Ballarino T, Ballarino E, Pretelli I (2016) Manuale di diritto internazionale privato, 8th edn. CEDAM, Milano

Barrett E (1947) The Doctrine of Forum Non Conveniens. California Law Rev 35:380–442

Beaumont P (2018) Forum non conveniens and the EU rules on Conflicts of Jurisdictions: A Possible Global Solution, Revue critique de droit international privé 447–457

Braun J (2014) Lehrbuch des Zivilprozeßrechts, 1st ed. J. C. In: B. Mohr, Tübingen

Briggs A (2013) The conflict of laws, 3rd edn. Oxford University Press, Oxford

Brown JP (2008) Seeking recognition of Canadian class action judgments in foreign jurisdictions: perils and pitfalls. Can Class Action Rev 4:220–257

Bureau D, Muir Watt H (2010) Droit international privé, Tome I, Partie générale. Presses universitaires de France, Paris

Cappelletti M (1975) La protection d'intérêts collectifs et de groupe dans le procès civil (Métamorphoses de la procédure civile). Revue internationale de droit comparé 27:571–597

Carballo Piñeiro L (2009) Las acciones colectivas y su eficacia extraterritorial: problemas de recepción y transplante de las "class actions" en Europa, Universidad de Santiago de Compostela. Servicio de Publicaciones e Intercambio Científico, Santiago de Compostela

Chabrny J (2019) Grenzüberschreitende Sammelklagen, Verlag Dr. Kovač, Hamburg

Clermont KM (2015) Solving the puzzle of transnational class actions. Indiana Law J Suppl 90:69–77

Clopton ZD (2015) Transnational class action in the shadow of preclusion. Indiana Law J 90:1387–1428

Clopton ZD (2018) The global class action and its alternatives. Theoret Inq Law 19:125–150

Coester-Waltjen D (2017) Das Spannungsverhältnis zwischen Privat – und Parteiautonomie einerseits und staatlichen Schutz – und Ordnungsinteressen im Privatrecht andererseits. Juristenzeitung 72:1073–1080

de Miguel Asensio PA, Cuniberti G, Franzina P, Heinze C, Requejo Isidro M (2018) Study: the Hague conference on private international law "Judgments Convention". European Parliament, Brussels 2018. Available at http://www.europarl.europa.eu/thinktank/en/document.html?reference=IPOL_STU(2018)604954

Dodge J (2014) Facilitative judging: organisational design in mass-multidistrict litigation. Emory Law J 64:329–382

Dowers NA (2013) The anti-suit injunction and the EU: legal tradition and Europeanisation in international private law. Cambridge J Int Comp Law 2:960–973

Duquette MB (2003) Les questions de compétence des tribunaux québécois soulevées par le recours collectif multi-jurisdictionnel: pragmatisme ou cohérence théorique. LL.M. Thesis University of Montreal, Montreal. Available at https://papyrus.bib.umontreal.ca/xmlui/handle/1866/2365

Egea V (2014) La résolution des conflits de procédures dans le règlement Bruxelles I bis. In: Guinchard E (ed) Le nouveau règlement Bruxelles I bis Règlement n° 1215/2012 du 12 décembre 2012 concernant la compétence judiciaire, la reconnaissance et l'exécution des décisions en matière civile et commerciale. Buylant, Brussels, pp 147–165

Erk-Kubat N (2014) Jurisdictional disputes in parallel proceedings: a comparative European perspective on parallel proceedings before National Courts and Arbitration Tribunals. Ph.D. Thesis. University of St. Gallen, School of Management, Economics, Law, Social Sciences and International Affairs, St. Gallen. Available at www1.unisg.ch/www/edis.nsf/SysLkpByIdentifier/4226/$FILE/dis4226.pdf

Franzina P (2014a) L'universalisation partielle du régime européen de la compétence en matière civile et commerciale dans le règlement Bruxelles I bis: une mise en perspective. In: Guinchard E (ed) Le nouveau règlement Bruxelles I bis Règlement n°1215/2012 du 12 décembre 2012 concernant la compétence judiciaire, la reconnaissance et l'exécution des décisions en matière civile et commerciale. Buylant, Brussels, pp 39–82
Franzina P (2014b) Lis pendens involving a third country under the Brussels I-bis regulation: an overview. Rivista di diritto privato e processuale 2014:23–42
George JP (1999) Parallel litigation. Baylor Law Rev 51:669–986
George JP (2002) International parallel litigation – a survey of current conventions and model lawS. Texas Int Law J 37:499–540
Glenn HP (1999) L'affaire Bre-X et les recours collectifs transfrontaliers. Revue québécoise de droit international 12:33–45
Goldstein G (2016) Le forum non conveniens en droit civil: Analyse comparative à la lueur du droit international privé du Québec et du Japon. Revue critique de droit international privé 111:51–83
Halfmeier A (2012) Recognition of a WCAM settlement in Germany. Nederlands Internationaal Privaatrecht:176–184
Heß B (2000) Die Anerkennung eines Class Action Settlement in Deutschland. Juristenzeitung 55:373–382
Hess B (2010) Cross-border Collective Litigation and the Regulation Brussels I. Praxis des Internationalen Privat - und Verfahrensrechts (IPRax) 30:116–121
Hess B, Mantovani M (2019) Current developments in forum access: comments on jurisdiction and forum non conveniens – European perspectives on human rights litigation. MPILux Research Paper Series 2019 (1). Available at www.mpi.lu
Johnson GW (2012) Rule 23 and the exclusion of foreign citizens as Class Members in US class actions. Va J Int Law 52:963–993
Kafi-Cherrat O (2018) La class action s'approche: à propos de la reconnaissance en Belgique des class action settlements américaines (Aff. Lernout & Hauspie). Journal du droit international (Clunet) 145:81–95
Kastanidis AT (2015) La litispendance internationale au regard du règlement (UE) 1215/2012. Revue critique de droit international privé 104:579–588
Klauser A (2005) Von der "Sammelklage nach österreichischem Recht" zur echten Gruppenklage. ecolex 16:744–747
Lahav AD (2011) Two views of the class action. Fordham Law Rev 79:1939–1963
McLachlan C (2008) Lis Pendens in International Litigation. Recueil des cours de l'Academie de droit international de la Haye / Collected Courses of the Hague Academy of International Law, vol 336. Nijhoff, Leiden, Boston, pp 199–553
Michaels R (2006) Two paradigms of jurisdiction. Mich J Int Law 27:1003–1069
Monestier T (2010) Personal Jurisdiction over Non-Resident Class-Members: Have We Gone Down the Wrong Road. Texas International Law Journal 45:537–572
Monestier TJ (2011) Transnational class actions and the illusory search for Res Judicata. Tulane Law Rev 86:1–79
Nagareda RA, Bone RG, Chamblee Church E, Silver C, Woolley P (2013) The law of class actions and other aggregate litigation, 2nd edn. West, St. Paul
Nagel H, Gottwald P (2013) Internationales Zivilprozessrecht, 7th edn. Verlag Otto Schmidt, Cologne
Oquendo ÁR (2017) Justice for all: Certifying Global Class Actions. Washington University Global Studies Law Rev 16:71–124
Perucchi L (2008) Anerkennung und Vollstreckung von US class action – Urteilen und – Vergleichen in der Schweiz. Schulthess, Zurich, Basel, Geneva
Picardi N (2010) Le juge naturel – Principe fondamental en Europe. Revue internationale de droit comparé 62:27–73

Piché C (2016) L'emprise des cinq doigts de Frankenstein: réflexions en cinq temps sur l'action collective. Revue internationale de droit comparé 68:291–317
Piché C, Saumier G (2019) Consumer collective redress in Canada. Jpn Yearb Int Law 61:231–259
Romy I (1999) Class actions américaines et droit international privé suisse. Aktuelle juristische Praxis / Pratique actuelle juridique 1999:783–801
Schack H (2017) Internationales Zivilverfahrensrecht, 7th edn. CH Beck, Munich
Schütze R (2009) Rechtsverfolgung im Ausland, Prozessführung vor ausländischen Gerichten und Schiedsgerichten, 4th edn. De Gruyter, Berlin
Segovia González MJ (2018) Les accords judiciaires de coopération internationale. Larcier, Brussels
Shapiro DL (1998) Class actions: the class as party and client. Notre Dame Law Rev 73:913–962
Sherman EF (2008) The MDL model for resolving complex litigation if a class action is not possible. Tulane Law Rev 82:2205. Public Law and Legal Theory Research Paper Series Research Paper No. 08-12, June 2008, http://ssrn.com/abstract=1407588
Sladič J (2013) The remedies and recourses in European civil procedure after the intended abolition of the exequatur. Zeitschrift für europarechtliche Studien 16:329–358
Sladič J (2017a) Conditions of admissibility and access to Justice – A Slovenian perspective. In: Uzelac A, van Rhee CH (eds) Revisiting procedural human rights. Intersentia, Cambridge, pp 209–239
Sladič J (2017b) Das slowenische Gesetz über Sammelklagen. Zeitschrift für Zivilprozess International 22:137–186
Štempihar J (1953) Uvod v mednarodno zasebno pravo. Pravna fakulteta Univerze vLjubljani, Ljubljana
Stürner M, Wendelstein C (2018) Datenschutzrechtliche "Sammelklagen" im Zuständigkeitsregime der Brüssel Ia-VO. Juristenzeitung 73:1083–1092
Symeonides SC (2008) Choice of Law in the American Courts in 2007: Twenty-First Annual Survey. http://www.ssrn.com
Telfer RTC (2017) Forum shopping and the private enforcement of EU competition law: Is forum shopping a dead letter?. Ph.D. Thesis. University of Glasgow, Glasgow. http://theses.gla.ac.uk/8002
Tzankova I, Kortmann J (2010) Remedies for consumers of financial services: collective redress and improvement of class representation. Eur Rev Consum Law / Revue europénne du droit de la consommation 117–140
van Lith H (2010) The dutch collective settlements act and private international law. Aspecten van Internationaal Privaatrecht in de WCAM
Virgós Soriano M, Garcimartín Alférez FJ (2007) Derecho Procesal Civil Internacional (Litigación internacional), 2nd edn. Thomson Reuters, Madrid
Voet S (2017) Chapter 4: Actions for Collective Redress. In: An evaluation study of national procedural laws and practices in terms of their impact on the free circulation of judgments and on the equivalence and effectiveness of the procedural protection of consumers under EU consumer law, Report prepared by a Consortium of European universities led by the MPI Luxembourg for Procedural Law as commissioned by the European Commission, JUST/2014/RCON/PR/CIVI/0082, European Commission, Brussels. Available at https://ec.europa.eu/newsroom/just/document.cfm?action=display&doc_id=49503
Wasserman R (2011) Transnational class action and interjurisdictional preclusion. Notre Dame Law Rev 86:313–380
Wautelet P (2002) Les conflits de procédures: étude de droit international privé comparé, Ph.D. Thesis. Catholic University in Leuven, Leuven. Available at http://hdl.handle.net/2268/193
Westbrook JL (2003) International judicial negotiation. Texas Int Law J 38:567–586
Winters BA (1985) Jurisdiction over unnamed plaintiffs in multistate class actions. Calif Law Rev 73:181–211

Jorg Sladič PhD. at the University of Saarland (Germany), assistant professor at the European Faculty of Law, Ljubljana, Slovenia, where he specializes in private international law and in comparative law and attorney at law in a law firm Sladič-Zemljak. From 2004 to 2007, he was a EU official at the European Court of Justice in Luxembourg (first as a legal secretary of a judge and latter of advocate general Trstenjak) in 2018 he was a member of the European Commission's Expert group on Modernisation of Judicial Cooperation in Civil and Commercial Matters.

Collective Redress in the EU: Will It Finally Come True?

Alexandre Biard and Stefaan Voet

Abstract On 22 June 2020, the European institutions reached a historical deal on a new Directive for representative actions for consumers, which was finally adopted on 25 November 2020 New EU Directive 2020/1828 allows Qualified Entities across the EU to seek compensation on behalf of consumers affected by mass harm situations. Presented by the European Commission in April 2018 as part of its "New Deal for Consumers" package, the Directive intends to strengthen the enforcement of consumer rights and to ensure access to justice when large-scale damage arise. It also gives considerable leeway to the Member States when implementing the new rules into their national legislations. Therefore, the effectiveness of the new EU instrument will strongly depend on the choices made by Member States at national levels. These issues are pivotal to ensure that the new EU collective redress instrument meets its objectives and fully delivers for all harmed individuals.

1 Introduction

Monday evening 22 June 2020, Brussels. White smoke finally emanates from the building where the negotiators of the European Commission, the Parliament and the Council have been gathering to discuss the proposal for a new EU Directive on Representative Actions for Consumers (hereafter 'Representative Action Directive' or 'RAD').[1] After decades of controversies, a historic political deal was finally

[1]Council of the European Union (26 June 2020) Directive of the European Parliament and of the Council on representative actions for the protection of the collective interests of consumers, and repealing Directive 2009/22/EC—Analysis of the final compromise text with a view to agreement.

A. Biard
Erasmus University Rotterdam, Rotterdam, The Netherlands
e-mail: biard@law.eur.nl

S. Voet (✉)
KU Leuven, Leuven, Belgium
e-mail: stefaan.voet@kuleuven.be

A. Uzelac, S. Voet (eds.), *Class Actions in Europe*, Ius Gentium: Comparative Perspectives on Law and Justice 89, https://doi.org/10.1007/978-3-030-73036-9_12

reached between the EU institutions, which will soon allow Qualified Entities across the EU to claim compensation on behalf of consumers involved in mass harm situations.

Presented by the European Commission in April 2018 as part of its "New Deal for Consumers" package,[2] and finally formally adopted in November 2020, the new Directive 2020/1828 on representative actions for the protection of the collective interests of consumers intends to strengthen the enforcement of consumer rights and to ensure access to justice when large-scale damage arise. The Commission was urged to act as a result of the multiplication of mass damage cases in recent years (Volkswagen Dieselgate, Ryan Air tickets mass cancellation, just to name a few), combined with the absence of adequate tools for compensating harmed individuals, and the failure to secure a coherent legal framework for collective redress. For 2 years, the Commission proposal went through many debates, controversies, and re-writing by the Parliament and the Council. In March 2019, the Parliament finally adopted its resolution on the text,[3] followed by the Council in November of the same year.[4] When the Croatian presidency finally took over in January 2020, everything was set for the start of the Trilogue negotiations.[5] Given the complexity of the issues and the diverging views between Member States, interinstitutional discussions were expected to be long and difficult. For Member States where no collective redress instruments were available, the new proposal implied heavy procedural changes into their national systems. For Member States where collective redress instruments were already in place, stakeholders were worried that the new rules could undermine their existing national mechanisms. On top of this, the proposal also faced strong resistance and criticisms from businesses and the industry, using the fears of abusive litigation and excesses based on the US experience with class actions to slow down negotiations.[6]

---

file:///C:/Users/u0103885/AppData/Local/Microsoft/Windows/INetCache/Content.Outlook/EUEB0OYU/clean_texteconseil.pdf. Accessed 24 Aug 2020.

[2]European Commission (11 Apr 2018) Press Release A New Deal for Consumers: Commission strengthens EU consumer rights and enforcement. https://ec.europa.eu/commission/presscorner/detail/en/IP_18_3041. Accessed 15 Mar 2020.

[3]European Parliament (26 Mar 2019) European Parliament legislative resolution of 26 March 2019 on the proposal for a Directive of the European Parliament and of the Council on representative actions for the protection of the collective interests of consumers, and repealing Directive 2009/22/EC. https://www.europarl.europa.eu/doceo/document/TA-8-2019-0222_EN.html?redirect. Accessed 24 Aug 2020.

[4]Council of the European Union (21 Nov 2019) Proposal for a Directive of the European Parliament and of the Council on representative actions for the protection of the collective interests of consumers, and repealing Directive 2009/22/EC – General approach. https://data.consilium.europa.eu/doc/document/ST-14210-2019-INIT/en/pdf. Accessed 24 Aug 2020.

[5]Not less than 5 presidencies—the Bulgarian, Austrian, Romanian, Finnish and finally Croatian presidencies—where involved in the negotiation of the directive.

[6]See e.g. US Chamber Institute for legal Reform, The growth of collective redress in the EU, 21 March 2017 (www.instituteforlegalreform.com/research/the-growth-of-collective-redress-in-the-eu-a-survey-of-developments-in-10-member-states-).

After the two first Trilogue meetings organised in January and March 2020, the Covid-19 pandemic outbreak hit Europe. It slowed down the process by adding organisational complexity to an already difficult situation. The crisis led to the cancellation of in-person meetings and forced the EU institutions to work in a lockdown mode for several weeks. At the start of June, whereas the health situation started to show signs of slow improvements in Europe, few people thought that a deal could realistically still be achieved before the Summer break. Negotiations were thus expected to continue under the German presidency starting in July. It is in this very unusual context that a political agreement was reached during the third Trilogue meeting. For many, this came as a welcome surprise. A few days earlier, the industry was still actively lobbying and urged the EU institutions to not 'rush' the adoption of collective redress in the EU (somehow disregarding the fact that collective redress had already been a topic discussed for more than 30 years in Europe. . .).[7]

Although Directive 2020/1828 undoubtedly constitutes an important milestone putting an end to several unsuccessful initiatives (Sect. 2), several important steps now need to be taken by Member States to ensure that consumers can trully benefit from effective and useful instruments for obtaining compensation in mass harm situations (Sect. 3).

2 Habemus EU Collective Redress!

The road to collective redress in Europe has been a bumpy and thorny one with many unsuccessful attempts to secure a coherent framework (Sect. 2.1). In 2018, the European Commission finally made a proposal introducing representative actions in all Member States (Sect. 2.2). After complex interinstitutional negotiations (Sect. 2.3), a political deal was finally reached on the new EU Directive (Sect. 2.4).

2.1 Unsuccessful Previous EU Initiatives

In 2011, after many patchy initiatives within the European Commission and numerous Green and White Papers,[8] former Commission President Barroso called on his Commissioners in charge of Consumer Affairs, Justice and Competition to come up

[7]Joint business statement on the proposal on representative actions, "rushing collective redress will not get it right", 2 June 2020 (https://www.gsma.com/gsmaeurope/wp-content/uploads/2020/06/02062020_Joint-Business-Statement-on-the-Proposal-on-Representative-Actions-Collective-Redress.pdf).

[8]Commission of the European Communities (27 Nov 2008) Green Paper On Consumer Collective Redress. https://eur-lex.europa.eu/legal-content/EN/TXT/PDF/?uri=CELEX:52008DC0794&from=en. Accessed 25 Aug 2020 and Commission of the European Communities (2 April 2008) White Paper on Damages actions for breach of the EC antitrust rules. https://ec.europa.eu/

with a joint and coherent approach to collective redress. In a collaboration note published in 2010, the three Commissioners announced the launch of a public consultation on a 'European approach to collective redress in order to identify which forms of collective redress could fit into the EU legal system and into the legal orders of Member States'.[9] In 2012, the Parliament also called on the Commission to adopt a horizontal approach to collective redress to avoid any further fragmentation within the EU and additional uncoordinated actions.[10] In 2013, the process led to a package of three documents: a Communication where the Commission explained its approach to collective redress,[11] a Recommendation listing eleven criteria that should guide Member States when establishing their respective national legislations on collective redress,[12] and a draft Directive on damages for breach of EU competition law.[13] As the second document was only a Recommendation, the rules were not binding for the Member States. Albeit disappointing, this was the only outcome that could reasonably be expected on such a controversial topic before the end of the Commission mandate. The Recommendation did not intend to promote harmonisation between Member States but aimed at promoting some coherence and consistency between national collective redress mechanisms.[14] In addition, it intended to promote a balanced framework ensuring both an effective access to justice for harmed individuals and sufficient safeguards to avoid abusive litigation.[15]

The Recommendation of 2013 however, fell short of meeting the expectations. In 2016, a research conducted by the Universities of Leuven and Oxford pointed out that 'each national system is tailored to domestic needs, often uninfluenced by the Commission's blueprint, and the overview is of piecemeal development which is

competition/antitrust/actionsdamages/files_white_paper/whitepaper_en.pdf. Accessed 25 Aug 2020.

[9]European Commission (5 Oct 2010) Joint information note 'Towards a Coherent European Approach to Collective redress: next steps. https://ec.europa.eu/competition/antitrust/actionsdamages/Commission_2010_information_towards_european_collective_redress.pdf. Accessed 25 Aug 2020.

[10]European Parliament (2 Feb 2012) Towards a coherent European approach to collective redress, www.europarl.europa.eu/sides/getDoc.do?pubRef=-//EP//TEXT+REPORT+A7-2012-0012+0+DOC+XML+V0//EN. Accessed 25 Aug 2020.

[11]European Commission (11 Jun 2013) Towards a European Horizontal Framework for Collective Redress. https://eur-lex.europa.eu/legal-content/EN/ALL/?uri=CELEX:52013DC0401. Accessed 25 Aug 2020.

[12]Recommendation of the European Commission of 11 June 2013 on common principles for injunctive and compensatory collective redress mechanisms in the Member States concerning violations of rights granted under Union Law, 2013 O.J. (L 201).

[13]European Commission (11 Jun 2013) Proposal for a Directive of the European Parliament and of the Council on certain rules governing actions for damages under national law for infringements of the competition law provisions of the Member States and of the European Union. https://eur-lex.europa.eu/LexUriServ/LexUriServ.do?uri=COM:2013:0404:FIN:EN:PDF. Accessed 25 Aug 2020.

[14]Voet (2014).

[15]Biard (2018a), pp. 189–204.

uncontrolled'.[16] In the wake of Dieselgate, the European Parliament called on the Commission to make 'a legislative proposal for the establishment of a collective redress mechanism in order to create a harmonised system for EU consumers, thus eliminating the current situation in which consumers lack protection in most Member States'.[17] In October 2017, thirty-eight Members of the European Parliament and the European Consumer Association (BEUC) wrote to President Juncker and Justice Commissioner Jourová asking for measures to compensate individuals involved in mass harm situations.[18] Finally, in January 2018, the Commission published its evaluation report on the 2013 Recommendation.[19] Unsurprisingly, the report noted that the impact of the Recommendation had been overall fairly limited. Nine Member States still had no compensatory collective redress mechanism while seven had adopted instruments which were not fully in line with the Recommendation. The Commission also noted persistent divergences between the existing instruments (concerning for example the use of opt in or opt out systems).[20]

2.2 *The "New Deal for Consumers" and the RAD Proposal*

In April 2018, the Commission published its New Deal for Consumers package.[21] It aimed at stepping up the enforcement of EU law in a holistic way and securing more effective consumer redress in mass harm situations. The package was built upon the collective redress evaluation report of January 2018 and upon the results of the Fitness check of EU consumer and marketing law of 2017, which covered 6 Direc-

---

[16]Hodges and Voet (2017), p. 7.

[17]European Parliament, Recommendation following the inquiry into emission measurements in the automotive sector, P8-TA (2017)0100, 4 April 2017, para. 59, www.europarl.europa.eu/sides/getDoc.do?pubRef=-//EP//TEXT+TA+P8-TA-2017-0100+0+DOC+XML+V0//EN (accessed August 2020).

[18]BEUC Letter sent to Commission President Juncker and Justice Commissioner Jourova 'Time for the European Commission to legislate on Collective Redress', 10 October 2017, www.beuc.eu/publications/beuc-x-2017-107_time_for_the_european_commission_to_legislate_on_collective_redress.pdf (accessed August 2020).

[19]European Commission (25 Jan 2018) Report on the implementation of the Commission Recommendation of 11 June 2013 on common principles for injunctive and compensatory collective redress mechanisms in the Member States concerning violations of rights granted under Union Law. www.ec.europa.eu/newsroom/just/document.cfm?action=display&doc_id=49502. Accessed 26 Aug 2020.

[20]Voet (2017).

[21]https://ec.europa.eu/newsroom/just/item-detail.cfm?item_id=620435. Accessed 26 Aug 2020.

tives (including the 2009 Injunctions Directive[22]).[23] It included a Communication from the Commission[24] as well as two legislative instruments: a proposal for a Directive on better enforcement and modernisation of EU consumer protection (also called "omnibus Directive)[25] and a proposal for a Directive on representative actions for the protection of collective interests of consumers.[26] The latter intended to modernise the framework for injunctions. As the 2017 Fitness Check had revealed, the length and costs of the procedures, their limited use to stop cross-border infringement, and the absence of compensatory effects for consumers had been the main shortcomings of the existing rules on injunctions. The new proposal was thus aimed at remediating the situation and introduced a new instrument providing harmed individuals with the possibility to obtain redress in mass harm situations.

The scope of the proposed RAD proposal was detailed in an Annex. Member States were free to decide whether the procedure had to be a judicial or administrative one, or both. The proposal kept the general architecture of the Injunctions Directive and provided that only Qualified Entities were allowed to initiate representative actions on behalf of consumers. Consumer organisations and independent public bodies would be eligible for such a status. The proposal imposed several designation criteria for Qualified Entities (e.g. they must have a non-for-profit nature, be properly established, have a legitimate interest to act, etc.). Member States could also decide to appoint Qualified Entities on an *ad hoc* basis for the purpose of bringing a specific action.

Qualified Entities may request injunctive redress measures and compensatory measures. Where the quantification of the damage would be complex, Member States would be able to allow courts or administrative bodies to issue a declaratory decision instead of a redress order. For injunctions measures, an opt-out system would be introduced, and Qualified Entities would not have to collect the individual

[22]Directive 2009/22 of the European Parliament and of the Council of 23 April 2009 on injunctions for the protection of consumers' interests, 2009 O.J. (L 110) (EC).

[23]European Commission (23 May 2017) Report of the Fitness Check. file:///C:/Users/u0103885/AppData/Local/Microsoft/Windows/INetCache/IE/2YQ1B76B/FitnessCheckStaffworkingdocument.pdf. Accessed 24 Aug 2020.

[24]European Commission (11 Apr 2018) Communication from the Commission to the European Parliament, the Council and the European Economic and Social Committee A New Deal for Consumers. https://eur-lex.europa.eu/legal-content/EN/TXT/?qid=1573718927782&uri=CELEX%3A52018DC0183. Accessed 24 Aug 2020.

[25]European Commission (11 Apr 2018) Proposal for a Directive of the European Parliament and of the Council amending Council Directive 93/13/EEC of 5 April 1993, Directive 98/6/EC of the European Parliament and of the Council, Directive 2005/29/EC of the European Parliament and of the Council and Directive 2011/83/EU of the European Parliament and of the Council as regards better enforcement and modernisation of EU consumer protection rules. https://eur-lex.europa.eu/legal-content/EN/TXT/?qid=1523880940100&uri=COM:2018:185:FIN. Accessed 24 Aug 2020.

[26]European Commission (11 Apr 2018). Proposal for a Directive of the European Parliament and of the Council on representative actions for the protection of the collective interests of consumers, and repealing Directive 2009/22/EC. https://eur-lex.europa.eu/legal-content/EN/TXT/?uri=COM:2018:184:FIN. Accessed 24 Aug 2020.

mandates of consumers for acting. However, when it comes to redress measures, Member States would have the possibility to chose between opt-in and opt-out. Furthermore, to facilitate cross-border actions, any Qualified Entity would be allowed to bring actions in any other Member States and several Qualified Entities from different Member States would also be allowed to join to bring a single action in one Member State.

Importantly, the proposal also introduced measures to support Qualified Entities. First, Qualified Entities would be financially supported through easier access to funding. Member States would have to take the 'necessary measures' to ensure that the procedural costs do not constitute financial barriers for Qualified Entities. Second, their access to evidence would be facilitated. The proposal also introduced specific rules on funding; to avoid conflicts of interests, Qualified Entities would have to declare the origins of their funding at an early stage. Third-party funding would be prohibited from influencing the decision of the Qualified entities or could not be used to finance actions against competitors. The proposal also included rules on mass settlement. Scrutiny of the court or the public authority over the settlement agreement would be required to assess the fairness of the settlement taking into consideration the rights of all interested and represented parties.

Throughout 2018 and 2019, the Commission organised a series of 'Consumer Dialogues' in the EU Member States to present the New Deal package. The RAD proposal raised many reactions from stakeholders. From the consumer side, the European Consumer Association strongly welcomed the proposal. Although it pointed certain limitations, it overall considered that the Commission had 'come up with a balanced system with procedural norms and safeguards to ensure that both the interests of consumers and of traders can be taken into account'.[27] On the contrary, businesses expressed strong criticisms and argued that the proposal did not contain sufficient safeguards likely to preventing abusive litigation from happening.[28] Some national parliaments also sent detailed opinions and took the view that some aspects of the proposal were incompatible with the principle of subsidiarity.[29]

2.3 The Interinstitutional Negotiations

Once in the hands of the European co-legislators, a fierce and long battle was to begin. At the European Parliament, the proposal was referred to the Committee on

[27]BEUC, "New deal for consumers"—clear improvement but not the needed quantum leap', 11 April 2018.

[28]Eurochambres, 'The New deal for consumers or how to open the door for abuses: an example of needless overshooting', 11 April 2018; EDiMA, 'EDiMA's reaction to the Commission's New deal for consumers', 11 April 2018.

[29]E.g. the Austrian and Swedish Parliaments.

Legal Affairs in May 2018. The Parliament adopted its final resolution in March 2019 and made several changes into the Commission's proposal.[30] In particular, the scope of the Directive was extended to cover *inter alia* the General Product Safety Directive (GPSD) as well as some other pieces of EU legislation. In particular, data subjects were also added into the definition of who can bring collective actions. Moreover, the possibility to derogate from collective redress and only allow the judge to issue a declaratory judgement instead was removed. The necessity to have an injunction order before seeking a redress order was also removed. The Parliament also adopted a new provision with an obligation for Member States to provide structural support to Qualified Entities to enable them to initiate representative actions.

In parallel, discussions before the Council started in April 2018. In November 2019, the Council finally agreed on its general approach, which also included significant changes into the Commission's proposal.[31] One of the most important changes regarded the distinction between domestic and cross-border actions and the split in the designation criteria for Qualified Entities. Only the criteria for being able to initiate cross-border representative actions were to be regulated by the Directive. For domestic actions, Member States were free to set up their own criteria provided that they comply with the objectives of the Directive. The split was pushed by Member States who did not want the EU to meddle in their existing collective redress procedures. Discussions before the Council also revolved around the scope of the Directive (by adding, for example, the Medical Devices Regulation into the Annex of the Directive) and rules on the assistance to Qualified Entities. Furthermore, the effects of the final decision watered down. It was for instance decided that previous decisions or judgements establishing an infringement may only be used as evidence in the follow-on redress cases, but not as rebuttable presumptions.

2.4 *The Political Deal of June 2020*

The final deal agreed between the EU institutions[32] kept the distinction between domestic and cross border cases and the split between designation criteria for

[30]European Parliament (26 Mar 2019) European Parliament legislative resolution of 26 March 2019 on the proposal for a Directive of the European Parliament and of the Council on representative actions for the protection of the collective interests of consumers, and repealing Directive 2009/22/ EC. https://www.europarl.europa.eu/doceo/document/TA-8-2019-0222_EN.html?redirect. Accessed 24 Aug 2020.

[31]Council of the European Union (28 Nov 2019) Proposal for a directive of the European Parliament and of the Council on representative actions for the protection of the collective interests of consumers, and repealing Directive 2009/22/EC – General Approach. https://data.consilium.europa.eu/doc/document/ST-14600-2019-INIT/en/pdf. Accessed 24 Aug 2020.

[32]Council of the European Union (26 June 2020) Directive of the European Parliament and of the Council on representative actions for the protection of the collective interests of consumers, and

Qualified Entities (Art. 3.6–7). Member States will therefore be able to decide on their own criteria for the designation of Qualified Entities for the purposes of bringing domestic actions, provided that these criteria are compliant with the objectives of the Directive. *Ad hoc* Qualified Entities will also be authorised but only for domestic actions (Art. 4.6). Conversely, for cross-border actions, the criteria will be the same across the EU (e.g. Qualified Entities will have to demonstrate at least 12 months of activity in the protection of consumer interest, have a non-profit character, etc) (Art. 4.3). Although one set of clear rules covering both domestic and cross-border representative actions would certainly have simplified the situation and facilitated legal certainty, the split was strongly defended by the Council which made it a *conditio sine qua non* for giving its consent to the proposal. Member States will have to ensure that in particular consumer organisations can get a Qualified Entities status (Art. 4.2). The list of Qualified Entities will need to be communicated to the European Commission and made public at both national and European levels (Art. 5.1).

Another controversial issue regarded the effects of final decisions and whether liability is presumed in all Member States if it has already been determined by a court or administrative body in another Member States. The positions of the Commission, the Parliament and the Council diverged on this point. Ultimately, the provision has been watered down as previous decisions or judgements establishing an infringement can only be used as evidence but not as rebuttable presumption (Art. 15). This is a missed opportunity to ensure legal certainty and coherence across the EU: if the infringement has already been established in a final decision or a court judgement, it should be possible to rely on it in the subsequent redress action, without the need to prove the infringement again.

Member States will have the possibility to chose between opt-in and opt-out systems (Art. 9.2). However, for consumers residing outside the Member State in which the action is brought, the opt-in system is mandatory (Art. 9.3). If there are outstanding amounts (i.e. amounts not collected by harmed individuals), Member States will be entitled to decide where those funds should go (Art. 9.7). As regards the assistance for Qualified Entities, Member States will have to take measures to ensure that the procedural costs do not preclude Qualified Entities from bringing representative actions. This may be done through public funding or other structural support (Art. 20). The deal also contains several rules regulating third-party funding (Art. 10). Third-party funding is possible provided that it complies with several safeguards preventing conflicts of interests.

---

repealing Directive 2009/22/EC—Analysis of the final compromise text with a view to agreement. file:///C:/Users/u0103885/AppData/Local/Microsoft/Windows/INetCache/Content.Outlook/EUEB0OYU/clean_texteconseil.pdf. Accessed 24 Aug 2020.

3 Converting the Collective Redress Try at Member States Levels

Let's use a comparison that sport amateurs may appreciate: in rugby, the complex scoring system used to calculate points has two main steps: after a 'try' (meaning that a player has successfully managed to bring the ball in the 'in-goal' area of the other team), the scoring team has the possibility to add additional points by the means of a so-called 'conversion kick'. In rugby jargon this means that the team has the opportunity to 'convert the try'. Although this might seem far away from the field of collective redress at first sight, the comparison remains useful to depict the current situation. The political agreement on the RAD has indeed been the 'try' scored at the EU level which Member States will now have to 'convert' at their national levels. As the Directive gives leeway to Member States for implementing the Directive into their national legislations, the effectiveness of the new EU instrument will strongly depend on the procedural choices at national levels (Sect. 3.1). In addition, the expected multiplication of cross-border damage in the years to come will require changes in the EU private international rules framework. These issues are pivotal to ensure that the EU collective redress instrument fully meets its objectives and delivers for harmed individuals (Sect. 3.2.).

3.1 Directive 2020/1828 and its Implementation at the National Levels

Now that the battle for collective redress at the European level is coming to an end, another one is about to begin, this time at the national levels. Directive 2020/1828 was finally adopted on 25 November 2020 and Member States have until 25 December 2022 to transpose it into their national legislations. The new provisions will apply as from 25 June 2023. The Directive has given important leeway to the Member States for implementing the new rules. This means that the added value and the effectiveness of the new instrument will strongly depend on the choices made by the Member States. There are for instance no harmonised criteria for Qualified Entities when bringing domestic representative actions. Member States will therefore be free to choose the criteria that they deem necessary. They may use the same criteria as for cross-border cases but are not compelled to do so and may choose stricter requirements. The only obligation for the Member States will be to ensure that the criteria used for domestic cases comply with the objectives of the Directive. Ultimately, the set of criteria adopted by Member States for the purpose of bringing domestic representative actions should not be unduly complicated or too burdensome to not prevent Qualified Entities from bringing domestic representative actions.

National measures aimed to provide financial support to Qualified Entities will also need to be scrutinized carefully. Attention will have to be paid to the applicability of the cost rules in representative action procedures. In most Member States there is no legal aid or public funding for Qualified Entities to bring representative actions. The question arises whether Member States will be willing to provide public funding or set specific funds supporting these kind of procedures.

In some Member States where existing collective redress instruments have so far brought limited results (e.g. in France and Belgium),[33] the RAD can be a useful opportunity to upgrade the existing rules. Let's hope that Member States will seize this chance to introduce mechanisms that are adapted and useful for the resolution of mass claims.

3.2 Upgrading the EU Private International Framework

The RAD intends to facilitate cross border litigation in case of mass harm situations. For example, several Qualified Entities may jointly bring a representative action to the court or administrative authority of a Member State (Art. 4b). However, the Directive does not touch upon EU private international rules.[34]

The application of the Brussels I*bis* Regulation in the context of mass claims has raised several interpretative issues.[35] This is because EU private international rules have been drafted with the tradition 'one-on-one' litigation model in mind and are not adapted to multicentred disputes where damage and harmed individuals may spread over several jurisdictions. In 2013, stakeholders asked for additional guidance on the application of EU private international rules to mass litigation. However, no agreement could be achieved between the EU institutions and the Commission finally took the view that the 'existing rules laid down in the Brussels I*bis* Regulation should be fully exploited'.[36] As many observers pointed out at that time, the absence of rules was a missed opportunity to clarify the situation.[37]

In 2018, in the context of the ECJ ruling *Schrems v. Facebook*, Advocate General Bobek also highlighted the limits of the Brussels I*bis* Regulation in the context of collective redress and argued that the issue is 'too delicate and complex' and cannot be solved on the basis of an instrument that is 'clearly unfit' and is 'in need of comprehensive legislation'.[38] In 2020, in the context of the Dieselgate litigation, an Austrian court sought clarification on the notion of 'place where the harmful event

[33]See the chapters about France and Belgium in this book; see also Assemblée nationale (2020) and Biard (2018b).

[34]Biard and Kramer (2019).

[35]See e.g. Bosters (2017).

[36]European Commission (11 Jun 2013) Towards a European Horizontal Framework for Collective Redress. https://eur-lex.europa.eu/legal-content/EN/ALL/?uri=CELEX:52013DC0401. Accessed 25 Aug 2020.

[37]Stadler (2013).

[38]Opinion of Advocate General Bobek 14 Nov 2017. Case C-498/16. *Schrems v Facebook*. https://www.politico.eu/wp-content/uploads/2017/11/C0498_2016-EN-AGO.pdf. Accessed 21 Aug 2020.

occurred' laid down in Article 7.2 the Brussels *Ibis* Regulation and referred a question to the European Court of Justice for a preliminary ruling. This case was about an action brought by the Austrian consumer organisation Verein für Konsumenteninformation (VKI) which had brought several actions representing 16,000 consumers affected by the Dieselgate scandal before Austrian courts. Volkswagen had challenged the competence of Austrian courts as the company is seated in Germany. In its decision of 9 July 2020, the Court held that Art. 7.2 of the Brussels *Ibis* Regulation must be interpreted as meaning that, in the context of the Dieselgate, where a manufacturer in a Member State has unlawfully equipped its vehicles with software that manipulates data relating to exhaust gas emissions before those vehicles are purchased from a third party in another Member State, the place where the damage occurs is in that latter Member State.[39]

With the multiplication of cross border damage, it can be expected that the number of similar questions relating to the interpretation of EU private international rules will multiply in the future. During the preparatory discussions of the RAD, the Parliament suggested to use the domicile of the defendant to determine the competent jurisdiction.[40] However, this idea was dismissed. Ultimately, the agreed RAD provides that 'this Directive should not affect the application of nor establish rules on private international law regarding jurisdiction, the recognition and enforcement of judgments or applicable law. The existing Union law instruments apply to the representative actions set out by this Directive' (Recital (21)). Moreover, the Commission should, within 5 years after the date of application of the Directive, assess whether a 'European Ombudsman' should be created for the purposes of solving cross-border mass claims (Art. 23). There is however uncertainty as to what this 'European ombudsman' should look like or how it should handle cross-border mass claims. Finally, in its Communication on collective redress of 2013, the Commission considered that 'in the light of further experience involving cross-border cases, the report foreseen on the application of the Brussels *Ibis* Regulation should include the subject of effective enforcement in cross-border collective actions'.[21] This report is expected for January 2022 and hopefully should guide regulatory changes at the EU level.

---

[39]CJEU 9 July 2020. Case C-343/19. *VKI v Volkswagen*. https://eur-lex.europa.eu/legal-content/EN/TXT/?uri=CELEX:62019CJ0343. Accessed 25 Aug 2020.

[40]European Commission (11 Jun 2013) Towards a European Horizontal Framework for Collective Redress. https://eur-lex.europa.eu/legal-content/EN/ALL/?uri=CELEX:52013DC0401. Accessed 25 Aug 2020.

4 Conclusion

EU Member States have now until the end of 2022 to implement the rules laid down in Directive 2020/1828 into their national legislations. The EU Directive on representative actions for consumers is likely to profoundly change the European civil litigation landscape. However, today it is still too early to assess whether the RAD will be the promised game-changer enhancing the rights of individuals involved in mass harm situations. Now settled at the EU level, the EU Member States have a key role to make this ultimately happen.

Let's wait and hope.

References

Assemblée nationale (France), Rapport sur le bilan et les perspectives des actions de groupe par L. Vichnievsky and P. Gosselin, June 2020 (www.assemblee-nationale.fr/dyn/15/rapports/cion_lois/l15b3085_rapport-information#) Accessed August 2020

Biard A (2018a) Collective redress in the EU: a rainbow behind the clouds? ERA Forum 19:189–204

Biard A (2018b) Sale temps pour l'action de groupe...la nécessaire recherche d'outils alternatifs pour résoudre les litiges de masse. Revue Lamy Droit Civil 157:21–26

Biard A, Kramer X (2019) The EU directive on representative actions for consumers: a milestone or another missed opportunity?, Zeitschrift für Europäisches Privatrecht (ZEuP), 249–259

Bosters M (2017) Collective redress and private international law in the EU. Asser Press, p 268p

Hodges C, Voet S (2017) Delivering collective redress in markets: new technologies. https://www.fljs.org/sites/www.fljs.org/files/publications/Delivering%20Collective%20Redress%20in%20Markets-New%20Technologies.pdf. Accessed 15 Aug 2020

Stadler A (2013) The commission's recommendation on common principles of collective redress and private international law issues. Ned Int Privaatr, 483–488

Voet S (2014) European collective redress: a status quaestionis. Int J Proc Law 1:97–128

Voet S (2017) Where the wild things are. Reflections on the state and future of European collective redress. In: Waves in contract and liability law in three decades of Ius Commune. Intersentia, pp 105–140

Alexandre Biard Affiliated senior researcher at Erasmus University Rotterdam. His research focuses on consumer rights, enforcement and access to justice.

Stefaan Voet Associate professor of civil procedure at the University of Leuven and a host professor at the University of Hasselt. Programme Affiliate at the CMS/Swiss Re Research Programme on Civil Justice Systems at the Centre for Socio-Legal Studies at the University of Oxford. Member of the Class Actions Exchange Network spearheaded by the universities of Stanford, Oxford and Tilburg and affiliate at the Class Action Lab of the University of Montréal. He is also a member of different working groups of the European Law Institute.

Part IV
Global Perspectives on Collective Redress

The State of Reform in First and Second Generation Class Action Jurisdictions

Jasminka Kalajdzic

Abstract While collective redress mechanisms continue to develop in much of Europe and in pockets around the world, the oldest class action regimes are undergoing reform. This contribution explores the state of reform in the first and second generation class action jurisdictions: the United States, Australia, Israel and Canada. Their respective class action procedures are outlined in Sect. 2. Section 3 discusses the reform initiatives of the past 3 years in each of the four countries. In Sect. 4, common areas of concern as well as areas of divergence are explored. Comparing and contrasting these reform efforts illustrates the evolution of class actions in these countries and provides useful insights for those studying and contributing to the development of newer collective redress systems.

1 Introduction

Collective redress mechanisms have emerged in dozens of jurisdictions around the world in the past decade. At last count, 38 countries allow some form of collective litigation.[1] The debates about the virtues and vices of class actions play out in all of these jurisdictions with several common themes: Should group members have to opt in? Are class actions suitable for all types of legal wrongs? Ought lawyers be able to work on a contingency fee basis? Many scholars all over the world, including contributors to this book, have helpfully explored these debates, revealing that the state of investigation in these so-called third-generation class action jurisdictions is still very much in flux.[2]

But what of the first and second generation regimes? The United States is the birthplace of the modern class action and is viewed as either the model or the

[1] Hensler (2017), pp. 965–966.

[2] See, e.g., Voet (2014).

J. Kalajdzic (✉)
University of Windsor, Windsor, ON, Canada
e-mail: kalajj@uwindsor.ca

A. Uzelac, S. Voet (eds.), *Class Actions in Europe*, Ius Gentium: Comparative Perspectives on Law and Justice 89, https://doi.org/10.1007/978-3-030-73036-9_13

cautionary tale for collective redress procedures in states that have recently introduced them. Canada, Australia and Israel adopted class actions about 25 years after the United States, in the early 1990s. These second-generation jurisdictions are very much modelled on the American procedure, albeit with important distinctions, primarily on the issues of costs, fees and standards for certification.

While class actions are indisputably entrenched in these older, common law jurisdictions, the extent to which they are perceived as 'successful' is contested. Moreover, in each jurisdiction reform efforts have been underway in recent years. In this contribution, I explore the state of reform in first- and second-generation class action regimes. I start by briefly summarizing the basic contours of the class action procedure in the United States, Australia, Israel and Canada. In Sect. 3, I describe the recent reform initiatives in each of the four countries. In Sect. 4, I analyze the common areas of concern as well as areas of divergence. By comparing and contrasting these reform efforts, I hope to provide observations from 'mature' class action jurisdictions that both illuminate the evolution of class actions in these countries and provide useful insights for those studying and contributing to the development of newer collective redress systems.

2 Procedural Frameworks in the U.S.A., Australia, Israel and Canada

The United States is the birthplace of the modern class action with roots in medieval English group litigation.[3] Federal Rule 23[4] was drafted in 1966 in order to facilitate group litigation on behalf of consumers, shareholders and environmental causes.[5] It was followed about 25 years later by the first common law province in Canada[6] and the Federal Court in Australia. In the US, class action procedure is codified by way of the Federal Court rules and analogous state court rules. In Australia, representative proceedings are governed by provisions in the Federal Court Act and comparable statutes in two Australian states.[7] In Ontario and all but one of the other eight common law provinces, self-standing class action statutes were enacted between

[3]Yeazell (1987).

[4]Fed. R. Civ. P. 23.

[5]See "An Oral History of Rule 23," a transcript of an interview conducted by Issacharoff with Arthur Miller, who was the assistant to Professor Benjamin Kaplan, the Reporter for the Advisory Committee, Issacharoff and Miller (2018), p. 105, 109–110, cited in Hensler (2020), n. 14.

[6]The very first province in Canada to permit class actions was Québec, a mixed civil and common law jurisdiction, by way of amendments to its Civil Code of Procedure in 1979. Its procedure has many similarities to the American Rule 23 but also significant departures, including a different certification test and a presumption that no evidence will be filed by the parties.

[7]Federal Court of Australia Act 1976, No. 156, 1976, Part IVA.

1992 and 2011,[8] while the Federal Court rules were amended to include class action provisions in 1998.[9] Class action mechanisms were first introduced in Israel by way of amendments to their securities legislation in 1988 and similar amendments to consumer protection law in 1994, and subsequently in other statutes. In 2006, the Knesset enacted a new, trans-substantive class action statute that replaced all previous specific statutory arrangements.[10]

In the main, these first- and second-generation jurisdictions are very similar in providing a procedure for collective action that is trans-substantive, opt-out and subject to close judicial supervision. All allow representative plaintiffs to sue for damages on behalf of the class, in addition to non-monetary relief. All acknowledge that class members are largely absent in representative proceedings, but permit class members to participate by objecting to proposed settlements. As I will explain later, many reform efforts are directed to making court oversight on behalf of the class more meaningful.

Finally, the United States, Canada and Israel share fairly similar certification procedures, pursuant to which a proposed representative plaintiff must satisfy a judge that their claims are appropriately prosecuted on a collective basis. There must be a commonality of claims and an absence of conflicts of interest between class members, as well as a suitable representative with competent counsel.

Although Australia does not have a certification requirement, and therefore a lawsuit can be initiated as a class action, rather than as an individual lawsuit that is then certified or converted into a class action, Australia's rules allow for a defendant to move to decertify litigation using many of the same criteria employed in the other countries' certification procedure—that is, on the basis, for example, that there is no commonality, there are conflicts of interest, or that the proceeding is no longer an efficient method of resolving the claims.[11]

There are also significant differences between these four jurisdictions.

Evidentiary Rights/Certification Requirements Only the United States has extensive pre-certification discovery rights. That said, a not insignificant amount of evidence is filed at certification in Canada and Israel. The threshold for certification has also become stricter in the United States than elsewhere in recent years, as a result of more conservative judicial interpretations of Rule 23.

Contingency Fees Contingency fees have always been allowed for plaintiff attorneys in class actions in the United States, Canada and Israel. They are prohibited

---

[8]Alberta: Class Proceedings Act, SA 2003, c. C-16.6; British Columbia: Class Proceedings Act, RSBC 1996, c. 50; Manitoba: Class Proceedings Act, CCSM c. C.130; New Brunswick: Class Proceedings Act, RSNB 2011, C. 125; Newfoundland and Labrador: Class Actions Act, SN 2001, c. C-18.1; Nova Scotia: Class Proceedings Act, SNS 2007, c. 28; Ontario: Class Proceedings Act, 1992, SO 1992, c. 6; Québec: Code of Civil Procedure, RSQ c. C-25.01, Book VI, articles 571 to 604; Saskatchewan: Class Actions Act, SS 2001, c. C-12.01.

[9]Federal Court Rules, SOR/98-106, enacted pursuant to Federal Courts Act, RS, 1985, c. F-7.

[10]Klement and Klonoff (2018), p. 172.

[11]Federal Court of Australia Act, n. 7 above, sections 33L, 33M & 33N.

in Australia, which has resulted in a very robust third-party litigation funding industry.

Cost-shifting The English rule (the loser pays the successful party's legal costs) exists in half of the Canadian provinces, in Israel and in Australia. In the United States and four Canadian provinces, each party bears its own costs. The exposure of the representative plaintiff to very high adverse costs has led to class counsel providing indemnities to representative plaintiffs. Such indemnities are prohibited in Israel. And in Australia, commercial litigation funders take on that risk and are therefore responsible for paying the successful defendant's cost awards.

Third-party Funding Commercial litigation funding is most pronounced in Australia, far less so in Canada and Israel, and non-existent in class actions in the United States.[12] The role of funders in the litigation, and the court's function in supervising the funder-lawyer relationship, are the topics of much judicial discussion and reform attention.

3 State of Reforms

In this section, I describe the specific reform efforts that have taken place over the past 3 years in each of the four countries under examination. As will become evident, class actions have been the subject of considerable attention and give rise to some similar concerns.

3.1 The United States

Class action reform in the United States can take place in three different ways: by the courts' rulemaking committees; in the development of case law as issues percolate in the appellate courts; and through Congress. Procedural reforms linked to federal substantive statutes are within the institutional role of Congress. Procedural reforms not connected to subject-matter jurisdiction, however, are more properly the purview of deliberative rulemaking bodies or appellate consideration in the context of live disputes.[13] Reform efforts in the United States have taken place at all three levels: a new law was drafted to significantly restrict the availability of class actions; the Rules Committee amended Rule 23; and one of the busiest circuits introduced guidelines for class action settlements. Only the latter two initiatives were ultimately enacted, but the proposed statute is worthy of attention, if for no other reason than that it is possible a new Congress will seek to re-introduce it, depending on the outcome of the next American election.

[12]Kalajdzic et al. (2013).

[13]Erichson (2018).

3.1.1 FICALA

In February 2017, less than three weeks after President Trump took office, sweeping changes to class action procedure were introduced by a Republican Congress in the Fairness in Class Action Litigation Act of 2017 (FICALA).[14] The bill was passed by the House of Representatives along party lines, but failed to advance in the Senate.

Had FICALA become law, the availability of class actions in federal courts would have become far more limited. For example, provisions would have prohibited class certification for personal injury or economic loss unless the plaintiff "affirmatively demonstrates that each proposed class member suffered the same type and scope of injury as the named class representative".[15] Requiring identical harm among class members would have eliminated many appropriate class actions, such as those on behalf of consumers and employees, simply because the degree of harm between them may differ. Another provision would have prohibited determining or paying class counsel fees until all class members were paid. An absolute prohibition on the payment of even interim fees would create problematic incentives to negotiate settlements with short claims processes even where a longer process would be appropriate.

By all accounts, FICALA appeared to be less about improving judicial efficiency or updating an outmoded procedure than a "defendant-driven effort to reduce liability exposure by making it difficult for plaintiffs to aggregate claims".[16] That said, while critical of some of the more draconian aspects of FICALA, commentators did find some proposals to be laudable.

For example, one provision would have required class counsel to submit an accounting of class action payouts to the Federal Judicial Center, a neutral body, which would then compile the data and report it annually. Such an accounting would bring transparency to the total value paid to class members, the median and average recoveries, the number of class members who received payments and all payments to anyone outside the class. Reporting back to the courts in this way would allow for comprehensive and systematic evaluation of the effectiveness of the class action device, rather than debate anecdotal evidence of extreme cases of abuse or poor results.

FICALA would also have required disclosure of any litigation funding in order to address concerns about who controls the decision to settle. This increased transparency would ensure that class members' interests are protected, particularly with respect to commercial funding arrangements which are otherwise unregulated in the United States.[17]

---

[14]H.R.985—Fairness in Class Action Litigation and Furthering Asbestos Claim Transparency Act of 2017, available online: https://www.congress.gov/bill/115th-congress/house-bill/985. Accessed in January 2020.

[15]*Ibid.* §1716.

[16]Erichson (2018), p. 20.

[17]Kalajdzic et al. (2013).

No doubt to the considerable relief of the plaintiff bar, FICALA did not become law, as the bill failed to advance in the Senate prior to the end of the previous Congress; Democrats, who are more supportive of class actions, took control of the House of Representatives in the new Congress at the end of 2018. There is good reason to believe, however, that Republicans will reintroduce FICALA or similar legislation in the future: Lindsey Graham, the Republican Chair of the Senate Judiciary Committee, said in 2019 that "litigation abuse is real" and that class action reform should be explored.[18]

3.1.2 Rule Amendment

While legislative reform may be dead for the time being, other reforms are taking place at the court level and by the Federal Rules Committee. Federal Rule 23 was amended in 2018 after several years of study and deliberation by the Rules Committee. The changes are designed to provide a more streamlined class action process that is fairer to both the class and defendants. The five main areas of amendment are:

- *Notice*: the Rule now explicitly recognizes additional forms of notice beyond newspapers and mail, namely, electronic means;
- *Preliminary approval of proposed settlement*: the Rule formalizes long-standing practice of seeking preliminary approval of a proposed settlement from a judge prior to issuing notice of the settlement approval hearing;
- *Specific criteria for settlement approval*: Rule 23(e)(2) now requires that courts analyze four factors in determining whether the settlement is fair and in the best interests of the class: adequacy of class representation and counsel, arm's-length settlement negotiation, adequacy and terms of settlement, and equity of treatment as between class members. Courts will balance these factors against the risks, delay and costs of a trial;
- *Objectors*: Rule 23(e)(5) now requires more specificity from objectors to discourage bad-faith objections, and requires approval of any payment connected to an objection, to discourage extortionist behaviour;
- *Appeals*: the Rule prohibits appeals from a preliminary approval of settlement.

3.1.3 Court Guidance

Official court guidance can also be responsive to concerns and trends in class action practice, and is a faster method of reform than either amendments of Rule 23 or enactment of statutes. One of the most active class action jurisdictions in the United States, the Northern District of California, issued comprehensive guidance for class action settlements in November 2018, both to implement the 2018 amendments to

[18] O'Brien (2019).

Rule 23 and to give additional information to assist both the parties negotiating settlements and the courts in approving them.[19] The court now requires much more detail on a motion for preliminary approval of a proposed settlement. For example, counsel must:

- Explain any differences between the settlement class and the class originally proposed in the complaint;
- Explain any differences between the claims to be released and the claims in the complaint;
- Set out the factors bearing on the compromise between anticipated class recovery and the potential recovery if plaintiffs had fully prevailed at trial;
- Estimate the number of class members and the percentage of the class that are expected to submit claims; and
- Provide much more detail about how the claims administrator was selected, the fees being requested, how any *cy près* award recipients were selected and a post-distribution accounting within 21 days of final distribution of settlement funds which must be posted on the settlement website.

All of these directives are aimed at reducing the possibility of improvident settlements by requiring more scrutiny of the work done, the compromises made and the manner in which the settlement, once approved, will actually be distributed to the class members. It is a theme we will see repeated in the reform efforts of the other jurisdictions.

In addition to these reforms, many American academics, including Professor Linda Mullenix whose work appears in this volume, have written on developments and have proposed reforms of their own.[20]

3.2 Australia

Two major law reform studies concluded in 2018 in the two most active class action jurisdictions in Australia. The Attorneys General of the State of Victoria and the Commonwealth launched inquiries and set terms of reference for their respective law reform commissions in late 2016 and 2017, respectively.[21] Both Commissions engaged in extensive consultations and convened advisory committees with academics as well as representatives of the judiciary and the bar. And both studies

[19]Northern District of California (2020).

[20]Mullenix (2014), Klonoff (2013), Fitzpatrick (2019).

[21]In December 2016, the then Attorney-General, the Hon. Martin Pakula MP, asked the Victorian Law Reform Commission "to report on access to justice by litigants who seek to enforce their rights using the services of litigation funders and/or through group proceeding": Victorian Law Reform Commission (2018), p. 2. In December 2017, the Commonwealth Attorney-General announced that he had asked the Australian Law Reform Commission (ALRC) to inquire into class action proceedings and third-party litigation funders: Australian Law Reform Commission (2017).

resulted in extensive recommendations that would make class proceedings more readily available in Victoria and in the Federal Court.

3.2.1 The Victorian Law Reform Commission

The Victorian Law Reform Commission (VLRC) was charged with studying access to justice by focusing on three principal issues:

- Whether there is scope for the supervisory powers of Victorian courts or Victorian regulatory bodies to be increased in respect of litigation funders;
- Whether removing the existing prohibition on law firms charging contingency fees (except in areas where contingency fees would be inappropriate, including personal injury, criminal and family law matters) would assist to mitigate the issues presented by the practice of litigation funding;
- In respect of group proceedings commenced under the provisions of Part 4A of the Supreme Court Act 1986 (Vic) and similar proceedings, whether there should be further regulation of such proceedings.[22]

The terms of reference noted the specific concern that while litigation funding, contingency fees and class proceedings can improve access to justice, there is the parallel concern that "litigants are not exposed to unfair risks or disproportionate cost burdens" when availing themselves of these procedures.

In its Final Report issued in March 2018, the VLRC made many recommendations for statutory reform, and called on the Victorian government to advocate for national regulation and supervision of the litigation funding industry. With respect to group proceedings, the VLRC recommended stronger case management, to ensure that the class actions are conducted efficiently, to reduce cost and delay, and to manage competing actions.[23] To improve the court's oversight of class settlements, the VLRC recommended that the Supreme Court "consider amending its practice note on class actions to include guidance for the appointment of an independent representative (commonly known as a contradictor) to assess the terms of settlement, or the terms of the settlement distribution scheme, on behalf of class members".[24]

Accountability and transparency were also at the heart of the recommendation to require that settlement administrators report regularly to the court during the course of a settlement administration, and to submit a final report "outlining the distributions made to class members, the time taken for such distributions, the amounts charged each class member for distribution, and any outstanding amounts that were unclaimed by class members, including what was done with these outstanding amounts".[25] This recommendation is strongly reminiscent of reporting obligations

[22]Victorian Law Reform Commission (2018), p.v.

[23]Victorian Law Reform Commission (2018), pp. 79–86.

[24]Victorian Law Reform Commission (2018), p. 102.

[25]Victorian Law Reform Commission (2018), p. 107.

recommended in FICALA and mandated in the Northern District guidelines. The common thread: a recognition of the unique conflicts of interest that arise in representative litigation, especially during the settlement phase, and a desire to manage them.

Management of conflicts of interest was central in other recommendations. Because "[t]he involvement of a litigation funder creates conflicts of interest and can affect the rights of all class members", courts' oversight responsibilities are heightened in funded class actions.[26] Further, conflicts of interest for lawyers in class actions are more complex than in single-party litigation, and they may be exacerbated with funder involvement. As a consequence, the VLRC recommended that professional guidelines be produced for lawyers on their duties and responsibilities to all class members in class actions.[27]

Finally, among the most significant recommendations in the Report was a call to liberalize the rules prohibiting contingency fees and to allow courts to order a common fund whereby counsel fees and litigation funders' fees are calculated as a percentage of any recovery. While acknowledging the historical reticence to allow contingency fees, the VLRC concluded that such fees "provide another avenue of funding for clients who may be otherwise unable to pursue proceedings due to costs".[28] Further, allowing lawyers to work on contingency would increase competition with litigation funders which may reduce costs in some cases and enable claims to be pursued that are not attractive to funders. In early 2020, the Victorian Parliament appeared certain to pass legislation permitting contingency fees, as recommended by the VLRC.[29]

3.2.2 Australian Law Reform Commission

In December 2017, the Australian Law Reform Commission (ALRC) inquiry was commissioned by the Commonwealth Attorney-General to study the efficacy of the class action system and the integrity of third-party funded class actions. The study was inspired by the increased prevalence of class actions and the role of litigation funders. The inquiry was guided by three fundamental principles:

- It is essential to the rule of the law that citizens should be able to vindicate just claims through a process characterized by fairness and efficiency to all parties, that gives primacy to the interests of the litigants, without undue expense or delay;
- There should be appropriate protections in place for litigants who wish to avail themselves of the class action system and the variety of funding models that facilitate the vindication of just claims;

[26]Victorian Law Reform Commission (2018), p. xv.

[27]Victorian Law Reform Commission (2018), p. xvi.

[28]Victorian Law Reform Commission (2018), p. xvii.

[29]Mills (2020). As of late May 2020, the bill had not yet passed but remained on the legislative agenda. Eveleigh (2020).

- The integrity of the civil justice system is essential to the operation of the rule of law.[30]

The ALRC study spanned 12 months and engaged numerous stakeholders as well as an expert panel of both Australian and foreign academics.[31] The Final Report included extensive discussion of the evolution of class proceedings and third-party litigation funding and made 24 recommendations for reform. Several recommendations overlap with those of the VLRC, including disclosure requirements for lawyers and funders; support for contingency fees; and further regulation of settlement approval. The ALRC recommended amendments to provide the court with an express statutory power to make common fund orders and to resolve competing class actions (Recommendations 3 and 4). It further recommended an amendment to the Federal Court's Class Actions Practice Note to "require settlement administrators to provide a report to the class on completion of the distribution of the settlement sum" and that the report be published on a national database to be maintained by the court.[32]

Again we see a common refrain: address potential abuse in a mechanism where those affected are largely absent. "It is important that there are appropriate protections in place for litigants involved in class actions, including passive class members who are nevertheless reliant on the representative plaintiff, and the solicitor acting for the representative plaintiff, to act in their interests."[33]

With respect to litigation funders, the ALRC proposed a statutory presumption that funders provide security for costs and an amendment that would expressly empower the courts to award costs against funders. Most importantly, the ALRC recommended a provision that would make all third-party funding agreements in representative proceedings enforceable only when approved by the court, a position consistent with the current law of Ontario.[34]

Finally, the ALRC also recommended that class attorneys be permitted to work on a percentage-of-recovery basis, with leave of the court and subject to strict judicial scrutiny, including as to the terms of the contingency arrangement (Recommendations 17–19). This method of financing class actions has long been in place in the United States, Canada and Israel.

The ALRC Report was tabled in Parliament in December 2018 but most of its recommendations are unlikely to be taken up in light of the current government's expressed aversion to litigation funders and class proceedings. Statements attributed to the Attorney-General in late 2019 suggest that the government may choose to ignore many of the ALRC's recommendations in favour of a more restrictive class

---

[30]Australian Law Report Commission (2018), p. 16.

[31]I served on the ALRC's Academic Expert Panel.

[32]Australian Law Report Commission (2018), p. 10.

[33]Australian Law Report Commission (2018), p. 31.

[34]JB & M Walker Ltd/1523428 Ontario Inc. v. TDL Group, 2019 ONSC 999.

action regime to protect businesses from 'lawfare'.[35] The COVID pandemic may prove to be a catalyst for reform in this regard: in May 2020, the Attorney-General announced a wide-ranging Parliamentary inquiry on class actions and litigation funding. The purpose of the inquiry is two-fold: to determine whether the outcomes in the litigation funding-fueled industry are in the interests of the people that are meant to be represented, and whether the operation of the class action system is consistent with principles of justice.[36] The Joint Committee on Corporations and Financial Services is to report its findings by 7 December 2020.[37]

3.3 Israel

In 2016, several reforms were introduced to Israeli class proceedings by way of statutory amendment. These focused principally on three areas: settlement, objectors and *cy près* awards.

In response to a high incidence (57%) of claims dismissed before certification in which the class representative and counsel were still compensated, new provisions now require the judge to consider both whether the claim showed a valid cause of action and the benefits that accrued to class members, if any, after the action was filed. These provisions aim to deter plaintiffs from filing meritless actions. "Courts are expected to examine the merits of the alleged claims and reject any settlement in which those merits are questionable. This would mark a significant change from past court decisions, which justified approval of low settlements by referring to the claims' low likelihood of success."[38]

Israeli scholars attributed a low rate of objections by class members and non-profit organizations at settlement approval to an absence of information regarding settlement and to the lack of incentives and resources for filing objections.[39] As a result, amendments were introduced to expand standing to any "person who acts in the interest of class members". New provisions would also allow for compensation of successful objectors.

Finally, as in the United States and Canada, *cy près* payments are common in Israel. Amendments to Israeli procedures for approving *cy près* awards recognized such awards have neither a deterrent effect if the defendants get reputational gains when making public donations, nor a compensatory function if there is no proximity between the recipient and the class or the cause of action. The amendments thus designated a public fund responsible for the administration and distribution of *cy près* awards and any unclaimed damages. This public fund is overseen by a

---

[35]Butler (2019).

[36]Hansard Report (2020), p. 85.

[37]Hansard Report (2020), p. 84.

[38]Klement and Klonoff (2018), p. 180.

[39]Klement and Klonoff (2018), p. 184.

committee with a number of representatives appointed by the Attorney-General and from public organizations.[40]

3.4 Canada

Finally, in Canada we saw both statutory changes in British Columbia and a large-scale law reform inquiry in Ontario in 2017–2019.

British Columbia is now, like Ontario, a full opt-out jurisdiction, including for non-residents.[41] Like Israel, British Columbia has made specific provisions regarding *cy près*, by mandating that 50% of unclaimed money be given to the Law Foundation, a non-profit organization that supports a variety of access to justice projects.

In July 2019, the Law Commission of Ontario (LCO) concluded a 2-year study of the most active class action jurisdiction in Canada, with its release of a Final Report and 47 recommendations for reform.[42] In light of the continuing spread and evolution of class actions around the globe, the LCO's proposals for improving class actions are worthy of consideration both in existing class action jurisdictions and in those contemplating their introduction.

The LCO framed its review of Ontario's Class Proceedings Act (CPA)[43] around three fundamental questions:

- Are class actions in Ontario fulfilling their three-part promise to improve access to justice, foster judicial efficiency and promote behaviour modification?
- Does the CPA reflect contemporary class actions issues and practice?
- Does the CPA reflect contemporary priorities in Ontario's justice system and public administration?

The LCO project team[44] announced early on its intention to conduct an independent, comprehensive and evidence-based study of class actions, free of partisan agendas. The team engaged in extensive public consultations with a broad cross-section of class action stakeholders, conducting well over 100 interviews with plaintiff and defendant litigators, judges, class members, NGO representatives, court administrators, academics, claims administrators and in-house counsel. While the LCO received 32 written submissions from industry groups, non-profit organizations and lawyers from both sides of the bar, the majority of the submissions represented defendant interests.

[40]Rozent et al. (2020).

[41]Class Proceedings Amendment Act, 2018, S.B.C. ch-16.

[42]Law Commission of Ontario (2019).

[43]Class Proceedings Act, 1992, S.O. 1992, ch-6.

[44]I was a co-principal researcher and co-author of the Final Report.

The LCO's recommendations focused on improving the class action system for its users (principally, but not exclusively, class members), and on updating the CPA to reflect current best practices. The bulk of the proposed reforms aimed to improve access to justice and judicial efficiency, two of the three principal objectives of class actions. By way of example, the LCO recommended:

- The introduction of explicit procedures for multi-jurisdictional class actions that are consistent with several other provinces, to improve the cumbersome process of adjudicating overlapping and parallel litigation in a country where a procedure akin to the American Multi-District Litigation process is not possible;
- Explicit provisions for the determination of carriage when there are competing class actions, including the requirement to bring a carriage motion within 60 days of the filing of the first action and a claims bar precluding any subsequent class actions;
- The creation of administrative dismissal for delay to weed out dormant cases;
- The requirement that court-approved notices be written in plain language and be disseminated electronically where feasible;
- The mandatory registration of all new class actions to create a more orderly, comprehensive database of cases;
- The elimination of two-way costs for the certification motion, to reduce barriers to class actions for smaller claims and those on behalf of vulnerable populations;
- The introduction of explicit powers to make *cy près* awards, and a stipulation that *cy près* distributions should only be approved when it is not practical or possible to compensate class members directly, using best but reasonable efforts;
- The requirement that parties file formal reports with the court at the end of a settlement in order to make lawyers and administrators accountable for settlement monies; and
- More streamlined appeal routes from certification by eliminating the need to go to the Divisional Court (an intermediate court between the trial court and the Court of Appeal) and dispensing with the leave requirement for both plaintiffs and defendants.

Few recommendations related to the behaviour modification objective of class actions: the LCO proposed codifying the authority to make *cy près* distributions only when compensation is not feasible, and suggested that parties report on any changes in defendants' practices as a result of a class action settlement. Not surprisingly, the LCO had difficulty finding evidence (other than anecdotal) of the deterrence effect of class actions. The Final Report concluded, however, that class actions as a whole provide incentives for increased compliance with the law. Even the most ardent advocates for defendant interests acknowledged that the "mere existence of the class action regime forces defendants to consider the risk of class actions when considering any course of business activity, and itself provides a deterrent effect".[45] Representatives from automobile manufacturers conceded that the risk of class action

[45]Law Commission of Ontario (2019), p. 89.

litigation has a deterrent effect in that it forms part of the advice given internally with respect to appropriate marketing practices.

The balance of the recommendations involved codifying existing best practices related to fee approval, certification and settlement approval. Notably, the LCO did not agree with defendants who argued for a stricter certification test. The LCO devoted the biggest chapter of the Report to the question of whether a higher evidentiary burden or a preliminary merits test ought to be introduced, and concluded that both proposals would undermine access to justice and increase costs and delay.

The LCO decried the poor state of court records in Ontario and the resulting lack of empirical data about the initiation and outcomes of class proceedings. As a result, the Report devoted considerable attention to the reforms necessary to improve data collection and support evidence-based policymaking in class actions. The most significant of these recommendations is one that requires reports back to the court, and made publicly available thereafter, of the outcomes of settlement distributions. The recommendation is very similar to reforms in the Province of Quebec[46] and the Northern District of California guidelines discussed earlier.

The appetite for reform of the CPA 25 years after its introduction was confirmed less than six months after release of the Report: in December 2019 the Attorney General introduced a bill[47] to significantly amend the CPA that incorporates the vast majority of the LCO's recommendations. Two notable exceptions: the Attorney General did not accept the no-costs amendment, and he introduced superiority and predominance requirements as part of certification. The latter requirement is virtually identical to the predominance test under U.S. Federal Rule 23(b)(3) and was proposed by the Canadian Bankers Association and the Canadian Life and Health Insurance Association as a less radical change of the certification test than amendments proposed by other defendant groups. Provisions that make certification more stringent and class actions less accessible were welcome by industry participants and criticized by public interest and consumer groups.[48]

The bill is still being debated in the legislature as of the time of writing but is expected to be passed into law in the summer of 2020.

The LCO's Class Action Report should be of considerable interest to policymakers examining the experience of second-generation class action regimes. In describing Ontario's quarter-century development of class actions and suggesting improvements, the Report serves as both inspiration and a cautionary tale for those nascent systems currently contemplating the enactment of collective redress

[46]Code of Civil Procedure, ch. C-25.01, s. 59.

[47]Bill 161, Smarter and Stronger Justice Act, 2019, online: https://www.ola.org/en/legislative-business/bills/parliament-42/session-1/bill-161.

[48]Debates on the proposed changes were held by the Standing Committee on Justice Policy on June 10-12, 2020. Witnesses from industry groups, class action firms, the Law Commission of Ontario and the author appeared before the Committee.

mechanisms, and helps Ontario join a growing list of jurisdictions reforming class action procedures.

4 Comparative Law Reform

Several areas of convergence appear in the four jurisdictions examined in this chapter. Most notably, the improvements to class action systems all aim to strengthen court oversight, especially at the settlement approval stage, and improve accountability. The need for robust court scrutiny is the product of a universal recognition of the inherent conflicts of interest in a procedure where the interests of absent class members are implicated.[49] Reforms in Canada, Australia and the United States all require the parties to file final reports with the court after a settlement has been distributed. This practice not only provides an incentive for counsel to do their best to distribute money directly to as many class members as possible, it also gives valuable information to judges in future settlement approval hearings, in terms of how successful counsel have been and which settlement distribution schemes work best. Such reports also constitute much needed empirical data for future evidence-based policymaking.

Israel, Canada and the Northern District of California addressed the use of *cy près* in distributing settlement funds. At the time that class actions were introduced in each of these jurisdictions, distributing settlement funds to third-party charities was barely contemplated and neither Federal Rule 23 nor any of the Canadian class action statutes contained explicit provisions for their use.[50] The practice of distributing settlement money that was unclaimed or too difficult to direct to class members developed over time and is now commonplace. Reforms in all three jurisdictions respond to the rise of *cy près* and concerns that they are awarded in unprincipled ways.[51] The introduction of explicit *cy près* provisions, a requirement that *cy près* be used only when necessary and the transparent selection of a *cy près* recipient replace opaque practices that had developed in these jurisdictions over the years. Again, such measures improve accountability at the critical settlement stage.

Both the Ontario and the two Australian law reform commissions recommended explicit regulation of third-party funding agreements by the courts. Unless approved by the courts to ensure class members' interests are protected, these agreements are not enforceable.

Ontario and Australia also share similar recommendations to address competing and overlapping class actions. In the United States, such cases are managed through

[49]For a discussion of the role of the courts in protecting class members' interests and the inherent conflicts between class counsel and the class, see Piche (2011), ch. II.

[50]Only Israel explicitly addresses the substitution of *cy près* payments for direct compensation in section 20(c) of the Class Action Law, 5776-2016, SH No. 2054 p. 264 (Isr.).

[51]For an empirical and critical examination of *cy près* in Canada, see Kalajdzic (2014).

the multi-district litigation procedure. The need for explicit powers to manage competing actions arises from the growth of the class counsel bar and an increase in class action filings.

Reforms in the four jurisdictions also share what was *not* present: there was no serious call for the abolition of class actions, although there are moves to limit them. Ironically, whereas jurisdictions all over the world usually state forcefully that they wish to fashion class action regimes that are *not* like the Americans, the most organized and vocal ideological campaign to restrict class actions severely is operated by an American organization.[52] With the American class action under assault by conservative lobbyists and interest groups, the true 'American-style' class action is easier to find in Canada and Israel than in the United States itself.

Not all reform recommendations are shared with another jurisdiction. For example, Israel's introduction of a requirement that judges examine the merits of alleged claims and reject any settlement in which those merits are questionable is peculiar to that country, where there is a very high rate of claims dismissed before certification but in which class counsel are still paid a fee. This phenomenon is not present in Canada, Australia or the United States.

The Law Commission of Ontario's recommendation that the province move from a cost-shifting to a no-costs regime is also unique to that jurisdiction. The United States is, of course, already a no-costs jurisdiction, and Australians are only now showing some willingness to allow contingency fees; the abandonment of cost-shifting would be too radical a departure from existing norms in Australian civil procedure. Israel also shows no sign of abolishing costs, and, in fact, the trend has been to order significant costs against a plaintiff whose claim is determined to be 'unjustified'.[53]

Also unique is the amended U.S. Federal Rule 23(e)(5) which proscribes payments to objectors without court approval; this revision responds to the unique American phenomenon of 'professional objectors'—lawyers who attempt to scuttle a proposed settlement and then extract a payment from class counsel in order to stand down. Such extortionist activity on the part of objecting class members is not evident in the other jurisdictions. Indeed, Israel introduced amendments to expand standing requirements for objectors in order to encourage *more* objections.

[52]The U.S. Chamber of Commerce's Institute for Legal Reform is a well-funded Conservative organization which extends its lobbying against class actions and third party litigation funding beyond America. In fact, it made written submissions to both the Law Commission of Ontario and the Australian Law Reform Commission. See https://www.instituteforlegalreform.com/global/australia for details of its lobbying efforts in Australia, and https://www.instituteforlegalreform.com/global/canada regarding its Canadian activities.

[53]Rozent et al. (2020).

5 Conclusion

As class actions spread across the globe in varying forms, the places where class actions have taken root over the past several decades continue to evolve. By examining recent reforms in the United States, Canada, Australia and Israel, important themes emerge that may prove instructive to policymakers developing newer systems in other parts of the world.

While the entrepreneurial and representative nature of class actions is such that there is a common risk of self-interest and conflict of interest, all four first- and second-generation jurisdictions rely heavily on the courts to exercise a protective function and preserve the integrity of the class action system. Most significantly, because class action settlements are both commonplace and challenging to scrutinize, all four jurisdictions introduced reforms to improve the settlement approval process and to require an accounting of the settlement distribution.

Continued tweaking in second-generation regimes may actually move them closer to the American model—potentially no costs in Ontario, a greater role for objectors in Israel, and both contingency fees and a true opt-out system in Australia.

The recent celebrations of the 25th and 50th anniversaries of the oldest class action regimes in the common law world were cause for introspection and a recognition of their imperfections. Through their reform efforts, these same jurisdictions continue their quest for the Holy Grail of civil procedure for collective redress.

References

Australian Law Reform Commission (2017) Terms of Reference—Inquiry into Class Action Proceedings and Third Party Litigation Funders. 15 December 2017). https://www.alrc.gov.au. Accessed 19 Feb 2020

Australian Law Report Commission (2018) Integrity, Fairness and Efficiency – An Inquiry into Class Action Proceedings and Third-Party Litigation Funders, Final Report

Butler B (2019) Australian Litigation Funding Giant Rejects Christian Porter's 'Lawfare' Claim". The Guardian, 14 November 2019. https://www.theguardian.com/australia-news/2019/nov/15/australian-litigation-funding-giant-rejects-christian-porters-lawfare-claim. Accessed 19 Feb 2020

Erichson H (2018) Searching for salvageable ideas in *FICALA*. Fordham Law Rev 87(1):19

Fitzpatrick BT (2019) The conservative case for class actions. University of Chicago Press

Hansard Report (2020) Australian Parliament, House of Representatives, 46th Parl, 1st Sess, 1st Per (13 May 2020)

Hensler D (2017) From sea to shining sea: how and why class actions are spreading globally. Kansas Law Rev 65:965

Hensler D (2020) Foreword. In: Fitzpatrick BT, Thomas R (eds) Cambridge international handbook of class actions. Cambridge University Press

Issacharoff S, Miller A (2018) An oral history of rule 23. NYU Ann Surv Am Law 74:105

Kalajdzic J (2014) The illusion of compensation: Cy près distributions in Canadian class actions. Can Bar Rev 92(2):173

Kalajdzic J, Cashman P, Longmoore A (2013) Justice for profit: a comparative analysis of Australian, Canadian and U.S. Third party litigation funding. Am J Comp Law 61(1):93
Klement A, Klonoff R (2018) Class actions in the United States and Israel: a comparative approach. Theor Inq Law 19:151
Klonoff E (2013) The decline of class actions. Wash Univ Law Rev 90:729
Law Commission of Ontario (2019) Class Actions: Objectives, Experiences and Reforms. https://www.lco-cdo.org/en/our-current-projects/class-actions/final-report/. Accessed 19 Feb 2020
Mills T (2020) US-style class action fees poised to come to Victoria. Brisbane Times, 2 February 2020. https://www.brisbanetimes.com.au/national/victoria/us-style-class-action-fees-poised-to-come-to-victoria-20200202-p53wxo.html. Accessed 19 Feb 2020
Mullenix L (2014) Ending class actions as we know them: rethinking the American class action. Emory Law J 64:399
Northern District of California (2020) Guidance for Class Acrion Settlements, 5 December 2018. https://www.cand.uscourts.gov/forms/procedural-guidance-for-class-action-settlements/. Accessed 19 Feb 2020
O'Brien J (2019) Lindsey Graham says 'litigation abuse is real,' class action reform should be considered, Legal Newsline, 3 April 2019. https://legalnewsline.com/stories/512401974-lindsey-graham-says-litigation-abuse-is-real-class-action-reform-should-be-considered. Accessed 19 Feb 2020
Piche C (2011) Fairness in class action settlements. Carswell
Rozent G et al (2020) Class/collective actions in Israel: overview, practical law. Thomson Reuters. https://uk.practicallaw.thomsonreuters.com/8-617-6659?transitionType=Default&contextData=(sc.Default)&firstPage=true&bhcp=1. Accessed 19 Feb 2020
Victorian Law Reform Commission (2018) Access to justice — litigation funding and group proceedings: report
Voet S (2014) European collective redress: a *Status Queaestionis*. Int J Proc Law 4(1)
Yeazell S (1987) From medieval group litigation to the modern class action. Yale University Press

Jasminka Kalajdzic Associate Professor of Law at the University of Windsor (Ontario, Canada) where she teaches Class Actions, Evidence Law and Legal Ethics. Founder and Director of the Class Action Clinic, the first legal clinic in the world focused on representing and advocating for class members. Canadian representative in an International Research Collaborative on Collective Litigation and teaches a comparative class action course with colleagues in the U.S., Germany and the Netherlands. A frequent speaker on class actions domestically and abroad.

Empirical Data and the Powerful Lessons Learnt About Class Actions in Quebec

Catherine Piché

Abstract This contribution evaluates the economic utility and effectiveness of class actions in Quebec based on empirical data obtained at the Class Actions Lab over a period of 25 years. The University of Montreal Faculty of Law's Class Actions Lab is conducting this study in the course of its "Class Action Compensation Project". The Project began in the summer of 2015 and is scheduled to conclude in 2022. The Project seeks to compile and compare take-up rates in various class action files, as well as per-plaintiff recovery data. Ultimately, it measures the end product of class action litigation, the value and benefit of this kind of litigation, and, incidentally, its costs as assumed by the parties and the system. The Project has identified specific parameters that can be used to evaluate empirically class action costs and benefits, and a significant list of criteria directly associated with higher rates of participation and compensation. This is the first Canadian study of its kind. The contribution shows that class actions are instruments of compensation of class members, but that this compensation remains imperfect by way of the number of members compensated, the extent to which they are compensated and the exorbitant costs of bringing such actions.

This contribution reproduces in part an article published in Piché (2019a). This research was made possible thanks to the Fonds québécois de recherche—Société et culture, the Fondation Claude Masse, as well as to the Project Access to Law and Access to Justice (ADAJ), funded by the Social Sciences and Humanities Research Council. I am extremely grateful to each of these six students, Shana, Alex, William, Andrea, Charles-Antoine, and Hugo. Without your precious work I would not have been able to gather such interesting results. All results included in this report are being published in Piché (2019b).

C. Piché (✉)
University of Montreal, Faculty of Law, Montreal, QC, Canada
e-mail: catherine.piche@umontreal.ca

A. Uzelac, S. Voet (eds.), *Class Actions in Europe*, Ius Gentium: Comparative Perspectives on Law and Justice 89, https://doi.org/10.1007/978-3-030-73036-9_14

1 Overview of Class Actions in Quebec

As a federation, Canada divides legislative competency between its federal government and the provincial and territorial governments.[1] Accordingly, the provinces hold jurisdiction over questions of private law and civil procedure and, therefore, collective redress in the form of class actions is determined by provincial law.

The introduction of the class action in Canada dates back to 1978, when Quebec became the first province to adopt class action legislation and a procedure initially called the "recours collectif".[2] Following Quebec, 14 years later, Ontario became the first common law province to enact class proceedings legislation in 1992.[3] Now, with the exception of Prince Edward Island, all the provinces in Canada have a class action procedure.[4] Moreover, the Federal Court of Canada provides for class proceedings within its federal law jurisdiction.[5]

In Quebec, the class action begins with an application for authorization, whereby a representative plaintiff may apply to bring a case before the court on behalf of other class members who find themselves in a similar situation.[6] No class action may be heard without the authorization of the court. As such, this preliminary hearing is a process that serves to filter frivolous or unfounded cases and permits defendants to avoid having to answer "untenable claims on the merits".[7] This first stage of the class

[1]The Constitution of Canada defines the powers of the federal and provincial governments.

[2]*An Act respecting the Class Action*, R.S.Q., c. R.2-1. Also see Walker and Watson (2014), p. 33; Piché (2009), p. 44.

[3]*Class Proceedings Act*, 1992, S.O. 1992, c. 6 (hereinafter "Ont. C.P.A.").

[4]See *Class Proceedings Act*, R.S.B.C. 1996, c. 50 (British Columbia) (hereinafter "B.C.C.P.A."); *Class Proceedings Act*, S.A. 2003, c. C-16 (Alberta) (hereinafter: "Alta. C.P.A."); *The Class Proceedings Act*, C.C.S.M. c. C. 130 (Manitoba) (hereinafter "Man. C.P.A."); *Class Proceedings Act*, R.S.N.B. 2011, c. 125 (New Brunswick) (hereinafter "N.B.C.P.A."); *Class Actions Act*, S.N.L. 2001, c. C-18-1 (Newfoundland and Labrador) (hereinafter "N.&L.C.P.A."); *Class Proceedings Act*, S.N.S. 2007, c. 28 (Nova Scotia) (hereinafter "N.S.C.P.A."); Ont. C.P.A.; *Code of Civil Procedure*, C.Q.L.R. c. C-25.01, arts. 574ff. (Quebec) (hereinafter "C.C.P."); *The Class Actions Act*, S.S. 2001, c. C-12.01 (Saskatchewan) (hereinafter "Sask. C.P.A."). Also see Walker and Watson (2014), p. 33, n. 3. In Prince Edward Island and the Canadian territories, class proceedings may be brought in accordance with the local rules of court. See *Western Canadian Shopping Centres Inc. v. Dutton*, 2001 SCC 46, [2001] 2 SCR 534, para 27 (hereinafter "*Dutton*").

[5]*Federal Court Rules*, SOR/98-106, enacted pursuant to *Federal Courts Act*, R.S.C. 1985, c. F-7 (hereinafter "F.C.R.").

[6]See Art. 571 to 604 C.C.P. According to Art. 571(2) C.C.P., the definition of "class member" extends beyond natural persons, including legal entities established for a private interest, partnerships and associations, or other groups that may not have juridical personality.

[7]*Infineon Technologies AG v. Option consommateurs*, 2013 SCC 59, paras 37 and 59 (hereinafter "*Infineon*"]: *Vivendi Canada Inc. v. Dell'Aniello*, 2014 SCC 1, para 1, [2014] 1 SCR 3, para 37 (hereinafter "*Vivendi*"): "The judge's function at the authorization stage is one of screening motions ... The judge must not deal with the merits of the case, as they are to be considered only after the motion for authorization is granted."

action is referred to as "certification" in the common law provinces.[8] The court of exclusive jurisdiction on class actions in Quebec is the Superior Court of Quebec.[9]

At the authorization stage, the application for authorization must state the facts on which it is based and explain the nature of the class action, and the application must describe the class on whose behalf the person intends to act.[10] It must be filed no later than 3 months after authorization;[11] and judgments denying authorization may be appealed as of right, while those authorizing a class action, only with leave.[12] In conformity with the principle of proportionality,[13] the application for authorization can only be contested orally, and cannot include any evidence without permission from the court. The chief justice must assign a judge as a special case management judge responsible for presiding over the proceeding, and hearing all procedural matters regarding the class action.[14]

The court must authorize a class action procedure and designate the status of a representative to a member of the class when convinced that the four criteria for authorization are met.[15] These criteria are:

(1) The claims of the class members raise identical, similar or related issues of law or fact;
(2) The facts alleged appear to justify the conclusions sought;
(3) The composition of the class makes it difficult or impracticable to apply the rules for mandates to take part in judicial proceedings on behalf of others or for consolidation of proceedings;
(4) The class member appointed as representative plaintiff is in a position to adequately represent the class members.[16]

The "common questions" criterion in Article 575(1) of the C.C.P. aims to determine "[w]hether allowing the suit to proceed as a class action will avoid duplication of fact-finding or legal analysis".[17] This "commonality" test is interpreted broadly; it is sufficient to identify one common question between

[8]See, in sec. 5, Ont. C.P.A.; sec. 5, Alta. C.P.A.; sec. 5, B.C.C.P.A.; sec. 4, Man. C.P.A.; sec. 6, N. B.C.P.A.; sec. 5, N.&L.C.P.A.; sec. 7, N.S.C.P.A.; Art. 575, C.C.P.; sec. 6, Sask.C.P.A.

[9]See Art. 33, para 2 C.C.P. that outlines the Superior Court of Quebec as the only competent court to hear class actions.

[10]Art. 574 C.C.P. The motion must be served on the defendant, with at least 30 days' notice.

[11]Art. 583, para 1 C.C.P.

[12]Arts. 578 and 602 C.C.P. (appeal of the case on the merits).

[13]Art. 18 C.C.P; see also Piché (2019b), p. 359.

[14]Art. 572, para 2 C.C.P.

[15]*Vivendi*, para 67.

[16]Art. 575 C.C.P.

[17]*Dutton*, para 39. "An issue will be 'common' only where its resolution is necessary to the resolution of each class member's claim."

potential class members.[18] As such, Quebec's interpretation of "common issues" allows for more flexibility than the common law provinces.[19]

The second criterion in Article 575(2) C.C.P., whether "the facts alleged appear to justify the conclusions sought", requires courts to ensure that there is a reasonable cause of action. This criterion is not meant to be "a test of the merits of the action"; the potential representative plaintiff must merely demonstrate that the claim has "some basis in fact".[20] In other words, only a "*prima facie* case", or an "arguable case" must be established.[21] Thus, and as previously mentioned, the authorization step in Quebec seeks to avoid class actions that are frivolous or clearly unfounded in law.[22] Furthermore, Article 575(3) C.C.P. requires the judge to be given information regarding the potential size of the class and its characteristics.[23] This criterion is satisfied if the judge considers that the composition of the class renders another procedural channel impractical.

Lastly, in accordance with Article 575(4) C.C.P., the appointed representative plaintiff must be judged to adequately represent the interests of class members, according to three factors: whether or not he or she (a) has an interest in the suit, (b) is competent and (c) has a conflict of interest with the other class members.[24] The authorization judgment designates the member who will act as representative plaintiff (Art. 576, para 1 C.C.P.). Under Quebec's C.C.P., the definition of who can be considered a representative plaintiff has broadened to include non-profit organizations.[25] In *Dutton*, the Supreme Court of Canada listed various factors that the court may look to when assessing whether the proposed representative plaintiff is adequate, including "the motivation of the representative, the competence of the representative's counsel, and the capacity of the representative to bear any costs that may

[18] *Sibiga v. Fido Solutions inc.*, 2016 QCCA 1299, at para 122 (available on CanLii) (hereinafter "*Sibiga*").

[19] *Sibiga*, para 54.

[20] *Hollick v. Toronto (City)*, 2001 SCC 68, at para 16 (available on CanLii) (hereinafter "*Hollick*").

[21] *Infineon*, paras 64–67, 79–80, 100–101.

[22] *Vivendi*, para 37: "The judge's function at the authorization stage is one of screening motions to ensure that defendants do not have to defend against untenable claims on the merits. ... In considering whether the criteria are met at the authorization stage, the judge is therefore deciding a procedural question. The judge must not deal with the merits of the case, as they are to be considered only after the motion for authorization is granted."; See also *Infineon*, para 59: "At the authorization stage, the court plays the role of a filter. It need only satisfy itself that the applicant has succeeded in meeting the criteria set out in Art. 1003 of the *CCP* [now Art. 575 C.C.P.], bearing in mind that the threshold provided for in that article is a low one. The authorizing court's decision is procedural in nature, as it must decide whether the class action may proceed."

[23] *Catucci v. Valeant Pharmaceuticals International Inc.*, 2017 QCCS 3870, at para 327 (available on CanLii).

[24] *Infineon*, para 149; *Sibiga*, paras 97–129.

[25] However, legal persons established for a public interest such as religious corporations, government organizations, professional orders, etc., cannot become class members nor representative plaintiffs.

be incurred by the representative in particular".[26] In addition, the representative is not required to be the "best" possible representative, nor to be "typical" of the class.[27]

At the authorization stage, in contrast to the Canadian common law provinces, the Quebec judge cannot consider whether the class action is the "preferable procedure" for the case. Nevertheless, the judge can deny authorization on the basis of the principle of proportionality (Art. 18 C.C.P.), which must also be taken into account within the class action context.[28] If the judge is uncertain on whether to approve the class action, authorization should be granted in order to achieve a greater access to justice.

Once a case is authorized to proceed as a class action, the court will thereafter consider the merits of the case, at which point the case proceeds like any other civil action. If a favourable final judgment is issued after the trial on the merits, the court determines either the compensation that members are entitled to or the means to determine the compensation as well as the manner in which class members can make their claim.

In 2001, the Supreme Court of Canada issued a fundamental trilogy of class action cases in *Dutton, Rumley* and *Hollick.* In *Dutton,* the Court held that the three quintessential public policy objectives and purposes underlying the class action are access to justice, judicial economy and behavior modification of potential wrongdoers.[29] The Court explained that the class action offers great access to justice, as it gives a recourse to those individuals whose claims are not worth pursuing economically on an individual basis, keeping in mind that access to justice is understood by class action academics to mean access to a form of compensation.[30] In addition, the Court held that class actions provide judicial efficiency and aim to deter actual and potential wrongdoers from inflicting "small amounts of damage on a larger number of people".[31]

A new Code of Civil Procedure came into force on January 1, 2016,[32] and provided some interesting changes to class actions law in Quebec. One of these changes is the defendants' right to appeal an authorization decision with leave from a judge of the Court of Appeal. Three decisions from the Court of Appeal shed light on this "leave test".[33] The Court held that leave to appeal may be granted in the

---

[26] *Dutton,* para 41.

[27] Ibid.

[28] *Lorrain v. Petro-Canada,* 2013 QCCA 332. See also *Marcotte v. Longueuil (City),* 2009 SCC 43, [2009] 3 S.C.R. 65, paras 129–130.

[29] *Dutton.* See also *Vivendi,* para 1: "This procedural vehicle has several objectives, including facilitating access to justice, modifying harmful behavior and conserving judicial resources."

[30] *Dutton,* para 28 and 119. See also, e.g., Piché (2019c), pp. 273–275; Iacobucci (2011), p. 20.

[31] *Dutton,* para 29.

[32] *Loi instituant le nouveau Code de procédure civile* (2014, chapitre 1).

[33] *Centrale des syndicats du Québec v. Allen,* 2016 QCCA 1878, *Énergie éolienne des Moulins, s.e.c. v. Labranche,* 2016 QCCA 1879 and *DuProprio inc. v. Fédération des chambres immobilières du Québec (FCIQ),* 2016 QCCA 1880.

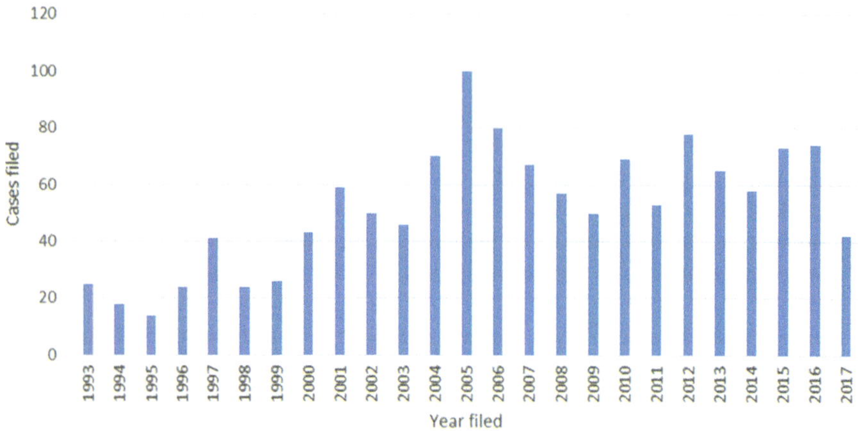

Fig. 1 Quebec class action filings in the past 25 years

situations where there is either a "significant error" in relation to the authorization criteria or to the facts pertaining to their application, or where there is a flagrant jurisdictional issue.

2 Volume of Class Action Litigation

This section will serve to provide data with respect to the total number of annual case filings in the Canadian province of Quebec over a 25-year period, from January 1993 to July 2017. These filings are interesting to understand the volume and evolution of case filings in the province, but they are even more revealing when compared to the annual case filings in the most important province in Canada—Ontario—in terms of population (more than 14 million in 2017, as compared to a little more than 8 million for Quebec that same year) and class action litigation volume.

I identified 1,306 cases filed in Quebec since 1993. This number constitutes an average of 50 cases per year.

As seen in Fig. 1, there was an increase in the number of class actions in 2005, as well as peaks in 2010, 2012 and 2016. These years mark important events related to the implementation in Quebec of a new regime for class actions providing lessened rights to the defendant by way of the disappearance of a right to contest by writing and a lesser amount of evidence required at authorization.

For the same period of time, it is useful to compare the data in Fig. 1 with the number of case filings in the province of Ontario (Fig. 2 below).[34] A total of 1459

[34]For this task, I referred to the Ontario Law Commission compilation of case data arising from Ontario courts in 1993–2018, which our team of lawyers and researchers at the Class Action Lab has worked on.

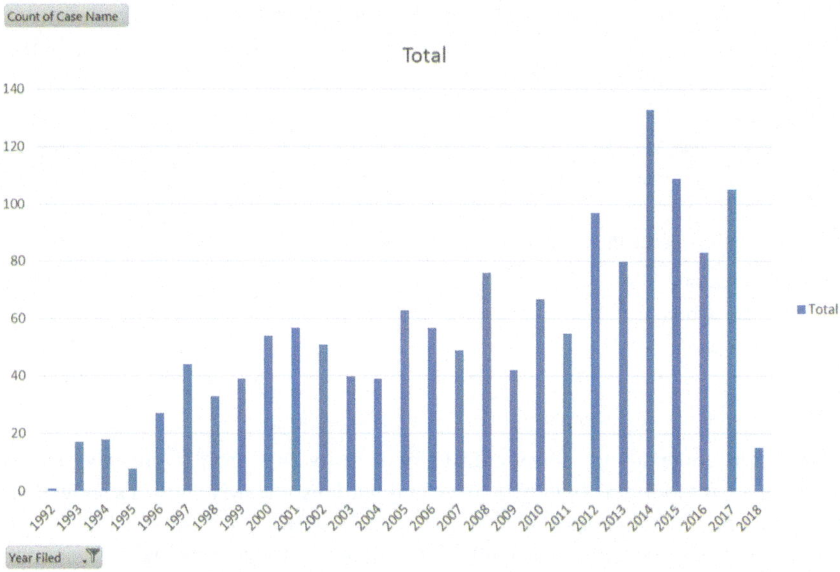

Fig. 2 Ontario class action filings in the past 25 years (This chart was created by the Law Commission of Ontario for the LCO's Class Actions Project)

cases were filed in Ontario in the same period, for an average of 54 cases per year. Ontario, by way of comparison, has seen a steady increase in the number of class action case filings, with 2014 topping at 130 cases, 2015 at 110 cases, and 2017 at 108 cases. One hypothesis for the greater number of case filings in these years is the existence and prevalence of carriage motions in the province.

In both provinces, a steady increase in class action activity is noticeable, with peaks in recent years. In my view, these peaks coincide with some important decisions having been issued by the Ontario courts in recent years,[35] as well as the Supreme Court of Canada's recent support of multi-jurisdictional proceedings and class actions more generally as means for providing increased access to justice.

3 Probability of Class Actions Settling Out of Court

There is a general consensus amongst lawyers, academics and judges, as well as all jurists, that once a class action is filed, it is almost certain to conclude by way of settlement, similarly to other types of civil litigation. Civil trials—especially in the

[35]Such as *Cloud v. Canada (Attorney General)* (2004), 247 DLR (4th) 667 (Ont CA) (hereinafter "Cloud"); *Pearson v. Inco* (2005), 78 OR (3d) 641 (CA) (hereinafter "Pearson"); *Markson v. MBNA Canada Bank*, 2007 ONCA 334 (hereinafter "Markson"); and *Cassano v. The Toronto-Dominion Bank*, 2007 ONCA 781 (hereinafter "Cassano").

Table 1 Outcome of Quebec class actions and probability of settlement

Outcome	% of Files
Judgment on the merits	15.65%
Settlement	82.58%
Special cases—grey zone	1.76%

Table 2 Timing of settlements in Quebec

Time of settlement	% of Files
Before authorization	60.97%
After authorization	39.03%
Total	100%

class action context—are considered to be a rarity in Canada,[36] in part because litigating a case to trial is both expensive and burdensome. My statistics show that it is true that the great majority of class action cases settle, at least in Quebec. I found that while Quebec has a greater number of cases being tried on the merits than in the rest of Canada with a 15.65% rate of judgments being issued on the merits, close to 83% of class action cases are settled (Table 1 above). Some cases are hybrid cases that lie in a "grey zone", given that they are cases where both a settlement and a judgment are present in the case file.

In addition, this data is important to demonstrate that the law is still being developed in class actions in Quebec by way of decisions on the merits.

In Table 2 above, I sought to determine the most prevalent timing of settlements in Quebec. There is a general informal consensus amongst practitioners that authorization or certification is the last nail in the coffin for the class action. What I demonstrate below is that this consensus is ill-founded and incorrect. Settlements in Quebec occur largely before authorization, at a 60% rate, which suggests that it might instead be the initial motion to authorize that incites the defendants to agree to settle the case. It is worth noting that 38% of these settlements occur in multi-jurisdictional cases, with the result that the settlement may occur in a jurisdiction different from that in which the certification occurred.

While settlements account for a large part of Quebec class actions outcome, there are many other types of resolution to be considered. Table 3 below provides a complete overview of class actions resolutions in Quebec.

Table 3 shows that 23% of all cases filed in Quebec from 1993 to 2017 are still ongoing. This is due, at least in part, to the serious delay inherent in class actions. Ongoing cases range from cases that have not yet been authorized to cases where an appeal on the merits is still pending.

Ongoing cases aside, discontinuances are the second most common type of resolution in Quebec class actions, with a rate of 16%. In fact, I found more discontinued cases than cases that were denied authorization over the 25-year period

[36]See, e.g., Foreman and Meisenheimer (2014).

Table 3 Outcome of class actions in Quebec from 1993 to 2017

Outcome	Number of files	% of Files
Settlement approved	345	26.42
Ongoing	301	23.05
Discontinuance	208	15.93
Authorization denied	149	11.41
Decision on the merits	71	5.44
Uncertain	52	3.98
Transferred	48	3.68
Continued *sine die*	38	2.91
Stayed	37	2.83
Preliminary motion	33	2.53
Summary dismissal	24	1.84
Total	1306	100

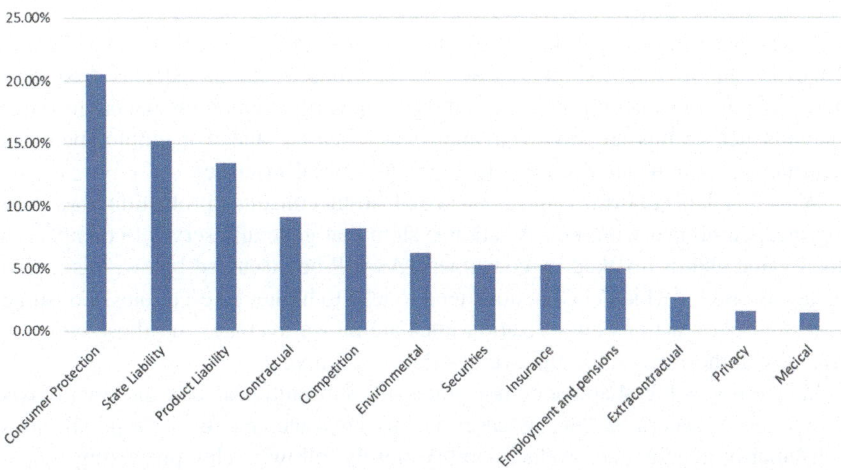

Fig. 3 Substantive claims advanced in class actions filed in Quebec between 1993 and 2017

examined. The reasons motivating discontinuances vary, but they are not always detrimental to class members. For example, discontinuance of the Quebec proceedings may be necessary to settle a multi-jurisdictional case nationally. Further research will be necessary to explain the reason for such a high number of discontinuances in Quebec class actions.

4 Substantive Claims Pursued in Class Actions

Figure 3 above provides statistics with respect to the substantive areas of the law involved in class actions filed in Quebec. The data shows that consumer protection cases are overwhelmingly present and frequent in Quebec class action practice, at a

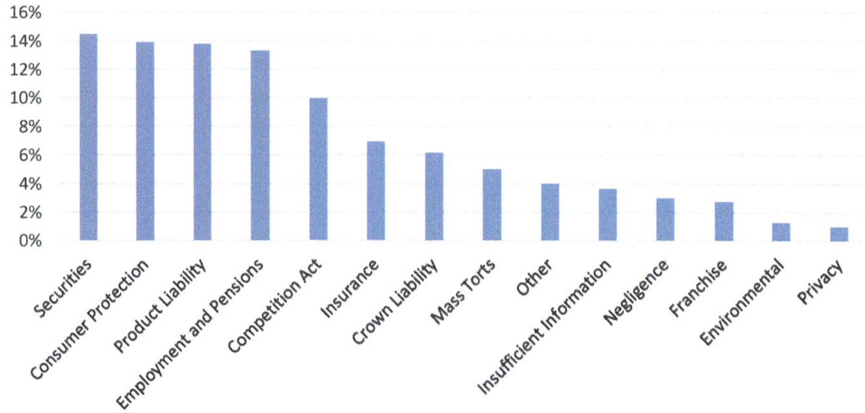

Fig. 4 Substantive claims advanced in class actions filed in Ontario between 1993 and 2017 (This chart was created by the Law Commission of Ontario's research team for the LCO's Class Actions Project)

rate of 20.52% of cases, followed by state liability (15.15%) and product liability (13.40%). In product liability cases, the pharmaceutical industry is frequently involved, but consumer products even more. It is worth mentioning that environment and nuisance claims are involved in 6.19% of cases, and that employment and securities law claims are each invoked in 5.26% of all instances.

What this data confirms is the existence of strong consumer protection laws in the province, combined with a class action system that generally serves to compensate small-value claims invoked by consumers. As will be discussed below, this area of the law is one for which class actions tend to lead to higher take-up rates. Consumer protection class actions authorization rates are above average, and those cases are generally authorized within the average delay of 2.5 years.

In Ontario, as Fig. 4 above demonstrates, the substantive area of the law invoked most often is securities law, as cases in this area account for 15% of all cases. Consumer protection and product liability closely follow, each representing 14% of all cases. This data is interesting to compare with that of Quebec, where securities cases represent only 5% of all cases. This trend is most likely due to the fact that Ontario is the heart of financial services in Canada.

Interestingly, the Quebec welfare state is likely responsible for the 15% of state liability cases in Quebec, as opposed to 6% of all cases only in Ontario. Moreover, 13% of class actions in Ontario are employment and pensions cases, as compared to only 5% in Quebec. This low rate may result from the mandatory arbitration policy provided in the Quebec Labour Code (R.S.Q., c. C–27, s. 100) for employees whose employment is governed by collective bargaining agreements. This provision has kept a number of cases from proceeding as class actions in front of civil courts in Quebec.[37]

[37]The most well-known case is *Bisaillon v. Université Concordia,* 2006 CSC 19.

5 Average Duration and Inherent Delays in Class Actions

Delay is a tremendously important issue in class actions law and practice. Indeed, it is the primary consideration and preoccupation for stakeholders in class actions in Canada.[38] Furthermore, delay is important because it has the potential of impacting the rights of the parties. With the passage of time, the likelihood and levels of compensation are reduced. For as months and years go by, there is increased risk of members' personal information and contact details being lost, and so too increased risk of members moving or even dying, but also one notices the dampening effect that delay has on the feelings of potential benefiters of the class action who will become incentivized to participate in any potential distribution. In addition, delay is an administration of justice issue, as class action cases take up a lot of time and "space". Indeed, cases brought as class actions fill a judicial "space" that could have been used for other types of civil cases.

Delay in class actions is often thought to be a consequence of the importance and complexity of procedures and of the evidence (notably by way of expert reports and testimonies), the number of lawyers involved in the case—often amounting to a true "band of suitcases"—and the lack of efficient management by judges. In Quebec, the amount of evidence presented at authorization is much more limited than it is elsewhere in Canada, but the fact remains that building a class action case is lengthy and burdensome.

Some judges have recently questioned the legitimacy, necessity, and efficiency of authorization. In the *Boiron* case, Justice Bich explained:

> [72] [T]he preliminary class authorization process, in its actual state, consumes important judicial resources, and the scarcity of these resources does not accommodate itself to the often unreasonable efforts made by the parties, at the price of an intolerable engorgement of the courts. It also constitutes a costly process for the parties, slow (sometimes never-ending), generating debates and interlocutory motions. This is without mentioning the right of appeal, recently broadened by the legislator for an unbeknown reason, which multiplies the occasions to slow down preliminary stages of the action. [my translation][39]

Judges have cited delays of 2, even 3 years in Quebec before the case is authorized. Are they correct to say that it takes this long?

The length of time until resolution must also be examined, in an access to justice perspective. Here, the issue is how long it takes to see a settlement executed, and the moneys distributed. It may be helpful to make a comparison with the regime in Australia, even if its one-step class regime with no preliminary screening of the action is necessarily very different. There, the average delay to see a case resolved by way of a settlement in consumer cases is 2.5 years. As will be shown below, the authorization procedure adds considerable delays to class actions in Quebec.

---

[38] I found this issue to be a primary consideration during consultations I held with stakeholders involved in class actions in Ontario as a co-principal researcher for the Law Commission of Ontario's Class Actions Project, https://www.lco-cdo.org/en/our-current-projects/class-actions.

[39] *Charles* v. *Boiron Canada inc.*, 2016 QCCA 1716, para 72.

Table 4 Average delay to authorize a class action in Quebec

Average delay	Length of time
Until a Superior Court authorization decision	2 years, 45 days
Until a Court of Appeal authorization decision	3 years, 308 days
Until a Supreme Court of Canada authorization decision	6 years, 228 days
Average (total)	2 years and 185 days

Table 5 Outcome of motions for authorization filed in the Quebec Superior Court

Outcome	Number of cases	%
Authorization granted	306	63.22
Authorization denied	178	36.78
Total	484	100

5.1 Class Action Certification Delays

In Table 4 above, I present data showing that authorizing (or certifying) a case as a class action in Quebec takes 2 years and 185 days, on average, as based upon a dataset of more than 400 cases filed in the province. In other words, it takes more than 2 years in Quebec to filter cases appropriately, in view of fulfilling the overarching objective of authorization, which is to reject cases that appear to be frivolous and/or unmeritorious (i.e. to lack merit).[40] This delay is comparable to Ontario's, anecdotally sitting at roughly 2 years until certification. Given the fact that authorization—and certification—are meant to be procedural tools to screen out unmeritorious and/or frivolous cases, ways should be found to proceed faster onto the merits of the case.

In the debate about the legitimacy of authorization or certification, it is often argued that this stage is necessary to filter out cases and verify that the case meets the criteria provided in Article 575 C.C.P. (which sets out the list of authorization criteria in Quebec). Two questions arise here. First, are cases generally authorized, and how rigorous is the screening of cases? Second, on what grounds are applications for authorization denied?

In Table 5 above, I demonstrate that authorizations are more likely to be granted than not in Quebec, with a 63.22% rate of applications granted by the Superior Court. This rate, based on a subset of 484 cases, is representative and persuasive.

The likelihood of authorization is confirmed when an additional fact is added to the equation. In those authorization decisions that are appealed, only 43.02% of the Superior Court decisions are overturned, thereby bringing the overall rate of authorizations to 71%.

The data compiled in Table 6 shows that authorization was denied by the courts in 29% of the cases (including appeals from authorization). While it is now clear that

[40]See, e.g., *Infineon Technologies AG v. Option consommateurs*, 2013 CSC 59, para 61.

Table 6 Overall outcome of motions for authorization in Quebec (considering appeals from authorization decisions)

Outcome	Number of cases	%
Authorization granted	343	70.87
Authorization denied	141	29.13
Total	484	100

Table 7 Outcome of authorization motions after appeals

Outcome	Number of cases	%
Appeal granted	37	43.02
Appeal dismissed	49	56.98
Total	86	100

Table 8 Authorization criteria justifying denial of authorization

	1003a)	1003b)	1003c)	1003d)
Number of instances the criterion is cited by the court	64	124	36	70

authorization is principally meant to filter frivolous cases, judges are far from granting authorizations automatically. It is worth noting that prior to 2016, only decisions denying authorization to institute a class action could be appealed as of right.

Our data shows that appeals of class action authorization decisions have led to an increase of authorization rates of more than 7%, which is considerable.

Table 7 shows the outcomes of appeal decisions on authorization. Appeals judges have maintained Superior Court decisions 57% of the time. It is worth mentioning that the Supreme Court of Canada did not overturn the Quebec Court of Appeal on the authorization of a class action during the time period reviewed.

Since the 2016 reform of the Quebec Code of Civil Procedure, decisions granting authorization may be appealed with leave by the defendant (Art. 578(1) C.C.P.). To my knowledge, only one appeal was heard by the Court of Appeal during the time period covered by this empirical study.[41] However, some cases were granted leave and are still pending before the Court.[42] We have yet to see whether these legislative amendments will impact delays at the authorization stage, as well as overall rates and the likelihood of authorization.

[41] *Ameublements Tanguay inc. v. Cantin,* 2017 QCCA 1330. An appeal of an authorization judgment was also heard and dismissed in 2018 in *Union des consommateurs v. Magasins Best Buy Ltée,* 2018 QCCA 445, after the leave was retroactively granted (*nunc pro tunc*) in the same decision.

[42] *Maruyasu Industries Co. Ltd. v. Asselin,* 2018 QCCA 526 (leave granted for only one defendant); *Procureure générale du Canada v. Sarrazin,* 2017 QCCA 147.

Table 9 average delay until settlement approval

Time of settlement	Length of time
Settled before authorization	3 years and 125 days
Settled after authorization	6 years and 327 days
Average	4 years and 243 days

Table 8 shows the number of instances in which each of the Quebec authorization criteria was used by Superior Court judges to deny authorization of a class action. These criteria have not changed with the new Code of Civil Procedure. As explained earlier (Sec. 1), it must first be demonstrated that the claims of the members of the class action raise identical, similar or related issues of law or facts ("the related issues criterion") [1003a)]. Second, the facts included in the authorization motion need to justify the conclusions sought ("the appearance of law criterion") [1003b)]. Third, the composition of the class must make it difficult or impracticable to apply the rules of mandate, to take part in judicial proceedings on behalf of others or for a consolidation of proceedings ("the composition of the class criterion") [1003c)]. Fourth, the representative plaintiff must be in a position to properly represent the class members ("the adequate representation criterion") [1003d)].

Our data shows that the majority of class action cases are denied authorization based on the appearance of law criterion. I also found that this criterion is used alone by judges to deny authorization much more frequently than other criteria. The related issues of law or facts and adequate representation criteria are invoked equally frequently as second most important by judges in their authorization decisions. However, while the use of the adequate representation criterion has increased over time, the related issues criterion is referred to less frequently, most likely due to a more liberal approach advocated by the Supreme Court of Canada and the Quebec Court of Appeal regarding this criterion.[43] Finally, the composition of the group criterion is not frequently invoked by the Superior Court. It is noteworthy that a few class actions with low numbers of potential members were authorized in recent years.[44]

[43] *Vivendi*; *Collectif de défense des droits de la Montérégie (CDDM) v. Centre hospitalier régional du Suroît du Centre de santé et de services sociaux du Suroît*, 2011 QCCA 826.

[44] See, e.g., *Protection environnement Boisbriand v. Boisbriand (Ville de)*, 2007 QCCS 484, with only 100 potential members. *Lassonde v. Québec (Procureur général)*, 2016 QCCS 569, with only 85 potential members. Also, of note is the Rozon sexual abuse authorization decision, with 20 members: *Les Courageuses v. Rozon*, 2018 QCCS 2089; confirmed on appeal at 2020 QCCA 5; motion to appeal in Supreme Court of Canada denied.

Table 10 Average delay until a decision is issued on the merits

Court decision	Length of time
To a Superior Court decision	5 years and 290 days
To a Court of Appeal decision	7 years and 242 days
To a Supreme Court of Canada decision	11 years and 124 days
Average	7 years and 30 days

5.2 *Settlement Approval Delays*

Table 9 above shows that it takes on average 4 years and 243 days for a case to be settled in Quebec. However, it is important to distinguish cases where authorization and settlement approval are granted simultaneously from those where the settlement is concluded and approved after the authorization decision.

Table 9 shows that authorized cases take twice as long to be settled as those settled before authorization.[45] The authorization process itself causes some of this delay, but a considerable part of it occurs after the authorization decision itself. In fact, it takes on average an additional 4 years and 157 days after the authorization decision to settle the case. Contrary to popular belief, class actions do not appear to settle directly after the authorization decision, and a lot of time is evidently "wasted" between the authorization decision and the decision to settle. Agreeing on the terms of a settlement and negotiating its details and clauses assumingly takes time, yet I cannot help but presume that the lawyers on both sides take advantage of the pressure of time to strategize and wait for the best time to resolve the case. Meanwhile, time passes, and the likelihood of compensation diminishes, as I will further address below.

As mentioned before, I compared delays until settlement approval in Quebec and in Australia, a jurisdiction where no systematic preliminary screening of cases is conducted. Australian class actions take, on average, 2 years and 248 days to settle.[46] By contrast, in Quebec, class actions settle before authorization after 3 years and 125 days. Accordingly, even without the authorization step, actions take much longer to settle in Quebec on average. The picture gets even darker when one considers the authorization step in Quebec, as class actions are settled after authorization there at an average of 6 years and 327 days, and the majority of this delay occurs after the authorization decision. All of this demonstrates that, using Australian data for comparative purposes, authorization does in fact generate important delays. Furthermore, considerable time is spent to reach a settlement after the authorization decision.

[45] To be clear, these are cases where authorization and settlement approval are granted at the same time. However, in practice, the settlement is concluded before the authorization itself.

[46] Morabito (2017), p. 31.

5.3 Overall Delays and Going to the Merits

As presented earlier, only a small fraction of class actions started in Quebec reach the decision on the merits milestone. In fact, only 71 cases went to trial over a 25-year period, according to our data. Nevertheless, the statistics I gathered on delay to the decision on the merits can be compared with those obtained on settlement approval.

Table 10 shows that it takes on average 5 years and 290 days to reach a decision on the merits in the Superior Court. When a decision is appealed, it will take on average 7 years and 30 days to see a decision issued on the merits. It is worth highlighting here that it takes less time on average to reach a decision on the merits in the Superior Court (5 years, 290 days) than to have the case authorized and thereafter settled (6 years, 327 days).

Still, going to trial is risky for class members and their counsel. I was able to determine that in the Superior Court there is an overall 39.72% chance that the Court will decide in favour of the defendants. In addition, the Court finds in favour of the plaintiff 38.35% of the time, and in part for the plaintiff 21.91% of the time. These two numbers change to 31.51% and 28.77% when appeals are considered. All in all, this data means that in 40% of the cases no compensation is provided to class members, and lawyers paid on contingency are not paid for their efforts.

Once a settlement is approved, or a decision on the merits is issued, the quintessential process of distributions and implementing the settlement begins. The distributions process itself is crucial for class members' compensation, but, unfortunately, it often falls outside of the court's scrutiny. Consequently, closing judgments are scarce and hard to find, and are often only available within the physical case files. Nonetheless, these judgments are a sort of confirmation of the class action's "end", and they allow the judges to review the distributions process, and verify the actual levels of compensation of class members.[47] I found that it takes, on average, 8 years and 92 days to see a closing judgment issued.

6 Class Action Distributions: How Much Members Are Receiving

6.1 Challenges in Measuring Compensation

Compensation of class members is without doubt the most difficult aspect to measure in class actions.

First, distribution reports that contain information about the number (and sometimes identity) of members compensated are rarely communicated to the courts or disclosed/published on firms' or case websites, or otherwise. When they are so

[47] See Piché (2019c).

disclosed, they are almost systematically left in the physical court files. Although one has the right to access court files individually, reviewing a large quantity of files, in order to work more efficiently and obtain a broad and true appreciation of distributions, requires a special authorization from the court clerk.[48] Fortunately, a 2016 regulation now makes it mandatory in Quebec to file a report on the administration to the court in collective recovery cases made with individual payments,[49] which likely will bring more systematic disclosures of distributions.

Second, there is a theoretical debate to be had on what constitutes class members' compensation and on how to measure it. Settlement reliefs can take a number of shapes, ranging from the commonly used cash payments to a permanent injunction. Furthermore, indicators of success in the distribution process—and overall class action outcome—are numerous and varied, each having its strengths and weaknesses. For instance, while I believe the take-up rate or rate of distribution to be the ultimate indicator of success in class distributions, the total amount disgorged by the defendant is another such indicator, as well as individual recoveries and indirect recoveries (by way of *cy-près* or otherwise).

Interestingly, the nature of the compensation obtained by the class members in my chosen dataset was varied. While the majority of compensations is monetary (73.27%), *cy-près* distributions are prevalent (22.12%), as well as special measures (28.11%) (such as environmental measures seeking to repair some of the damage done to the environment, or physical installations built on the premises to enhance their accessibility). Coupons or rebates are not very prevalent in Quebec, at least not in our dataset.[50]

6.2 *Total Disgorgements by the Defendants*

As such, I found that the average total amount granted by way of settlement or decision on the merits in Quebec class proceedings is CAN$11,712,079.80. This amount is based on a dataset of 135 cases that either reached the settlement stage or a decision on the merits.[51] While this amount does not show how much money goes to each class member, it is an impressive figure that confirms that considerable amounts of money are being disgorged by the defendants through the class action mechanism.

Using the same dataset, I found that the median total amount granted by way of settlement or a decision on the merits stands at $960,540.00. The settlements

[48]This is how I was able to gather such a large volume of information about distributions, over a 3-year period.

[49]*Regulation of the Superior Court of Québec in Civil Matters*, RLRQ, c. 25.01, r. 0.2.1., sec. 59.

[50]It is worth noting here that these forms of compensation were sometimes present in two cases, thereby leading to dual measures and enhanced percentages.

[51]Some of the cases in this dataset are multi-jurisdictional cases, whereby the total amount is allocated to all class members in Canada.

concluded in *Honhon v. Canada (Procureur général)*[52] and *Desjardins v. Canada (Procureur général)*,[53] which were a part of the national tainted blood class action, were each valued at more than a billion dollars. A national settlement potentially valued at $2,1 billion, including $550 million in cash payments, was approved in *Grondin* c. *Volkswagen Group Canada Inc.*, following the diesel emissions scandal in the auto industry. Of note, however, is the fact that the class action against the tobacco industry[54] was not considered. These high-profile cases probably help inflate the impressive average total amount noted above.

6.3 Take-Up or Distributions Rates

In order to measure how often class members are compensated, I used an indicator called the distributions rate or "take-up" rate. Consistent with the Class Action Lab's research methods as well as its previous publications,[55] the take-up rate measures the ratio between the number of class members who received a form of compensation and the estimated number of members at trial or settlement. I managed to obtain such take-up rates in 94 files. The calculated average take-up rate is 55.64%, which means that more than half of the members are compensated, on average. In addition, in 48 of the 94 files for which take-up rates were calculated, the take-up rate is higher than 50%; thus, the proposition that only a minimal number of members are compensated within the class is no longer plausible. In my view, this rate in itself is a strong indication that class actions do meet their compensatory objective in Quebec.[56]

There is, however, a great disparity in take-up rates. While the rate is lower than 25% in 26 files, it is well above 75% in 32 files, with five at a rate greater than 100%. Several factors can explain the disparity: the total amount disgorged, the average amount distributed to the members, the recovery process chosen by the parties, the presence (or not) of a claims administrator, the class notices, etc.

6.4 Compensation (or Recovery) Rates

The take-up rate does not measure the proportion between the damages caused by defendants' action and the reparation provided by the settlement or the decision on the merits. This rate, which I refer to as a "compensation rate", has also been studied

[52] *Honhon v. Canada (Procureur général)*, C.S. 500-06-000016-960.

[53] *Desjardins* v. *Canada (Procureur général)*, C.S. 500-06-000065-983.

[54] *Létourneau v. JTI-MacDonald Corp.*, 2015 QCCS 2382.

[55] Piché (2019c), pp. 288–289.

[56] Piché (2019c), pp. 292–293.

by others as a "recovery rate".[57] It is challenging to calculate, since damages are difficult to assess at the authorization stage, especially when each class member's damages vary. I was nevertheless able to calculate such rates in 21 cases. I found that the median rate of recovery, or median compensation rate, is 65.52%, which means that when the loss or prejudice is clearly identifiable, class members are well compensated. In 13 of the 21 cases, members received back more than half of their loss. Thus, in these instances, the class action works very well, and is very much worthwhile.

In class actions, distributions processes are many and varied. The norm is collective recovery, whereby the defendants are obliged to deposit a lump sum in order to compensate members. Individual recovery, somewhat more exceptional, allows the defendant to keep the monies owed in his or her bank account and grant relief only through presentation of a valid, formal claim. Mixed recovery may also be ordered in special cases where some parts of the funds are more easily distributed collectively, and others will require individual recovery processes. As I have written elsewhere, collective recovery is known to result in the highest rates of participation and compensation.[58]

There are subtle differences between collective and individual recovery processes. In individual recovery, claimants will likely (and logically) come forward when there is more at stake. Very few individuals will claim when amounts to be recovered are less than $100. This $100 (or a few hundred dollars) thus appears to be a threshold amount, below which claiming does not appear to be worthwhile for the members. Actually, for smaller amounts, parties will prefer automatic or collective recovery processes to individual recovery processes.

More largely, there generally appears to be a trend—in all distributions (whether collective or individual) —towards lower distributions rates when the average individual amount paid to members is higher. While this correlation may appear contradictory, it is tributary of the mode of recovery chosen. When small amounts are at stake, automatic recovery processes are privileged, and distributions rates are higher. These cases often coincide with consumer cases that generally fare very well in Quebec.

Furthermore, I found that in cases that lead to a judgment on the merits, the distributions rate on average is 59.85%, and is lower in the case of settlements, at 53.96%. I found that the likely reason for this is that settlements are often concluded for the sake of making peace. Reaching an agreement is often done at the risk of losing some form or amount of compensation. Judges are often found to have no choice but to approve a settlement in the face of an adversarial void, and this settlement proposal, while imperfect and likely to provide only rough justice, is often found to be better than "nothing". The unfortunate consequence of this "rough justice" approach is that distributions are reduced in settlements.

---

[57]Fitzpatrick and Gilbert (2015). The authors obtain an average recovery rate of 37.67% and a median recovery rate of 40.32% for 13 files.

[58]Piché (2016).

In the settlement context, distributions rates are higher when the case is settled before authorization, and the distributions process is concluded before authorization. Indeed, before authorization, the rate of distributions is 57.14%, while after authorization it is lower, at 51.26%. In addition, members are better compensated when distributions happen earlier, with a global compensation rate much higher at 75.39% before authorization, than before authorization, at 47.73%. Finally, it is worth noting that more than four times more money is paid to the members by the defendants when distributions happen before authorization. Accordingly, all in all, "the earlier, the better", in terms of distributions.

7 Costs of Class Actions in Quebec

7.1 Class Counsel Fees

Completing a survey of counsel fees has proved challenging for a series of reasons. First, counsel fees are not generally disclosed when the case is resolved by way of a decision on the merits, leaving a good amount of data missing. Adding to the complexity is the fact that counsel fees are sometimes allocated as a percentage of each claim, instead of being calculated based on a total settlement amount. Furthermore, the amount of counsel fees approved by the court sometimes includes disbursements and sales tax, making it difficult to isolate the net fees. Still, counsel fees were calculated in 186 files.

An appreciation of counsel fees cannot be complete without a comparison of how those fees fare in comparison with distributions to class members. Based on 146 files for which both a total award and an amount for counsel fees were available, I was able to estimate that counsel fees represent on average 27.45% of the total settlement award. This rate includes taxes and disbursements, as those are often included in the amount approved by the court, and because it is not possible to single them out. Ultimately, counsel fees are not always proportionate to the results achieved for the class and the risks undertaken by class counsel, as they should be. Nonetheless, this rate is typical of the 30% going rate for class counsel fees, and is not excessive in the circumstances per se, but must still be found by the court to be fair and reasonable.[59] The fairness and reasonableness of the fee awarded in respect of class proceedings is to be determined in light of the risk undertaken by the lawyer in conducting the litigation and the degree of success or results achieved.[60]

---

[59] *Option Consommateurs v. Infineon Technologies, a.g.*, 2013 QCCS 1191. Also see: *Pellemans v. Lacroix*, 2011 QCCS 1345 (CanLII); *Sony BMG Musique (Canada) inc. v. Guilbert*, 2099 QCCA 231; *Guilbert v. Sony BMG Musique (Canada) inc.*, 2007 QCCS 432 (CanLII).

[60] *Parsons v. Canadian Red Cross Society (2000)*, 2000 CanLII 22386 (ON SC), 49 O.R. (3d) 281 (S.C.J.).

7.2 *Administration Fees*

Another cost that diminishes class members' compensation is administration fees. External claim administrators are often used by parties to review claims and their supporting documentation. Notice programs also generate costs, as they can include measures to target and locate class members. Some settlements also include an arbitration process for complex claims, which generates additional costs. We considered all the fees incurred during the distributions process to be administration fees.

Our dataset on administration fees is most likely incomplete. We only gathered this piece of data for 50 settlements. This is most likely due to the fact that administration fees are not always disclosed at the settlement approval milestone. Administration fees are often paid as a percentage on each claim or calculated and disclosed at the end of the distributions process.

On average, I found that the administration fees appear to represent 7.80% of the total settlement award. This figure should be used carefully, since many cases do not require the use of an external administrator or an extensive notice program. These cases do not appear in our dataset and would lower the administration fees' percentage.

7.3 Public Funding: The *Fonds D'aide Aux Actions Collectives*

The *Fonds d'aide aux actions collectives* finances approximately 45% of class actions in Quebec. To accomplish its mission, the *Fonds* withholds a regulatory percentage on each liquidated claim and on the balance remaining after payments are remitted.[61] This amount ranges from 2% to 10% for each liquidated claim, from 50% to 90% for the balance remaining after an individual liquidation and from 30% to 70% for the balance remaining after a collective liquidation. Furthermore, settlements often allocate an additional amount to the *Fonds* as a reimbursement for sums advanced for expert fees, counsel fees as well as judicial fees. These sums are often included in class counsel fees or paid directly by the defendant.

As a side note, I found only one case involving third party funders in Quebec for the given timeframe.[62] In this case, third-party financing represented $7,335,862 and was paid using the settlement amount in addition to counsel fees.

---

[61]*Regulation respecting the percentage withheld by the Fonds d'aide aux actions collectives*, RLRQ c. F-3.2.0.1.1., r. 2, sec. 1.

[62]See Marcotte v. Banque de Montréal, 2015 QCCS 1915, paras 39–50.

7.4 Awards to Class Representatives

Representative awards are usually allocated to compensate the representative for the time and resources spent on the case. In Quebec, a large number of class actions are instituted by associations. Out of a dataset of 745 cases where the representative plaintiff was identified, I found that 141 cases involved an association as representative of the class, which represents 18% of the dataset. Awards allocated to these associations at the end of the proceedings can be quite high. For example, in *Lavergne* c. *Union canadienne,* a case conducted against insurance companies following the 1998 ice storm, two settlements allocated in total $200,000 to the representative Option Consommateur as representative awards.[63] In many instances, representative associations also received a part of the residual fund by way of *cy-près*. We did not consider these amounts to be representative awards.

Based on 59 files where representative awards were allocated, we found the average award to be $25,830.07. Leaving representative associations aside, the average representative award drops to $4822.98, based on 34 files.

8 Conclusion

The Class Actions Lab Compensation Project and empirical analysis of class action files has shown that a majority of class actions within our case sample serves to compensate Quebec citizens, given the 55.64% take-up rate. Accordingly, a collective approach to compensation[64] applied to the data analysis has served to support a conclusion that class actions serve to compensate people. If class actions serve to compensate, then access to justice can be said to be provided to the citizens of the province. With enhanced access to justice and accomplishment of at least one goal of the action, the goal of compensation, the class action can further be affirmed to be a legitimate, desirable and effective procedural tool.

References

Fitzpatrick BT, Gilbert RC (2015) An empirical look at compensation in consumer class actions. NY Univ J Law Bus 11(4):767–792

Foreman J, Meisenheimer G (2014) The evolution of the class action trial in Ontario. West J Legal Stud 4(2). http://ir.lib.uwo.ca/uwojls/vol4/iss2/3. Accessed 26 Mar 2020

Iacobucci F (2011) What is access to justice in the context of class actions? In: Kalajdzic J (ed) Accessing justice – appraising class actions ten years after dutton, Hollick & Rumley. LexisNexis Canada, Markham

[63] *Option Consommateurs v. Union canadienne (L'), compagnie d'assurances*, 2013 QCCS 5505.

[64] Piché (2019c).

Morabito V (2017) An Empirical Study of Australia's Class Action Regime, Fifth Report. The First Twenty-Five Years of Class Actions in Australia, July 2017. online: http://globalclassactions.stanford.edu/sites/default/files/documents/Morabito_Fifth_Report.pdf. Accessed 26 Mar 2020

Piché C (2009) The cultural analysis of class action law. J Civil Law Stud 2(1):102–145

Piché C (2016) Le recouvrement et l'indemnisation des membres dans l'action collective. Canadian Bar Rev 94:171–207

Piché C (2019a) Understanding class actions through a historical overview and empirical data from Quebec from the past twenty-five years. Canadian Class Action Rev 15(1):201

Piché C (2019b) L'action collective: ses succès et ses défis. Éditions Thémis, Montreal

Piché C (2019c) Class action value. Theor Inq Law 19(1):261–302

Walker J, Watson GD (2014) Class actions in Canada. Emond Montgomery, Toronto

Catherine Piché Professor of civil evidence and procedure, complex litigation, comparative law and private international law at the University of Montreal where she also serves as Vice-Dean Research and International Affairs, Director of the Class Actions Lab, and Scientific Director of the Quebec Law Reform Commission (the "Institut québécois de réforme du droit et de la justice"). As a member of the Quebec Bar and New York Bar, she practiced commercial litigation for national law firms in New York City and Montreal for more than 6 years. She is the author of numerous articles on procedural law civil evidence and class actions.

Collective Redress in Brazil: Success or Disappointment?

Hermes Zaneti Jr

Abstract It is recognized that the Brazilian experience with class actions is one of the most developed in the civil law world. However, this experience is not only successful. After a long period of broad access to justice, for pragmatic reasons, new techniques are coming to the fore. This chapter focuses on the traditional Brazilian class actions, addressing some new trends and risks. The goal is to sketch a broad and realistic view of Brazilian class action landscape, highlighting the good experiences and new trends, as well as the evolution of the Brazilian system. An analysis of quantitative and qualitative data from more than 286,000 class actions filed between 2014 and 2018 is provided. The most important features of the Brazilian class action system: standing, *res judicata*, *lis pendens*, costs and fees, etc. will be presented, showing how new Civil Procedure Code applies to the collective redress schemes. The focus will be on the emergence of aggregate litigation as a form of collective redress, in combination with Brazilian class actions. Finally, we will deal with "the procedural law of disasters".

1 Introduction

It is recognized that the Brazilian experience with class actions is one of the most developed in the civil law world. However, this experience is not only successful. After a long period of broad access to justice, for pragmatic reasons, new techniques are coming to the fore. In this chapter we will focus on the traditional Brazilian class actions, addressing some of the new trends and risks they present. The goal is to sketch a broad and realistic view allowing us to preserve the good experiences, to take into account the new trends and to be aware of the evolution of the Brazilian system.

This chapter will first describe how the Brazilian collective redress scheme is currently shaped, with its quantitative and qualitative success and its forthcoming

H. Zaneti Jr (✉)
Federal University of Espírito Santo, Vitória, Brazil
e-mail: hzaneti@mpes.mp.br

A. Uzelac, S. Voet (eds.), *Class Actions in Europe*, Ius Gentium: Comparative Perspectives on Law and Justice 89, https://doi.org/10.1007/978-3-030-73036-9_15

future. The traditional model of US-style *opt out* class actions is changing to a combined model with *opt in* aggregation techniques and a wide use of procedural legal agreements and collective settlements, many of which were a direct result of the new Code of Civil Procedure of 2015.[1]

Finally, and following a recent controversial case, the Case of Rio Doce, the biggest environmental disaster in the history of Latin America, we will address the next generation of collective redress techniques, with special concern for public interest litigation, structural injunctions and "the procedural law of disasters."

1.1 The Brazilian Model

It should be made clear from the outset that Brazil faces the risk of transforming individual actions into collective actions, thus binding everyone to a singular judicial decision, without the procedural guarantees of a traditional collective redress procedure. One of the goals of this chapter is to clarify the predominance of the Brazilian class action system and the protection of the public interest in collective redress proceedings.

The only way to deal with this risk is to understand the collective redress scheme as a genre, composed of various techniques and procedures, modelled to the needs of collective protection in active and passive legal situations where the stakeholders are groups of people.[2]

Departing from this perspective it is wrong to think that only *opt out* class actions serve the objective of group protection of individual and collective rights. There is no single model.

Next to judicial remedies, there are also effective extrajudicial remedies, governmental agencies and ombudsmen. These technologies need to be addressed together with a focus on redress via regulatory agencies and ombudsmen. In Europe, regulatory redress, ombudsmen and collective ADR predominate judicial redress.[3]

---

[1]Zaneti (2017a), pp. 583–614.This article is a result of the project Grounds of Contemporary Civil Procedure ("Fundamentos do Processo Civil Contemporâneo"—FPCC), funded by the Foundation for Research Support and Innovation of the State of Espírito Santo (FAPES). The FPCC Research Group is the founder of ProcNet—an International Research Network on Civil Justice and Contemporary Procedural Law (https://bit.ly/3349S1a). Earlier versions of this work has been published in: Zaneti (2019a), pp. 11–40; Zaneti (2019b); Zaneti (2019c), pp. 293–330. I would like to thank Antonio do Passo Cabral, for discussions and improvements to the former versions of the text. I would especially like to thank Halvard Haukeland Fredriksen for his careful reading, debates and many suggestions for making the text more readable to non-Brazilians. The problems of the text are not attributable to these colleagues, but some of their qualities—if any—are.

[2]Didier and Zaneti (2017).

[3]Hodges and Voet (2018).

The best solution allows a combination of all tools. This is also the case in court proceedings, with *opt out* and *opt in* techniques, with class actions protecting the group rights collectively and with aggregated litigation allowing individual *opt in* protection for group members. In all cases, before and during the judicial process, collective settlements should be stimulated.[4]

Furthermore, the combination of various collective redress means, seeking to find the most effective design, is the one that best meets the economic demands. A smarter, market-oriented institutional design and an architecture which offers various choices allows to establish a more efficient *default* option for every group of cases.[5]

The combination of these techniques is, as we will see, a characteristic of the Brazilian collective redress system. Brasil escaped many of the problems pointed out by European and American doctrine. The *opt out* class actions are not the "Big Bad Wolf". Brasil does not have entrepreneurial lawyering, contingency fees and punitive damages imposed in a jury trial. On the other hand, there is a unified judicial system and judicial review of the legislative and executive acts and decisions.[6]

The public good and the deterrence of wrongful conduct are important goals in the Brazilian system. Although criticism can be made, it is the role of the Public Prosecutor's Office as ombudsman of fundamental rights which allows greater integration between all the mechanisms. Even when the prosecutor does not function as a plaintiff, it is always mandatory for the prosecutor to intervene in each procedure as *custos legis*.

1.2 Past

Brazilian civil procedure has been under significant influence from Italian legal scholarship. As far as collective judicial redress is concerned, Brazilian scholars read the studies of many icons of Italian proceduralism that used to describe other models of collective actions in a comparative perspective, especially the American

[4]"The bottom line is to connect the different dots. To put it simply, the approach should be 'and ...and' and not 'or ... or'. It is not choosing between white or brown bread, it is looking at how it is baked. The ultimate goal should be an integrated and holistic framework, or, as was mentioned above, a 'multilayered framework of regulation, lawmaking and law application (...) The focus should be on exploring and optimizing all options for mass harm situations. Even more important, is to connect these options so they can form an integrated (dispute resolution) framework. Only a broad and integrated instrumentarium, as a 'dispute resolution continuum', which can avoid empty enforcement gaps, can tackle mass harm situations effectively and efficiently", Voet (2017), pp. 138–139; Hodges and Voet (2018); Dodson (2016).

[5]Roth (2016), Thaler and Sunstein (2008), Sunstein (2013).

[6]For the European and American criticism *see* Hess (2014), pp. 3–4; Marcus (2014), pp. 35–49. For a criticism regarding the goals of public interest in class actions *see* Uzelac (2014), pp. 53–69.

class action model.[7] Maybe because of the language proximity, it was through these indirect sources that U.S. style class actions were studied and ultimately ended up in serving as a model for the Brazilian collective redress scheme. But Brazil did not only look at U.S. class actions. The truth is that Brazilian paternity and originality made a double process of cross-reception. On one hand it took advantage of the existence in Brazil of the *actio popularis* (public interest action, 1965), interpreting it as a mechanism for the protection of diffuse societal rights.[8] On the other hand, it developed concepts broadly by extending the their scope to a broader spectrum of rights and types of action.

Between 1977 and 1982, José Carlos Barbosa Moreira,[9] Ada Pellegrini Grinover[10] and Waldemar Mariz de Oliveira Júnior[11] published the first essays paving the way for the civil protection of collective rights in statutory law in 1981 (class action to protect environmental rights), 1985 (transubstantive class actions), and 1988 (constitutional guarantees). Nevertheless, it was the 1990 Consumer Code (CDC) that became the base for the Brazilian model of collective redress. Atypical and transubstantive actions not only aim at the tutelage of the rights of consumers, but also at every other right that might be seen as collective in the broadest sense of the word. Intermediate categories have been created by statutory law, in between substantive and procedural law, in order to protect group rights and by defining collective rights as diffuse rights (an undertermined group of people), strictly collective rights and homogeneous individual rights (Art. 81 CDC).

The judicial collective redress scheme is an example of how procedural law evolved through private and public phases, related to the action, its autonomy and the role of jurisdiction in affirming the "concrete will of the law" ("*concreta volontà della legge*"), to the centrality of the process itself in the solution of the conflict.

Brazilian class actions work in the perspective of guaranteeing access to justice and the resolution of conflicts for substantantive rights of the group (rights precede remedies which is the most common situation) and for situations that are worthy of the protection of group rights (remedies precede rights, exceptionally applying constitutional law).[12]

---

[7]This is true in regards of the doctrine developed in the 1970s, in Italy, which influenced Brazilian doctrine and legislation, but unfortunately does not correspond to the current situation in Italy. For the most cited Italian doctrine in Brazil *see* Denti (1976), Pisani (1976), Vigoritti (1979), Cappelletti (1976, 1977, 1983), Costantino (1974), p. 817; Costantino (2010), p. 1130; Chiarloni (2007, 2008), Taruffo (1976, 2003), Santis (2013), Donzelli (2011), Giussani (2008).

[8]Barbosa Moreira (1981)(1977), pp. 110–123, dedicated to E.T. Liebman.

[9]Barbosa Moreira (1981), first published in (1977), pp. 173–181, Barbosa Moreira (1984a), first published in Barbosa Moreira (1980), pp. 183–192, Barbosa Moreira (1984b), first published in Barbosa Moreira (1981), pp. 193–221, (1984c) first published in Barbosa Moreira (1982).

[10]Grinover (1979).

[11]Oliveira Júnior (1984).

[12]According to the doctrine and the decisions of the European Court of Human Rights (ECHR), a proper combined model of rights and remedies is necessary for an adequate and fair protection, giving access to justice to situations that are worthy of protection: *remedium ibi ius* or *remedies*

2 A History of Success? Quantitative and Qualitative Effectiveness of the Collective Redress Actions in Brazil and The New Code of Civil Procedure (CPC/2015)

Collective redress in Brazil has a long history of success. Of course, there were not only successes. Compared to to other self-proclaimed civil law systems that tried to implement the system of judicial collective redress, Brazilian civil procedure represents one of the most advanced models, perhaps the one that produced most cases and relevant changes in society.

In the absence of more in-depth empirical and compared research, we will simplify the data. We use two two basic criteria: the number of lawsuits filed and admitted in court and the effectiveness of the procedural system to ensure the substantive rights defined by a judgement.

2.1 *Number of Collective Actions Filed and Admitted to Judgment*

We have an impressive number of class actions on a wide range of issues. The official numbers between 2014 and 2018 reach 286,282 pending class actions in the judicial system.[13,14] There are also other data contained in the Collective Actions Report of the National Council of Justice (RAC/CNJ)[15] and the Public Prosecution

---

precede rights. *See* Taruffo (2002), pp. 67–97; Trocker (2011), pp. 302–303; Mazzamutto and Plaia (2012), Pino (2003), Di Majo (2003), p. 72; Varrano and Barsotti (2010), Zaneti (2016), pp. 175–196.

[13]These data refer to the official monitoring panels of the National Counsel of Justice, regarding the four types of collective actions: "ação civil pública", "ação popular", "ação de improbidade administrativa" e "ação coletiva" (based on the CNJ/CNMP unified taxonomy). *See* https://bit.ly/2Mjgr7Y. The data can be inaccurate, since they include expressions used in research and depends on the accuracy of the people who informed the system. Moreover, it is possible to register more than once the same process according to the existence of more than one resource in the same demand. However, the database is collected and compared in this chapter with the Public Prosecution Service database, fed by another system. Therefore, even if inaccurate, the data proves the volume of class actions in Brazil. This tool is powered by all organs of the Brazilian Judiciary and represents a growing source of monitoring and research to improve the judicial system. For more data and the total number of pending proceedings in Brazil (in 2018 78.7 million actions) *see* CNJ (2019). Similar problems of methodology have been pointed out in other studies, such as: Mendes (2018). The research related to the EU reveals a significant lower number of cases: Hodges and Voet (2018), pp. 284–285; Vitorelli and Zaneti (2019), pp. 195–233.

[14]Only in the Superior Court of Justice (Superior Tribunal de Justiça), the equivalent of the Italian Court of Cassation, there are 18,881 decisions for the term "ação civil pública", and there are 1929 decisions for the term "processo coletivo", using the official survey tools of the Court. The number of actions filed and judged in higher courts is therefore a positive outcome indicator. However, it is relevant to note that not all collective procedures end with a judgment or even reach the Superior Court of Justice.

[15]Mendes (2018).

Report: A Portrait.[16] The latter is based on information coming from the various branches of the Public Prosecution Service in the year 2017.[17]

The RAC/CNJ report was prepared by academics who lack practical experience. However, the initiative is commendable. The criticism of the Collective Actions Report points to a discrepancy in the number of "*ações civis públicas*", affirming that the actions in the health area are often individual and not collective and that there would be a distortion of these actions by the Public Prosecutor's Office itself rather than seeking structural solutions with social reach; individual actions are being priviliged, even by judges who think these actions are the most effective ones. The same research affirms, without proving it, that some collective actions are unsuccessful due to structural difficulties, for example, environmental actions are unsuccessful due to deficiencies in the production of the expert evidence required for trials, which are very costly and difficult to produce. The same would be true regarding actions to fight corruption with difficulties of proving fraud in the conduct of public agents.

From a methodological point of view, the research data can be challenged. Inefficient robots (crawlers) were used for the searches—which were for example unable to access the diverse and well-known class action decisions of the Superior Court of Justice in environmental matters.[18] The number of STJ decisions is very large, both in procedural matters and regarding substantive law; several of them resulted in *pro-environment* decisions. Another aspect is that the research was also not efficient in collecting the profile of the magistrates, either by the biased wording of the questions in the survey or by the sample problems. For example, only 1 of the 11 ministers of the Federal Supreme Court (Supremo Tribunal Federal—STF) answered the questionnaire, which is insufficient to affirm how the Court thinks. The results, due to these problems in data collection, are not conclusive and are clearly biased.[19]

---

[16]Conselho Nacional Do Ministério Público. Ministério Público (2018).

[17]Both need to be read critically. The RAC can be criticized for being a random search carried out by robots (crawlers) and interviews with judges (survey). The CNMP's report can be criticized as a data collection carried out by the various public prosecutors throughout the country, being a recent experience based on the CNMP/CNJ unified taxonomy, that describes the type, classes and movements of the judicial and administrative proceedings. On the other hand, there is the possibility that an overlap of information occurs. As we will see later, this methodology presents room for improvement. For a broad criticism of the methodology used *see* Vitorelli and Zaneti (2019).

[18]Vitorelli and Zaneti (2019), demonstrating several important decisions regarding substantive and procedural law in the Brazilian higher Courts.

[19]Recent research in behavioral psychology has identified a series of biased postures as the heuristic of availability, which can be implicated here. We tend to evaluate with mental shortcuts and predict the frequency of an event from examples that are most easily accessible to our mind. This form of heuristics may result in the confirmation bias that deals exactly with the phenomenon of validating results in accordance with what was previously thought. Thus we easily overestimate the probability of an event and give excessive weight to findings in a survey because our attention is focused on a particular outcome, we wait for the confirmation of our preconceptions or simply for cognitive comfort. Kahneman (2011), pp.130–131; Tversky and Kahneman (1973), pp. 207–232.

On the other hand, the CNMP data in the "Public Prosecution: A Portrait" (2018) report indicates that in 2017 alone, 39,496 new actions were filed, and 12,627 Conduct Adjustment Agreements were made with the Public Prosecutor's Office. If we look at the period 2014–2017 in the National Council of Justice system more than 80 percent of the class actions have been filed by Public Prosecutors.

Moreover, the report states that 256,678 preparatory procedures and civil investigations have been initiated in matters relating to collective rights or group rights.[20] There is clear proof that many of the Brazilian class actions are filed by Public Prosecutors against public bodies. It should not need to be said that this is a by-product of the lack of efficiency of public authorities to guarantee the rights ensured by the legal order to all citzens.[21] According to the table below, the Federal Public Prosecutor's Office and the State and Federal District Public Prosecutors' Offices in 2017 worked primarily in the following areas:

Subject	Number of Preparatory Procedures and Civil Inquiries in 2017
Administrative dishonesty (corruption fighting)	31,476 (MPE and MPDFT) and 15,475 (MPF)
Environment	27,238 (MPE and MPDFT) and 3594 (MPF)
Public Patrimony	19,746 (MPE and MPDFT) and 4934 (MPF)
Child and Adolescent Law	18,405 (MPE and MPDFT) and other subjects (MPF)[22]
Health	18,130 (MPE and MPDFT) and 4448 (MPF)
Consumer Rights	9362 (MPE and MPDFT) and 2100 (MPF)
Urban Order	8139 (MPE and MPDFT) and other subjects (MPF)
Education	6458 (MPE and MPDFT) and 3670 (MPF)
Elderly	5292 (MPE and MPDFT) and other subjects (MPF)
Other Subjects	46,989 (MPE and MPDFT) and 24,784 (MPF)
Subtotal MPE and MPDFT	191,235
Subtotal MPF	65,443
Total	256,678

[20]The total number of investigations shows the extent of collective redress in Brazil and the performance of the Brazilian Public Prosecution service in collective redress. It should be noted that at the end of the investigation carried out by such authorities, three hypotheses are possible: (a) they may discontinue the procedure if it is understood that the issues are resolved or that there is no damage; (b) a settlement; a Conduct Adjustment Agreement (by private parties, individuals and/or the Government) could be carried out resolving the conflict and leading to the dropping of charges, as determined by law; (c) or a class action procedure might be filed.

[21]Maybe this is not a problem only in Brazil, or in South America: "only a minority would suggest that in Europe public regulation works really effectively", Silvestri (2010), pp. 99–112.

[22]The MPE, MPDFT and MPF tables do not correspond in all matters. The MPE and MPDFT tables are adopted as the most representative of the number of preparatory procedures and civil investigations. In the event of non-correspondence we will note "other subjects", as in this case. The subjects and quantities of procedures related to public domain (2236), public civil servant (2207) and civil responsibility (1995), existing in the MPF table, were added to the overall computation. We emphasize that the research itself informs the possibility of registering more than one topic by procedure, where the topics overlap.

This model—the standing of the Brazilian Public Prosecutor—was analyzed by Mauro Cappelletti in the following terms. Various models have come to the attention. In one model, in which diffuse interests are considered as public, the Public Prosecutor is given the right to act for their protection. This is made possible by Art. 129, III of the Brazilian Constitution. In Europe, however, this solution has proven not to be very efficient. However, independence and specialization are two vital conditions for the success of the solution considered here.[23]

2.2 *Termination of Lawsuits by Judicial or Non-Judicial Settlements as an Element Due to the Existence Of Judicial Protection*

Regarding the effectiveness aspect, a practical consideration must be added. Brazil followed the Multi-Door Courthouse movement, with the CPC providing for a general duty to encourage alternative dispute resolution (Art. 3, § 3, CPC). In collective redress, since 1985, collective settlements exist and many cases are resolved extrajudicially.[24]

Class actions in Brazil have allowed the evolution of self-regulation. In such cases, there is a reinforcement of BATNA (Best Alternative to a Negotiated Agreement),[25] because the Public Prosecutor's Office and the parties facing a collective negotiation in a civil proceeding know that if there is no search for common interests and compliance with legal requirements, the issue will be referred to litigation—often with provisional injunctions and interlocutory reliefs against the wrongdoer.

Anyone having experience in civil litigation knows that there are only agreements and one can only speak of self-regulation when the judicial procedure represents a concrete threat of a decision contrary to the interests of the defendant. Experience shows that when a provisional measure is granted in a class action, the agreement is more easily facilitated. This occurs because there are not only psychological elements, but also legal ones since there is already an indication that the court is likely to acknowledge the right. Thus, agreements have shown significant growth, and

[23]Cappelletti (1994), pp. 109–110. Recently Chinese Law recognized class action standing for public prosecutors: Fu and Meng (2016), pp. 117–118.

[24]The Conduct Adjustment Agreement can be made by a public agency and is regulated by Art. 5, § 5, of Law number 7,347/1985 (LACP) and, currently, by CNMP Resolution number 179/2017. The trend is worldwide. Van Rhee and Tzankova (2014); Silvestri (2014), p. 200, Harsàgi & Van Rhee (2014).

[25]Judicialization has been mentioned as an alternative for the possibility of no agreements on complex issues. On the other hand, judicialization also leads to objectification of the conflict and a delineation of the conflict in a more precise way, with the impossibility of an alternative after the filing of the action. It eliminates BATNA referring to the exit from the negotiations. If it is not possible to negotiate, after the filing of the suit, the alternative becomes the adjudicated decision. Pigman (2016), pp. 187–215.

even judicial proceedings are often concluded or addressed by self-regulation, as the Rio Doce case (as discussed below) illustrates.[26]

2.3 Results of Judicial Collective Redress in Brazil

Judicial collective redress as described above can result in "any type of action to provide an adequate and effective protection" (Art. 83 CDC). Declaratory judgments, injunctions, compensatory and monetary judgments and others to protect diffuse, collective and individual homogeneus rights.

Judicial cases and settlements can result in: payment of damages to consumers who have faced a loss; reimbursement of overpaid amounts; obligations of acting or not to act that are related to the environment, including destruction of consolidated properties, installation of anti-pollution equipment and the prohibition of installing certain enterprises, as well as the recovery of degraded areas and public policies for the returning of the natural environment to the *status quo ante*; the obligation to carry out facility enhancement works in prisons, hospitals and schools and changing the practices in the same institutions supervised by the Public Prosecutor or/and the judiciary; supplying hospital beds and vacancies for children in preschool day care centers; etc.[27]

The impact of positive actions is also cultural. Just to illustrate with another recent and worldwide known case. In the Brazilian fight against corruption, figures related to the "Car Wash" Operation are not only impressive, but also self explanatory. More than 14.5 billion Reais—4.5 billion dollars—is claimend as civil damages in collective procedures.[28] It should be noted that only the combination of criminal and civil court procedures allows for such results.

Another illustration is the Diesel Gate case. In Brazil the action was filed by a consumer association and resulted in a total of 1 (one) million Reais (215,640.87 euros) in collective damages for the diffuse rights of Brazilian consumers (nonpecuniary losses) and 64,000 Reais (13,801.02 euros) of individual damages for each of the 17,057 buyers of the Amarok Diesel 2011/2012 vehicle (54,000 Reais for material damages and 10,000 Reais for nonpecuniary losses). The Public Prosecutor intervened as *custos legis* and appealed to increase the damages, without success.[29]

---

[26]*See* above the comments on the survey "Public Prosecution: A Portrait". The "winning consumer" website, linked to the Public Prosecutor's Office, which exists in the various state and federal units, has reported more than 4000 occurrences of consumer conduct adjustment agreements, many with national coverage. The website gives access to more than 2000 decisions and national conduct adjustment agreements for the benefit of Brazilian consumers. *See* https://bit.ly/2Nv7ZUo.

[27]In the future, with the growing use of electronic proceedings, it will be possible to have more data about the specific results of class actions, the money collected and received by the group members and the effectiviness of the institutional and social changes (see Sect. 2.1).

[28]*See* https://bit.ly/333xAtV.

[29]TJRJ – APC n° 041231820.2015.8.19.0001.

2.4 *Legal Standing in Brazilian Class Actions: Public and Private Parties*

On the other hand, these experiences are not limited to the Public Prosecutor's Office. Civil associations, legal entities of public law such as the Federal State, the Member States of the Federation and Municipalities and, in the case of the *actio popularis*, also the ordinary citizen may have class action standing. In all cases, the Public Prosecutor's Office, in the event that it does not function as the author, will intervene to protect the public interest (*custos legis*). Non-intervention of the Public Prosecutor's Office will result in the end of the procedure in cases in which it considers that there is a loss (Art. 279, § 1 and § 2 CPC—*pas nullité sans grief*).

The characteristic of broad legal standing, with many co-plaintiffs, is another peculiarity of the Brazilian collective redress scheme. This standing is autonomous, exclusive, concurrent and disjunctive or simple and, although there is some conceptual divergence in doctrine, it is a kind of procedural substitution (representative proceeding[30]) in which the group (holder of the right) is replaced by an authorized party by statutory law (*ope legis*) and its standing (adequacy of representation) can later be judicially controlled later in the case (*ope judicis*).[31]

2.5 *Res Judicata Secundum Eventum Litis*

Another characteristic element of Brazilian class actions is the *res judicata erga omnes secundum eventum litis*. But this matter must be well understood, bearing in mind that *secundum eventum litis* is not the *res judicata* but the subjective extension of the *res judicata* to benefit the individual claimants.

Once the *res judicata pro et contra* is formed, one cannot file a new class action (regardless the plaintiff bringing the action and the name given to it, e.g., collective "mandado de segurança", *actio popularis* or "ação civil pública") under the basis of the same cause of action and the same claim. However, there is no binding effect against the individuals. A class action that might have been dismissed does not prevent the holders of individual rights from filing their individual actions or

[30]In civil law the term "representation" can be problematic, as pointed out by Jeuland: "The idea is that a person - usually in a weak or a dependent situation - might be substituted by another one who is not a representative. A distinction is to be made between representation and substitution: in the mechanism of substitution, the one who brings the action is a party indeed, even though the interest of another person, a third party, is taken into account. The third party does not become a party [...] To be consistent and give only one meaning to the notion of representative action, we consider that it applies only to the situation where a party is represented in a civil action and remains a party. In a collective redress action, the party who brings the action is the actual party while group members do not become parties. So, s/he is not a representative party but a qualified claimant.". Jeuland (2019).

[31]The evolution of the Brazilian model is still in the sense of recognizing defendant class actions, in which the group is the actual defendant. Didier and Zaneti (2019a).

continuing until there is a judgment of the actions that were already filed (Art. 103 CDC). For the same reasons it is stated that there is no *lis pendens* between individual actions and class actions (Art. 104 CDC; Art. 22 Federal Law n° 12.016/2009). Because the cause of action related to a group right may not be deemed the same as the cause of action related to the individual right, there is no *lis pendens* nor *res judicata* against the individual claimants.

This original formulation has always represented one of the most criticized aspects by Brazilian and also international doctrine.[32] That is because the US-style *opt out* class action is characterized by the *pro et contra* binding effect, even against the holders of individual rights. Nowadays, these criticisms have lost some of their strength because of some new case management strategies in Brazilian law, which allow that issues that affect collective redress and mass litigation to be set with some degree of "binding force" for all other cases in progress or future actions, as we will see below.

2.6 Public Interest Actions and Emphasis on the Judgement of the Merit: Collective Redress Microsystem

Finally, Brazilian class actions are characterized by the strong presence of public interest and the principle of merit judgement primacy. The public interest is the result of the legislator's concerns of defending the diffuse interests of society in class action procedures. It also unbalances the procedural relationship for the benefit of collective redress (public interest actions).[33]

There are many laws that regulate collective actions, but the statutes are interpreted as a single body, a collective process code, a collective civil procedure microsystem with several laws that are strongly interconnected. There are several examples, in doctrine and precedents, of the application of this microsystem.[34] In

[32]Gidi (2008), Gidi (2007), pp. 374–380.

[33]The concept of primary public interest results from the Italian influence of Alessi (1953), pp. 148–155, cited in Mello (2003), Mazzilli (2003), Didier and Zaneti (2019b), p. 42. Italian doctrine also helped to build a normative phenomenon in Brazilian class actions: the formation of a collective civil procedure microsystem with several laws that interpenetrate and subsidize each other, as they are mutually applied, due to the influence of Natalino Irti and due to total oblivion of the CPC/1973 in relation to collective proceedings. Irti (1999).

[34]It is enough to remember here that: (a) when in the position of the defendant, companies and government authorities may respond to the initial claim by choosing to defend themselves, by changing for the active pole or by not responding at all, this triple option often is called depolarization of the demand or mobile intervention (STJ, 1ª, T T., REsp n. 791.042/PR, Rel. Ministro Luiz Fux, j. em 19.10.2006, publicado no DJ de 09.11.2006, p. 26; (b) the enforcement of judgments against a defendant who is a debtor of the State may be carried out by means of a payroll-deduction (which is an exception to the principle of non-leviable salaries or wages, *see*, art. 14, § 3° LAP; art. 833 CPC); the necessary remittance to the court of appeal in the judgments of dismissal of merit and in the judgments of extinguishment of the case without resolution of the merit (REsp 1447774/SP,

judicial collective redress, it also results from the primacy of the merit judgment, a judgment that exhausts all matters related to evidence (*res judicata secundum eventum probationis*).

Thus, actions dismissed for lack of evidence may be re-submitted, since the new evidence is capable of, on its own, altering the outcome of the judgment. This institute is called *res judicata secundum eventum probationis*. The exception of *res judicata* cannot be enforced when the proposed (new) evidence may result in a new judgment on the merits.[35]

The microsystem serves as a shield for the rather individualist approach to the CPC from 1973 until 2015, which was only applied in residual collective redress procedures. The 2015 CPC changed the relationship between collective redress and individual procedures. The relationship between the CPC and the microsystem ceased to be a residual one. The relationship became more direct direct and collective redress gained another jurisdictional type of protection, namely aggregate litigation (or repetitive cases) that interacts with the class action model, as we will see below.

3 Collective Redress in Brazil: Towards a Combined Model with Brazilian Class Actions (Opt Out) and Aggregate Litigation (Opt In)

From a dogmatic point of view the success of the Brazilian collective redress process is characterized by its flexibility and adaptation; as described previously, the model evolved by statutory law, precedents and doctrinal interpretation. The new CPC expressly refered to the existence of the class actions, even though it did not bring its own topic on the matter, leaving it to additional statutory legislation.

However, it applies directly to the interpretation and application of the microsystem rules. Since new CPC, the entire collective redress scheme will be regulated by the basic norms and rules of civil procedure as mainly laid down in the

---

Rel. Ministro Francisco Falcao, Segunda Turma, julgado em 21/08/2018, DJe 27/08/2018; REsp 1.108.542/SC, Rel. Ministro Castro Meira, Segunda Turma, DJe 29/5/2009); (d) jurisdiction of the place where the damage occurred (CC 97.351/SP, Rel. Ministro Castro Meira, Primeira Seção, julgado em 27/05/2009, DJe 10/06/2009); (e) the principle of the primacy of merit in the collective process, which among other things determines, for example, the procedural succession, with the call of other party with legal standing rather than the decision of the case without ruling on the merits for lack of *legitimatio ad causam* (REsp 1177453/RS, Rel. Ministro Mauro Campbell Marques, Segunda Turma, julgado em 24/08/2010, DJe 30/09/2010).

[35]It should be noted that although the law is clear in relation to diffuse and collective rights, there is not the same clarity regarding homogenous individual rights, see art. 103, I, II (diffuse and collective) and III (homogenous individual rights) CDC. For these, there is no explicit prediction of *res judicata secundum eventum probationis*. There is at least one decision of the STJ in the sense that the rule does not apply in these cases (REsp 1.302.596-SP, Rel. Min. Paulo de Tarso Sanseverino, Rel. para acórdão Min. Ricardo Villas Bôas Cueva, julgado em 9/12/2015, DJe 1°/2/2016). Criticizing the STJ ruling *see* Didier and Zaneti (2019b), 478–482.

new General Part of the 2015 CPC. All these basic norms are fully applicable to collective redress procedures. Moreover, a number of other norms, which are not laid down in the General Part, are also applicable. The conclusion is that the 2015 CPC is no more of a residual nature. Instead it now focuses directly on the microsystem of Brazilian class actions. There are several examples of this applicability, but special emphasis is given on class actions in Art. 139, X dealing with the obligation to communicate authorized legal standing parties about the existence of individual actions with potential for collectivization.

Therefore, the current Brazilian judicial collective redress system is a genre composed of at least two species: on the one hand, *opt out* class actions as described above, and of which the main example is the public civil action, and on the other hand, aggregate litigation (repetitive cases).[36] Class actions and repetitive cases converge by bringing an active or passive collective legal situation concerning a group of people.

The doctrine claims that in class actions the group is formed on an *opt out* basis by including all who are in the same situation, without demanding any active behavior. In repetitive cases the group is formed on an *opt in* basis, which requires the filing of an action by each individual. Although the use of this classification is connected with the impact of the *res judicata* or binding effect, it is necessary to look at this differently.[37] The traditional classification concerns the binding nature of *res judicata* because it is understood that only an *opt out* can deal with the whole claim binding every individual in the class. Part of Brazilian doctrine inverts the classification to objectify not the end (the stability of the decision), but rather the beginning (the formation of the group); using this formation, to extract some consequences, as we will see ahead.[38]

Although the use of the expressions *opt in* and *opt out* is common in economics and medicine, there is no natural or correct form, and the classification might be made by stipulation to explain the *default formula*.[39]

---

[36]Didier and Zaneti (2017). These repetitive cases are a kind of aggregation of litigation, in which actions are suspended for the processing of an incident resolution of repetitive demands in the court of appeal, or for the judgment of a "especial" or/and "extraordinário" repetitive appeals in matters of substantive law or procedural law (Art. 928 CPC). The inspiration for this was found in the *Musterverfahren* (KapMuG, *Kapitalanleger-Musterverfahrensgesetz*), as expressly mentioned in the explanatory memorandum by the CPC/2015 draft rapporteurs, the *Pilotverfahren*, the Group Litigation Order (GLO) and the Multidistrict Litigation model (MDL). The doctrine and judicial precedents about this new technique is still evolving.

[37]There is also a tendency in the doctrine to propose mixed models of *opt in* and *opt out*. *See* Voet (2017).

[38]Didier and Zaneti (2017), pp. 266–275.

[39]*See*, for example, the debates about organs donations, clear energy, retirement plans *etc* in Thaler and Sunstein (2008), Roth (2016), showing that automatic enrollment dramatically increases participation and must be treated as an option to enforce public policies.

3.1 Fair Process in a Combined Model: Preference for the Broader Protection

The need to combine methods of collective redress, so that there is no excess in the purposes of the process, is notable. It is understandable that the guarantee of protection of persons and rights is achievable in an adequate, effective and timely manner through a fair process that can deal with the conflict.

In collective redress proceedings it would not be fair that the proceedings do not present a solution of the conflicts beyond the individual pretensions. The structure of the collective fair process should contain the following minimum procedural guarantees: (a) adequacy of representation of the stakeholders (in most cases members or groups of the process who are absent); (b) the right of influence by the appropriate representatives of the group and the duty of the judge to discuss the factual and legal grounds in the case, including the participation of interest groups by means of the *amici curiae* institute or by public hearings for the reinforcement of argumentative representativeness; (c) a result that is effective to resolve the collective conflict as a whole, as stated above, in addition to individual pretensions.

For these reasons, it is necessary to think about the balance between the various available forms of collective redress, and more concrete between the use of class actions and aggregate litigation.[40] Therefore, it can be said that it is "possible to create a guideline for the incident of aggregate litigation of repetitive demands (. . .) and the existence of class actions (. . .); the pending collective action should lead to the suspension, even *ex officio*, of individual cases."[41] The Superior Court of Justice also decided in that way.[42] It prevents contradictory decisions, facilitates the management of cases and results in procedural economy.

---

[40]An example of this concern is reflected in the relationship between class actions and repetitive cases. "In addition, if the objects of collective action and the incident of a judgment of repetitive cases are different – what may occur frequently when the judgment of repetitive cases has as its object a procedural question –, there being a collective action among the repetitive causes, it should be chosen as the pilot case (representative cause of the controversy, under the terms of Para 6 of Art. 1036 of the CPC)." In the same sense, the statement n. 615, FPPC: "In the choice of the paradigm cases, collective demands should be preferred, as representative of the controversy, to the individual ones, observing the requirements of Art. 1036, especially of the respective § 6°". This results from the application of due collective legal process, from the notion of collective fair process. There is, therefore, a normative guideline in the sense of prioritizing collective tutelage by collective action. This option is shown with some clarity in Art. 139, X CPC. Didier and Zaneti (2019a), pp. 101–105.

[41]Didier and Zaneti (2019a), pp. 101–105.

[42]In the lawsuit, which discussed inflationary purges and consumer law in the face of bank conduct, the staying of individual judgments was granted (Art. 313, V, a CPC) because it was understood that the judgment of merit in individual cases "would depend" on the judgment of the class action in order to prevent contradictory decisions and to achieve what are considered to be the general objectives of contemporary civil justice, joint and shared responsibility for the fair, efficient, (timely) swift and proportional solution of civil disputes (REsp. n. 1.110.549-RS, rel. Min. Sidnei Beneti, j. em 28.10.2009). The decision is a clear hypothese of case management by force of judicial precedent, being applied many times by the Courts (REsp 1353801/RS, Rel. Ministro Mauro

3.2 *Innovations Regarding Stability from Repetitive Cases, Precedents and Case Management in Collective Processes*

Repetitive cases, case management and binding precedents still have the possibility to resolve one of the problems raised by Brazilian doctrine regarding the model of *res judicata secundum eventum litis* in Brazilian class actions.

As we have seen above, the *res judicata* effect in class actions proceedings only affects the holders of individual rights to benefit them. Numerous individual actions can be proposed, which might lead to contradictory decisions and legal uncertainty. The option of the CPC is clear, although such risk does exist, class actions and individual actions are not to be confused as they do not lead to *lis pendens* and the *res judicata* of collective judgments does not affect, in case of a denied relief, the proposal of an individual action. There is no claim preclusion for individual right claims.

There are however three new issues that address, in a pragmatic way, the binding effect of class actions for individual plaintiffs, even though not with the same force of *res judicata*: (a) the binding effect of the thesis in a judgment of repetitive cases; (b) normatively binding precedents and; (c) collective actions in relation to individual actions in the "macro litigation generating multitudinous litigations".

The first two are derived from an analysis of CPC dogmatics:

(a) First, by the advent of repetitive cases, the technique of judgment and management of aggregate litigation, which allows the suspension of all individual and collective actions for the application of the legal thesis formed, be it favorable, or contrary to the individual litigant. Once the thesis is judged it will apply to all pending actions that deal with an identical point of law (Arts. 985, I and 1.040, III CPC).
(b) Second, by legally binding precedents.[43] Even if it is not a repetitive case, the class action may form a precedent binding all those who have a similar case (Arts. 926 and 927 CPC) and authorizing the preliminary denial of any future claim using the same *ratio decidendi* (Art. 332 CPC).
(c) Third, the judicial construction of the Superior Court of Justice. The STJ extended the effects of the stay of judgments to individual claims when in relation to class actions generated from the same macro litigation. The Court granted the stay of all individual actions related to the class action during 1 (one) year. After the judgment, those individual actions, in case their claims are deemed to be fully or partially granted, can be converted into liquidation and

---

Campbell Marques, Primeira Seção, julgado em 14/08/2013, DJe 23/08/2013). In the litigation originating from a precedent, the individual actions were deemed to have arisen and converted from cognitive proceedings into liquidation and execution proceedings (REsp 1189679/RS, Rel. Ministra Nancy Andrighi, Segunda Seção, julgado em 24/11/2010, DJe 17/12/2010).

[43]For an overall analysis of binding precedentes in Brazil *see* Zaneti (2017b).

enforcement proceedings. In case the class action claim is denied, the detrimental effect thereof could also affect the individual actions.[44]

4 Collective Process in Brazil: Next Generation? Design of Dispute Resolution, Structuring Processes and the Rio Doce Case (Procedural Law of Disasters)

The Rio Doce case is a complex litigation case that can be considered or as a proof of strength for this new model of collective redress and a confirmation of its effectiveness, or as a demonstration of its insufficiency.[45]

The complexity of collective litigation requires that every generation anticipates problems and looks for solutions that may prove themselves adequate for the solution of new conflicts that, although occurred in the past, due to systemic failures of a rigid civil procedural model, have been left out without a proper solution.

The need to resolve complex conflicts involving issues such as the environmental disasters of Mariana (Rio Doce) and Brumadinho, the air crashes of TAM and Air France in Brazil, *apartheid* in Africa, the truth and reconciliation commissions in Canada, online resolutions made in the case of savers,[46] judicially, or extrajudicially e.g. by eBay and consumer.gov and many other examples, stimulate us to look for the best suitable *dispute resolution design*.[47]

---

[44]In the terms of binding precedent, Theme 60: "As a result of collective action concerning the macro litigation that generates multitudinous litigations, individual actions are suspended, awaiting the judgment of collective action." REsp 1110549/RS, Rel. Ministro Sidnei Beneti, Segunda Seção, julgado em 28/10/2009, DJe 14/12/2009. The theme was already applied in other situations (REsp 1353801/RS, Rel. Ministro Mauro Campbell Marques, Primeira Seção, julgado em 14/08/2013, DJe 23/08/2013) and the STJ has already defined that after the collective decision, the individual cognitive actions that are suspended may be converted *ex officio* into liquidation and enforcement of the judgment.

[45]"Unfortunately, lessons are learned from catastrophes and in turn they play a prominent role in the evolution of Environmental Law by way of response instead of anticipatory action. In order for disasters to spur changes in human response, information and statistical data about their causes and consequences must be produced and assimilated. This collective energy must necessarily be channeled into the production of constructive reflections on the role of the Law in imposing disaster prevention duties [...] regulatory deficit largely correlates with a lack of conscious imposition of standards of care implementing reasonable legal duties upon organizations, governamental entities, and the judiciary in an attempt to incorporate circular risk management into the societal structure." Carvalho (2019), pp. 281–300.

[46]The case of the savers lasted 30 years and the agreement was ratified only when the lawsuits were being processed by the Federal Supreme Court. There are many doubts about the effectiveness of the solution taken by agreement. The decision by the STF suspends individual and collective actions for the individual adhesion of each consumer to the agreement of an online platform (https://www.pagamentodapoupanca.com.br/).

[47]*See* Rogers et al. (2013); Faleck (2018).

The objectives of dispute resolution design can be summarized as follows: (a) identifying and absorbing opportunities for mutual gains; (b) building and strengthening relationships between individuals, representatives, groups of people and communities; (c) favoring the objectives of justice; (d) promoting peace and reconciliation; (e) ensuring adequate structural reforms through the rule of law by identifying the interests and rights of the most disadvantaged (less powerful stakeholders) and by curing deficiencies in traditional dispute resolution practices; and (f) adapting to time changes and focusing on the needs of victims and interested groups.[48]

The adequate solution of complex litigation goes through planning and design activities that allow the adequacy of procedures to the end of conflict resolution and application of the right to the case with the lowest cost and the highest benefit and effectiveness.

Structural changes or creation of new structures are often necessary, through structuring processes, for the effectiveness of public policies and public interest; whether these policies are carried out by the public power, by joint action or even by the initiative of those private entities responsible for the conflict, either individuals or companies. The doctrine also focuses on the creation of entities with specific purposes for the resolution of conflicts, so-called claim resolution facilities.[49]

In order to achieve this objective, structural injunctions have altered the traditional collective procedural law to allow new forms of discussion, self-regulation, delimitation of the litigation, definition of jurisdiction, decision and enforcement of judicial measures.

The main characteristic of these proceedings is the need for adequacy and flexibility to reach a certain goal: identifying a structural problem and determining the implementation of the structural modification of reality for dealing with the conflict.

There are numerous case studies, and in Brazil the examples are related to the end of the policy of racial separation, environmental pollution (Mendonça Case[50] and ACP Coal Case[51]), the reform of prisons (FUNPEM case) and the guarantee of pre-school education (Case of Day Cares in São Paulo).[52]

The Rio Doce case is another example of the growing use of structural redress and the importance of collective protection of groups in Brazil. In this case, a worldwide documented environmental disaster and one of the largest in Latin American history; more than 60 collective actions were filed, along with thousands of individual

---

[48] *See* Rogers et al. (2013), p. xvii.

[49] *See* Cabral and Zaneti (2019), pp. 445–483.

[50] Verbic (2013), pp. 267–286; Verbic (2017), p. 275 ff.

[51] Arenhart (2015), p. 7, defending the structural injuctions in Brazil and departing from Fiss (1978) and Fiss & Resnik (2003).

[52] Grinover (2017), Costa and Fernandes (2017), Mendes et al. (2018), pp. 203–209.

actions and the establishment of incidents of aggregate litigation in the State of Minas Gerais, Espírito Santo, and in Brasília, the Federal District.[53]

One of the first problems was the need to identify the right jurisdiction in order to avoid conflicting decisions. The actions were brought together by a decision of the Superior Court of Justice that established the jurisdiction of the Federal Court of the capital of the State of Minas Gerais, Belo Horizonte. The decision complies with the idea of adequate jurisdiction for two reasons: it shifts the competence to one of the affected states, avoiding the Federal District, and preserves actions that deal with local impacts, even if collective, on affected cities. Thus, it preserves the main rule of Brazilian class actions, that is the jurisdiction of place where the damages occurred.

There were two important class actions: a class action brought by the Federal Union and other executive branches, and a class action brought by the Federal Public Prosecutors, later joined by the State branchs affected.

A collective action brought by the Federal State, the States of Minas Gerais and Espírito Santo, the Municipalities affected and the environmental authorities responsible for inspection, for a total amount of 20 billion Reais (4.3 billion euros). This led in early 2016, shortly after the Disaster, to a Conduct Adjustment Agreement, that created the Renova Foundation—a claim resolution organism to address the disaster issues.

The entity is financed by private resources coming from the companies that caused the disaster (Samarco S.A. and its parent companies, Vale S.A. and BHP Billiton of Brasil) and it has 42 socio-environmental and socio-economic programmes aiming at full recovery of the damage. It is important to mention that there was an attempt to have it ratified in court, which was successfully done at the Regional Court of the 1st Region. However, this homologation was later annulled. One of the arguments was the lack of participation of the Public Prosecutor's Office in the elaboration of the agreement and the lack of participation of the affected groups.

At the same time as the attempted approval, the Public Prosecutor's Office filed a public civil action with an estimated value of 155 billion Reais (33.4 billion euros) aiming at full reparation. As the agreement continued to be valid even without the homologation, but only for the parties, the collective actions of the Federal Government and the MPF (Federal Public Prosecutor's Office) were joined together to be judged by the 12th Civil Court of the District of Belo Horizonte, Minas Gerais. The novelty from an institutional point of view was the joing up of the Federal Prosecutor's Offices, the Public Prosecutor's Office of the State of Minas Gerais and the Public Prosecutor's Office of the State of Espírito Santo, as well as the Public Defender's Office at the same Federal and States levels.

It was possible to adjust the production of independent and impartial evidence on the programs of the Renova Foundation and to restructure the Foundation's governance, creating more decision-making instances for deliberation and increasing the participation of those affected. The Public Defenders and the Public Prosecutors

[53]Carvalho (2019), pp. 281–300.

were added to the management and control of the Renova Foundation and the Interfederative Committee, which acts as a technical supervision chamber. Governance renegotiation also included the invitation of institutions of civil society to form an Observer Forum. On the level of collecting evidence, independent technical audits were ordered by the Public Prosecutor's Office.[54]

To carry out this reengineering, new concepts of the CPC were used; in particular the duty of cooperation, the permanent stimulus of self-regulatory solutions and procedural agreeements (Art. 190 CPC).[55] There was also room for other initiatives such as the possibility of internal judicial cooperation between the Federal Justice and the State Courts (Art. 69 CPC). The terms of the agreement still determined the general reorganization of the collective lawsuits, including the 20 billion Reais lawsuit filed by the Federal Union and the deadlines for reviewing claims.

Another issue was the possibility of limiting individual claims of people who had not yet filed their lawsuits. As the disaster occurred on November 5, 2015 and the Civil Code provides a time limit of three (3) years to file an action seeking civil damages for liability (Art. 206, § 3 V, CC), a discussion was triggered pushing for the new filings of thousands of individual actions. The point is that Brazilian doctrine and jurisprudence have understood that when the class action is filed, the time limit is interrupted for individual actions, precisely to avoid a rush to the courts once the affirmative judgment will benefit the holders of individual rights.[56] Finally, by a joint action of the Public Prosecutor's Office and the Public Defender's, the time limit was conventionally dismissed, with the agreement of the companies and the Renova Foundation.[57]

This last example shows the importance of the role of the judge as a "judge of guarantees" (as a manager and a facilitator). He must resolve conflicts that arise in the course of the implementation of his decisions. The judge also ordered the suspension of the 155 billion Reais action for general pre-trial arrangements such as the realization of audits of the Renova Foundation's programs, including the

[54]This review of governance and external audit was based on two terms of conduct adjustment called TAC GOV and TAP.

[55]"When the action deals with rights that permit the resolution of the dispute by the parties themselves, the competent parties can lawfully stipulate changes in the procedure to adapt it to the specific requirements of the action and to agree upon their burden, powers, procedural rights and obligations, before or during the proceedings. Sole paragraph. Whether ex officio or upon request, the judge shall control the validity of the agreements set forth in this article, denying their application only in the case of nullity or inclusion of unconscionable terms in adhesion contracts or in cases where any of the parties is in a manifest position of weakness."

[56]Cf. Zaneti et al. (2019).

[57]The term expressly stated that "The COMPANIES and the RENOVA FOUNDATION reaffirmed, in accordance with Brazilian legislation, the TTAC, the TAP and its additive, and the TAC GOV, its obligation to fully repair the people affected by the DAM RUPTURE OF FUNDÃO (...) There will be no loss of rights and pretensions of people affected, based on time limit, on November 5, 2018". Cf. http://laprocon.ufes.br/principais-termos-de-ajustamento-de-conduta. Accessed November 14, 2018.

Mediated Indemnity Program (PIM), which deals with the compensation for lack of water and general damages.

The time limit was no issue because of the fact that the filing of the general collective action aiming at the compensation of all victims, what was requested in the ACP of 155 billion Reais, interrupted the time limit, as recognized by precedent of the Superior Court of Justice followed by more than 50 (fifty) decisions of that court. Ideally, the original judge of the case should bring the parties together for clarifying the issue.

After all, if the environment is created for self-regulation as the best alternative for the full protection of the rights affected, it would be contradictory behavior of the companies to insist on the time limit thesis. The matter was resolved via consensus, after a long debate and the filing of thousands of individual actions.

The aforementioned situations that arise in a litigation of such a complexity demand an expansion in the cause of request and the petition to comply with the new relevant legal situations to resolve the conflict. All these solutions are possible because the new Code allows flexibility regarding the subject matter of the claim and consistence with the limits of the claim and cause of action, so that the interpretation of the claim (Art. 322, § 2 CPC) takes into account the complexity of the structural litigation.

According to this perspective, it is also possible to talk about a cascade of decisions and an amplification of *thema in decidendum* to take into consideration the facts that arise in the course of instruction, as long as the *audi alteram partem* principle is preserved (Art. 493, sole paragraph, CPC). It becomes a fundamental tool for the judge, at the stage of effective structural decisions, to correct the directions of executive tutelage in order to contemplate the current needs of the interested parties. While the implementation of decisions made in non-structural processes usually takes place in an impositive manner, it is common for the structural decisions to become effective in a dialectical way, "from a broad debate in which the only premise consists in taking the conflict as a result of a social structure to be reformed."[58] It is the conflict that is treated, not only the initial intended claim.

In Brazilian procedural law, the normative basis for the execution of structural decisions is derived from the combination of Art. 139 IV[59] and Art. 536, §1 both CPC. The provisions are executive general clauses, from which the power to promote the execution of decisions by atypical measures is granted to the judge.

But in addition to this, a refoundation of the principle of orality must also be observed for the solution of complex issues, with the possibility for the judge to determine the attendance of the parties at any time (Art. 139, VIII CPC) and to

[58]Violin (2013), p. 151. Sérgio Cruz Arenhart also points out that, since the structural decision aims at a substantial change for the future in relation to a particular practice or institution, it is extremely important to guarantee the participation not only of the community that will be affected, through public hearings and *amici curiae*, but also of experts who "can contribute both to the proper dimensioning of the problem to be examined and to alternatives to the solution of the controversy". Arenhart (2015), p. 4.

[59]Jobim (2016), pp. 230–232, Jobim (2013).

convene a hearing for clarifications in complex cases by inviting the parties to complete or clarify their allegations (Art. 357, § 3 CPC: "If the case reveals complexities on points of fact or of law, the judge must schedule a hearing for the clarification of these points to be carried out with the cooperation of all the parties, at which time the judge shall, if necessary, invite the parties to complete or clarify their allegations").

The reestablishment of the principle of orality requires that the judges and the parties have a new behavior in the proceedings, the attendance at these hearing sessions must be carried out with knowledge of the issues discussed and in order to allow the commitment of the parties towards the object of the process, the solution or the construction of a procedure which allows the clearest possible discussion of facts and law under discussion.

Finally, because of the complexity of the matters discussed in the structural procedures and the possibility that the decisions originated thereof may affect a significant number of people, it is necessary to think about new ways of involving interested parties in the process, such as the admission of the *amicus curiae* and convening public hearings.[60] The traditional formulas of intervention thought for the individual processes are not sufficient to guarantee broad participation in the structural processes that require a qualified argumentative representation in order to reach their purpose.

This aspect of argumentative representation must reach all new forms of collective redress. It is necessary that the compliance with the *audi alteram partem* principle should be strengthened, especially in cases in which a group of people who will not participate in the process but who will be affected by judicial decisions, as is the case in for example class actions and repetitive cases.[61]

References

Alessi R (1953) Sistema istituzionale del diritto amministrativo italiano. Giuffrè, Milano

Arenhart SC (2015) Processos estruturais no direito brasileiro: reflexões a partir do caso da ACP do Carvão. Revista de Processo Comparado, v. 2

Barbosa Moreira JC (1981) A ação popular do direito brasileiro como instrumento de tutela dos chamados "interesses difusos" (1977). In: Moreira B, Carlos J (eds) Temas de direito processual civil: primeira série. Saraiva, São Paulo

Barbosa Moreira JC (1984a) A legitimação para a defesa dos "interesses difusos" no direito brasileiro. In: Barbosa Moreira JC (ed) Temas de direito processual civil: terceira série. Saraiva, São Paulo

Barbosa Moreira JC (1984b) A proteção jurídica dos interesses coletivos. In: Barbosa Moreira JC (ed) Temas de direito processual civil: terceira série. Saraiva, São Paulo

Barbosa Moreira JC (1984c) Tutela jurisdicional dos interesses coletivos ou difusos. In: Barbosa Moreira JC (ed) Temas de direito processual civil: terceira série. Saraiva, São Paulo

[60] In the same sense: Grinover (2015), p. 26.

[61] Didier and Zaneti (2019a), p. 110.

Cabral AP, Zaneti H Jr (2019) Entidades de Infraestrutura Específica para a Resolução de Conflitos Coletivos: As Claim Resolution Facilities e a sua Aplicabilidade ao Brasil. Revista de Processo. 287:445–483
Cappelletti M (1976) Appunti sulla tutela giurisdizionale di interessi coletivi o diffusi. In: Le azione a tutela di interessi collettivi: atti del convegno di studio di Pavia, 11-12 giugno 1974. CEDAM, Padova
Cappelletti M (1977) Formações sociais e interesses coletivos diante da justiça civil. Revista de Processo 2(4), São Paulo
Cappelletti M (1983). Acesso a la justicia – programa de accion reformadora y nuevo método de pensamiento. Trad. Silvia Virgínia Leo Vidaña. Boletin mexicano de derecho comparado: Instituto de Investigaciones Jurídicas. Universidad Nacional Autônoma de México. Nueva Serie, Año XVI, n. 48
Cappelletti M (1994) Dimensione della Giustizia nella Società Contemporanee. Il Mulino, Bologna
Carvalho DW (2019) The Ore Tailings Dam Rupture Disaster in Mariana, Brazil 2015: what we have to learn from anthropogenic disasters. Nat Resour J 59(2):281–300
Chiarloni S (2007) Per la chiarezza di idee in tema di tutele collettive dei consumatori. Riv Dir Proc
Chiarloni S (2008) Il nuovo articolo 140 bis del codice del consumo: azione di classe o azione collettiva? In: Analisi Giuridica dell'Economia
CNJ (2019) Justiça em Números. Conselho Nacional de Justiça, Brasília
Conselho Nacional Do Ministério Público. Ministério Público: um retrato (2018) CNMP, Brasília
Costa SH, Fernandes DC (2017) Processo Coletivo e Controle Judicial de Políticas Públicas – Relatório Brasil. In: Grinover AP, Watanabe K, Costa SH (eds) O Processo para solução de conflitos de interesse público. Juspodivm, Salvador
Costantino G (1974) Brevi note sulla tutela giurisdizionale degli interessi collettivi davanti al giudice civile. Diritto e Giurisprudenza.
Costantino G (2010) L'azione di classe ai sensi dell'art. 140 bis del codice del consumo. La sentenza di accoglimento. Il giudizio preventivo di ammissibilità. Diritto ed Economia dell'Assicurazione
Denti V (1976) Relazione introduttiva. In: Le azione a tutela di interessi collettivi: atti del convegno di studio di Pavia, 11-12 giugno 1974. Cedam, Padova
Di Majo A (2003) La Tutela Civile dei Diritti. 4ª ed. Giuffrè, Milano
Didier Jr F, Zaneti Jr H (2017) Las Acciones Colectivas y el Enjuiciamento de Casos Repetitivos: dos Tipos de Proceso Colectivo en el Derecho Brasileño, International Journal of Procedural Law, vol. 7. Intersentia, Cambridge
Didier Jr F, Zaneti Jr H (2019a) Curso de Direito Processual Civil. Processo Coletivo, 13ª ed. Vol. 4. JusPodivm, Salvador
Didier Jr F, Zaneti Jr H (2019b) Proceso Colectivo. Tutela Procesal de los Derechos Difusos, Colectivos e Individuales Hmogéneos. Palestra, Lima
Dodson S (2016) An opt-in option for class actions. Mich Law Rev 115(2)
Donzelli R (2011) L'azione di classe a tutela dei consumatori. Jovene, Napoli
Faleck D (2018) Manual de Design de Sistemas de Disputas. Criação de Estratégias e Processos Eficazes para Tratar Conflitos. Lumen Juris, Rio de Janeiro
Fiss OM (1978) The civil rights injunction. Indiana University Press, Bloomington
Fiss OM, Resnik J (2003) Adjudication and its alternatives. An introduction to procedure. Foundation Press, New York
Fu Y, Meng X (2016) Civil Justice in China. Brics Law J III(4):117–118
Gidi A (2007) A class action como instrumento de tutela coletiva dos direitos. RT, São Paulo
Gidi A (2008) Rumo a um Código de Processo Civil coletivo: A codificação das ações coletivas no Brasil. Forense, Rio de Janeiro
Giussani A (2008) Azioni collettive risarcitorie nel processo civile. Il Mulino, Bologna
Grinover AP (1979) A tutela dos interesses difusos. Revista da Procuradoria-Geral do Estado de São Paulo 12:1979
Grinover AP (2015) Seoul Conference 2014 – Constitution and proceedings – The Judiciary as an Organ of Political Control. Revista de Processo, vol 249. RT São Paulo

Grinover AP (2017) Caminhos e descaminhos do controle jurisdicional de políticas públicas no Brasil. In: Grinover AP, Watanabe K, Costa SH (eds) O Processo para solução de conflitos de interesse público. Juspodivm, Salvador

Harsàgi V, Van Rhee CH (eds) (2014) Multi-party redress mechanisms in Europe: squeaking mice? Intersentia, Cambridge

Hess B (2014) European perspectives on collective litigation. In: Harsàgi V, Van Rhee CH (eds) Multi-party redress mechanisms in Europe: squeaking mice? Intersentia, Cambridge

Hodges C, Voet S (2018) Delivering collective redress. New technologies. Hart, Oxford

Irti N (1999) L'Età della Decodificazione Vent'Anni Dopo. In: Irti N (ed) L'Età della Decodificazione. 4ª ed. Giuffrè, Milano

Jeuland E (2019) Class Action: Representation or Substitution? The ELI-UNIDROIT Project Example, hal-02129656

Jobim MF (2013) Medidas estruturantes: da Suprema Corte Estadunidense ao Supremo Tribunal Federal. Livraria do Advogado Editora, Porto Alegre

Jobim MF (2016) "A previsão das medidas estruturantes no artigo 139, IV, do novo Código de Processo Civil brasileiro". Repercussões do novo CPC – processo coletivo. Zaneti Jr. H (coord.). Editora JusPodivm, Salvador

Kahneman D (2011) Rápido e devagar, duas formas de pensar (Thinking, fast and slow). Objetiva, Rio de Janeiro

Marcus R (2014) The big bad wolf: American class actions. In: Harsàgi V;, Van Rhee CH (eds) Multi-party redress mechanisms in Europe: squeaking mice? Intersentia, Cambridge

Mazzamutto S, Plaia A (2012) I Rimedi nel Diritto Privato Europeo. Giappichelli, Torino

Mazzilli HN (2003) A defesa dos interesses difusos em juízo. 15ª ed. Saraiva, São Paulo

Mello CAB (2003) Curso de direito administrativo. 15ª ed. Malheiros, São Paulo

Mendes CH et al (2018) Ações coletivas no Brasil: temas, atores e desafios da tutela coletiva. CNJ, Brasília

Oliveira Júnior WM (1984) In: Grinover, Ada Pellegrini (Coord.). A tutela dos interesses difusos: doutrina, jurisprudência e trabalhos forenses. Max Limonad, São Paulo, first published in 1978

Pigman GA (2016) Judicialization: the third transformation. In: Trade diplomacy trasformed. Palgrave Macmillam, London

Pino G (2003) Il Diritto All'Identità Personale: Interpretazione Costituzionale e Creatività Giurisprudenziale. Il Mulino, Bologna

Pisani AP (1976) Apuntti preliminari per uno studio sulla tutela giurisdizionale degli interessi colletivi (o piu esattamente: superindividuali) innanzi al giudice civili ordinario. In: Le azione a tutela di interessi collettivi: atti del convegno di studio di Pavia, 11-12 giugno 1974. Cedam, Padova

Rogers NH, Bordone RC, Sander FEA, Mcewen A (2013) Designing systems and processes for managing disputes. Wolters Kluwer, New York

Roth A (2016) Who gets what – and why. The new economics of matchmaking and market design. Mariner Books, New York

Santis AD (2013) La tutela giurisdizionale collettiva. Jovene, Napoli

Silvestri E (2010) The difficult art of legal transplants: the case of class actions. Revista de Processo, vol. 218. RT, São Paulo

Silvestri E (2014) Class actions in Italy. In: Harsàgi V, Van Rhee CH (eds) Multi-party redress mechanisms in Europe: squeaking mice? Intersentia, Cambridge

Sunstein CR (2013) Simpler. The future of government. Simon & Schuster, New York

Taruffo M (1976) Interventi. In.: Le azione a tutela di interessi collettivi: Atti del convegno di studio di Pavia, 11–12 giugno 1974. Cedam, Padova

Taruffo M (2002) Sui Confini. Scritti Sulla Giustizia Civile. Il Mulino, Bologna

Taruffo M (2003) Modelli di tutela giurisdizionale degli interessi collettivi. La tutela giurisdizionale degli interessi collettivi e diffusi. Lucio Lanfranchi (org.). Giappichelli, Torino

Thaler RH, Sunstein CR (2008) Nudge. improving decisions about health, walth, and happiness. Penguin Books, New York

Trocker N (2011) La Formazione del Diritto Processuale Europeo. Giappichelli, Torino
Tversky A, Kahneman D (1973) Availability: a heuristic for judging frequency and probility. Cogn Psychol 5
Uzelac A (2014) Why no class actions in Europe? A view from the side of dysfunctional justice systems. In: Harsàgi V, Van Rhee CH (eds) Multi-party redress mechanisms in Europe: squeaking mice? Intersentia, Cambridge
Van Rhee CH, Tzankova I (2014) Collective redress in the Netherlands. In: Harsàgi V, Van Rhee CH (eds) Multi-party redress mechanisms in Europe: squeaking mice? Intersentia, Cambridge, pp 209–224
Varrano V, Barsotti V (2010) La Tradizione Giuridica Occidentale, 4ª ed. Giappichelli, Torino
Verbic F (2013) El Remedio Estructural de la Causa 'Mendoza'. Antecedentes, Principales Características, y Algunas Cuestiones Planteadas Durante los Primeros Tres Años de su Implementación. Revista Anales n° 43, Facultad de Ciencias Jurídicas y Sociales de la UNLP, pp 267–286
Verbic F (2017) Manual de Introdución a los Processos Colectivos y las Acciones de Clase. In: González L, Fandiño M (eds) Diálogo Multidisciplinario sobre la Nueva Justicia Civil de Latinoamérica. Centro de Estudios de Justicia de las Américas, Santiago
Vigoritti V (1979) Interesse collettivi e processo: la legitimazione ad agire. Giuffrè, Milano
Violin J (2013) Protagonismo Judiciário e Processo Coletivo Estrutural. Juspodivm, Salvador
Vitorelli E, Zaneti H Jr (2019) O Futuro do Processo Coletivo: Considerações sobre o Relatório Analítico Propositivo do Conselho Nacional de Justiça. Revista de Processo 295:195–233
Voet S (2017) 'Where the wild things are': reflections on state and future of European collective redress. In: Keirse ALM, Loos MBM (eds) Waves in contract and liability law in three decades of Ius Commune. Intersentia, Cambridge
Zaneti Jr H (2016) A Legalidade na Era da Proteção das Necessidades de Tutela: Princípio da Constitucionalidade e Legalidade Ampla. In: Didier Jr F, Nunes D, Freire A (eds) Normas Fundamentais. JusPodivm, Salvador
Zaneti H Jr (2017a) El Nuevo Código de Proceso Civil brasileño de 2015 y los conflictos jurídicos: el Derecho Procesal como un camino para la paz social. Revista de Derecho Procesal. Buenos Aires, Rubinzal-Culzoni
Zaneti Jr H (2017b) O Valor Vinculante dos Precedentes. 3ª ed. JusPodivm, Salvador
Zaneti H Jr (2019a) Processo Coletivo no Brasil: Sucesso ou Decepção? Civ Proced Rev 10:11–40
Zaneti H Jr (2019b) Processo Coletivo no Brasil: Sucesso ou Decepção? In: Jobim MF, Reichelt LA (eds) Coletivização e Unidade do Direito. Thoth. This version has been improved with new data and some further developments
Zaneti H Jr (2019c) Proceso Colectivo en Brasil: éxito o decepción? Revista de Derecho Procesal 2:293–330 (Rubinzal-Culzoni, Buenos Aires)
Zaneti H Jr, Lino DB, Sobral MA, Campos RMP, Trazzi P (2019) Ações Individuais no Caso Rio Doce: Interrupção da Prescrição, Suspensão da Prescrição e Comportamento Contraditório dos Litigantes no Processo de Autocomposição. Revista de Processo 298:193–217 (RT, São Paulo)

Hermes Zaneti Jr Tenured Professor of civil procedure at the Federal University of Espírito Santo, Vitória, Brazil. Member of the International Association of Procedural Law. Public Prosecutor and Dean of the Public Prosecutor's School of the State of Espírito Santo.

Class Actions and Public Interest Litigation in China

Yulin Fu

Abstract China has two major judicial reliefs against large-scale rights' infringements. One, established in 1991, is a mass private interest action under which the victims of mass harm can opt-in and join the plaintiff class in representative litigation. The plaintiff class selects their representatives who participate in the trial. The plaintiffs are bound by the judgment. The victims who did not join the plaintiff class may sue separately, but in separate litigation the class judgment is usually applied as a 'model-litigation'. This type of judicial relief was not sufficiently effective, which led to legislative changes and the establishment of another type of collective relief. In 2012, a new form of collective relief, called 'public interest litigation' was established. In public interest litigation the procurator and some other legally authorized social organizations act as plaintiffs in cases of environmental harm and mass infringement of consumer rights. An individual consumer is not allowed to file a public interest lawsuit, in spite of the fact that the legally authorized plaintiff entities often lack motivation to file such claims. Apart from these two means of collective redress, this contribution also addresses the main features of a new, opt-out type of class action established by the Securities Law at the end of 2019.

1 Introduction

In China, there are two main types of judicial action for collective redress caused by mass harm situations. One was established in 1991 as 'representative action' (sometimes also referred to as 'class action'). Currently, it is regulated by articles 53 and 54 of the Civil Procedure Law (CPL):

Art 53

Where there are numerous parties on one side of a joint action, such parties may propose a representative or representatives to participate in the action. The litigation conducted by such

Y. Fu (✉)
Peking Law School, Beijing, China
e-mail: fuyulin@pku.edu.cn

A. Uzelac, S. Voet (eds.), *Class Actions in Europe*, Ius Gentium: Comparative Perspectives on Law and Justice 89, https://doi.org/10.1007/978-3-030-73036-9_16

> representatives shall bind all the represented parties. However, to modify or relinquish any claims, admit any claims of the opposing party or reach a settlement, such representatives must obtain a consent from the represented parties.

Art 54

> Where the exact number of such parties is uncertain when the action is instituted, the court may publish a notice describing the case and claims filed, and invite the potential right holders to register with the court within a certain period of time. The judgment or ruling issued by the court shall bind all right holders which have registered with the court, and shall also apply to actions instituted during the time limitation by rights holders which have not registered with the court.

The other type of collective redress is known as 'public interest litigation' (PIL). It was established in 2012 by an amendment to CPL which was again amended in 2017.

Under Article 55 CPL,

> ... [f]or conduct that pollutes environment, infringes upon the lawful rights and interests of many consumers or otherwise damages the public interest, an organ or relevant organization as prescribed by law may institute an action in a people's court. Where the people's procuratorate finds in the performance of its functions any conduct that undermines the protection of the human environment and natural resources, infringes upon consumers' lawful rights and interests in the field of food and drug safety, or any other conduct that damages social interest, it may file a lawsuit with the court if there is no organ or organization prescribed in the preceding paragraph authorized to do so, or such organ or organization fails to file a lawsuit.

The main differences between the two types of judicial relief are the following:

(1) **Interests.** A representative action is a form of litigation for *private interests* of a group with more than 10 joint parties represented by designated representative (s). In contrast, the PIL is a form of litigation for the protection of *public interests* so that the plaintiff should not pursue private interests in the litigation.
(2) **Subjects in the procedure/Standing to sue**. The plaintiffs of a representative action *must be the holders of disputed rights*. Just like in one-on-one litigation, standing to sue is required for the designated representative(s) who can only be selected or appointed from the group of joint plaintiffs. In contrast, the plaintiff of PIL must be one of the authorized governmental bodies (mainly the state prosecutor or procurator) or an authorized organization prescribed by law (e.g. a consumers' association).
(3) **Object of litigation**. Representative litigation is applied to a *broad scope of disputes* related to mass harm situations arising from torts or contracts. In contrast, PIL is *more narrowly applied* to harms related to environmental pollution or damages caused to a large number of consumers, or otherwise damages that would be covered by the definition of "public interest".

The substantive laws that authorize an organization to file a PIL are the legal base for the plaintiff's right to file an action in a specific field. By now, organizations authorized to file a PIL include:

(1) for damages caused to a large number of consumers—consumer associations under Art. 37 and Art. 47 of the Law on the Protection of Consumer Rights and Interests (Consumer Law);
(2) for damages caused by acts of pollution or other ecological damage—social organizations legally registered with the civil affairs department of the government if they were engaged in environmental protection for the public good for five or more consecutive years, provided that they do not have any recorded violation of law (Art. 58 of the Environmental Protection Law (2015));
(3) for damages caused to marine environment—the interested department empowered by the provisions of the Marine Environmental Protection Law (2017).

The CPL and most legal textbooks do not specifically distinguish regular ("one-on-one") litigation, joint litigation, representative (class) action and PIL. Instead, the CPL regulates all these forms of litigation jointly in the chapter "Litigants". Thus, many issues that arise in addition to the issue of standing to sue are regulated by so-called judicial interpretations or judicial opinions issued as abstract rules by the Supreme People's Court (SPC) and sometimes also by the Supreme People's Prosecution (SPP). These judge-made regulations are very important sources of law in China. In particular, the SPC provides procedural rules for the conduct of both major forms of collective redress.

Furthermore, the Administrative Procedure Law was revised in 2017, at the same time of the revision of the CPL, and added Article 25:

> Where the people's procuratorate finds in the performance of functions that any administrative organ assuming supervision and administration functions in such fields as the protection of the human environment and natural resources, food and drug safety, protection of state-owned property, and the assignment of the right to use state-owned land exercises functions in violation of any law or conducts nonfeasance, which infringes upon national interest or public interest, it shall offer procuratorial recommendations to the administrative organ, and urge it to perform functions in accordance with the law. If the administrative organ fails to perform functions in accordance with the law, the people's procuratorate shall file a lawsuit with the people's court in accordance with the law.

This means that parallel litigation may arise regarding the same event both in the form of civil PIL and in the form of administrative PIL. A department of the government can file a civil PIL as plaintiff against a specific company, and in the meantime the same company can become a defendant of administrative PIL by the prosecutor's charge.

In practice, the situation can be even more complicated. As already stated, an individual may not file a PIL under Art. 55 of the CPL. But consumers frequently file suits not only in their private interest, but also in public interest cases. On the other hand, authorized consumer associations have filed only a few cases, though illegal conduct and mass damages happen frequently. Against such a background, together with the judicial reform of registration/docketing, some courts accept the cases filed by individual plaintiffs and grant their claims for relief in public interest, overturning the long-standing practice where the parts of the individual's claims related to public interest were regularly dismissed. New case law was welcomed by society and supported by the appellate courts. The SPC might accept this practice and turn it into "judicial guidelines", recognized under the Chinese system of case law.

2 The Rise and Fall of Representative (Class) Actions

A class action procedure, also known as a representative action, was provided in the CPL as early as in 1991. It was a hot topic in the early 1990s. But this mechanism of collective redress did not function well in the following years. Though the regulation of representative action remained untouched by the amendments of the CPL in 2007, 2012 and 2017, there was a need for new, more effective mechanisms. One of them is to be found in the newly amended Securities Law of 2019, which provides institutional development of the class action system. Now, China has a general system of *opt-in* class actions and a special system of *opt-out* class actions. In this chapter, the development of representative actions will be discussed, as well as the limitations and practical failures of this form of collective redress.

2.1 Background

The CPL of China was enacted in 1982 as a test law ('Test CPL 1982'). Under Test CPL 1982, there were only three kinds of litigants: (1) a plaintiff and a defendant (individual litigation); (2) joint litigants (multiparty litigation); and (3) the third party (intervener). Joint litigants were conceived as the aggregate of an individual litigant instead of a 'group' or a 'class', even when in some cases the list of plaintiffs in the judgement stretched over several pages. All parties had to attend the trial in person.

In the late 1980s, Chinese courts faced an increasing number of multiparty disputes but lacked an appropriate procedure to handle them. The courts' difficulties stemmed from the complexity of cases involving large numbers of litigants, and from the courts' own lack of resources, as judges had only informal legal education and the courts were underfunded. In that period, it was very fashionable to learn from Western countries, especially from the experience of the US.

In 1988, an influential case attracted the attention of scholars and stimulated the legal community to study US class actions. More than 1.600 farmers filed suits before the Court of Yueyang County for damages caused by artificial seeds sold by a company. The number of potential parties was still uncertain.[1] After consulting the class action models from the US, the UK, Germany, Japan, and Taiwan of China, China created its own system of 'representative action' or 'class action', mainly

[1]The case of Yue-Yang seed, see Wei and Changchun (1988), pp. 84–91.

modeled after Japanese law. Accordingly, a new type of litigant, called 'joint representative of the parties' was inserted in the CPL when it was amended in 1991.[2]

2.2 Features and Limitations

Under Articles 53 and 54 of the CPL, which were amended by a series of SPC's judicial interpretations, the representative litigation is an extension of the joint litigation. The applicable provisions classify class actions into two types: litigation with a certain number of parties (Art. 53) and litigation with an uncertain number of parties (Art. 54). The former is just a typical multi-party litigation in which more than ten parties participate on the plaintiff's or defendants side. It differs from general multi-party litigation insofar that the parties may not conduct litigation in person. Instead, they have to propose a representative or representatives (normally not more than 5) from the group of joint parties. Their actions bind all other represented parties. If the group fails to agree on the joint representatives, the court will appoint them. But, for modification or relinquishment of claims, admittance of the claims of the opposing party or a settlement, the representatives must obtain a consent from all represented parties. Accordingly, the representative action with a certain number of parties has few substantial differences from ordinary joint litigation. Later in this text I will disregard it while discussing class actions.

The second, more interesting form is the representative action with an uncertain number of parties. It largely matches the concept of class action from a comparative law perspective. Under Art. 54 CPL,

> [w]here the subject matter of dispute for each party is of the same kind, and the parties on one side of an action are numerous, but the exact number of such parties is uncertain when the action is instituted, the people's court may publish a notice describing the case and the submitted claims and instruct right-holders to register with the people's court within a certain period of time.

From this provision we can conclude that China's main form of class action is an *opt-in* action.

The appointment of representatives in class actions with an uncertain number of parties is similar as in litigations with a certain number of parties. The right-holders that have registered with the court may nominate a representative or representatives who will actively participate in the litigation. If no representative is nominated, the court may designate a representative or representatives in consultation with the registered right-holders. The actions of the representatives bind all represented parties. Again, to modify or relinquish any claims, admit any claims of the opposing

[2]In the late 1980s American experience kickstarted the adoption of class action procedures in the CPL. However, China's class action institution mainly took Japanese law as model. See Wei and Jianguo (1994), pp. 3–4.

party or conclude a settlement, the representatives must obtain a consent from the represented parties.

The binding force of the judgment is peculiar, insofar that it combines the opt-in model with some features of model litigation regarding the parties who have not joined the group litigation. Under Art. 54 CPL, the judgment or ruling issued by the court in a representative action binds all right-holders that have registered with the court. The right-holders who have not registered with the court may file a separate action with the court (subject, however, to the statute of limitations). However, the judgment or ruling made in the class action should also apply to the independent litigants. I will discuss this feature in more length later.

From the above, we can conclude that China's class action model is limited in several aspects: the plaintiff's class is limited to opt-in members; the representatives are limited to the class members; the representatives' rights to dispose of or settle the claim are limited by approval of all class members; the binding force of the judgment is limited to the representatives' actions authorized by the class's agreement. These limitations are justified by the due process principle, i.e. the need to guarantee the control over their substantive rights to class members who have no opportunities to personally participate in the trial.

However, with so many limitations, one may wonder what are the benefits of representative litigation and the advantages of this form of class action compared to simple multi-party litigation? And in how many cases can a huge class with e.g. 1600 members conclude an agreement on modification, admittance or waiver of the claims, which is a common form of settlement of civil cases in China? On the other hand, the class members who do not join the class are actually also bound by the class action judgment under the so-called 'model litigation' trial mode, though they only need to prove that they fall within the scope of the class description. This puts into question the benefits for the members of the group who initially filed the class action and for the representatives who usually organize the class to file the action. The practical experiences from the application of the representative litigation system confirmed these doubts and showed that it was not achieving the desired goals.

2.3 *Modest Practice of Class Actions and Their Chinese-Style Alternations*

As a legal innovation aimed to facilitate the resolution of complicated disputes that are not uncommon in Chinese society, the representative action became a hot topic for both practitioners and legal scholars. As a mixture of the features of various collective redress mechanisms from different jurisdictions (e.g. U.S., Germany and Japan), there were big expectations from the very beginning when it was introduced by 1991 CPL amendments. However, the big thunder did not produce a lot of rain.

The limitations of the system as described above were not the only cause which discouraged representative litigation. Some other factors particular to Chinese circumstances demotivated the courts from making use of it.

The first factor is the political rejection of any group action, particularly in the period since the late 1990s when the construction of a harmonious society became the preeminent political goal. In that light, any organized collective action has a potential to become a hot potato, a so called 'sensitive event'. When a court accepts a class action into its judicial docket, it is likely that the complicated proceedings and its result (be it a judgment, or a conciliated settlement, or a withdrawal) may cause mass petitions against the judges, the tribunal, the (higher) court and probably the whole court system in the following several years. To calm down the situation, it is also likely that a scapegoat would need to be found, and that some judges or leading judicial figures will have to be found accountable.

The second discouraging factor is the judicial evaluation system. A judge's performance is mainly assessed by the number of processed cases and by the time spent on each case. For the individual quantitative assessment of a judge, a case resolved in class litigation is not evaluated very differently from an ordinary case, in spite of the fact that it obviously needs much higher engagement of judges' time and work in comparison to ordinary judicial cases. Therefore, while class actions may be helpful to improve the efficiency of the judicial system, for the individual judge they are rather inefficient as a means to improve his or her individual assessment index. Thus, the aversion of class actions exists not only on the side of the courts as institutions, but also on the side of the individual judges.

As a result, both the judges and the court administration tend to split group action cases into a series of individual cases, handled in a form of so-called 'string cases' proceedings. The court sends all cases to a group of judges (sometimes further dividing them among several tribunals in the same group of judges). The designated tribunals select one case or one group of cases and hear them under ordinary procedural rules. After rendering a decision in such a 'model trial', the other similar cases will be tried under summary procedure one by one, in a very brief way. If all the cases are represented by the same lawyer, there is no need to hold a hearing or other procedure, the only necessary step is to modify the information that differs from the model case before copy-pasting the draft judgment. If a mediated settlement has been reached in the model case, the court will try to persuade the litigants in the other cases to accept the same criteria of compensation; but if the litigants refuse to accept such a suggestion, the court will have to make its judgment after conducting a full procedure.

Moreover, the political aversion to organized collective action led to the handling of mass harm situations by other means, beyond the forms regulated by the CPL. They cannot simply be called 'alternative dispute resolution' (ADR) if ADR is defined as a dispute resolution method beyond judicial involvement. Actually, in the Chinese style of political handling of disputes, the court usually plays an important role by participating directly or indirectly in the process of political negotiations. The example of the Sanlu Toxic Milk Powder Scandal[3] illustrated how mass infringement of consumers' rights can be handled.

On 12 September 2008, it was revealed that around 50,000 cases of urinary stones in infants were caused by Sanlu brand milk which had been contaminated with melamine.[4] Soon thereafter, the General Administration of Quality Supervision Inspection and Quarantine (AQSIQ) announced that 22 milk powder brands, including the three most famous brands, were found to contain melamine, with Sanlu holding the highest level. According to the Statistics of the Ministry of Health, Sanlu poisoned nearly 300,000 infants and six infants died.

More than 100 lawyers from 23 provinces gradually organized the 'Sanlu Milk Powder Incident Volunteer lawyers group' to provide free legal advice and guidance to the families of infants and children affected.[5] The State Council set up the Emergency Department of Sanlu Milk Powder Safety Accident ('the Emergency Department') and directed the national hospitals to guarantee free treatment of the infants, which would be reimbursed by the government. The first lawsuit was filed by baby Zhang Zuoyu's father against Sanlu Company and the China Dairy Association before the Guanzhou Intermediate Court, claiming 900,000 RMB (yuan) for damages. However, this lawsuit was not accepted for processing for two months, though the CPL provided that the court had to decide on this issue within 7 days. During that waiting period, all other similar cases in the other local courts were also not accepted, either as individual actions, joint actions or as a class action.

In the meantime, the Emergency Department of the State Council organized the settlement negotiations as a process in which four groups participated: (1) the lawyers as representatives of the victims, (2) the Consumer Association as the representative of the consumers as a whole, (3) Sanlu Company as the defendant, and (4) the China Dairy Association as representative of the milk enterprises. A special novelty in this process was that the judges and officials of the Docketing Department of the Supreme Court formed a part of the Emergency Department team. By the end of 2008, the official compensation plan was announced, offering 200,000 yuan for death, 30,000 yuan for severe cases and 2000 yuan for common symptoms. However, at least 10,000 parents were not satisfied with the plan and decided to

[3]Xinhuanet (2020) Sanlu infant milk powder incident tracking report. http://www.xinhuanet.com/newscenter/ztnfsj/sjjj.htm; Baidu Baike (2020) Contamination of Dairy products in China. https://baike.baidu.com/item/%E4%B8%AD%E5%9B%BD%E5%A5%B6%E5%88%B6%E5%93%81%E6%B1%A1%E6%9F%93%E4%BA%8B%E4%BB%B6/86604?fr=aladdin.

[4]This scandal led to serious criminal punishment of the senior managers of Sanlu company, removal of the head of Hebei province in which company was located and the removal of the head of the AQSIQ, apology of the head of China, and enactment of a series of laws including the Regulations on Supervision and Administration of Quality Safety of Dairy Products and the Food Safety Act.

[5]According to Hong Kong-based Ta Kung Pao, on September 14 the lawyers were required not to get involved in the contaminated milk case, stressing that the government has done a lot of work and asked them to "obey the overall situation and maintain stability", and not to get too involved in the Sanlu milk powder incident.

'pursue it to the end'. The other victims opted to enter the agreement and accordingly waived their right to initiate litigation.[6]

Most of the victims decided to accept the settlement and to waive any form of litigation, despite the fact that the amount of compensation that was offered was far below the victims' real damages, especially in cases where children had died. Some victims were satisfied with the compensation because their babies were apparently cured, and the continuing side effects seemed to be light at that time. Others were happy as they did not have sufficient proof for filing an individual lawsuit. However, the most important reason why a large part of the victims waived their right to sue was that they were informed by their lawyers that a class action procedure would most likely not be accepted and that the judgments in individual lawsuits would take the political settlement as a reference point, so that investment of plaintiffs' time and money for the individual lawsuit would not pay off.

This assessment proved to be true. On February 19, 2009, one week after the local court formally announced Sanlu bankruptcy, 117 victims of the incident filed civil lawsuits against the defendant Sanlu in order to receive compensation for their medical treatments. The claimed amount was 25.174.400 yuan, but it was not accepted by the court. A news reporter stated: 'Previously, Sanlu milk powder victims have repeatedly filed joint or class lawsuits with courts at all levels, but so far none has been accepted.'

2.4 *Successful Cases and Institutional Development of Class Actions*

Although the class action system in practice has been neither as broadly used as legal scholars expected, nor organized as successfully as the legislation provided, it has been utilized in some large scale disputes with some success. E.g. in 2005, 1013 farmers sued a flour mill before the Henan court[7]; more than 3000 peach farmers sued a middleman for payment under oral contract and won the case[8]; 1721 people won a judgment against a chemical plant for compensation of pollution damage before Hunan court,[9] and 4535 farmers and herdsmen in Qinghai Province sued

[6]China Enterprise Advisory Network (2009) Sanlu defective milk powder compensation plan unveiled. http://www.cction.com/info/200901/10684.html.

[7]Court of China (2005). The Court of China has settled a lawsuit involving a group of farmers. https://www.chinacourt.org/article/detail/2005/05/id/162430.shtml.

[8]Sina net (2005). 4000 Peach farmers suing 'peach vendors' for debt. http://news.sina.com.cn/s/2005-01-11/21474795014s.shtml.

[9]Database of Chinese Trial Cases. http://www.chncase.cn/case/bulletin/1085566.

several aluminum companies for environmental pollution damage and settled under judicial mediation.[10]

The 'old' class action system may be rejuvenated by recent legislative changes. At the end of 2019, the Securities Law activates class actions again, though by a different mode of litigation. In the securities class actions, the class representative may be appointed by the Investor Protection Agency upon application of more than 50 investors, and the class action adopts the *opt-out* principle. This new mode should overcome the defects of the current system and the difficulties in selecting representatives and the confirmation of the class. For specific procedural rules regarding the new form of class action, it is expected that the Supreme Court will soon issue its judicial interpretation. On 24 March 2020, the newly established specialized financial court, the Shanghai Financial Court, issued a regulation on representative litigation mechanism for securities disputes, including specific provisions on the conduct of the process, confirmation of the representative, the trial and the enforcement of the lawsuit. Under this regulation, the investors can be registered through an online platform hereby solving the problem of numerous and dispersed securities investors; the enforcement of the decision may be paid in the form of a deposit to the Investor Protection Agency, which will make a secondary distribution to successful plaintiffs through the securities exchange settlement system. The previously existing regulation on model judgments in securities disputes remained untouched and may continue to be used under the CPL in parallel with the new securities class action rules.

3 Origin and Development of Public Interest Litigation

The public interest litigation (PIL) system was established in 2012, by Article 55 CPL. Under Art. 55, a public interest action in environmental pollution, consumer protection or similar cases may be brought by 'an organ or relevant organization prescribed by law'. In 2017, in order to demonstrate that the procuratorate is the one (if not the only one) 'organ prescribed by law' the Standing Committee of the National Congress specifically amended paragraph (2).

3.1 Background and Brief Overview of the PIL System

As described *infra* in para. 2, the existing representative action system has been unable to effectively respond to frequent violations of social and public interests because of its limitation in the standing to sue and extremely low utilization rate.

[10]China Court Website (2005).Qinghai province successfully mediated a lawsuit brought by an environmental pollution group. https://www.chinacourt.org/article/detail/2005/05/id/161755.shtml.

Even before the introduction of the PIL, in order to avoid the 'tragedy of the commons' in the field of public welfare protection, some non-governmental organizations (NGOs) and local prosecutors filed representative actions in local courts but were repeatedly denied.

On December 3, 2005, the State Council issued the Decision on Strengthening Environmental Protection (Guo Fa [2005] No. 39), which explicitly and for the first time stated that '[t]he role of social organizations should be brought into full play, various illegal environmental behaviors should be discouraged and disclosed, and environmental public interest lawsuits should be promoted'. Since then, the public interest environmental litigation pushed by civil organizations for many years finally became officially accepted. In 2007, Guiyang took the lead in setting up an environmental court to adjudicate environmental cases. At least 17 environmental public interest lawsuits were filed by social organizations, procuratorial and administrative organs before the amendment of the CPL which formally introduced the PIL system.

These PILs were filed and disposed of under the existing legal framework, as the CPL provides in Article 15 that 'any state organ, public organization, enterprise or institution may support the injured body or individual in bringing an action in a people's court with respect to an act that harms civil rights and interests of the State, a collective or an individual.' Obviously, Article 15 or 'the principle of supporting prosecution' did not qualify these public interest plaintiffs to submit an independent *actio popularis* as Article 108 (now 119) CPL provides that the plaintiff should be someone "with a direct interest in the case". However, under frequent and urgent pressure from practice, some local courts accepted and decided such public interest lawsuits regarding a diverse range of claims.[11] Some of their judgments were greeted and praised by the public for their sound substantive reasoning, but the defendants regularly challenged them on procedural grounds, alleging that plaintiffs lacked the required standing to sue.[12] Although most of the challenges raised on this ground were denied by the appellate courts that supported PILs, this issue has been presented to the Congress again and again over a long period of time.

As a result, in the first comprehensive amendments since the CPL was enacted, there was an agreement on the necessity for establishing a PIL system which would function in parallel with the existing class action system. However, as the draft process started, almost all issues were contested. There was a divergence of views regarding the definition and the scope of the 'public interest' notion, the authorized bodies, the limitation of claims, effects of the actions brought on the plaintiffs (including the potential ones) and the (mandatory or not) joinder of PILs filed against the same defendant, the separation or joinder of the PILs and the class actions arising

[11]Civil Judgment No. 1216 of Xishan District People's Court of Wuxi City, Jiangsu Province (2009); Civil judgment No. 587 of Fushun Zhongfa Zhongfa Zhongzi No. 1 of Intermediate People's Court of Foshan City, Guangdong Province (2010).

[12]Kunming Municipal Environmental Protection Bureau (supported by the Kunming People's Procuratorate) vs. Kunming Sannong & Agriculture and Animal Husbandry Co., LTD. for environmental pollution infringement, See Civil Judgment No. 41 of Yunnan Higher People's Court (2011).

from the same infringement event, the rules on the burden of proof, and the financial management of compensation. No consensus was reached on these issues.

The legislation tried to circumvent the missing consensus by restricting the rules to the general points i.e. the recognition of the plaintiff's qualification which has been urgently called for by the public, leaving the debated issues to be developed in practice. The special public interest plaintiff was added in the form of 'an organ or relevant organization prescribed by law' but only 'for conduct that pollutes environment, infringes upon the lawful rights and interests of a large number of consumers or otherwise damages the public interest'. This provision, and its subsequent judicial interpretations, provided the legal base to overcome the obstacles contained in the conditions for ordinary plaintiffs as stipulated under Article 119.

However, the CPL amendment in 2012 left the main issue—who will be a qualified plaintiff—to other laws. At that time, there was no theoretical agreement on government branches or social organizations that are the proper deputy of the 'public interest', and the procuratorates who were often regarded as the proper organ by the experts were reluctant to undertake this hard mission. At the same time, the Administrative Procedure Law was revised in 2014 to provide the procuratorates with plaintiff qualification to file public interest claims against administrative departments.[13]

The turning point was in 2014, when the 4th Plenary Session of the 18th CPC Central Committee made major adjustments to the functions of procuratorate organs and proposed to explore the 'PIL system initiated by the procuratorate organs'. With this political mission, the SPP launched the pilot project of instituting PIL by the procuratorial organs,[14] which allowed procuratorial organs in 13 provinces, from 2015 to 2017, to file civil PIL against public interest infringers and to file administrative PIL against administrative organs that were negligent in performing their duty of protecting the public interest.

As a result, it was found that the number of cases and the effectiveness of public welfare relief proved that procuratorial organs could shoulder the responsibility of safeguarding public interest. Then in 2017, the Standing Committee of the National Congress specially amended Paragraph (2) of Article 55 of the CPL to manifest the procuratorate to apply the PIL against the conduct that damages public interest, while the procuratorate maintains discretionary power whether it 'may file a lawsuit' and the precondition 'if there is no organ or organization prescribed' in the paragraph

[13]Article 25(4) of the Administrative Litigation Law (ALA): 'Where the people's procuratorate finds in the performance of functions that any administrative authority assuming supervision and administration functions in such fields as the protection of the ecological environment and resources, food and drug safety, protection of state-owned property, and the assignment of the right to use state-owned land exercises functions in violation of any law or conducts nonfeasance, which infringes upon national interest or public interest, it shall offer procuratorial recommendations to the administrative authority, and urge it to perform functions in accordance with the law. If the administrative authority fails to perform functions in accordance with the law, the people's procuratorate shall file a lawsuit with the people's court in accordance with the law.'

[14]Provision of the SPP, 2015.7.2.

(1) or the organ or organization does not file a lawsuit. The procuratorate would like to maintain its discretion that if the organ or organization prescribed in paragraph (1) files a lawsuit, they 'may support' the filing of a lawsuit.

In contrast to the hesitant attitude of the procuratorates, the social organizations who have been very active and successful in promoting the PIL system were more or less discouraged by the enacted laws. The CPL opened the option that 'a relevant organization prescribed by law' be authorized to sue in respective field by special legislation. At present however there are only two types of authorized associations: one is provided by the Law on the Protection of Consumer Rights and Interests (2013 Amendment), which authorizes the Consumers Association of China and the consumer associations formed directly by the Central Government in provinces, autonomous regions, and municipalities to sue in people's courts on behalf of a large number of consumers (Article 47). The second type is provided in the Environmental Protection Law that authorizes for environmental suits those social organization that satisfy several criteria, among other (1) registration with the civil affairs department of the people's government of specific level (2) a proved history of engagement in environmental protection for the public good for five consecutive years or more, and (3) no recorded violation of law. A social organization may not seek any economic benefit from an action instituted by it.

There were also proposals to include individuals (citizens of China) as plaintiffs authorized to file PIL, but these proposals were finally not accepted. Before their rejection, there were several influential cases filed by individual citizens against monopolist companies, challenging their illegal or unfair policies. One of such cases was filed by Mr. Qiu Jiandong against the post office for '1.2 yuan telephone charges'. Mr. Qiu claimed for (1) double compensation for the overpaid phone bill of 1.2 yuan, and (2) taking off the misleading price table in all the public telephone booths. The claim (2) was obviously for public interest, and it was dismissed because Mr. Qiu had no 'direct interest in the litigation' i.e. no standing to sue regarding such a claim. Mr. Qiu withdrew his first lawsuit in 1996 in Longyan county court after the defendant Longyan Post Office corrected all the price tables in its region to satisfy the plaintiff's claim.[15] But this public interest litigation had no impact on the rest of the national half-price telephone policy and transparent notice of price, so in the following years Mr. Qiu continued to file lawsuits in other places raising the same claim. No court could, however, accept his suit and rule in support of his public interest claims.

Another famous case filed by individuals dates from 2005. Six professors and students of Peking University Law School filed as joint plaintiffs the first environmental public interest lawsuit to the High Court of Heilongjiang Province. The court, however, dismissed the case.

It was also debated whether an administrative department may be a plaintiff filing suits for infringement of lawful rights and interests of other people, because the

[15] Economic Daily (1996), front page.

existing Marine Environmental Protection Law[16] provides that the interested department, empowered to conduct marine environment supervision and control may, on behalf of the State, claim compensation from those held liable for the damages. However, the overwhelming view has been that, as a principle, administrative departments may not be a plaintiff in a civil PIL in China because it would be in conflict with its general role as a defendant of administrative PIL. Still the CPL left some space for this by providing that the plaintiff's role can be granted to 'an organ prescribed by law' without qualifying any specific organs. By now, the marine environmental supervision and administration organs as prescribed by the Marine Environmental Protection Law make the only exception in two respects: (1) they are the only administrative organs qualified to file a civil PIL; (2) they are the only qualified plaintiffs for marine environment ecological damage, i.e. the procurators or social organization that may file a general PIL are in this field excluded.[17]

3.2 Open Nature of Public Interest Litigation Under Art 55 CPL

The regulation of PIL under Civil Procedure Law is open-ended and somewhat vague. It is still more than nothing, but the rules enacted obviously rely upon further development through practical use of the system.

As to the scope of application of PIL, the law does not define what 'infringing public interest' means. The examples listed in the law include environmental pollution and mass harm caused to consumers, but other forms of infringement of public interest are not excluded, leaving room for other applications. In fact, judicial practice is gradually expanding the scope of civil PIL. For example, there have been cases of PIL in Henan province, which dealt with endangering public traffic safety.

In terms of parties in PIL, the CPL clearly excludes individuals from the list of potential plaintiffs. They are excluded because it was regarded that they may easily confuse public interest with their private interest or motivation. However, for legal entities—'organs or relevant organizations'—it is left to special legislation to define what entities could file particular types of PIL. Such special legislation was not always coherent.

For example, under the Marine Environmental Protection Act the relevant plaintiff entities are administrative organs for environmental protection, but no social organization is eligible to file suits in PIL. On the contrary, under the Environmental Protection Act an 'organ or relevant organization prescribed by law' refers to

[16]The Marine Environmental Protection Act was enacted in 1982 and amended in1999, 2013, 2016, and 2017.

[17]See Provisions of the Supreme People's Court on Several Issues concerning the Trial of Cases Involving Disputes over Compensation for Damage to Marine Natural Resources and Ecological Environment (taking effect on Jan 15, 2018).

specific social organizations (such as environmental protection NGOs) but does not authorize government departments to file PIL.

However, such open nature of the CPL regulation of PIL should not be viewed as a form of flexibility, but mainly as a transfer of regulation to existing and future substantive laws and regulations. Sometimes these sources of law can overlap. For example, a consumer association has no universal qualification to file PIL for environmental infringements, unless the damage is related to the mass violation of consumers' rights and interests prescribed by the Consumer Protection Act. The scope of action and the types of conduct that a consumer association can challenge are both regulated by Article 55 CPL and by detailed provisions of Consumer Protection Act. Moreover, an institutional practice in China is that the SPC issues legislative interpretations or regulations in various documents, usually combining substantive and procedural issues. And the PIL system, as an innovative and open-ended institution, has been very much construed in the light of many interpretative acts issued by the SPC. All in all, the regulation of PIL is complicated and full of ambiguity and conflicts, as we will show later in this paper.

One key provision of the CPL is granting the right to sue in PIL to the procuratorate organs. This is also somewhat unusual. Usually, the functions and powers of the procuratorate are prescribed in the Organic Law on Procuratorate that forms a constitutional base for the CPL (or other law) to provide in detail what role the procuratorate should have in the process. However, urgent calls for strengthening the procurator's role in PIL urged the National Congress to add this qualification first into the Civil Procedure Law and Administrative Litigation Procedure Law, and only later into the amended Organic Law (which happened in 2018).[18]

As the only named plaintiff of PIL in the CPL (in contrast to others that need to be authorized by other laws in limited fields), the procuratorates have a general mandate to file PIL in respect to all types of public interest actions prescribed in Article 55 CPL, irrespective of the right to sue awarded by respective substantive laws and judicial interpretations of the SPC to particular government organs or social organizations. This means that, theoretically, procuratorates could file all PILs which could overlap with other entities' rights and discourage the other qualified PIL plaintiffs to take action.

In order to spare the procuratorates from having unlimited discretionary rights and full burden of filing all PILs, the second paragraph of Article 55 CPL makes

[18]In China, several amendments of the Organic Law of Procuratorate have been always at the same time; and the amendments in 2018 were considered systematic revisions which adopted the achievements of the judicial reforms of the past 20 years. The new authority of PIL for the procuratorate is very important to civil litigation because it substantially changed the traditional structure that the civil litigation are private action and had never been filed by a public organ; but it may not so important as compared with the other amendments in of the Organic Law of Procuratorate. In addition, regarding the constitutional position of the procuratorate and its role in civil litigations, see Yulin (2012), pp. 176–185. For the discussion on the suitability of the procuratorate as a plaintiff in civil public interest litigation, see Hao (2017), pp. 168–181; Liming (2011), pp. 134–140.

prosecutorial intervention conditional upon actions of the two other types of eligible plaintiffs. A procuratorate organ may file a PIL only if there is no other organ or organizations authorized to do so, or if such entities fail to act. This is known in theory as the prosecution's 'modesty'. The order and joinder of PIL will be discussed later in this contribution.[19]

3.3 *Establishing Special Procedural Rules for the PIL*

The PIL emerged in August 2012 when Art. 55 CPL was enacted[20] but was only gradually developed through laws and 'judicial interpretations'. We should specifically note the amendment of the Consumer Protection Act,[21] the Environmental Protection Act,[22] and the Marine Environmental Protection Act,[23] and several 'judicial interpretations' issued by the SPC and the SPP establishing procedural rules of PIL.

It has been the only time in the history for the SPC and the SPP to issue 'judicial interpretations' on the same matter in such a number and in such a frequency. Apart from the conventional interpretation of the SPC on the Application of the CPL,[24] the more important judicial regulations include:

- Interpretations on Several Issues Concerning the Application of Law in the Trial of Environmental Civil PIL Cases;[25]
- Plan for the Pilot Project of Reform of Instituting PIL by the Procuratorial Organ;[26]
- Interpretation on Several Issues Concerning the Application of Law in the Trial related to Civil PIL of 2016;
- Interpretation on Several Issues Concerning the Application of Law in the Trial of Civil PIL regarding Consumption;[27]
- Work Standard for Trial of Environmental PIL Cases;[28]
- Interpretation on Several Issues Concerning the Application of Law for Cases Regarding Procuratorial PIL;[29]

[19]See Yanmin (2000), pp. 161–175.

[20]Art. 55 CPL was enacted on 31 August 2012 and amended again on 27 June 2017. The coming into force was several months later.

[21]Enacted on 25 October 2013.

[22]Enacted on 24 April 2014.

[23]Enacted on 4 November 2017.

[24]SPC, 4 February 2015. See Arts 284–291.

[25]SPC, 7 January 2015.

[26]SPP, 2 July 2015.

[27]SPC, 24 April 2016.

[28]SPC, 1 April 2017.

[29]SPC & SPP, 1 March 2018.

- Several Provisions on the Trial of Cases on Compensation for Damage to the Ecological Environment;[30]
- Official Reply on Whether the Pre-litigation Public Announcement Procedures Shall Be Performed for a Civil PIL Incidental to Criminal Proceedings Filed by a People's Procuratorate.[31]

The provisions of these 'judicial interpretations' mainly focus on the issues of jurisdiction, the types and causes of the claims, mandatory joinder of the plaintiffs, disclosure of evidence and burden of proof, judicial mediation and decision-making.

3.3.1 Limit of Disposition Right and Intervention of the Court

Since the target of PIL is not the protection of private but of the public interest, there is agreement that, in principle, the plaintiff in PIL is not entitled to freely dispose of its claims. Instead, the trial is conducted under the rules of an inquisitorial system.[32] In contrast to the adversarial style of proceedings, in PIL there is an increased judicial intervention in the process, as the court should closely monitor the plaintiff's conduct in the process, and review any parties' attempt to admit or withdraw the claims, or 'compromise' the process by concluding a settlement.

If the judge considers that the plaintiff's claim is insufficient to protect the public interest, he has to suggest to the plaintiff to amend or supplement the claim. If the plaintiff admits facts or evidence presented by the other party, the judge will disregard such disposition if he considers it harmful for the public interest. If the plaintiff is unable to obtain evidence important for the assessment of the facts in the case, the judge may lead the investigation and collect evidence *ex officio* or upon plaintiff's request and may also engage a qualified expert assessing specific facts. This is also applicable in the cases filed by the procuratorates. Where a court deems that the claims raised by a procuratorate are insufficient to safeguard the public interest, it may amend or increase them or impose its own remedies for infringement and restoration of the ecological environment to the original state.

The plaintiff's right to settle or withdraw his claims is in civil public interest litigation limited. If a plaintiff applies for the withdrawal of the suit after the conclusion of the examination, the court shall not grant permission, unless the plaintiff's claim has been fully realized by administrative enforcement. Moreover, if a plaintiff and a defendant reach a settlement (including settlements arising out of mediation/conciliation), the content of the settlement needs to be publicly announced for no less than 30 days. After the expiration of the announcement period, if the court, after review, considers that the content of the settlement does not harm social and/or public interests, it shall confirm the settlement.

---

[30] SPC, 5 June 2019.

[31] SPC & SPP, 25 November 2019.

[32] Weiping (2013), pp. 17–20.

3.3.2 Compulsory Joinder of the PIL Plaintiffs and Notice to the Administrative Authority

After a court accepts a PIL and before the main hearing, any other organ or relevant organization which is eligible for initiating an action in accordance with the law, may announce to the court its wish to participate in the process. Where the court allows the organ or organization to participate in the process, such organ or organization may be listed as a co-plaintiff.

When one of the qualified plaintiffs files a lawsuit with the competent court, this court shall announce the civil PIL to the public and invite potential plaintiffs to participate in the lawsuit within 30 days from the date of the announcement. If other potential plaintiffs join, they will become ‘co-plaintiffs’. If they do not apply to the court within 30 days, they will not be allowed to sue over the same facts. Such ‘compulsory joinder system’ for plaintiffs in civil public interest litigation wants to avoid the defendant’s litigation burden and to save judicial resources.

At the same time, a court shall, after accepting a PIL, notify the relevant administrative department within 10 days. This provision is meant mainly to inform the administrative organs of the government and urge them to solve the public interest infringement cases through administrative enforcement in a timely manner, because the latter is often faster and more effective. The other consideration is that some of the notified administrative organs may fall under the category of ‘qualified organs’ that can be plaintiffs under Article 55 of the CPL, while others may fall into the category of potential defendants in an administrative PIL.

Where a procuratorate files a criminal prosecution against those liable for damages caused to the human environment and resource protection, or for mass harms caused to consumers in the food and drug safety field, the procuratorate may file with a court an incidental civil PIL, which shall be tried by the same court panel.

After the judgment in a civil consumer PIL comes into force, all other authorities or social organizations qualified as plaintiffs cannot institute a separate civil PIL for the same infringement.

3.3.3 Relation Between Private and Public Interest Proceedings: Distinct Proceedings with an Option of Evidence-Sharing

The above mentioned mandatory joinder is applicable only in public interest litigation. On the contrary, private litigants against the same defendant cannot join the PIL proceedings. According to the relevant rules and civil procedure doctrine, a victim who seeks compensation for damages as a private party must file a separate lawsuit, as a single litigant, as an ordinary co-plaintiff, or as a member of a class action. A PIL accepted by the court does not affect an action filed by victims of the same tort in accordance with the provisions of Article 119 of the CPL.

However, private plaintiffs in all kinds of private proceedings arising from the same subject-matter that led to a civil PIL may share the proof of infringement with the PIL. Moreover, where consumers suffering damage from the same infringement institute an action in accordance with the provisions of Article 119 of the CPL, it is unnecessary for both the plaintiff and the defendant to assume the burden of proof for the facts that have been identified in a binding judgment issued in a civil PIL, unless the party involved raises an objection to such facts and provides contrary evidence sufficient to reverse such findings.

In such situations, the positions of the plaintiffs and of the defendants are not equal: if a judgment in a civil consumer PIL finds business operators liable, the consumers who suffered damages may sue under Art 119 CPL and allege that such effective judgment is applicable. In such a case, the court shall take the allegation of the plaintiff as proven, unless the defendant produces evidence to the contrary sufficient to reverse the allegation. On the other hand, where the defendant contends that the judgment in a civil PIL is favorable to him, the court in private litigation can raise doubts regarding such contention of the defendant, so that the defendant still has to meet the corresponding burden of proof.[33]

3.4 *Debates and New Problems*

The gradual formation of the above rules in practice partially resolved some issues that had been controversial before the enactment of the Civil Procedure Law 2012, for instance the definition of 'public interest'. On the other hand, some key questions still remain unanswered, such as the qualification of the plaintiffs. In addition, as the practice unfolds, new problems arise.

3.4.1 Remaining Controversial Issues Regarding Plaintiff's Qualification

In two aspects the problems of the plaintiff's qualification to file a PIL still remain: first, the right of social organizations to initiate PIL in cases of harm caused to the human environment ('environment PIL') is seriously restricted, while on the other hand the procuratorates' right to initiate action in cases of mass harm caused to consumers ('consumer PIL') is narrow in scope and rather discretional. It is a paradox that social organizations were in the past important promoters of the PIL system and that they possess general capacity to be recognized as PIL plaintiffs, but they are still prevented from taking action by substantive laws whose content was under the influence of the lobbying by administrative departments and some large enterprises. Political hesitation *vis-a-vis* any organized action from society also played a role.

[33]Interpretation of the Supreme People's Court on Several Issues concerning the Application of Law in the Trial of Civil Public Interest Actions regarding Consumption, No. 10 [2016] of the SPC.

It has already been stated that as a plaintiff of environmental PIL, a social organization needs to satisfy several conditions in order to be eligible to institute an action in a people's court. Additionally, a social organization may not seek any economic benefit. In practice, it has been hard to determine whether an environmental organization meets the requirement of 'specialization in environment protection activities for more than five consecutive years. The judicial interpretation of the SPC on Environmental PIL of 2015 stated that an organization meets the criteria of environmental specialization from Art. 58 Environmental Protection Act (EPA) if 'the purpose and main business scope of [its] articles of association are related to the public good and the organization is engaged in environmental protection activities for public benefit'. Nonetheless, the lower courts are still puzzled with the definition of 'engaged in environmental protection activities' from the SPC's ruling.

As an example, in the PIL submitted by China Biodiversity Conservation and Green Development Foundation against Ningxia Ruitai Materials Technology Co., Ltd for polluting the environment,[34] the plaintiff was an active and well-known environmental protection organization. Yet, it never conducted public activities of environmental welfare protection, and therefore both the first instance and second instance courts ruled that the plaintiff engages in environmental seminars and ecological investigations, carries out public educational campaigns on environmental protection; but this does not directly belong to the activities of environmental public protection for the public benefit, and therefore cannot be regarded as sufficient to meet the 'five years specialization in environmental protection activities' criterion. Consequently, the courts dismissed the plaintiff's claims for lack of standing to sue.

Fortunately, this case was retried by the SPC and the rulings of the lower courts were overturned. The SPC held that the plaintiff's foundation is qualified to sue in PIL and ruled that the original first-instance court must accept the case. In its ruling, the Supreme People's Court stated:

> Although the articles of incorporation of this social organization do not specifically mention the protection of environmental public interests, its work in protecting the environment and preserving ecosystems should be recognized. Public welfare activities of environmental protection include not only activities that directly improve the human environment, but also activities related to environmental protection that are conducive to improving the governance of the environmental system, and promote the formation of a broad consensus on environmental protection in the whole society. Where a matter brought by a social organization corresponds to its legal purpose and scope of business, or has a certain connection with environmental elements and ecosystems it aims to protect, it shall be recognized as 'specialized in environmental protection public benefit activities'.

Since this case was awarded the status of Guiding Case No. 75 of the SPC, it factually gained a binding force as a judicial precedent unifying the recognition standards of environmental organizations as PIL plaintiffs by courts at all levels.

[34]Civil Ruling of Petition No. 3377 of the Supreme People's Court (2015).

This sent a positive signal encouraging environmental organizations to file environmental civil PIL.

However, the consumer PIL has not been so lucky as its environmental counterpart. The Consumer Law provides the right to file a consumer PIL to the China Association of Consumers and the consumer associations established in the provinces, autonomous regions, and municipalities directly under the Central Government.[35] The same law provides in Article 37(7) that consumer associations discharge a public duty of 'filing lawsuits for the infringement of lawful rights and interests of consumers'. However, the judicial interpretation of the SPC on Consumer PIL[36] only grants qualification for filing a PIL to the China Consumers' Association ('CCA') and consumers' associations set up at the provincial level if they 'institute civil PIL regarding consumers' rights against business operators that infringe lawful rights and interests of many unspecified consumers or have acted by endangering the safety of people and their property and impairing public interests', though it is still open to other civil consumer PIL instituted by authorities and social organizations as prescribed by the CPL.

While Article 55(2) CPL authorizes procuratorial organs to act against infringements of lawful rights and interests of consumers in the field of food and drug safety, as well as 'any other conduct that damages social interests', considering the passive attitude of the procuratorial organs to PIL as a whole, the consumer PIL system mainly relies on the consumer associations. However, there are only 31 qualified consumer associations nationwide in Mainland China. Moreover, the precondition of the procuratorial action is that none of the other authorized plaintiffs file a lawsuit. But, in contrast to consumer associations, procuratorial organs authorized to file PIL exist in each province both at county, city, district and provincial level. Considering the complicated procedure for a procuratorate on the lower level to institute PIL cases that have not been launched by provincial consumer associations, the likelihood that a procuratorate will institute proceedings is very low.

3.4.2 Claims for Compensation and Management of Compensation Funds

Since the PIL plaintiffs are prohibited to advance their own interest, the formulation of claims and the relief sought may pose serious problems. The controversy is focused on claims for compensation and their regulation in the environmental civil PIL. According to Articles 18–22 of the judicial interpretation of the SPC on Environmental PIL, the plaintiff may request the court to impose on the defendant 'civil liabilities such as the cessation of the infringement, removing the obstruction,

---

[35]See Art 47 Consumer Law. The autonomous regions (such as Tibet and Xinjiang) and the municipalities which are directly under the Central Government (such as Beijing and Shanghai) are on the same level of provinces.

[36]SPC, 24 April 2016.

eliminating the danger, restoring the original state of affairs, compensating the loss and providing an apology'. Compensating the loss includes 'undertaking preventive or remedial measures at reasonable cost', 'paying of costs for restoration of healthy environment', 'bearing costs of implementation of the repair plan and monitoring' as well as 'supervision fees', 'costs of actions needed to restore the loss of function', and 'the costs of plaintiff's inspection, appraisal charges, reasonable legal fees and other reasonable expenses'.

Among all these claims involving monetary compensation, the most difficult to manage are ecological restoration funds and charges for the restoration of healthy environment and function losses. Because a healthy environment is in the interest of society, and its owner is an unspecified subject, 'the public', compensation cannot be paid directly. Moreover, the restoration of a healthy human environment often takes a long time and demands professional input, making it difficult for the ordinary residents to monitor and assess its effects and daily progress. Therefore, in order to truly use the compensation funds for recovering environmental damage and benefit the local public, it is vital to formulate the management rules for compensation funds.[37] At present, each region has different management methods. Some provinces put the compensation into a special account of the government finances, others deposit it into a special account of the environmental protection bureau, and others open a special account of procuratorate or put it into a special management fund.[38] Varying approaches are not conducive to the overall management of compensation funds, and they also cause difficulties for the plaintiffs and the public in supervising the use of these funds. Therefore, there have been lively discussions on how to effectively manage the compensation paid for environmental and ecological damages.

Additionally, facing the high costs of time-consuming expert opinions, on which environmental cases often rely on, delays in the litigation process are likely that, in turn, discourage plaintiffs to file an environmental PIL.[39] The 2016 judicial interpretation of the SPC suggests, in Article 24, that a mechanism should be established for the mutual use of ecological damage compensation funds in environmental civil PILs nationwide. If the compensation paid in one case generates a surplus after being used to repair the environment, it could be used for the assessment and the expert consultation in other environmental public interest litigation cases. Recently, some scholars have called for the establishment of a special national fund for public interest litigation to be used to advance the plaintiff's costs and expenses for filing environmental civil PIL and to be paid back in full by the defendant after the plaintiff wins the lawsuit. According to this suggestion, if the plaintiff would lose the lawsuit, the plaintiff and the fund would each bear half of the costs.[40]

---

[37]Xiaoren (2018), 005 edition.

[38]Shuya (2017), 003 edition.

[39]Gu (2015), pp. 16–33.

[40]The problem of judges relying too much on expert opinions in environmental civil public interest litigation is also a serious problem, see Dun (2018), pp. 344–345; Gu (2015), pp. 16–33.

4 The Practice of Civil PIL

Since the establishment of the civil PIL system in 2013, thousands of such cases were brought. The data is not always accurate as it is affected by the different approaches of statistical monitoring. Even so, in two aspects there are no doubts: the number of environmental civil public interest lawsuits is significantly higher than consumer civil public interest lawsuits; and, the number of civil public interest litigation cases brought by procuratorial organs is obviously higher than that brought by social public interest organizations. In this chapter we will present and evaluate some statistics regarding the civil PIL practice.

4.1 Improving PIL Practice in Environmental Cases and the Role of the Procuratorates

In practice, PIL in procuratorial organs is divided into two stages. Although the procuratorial organs have had different functions and priorities in these two stages, during the pilot period from July 1, 2015 to June 30 of 2017, and after the formal legislation in 2017, the practice shows that the procuratorates' role in improving environmental practice has been dominant, focusing on environmental (especially administrative) PIL, but mainly via 'pre-trial procuratorial supervision'.

4.1.1 The Procuratorates' PIL Practice During the Pilot Period (2015–2017)

In the first stage, when procuratorial organs instituted PIL in the 13 pilot provinces, they were authorized to file both civil PIL and administrative PIL in the field of environmental protection, while their functions in the field of consumer protection was limited to filing civil PIL. The approaches in procuratorial supervision of suspected harmful conduct included (i) filing a procuratorial civil PIL; (ii) issuing a procuratorial suggestion to the qualified organs or organizations to file a civil PIL under Article 55 the CPL or (iii) file an administrative PIL under Article 25 (pre-suit *exigi facias*). In the practice, they mainly opted for administrative PIL and suggested other organs to bring PIL. Before filing lawsuits, the procuratorates who identify potential mass harm under Article 55(2) CPL need to make a public announcement according to the law. If within 30 days after public announcement the organ or organization prescribed by law does not file a lawsuit, a procuratorate may file a civil lawsuit.

As already noted, the procuratorates were much more inclined to file or support the filing of administrative PIL than civil PIL. Between July 2015 and March 2017, procuratorial organs initiated 653 public interest lawsuits but they included only 71 civil PIL (10.88%), together which 7 consumer cases related to food and drug safety. At the same time, procuratorial organs issued 5.218 pieces of pre-suit *exigi facias* to urge the other authorities or social organizations to initiate PIL but only 144 (2.76%) for civil PIL, among which 33 cases (0.63%) were related to mass harm to consumers related to food and drug safety. In the cases where procuratorates urged social organizations to file a PIL, 29 cases (20.14%) were filed; in 48 cases (33.33%) the social organizations decided not to file a claim or provided no reply; and in 64 cases (44.44%) there was no eligible qualified social organization within the respective jurisdictions of the procuratorate.[41]

This set of data shows that the social organizations were not as enthusiastic to file PIL as expected. However, the procuratorates' pre-trial recommendations were very instrumental in changing the passive attitude of administrative organizations. According to the report, the procuratorial organs sent 5.074 procuratorial suggestions to administrative organs, and as a result, about 90 percent of the pre-litigation prosecutorial recommendations were accepted. Procuratorial organs formally filed 580 administrative PIL with the courts.[42]

4.1.2 The Practice of Procuratorates' PIL after 2017

Based on the successful pilot practice in 2015–2017, new functions of the procuratorate were converted into legislation—Art. 55(2) CPL and the Art. 25 (4) ALA—but with an adjusted scope and new types of action. In the environmental protection field, the procuratorates may file a civil and/or administrative PIL; for the protection of state-owned assets and the transfer of rights of state-owned land use, only an administrative PIL may be filed; for large scale consumer cases, not only a civil PIL but also an administrative PIL can be filed, however limited to food and drug safety. Meantime, the two approaches of procuratorial supervision were maintained: (i) urging administrative authorities or social organizations to take action to remedy harmful activities, or to file a civil or administrative PIL, or (ii) filing a procuratorial PIL with the court, if step (i) failed and if the lawsuit is regarded as necessary.

Soon after the above amendments of CPL and ALA, the SPC and the SPP issued their joint mandatory interpretation on procuratorial PIL cases,[43] which regulates specific matters such as jurisdiction, the procuratorial organs' right of discovery, the judges' power of intervening into the procuratorate's claim, procedural arrangements, etc. From then on, the procuratorates have been playing an overwhelming role in PIL, especially in administrative PIL for environmental protection. For example, in 2018, the procuratorial organs nationwide initiated 108,767 cases related to administrative PIL, accounting for 96.12% of all PIL cases. Most of these cases

[41]Civil Administrative Procuratorate of the Supreme People's Procuratorate (2017), pp. 69–78. The remaining 2.1% relate to incomplete replies.

[42]Civil Administrative Procuratorate of the Supreme People's Procuratorate (2017), pp. 69–78.

[43]SPC & SPP, 1 March 2018.

were disposed of by issuing procuratorial suggestions and pre-suit announcements, among which 101,254 cases (97.2%) were terminated by administrative pre-litigation procedures.[44] Thus, only few administrative PIL were effectively filed with the court. In contrast, the procuratorates dealt with civil cases mainly by filing civil PIL with the court, but in general the procuratorial role in civil cases is obviously limited. From 2013 to 2017, the courts heard 1383 cases brought by procuratorates and 252 cases brought by social organizations.[45]

In 2019, the PIL experienced an expansion of its scope and diversity. In addition to 69,236 cases in the field of environmental protection (an increase of 16.7% compared to 2018), there were 35,778 consumer protection cases related to food and drug safety. The procuratorates also handled 2829 PIL cases involving epidemic prevention materials related to masks, medical waste disposal, wildlife protection and other issues. In contrast to administrative PIL which contributed to 119,787 cases (an increase of 62.2%), the share of civil PIL cases (7.125, or an increase of 10.1%) was still insignificant. However, the number of PIL filed with the courts was 4778, 48% more than 2018. It shows that the procuratorates are getting more powerful and active in litigation after several years where pre-suit dispute resolution attempts dominated.

In 3238 cases tried by the courts, the plaintiff procuratorates won 3225 cases.[46]

4.2 *The Slow-Moving Consumer PIL Practice and the Role of Social Organizations*

In contrast to the steady growth of environmental PIL, the practice of consumer PIL has been very limited. Neither the procuratorial organs nor the consumer associations are very active in this area, and the active individuals who could fill in the void are, by law, excluded from launching PIL.

4.2.1 Sluggish Practice Despite Urgent Social Need

For establishing data about consumer PIL, we have consulted the reports of the SPC and the SPP, as well as the China Judicial Judgment Website of the SPC and the two major legal case databases Fabao and Wusong. According to these sources, from

---

[44] Jun (2019) Report of the Supreme People's Procuratorate on the Procuratorial work on public Interest Litigation—delivered at the 2nd Session of the Standing Committee of the 13th National People's Congress on October 23, 2019. http://cpc.people.com.cn/n1/2019/0320/c64094-30984797.html.

[45] Zhou Qiang (2018) Report of the Supreme People's Court – delivered at the first session of the 13th National People's Congress on March 9, 2018, http://www.court.gov.cn/zixun-xiangqing-84292.html; https://www.spp.gov.cn/tt/201903/t20190312_411422.shtml.

[46] http://www.china-cer.com.cn/guwen/202006025548.html.

2013 to 2019 the courts at all levels nationwide only accepted 12 consumer PIL cases brought by consumer associations. This data is roughly consistent with findings of another researcher who established that, from 2012 to 2016, consumer associations initiated a total of 6 consumer PIL nationwide.[47] It is also compatible with the data of the SPP showing a similar picture: 7 consumer PIL between 2015 and 2017. In the same period, according to the same source, 71 civil PIL cases were included in the total of 653 PIL cases that were filed nationwide in the pilot project.[48]

On the other hand, the mass infringements of lawful rights and interests of consumers were happening so frequently that thousands of criminal sentences, including those in the field of food and drug safety, were issued within the scope of procuratorial PIL. The typical case is the notorious Changsheng Illegal Vaccine Event which happened in March 2016 in Shandong province and influenced 24 provinces. By March 26, 2018, this event led to 91 criminal judgments with 137 people being sentenced guilty, 64 of whom were public officials, for illegal business operation, abuse of power, destruction and falsification of evidence, corruption and intentional disclosure of state secrets. However, there were no reports about civil PIL filed with the courts either by a procuratorial organ or by a consumer association, though some procuratorial organs on the county or city level in several provinces such as Shanxi, Guizhou, Yunnan and Shenzhen city were involved in 'PIL investigation' and issued 'procuratorial suggestions' to the respective local administration urging them to undertake measures against illegal conduct.

4.2.2 The Role of Consumers Associations and 'Procuratorial Suggestions'

By law, 31 existing consumer associations at the provincial level are the only qualified plaintiffs in PIL for mass harm caused to consumers.[49] The law states that they 'may' (and not 'shall' or 'should') file PIL, and for that they do not need a complaint or request by a consumer.

Moreover, consumer associations are established nationwide as social organizations having the approval of the State Council that grants them the right to protect the legitimate rights and interests of consumers through social supervision of commodities and services. The consumer associations are semi-official entities, they are funded by the government and have political sponsorship comparable to support given to administrative organs. However, a consumer association that does not fulfill its duties cannot be challenged by administrative suits. The courts' rulings on various levels and in different regions have repeatedly confirmed that consumer associations

[47]Liu Wenhui (2017) Consumer Public Interest Litigation: Declaring War on Dishonest Enterprises. http://www.spp.gov.cn/zdgz/201703/t20170322_185995.shtml.

[48]Civil Administrative Procuratorate of the Supreme People's Procuratorate (2017), pp. 69–78.

[49]China Consumers Association (2020) Map of the Association. http://www.cca.org.cn/map/index.html.

are not administrative organs, and do not fall under laws and regulations that authorize the exercise of administrative functions. Thus, consumer associations cannot be sued in administrative lawsuits.[50]

Since consumer associations are neither governmental organs nor non-governmental organizations (NGOs) or bodies of self-government, as exclusive organizations qualified to file a consumer PIL, they have little motivation or resources, as they are not subject to official evaluations or pushed to make market profits, or subject to peer competition. This situation has not been changed much with the establishment of the mechanism of 'procuratorial supervision'. Instead, when the ball is kicked to the consumer association by means of the 'procuratorial suggestion', it is usually, after a long delay, kicked back to the procuratorate with all sorts of excuses. The Consumer Association of Jilin Province provided two examples. When it received Changchun procuratorate's PIL suggestion in the case of Jiang Guiling who sold fake drugs and was convicted on November 10, 2016, and Tonghua procuratorate's PIL suggestion in the case of Dong Chunmeng who was sentenced to 3 years' imprisonment for producing and selling toxic and harmful food, it directly refused the procuratorial suggestions to file a civil PIL against the criminal defendants. The consumer association informed the procuratorate that it would rather institute a PIL on its own motion. The procuratorate had no choice but to follow this advice and filed a civil PIL on their own. [51]

This situation evokes the debates as mentioned above about the role of the procuratorates in consumer PIL. By adopting the doctrine of 'modesty' of the procuratorial organs, Article 55(2) CPL limits the procuratorial authority with the consequence that the other qualified plaintiffs have priority to file a civil PIL. In order to encourage social organizations to actively file civil PIL, and remind the procuratorial organs to restrain the use of their public power in civil litigation, the SPP regulations direct that a procuratorial organ should make a public announcement before filing a civil PIL. However, the consumer associations, who occupied the space left for the social organizations by the CPL, are not real 'social organizations' (NGOs) but quasi-governmental organs, with no financial support and functional pressure as well as with strong power to resist pressures to act.

As a result, some local procuratorates and legal scholars are calling for the promotion of procuratorial involvement in consumer PIL, by giving them the right to directly file lawsuits without waiting for other entities to act. The opposite view maintains that the political and financial power of procuratorial organs is exactly the reason why they should exercise restraint in their involvement in civil litigant; as this could have an adverse impact on equal treatment of parties and undermine the core

[50]See Chen Hongwei (2015). One typical case which demonstrates this view is the case submitted by the owner of Volkswagen Sagitar against China Consumer Association, that was rejected by Haidian Court, http://www.china.com.cn/legal/2015-03/26/content_35160989.htm; see also Huang Che v. the Inner Mongolia Autonomous Region Administration for Industry and Commerce, Administrative confirmation of the final judgment No.61 of Huhehaote Intermediate People's Court (2017).

[51]Civil judgment No. 86 of Tonghua Intermediate People's Court (2017).

values of civil procedure. In China, this is even more dangerous as the procuratorate has special function as 'judicial supervisor' who monitors the functioning of the courts. China's criminal procedure system has already provided such lessons and is still struggling to establish appropriate balance for the defense.

On the other hand, it can be cautiously stated that 'procuratorial suggestions' sometimes reach remarkable results. In 2018, affected by the political attention of the CCP and the special encouragement of the SPP, the procuratorial PIL in the field of the production and the sale of counterfeit and substandard medicines, as well as poisonous and harmful food, made out more than 33% of the total number of PIL cases in the procuratorial organs,[52] as a dramatic contrast to less than 1% during the pilot period. However, most of the cases were not filed with the courts but were settled after the procuratorate's early involvement. Such 'soft' procuratorial intervention into the civil field might be more suitable to Chinese circumstances, especially in the early stage of the PIL's institutional development.

4.2.3 PIL Cases Filed by Consumer Associations

Although consumer associations have rarely filed PIL with the courts, they substantially won all the cases which they initiated. The following six PIL cases filed by consumer associations attracted considerable attention due to their success.

Case I (2014) was filed by the Zhejiang Consumer Association before the Shanghai Railway Transportation Court against the Shanghai Railway Bureau[53] claiming the reversal of its policy of forcing consumers who lost the ticket issued on their name to buy a new ticket after embarking on the train.[54] But this milestone PIL case, which was a reaction to the newly amended Consumer Law and the fresh PIL system and that was publicly supported by the National Consumer Association, was surprisingly dismissed by the court, on January 30, 2015, with the ruling that the plaintiff 'lacks the necessary proof (of standing) required under Article 119 of the CPL'. During the appeal process, another plaintiff, Mr. Qiu Jiandong, who is the 'hero' in the PIL field as mentioned above, filed an ordinary private litigation

[52]Zhang Jun (2019) Report of the Supreme People's Procuratorate on the Procuratorial work on public Interest Litigation—delivered at the 14th Session of the Standing Committee of the 13th National People's Congress on October 23, 2019. http://cpc.people.com.cn/n1/2019/0320/c64094-30984797.html

[53]The 'Railway Bureau' was a government organ before it was transformed into free market institution in 2010s.

[54]From May to July 2014, Zhejiang Province Consumer Association received complaints from several customers who bought tickets under their real names and were forced by station staff to buy another ticket after they lost their tickets accidentally. The association contacted the Shanghai Railway Bureau by telephone and mail to investigate and verify consumer complaints and the basis of the policy and requested a refund for the consumers, but was responded that, according to Article 43 of the Railway Passenger Transport Regulations, the policy is compliant to relevant regulations.

procedure for the sake of the public interest as he had done frequently before, challenging the Shanghai Railway Bureau for the same policy but by presenting the 'necessary proof (of standing) required under Article 119 of the CPL'. His claim was also not accepted by the court which ruled that the individual is not qualified to be a PIL plaintiff according to Article 55. However, pressed by these two cases and pressure from society and the potential reversal in the appellate proceedings, the Shanghai Railway Transportation Intermediate Court corrected its judgment on its own. On November 30, 2015, the consumer association withdrew the appeal on the grounds that an understanding was reached with the defendant and that there was no need to continue the lawsuit.

The following cases had less complications. Case II (2015) was filed by the Shanghai Consumer Association before the First Intermediate Court of Shanghai against two communication technology companies for unwillingly installing software on cellphones that consumers had purchased without them being notified. Case III (2016) was filed by the National Consumer Association before the Fourth Intermediate Court of Beijing for a company's illegal sales of motorcycles. Case IV (2016) was filed by the Jiangsu Consumer Association against the Nanjing Water Supply Group Company for unfair standard terms regarding water supply. Case V (Jilin, 2016) and Case VI (Guangdong, 2017) were filed by the consumer association that adopted the local procuratorate's suggestion. The defendants were the criminal offenders sentenced for the infringement of consumers' rights after a criminal investigation of the procuratorate that issued the suggestion.

In the above cases, the PIL claims and the following proceedings were diverse. In Case III the National Consumer Association claimed a declaratory judgment finding that the defendant had committed 'fraudulent conduct' so that the consumers later could seek damages by filing private civil lawsuits. In Case VI, the PIL plaintiff directly presented a claim for damages. By the end of September 2018, the Guangzhou Consumer Association won all four PILs for the fake salt sold to consumers. The 15 defendants, including those who provided production sites and employed labor, were ordered to pay a total of 1.314 million yuan as compensation and publicly apologized on the provincial media.[55]

4.2.4 The Persistent Struggle for the Citizens' Right to File Consumer PIL

Even after the CPL clearly denied the individual citizens' right to file PIL, cases in which individuals submitted PIL occurred year after year and were repeatedly rejected by the courts. A good example is the case of You Muchun vs. Guangzhou Bus Company for elderly's welfare (2014).[56] In 2014, You Muchun filed a suit

[55]Liu Wenhui (2017), Consumer Public Interest Litigation: Declaring War on Dishonest Enterprises. http://www.spp.gov.cn/zdgz/201703/t20170322_185995.shtml.

[56]Civil judgment No. 1723 of Guangzhou Intermediate People's Court (2015).

against the Guangzhou Bus Company for being charged 2 yuan instead of letting him ride the bus for free with his senior citizen ID. Free transportation for the elderly was a local welfare policy under the Law on the Protection of the Rights and Interests of the Elderly. He claimed that the defendant had to return the 2 yuan and had to apply the same policy to all other elderly people who suffered the same harm. This illustrates that, contrary to the sometimes reluctant attitude of consumer associations, consumers often have a personal urge to act as a representative of other people in the same circumstances and with the same problems and interests.

A reasonable option for the institution of PIL is to open the possibility for claims for declaratory relief to be submitted by individuals in a way that other people in the same situation can ride on the 'public interest bus', sharing the fruits of the brave legal efforts of their peers without a risk of private or institutional loss when raising claims for compensation.

5 Conclusion

The legal boundary between public interest litigation and private interest litigation should be predominantly determined according to the objective of each of these actions; procedural technology must only serve these objectives. China has attempted a form of institutional merger of two forms of collective redress, either in a mass private lawsuit for 'public interest' such as the ordinary representative action under Article 54 of the CPL, or in a 'public lawsuit' for private interest such as the one under the Securities Law—the latter being not much different from the PIL under Art 55 CPL.

At the level of their social function, irrespective of the plaintiffs' status, all forms of collective redress in China have similar purposes, which include both private and public perspectives. They are aimed at overcoming the deficiencies of dispersed and uncoordinated litigation, at the effective and rational use of public resources, at compensating victims for the violation of their rights and interests and at sanctioning the illegal conduct of various tortfeasors.

The civil litigation system is essentially a form of procedure where private litigants seek relief for their own allegedly violated rights and interests. Thus, in conventional litigation the capacity to sue is connected with the private interest of private litigants who seek to protect their own rights.

As a contrast, in public interest litigation, civil lawsuits are brought by plaintiffs who do not seek to protect their own private rights and interests. These plaintiffs need to have a special legal basis for their claims in favor of others, which authorizes them to bring a suit when a particular type of public interest is infringed. It can be stated that all forms of public interest litigation at the normative level are special vehicles attached to the traditional mechanisms of civil procedure.

However, the success of any form of class action inserted into the conventional system of civil procedure depends on its particular context and systemic operation. For example, a class action system established to protect the public interest must balance the protection of individual rights with the efficiency in solving mass disputes.

The rules on costs and their distribution, the risk of losing the case, as well as the corresponding legal culture, directly affect the motivation of interested persons and entities to bring collective actions. This is decisive for their effectiveness—not to mention the influence of the political system. In the context of the specific features of China's political system and legal culture, it is hard to talk about a private system of enforcement of public law. The social organizations entitled to bring actions are also supported and financed by the government (e.g. the consumer associations and the Environmental Protection Fund). They do not have full autonomy regarding the enforcement of private rights and do not object to the intervention of public powers in private rights. In a system in which private autonomy is not a key principle of the civil litigation system, but where public power and political intervention permeate all pores of society, public interest obviously relies a lot (too much) on 'public interest litigation' conducted by public governmental bodies or quasi-governmental social organizations. However, this puts a heavy burden on the system and jeopardizes the core values of civil litigation such as procedural equality and the adversarial principle. And since the concept of 'public interest' is too fuzzy to be defined by legislation, the indifferent governmental organs or bureaucratic semi-governmental organizations are the gatekeepers of the interests to be protected, while those who really matter—ordinary citizens whose lives, health and other vital interests are at stake—are left excluded and abandoned.

References

Baike B (2020) Contamination of Dairy products in China. https://baike.baidu.com/item

China Consumers' Association (2020) Map of the Association. http://www.cca.org.cn/map/index.html

China Court Website (2005) Qinghai province successfully mediated a lawsuit brought by an environmental pollution group. https://www.chinacourt.org/article/detail/2005/05/id/161755.shtml

China Enterprise Advisory Network (2009) Sanlu defective milk powder compensation plan unveiled. http://www.cction.com/info/200901/10684.html

Civil Administrative Procuratorate of the Supreme People's Procuratorate (2017) Practice and exploration of public interest litigation by procuratorial organs. China Procuratorial Publishing House, pp 69–78

Court of China (2005) The Court of China has settled a lawsuit involving a group of farmers. https://www.chinacourt.org/article/detail/2005/05/id/162430.shtml

Datebase of Chinese Tiral Cases. http://www.chncase.cn/case/bulletin/1085566

Dun L (2018) Observation Report on Environmental Public interest Litigation, vol 2016. Law Publishing House, pp 344–345

Economic Daily (1996) A 1.2 yuan lawsuit worth fighting? October 30th: the front page

Gu G (2015) An empirical analysis of environmental civil public interest litigation in China in 2015. Law 9:16–33

Hao L (2017) On the status of procuratorial organs in civil public interest litigation. Law Sci 11:168–181

Hongwei C (2015) The owner of Volkswagen Sagitar sued China Consumers Association, which was rejected by Haidian Court in the first instance. http://www.china.com.cn/legal/2015-03/26/content_35160989.htm

Jun Z (2019) Report of the Supreme People's Procuratorate on the Procuratorial work on public Interest Litigation -- delivered at the 2nd Session of the Standing Committee of the 13th National People's Congress on October 23, 2019. http://cpc.people.com.cn/n1/2019/0320/c64094-30984797.html

Liming Z (2011) Procuratorial organs should not be the plaintiffs in environmental public interest litigation. Law Sci 6:134–140

Qiang Z (2018) Report of the Supreme People's Court-- delivered at the first session of the 13th National People's Congress on March 9, 2018. http://www.court.gov.cn/zixun-xiangqing-84292.html

Shuya M (2017) How to manage and spend the environmental public interest litigation compensation. The Procuratorial Daily, April 23rd:003 edition

Sina net (2005) 4000 Peach farmers suing 'peach vendors' for debt. http://news.sina.com.cn/s/2005-01-11/21474795014s.shtml

Wei J, Changchun G (1988) On class action. China Legal Sci 6:84–91

Wei J, Jianguo X (1994) Some issues regarding representative litigation. Jurists' Rev 3:3–4

Weiping Z (2013) Research on the institutionalization and Implementation of civil public interest litigation principles. Tsinghua Law Rev 4:17–20

Wenhui L (2017) Consumer Public Interest Litigation: Declaring War on Dishonest Enterprises. http://www.spp.gov.cn/zdgz/201703/t20170322_185995.shtml

Xiaoren L (2018) How to use the huge ecological restoration costs. Audit report in China April 9th:005 edition

Xinhuanet (2020) Sanlu infant milk powder incident tracking report. http://www.xinhuanet.com/newscenter/ztnfsj/sjjj.htm

Yanmin C (2000) From regulation to operation: on procuratorial supervision in civil litigation. Law Rev 3:161–175

Yulin F (2012) The power and procedure configuration of civil procuratorial power. Legal Sci 5:176–185

Yulin Fu Professor of Law at Peking University, China, where she teaches Civil Procedure, Evidence, Arbitration, Dispute Resolution. Vice-president of China Civil Procedure Society. Counsel expert of the Supreme Procuratorate. Council member of International Association of Procedure Law.

The manufacturer's authorised representative in the EU is Springer Nature Customer Service Centre GmbH, Europaplatz 3, 69115 Heidelberg, Germany. If you have any concerns regarding our products, please contact ProductSafety@springernature.com

Printed and bound by CPI Group (UK) Ltd, Croydon, CR0 4YY
30/09/2026
02225294-0015